THE CROWD IN THE EARLY MIDDLE AGES

HISTORIES OF ECONOMIC LIFE

Jeremy Adelman, Sunil Amrith, Emma Rothschild, and Francesca Trivellato, Series Editors

The Crowd in the Early Middle Ages by Shane Bobrycki

A Third Path: Corporatism in Brazil and Portugal by Melissa Teixeira

Power and Possession in the Russian Revolution by Anne O'Donnell

Toward a Free Economy: Swatantra and Opposition Politics in Democratic India by Aditya Balasubramanian

No Return: Jews, Christian Usurers, and the Spread of Mass Expulsion in Medieval Europe by Rowan Dorin

Desert Edens: Colonial Climate Engineering in the Age of Anxiety by Philipp Lehmann

Distant Shores: Colonial Encounters on China's Maritime Frontier by Melissa Macauley

A Velvet Empire: French Informal Imperialism in the Nineteenth Century by David Todd

Making It Count: Statistics and Statecraft in the Early People's Republic of China by Arunabh Ghosh

Empires of Vice: The Rise of Opium Prohibition across Southeast Asia by Diana S. Kim

Pirates and Publishers: A Social History of Copyright in Modern China by Fei-Hsien Wang

Sorting Out the Mixed Economy: The Rise and Fall of Welfare and Developmental States in the Americas by Amy C. Offner

Red Meat Republic: A Hoof-to-Table History of How Beef Changed America by Joshua Specht

The Promise and Peril of Credit: What a Forgotten Legend about Jews and Finance Tells Us about the Making of European Commercial Society by Francesca Trivellato

A People's Constitution: The Everyday Life of Law in the Indian Republic by Rohit De

A Local History of Global Capital: Jute and Peasant Life in the Bengal Delta by Tariq Omar Ali

The Crowd in the Early Middle Ages

SHANE BOBRYCKI

PRINCETON UNIVERSITY PRESS
PRINCETON & OXFORD

Copyright © 2024 by Princeton University Press

Princeton University Press is committed to the protection of copyright and the intellectual property our authors entrust to us. Copyright promotes the progress and integrity of knowledge created by humans. Thank you for supporting free speech and the global exchange of ideas by purchasing an authorized edition of this book. If you wish to reproduce or distribute any part of it in any form, please obtain permission.

Requests for permission to reproduce material from this work should be sent to permissions@press.princeton.edu

Published by Princeton University Press
41 William Street, Princeton, New Jersey 08540
99 Banbury Road, Oxford OX2 6JX

press.princeton.edu

All Rights Reserved

Library of Congress Cataloging-in-Publication Data

Names: Bobrycki, Shane, 1985- author.
Title: The crowd in the early Middle Ages / Shane Bobrycki.
Description: Princeton : Princeton University Press, [2024] | Series: Histories of economic life | Includes bibliographical references and index.
Identifiers: LCCN 2024001062 (print) | LCCN 2024001063 (ebook) | ISBN 9780691189697 (hardback) | ISBN 9780691255590 (ebook)
Subjects: LCSH: Crowds—History—To 1500. | Collective behavior—To 1500. | BISAC: HISTORY / Europe / Medieval | SOCIAL SCIENCE / Anthropology / Cultural & Social
Classification: LCC HM871 .B54 2024 (print) | LCC HM871 (ebook) | DDC 302.330903—dc23/eng/20240312
LC record available at https://lccn.loc.gov/2024001062
LC ebook record available at https://lccn.loc.gov/2024001063

British Library Cataloging-in-Publication Data is available

Editorial: Priya Nelson and Emma Wagh
Production Editorial: Sara Lerner
Jacket Design: Felix Summ
Production: Lauren Reese
Publicity: William Pagdatoon and Charlotte Coyne
Copyeditor: Lachlan Brooks

Jacket Credit: Stuttgart Psalter, 9th century, Saint-Germain-des-Prés, Bibl. fol. 23. Courtesy of Württembergische Landesbibliothek, Stuttgart, Germany

This book has been composed in Arno

10 9 8 7 6 5 4 3 2 1

CONTENTS

Preface ix
Acknowledgments xiii
Abbreviations xvii

	Introduction	1
	The Early Middle Ages: A World without Crowds?	1
	The Crowd as Historical Subject	3
	The Crowd Regime of the Early Middle Ages	10
	Sources and Structure	12
1	The Roman Legacy	15
	Crowds in Roman Antiquity	15
	The Crowd from the Republic to the Principate (c. 400 BCE–300 CE)	17
	The Crowd in Late Antiquity (c. 300–600)	19
	Scale	23
	Functions	25
	Ambivalence	27
	The End of the Roman Crowd Regime in the West	31
	The Legacy of Roman Crowds	33
2	Numbers	35
	Number and Scale	35
	Early Medieval Demography: Evidence, Causes, Trends	36
	Regional Heterogeneity	40
	Population Pools and Carrying Capacities	44

	Sizes of Gatherings	51
	Numbers and Crowds	63
3	Peasants and Other Non-Elites: Repertory and Resistance	64
	The Problem of Non-Elite Crowds	64
	Peasants: Far from the Madding Crowd?	65
	Horizontal and Vertical Coordination	71
	Spirituality and Recreation	75
	Resistance	78
	Repertory and Resistance	91
4	The Closed Crowd: Elite Venues and Occasions for Gathering	93
	Predictability, Hierarchy, Unity	93
	Religious Gatherings	94
	Gatherings in "Public" Life	104
	Intra-Elite Competition and Conflict: The Case of Tours	110
	The Solemn Assembly	112
	Ramifications of the Closed Crowd	116
5	Words	119
	Semantic History	119
	Crowds across Languages	120
	Blurring Distinctions: Populus	128
	Christianization: Contio	132
	Erosion of Negative Connotations: Turba	135
	Crowd Words Transformed	141
6	Representations	143
	Patterns of Representation	143
	Topoi, Type Scenes, and Their Sources	144
	Qualities of the Crowd in Early Medieval Discourse	148
	Crowds and Sanctity	152
	The Crowd as Witness	155
	Bad Crowds	158
	Epilogue: Into the Eleventh Century	168

Conclusion 171
The Crowd in the Early Middle Ages 171
Ramifications 174

Notes 179
Index 297

PREFACE

IN EARLY MEDIEVAL Europe (c. 500–1000), crowds underwent a sea change. In the Byzantine and Islamic Mediterranean, the West's fellow heirs to Roman Antiquity, old patterns of collective behavior persisted more recognizably, in societies less affected by depopulation and deurbanization. In a time when Europe's largest cities had fewer inhabitants than a poor showing at the Roman games, gatherings there were smaller and less spontaneous than they had been since perhaps the early Iron Age. This book is about a world in which crowds were harder to come by, in synchronic and diachronic comparison, but in which crowds remained vital.

It was written against the backdrop of crowds in the present day. The dissertation behind this book, from which it departs in many respects, was defended in 2016, a year marked by global populisms. Revisions were carried out in 2020–23, a time of crowds: the Black Lives Matter movement, COVID-19 rallies, climate protests, the storming of the US Capitol. It was eerie to pose questions about crowds and demographic decline while considering the crowds, constraints on gatherings, and concern with demographic crisis that filled the news.

The present offered a foil for my early medieval setting. Crowds then, as now, offered opportunities to pursue justice, power, legitimacy, and a sense of belonging. But there were profound differences in how early medieval Europeans experienced and described coming together in numbers. The crowds of seventh- through tenth-century Europe seemed orderly, almost tidy, compared to modern counterparts. They seemed to spend their time worshipping saints, marching in processions, and shouting acclamations.

In earlier iterations of this project, I was inclined to argue that early medieval Europe, with its predictable, circumscribed gatherings, was an age of "closed crowds," to use the phrase of Elias Canetti. For half a millennium, the crowd seemed logistically suited to elite control. Living through our crowd-filled times, I came to see that this framing did not capture the whole picture. The stage-managed gatherings of early medieval elites were vulnerable to passive or "slantwise" resistance. Rulers were at a loss to delegitimize crowds that did the wrong thing in the wrong place at the wrong time, because crowds became, by default, a proof of authority. The rules of the game altered, but crowds remained at the center of social conflict. Unexpectedly, the fraught discourse on crowds of the early 2020s helped me see this better.

Years of working on this protean subject have left me with a profound sense of gratitude to those in other specializations on whose shoulders I have climbed. My frame was demographic, so I used the proxy data, archaeological evidence, and statistics of that challenging field. In attempting to inventory the gatherings that made up everyday life in the early Middle Ages, I hunted for crowds across genres—hagiography, history, liturgy, law, poetry, charters—and accumulated great debts to the editors, commentators, and database-compilers who have made these sources available. Without searchable databases such as CETEDOC, Patrologia Latina, Acta Sanctorum, the Corpus Corporum, and Analecta Hymnica, which allowed me to search for hundreds of words across thousands of texts, this project would have been impossible in its present form. The digitization of manuscripts facilitated examination of crowd art and crowd-like phenomena (for instance, huge name-lists). For the philological and discursive side, I drew on literary studies, manuscript studies, art history, and philology.

None of that had been the plan, originally. My interest in this subject was sparked by the curiously ubiquitous crowds of hagiography: saints' lives, miracle stories, and relic-translation accounts. Initially my questions were limited to the discursive role of these hagiographical witness crowds. But I became convinced that my story would be wanting if I failed to investigate the wider context. That led me to questions about the relationship between structural change—demographic, economic, political, religious—and collective behavior writ large.

The result is a history that differs from the usual historiographical approach to crowds. Carefully circumscribed definitions of the "crowd" used by scholars I most admired—Georges Lefebvre, George Rudé, E. P. Thompson, Charles Tilly, Natalie Z. Davis—restricted the subject to atypical, contentious non-elite gatherings. In this tradition, crowds' unruly acts were justified by an immanent "moral economy" permitting common people to band together in numbers when the normal "repertory" of public life had failed them. If bakers refused to sell bread at a fair rate, and the law did nothing about it, crowds felt entitled to "set the price"; if magistrates were unable to accuse, instruct, and punish heretics, crowds felt a right to perform these functions through violence. This rationalizing approach to crowds, so illuminating for early modern Europe, broke down in the face of early medieval evidence, where public–private distinctions blurred and the dichotomy between "crowd" and "repertory" dissolved. I found I had to develop a broader, more neutral working definition: not "crowds" in the historiographical sense (collective behavior as part of non-elite contentious action), but "gatherings" of all kinds.

To my knowledge, this is the first book directly on that subject, but it is only a first step. In what follows, I have understated regional and chronological differences. Some settings are better represented (especially the Merovingian, Lombard, and Carolingian worlds). Above all, I have only touched upon the complex story of crowds in the West's sibling cultures—Byzantium and Islam—and I hope that this topic will attract the attention it deserves. For the present, I hope a single book treating 1) the demographic and economic basis for gatherings, 2) non-elite and elite venues and occasions, 3) the language of collective behavior, and 4) the representation of crowds in early medieval Europe will restore to scholarly attention a most unusual chapter of crowd history.

Vienna 2023

ACKNOWLEDGMENTS

ANY PROJECT OF LONG DURATION has its debts. Many friends, colleagues, and mentors have contributed to this book over the years. I feel both the difficulty and satisfaction of thanking this large and indispensable crowd. My first debt is to institutions that have sustained my research. The earliest stages of this project were supported by the Frederick Sheldon Fellowship, a "Visiting Scientist" Borsa at the Università degli Studi di Padova, the National Endowment for the Humanities, the Graduate School of Arts and Sciences at Harvard, and the Radcliffe Institute for Advanced Study. The Center for History and Economics (Harvard, MIT, Cambridge, Sciences-Po) was my academic home during my postdoctoral years, and I am grateful to colleagues at MIT for their encouragement while I was a lecturer there. At the University of Vienna, the Institut für Geschichte and the Institut für österreichische Geschichtsforschung have been the perfect home for the last stages of this project. Not every medieval historian gets to have an office inside a world-class medieval library surrounded by world-class medieval historians. Colleagues, staff, and librarians at these institutions have my heartfelt thanks.

My students at Harvard, MIT, and the University of Vienna have been a source of inspiration and delight. In its five iterations between 2015 and 2021, undergraduates in my seminar The Crowd in History: From the Hunting Band to the Social Network have taught me an enormous amount about my theme. I have yet to read a final paper on crowds of penguins in Antarctica, but I have now read student papers on crowds from all inhabited continents and most epochs from prehistory to the present day. I lack the words to describe my gratitude for all the insight my students have shared with me.

My gratitude to scholars and friends (often one and the same) puts me in mind of the early medieval monks and nuns who set out to list their spiritual brothers and sisters in confraternity books. No log of names can properly express my thanks for the encouragement, suggestions, criticism, institutional support, and good company I have enjoyed over the years. I would like to be able to dwell in depth on the different ways all of them have helped me, from those who furnished an academic home away from home (Cristina La Rocca, Geneviève Bührer-Thierry, Régine Le Jan, and the late, much-missed François

Menant), to grad school chums and nonspecialist colleagues who offered moral and intellectual support (too many to list here), to members of the world's finest work-in-progress reading group (Paige Glotzer, Melissa Teixeira, Annie Ruderman), to learned helpers in languages I do not know (Arafat Razzaque for Arabic, Jo Wolf for Old Irish), to folks who shared a tip that made a difference (Cam Grey, " slantwise resistance"; Erik Inglis, "icocephaly"). It feels a shame to congeal so many discrete contributions into one mass of names. But my gratitude toward all those who sustained my work is genuine, and for anyone I inadvertently omitted, I hope you can overlook my forgetfulness.

Thanks, then, to Claire Adams, Sunil Amrith, Colleen Anderson, Dimiter Angelov, David Armitage, Karole Armitage, Girolamo Arnaldi, Nate Aschenbrenner, Laura Ashe, Gideon Avni, Christine Axen, Lane Baker, Mou Banerjee, Rhae Lynn Barnes, Richard Barton, Adrien Bayard, Robin ("Boon") Beck, Peter Becker, Simone Bellini, Bob Berkhofer, Thomas Bisson, Ann Blair, Jamie Blasina, Philippe Buc, Geneviève Bührer-Thierry, Elise Burton, Ettore Cafagna, Claire de Cazanove, Alison Chapman, Paul Cobb, Kathleen Coleman, Elliott Colla, Jonathan Conant, Jenny Davis, Mayke De Jong, Emma Dench, Charles Donahue, Rowan Dorin, Tina Duhaime, Paul Dutton, Karin Einaudi, Francesca Fiaschetti, Robin Fleming, Luke Fowler, Stefano Gasparri, Laura Gathagan, Ross Gay, Patrick Geary, Mary Frances Giandrea, Sean Gilsdorf, Michael Gnozzio, Eric Goldberg, Peter Gordon, Cam Grey, Henry Gruber, John Haldon, Kyle Harper, Carla Heelan, Sarah Howe, Laurent Jégou, Kuba Kabala, Namrata Kala, Gregor Kalas, Diana Kim, Adam Kosto, Maryanne Kowaleski, Ian Kumekawa, Matthew Kustenbauder, Joe la Hausse de Lalouvière, Arnaud Lestremau, Mary Lewis, Thomas Lienhard, Kristen Loveland, Chris Loveluck, Tina Lutter, Alice Lyons, Simon MacLean, Lucie Malbos, Austin Mason, Stefano Massa, Youna Masset, Anne McCants, Rosamond McKitterick, Jamie McSpadden, Maureen Miller, John Mulhall, Maria Giuseppina Muzzarelli, Nikhil Naik, Piroska Nagy, Eric Nemarich, Jennifer Nickerson, James Norrie, Bill North, Steffen Patzold, Xiao Peng, Warren Pezé, Matthieu Pignot, Val Piro, Walter Pohl, Richard Pollard, Mircea Raianu, Kalyani Ramnath, Jake Ransohoff, Arafat Razzaque, Helmut Reimitz, Levi Roach, Andy Romig, Barbara Rosenwein, Evan Sadler, Jeffrey Schnapp, Jens Schneider, Ned Schoolman, Andreas Schwarcz, Kathryn Schwartz, Lesley Sharp, Stephen Shoemaker, Sarah Shortall, Josh Specht, Sallie Spence, Liat Spiro, Paolo Squatriti, Sita Steckel, Jo Story, Claire Tignolet, Heidi Tworek, Michael Tworek, David Ungvary, Giorgia Vocino, Jing Wang, Nicholas Watson, Jeff Webb, Tessa Webber, Herwig Weigl, Charles West, Stephen White, Chris Wickham, Ryan Wilkinson, Daniel Williams, Jo Wolf, Ian Wood, Julian Yolles, and Daniel Ziblatt. Among the names listed above, a few are no longer with us. To these, I add my beloved Aunt Marilyn, who would have read this book.

A few more drawn-out thanks are required. Collective thanks are owed to the 2015–16 cohort of the Radcliffe Institute for Advanced Study at Harvard, where I was incredibly lucky to be a graduate fellow in my last year of the PhD. My Center for History and Economics fellows have a special place in the next stage of the project. Both groups testify to the value of constant conversation with wise nonspecialists. Ippolita Checcoli and Simone Bellini, and the whole Checcoli family, have always treated me like family. Ippo, who is a trained medievalist, and Simone, who might as well be, endured several versions of this project, and made me feel at home at San Giusto. Rowan Dorin has been my brilliant friend for over a decade. I cannot say how grateful I am to have his rare combination of genius and diligence at my disposal. Nate Aschenbrenner, over many "Chez Paul" beers and in other pleasant settings, was a miraculous counselor as well as a canny guide to all things Byzantine and late medieval. Jake Ransohoff, Byzantinist and medievalist extraordinaire, has been a sounding board, a perceptive reader, and a too-generous friend. I have depended greatly on his knowledge and wisdom. To all these *amici* and *amicae*, my profound thanks: "Those friends thou hast, and their adoption tried, / Grapple them unto thy soul with hoops of steel."

Among scholarly mentors, Eric Goldberg first taught me medieval history at Williams College and, much later, a kindly turn of fate made us colleagues at MIT for two years of my postdoc. Eric has been a model of scholarship and a trusted friend. John Maddicott taught me medieval English history for two glorious terms at Exeter College, Oxford, and this book owes much to his infectious enthusiasm for medieval assemblies. Rosamond McKitterick advised my MPhil at Cambridge and profoundly influenced my understanding of the early medieval world. In my second year at Cambridge, Rosamond and I spent several weeks discussing Einhard's *Translatio Petri et Marcellini*, and it was then that I first took note of early medieval crowds.

Among my mentors at Harvard, special thanks go to Jan Ziolkowski, Emma Rothschild, Daniel Lord Smail, and Michael McCormick. Jan made me a closer, better reader of medieval Latin. I have drawn on his encyclopedic knowledge, his perspective as a literary scholar, and his generous wit and good humor. Emma has been a supporter of my work since we met. Her perspective as an economic historian and an early modernist has been indispensable. Her humane fascination with the inner lives of everyday people in the distant past has been a polestar for my work. I lack the words to express my thanks for her encouragement and support. Dan has a mind like no other. He has always pushed me to think bigger and better. In academic settings, over beers, in witty emails, and in brilliant comments, he has been an endless source of exciting ideas and trenchant criticism. Mike is a force of nature. He was *der allerbeste Doktorvater überhaupt*. I cannot understand how one person can possess

Mike's minute attention to detail and his devotion to the big picture, but I am grateful to have benefitted from both. All the Chimay in the world cannot express my thanks.

At Princeton University Press, I extend my thanks to my skillful and very patient editorial team, especially Priya Nelson and Emma Wagh. The series editors showed interest in this project and offered their intellectual support as well. Finally, I am grateful for the generous and critical comments of my anonymous readers, who saved me from errors and infelicities. Of course, the flaws that remain are my own.

My family has put up with my vocation for years, and I am thankful for their trust, love, and support. My little brother Max, the best of brothers, has always believed in me. I hope he knows how proud I am of his successes, how much they sustain me, and how happy I am to be Harry's uncle and Bre's brother-in-law. My father taught me my oldest and best lessons about writing, and his true love of learning has been an inspiration. My mother has been a rock of support, and her love of poetry and history encourage my own. All the Bobryckis and Pezzulos have my love. To my mother-in-law Bogusia and father-in-law Romek, infinite thanks for welcoming me into your family. Maybe it goes without saying, but without babcia, dziadziuś, and grandma to take care of Sophie, I would owe my publishers far more apologies and thanks for their patience.

My daughter has brought more joy to my life than I thought possible. A toddler is not always conducive to book-finishing, even if Sophie did occasionally command me: "Daddy, you work!" But Sophie has enriched my world beyond measure, and I believe my work is better for the new perspective she has given me. My wife Ania gets the last word. Medieval history is a world away from pediatric neurology, but this book would be so much less without her. Ania has been a source of joy, fun, and strength, both when things have been easy and when things have been hard. I am lucky she has borne so patiently with early medieval crowds. This book is dedicated to her, with all my love.

ABBREVIATIONS

AASS   *Acta Sanctorum*, ed. Jean Bolland et al., 3rd ed., 67 vols. (Paris and Brussels, 1863–1940).

AB   *Annales Bertiniani*, ed. Félix Grat, Jeanne Vielliard, and Suzanne Clémencet, with introduction and notes by Léon Levillain, *Annales de Saint-Bertin* (Paris, 1964).

AF   *Annales Fuldenses*, ed. F. Kurze, MGH SRG 7 (Hanover, 1891).

AH   *Analecta hymnica Medii Aevi*, ed. G. M. Dreves, C. Blume, H. M. Bannister, et al. 55 vols. (Leipzig, 1886–1922).

AMMIANUS   Ammianus Marcellinus, *Res Gestae*, ed. W. Seyfarth, L. Jacob-Karau, and I. Ulmann (Leipzig, 1978).

ARF   *Annales Regni Francorum*, ed. F. Kurze, MGH SRG 6 (Hanover, 1895).

AUG. CIV. DEI   Augustine, *De civitate Dei*, ed. B. Dombart and A. Kalb, *Sancti Avrelii Avgvstini De civitate Dei*, 2 vols., CCSL 47–48 (Turnhout, 1955).

AWB   *Althochdeutsches Wörterbuch: Auf Grund der von Elias v. Steinmeyer hinterlassenen Sammlungen im Auftrag der Sächsischen Akademie der Wissenschaften zu Leipzig*, ed. Elisabeth Karg-Gasterstädt und Theodor Frings (Leipzig, 1952–).

AX   *Annales Xantenses*, ed. B. von Simson, MGH SRG 12 (Hanover, 1909).

BAV   Biblioteca Apostolica Vaticana (Vatican City)

BEDE, HE   Bede, *Historia Ecclesiastica gentis Anglorum*, ed. Michael Lapidge, *Histoire ecclésiastique du peuple anglais*, SC 489–91, 3 vols. (Paris, 2005).

BHG   *Bibliotheca hagiographica graeca*, ed. F. Halkin, 3rd ed., Subsidia hagiographica 8a (Brussels, 1957); *Novum auctarium Bibliothecae hagiographicae graeca*, ed. F. Halkin, Subsidia hagiographica 65 (Brussels, 1984).

BHL *Bibliotheca hagiographica latina*, Subsidia hagiographica 6 and Subsidia hagiographica 12 (Brussels, 1898–1911); H. Fros, *Novum supplementum*, Subsidia hagiographica 70 (Brussels, 1986).

BNF Bibliothèque nationale de France (Paris)

c. *capitulum*; *caput*; *canon*; chapter; *circa*

CARM. *carmen*; *carmina*

CCCM Corpus Christianorum, Continuatio Mediaevalis (Turnhout, 1966–).

CCM Corpus Consuetudinum Monasticarum (Siegburg, 1963–).

CCSL Corpus Christianorum, Series Latina (Turnhout, 1952–).

CIL Corpus inscriptionum latinarum (Berlin, 1862–).

CLM Codices latini monacenses = Latin manuscripts at the Bayerische Staatsbibliothek (Munich)

COL. column; columns

CSEL Corpus Scriptorum Ecclesiasticorum Latinorum (Vienna, 1866–).

DEKKERS, CPL E. Dekkers, *Clavis patrum latinorum*, 3rd ed. (Steenbrugge, 1995).

DEUTSCHES ARCHIV *Deutsches Archiv für Erforschung des Mittelalters*

DÍAZ Y DÍAZ Manuel Cecilio Díaz y Díaz, *Index scriptorum Latinorum medii aevi Hispanorum*, 2 vols., Acta Salmanticensia, Filosofía y Letras 13 (Salamanca, 1958–59).

DIG. *Digesta Iustiniani*, ed. Theodor Mommsen, *Corpus iuris civilis* (Berlin, 1872), vol. 1.

EP. *epistola*; *epistula*

FASC. fascicle; fascicles

FOL. / FOLS. folio / folios

GREGORY OF TOURS, HIST. Gregory of Tours, *Historiarum libri X*, ed. Bruno Krusch and Wilhelm Levison, MGH SRM 1.1 (Hanover, 1951).

ISIDORE, ET. Isidore of Seville, *Etymologiarum siue Originum libri XX*, ed. W. M. Lindsay, 2 vols. (Oxford, 1911).

LA III	Karl Wendt, Johanna Hilpert, and Andreas Zimmermann, with Sonja Ickler, Hans Nortmann, Bernd Päffgen, Frank Siegmund, and Petra Tutlies, "Landschaftsarchäologie III: Untersuchungen zur Bevölkerungsdichte der vorrömischen Eisenzeit, der Merowingerzeit und der späten vorindustriellen Neuzeit an Mittel- und Niederrhein," *Bericht der Römisch-Germanischen Kommission* 91 (2010): 221–338.
LP	*Liber Pontificalis*, ed. Louis Duchesne, *Le Liber Pontificalis: Texte, introduction et commentaire*, 3 vols. (Paris, 1886–92); revised edition Cyrille Vogel (Paris, 1957).
MANSI	G. D. Mansi, ed., *Sacrorum conciliorum nova et amplissima collectio* (Venice, 1759–).
MGH	Monumenta Germaniae historica (Hanover, 1828–).
AA	Auctores Antiquissimi
CAPIT.	Capitularia regum Francorum
CAPIT. EPISC.	Capitula Episcoporum
CAPIT. N.S.	Capitularia regum Francorum, Nova series
CONC.	Concilia
DD	Diplomata
DD KAR. 1	Pippin, Karlmann und Karl der Große
DD KARL	Karl III
DD LO I	Lothar I
DD MER.	Merowinger
EPP.	Epistolae
EPP. SEL.	Epistolae selectae in usum scholarum separatim editae
FONT. IUR. GERM.	Fontes iuris Germanici Antiqui in usum scholarum
FORMULAE	Formulae Merowingici et Karolini aevi
GESTA PONTIF. ROM.	Gesta pontificum Romanorum
LDL	Libelli de lite imperatorum et pontificum
LIBRI MEM.	Libri memoriales
LIBRI MEM. N.S.	Libri memoriales et Necrologia, Nova series

LL NAT. GERM.	Leges nationum Germanicarum
NECR.	Necrologia Germaniae
ORDINES	Ordines de celebrando concilio
POETAE	Poetae Latini medii aevi
SRG	Scriptores rerum Germanicarum in usum scholarum separatim editi
SRG N.S.	Scriptores rerum Germanicarum, Nova series
SRL	Scriptores rerum Langobardicarum et Italicarum
SRM	Scriptores rerum Merovingicarum
SS	Scriptores
MLW	*Mittellateinisches Wörterbuch, bis zum ausgehenden 13. Jahrhundert*, ed. O. Prinz, et al. (Munich, 1959–).
MS / MSS	manuscript / manuscripts; manuscrit / manuscrits; manoscritto / manoscritti, etc.
NEW PAULY	H. Cancik and H. Schneider, eds., *Brill's New Pauly: Encyclopaedia of the Ancient World* (Leiden, 2002–10).
NO.	*numero*; number
OED	*Oxford English Dictionary*, 2nd ed., 20 vols. (Oxford, 1989).
OLD	*Oxford Latin Dictionary*, ed. P.G.W. Glare et al, 2nd ed., 2 vols. (Oxford, 2012).
PL	*Patrologia latina*, ed. J.-P. Migne, 221 vols. (Paris, 1844–64).
PRAEF.	*praefatio*; preface
RGA[2]	*Reallexikon der Germanischen Altertumskunde*, ed. H. Jahnkuhn et al., 2nd ed. (Berlin, 1968–2008).
S.A.	sub anno
SC	Sources chrétiennes (Paris, 1941–).
STOTZ	Peter Stotz, *Handbuch zur lateinischen Sprache des Mittelalters*, 5 vols., Handbuch der Altertumswissenschaft II.5.1–5 (Munich, 1996–2004).
SUPPL.	*Supplementum* / Supplement
S.V.	sub voce
TLL	*Thesaurus linguae latinae* (Leipzig, 1900–).
TYPOLOGIE DES SOURCES	Typologie des Sources du Moyen Âge Occidental (Turnhout, 1972–).

VERGIL, AEN. Vergil, *Aeneid*, ed. M. Geymonat, in *P. Vergili Maronis Opera*, 2nd ed., Temi e testi 4 (Rome, 2008); and *Vergilius Maro, Aeneis*, ed. Gian Biagio Conte (Berlin, 2011).

VOL. / VOLS. volume / volumes

WATTENBACH-LEVISON-LÖWE Wilhelm Wattenbach and Wilhelm Levison, *Deutschlands Geschichtsquellen im Mittelalter: Vorzeit und Karolinger*, ed. Wilhelm Levison and Heinz Löwe, 6 fasc. (Weimar, 1952–90).

WEBER-GRYSON R. Weber, B. Fischer, R. Gryson, et al., eds., *Biblia sacra iuxta Vulgatam versionem*, 5th ed. (Stuttgart, 2007).

Introduction

The Early Middle Ages: A World without Crowds?

What became of Roman crowds after Roman Antiquity? In the fifth and sixth centuries, a civilization famous for riots, triumphs, bread and circuses, and mass acclamations gave way to a quieter world. Urban and demographic decline meant that large and frequent gatherings grew rare. By 650, the ruins of the Colosseum, built in the first century to accommodate an audience of fifty thousand in a city of one million, could have held Rome's population twice over.[1] Across Europe and the Western Mediterranean, the crowds of old Rome became a memory. But they were not replaced all at once by the forms of collective behavior most commonly associated with the Middle Ages. Such quintessentially "medieval" crowds as acts of peasant unrest, mass preaching, popular heretical movements, pogroms against Jews, and collective armed pilgrimages to the Holy Land only arrived on the "stage of public events" much later, after the year 1000, when European populations and cities were expanding again.[2] This book is about gatherings in Europe during the five hundred years between an age of circuses and an age of crusades.

Scholars generally characterize c. 500–1000 as a time of quiescence in European collective life. The standard view is that the Western Roman Empire gave way to a largely rural, peasant-centered political economy, increasingly aristocrat-dominated by the 700s and 800s. Decentralization was still the rule when much of Western Europe came under the sway of the Carolingian empire (eighth to early tenth centuries). Compared to the north, southern Europe (coastal Spain, Provence, Italy, the eastern Adriatic) retained greater urbanism, population density, and integration with Byzantine and Islamic societies. But even city-rich Italy lacked the multitudes of Constantinople, Córdoba, or Baghdad. As a result, scholars see early medieval crowds as either epilogue to ancient Rome or preface to high medieval Europe.[3] The consensus, closer to a default than a position staked out, is that the de-urbanized, depopulated early

Middle Ages was a time in which masses did not play a decisive role in social, political, or economic life: a world without crowds.

There is some truth to this view, depending on how one defines the crowd. Urban riots were a statistical rarity in the early Middle Ages, though factional squabbles involving gatherings were not uncommon. Known peasant revolts across the whole period can be counted on the fingers of one hand. The mass entertainments and mass politics of old Rome, which lasted in the East, vanished in the West. But gatherings of many kinds retained their importance. Early medieval European sources are full of crowds—just not the sort historians have trained themselves to look for.

A gang of harvesters stands waiting for beer rations at the end of a long day in the fields. Merchants at a busy port jostle along the piers. A grumbling populace makes a count think twice about releasing a prisoner. Before a throng of grieving supplicants, a bishop resurrects a child thought to be dead. An abbess vindicates the chastity of her nuns against an accusation by processing before local onlookers. In an annual assembly, nobles hear decisions promulgated as troops muster for war. A town's multitudes clamor as magnates set out to the hunt. A ruler bathes in hot springs near his palace, surrounded by a hundred subjects. A priest asks God to protect and Mary to intercede on behalf of the people assembled in a church. Hundreds flock to see new relics of saints brought from distant lands, bringing gifts to the saints' earthly stewards. Supporters of rival candidates for bishop shout slogans and wave banners. As a pope takes power, crowds of clergy and laymen acclaim him as their chosen one. From the sphere of heaven, troops of angels and saints look down on the inhabitants of this world. At the end of time, "multitudes, multitudes" will gather in the valley of decision to be judged by the Lord.[4]

Crowds like these are ubiquitous in early medieval sources. In conceptual isolation, agricultural, mercantile, liturgical, ecclesiastical, monastic, elite, non-elite, and imaginary gatherings have enjoyed scholarly interest. But scholars have not brought these disparate crowds together to ask what unites them in this age of the crowd's scarcity. Indeed, some may doubt whether such gatherings, excepting rare acts of non-elite crowd resistance and the rowdy politics of southern cities, were really "crowds" at all.

The argument of this book is that the history of early medieval crowds, taken as a whole, tells a meaningful story: one of systemic, scalar change in economic and social life and of reorganization in the world of ideas and norms. In the early medieval West, gatherings became a scare resource, and this changed how people thought about them and what it was possible to do with them. At the same time, early medieval culture remained bound up with a Roman past marked by abundant multitudes. Crowds, being open to the imagination, escaped the confines of real-world demographic limits. The lens of the crowd allows us to see how reality and ideal responded to drastic change.

There were meaningful differences in how post-Roman crowds worked from setting to setting, particularly between the more urbanized south and the less urbanized north. But the crowd as subject illuminates early medieval Europe's structural coherencies in diachronic and synchronic comparison. By contrasting the early medieval European case to the Roman past and later medieval future, or to the Byzantine and Islamic present, a new crowd regime in Western Europe, c. 500–1000, comes into view.

What happened to collective behaviors—riots, assemblies, armed bands, violent groups, peaceful gatherings, religious processions, mass calamities, and laboring crowds—and the words, images, and ideas that stood for them between c. 500 and c. 1000?

In broad terms, in the wake of fifth- to seventh-century urban and demographic change, physical gatherings became smaller, less frequent, and less spontaneous. The uses to which they were put were circumscribed. Crowds were more predictable, more controllable. Ideas about their legitimacy changed. A negative discourse of mobs attenuated. Without regular riots, the word for a "riot" (*turba*) was given over to more peaceable assemblies.[5] This contrasts with contemporary Byzantium and Islam, where urban multitudes remained large, frequent, unpredictable, and discursively ambivalent.

Yet the early medieval European crowd regime, for all its peculiarity, was inventive and influential. Later European history owed more than has been recognized to this unusual chapter of crowd history. Laws of collective responsibility, politics of assembly, and the discourse of crowds, including both positive links between crowds and legitimacy and enduring negative associations between crowds and women, have early medieval roots. This book uses the crowd to situate the legacy of early medieval Europe in its wider history. But first, it is necessary to define what is meant by "crowd."

The Crowd as Historical Subject

The fact that there is no concerted study of the crowd in early medieval Europe makes this period exceptional. Innumerable settings across human history have been examined through this prism.[6] But what sort of scholarly subject is the crowd? The word alone casts a large semantic net.[7] Even by a narrow definition, like the *Oxford English Dictionary*'s ("large number of persons gathered so closely together as to press upon or impede each other; a throng, a dense multitude"), there are endless ways of tackling "the crowd" as a topic of investigation.[8]

First, there is the old crowd psychology, which defines the "crowd" as a gathering marked by shared mental alterity. Second, a sociological take on the psychological crowd focuses on collective effervescence as a component of ritual. Third, literary scholars and art historians pursue crowd representations in speech, writing, or art. Fourth—and most commonly in the discipline of history—crowds become proxies for the motives of the socially marginalized. Each of these approaches (barring the first, perhaps) has something to recommend it, but all, as we will see, are unsuited to the early medieval story. A new synthetic approach, influenced by a more recent sociology of crowds, is proposed instead.

Crowd Psychology: The "Open" Crowd

In classic psychological theory, a "crowd" is a gathering in a state of alterity. Participants lose their sense of self, decouple from normal social roles, and feel, say, or do things they never would in everyday life. The history of crowds by this definition is the story of how contingent values and institutions interact with a transhistorical psychotropic. Within this framework, there have been two ways of proceeding, one focused on collective behavior as the dissolver of social order, and the other focused on it as the servant of social order. Elias Canetti (1905–94) articulated this as the difference between "open" crowds (spontaneous, egalitarian, temporary), and "closed" crowds (nonspontaneous, hierarchical, perennial), a distinction to which we will return.[9]

The best-known account of the "open" crowd comes from nineteenth- and early twentieth-century crowd psychology.[10] Typical is Gustave Le Bon (1841–1931), author of the influential *Psychology of Crowds* (1894).[11] Le Bon insisted that numbers alone do not make a crowd.[12] Shared goals triggered a metamorphosis from mere gathering to "psychological crowd" (*foule psychologique*). He portrayed this shared crowd-mind as irrational, violent, and emotional, likening it to drunkenness, femaleness, childishness, and savagery, but acknowledging its power. Its natural impulse was to demolish, but its emotionality made it manipulatable.[13]

This approach casts an ambivalent shadow. Today, scholars are more inclined to study the antidemocratic, misogynistic, or racist politics Le Bon and his ilk smuggled into their ideas than to take them seriously.[14] But the traditional crowd psychology influenced the theories of Freud and Bernays, guided the policies of dictators and populists, and still informs the more palatable sociology and anthropology of the crowd.

Durkheim and Turner: The "Closed" Crowd

The "closed" crowd, in Canetti's terminology, is the domesticated version of the "open" one. Its theorists begin with the same premise that crowds trigger a state of giddy exception, but they ask how this state is used in the interests of social order. Festivals solidify group identity. Focal rites direct attention, veneration, or hostility toward a target. Reversal rituals, like the carnival as world-upside-down of Mikhail Bakhtin, offer release from the burdens of hierarchy.[15] This crowd breaks society apart in order to keep it going.

The foundational articulation comes from Le Bon's contemporary, the French sociologist Émile Durkheim (1858–1917). "As soon as individuals come together," he argued, "there arises from their interaction a kind of electricity that rapidly transports them to an extraordinary pitch of exaltation."[16] While this electricity was sometimes destructive, Durkheim believed "collective effervescence" provided stability to social realities.[17] It made change (relatively) safely. The norm-bending "liminality" of collective action, as Arnold van Gennep (1873–1957) called it, facilitated rites of passage.[18] The anthropologist Victor Turner (1920–83) developed an even rosier vision of this: crowd alterity as "communitas," whose effects "flood their subjects with affect."[19]

The Durkheimian or Turnerian approach, focused on the making of social order through controlled deconstruction, has proven more attractive to historians than the pejorative essentialism of Le Bon. Both reuse the same transhistorical claim: minds transform in a crowd. But there is a deeper functional point: whatever their stated purposes, crowds serve as a social maintenance project. Perhaps some Romans grasped that games and circuses functioned as a "safety valve" to hinder riots or as a "microcosm of empire" to induce solidarity; it hardly matters. The social scientist seeks the crowd's "etic" function (the outsider explanation), not its "emic" one (the insider explanation).[20]

Limitations of "Open" and "Closed" Crowds

There is something to all this. Experiments have detected raised levels of opioids and endorphins as well as coordinated heartbeats in those performing or just watching synchronized activities.[21] Societies doubtless adapted to changes in human physiology triggered by collective behavior. Nevertheless, there are problems with any definition of the crowd that stakes everything on mental transformation.

There are other, more fundamental, ways of characterizing collective behavior. Swarms of insects, schools of fish, flocks of birds, and herds of mammals perform coordinated behavior in which individual interactions add up to something greater. Although the mental or hormonal state of animals may alter when collective behavior is underway, that is not what defines the phenomenon. Instead, scientists stress an emergent problem-solving capacity, a kind of artificial intelligence arising from a cascade of individual stimuli.[22]

This emergent collective problem-solving serves many functions: risk mitigation, exchange of care, acquisition of information. Crowd theory's focus on altered mental states—put bluntly, how our one species reacts physiologically to collective behavior—is limited. After all, gatherings do more in human societies than to flood minds with affect. They offer strength in numbers, a venue for resource exchange, an efficient mechanism for sharing news, an occasion for deliberation, a chance for pleasure, and a public sphere. All these functions might be accompanied by the shared altered mental state that interested Le Bon, Durkheim, and Turner. None of them require it.

There is also an evidential problem. How can historians detect fleeting mental transformations from second-hand reports? Across the literature, there is a version of Potter Stewart's test for obscenity: "I know it when I see it." But what if participants are disengaged or faking it? Theodor Adorno argued that totalitarian crowds depend not on real mass unity, but on the coercive manipulation of its appearance.[23] The "function" of the crowd in societies may be a result of seeming rather than being. This speaks to the enduring importance of discourse.

The Crowd in Discourse

The "crowd" is an idea as much as a reality.[24] To cultural, literary, or intellectual historians, this makes it an important subject in its own right. One does not need to read the mind of dead participants or reconstruct ephemeral details of assembly, action, and dispersal. Discourse is revelatory on its own.[25]

For premodernists, an influential model is Erich Auerbach (1892–1957).[26] A historicist in the tradition of Vico, Auerbach believed representation was the key "to grasp the special nature of an epoch."[27] For him, crowd representations were particularly revelatory. Tacitus's motiveless crowd reflected his aristocratic worldview; Ammianus Marcellinus's grotesque crowd reflected late antique mannerism.[28] Although scholars quibble with Auerbach's historicism, his work has inspired studies of the literary crowd.[29]

That includes work on the later medieval crowd (c. 1000–1500). Several studies explore the figure of the crowd in sermons, exempla, and literature.[30] Alexander Murray has shown how twelfth-century university men nourished a snobbish discourse of mobs and rabbles.[31] Gary Dickson has probed the conception of crowds in later medieval spirituality, and the fears they awakened in thinkers like Roger Bacon, who worried that heresiarchs possessed a power of *fascinatio*, or "bewitchment," over crowds, just as Gustave Le Bon thought that leaders enthralled crowds by a sort of hypnotism.[32] Sara Lipton has explored the moral and civic significance of the crowd's gaze in late medieval art and society, particularly with respect to the depiction of Jews.[33] Two valuable articles on early medieval crowds, by Joaquín Martínez Pizarro and Hugh Magennis, were written in this literary mode.[34]

In discourse history, evidential vices become virtues. If a text copies a type scene from the Bible, this reveals an authorial filter. If it oscillates between concrete gatherings (a crowd) and abstractions (the people), this illuminates a thought-world. Nevertheless, most discourse histories share Auerbach's interest in the realities behind representations. They seek the economic, social, and political context behind crowds-in-texts.

The "Historical" Crowd: Rudé, Thompson, Davis

Since the mid-twentieth century, historians have approached that task in a particular way, focused on non-elite motivations. In the 1930s, the pioneer of bottom-up history Georges Lefebvre (1874–1959) attacked Le Bon's crowd as vague and stereotyped.[35] In 1961, the British Marxian historian George Rudé (1910–93) followed through with a definition of the crowd limited to "what sociologists term a 'face-to-face' or 'direct contact' group and not any type of collective phenomenon."[36] Rudé attacked scholars "preoccupied with mental states." He criticized the mission creep of theorists who used the term "crowd" to describe all imaginable collectivities. This, he argued, conflated analysis with judgment. "The crowd" became everything good or everything bad about (non-elite) collectivity: "the people" versus "the rabble."[37]

Rudé jettisoned "crowds" he felt were irrelevant to social history: casual onlookers, crowds assembled "on purely ceremonial occasions," event audiences whether passive or participatory, and "outbursts of mass hysteria." Such gatherings, he argued, may be "fascinating material for the student of crowd psychology, but they may be of only casual interest to the historian."[38] He limited himself to eighteenth- and nineteenth-century "strikes, riots, rebellions, insurrections, and revolutions."[39]

This pruning was the culmination of a long-term effort in sociology and history to rescue a social-scientific concept from metaphorical contamination.[40] In practice, it meant using prosopography and price/wage data to reconstruct the motives behind non-elite political crowds.[41] Strikes, riots, and the like were not the flailing rages of a disgruntled underclass, but reasoned reactions to socioeconomic stimuli, filtered through contemporary values and expectations. Just as Rudé recast eighteenth- and nineteenth-century workers' uprisings as reasoned actions, medievalists like Rodney Hilton, Michel Mollat, and Philippe Wolff found "real" socioeconomic causes for late medieval peasant revolts and heretical movements.[42] Common folk grabbed firebrands, followed millenarian leaders, or attacked minorities not because of a mob mentality, but for identifiable reasons rooted in class-based antagonisms and economic hardships.[43]

Still, something was missing. Rudé conceded that some crowds—moments of religious hysteria or pure rage, for instance—fell outside of the "historian's" (meaning the social or economic historian's) purview, and properly belonged to the psychologist or the scholar of religion. In the early 1970s, two historians, E. P. Thompson and Natalie Davis, reclaimed this *terra incognita* for history. In Thompson's 1971 article "The Moral Economy of the Eighteenth-Century English Crowd" and Davis's 1973 article "The Rites of Violence," and in their related articles on English and French charivaris, they altered the way historians talked about crowds for decades.[44]

The Moral Economy and the Rites of Violence: Thompson and Davis

At the heart of both contributions was the cultural turn. Instead of seeking socioeconomic explanations for crowd behavior, they sought what Thompson called a "legitimizing notion," the fact that "the men and women in the crowd were informed by the belief that they were defending traditional rights or customs; and, in general, that they were supported by the wider consensus of the community."[45]

Thompson criticized earlier historians for treating food riots as lurching reactions to hardship. Food riots were not "spasmodic" responses to grumbling stomachs, but the work of offended minds, responding in a culturally rooted fashion. Eighteenth-century rioters saw themselves as upholding a violated "moral economy" of price and distribution. They were "fixing" the price of bread (a quasi-legal procedure); they felt they had to do this because the government and gentry had failed to. In Davis, religious violence worked similarly. The crowd's exclamations mimicked the exhortations of pastors; its rough justice, the punishments of magistrates; its pageantry, routine liturgy, and folk tradition. For both, "the crowd" was a "curious continuation" of "repertory" under abnormal conditions: the people taking on the job of the authorities.[46]

These interventions prompted a shift. Formerly, non-elite crowds were seen as acting out of desperation. Doomed riots, orgies of violence, and ecstatic religious acts were quintessential "open" crowds. People suffering from what Durkheim called "anomie," the sense of being left out, turned to group unruliness out of alienation. The "economizing" explanation restored some of these crowds to a more precise rationality—their misrule being rooted in specific hardships—but Rudé's socioeconomic crowd was still saying a desperate "no" to a malign social order. Thompson and Davis, however, saw food riots and lynch mobs as would-be "closed" crowds. These crowds appealed to norms and aped official rituals. If people are primed by "repertory" (law, ritual) to think that the world is periodically made right by crowds, then riotous or ecstatic gatherings are not desperate rebellions against the status quo, but rational efforts to maintain it. This inversion—"open" crowds turn out to be "closed" crowds in anomic conditions—is central to Thompson's "moral economy of the crowd" and to Davis's "reasons of misrule" and "rites of violence," and has proven justly influential.[47]

Still, in Thompson, Davis, and those influenced by them (including some critics), a breach, or a perception of a breach, always separates crowd and repertory. Thompson's crowd defends a moral economy affronted. Davis's religious rioters act because order has not been defended "officially" and "formally."[48] Officialness or formalness becomes the absence that defines a crowd. But how should historians identify the border between norm and exception? In practice, historians look for non-elites acting unusually. If laborers take arms against their masters despite the inevitability of defeat, if commoners engage in ecstatic acts despite recriminations, if neighbors attack neighbors despite the social damage it causes—in short, if collective behavior is non-elite, anomalous, and maybe a little hopeless—that makes it a "crowd."

But the crowd–repertory dichotomy, for all its explanatory power, is as arbitrary and unprovable as Le Bon's distinction between the gathering and the "psychological crowd." If the distinction is between gatherings that resist public order (e.g., a riot that breaches a ruler's palace) and those that constitute it (e.g., a procession organized by the ruler), the deciding factor is a sense of public order.[49] But whose? If disruptive crowds turn out to be motivated by a desire to defend proper order after all, this distinction, as Suzanne Desan has noted, allows historians to have their cake and eat it too.[50] It is as if historians uphold the crowd–repertory distinction in order to be able to blur it.

Moreover, dividing collective behavior into repertory and crowds insists that the defining function of gatherings is to regulate order. In "repertory," order is shaped officially by elites; in a "crowd," unofficially by non-elites. Hence, the former tends to be associated with elite domination and the latter with non-elite resistance, or, at least, agency. Certainly, it is possible to categorize gatherings this way. But if we consider other functions, the limitations of this approach become clear. In all premodern societies, a crucial function of gatherings is to act as venues of information exchange. Yet historians do not draw a categorical distinction between gatherings in which information is shared vertically by design (sermons, assemblies) and those in which it is shared incidentally and horizontally (harvests, markets). Such a distinction might be analytically useful, but it would not occur to anyone to insist that the former are "real" crowds and the latter are some other kind of gathering.

The Crowd Regime of the Early Middle Ages

How then should we define the crowd in early medieval Europe? One way would be to use the restrictive definition of the historiography—the crowd as non-elite transgressive extension of normal social behavior—and to ask how this stably unstable subject was affected by post-Roman scale change. Applying this approach to the early Middle Ages would mean investigating an imbalance in domination and resistance. The period is known for orderly assemblies organized by elites, not for popular uprisings. One finds, in Davis's terms, "repertory" but not "the crowd," in Canetti's, "closed" but not "open" crowds. In 1980, Moore spoke for many when he argued that "the crowd" in its usual historiographical sense was largely absent in early medieval Europe.[51]

One could attempt to substantiate, explain, or add nuance to that observation. Did a lack of opportunities for resistant crowds deprive the marginalized of a means of asserting themselves? Did other weapons of the weak replace them? Hilton, Wickham, Goldberg, Rembold, and others have ably pursued these questions.[52] One could dwell on regional exceptions. For instance, Italian cities held onto rowdier crowds than other regions of post-Roman Europe. Brown, Herrin, and West-Harling have located the causes in Italy's greater urbanism and Byzantine political traditions.[53] These are valid perspectives, but they exclude the nonpolitical majority of early medieval gatherings.

Another way would be to focus on discourse, to conduct a literary history in the Auerbachian mode centered on the early medieval depiction of collective behavior. Here, one could question Moore's framing, and ask to what extent the apparent absence of historiographically familiar "crowds" is a mirage of the sources—and this is just what Moore himself wondered in a 2016 reconsideration of his 1980 argument.[54] One could ask how classical and Christian patterns of representation influenced writers c. 500–1000. This book certainly considers the extent to which biblical and hagiographical topoi inform the legitimizing crowd that predominates in surviving texts, even as classical contempt for unruly crowds did not entirely die out.

But the present study is more interested in how physical and discursive crowds interacted. To do this, it proposes the concept of an early medieval "crowd regime," a holistic ideal type of how collective behavior was organized and represented. In thinking about physical phenomena, it borrows the neutral term "gathering" from sociologist Clark McPhail.[55] A "gathering" is a crowd in the most neutral sense: active or passive, large or small, orderly or disorderly.[56] The term presupposes nothing about motivation, psychological state, or "officialness." It simply refers to numbers. This offers a way forward that depends on neither the "madding crowd" of crowd theory nor the self-effacing distinction between "crowd" and "repertory."

In thinking about the discourse history of crowds in this period—the blurring of technical differences, the attenuation of negative discourse, the tendency to associate crowds with legitimacy—this book balances two opposing tendencies. First, early medieval concepts drew upon classical and Roman models; second, they arose from new logistics of assembly. Instead of starting with prefabricated assumptions about what a "real" crowd must be, the goal is to trace the mutual interaction of gatherings and their representations.

The distinctive role of crowds in early medieval societies was a function of these different modalities. In diachronic and synchronic comparison, early medieval Europe was under-supplied with gatherings. Between c. 500 and c. 1000, many complex systems in the West—economies, social hierarchies, political regimes—adapted to a smaller demographic scale. But scale change, though it acts as a frame, does not fully explain the early medieval crowd regime. Post-Roman Europe was not much less densely populated than long stretches of the Iron Age before the Roman Empire. What sets this period apart is not downward scaling alone, but contraction alongside engagement with the Roman and Christian past.

In early medieval Europe, gatherings retained great importance. In economic and social life, they coordinated labor, information, and resources in seasonal venues. This made them easier to predict and manipulate by those controlling assembly. But although crowds ceased to be a weapon of the weak in the sense that non-elite uprisings were rare, as a tool of the strong, crowds had limits. Since resource extraction and authority depended on numbers, gatherings were an expensive necessity. They were vulnerable to resistance and misdirection too. In a world where taking dues, giving justice, providing pastoral care, and receiving political consent depended on the physical assembly of dependents or followers, refusal to assemble—or the choice to assemble on behalf of one lord as opposed to another—were effective tools of resistance and competition. A measure of this is a new pejorative discourse of rustic, foreign, and female crowds that arose from the 500s to the 800s, almost as a strategy of desperation, to replace the lost Roman language of rabbles and mobs. In discourse, crowds retained their electricity, but they were wired differently.

The dichotomy between crowd and repertory favored in the historiography—the religious riot versus the holiday procession—is not universal. It is best suited to demographically dense, economically complex societies with clear distinctions between public and private life, pronounced axes of domination and resistance, and regular non-elite recourse to crowd action in the form of riots and protests (complex anti-institutions whose existence cannot be taken for granted). These are the historical ecologies best known to crowd history. They include Greco-Roman Antiquity, the high and later Middle Age, the early modern West, the early industrial world, and our own times. But early medieval

Europe was a different environment. There was a blurrier distinction between public and private, so that differentiating "official" and "unofficial" crowds is difficult. While there are sometimes clear lines of domination and resistance, for most rural non-elites, passive resistance was a safer, more effective recourse than mass assembly. This meant that crowds served all the more powerfully as a source of legitimacy in this period, given the marshaling of resources and interclass cohesion it took to assemble them.

Sources and Structure

To trace this change, the present study uses texts, manuscripts, archaeology, artwork, and computational philology. The archaeology of churches, monasteries, palaces, cities, markets, and settlements in which gatherings assembled has improved markedly in the last half-century. It is easier than it once was to reconstruct a horizon of possibilities for gatherings in the post-Roman West. Early medieval narrative and literary sources are almost comprehensively word-searchable after decades of labor. Data-mining tools have enabled the comprehensive analysis of the early medieval language of crowds. Back in 1971, a valuable study focused on the use of the single term *populus* in two authors; now, with searchable databases rather than indices and concordances, it is possible to see at a glance, author by author, century by century, how thousands of texts used dozens of different crowd words.[57] Deluxe images of crowds in manuscripts and the visual arts are increasingly digitized and published.[58] Many of the logistical challenges of engaging upon a project of this purview have been eased by these developments. This book is aware of its debts: only thanks to decades of patient and skillful labor by others is it possible to ask these broader questions.

There are risks inherent to the sources of this period, which will be discussed in greater detail in the chapters below. Two should be foregrounded. First, early medieval written sources disproportionately represent the perceptions of elites, especially male ecclesiastical elites who monopolized (but never entirely) the written word. Second, such authors tended to use topoi inherited from the Roman and Christian literary past. One reason early medieval crowds seem so peaceful and pious is that early medieval texts were written by ecclesiastical authors copying hagiographical or biblical models. If we characterize these depictions as "typical" of early medieval perceptions of the crowd, we risk overstating or overinterpreting the evidence. It is not easy to say how typical one representation of the "crowd" really was in any given period.[59] This study attempts to overcome this difficulty by putting the written evidence in conversation with nonliterary sources, but the methodological difficulty should be mentioned at the outset.

The Crowd in the Early Middle Ages is roughly divided into two parts. The first examines gatherings as physical phenomena. The second turns to the crowd as idea. A background chapter (chapter 1) sets up the Roman legacy with which the early medieval crowd regime was in conversation. A chapter on numbers (chapter 2) uses archaeology and demography to reconstruct the size and density of crowds in the early medieval West, showing the downward scaling in the possibilities for post-Roman gathering. The subsequent chapters (chapters 3 and 4) examine the resulting ecology of gatherings, in non-elite and elite contexts. Despite constraints upon assembly generated by the new demographic regime, the seasonality of agricultural labor, warfare, political culture, and liturgy allowed for the regular assembly of large numbers. Crowds, it will be argued, played a central role in questions of domination, resistance (including "slantwise" resistance), and competition, but in new ways.

In the second part, a chapter on words (chapter 5) traces the semantic history of crowd words and expressions in early medieval Latin, looking also to Gothic, Romance, Old High German, Old English, and Greek. This shows a loss of specificity and negative connotations in the vocabulary of collective behavior. Finally, a chapter on representation (chapter 6) uncovers some of the patterns with which early medieval writers described collective behaviors: clichés and type scenes that repeat themselves in hagiography, history, liturgy, poetry, and other genres. Here, the focus is on a discursive elision between physical gatherings and the wider abstractions of community or group they can be made to stand for. Attention is given to negative exceptions: the rustics, foreigners, and women used by elite authors to account for "bad" crowds. It concludes with the political, religious, and legal institutions organized around mixture of reality and ideal. The book ends with a transformation around 1000: an age of mass pilgrimages, great assemblies, open-air sermons, and, ultimately, crusades that marked a departure.

The historiography on the topic of crowds in the early Middle Ages directly has, until recently, been small, limited to a handful of literary studies, essays on violence in early medieval Italian cities, and work on peasant collective action.[60] Yet the subject has ramifications for many spheres of interest for early medieval historians, and, in certain respects, has been touched on by many of them.[61] Early medieval Christianity, from churchgoing to the cult of relics to councils, is bound up with crowds.[62] Numbers were a scarce resource that elites struggled to control, making crowds a revealing vista onto early medieval social and political power.[63] Gatherings are at the heart of a vibrant historiography on assemblies.[64] Two excellent recent collections, on legal consensus and assembly culture, stress the order-making role of gatherings in the early Middle Ages.[65] The subject also touches upon the efficacy and mechanics of early medieval law.[66] Were crowds of witnesses called for in legal texts summoned in reality, or did they prove more effective in the breach (that is, in protecting elites from prosecution)? Finally, this subject speaks to the way later medieval collective forms—from liturgical gatherings to parliaments—arose from early medieval precedents.[67]

A wider view illuminates all these questions. Even in the face of logistical hurdles to assembly in the early Middle Ages, bishops, abbots, abbesses, counts, kings, and queens found ways to mobilize gatherings to assert power over or extract resources from subjects and to legitimize religious or political behavior. Non-elites too developed uses for crowds, including acts of resistance by nonparticipation and ways of getting by that resisted the intentions of elites in a more "slantwise" manner.[68] The prominence of the crowd in this period, its value as a way of organizing resources and legitimacy, was a reflection of the peculiar circumstances of early medieval Europe. This helps us grasp an essential truth about this period. Scholars have debated whether to understand Europe, c. 500 to 1000, as an extension of antiquity or as a prelude to the later Middle Ages.[69] The "crowd" helps us see how this period was its own entity, an age of demographic and logistical constraint committed to remaining as Roman as possible. The history of how a Roman way of crowds gave way to a distinctively early medieval one illuminates the slipperiness of ideas, historiographical and otherwise, about crowds. It is a story that helps us recognize the instability of "the crowd" as we know it now.

1

The Roman Legacy

Crowds in Roman Antiquity

If the centuries between 500 and 1000 were the "Long Morning of Medieval Europe," the party the night before was the history of the Roman Empire.[1] From the crops people cultivated, to the built environments they inhabited, to the languages they spoke and the beliefs they espoused, the legacy of Rome saturated early medieval Europe. This was true not only for regions that "stayed Roman" as much and as long as they could, such as Italy, southern Gaul, Spain, and North Africa, but for places outside the bounds of empire: the Celtic fringe, what is now northern and eastern Germany and Central Europe, Scandinavia, the Slavlands.[2] To understand the place of crowds in the early Middle Ages, it is necessary to begin with the place of crowds in Roman Antiquity.

The Roman world was full of gatherings. Crowds thickened the streets of the empire's multitude of cities.[3] They filled theaters, circuses, and amphitheaters.[4] They walked in processions, celebrated festivals, ate at public banquets, and marveled at triumphs.[5] They bathed together in prodigious numbers, and used the toilet together in grand imperial latrines.[6] They thronged around orators and religious leaders. They grieved at funerals, or interrupted them.[7] They united their voices in praise of leaders and officials, expressed formal grievances, and seized rocks or firebrands when their voices went unheard.[8] Crowds held a formal place in Rome's political ideologies, and wrenched power from the hands of its elites in practice.[9] Temples, roads, basilicas, forums, baths, entertainment buildings, and walls were constructed by and used by multitudes.[10] In the countryside, gangs of slaves and harvesters populated fields that fed millions.[11] Crowds perished together in Rome's disasters, when the bleachers of amphitheaters and circuses collapsed, in acts of mass punishment, in religious and political violence, in the course of wars, sacks, fires, famines, and invasions, and during the throes of epidemic disease.[12] After death, crowds of shades lined the roads that led to Roman cities, their ashes packed in *columbaria* ("pigeon-coops," the nickname for Roman family mausolea), their bones populating cities of the dead beyond the boundaries of settlement.[13]

The Roman crowd is an enormous topic, the subject of its own multifaceted and voluminous scholarship, and beyond the scope of this book. The present chapter restricts itself to three observations that inform the early medieval case. First, the urban-oriented Roman political, social, and economic world was capable of sustaining gatherings on a vastly larger scale than became possible in the early Middle Ages. Second, gatherings acquired an enduring place in Roman institutions; they did diverse political and cultural work in a consistent manner. Third, they were culturally productive in an ambivalent way; crowds provoked strong negative and positive discourse. To paraphrase Catullus, it was a case of *odi et amo*. Romans hated the crowd, and they loved it.

These three factors—scale, institutional importance, and discursive ambivalence—set the Roman crowd apart. To be sure, all human societies know crowds. The herds of extinct mammals painted tens of thousands of years ago in caves show that hunter-gatherers pondered the animal crowds around them and evoked them in firelit rituals. The world's oldest-known cities—Çatalhöyük, Mohenjo-Daro, Uruk, Nebelivka, and Jericho—preserve hints, in spatial organization, of the importance of collective behavior.[14] Long before Rome, Mediterranean cities had nurtured complex collective institutions and polarized sensibilities. Beyond the Mediterranean, crowds thronged Persian palaces, trailed processions of Maurya royal chariots, earned the scorn of Han intellectuals, and watched the ballgame in Mayan cities. Rome was not unique in making crowds important. But crowds were especially prominent and productive in Roman law, culture, and public life.

Why? First, the scale of Roman urbanism was rivaled only by ancient China.[15] Whole regional economies bent themselves to the task of maintaining cities and armies, agglomerations of humanity unrivaled in western Eurasia until early modern times. Second, Rome had once been a republic, in which the "common people," the *plebs* or *populus*, achieved a hard-won political role alongside the patricians. Distant as the days of tribunes and voting assemblies were in the last years of empire, the founding fiction of Roman law was that authority ascended from collective consent.[16] Third, the tensions within Roman society kept crowds electric. Factions marshaled crowds against each other, and the rights and wrongs of collective behavior were endlessly invoked, in fruitfully inconsistent ways.[17]

Rome was no monolith; across regions and over time, "Roman" crowds and discourse about them changed. That is particularly relevant in thinking about medieval Europe as an heir of Rome. Rome for seventh- to tenth-century Europeans was not the Rome of the Republic or the Principate, but the Rome of Late Antiquity (c. 300–600 CE). This period has been seen as an inflection point in the history of crowds.[18] One task of this chapter is to differentiate the late Roman story from the more familiar earlier one.

At the same time, as Anthony Kaldellis has stressed, Roman history had continuities that survived in Byzantium (the "Roman Republic," as it still called itself as Mehmet II's guns blasted the Theodosian walls).[19] From the vantage point of the European early Middle Ages, it can be necessary to squint to see differences between republican, imperial, and Byzantine crowds. The *contiones* and *comitia* (information-gathering and voting assemblies) of first-century BCE Republican Rome, the *circumcelliones* (slogan-shouting, club-wielding Donatists) of fourth-century CE rural North Africa, and the *demoi* (circus factions) of sixth-century Constantinople were worlds apart. But looking backward from the post-Roman centuries, their differences blur, as with distinct trees in a forest seen from the prairie. All were well-organized civilian gatherings, with durable group identities consolidated by ritual action. For all their diversity, Roman crowds had some commonalities from the age of Cicero to the age of Justinian.

The Crowd from the Republic to the Principate (c. 400 BCE–300 CE)

Between the fourth century BCE and the first centuries of the common era, Rome went from a relatively small settlement to a megalopolis at the center of an empire. Its vibrant crowd regime was part of a wider Mediterranean urban culture to which Rome was a relative latecomer. Rome had home-grown collective institutions in politics and religion. The senate, tribal assembly, the *comitia* and *contiones*, and plebeian council upheld the principle that public affairs were to be handled in assembly.[20] Processions, festivals, feasts, and pomps filled religious life with gatherings.[21] In law and politics, public speaking was a crucial elite skill.[22] The perfect orator, as Cicero argued, had to earn his "crown" (*corona*) of listeners by showing the facility of the famous actor Roscius:[23]

> Here is what I want to happen to my orator: when it is heard that he is going to speak, let every place on the benches be taken, the tribunal full, the scribes willing to grant or give up places, the crowd multitudinous [*corona multiplex*], the judge spellbound; when the man about to speak rises, silence is signaled for by the crowd [*corona*], next there are frequent acts of assent and much applause; laughter, when he wishes, when he wishes, tears; so that if someone should see it from afar, even if he did not know what was going on, he would nevertheless understand that he was pleasing [*placere*] and that a Roscius was on the stage.[24]

On the other hand, in the Republic, crowds had their bad side. Votives of foreign rites (like the bacchanals of the second century BCE) and sworn conspirators were to be prevented from assembling together.[25] Like most ancient civilizations, Rome faced urban riots from its plebeian and artisanal classes. The "symbolic actions" of these crowds developed around Roman institutions and spaces: attacking statues, targeting urban mansions, breaking *fasces*, disrupting court proceeding.[26] Roman law punished brawling (*rixa*), riot (*turba*), and sedition (*seditio*) with escalating severity.[27]

When the Republic ceded to monarchy in the first century BCE, new forms of mass communication and entertainment developed around the person of the princeps, the "first citizen," and his ministers. Euergetism, self-serving "do-goodery" by elites, had long taken the form of public munificence in the Greco-Roman world; emperors took up this philanthropic duty on an imperial scale.[28] In the second half of the first century CE, the Colosseum, that most enduring symbol of Roman crowds, rose on the site where Nero's engineers had built his artificial lake: here and at other "crowd containers," the people were courted and subdued.[29] Shows served as celebrations and microcosms of empire.[30] After his second war against the Dacians (105–106 CE), the emperor Trajan, according to a (possibly exaggerating) later historian, held 123 days of celebrations at Rome, with 10,000 gladiators and 11,000 beasts.[31] Such spectacles were seen by fabulously large audiences. The Colosseum's capacity was around 50,000, that of the Circus Maximus, around 150,000; these were the largest of many entertainment buildings in the capital. At hundreds of smaller theaters, amphitheaters, and circuses in cities around the empire, audiences of thousands and tens of thousands were titillated.

Crowds served as an important venue of communication between rulers and ruled. Staged provincial displays of collective consent or discontent at public ceremonies—as well as more spontaneous collective acts—were transmitted to authorities. Such displays took the form of acclamations (Latin *acclamationes*, Greek *phonai*), coordinated, rhythmical shouts meant to express either "applause, praise, and congratulations" or "reproach, imprecation, and demands."[32] From the first century onward, acclamations became, in Clifford Ando's words, "the primary vehicle through which the population of an entire city could ritually recognize the charisma of a particular ruler and the legitimacy of his government."[33]

Riots continued to be "a surprisingly common feature of life" in imperial Rome. Even in stable stretches of imperial history, they served "as a tacitly allowed informal institution for popular expression" when official lines of communication failed.[34] In the 200s, revolts, rebellions, and riots became more numerous, and punishments meted out to illicit gatherings took a turn for the harsher.[35] Still, they were given space. Riots centered on perceived injustices in the supply or pricing of food, what Cassiodorus later called the *querela panis*.[36] As with the "moral economy" of the eighteenth-century crowd, participants felt that they defended "traditional rights or customs," and authorities did not always disagree.[37]

Efforts to win over crowds by munificence continued. Despite Septimius Severus's (193–211 CE) advice to his sons to "enrich the soldiers, ignore the rest," Severus held grand *ludi saeculares* ("centurial games") in 204 to impress the masses. The baths built by his son Caracalla could accommodate more people than any yet constructed (he was eventually outdone by Diocletian). Caracalla's Antonine Constitution of 212 extended citizenship, and its rights, to all free men in the empire: a gift to millions. Amid the crises of a volatile century, Philip the Arab (244–249 CE) celebrated Rome's thousandth birthday (April 21, 248) with his own *ludi saeculares* featuring numerous animals and a thousand pairs of gladiators. This was a far cry from Trajan's Dacian celebrations 140 years earlier, but showed the same logic: Roman crowds were entitled to the best.[38]

The Crowd in Late Antiquity (c. 300–600)

Late Antiquity (c. 300–600) saw profound changes across the Roman world. The late third- and early fourth-century empire rebuilt itself as a more centralized, militaristic, and autocratic state: the dominate.[39] Christianity went from persecuted to state religion. The politics, culture, and economy of the eastern provinces overshadowed those of the West. At the end of the period, Roman administration in the West collapsed, except as a shadow of itself or an extension of Constantinople, and "barbarian" successor kingdoms—albeit Roman-looking ones—arose in its place. Historians have argued that these transformations marked a turning point in the history of crowds too.[40]

Crowd Violence and Late Antique Politics

This is because Late Antiquity has seemed, as Júlio César Magalhães de Oliveira writes, "an age of crowds."[41] Above all, violent ones. From the club-brandishing *circumcelliones* of North Africa, to the throngs of Alexandrian monks who murdered the pagan philosopher Hypatia, to the so-called *bacaudae* (peasant marauders) of Northern Spain and Southern Gaul, the "apparent increase in levels of collective violence" has attracted scholarly interest.[42] Historians disagree about the historical significance of the violent crowds of Late Antiquity. Some see them as a reflection of the military and political crises plaguing Roman society. Others see them as more of the same: traditional Roman dynamics with new protagonists in a new religious idiom. Still others see them as a mirage of the sources, highlighted because of new traumas or polemics.⁴³

It is not clear, numerically, that Late Antiquity saw more (or more violent) non-elite crowds than earlier moments of Roman history. Magalhães de Oliveira's catalogue of crowd actions from c. 300 to 600 CE finds about as much attested activity as Pekáry and Sünskes Thompson found for the period from 31 BCE to 235 CE—actually a little less.⁴⁴ But there may have been changes in how crowd violence worked. Magalhães de Oliveira argues for the crowd's "new political significance" as a "shift in the way in which ordinary people understood their role and power in local communities."⁴⁵ He sees this as a consequence of political centralization.⁴⁶ As with the pages of a book too tightly bound, the dominate threw wrinkles into local power structures. In a different way, Peter van Nuffelen roots a "virtue-based" model of late antique crowd behavior in the political expectations of Christian and Stoic concepts of leadership and justice.⁴⁷

The dominate also ramped up the political culture of ceremonial that connected legitimacy with orderly collective assent.⁴⁸ Few public events of the 300s and 400s—town council meetings, provincial assemblies, meetings of the senates of Rome or Constantinople, visits of luminaries, imperial proclamations—lacked performances of mass consensus. A famous case from December 25, 438 is the train of acclamations repeated by the Roman senate upon the ratification of the Theodosian Code in the West (which had been issued nine years before). The senators, assembled not at the senate house but in a magnificent private home at Rome, shouted slogans such as "Augustuses of Augustuses, greatest of Augustuses" (repeated eight times), "May it please our Augustuses to live forever!" (repeated twenty-two times), "These are the wishes of the senate, these are the wishes of the Roman people!" (repeated ten times), "Dearer than our children, dearer than our parents!" (repeated sixteen times), and "We give thanks for your regulation!" (repeated twenty-three times).⁴⁹ Ramsay MacMullen has calculated that the full performance of forty-three acclamations, each repeated between eight and twenty-eight times, for 748 speech acts in total, would have taken about two hours.⁵⁰ Doubtless it was planned and maybe rehearsed in advance. The confirmation of the Theodosian Code in 438 was particularly ornate, but staged consensus was a standard part of late Roman politics at nearly every level of society.

The senators who devoted Christmas Day to the otiose approval of a nine-year-old law code got something for their pains, even if it was only the feeling of senatorial self-importance. Emperors—really, the powers behind them, in this case Pulcheria in the East and Aetius in the West—understood the need to solicit recognition from "groups of acceptance."⁵¹ Unanimous assent from established parties, in the form of "lung power," was indispensable for Roman public legitimacy.[52] For those doing the shouting, collective performances, including stage-managed ones, opened a line of communication and a chance for self-assertion. Hence the paradoxical flavor of late Roman legitimacy, organized around strict hierarchy and pseudo-democratic consensus at the same time. This hot ice would endure in Byzantium.[53]

Christianity and Crowds

The most fateful novelty of the late antique period for crowd history was the fourth-century rise of Christianity to public prominence.[54] The late empire's Christians, after such recognition in the "Edict" of Milan (313 CE) and the Edict of Thessalonica (380 CE), worshipped openly, wielded coercive power, and controlled public space. Holy men, holy women, holy relics, and holy sites became public *loci* of charisma, their power (*virtus*) measured, in part, by the crowds they drew.[55] A bishop's strength, as with that of most urban elites, lay in his being a "controller of crowds."[56] The non-Christian Ammianus Marcellinus wryly remarked that Pope Damasus (366–384 CE), with his sprawling, factious retinue, cut the figure of a secular grandee.[57] But episcopal crowds, for believers, had the extra authority of the sacred. For Bishop Ambrose of Milan, episcopal suasion—backed up by chanting crowds—humbled an emperor.[58]

For Christians, crowds were doctrinally and historically ambivalent. Christ had preached to crowds, and done miracles for them, but crowds had also spurned and betrayed him. The Holy Spirit descended when Christians gathered together (Acts 2), but from Stephen onward, martyrs met death at the hands of crowds (Acts 7). As Christianity won recognition, divisions between Christians and non-Christians, and among Christian sects, were resolved by force of numbers, and contested in terms of them. Alexandria was notorious in the 300s and 400s for its sectarian street fights, though it had always had a reputation as a city of rabbles.[59] In 342, a violent scene unfolded in Constantinople among backers of rival bishops.[60] In 358, 366, 418–419, and 501–502, disputes over the papacy led to similar clashes in Rome. Conflicts over episcopal legitimacy caused a century of crowd violence between Catholics and Donatists in North Africa. A key question about this violence—a point on which scholars remain divided—is whether religiously motivated crowd violence differed fundamentally from its older secular equivalent, or whether the fault lines of "sacred violence" coincided with older "social cleavages."[61]

Numbers could resolve internal Christian disputes in more peaceable ways, in church councils presided over by bishops. These were one of the most important ancient legacies for the early medieval crowd. Church councils were closely modelled on the secular assemblies of the late Roman world, but imbued with authority by Christ's promise that he would be present whenever his followers assembled in his name (Matthew 18:20). Between the first ecumenical council of Nicaea (in 325) and the second ecumenical council of Constantinople (in 553), we know of some 255 church councils, with official attendance ranging between twelve and one thousand or more clerics (not counting retinues and lay attendees). In all likelihood, this is a fraction. According to the fifth canon of the council of Nicaea (325), provincial councils were to meet twice a year; this allows Ramsay MacMullen to calculate a theoretical count of fifteen thousand religious councils between 325 and 553.[62]

Admittedly, church councils could be an extension of crowd-against-crowd factionalism. Major ecumenical councils (Ephesus in 432, Chalcedon in 451) were rowdy affairs.[63] This risk of "tumult" remained into the early medieval period.[64] But most church councils were quieter events, stage-managed by protocol, like academic conferences shot through with sacred purpose. As with sacred violence, one can ask how much the sacred purpose of councils set such gatherings apart from secular assemblies (which, after all, also involved appeals to the divine), or how much secular and church assemblies informed one another. Later chapters will return to these questions, because this porous division marked the early medieval crowd regime.

The End of Roman Administration

Finally, the end of Roman rule was decisive to the future of crowds. The breakdown of imperial order in the West between the 400s and the 600s remains a controversial topic.[65] The decay of western urbanism, the rise of so-called "barbarian" successor states (the Sueves and Visigoths in Spain, the Vandals in North Africa, the Goths and Lombards in Italy, the Burgundians and Franks in Gaul, and the Angles and Saxons in Britain), the collapse of a unified Mediterranean exchange network, and demographic decline unraveled many threads of the crowd regime woven together by Roman imperial history. The incoming "barbarian" peoples had their own collective traditions, such as the military assemblies known (at least to us) by the Germanic name *Ding* or *Thing*.[66] Innovation accompanied unraveling.

The most conspicuous break was the end of Rome's culture of mass largess and entertainment. Euergetism lived on in the charity of the church and the pious, but on a humbler scale. There was little in early medieval Europe to match the state *annona*. As for games and spectacles, it is true that the Hippodrome at Constantinople, with its respectable capacity of around eighty thousand, remained the stage of Byzantine public life deep into the Middle Ages.[67] But in the West, mass entertainment sputtered out of existence by about 600, with few exceptions. What ended it was not so much a shift in tastes, but a lack of logistical wherewithal.

Scale

These are some of the big changes in the history of Roman crowds. Within this train of developments were continuities. The first of these was scale. By the Principate, the size of Roman gatherings could rival anything seen in the Hellenistic past or the contemporary world. Even China could not match ancient Rome for the density of its urban populations. Han Chang'an and Luoyang were cities of hundreds of thousands. Only under the T'ang did Chang'an achieve ancient Rome's apex of one million inhabitants.[68] The scale of Roman urbanism—not to mention Roman armies—enabled vast agglomerations on a regular basis. It was not out of the norm for the year to begin with 150,000 souls in the Circus Maximus, holding their breath simultaneously as they waited for the year's consul (often the emperor) to wave the *mappula* and kick off the New Year's Games.[69] It is unlikely that 150,000 persons ever assembled anywhere at one place and time in the European early Middle Ages.

That does not mean that collective life for most Romans occurred on the scale of the capital, or of the empire's largest cities: Carthage, Alexandria, Antioch, and Constantinople (each, at their height, cities of hundreds of thousands). But cities of tens of thousands and municipalities of thousands were sprinkled across the Roman West.[70] Local bigwigs offered scaled-down versions of imperial blandishments and spectacles. "Everywhere might be a little Rome," writes Peter Brown.[71]

Roman cities were designed to accommodate crowds. By the imperial period, urban topography across the empire's nearly 1,400 documented cities conformed to a more or less recognizable pattern. As A.H.M. Jones wrote, "A Roman citizen of the upper classes must have found himself at home wherever he traveled. The cities which he visited and the houses in which he stayed would have presented a very similar appearance to those he left behind."[72] This "similar appearance" included built environments that corralled, entertained, and amplified gatherings: amphitheaters, theaters, stadiums, thoroughfares, basilicas, forums, public baths, temples, and, by Late Antiquity, Christian churches and shrines. These spaces were mutually integrated. Colonnaded streets guided processions to forums or entertainment buildings. Circuses, theaters, and amphitheaters were venues for political action. The shaded portico of a theater might double as a dole-distribution center.[73] Rioters used these spaces as stages for resistance too—not the intention of ruling elites, but a stable use of the same topography. The ancient "urban armature," as Hendrik Dey has called it, came alive by dint of crowds.[74]

Similarly, the economics of empire depended on laboring masses. The state-supported alimentation system summoned workers in the thousands. One-off projects, like the building of entertainment facilities, temples, baths, or roads, entailed the work of thousands or tens of thousands. "The emperor as builder was the emperor as employer," writes one Roman historian.[75] Suetonius claims that the draining of the Fucine swamp employed thirty thousand workers over eleven years. It has been estimated that Caracalla's baths took nine thousand laborers to build.[76] In the third century, the construction of the Aurelian Walls—and thereafter their repair—summoned similarly large numbers.[77]

Admittedly, such vast crowds of the metropolis did not constitute daily experience for most ancient Romans. But rural Romans were no strangers to gatherings. In small municipalities, villages, and what archaeologists have termed "distributed habitations," the rhythm of agrarian and pastoral life also assembled regular gatherings.[78] Roman agriculture was greedy for labor. Brent Shaw estimates that the roughly 300,000,000 *modii* of cereal grains produced annually in Roman Africa required some half a million reapers at harvest.[79] It was from among these seasonal workers that the *circumcelliones* of North Africa recruited members. This scale was caused by the demand produced by interregional markets, urban and military agglomerations, and alimentary redistributions (the *annona*, the *coemptio*). Yet it was not only *latifundia*—large, landed estates—that demanded gangs of laborers; so did the small estates that characterized the bulk of agricultural production.[80] Small-scale farmers too hired or leased extra hands during harvest. Apart from labor, rural Romans enjoyed harvest festivals and winter festivals in labor-quiet months.[81]

Moreover, rural populations were never separated from city crowds. Ancient Romans, like the Greeks before them, loved to tell stories of country mice astounded by the big city. The poet Calpurnius Siculus imagined a rustic Corydon amazed by the sparkling games of the capital (Ecclesiastes 7). The orator Dio Chrysostom wrote a dramatic account of autarkic rustics who had never seen a forum nor heard of Rome.[82] To be sure, there must have been Roman peasants who could not tell a *secutor* from a *retiarius* or failed to grasp the significance of Blue–Green circus rivalries. But there were probably also farmers or herders who professed an exaggerated rusticity to men like Dio, like the twentieth-century peasants of Lucania who told Carlo Levi that "Christ stopped at Eboli."[83] There is an old debate in Roman economic history between those who see the Roman rural economy as primitive and nonintegrated and those who see it as dynamic and interconnected.[84] Outliers existed in both extremes. But Dio's autarkic folk are mostly a fantasy. City crowds were a part of daily rumor and economic life even for small farmers and herders.[85]

Moreover, the process cut both ways. Roman urban collective behavior was imprinted by the logic of the countryside. Rome's birthday, the *natalis urbis Romae*, April 21, celebrated by circus games, fell upon Parilia, the Feast of the Shepherds, in which men once leapt through burning straw and hay.[86] The

Roman upper crust always envisioned itself as so many Cincinnati ready to take up the plow, and Roman elites spent considerable time at villas outside of cities. Roman Christianity has sometimes been called a religion of cities, but its metaphors are dense with the logic of the fields: the parable of the sower, the lord's vineyards, the wheat and the chaff, the final harvest.[87]

Finally, where urbanism was not pronounced, there was also the Roman army: another vast, structuring conglomeration of people, animals, and things.[88] Perhaps some 600,000 served in the early fourth century.[89] At frontiers where semipermanent Roman camps looked out onto the "barbarians," rural economies on both sides of the border organized themselves around these stable eddies of demand, production, and exchange. A measure of armies' structuring influence is the way that border regions (Roman Britain, the Maghreb, the Danube frontier) experienced rapid material simplification, deskilling, and depopulation the moment the armies departed in the fifth century.[90] Military camps confronted rural communities with some of the largest human agglomerations in the Roman Empire. One way or another, denizens of the Roman world were exposed on a regular basis to gatherings of impressive scope.

Functions

Given the size and frequency of Roman gatherings, it is unsurprising that a complex social ecology should develop around them. Crowds performed multiple overlapping functions in Roman public life: providing households and individuals with provisions, enabling communication among classes, acting as a venue for justice (including street justice), and entertaining the people. Crowds were constitutive of identity, for in coming together, deliberating together, celebrating together, watching together, or shouting together, groups embodied collective personae. The success or failure of a leader, from the emperor down to the local patron, was measured by crowd control. This was one of the most durable features of Roman crowd discourse. Crowds were thus central to the Roman construction of legitimacy.[91]

This collective ecology was far from being static. There were oscillations in the relative popularity of crowd venues (chariot racing versus gladiatorial spectacle). There were modifications in crowd rituals. The *pompa circensis*, for instance, a procession through the streets of Rome culminating with races in the Circus Maximus, altered in itinerary, membership, and incidentals from its Republican origins to its late antique Christianization, as Patrizia Arena and Jacob Latham have explored.[92] Yet the essential logic of the procession never wholly changed. It remained, from the age of Cicero to the age of Gregory the Great, a visible, hierarchical expression of Roman order in microcosm moving along a meaningful topography. Riots too were never just atavistic upheavals, but motivated acts given meaning and shape by prevailing symbolic norms. Roman civilization was never without them. There were shifts in aim and appearance, from uprisings protesting against poor provisioning to uprisings in support of rival bishops. But their purpose—to give a voice to the disgruntled—abided.

Nowhere do the many uses of gatherings appear clearer than in Rome's "bread and circuses" (*panem et circenses*), to use Juvenal's phrase.[93] Mass alimentation and entertainment was deeply engrained in Roman civilization. It is true that most inhabitants of the empire never lined up to receive free *panis gradilis* ("step bread") or discounted *panis fiscalis* ("treasury bread"), nor caught a sponsored bout, show, or race on the grand scale.[94] But the logic of *munera* (the word tellingly means both "gifts" and "duties") and *spectacula* (the generic term for "show") was fundamental to Roman social order. Some iteration of these institutions marked every stage of Roman imperial history.

Largess to the masses became a special obligation of the state. Emperors, consuls, and officials sprinkled coins (*sparsio*) to crowds on ceremonial occasions. The state made gifts of bread, grain, wine, and pork to set constituencies. At Rome and other large cities (Constantinople, Antioch), an *annona civilis* was doled out to citizen families in public distribution centers on fixed dates. Enterprising elites, *collegia*, temples, and, eventually, churches also arranged public banquets, giveaways, and sales of food or drink at bargain rates, and received acknowledging acclamations in return. The duty of largess was maintained to the end of Roman Antiquity and beyond, though its scale diminished. In the sixth century, the Gothic king and then the pope took over the provisioning of the Western capital; in the East, grandiose rituals still accompanied the arrival of the *annona* into Constantinople. Early medieval kings, bishops, and aristocrats regularly performed the old duty of ostentatious charity. In that sense, this Roman practice of public charity never ended, it only shrank in scale.

Spectacles were a different matter. Shows before audiences were the most famous of all Roman crowd venues, and in the West, they did not last into the early Middle Ages. Even cities of modest size had spectacle venues. What took place upon the track, arena, or stage was subject to changes in fashion or law. By Late Antiquity, for example, the racetrack outshone the amphitheater, and staged hunts (*venationes*) supplanted gladiatorial fights. The punishment *ad bestias*, in which criminals were publicly exposed to animals, was banned in 325. Early in the next century, the emperor Honorius banned gladiators (so it was said) after a Christian monk was murdered by a rowdy audience for interrupting a bout.[95] But the *spectaculum*, as a genre, was fantastically durable.

There were many reasons for this durability. First and foremost, spectacles were thrilling. Historians, with their understandable interests in the deeper functions of closed crowds, should not forget Garrett Fagan's reminder about a tense match watched by tens of thousands at once: "In a nutshell, it is fun to watch."[96] As with other premodern sporting events (the Greek games, the Mesoamerican ballgame, Mississippian chunkey, Persian polo, Chinese cuju), spectacles occasioned gambling.[97] Moreover, fun served an array of social and political aims. The games were a public sphere, a space of gazes and judgments. As Tertullian wrote, "nobody going into a spectacle thinks of anything but being seen and seeing."[98] Famous attendees hoped to receive recognition upon their entry.[99] Seating arrangements expressed social hierarchies: the imperial family had their own box; senators sat close to the action; women, the poor, and foreigners made do with nosebleed seats.[100] Circus factions and other fan groups gave a space for self-expression and affinities.[101] Spectators knew from heralds, acclamations, and inscriptions who had paid for entertainments. A mutual "complicity," as Kathleen Coleman has termed it, bound audiences and sponsors.[102] It is no accident that emperors built their palaces adjacent to city circuses.[103]

In many ways, the games were quintessential "closed" crowds: gatherings as a tool of power. At the same time, crowds at games had known methods of airing opinions in entertainment venues, by applauding or booing a line, favoring a team, or chanting acclamations. Spectacles provided rulers with an informal opinion poll and "safety valve" for grievances.[104] The senatorial aristocracy reveled in offering shows, even as their ability to do so was carefully regulated. By the late empire, senators had lost political clout, but offering public entertainments remained a kind of Versailles.[105] Elites "greedy for civic favor" spent eyewatering sums on games.[106] While a middling level of elites could find this a burden, the ambitious and the rich saw it as conspicuous consumption par excellence. Boethius remembered the New Year's Games of his two consul sons (in 522) as his happiest day on earth—or at any rate, the earth ruled by Fortune.[107] It was the mass cheers of a huge crowd that fulfilled the worldly ambition of Roman elites.

Ambivalence

Despite the recognized utility of crowds, the ancient world never ceased to look down on them. "A 'crowd' [*ochlos*] is another name for anything lawless, disorderly, discordant, guilty," wrote Philo of Alexandria in the first century CE.[108] This was a common sentiment. For Rome's elites, crowds were a volatile necessity. It was the mark of a gentleman to hold them in contempt. But this made them a perfect foil. Control over crowds, or self-control in the face of crowds, required and embodied masculine virtue (*virtus*). The discursive opposite of a (free, elite) man (*vir*) was not only a woman, a slave, or a beast, but a crowd (*vulgus, turba*). Roman elites knew from their Vergil that a "man" (*vir*) ought to bridle the *ignobile uulgus*, the "ignoble rabble," whenever "sedition" (*seditio*) rose up in the hearts of the "people" (*populus*), just as the god of the sea once fettered the winds (tellingly, in Vergil's simile, a goddess's female rage unleashed them).[109] The more powerful the crowd, the more godlike the mastery. The result was a durable love–hate relationship between Roman elites and the crowds they needed for legitimacy.

This ambivalent disdain is best expressed in a famous letter by the first-century philosopher and statesman Seneca the Younger. Seneca told his young protégé Lucilius, a member of Rome's equestrian class, to avoid the *turba* (the crowd) "above all else." In particular, Lucilius was to be wary of the crowd at public spectacles. But this warning was addressed to Lucilius's youth. A man of mature years, like Seneca himself, had no choice but to make public appearances, notwithstanding the risk of becoming "less of a human" (*inhumanior*) by being "among humans" (*inter homines*).[110] A young Stoic, whose moral fontanelles had yet to fuse, needed the training of good models and diligent solitude to resist the crowd's corrupting influence.

For the have-nots of the Roman world, the crowd was a chance to have one's voice heard.[111] Acclamations offered a rare opportunity, respected by official authority, of being taken seriously in a world heavy with inequalities. When authorities had failed to right a wrong, more contentious gatherings were also a means of restoring justice. Despite a tendency among elite authors to depict such acts as mindless and meaningless—as Auerbach put it of Tacitus, "the whole thing is merely a matter of mob effrontery and lack of discipline"—Roman riots were as goal-oriented and symbolically complex as Thompson's eighteenth-century ones.[112]

It was a Roman truism that the common people—the *populus*—were in the thrall of Juvenal's "bread and circuses." The existence of fixed venues for crowd entertainment, to us a prototypical part of Roman civilization, was always fraught. Tacitus wrote of old men who believed that Pompey's establishment of a permanent stone theater caused the city's ruinous luxury. As late as c. 500, the Constantinopolitan historian Zosimos blamed centuries of "discords" (στάσεις) and "disorders" (ταραχαί) on Augustus's institution of mime dancing at Rome (admittedly, the shows were famous for political overtones).[113] Spectacles, races, and other popular entertainments were lambasted continuously through Roman history. Still, they continued to be held, at extraordinary cost, paid for by the very elites who mocked them.

One of the reasons emerges from a sixth-century letter of Cassiodorus, writing on behalf of King Theoderic to a Roman official that "Catos don't go to the circus."[114] In this letter, Cassiodorus identified a critical function of the games in Roman society: as an outlet for violent or antisocial behavior, like a

Bakhtinian carnival. A group of high-status individuals had complained to the Gothic king that their honor had been sullied by rowdy circus crowds. On Theoderic's behalf, Cassiodorus responded that senators should not be surprised to suffer *loquacitas popularis*, "talk-back from the crowd," at the circus.[115] The games had always been a safe space for "excess" (*excessus*):[116]

> Whatever is said there by a rejoicing crowd should not be considered a slight. That is a place which permits excess. Their freedom of speech, if it is patiently endured, is known to bring honor even to princes themselves.[117]

A law of Valentinian, Theodosius, and Arcadius in 398 had used the term *excessus* to describe the actions of a riot, a "violent multitude" (*multitudo violenta*), whose wrongdoing called for the severest action.[118] Thus, Cassiodorus invoked the worst a crowd could do. But the circus was a space where this dangerous collective mania was licit. More than this, indulging such behavior—again, the *vir*'s defining self-control—brought honor to great men. Cassiodorus's argument about permitted *excessus* reminds us that Roman elites were supposed to recognize the needs of the many, and, in the proper settings, endure *loquacitas popularis*.

This provided Theoderic, through his spokesman, an opportunity to out-Roman his Roman correspondents. A topos of good emperors was their politely concealed disinterest (Julian Caesar) or calculated indulgence (Augustus, Marcus Aurelius) at the games. Bad emperors like Nero or Commodus showed unhealthy fascination with chariot races, gladiators, or other mass entertainments. But it was also unnatural to ignore them entirely, as had the misanthropic Tiberius.[119] One of the criticisms Ammianus Marcellinus leveled at his hero Julian the Apostate—despite indulging in trendy criticism of the circus-addicted *plebs* himself—was that emperor's failure, out of boredom, to observe proper etiquette at the New Year's Games, thereby humiliating an incoming consul, though Julian repentantly fined himself.[120] A leader's ability to achieve the proper equipoise before a crowd in "excess" was a proof of his worth.

Elites feared, or pretended to fear, the corrupting effect of the crowd as it reveled in these moments of permitted excess. For that matter, there may have been working-class Romans who also shook their heads at spectacle crowds (we should not take elite sources at their word that all commoners loved them). "Nothing is more destructive to good morals than taking seats at some spectacle," Seneca had cautioned, "For there vices creep in more easily through the medium of pleasure."[121] But this came with a flip side: what young Stoic did not secretly relish the opportunity to test his mettle? A famous example of this is related by the Christian writer Augustine in the late fourth century.

Augustine's friend Alypius, later bishop of their shared hometown Thagaste, was a young Stoic and functionary in Rome, so noble-spirited that he resisted bribes and did not even take a government discount on books. He had once been a circus addict in his youth in North Africa, but he had overcome this weakness. At Rome, however, Alypius had a relapse, sparked by his own desire to resist the lure of the crowd:

> Clearly not deserting the earthly path, which his parents sang into him like a spell, [Alypius] had gone off to Rome to learn law, and there he was overtaken, to an unbelievable extent, by an unbelievable craving: for gladiatorial spectacle. For although he despised and recoiled from such things, some of his friends and fellow students, when by chance the amphitheater beckoned them as they returned from the mid-day meal, dragged him with companionable violence, as he vehemently refused and resisted, into the amphitheater, on days of cruel and deadly games, as he was saying: "even if you drag my body into that place and set me there, can you then draw my soul and my eyes into those spectacles? I will be present while absent, and that way I will defeat both you and them." This they heard, but still they dragged him along with them, maybe hoping to discover whether he could actually do what he said. When they came to their destination and took such seats as they might, everything was seething with savage pleasures. For his part, shutting the gates of his eyes, he forbade his soul to go forth into those evils. Would that he had stoppered his ears! For upon some fall in the battle, when the whole crowd's enormous clamor hammered vehemently against him, he, defeated by curiosity, though supposing he was about to conquer and defeat what he saw, whatever it might be, opened his eyes. And he was struck by a deeper wound upon his soul than was that other man, whom he wished to see, upon the latter's body, and he fell more pitiably than did the one whose fall produced the clamor. This clamor entered through his ears and unsealed his eyes, allowing his soul, till now bold rather than strong, and made all the weaker because he had presumed of himself what he owed from You [cf. Judith 6.15], to be struck and battered. For as soon as he saw blood, at once he drank up savagery and did not turn away, but fixed his gaze and swallowed furies and was unknowing, and he delighted in the sinful struggle and was intoxicated with gory pleasure. And now he was not that man who had come, but one from out the crowd to which he had come, and the true companion of those by whom he had been dragged. What more! He watched, he shouted, he burned, from there on in, he took away with him that madness by which he would be goaded to return, not only with those by whom he had been dragged, but even leading them, and dragging others beside. And yet even from there did You rescue him with a hand most potent and most merciful, and taught him to have trust not in himself but in You. But this was long afterwards.[122]

The key phrase of this riveting account is *et nesciebat*, "and he became unknowing." Alypius's fall rhymes with Augustine's own adolescent fall into sin, when he followed a band of unruly youths in their casual mindless vandalism, stealing pears and throwing them at pigs (*Conf.* 2.49). Augustine used all his rhetorical power to express his deeply Roman conviction that the power of the crowd was the most irresistible force in the world. God alone could bridle it. God's ministers—his bishops—held the impossible task of leading and correcting, of turning crowds into flocks. He who approached this task without God's help, like Alypius before "You taught him to have trust not in himself but in You," was doomed to be made *unus de turba*, "one from out of the crowd."

The End of the Roman Crowd Regime in the West

In the mid-seventh century, the bishop and polymath Isidore of Seville wrote that "a Christian should have no dealings with the circus's folly, with the shamelessness of the theater, with the amphitheater's cruelty, with the riotousness of the games."[123] By the time he was writing, Christian Westerners had little opportunity to violate his injunction. The games had outlasted Roman rule in the West. Theoderic promoted races in Gothic Italy, while mouthing pieties about their frivolity.[124] Circuses at Soissons and Paris were built (or rebuilt) in 577 by the Merovingian King Chilperic to "offer spectacles [*spectacula*] for the people."[125] It is likely there were other sixth-century spectacles that did not make it into the written record. After all, post-Roman rulers eagerly adopted many trappings of the Roman crowd regime.[126]

By the 600s, however, formal spectacles in purpose-built arenas were no more. While it is true that mass entertainments had undergone centuries of Stoic and Christian criticism, that is unlikely to have spelled their end. Augustine's writings on the dangers of games and circuses were informed by the anxieties of a bishop aware of the competition, and that competition remained strong throughout the Christian phase of the late Roman Empire.[127] Urban and economic contraction, not moral opposition, led to the decline of spectacles.[128] The bottom had to fall out for the system of mass entertainments to break down. The collapse of imperial infrastructure slowed the feats of masstransport that brought beasts from around the empire to the arenas of major towns.[129] Population decline and deurbanization, discussed in the next chapter, deprived them of audiences.

Theaters, amphitheaters, and circuses dissolved into new surroundings. Many settlements left old entertainment buildings outside new walls.[130] They became parts of battlements, churches, palaces, homes, granaries, and graveyards.[131] The amphitheater at Arles became a city unto itself.[132] In 673, the enemies of the Goths at Nîmes made their last stand against King Wamba in the city's old amphitheater (*intra arenas*).[133] A late eleventh- or early twelfth-century chronicle told a similar story in which inhabitants of Trier saved themselves during a Vandal siege by hiding "in the arena of the city, that is, in the amphitheater, which they fortified."[134] Faunal remains from the early eleventh-century Colosseum show the presence of domestic livestock; the exotic beasts that awed the multitudes in Cassiodorus's day were a memory.[135]

After 600, we rarely read of circuses and amphitheaters used for "spectacles" in the old sense, but they still appear from time to time as arenas of violence and power. In 604, a Lombard prince was raised to kingship in the circus of Milan before visiting ambassadors.[136] In 643 / 644, an exarch of Ravenna displayed a rebel's severed head in the city circus "as an example for the crowds."[137] In 768, one of the losers in a factional squabble for the papacy was dragged to a spot before the "Colosseum" (whether this refers to the amphitheater or to the statue of Nero outside is unclear), where his eyes and tongue were removed by "wicked men" who, papal sources protested a little too loudly, had no links to the pope who benefitted from this action.[138]

Were people conscious of the ancient sites of assembly in their midst? Did they feel a sense of numbers lost? In Italy, where the physical remains of the old entertainment buildings would have been most visible, the silence is deafening.[139] The *Liber pontificalis* is rich with Rome's topographical details (churches, oratories, gates, streets, bridges, and aqueducts). But the Colosseum, that most famous of Rome's ancient monuments, goes unmentioned until, suddenly and surprisingly, it appears as the backdrop to the brutal act of political violence mentioned above.[140] In the ninth century, Agnellus of Ravenna, otherwise minute chronicler of his city's architecture, mentions Ravenna's amphitheater in passing as a landmark.[141] The circus at Ravenna, where the exarch Isaac displayed a rebel's head, is otherwise unattested, and has not been recovered by archaeologists.[142] This is explicable. New urban fabrics were built into, against, around former entertainment buildings. They were no longer the open venues of old, but hemmed in and fragmented. Most mentions of "amphitheaters" or "arenas" from the early Middle Ages were spiritual in portent: a place of Christian memory or a metaphor for spiritual combat.[143] But the crowds that once filled them were gone. Moralists like Isidore cast barbs against a dead institution.

The eastern half of the empire was different. It is true that the frequency of chariot races decreased, from sixty-six annual holidays in the fifth and sixth centuries to less than a dozen by the tenth century.[144] Yet amid seventh-century depopulation, the Greek-speaking East retained much of the Roman crowd regime, including both "bread and circuses." Horse races continued to dominate Constantinopolitan life for centuries. Byzantine state ceremonial centered on the Hippodrome, the great racetrack, until the arrival of western jousts in the twelfth century.[145] Indeed, the Hippodrome in some ways became more central to public ritual in Byzantine than in Late Roman history.[146] Imperial politics played out there as if upon a stage. Public punishments were enacted there.[147] The Nika revolt began there.[148] The plot to kill Phocas (608), the mutilation and deposition of Justinian II (695), and Justinian II's vengeance upon his enemies (706) all took place at the racetrack.[149] In ceremonial, the factions (*demoi*) played a public role in delivering acclamations from their established places in the stands. As the West went its own way, much of the Roman crowd regime survived in the Byzantine East.

The Legacy of Roman Crowds

From the Republic to Byzantium, crowds played a prominent and multifaceted role in Roman civilization. That fact is so well known as to seem unremarkable. Crowds are among the first things people think of when they think of ancient Rome. But familiarity breeds misunderstanding. Rome was not wholly unique in how it mobilized collective behavior. Thanks to the Eurocentric gaze of the academy and the enduring popular fascination with Rome, gladiatorial audiences may be easier to picture in the mind's eye than, say, the (admittedly smaller) ballgame audiences of Maya Tikal or Chichén Itzá. Yet Roman public culture did possess unique features even within a global context, shaped by the demographic density, unique political history, and socioeconomic complexity of this ancient Mediterranean civilization.

In thinking about Rome's legacy in the West, this chapter has highlighted three aspects of Rome's crowd regime. First, Roman gatherings were large, frequent, and quotidian. Politics and religion were done in gatherings. Thousands or tens of thousands filled the stands of Roman entertainment buildings. Riots were an annual occurrence. The crowd was in no sense a rarity. Second, crowds did an enormous variety of work. Rome's economic needs were enabled by crowds of laborers. Acclamations provided ruling elites with legitimacy, and a degree of licit "excess" was afforded to those who shouted them. In Late Antiquity, the notion of a special crowd of believers—guided by the Holy Spirit—melded with older Roman ideas about numbers and legitimation. When amity broke down, crowds served as a factional bludgeon or a way to give a voice to the voiceless. Third, the result was a Janus-faced but productive discursive ambivalence about crowds. It was just as normal to use the crowd to bolster one's own legitimacy as it was to use it to deny the moral worth of one's enemies.

By the sixth and seventh centuries, this regime was breaking down in the West. After the dense populations and economies of scale of the Roman world disappeared, new venues for gatherings emerged, together with new ways of conceptualizing crowds. The city's preeminence as the site of gathering gave way, albeit never entirely, to new venues and means of enabling assembly. The coming early medieval crowd was, above all, a rural crowd. At the same time, mobile sites of assembly came to dominate political life ever more: the king and his court, entourages, extraordinary religious events, and armies. Orderly forms of gathering built around predictable patterns overshadowed spontaneous ones. Rare exceptions—urban riots, peasant revolts—proved the rule. Gatherings after Rome were better equipped to reinforce and express elite power, less volatile and less suited to the self-assertion of the humble. Yet behind all this change, there remained the inescapable legacy left behind by "the long glories of majestic Rome."

2

Numbers

Number and Scale

Between c. 500 and c. 1000, the Roman world transformed into the medieval world. Roman administration collapsed in the western provinces as new "barbarian" kingdoms arose in its place. Christianity triumphed over its competitors. The economy contracted, then slowly regrew. East and West parted ways, then warily reconnected. The size of populations and cities shrank, and then began their slow recovery.[1] Rome lived on too. Memory, belief, and ritual bound the early medieval world to the past. Ideals of political and religious legitimacy survived in institutions and little facets of life. Language, life, and death remained visibly Roman.[2] This mix of rupture and resilience, which too often divides scholars into "catastrophist" and "continuationist" camps, defines the ancient–medieval transition.[3]

The crowd traversed both continuity and change. Reasons for gathering and perceptions of gatherings remained Roman, even as new institutions and political economies altered the imperatives and means of assembly. But demographic downscaling also altered the rules of the game. The basic ingredient for gatherings—numerous human bodies in proximity—was now harder to achieve. This chapter addresses that scale change.

Early medieval Europe's population history can be divided into two broad phases, the first (c. 400–650) marked by decline and deurbanization, the second (c. 650–1000) by gradual recovery. Certainty is impossible; variation reigned; but it is reasonable to posit an overall thinning perhaps on the order of a third or more between the fifth and early seventh centuries. Recovery began almost as soon as mortality pressures (climate change, plague) ended, first in the north, and later in the south. But populations did not return to Roman levels of density until the high Middle Ages (c. 1000–1300).

In an age with few numerical records, precise quantification is impossible. What were the carrying capacities of countrysides, towns, and cities? What were salient regional and chronological differences? How big were gatherings?

What would have been typical, impressive, or humdrum? Were gatherings, in absolute terms, less frequent? The historian is in the frustrating position of being able to detect scale change without being able to measure it precisely. The evidence demands flexible strategies of investigation, and comfort with uncertainty.

This chapter argues that the scale of gatherings in the early medieval West significantly diminished in diachronic and synchronic comparison, while stressing that gatherings in absolute terms did not vanish. Gatherings in post-Roman Europe were smaller. Logistical restraints on them were higher. Crowds of tens of thousands were rare. Spontaneous crowds were rarer. But tens, hundreds, and thousands still regularly came together, especially in Mediterranean Europe. As with many aspects of life, the threads linking early medieval Europe to its Roman legacy were frayed, not severed.

Early Medieval Demography: Evidence, Causes, Trends

Demographic sparseness has been called the "fundamental characteristic" (Marc Bloch) if not the "most important fact" (Henri Pirenne) of post-Roman economic history.[4] Josiah Russell, the last to attempt a complete synthesis, saw the early Middle Ages as Europe's demographic "nadir."[5] Archaeology and specialist research have added nuance to the story since Russell made his calculations in the 1950s and 1960s. Scholars today stress regional asymmetries and exceptions; they no longer see the period c. 600–1000 as demographically stagnant. But a generalized post-Roman European thinning-out remains the consensus, and for good reason.[6]

Evidence

The data for this period cannot compare to the census reports of Roman Egypt, to later medieval hearth taxes, notarial documents (wills, marriage contracts, inventories, postmortems), and cadastral surveys, or to early modern parish registers and bills of mortality. Written evidence is patchy. "Cities in ruin, strongholds overthrown, fields despoiled; the land has gone back to nature," wrote Pope Gregory I in 593 or 594. "There is no farmer in the fields, almost no inhabitant remains in the cities."[7] Evocative as this lament is, it is better evidence for the pope's apocalypticism than for the demographic realities of sixth-century Italy.[8] Richer sources proliferate only in the 700s and 800s.

Polyptychs (or "Urbare"), lists of dependents and dues kept by lords, offer the best written evidence for early medieval Western demography.[9] The largest of them (not counting the Domesday Book, a late expansion of the genre) is the polyptych of Saint-Germain-des-Prés, which lists over nine thousand individuals living around the Seine River Basin in the early 800s.[10] Not many polyptychs survive.[11] A handful come down to us from parts of France, Germany, and Italy, most from the ninth century or later, all more fragmentary than Saint-Germain's, and most unusable for demography.[12]

As Toubert and Devroey have emphasized, it takes mediation to use polyptychs and other administrative sources demographically.[13] Only by filtering laconic data through informed assumptions, for instance, have Monique Zerner-Chardavoine and Irene Barbiera, Maria Castiglioni, and Gianpiero Dalla Zuanna been able to use the ninth-century polyptych of Saint-Victor, Marseille to address elusive questions of nuptiality and fertility.[14] Missteps are easy. The Saint-Germain polyptych displays marked, male-skewed sex-ratio imbalances, but most historians today doubt Emily Coleman's argument that this reveals widespread female infanticide.[15] To give another example, Ferdinand Lot reckoned there were about fifty inhabitants per square kilometer on average on the Saint-Germain estates, and by universalizing this figure, he concluded that ninth-century Gaul was as densely populated as the France of King Louis XIV (r. 1643–1715).[16] But the Saint-Germain lands, on the fertile and commercially active Seine, were a demographic exception, not the rule.[17] Even the twenty inhabitants per square kilometer on the lands of the polyptych of Saint-Bertin may have been especially dense by ninth-century standards.[18]

To fill in gaps, historians turn to archaeology.[19] Aspects of the big picture have changed as a result. The start of Western demographic decline is now placed earlier, as far back as the late second or third century in many regions.[20] In other cases, excavation has complicated old models: the brand-new sixth-century Visigothic royal city of Reccopolis near Toledo seems to have been a real city, not a Potemkin village.[21] Archaeology has also revealed the existence of category-defying settlements, like Italian ecclesiastical sites "combining qualities of the city, the villa, and the village" highlighted by Kim Bowes, for which written sources do not always prepare us.[22]

By and large, though, archaeology supports the picture of decline and recovery.[23] Demographic thinning is visible in settlement contraction and abandonment, agricultural reuse of urban space, flattening of settlement hierarchies, and simplification of material culture.[24] Field surveys show striking reductions in settlement density—in one from central Italy, a loss of four fifths.[25] A similar pace of abandonment occurred in sixth-century Puglia.[26] Across Europe, "cities" (*civitates*, *urbes*) endured as administrative and religious centers, but they saw less dense habitation and economic specialization. In other regions where large-scale surveys have been conducted, such as Lowland Britain and Northern France, there was a 50 percent decline of settlements.[27]

Archaeology also sheds light on the seventh- or eighth-century turnaround. This is first visible in northern Europe.[28] Villages, towns, centers specializing in mining or salt production, emporia, and monastic communities multiplied.[29] Cemetery populations expanded.[30] Southern Europe, possibly always more densely populated in absolute terms, recovered later and slower than the north.[31]

Newer methods are expanding our knowledge. Osteological, isotopic, and genetic analyses of human remains shed light on population health, structure, and mobility.[32] Large-scale cemetery inventories are underway.[33] Paleogeneticists' ability to estimate historical population size, mobility, and change is improving.[34] Reconstructions on these bases will still rely on assumptions built into models, so historians must make sure improbabilities are not smuggled in. But the old myth that early medieval population history is an evidential dead end is being revised.

Causes

This is not the place to discuss the causes of population change in any detail. Here, we can identify three causal phases—a Roman prelude (c. 165–400 CE) marked by demographic thinning in the West, a decline phase (c. 400–650), and a growth phase (c. 650–1000)—and briefly discuss their posited drivers.

1) Demographic decline and deurbanization in the late second and third centuries CE are thought to be driven by epidemic disease (Antonine Plague, Cyprian Plague), economic instability, and civil war.[35] But shifting migration trends also set the stage for the post-Roman demographic regime. During its imperial heyday (c. 200 BCE–200 CE), Rome's political and economic heft, combined with human trafficking on a massive scale, had allowed the West to outgrow the East by steady migration.[36] In the fourth century, this exception ended, as the East became the imperial center of gravity.[37] The "barbarians" who entered Europe in the fourth through sixth centuries probably did not make up for this *longue durée* shift; they certainly did not refill depleted cities.[38]

2) The marked decline of the fifth through seventh centuries was mostly the result of raised mortality factors.[39] In the fifth century, civil war and imperial collapse led to the breakdown of food-management institutions. In the sixth century, the Late Antique Little Ice Age (c. 536–660),[40] the First Plague Pandemic (c. 541–766),[41] continued warfare,[42] and other epidemics, endemic diseases, and zoonotics raised mortality rates.[43] Modeling climatic impact on demography is difficult and risky.[44] We must be mindful of Amartya Sen's dictum that famine—the main mechanism of decline—is driven by entitlements, not food availability.[45] Similarly, plague had asymmetric impacts, and

only where it struck repeatedly could it have had long-term impacts.[46] Nevertheless, extra mortality from climate and disease remains the best explanation for population collapse.[47] The main alternative is lowered fertility.[48] According to Chris Wickham, a transformation in the mode of production across Europe caused peasants, under less extractive pressure, to choose to have fewer children; over time, this supposedly reduced total population.[49] But it is unclear how sub-replacement fertility would have been a viable optimization strategy for primitive agriculturalists; nor is there evidence for Wickham's hypothesis.[50] By contrast, a growing body of hard evidence supports the theory of raised mortality and—admittedly regionally variable—high plague case load.[51]

3) Starting as early as the seventh century, patchy demographic recovery began across Europe. In part, this may be due to mortality factors vanishing. The Late Antique Little Ice Age ended in the 660s. Plague ceased to appear in the West after 766.[52] But precocious growth may reflect the health benefits of living in smaller, less crowded populations. For instance, in Italy the tendency to move to hilltop settlements probably reduced the risk of malaria. By the 700s and 800s, climatic conditions had improved, but social resilience played a role too.[53] A period of relatively few climatic forcing events (c. 725–1025) was succeed by the Medieval Climate Anomaly (c. 950–1250), which may have had its first stirrings perhaps in the 870s.[54] For European farmers, the warmer, wetter conditions of the MCA may have been agriculturally more forgiving.[55] The period saw improvements in agricultural and technological methods.[56] Extractive pressure may have pushed up birthrates (the flipside of Wickham's theory).[57] Growth of towns and cities at the end of the period encouraged additional demographic concentration. The year 1000 is an artificial cut-off, since growth and concentration continued into the 1200s.

Gross Estimates

The data suggest that, from c. 500 to c. 1000, European populations were smaller and less urban than their Roman forebears, but nor were they stagnant or immiserated.[58] Standards of living may have improved as density diminished.[59] Once mortality pressures lifted in the 600s, slow-moving growth was the rule for most regions. In some places, there was apparent stasis (e.g., in Italy) or reversal (e.g., Bavaria in the early 900s). By 1000 or 1100, populations across Europe matched or exceeded Roman levels.

It is not easy or wise to express this numerically. Russell provided one range of population estimates by region (probably too low) (see Table 2.1).[60] In 1979, Jean-Noël Biraben offered higher gross estimates (see Table 2.2).[61] It is equally hard to quantify deurbanization. One estimate places European

TABLE 2.1. European Population, 300–1000 (J. Russell), in millions

Year	Iberia	France	Italy	Britain	N. Europe	Total
300	4	5	4	0.3	3.5	16.8
600	3.6	3	2.4	0.8	2.1	11.9
1000	7	6	5	1.7	4	23.7

Source: F. Irsigler et al., "Bevölkerung," in *Lexikon des Mittelalters* (Munich, 1977–99), vol. 2, cols. 10–21, at col. 14 (by Josiah Russell).

TABLE 2.2. European Population, 200–1000 (J.-N. Biraben), in millions

Year (CE)	Total European Population
c. 200	44
c. 600	22
c. 1000	30

Source: Jean-Noël Biraben, "Essai sur l'évolution du nombre des hommes," *Population* 34 (1979): 13–25, at 16 (table 2); adopted with due warnings by Jean-Pierre Devroey and Anne Nissen Jaubert, "Family, Income and Labour Around the North Sea, 500–1000," in *Making a Living: Family, Income and Labour*, ed. Eric Vanhaute, Isabelle Devos, and Thijs Lambrecht (Turnhout, 2011), 1–40, at 9.

urban populations c. 700–750 at about 20 percent lower than they had been in 500 CE, and 40 percent lower than in 200 CE.[62] It is usually thought that until about 1000 only a few European cities numbered in the thousands, and only two or three counted tens of thousands. But such numbers are guesswork.[63] Trends, not figures, matter.[64] The population history of Europe c. 500–1000 can be imagined as a lopsided grin, from precipitous late antique decline to slow-moving growth leading gradually toward the high medieval takeoff.

Regional Heterogeneity

There were detectable variations in the carrying capacity of different regions, however.[65] Generally, the Mediterranean remained more urbanized, while (rural) growth may have been more pronounced north of the Alps. A brief survey is worthwhile.

Italy

Italy had been among the Roman Empire's most urbanized regions, but after 600 had much ground to recover.[66] An archaeological survey of territory near Siena and Grosseto found a diminishment from 2,521 "occupied sites" (one site per 1.27

square kilometers) in the first to fourth centuries, to 506 sites (one site per four square kilometers) in the fourth to sixth centuries, to a nadir of 201 sites (one site per ten square kilometers) in the sixth to seventh centuries.[67] By one estimate, Italy's population fell from 15.5 million (first century) to 8 million for much of the early Middle Ages.[68] Abandoning lowlands, communities of dozens or hundreds clustered on hilltops.[69] There may have been greater vibrancy in southern Italy.[70] But the overall impression is a stark diminishment of density.[71]

Post-Roman Italian cities were networks of garden-, orchard-, and farm-bound mini-towns, ensconced in reused ancient spaces.[72] Treating this as decay is misleading, as Caroline Goodson has stressed.[73] Italy was still Europe's urban hotbed. Milan, Pavia, Verona, and Ravenna remained vibrant ceremonial centers. Naples was a major entrepôt. Venice and Genoa rose from obscurity to vigor.[74] Rome, which experienced the most drastic decline of any western city, also remained the largest in Latin Europe.[75]

Rome's unusual status deserves attention.[76] Its population, a million strong in the first century, had dropped to 20,000–35,000.[77] It is astounding to think that the population of eighth- or ninth-century Rome may have been half that of its ancient port city Ostia at the latter's first-century zenith.[78] But this underestimates Rome's numerical power and relative crowdedness. Numbers fluctuated seasonally with pilgrims, and could be supplemented by the suburbs. While Rome was a shadow of its ancient self, early medieval northerners were struck by its size, and its frequent, raucous crowds.[79]

Iberia

Iberia saw waves of demographic loss (and recovery) from the third to the sixth century.[80] The Muslims later told stories of plague- and famine-driven demographic decline in Spain before the conquest.[81] But the Visigoths were among the most Roman of all post-Roman successors, a fact reflected in their ideological commitment to cities.[82] In a handful of cities from the 500s to the early 700s, urban life thrived in Iberia to a degree matched only in Italy.[83] Reccopolis, founded in 578 by Leovigild, previously thought to be a show-town, turns out to have been rich in dwellings beyond the ceremonial center.[84]

Toledo, once a mid-sized Roman city with an oversized circus, was the key site for high politics and religion before 711.[85] Eighteen major councils took place there between 400 and c. 702–3. At least twelve other cities were large enough to accommodate such councils.[86] Christian Spain after the Muslim conquest was less urbanized. Oviedo, the main city of the kingdom of the Asturias, was a shadow of Toledo; only later in the period did Barcelona became a city of importance.[87] On the other hand, demographic growth in Islamic Spain was pronounced. By the tenth century, perhaps a third of all European towns with populations over ten thousand were there.[88] Córdoba may have numbered 100,000 or more.[89] While some of this size was the result of in-migration from the Islamic Mediterranean, it is also a reminder that cultural differences as well as exogenous forces shaped European demographic asymmetries.

Gaul

The "Gauls" (France, Switzerland, Belgium, southwest Germany, and the Netherlands) faced waves of deurbanization long before the end of Roman rule. Before the 200s, Gaul had been among the empire's fastest-growing regions.[90] The third-century crisis saw demographic thinning and urban decay.[91] There was some recovery in the 300s, but the Lower Rhine and northern Switzerland remained depopulated; contraction began anew in the 400s.[92] Plague probably had asymmetric effects, worse in the South than the North.[93] Deurbanization was noticeable everywhere. Most Gallic *civitates* were more towns than cities, and even the exceptions like Paris, Bordeaux, Lyon, and Orléans probably only numbered in the thousands.[94] Marseille, the cosmopolitan port of southern Gaul, was prosperous in the 500s, but by 700 was a shell of itself.[95]

Still, the Franklands are thought to have experienced rural population growth from the seventh or eighth century onward.[96] By c. 800, Gaul possessed many densely populated river valleys. The Loire floodplain progressed toward its medieval future as an "urban ribbon."[97] The Seine, Rhône, Rhine, and Scheldt became densely populated by rural standards: estimates range from fifteen to thirty persons per square kilometer.[98] But density varied on the local scale. Palaiseau in the Seine valley was one of the largest estates in the Polyptych of Saint-Germain, with about six hundred dependents.[99] By contrast, Ennery near Paris counted eighty.[100] Despite what Lot thought, more Gallic settlements were probably like the latter than the former.

Northern Europe

Just prior to the fifth century, populations in northern Europe were growing.[101] From the 400s to the 600s, there are archaeological signs of settlement abandonment.[102] This thinning out, visible also in palynological evidence, is very marked in Schleswig-Holstein, hinting that sixth-century stories of recent mass migration of Goths and Vandals from "Scandza" may have some truth to them.[103] The Frisian coast underwent a similar diminishment between the fifth and seventh centuries.[104]

Such losses were later made good. The marshlands of the Ems and Weser show settlement recovery from the late seventh and eighth centuries.[105] Growth marks the archaeological record in Germany, the Netherlands, and the British Isles, suggesting demographic turnaround circa the late 600s.[106] In Scandinavia, populations grew after (climate- or migration-related) sixth-century decline.[107] Population pressure is an old explanation for the Viking invasions; true or not, by the 800s Scandinavian populations could supply impressively large "Great Armies" on the Continent and England.[108] Urbanism was muted. The eighth- and ninth-century emporia (or *wics*) were vibrant but not enormous. True urban development on the North and Baltic Seas took off only at the end of the tenth or beginning of the eleventh century.[109] As with Gaul, then, the general pattern is slow, rural growth from about 600.

British Isles

Bede (d. 735) thought that the history of the English began with fifth-century British demographic decline.[110] Depopulation in the 400s and 500s is indisputable.[111] One archaeological synthesis compares post-Roman Britain to modern Detroit.[112] As with other northern regions, recovery—boosted by in-migration—was underway by the 600s.[113] Ireland, not spared by plague, saw expansion from the 600s or 700s.[114]

By Bede's day, the largest agglomeration in the Isles was Lundenwic, the emporium situated just upstream from Roman London. By 800, it would have been one of the largest emporia-type cities north of the Alps, a home to thousands.[115] The Lundenwic site (around today's Aldwych) was abandoned by the middle of the next century, as London's center of gravity shifted back to the old walled site. Still, London remained Britain's great city.[116] York (*Eboracum, Eoforwic, Jorvik*), another Roman site turned *wic* turned Viking city, was a respectable second; excavations of its Viking-era Coppergate show dense habitation. Across the Irish Sea, the Viking port of Dublin, with its bustling market and Thingmote, grew from the mid-ninth century.[117] But most of the population of the islands lived in rural settlements.[118] The overall impression, as with the rest of northern Europe, is slow rural growth with few urban agglomerations.

Slavlands

The early Middle Ages were an important moment for demographic growth in Central and Eastern Europe.[119] Settlement density increased on Dnieper by the eighth century.[120] Ninth-century building at Pohansko (on the Czech border with Austria) has been associated with growth in Greater Moravia.[121] Deforestation and fortress-building in Poland signaled growth peaking in the 900s and 1000s.[122] Ibrāhīm ibn Ya'qūb, a Jewish visitor from Umayyad Spain, described the Poland of Mieszko I (d. 992) as a land swarming with people.[123]

It is hard to know how far to take the archaeological and written sources as marks of growth, however. Paleodemographic analysis of east European cemeteries in seventh- to tenth-century Latvia (Lejasbitēni) and ninth- to twelfth-century Poland (Wolin) suggests young populations afflicted by high mortality rates.[124]

The Byzantine and Islamic Mediterranean

A brief comparative glance at the demographic situation in the Byzantine and Islamic Mediterranean is worthwhile. The mortality drivers that faced western regions, particularly in the sixth and seventh centuries, did not spare the southern and eastern Mediterranean.[125] But they fell upon different economic conditions. Parts of Syria, for instance, were economically thriving when plague arrived; elsewhere in the Levant, urban decline was already underway.[126] The Eastern demographic nadir appears to have been the 600s, driven by a mix of climate-, disease-, and warfare-driven mortality factors.

The difference was in long-term outcome. While populations remained thin for centuries in the Latin West, dense populations and urbanism bounced back sooner in the Islamic and Byzantine worlds.[127] Reasons probably included agrarian innovation, persistent trade, the cultural importance of urbanism, and robust forced and unforced in-migration. Urbanism was altered—in the Islamic world, the shift from *polis* to *madina* is archaeologically visible—and new conurbations, like Kufa and Basra, rose as part of the Islamic experiment.[128] But by the 800s, cities like Constantinople, Baghdad, and Samarra numbered in the hundreds of thousands. These cities had stable palace bureaucracies that were better equipped to stage-manage collective rituals. The number of eunuchs in the imperial palace at Constantinople was likened to flies in a sheepfold.[129] The Latin West's sibling cultures much more quickly returned to a dense demographic regime and higher rates of urbanism.

Population Pools and Carrying Capacities

Having examined global and regional trends, how large were local pools from which gatherings could be assembled? Estimating settlement or regional population sizes from textual or archaeological evidence is tricky business. Sometimes archaeologists make carefully argued site or carrying capacity estimations.[130] Other times they offer conjectures. The various coefficients proposed for known city areas—150 to 250 people per hectare versus 70 to 140 people per hectare for Roman cities—produce alluring data.[131] But there is risk that such numbers will "take" just because they are to hand. In terms of numbers, then, nothing that follows is gospel.

Even where cemeteries have been largely surveyed, allowing rough estimates of population pools, early medieval cemeteries are missing bodies (especially of infants), hindering demographic reconstructions.[132] Noninvasive archaeology like aerial photography, ground-penetrating geomagnetic radar, and laser analysis (LIDAR) are helping scholars reconstruct settlements still under the earth, but ways of estimating population size on the basis of such data are still being developed.[133] In the future, Europeanists may turn to archaeologists of Native American settlements, whose inventive but supple models result in ranges rather than misleading exact numbers.[134]

There have been several attempts to taxonomize early medieval site-types by size. The seminal typologies of Max Weber, Henri Pirenne, Edith Ennen, and Martin Biddle have been modified by John Schofield and Heiko Steuer for early medieval archaeology. Their breakdown of settlements into ten (overlapping) categories is useful. We can consider them in rough descending order of size: 1) old Roman cities, 2) new trading emporia, and 3) midsized towns of other kinds; 4) royal and imperial palaces, 5) novel episcopal sees, 6) large and small monasteries, and 7) fortresses; 8) market sites, 9) sites of production or extraction, and 10) rural settlements.[135]

Large Pools (Thousands–Tens of Thousands): Cities, Emporia, Towns (1–3)

1) Old Roman cities remained the largest agglomerations of people in the early medieval West.[136] They shrank, admittedly. An eighth-century writer describes Metz as "abounding with crowds," but confesses that the city's amphitheater had been given over to wild snakes.[137] Several sites, like Tongeren or Tarquimpol, were abandoned or became hamlets.[138] But cities endured.[139] Many gained new life in the seventh, eighth, or ninth century as centers of production and exchange.[140] Rome, Milan, and Naples, Europe's largest cities outside of Islamic Spain, may have all had intramural populations over ten thousand during our period. Paris, London, Genoa, and Venice probably only reached that mark by the late 900s or later.

The majority of early medieval cities likely had populations in the low to mid thousands, though this is only a guess. Examples in Italy probably included places like Verona, Pavia, Pisa, Siena, Arezzo, and Lucca. Northern examples probably included Utrecht, Cologne, Worms, Speyer, Mainz, Trier, Strasbourg, Basel, Constance, Regensburg, Passau, and Vienna.[141] Many famous Gallic cities were probably on this order of magnitude. Gregory of Tours, raised in one venerable Gallo-Roman *civitas* (Clermont) and made bishop of another (Tours), contrasted the small *civitates* near to his heart with what seemed to him tawdry, oversized Babylons like Paris and Marseille.[142]

Yet small cities were symbolically and administratively central, with a power to pull in numbers.[143] Small cities boasted sacred and public spaces in which to assemble numbers on special occasions. Metz built no fewer than forty churches in the Carolingian period.[144] Urban carrying capacity extended beyond the intramural population. When numbers were called for, early medieval cities drew upon suburban settlements, rural hinterlands, and secondary sites. Inhabitants of the hills between Siena and Arezzo, perhaps only rare visitors to either city, felt so spiritually connected to the cathedral of Saint Donatus at Arezzo that over seventy of them trekked to Siena to testify to their loyalty to Arezzo.[145] Such extra-urban pools supplied the economic, ceremonial, and contentious gatherings that kept cities important.[146] In theory at least, rural communities were enjoined to come to their city church on major festivals such as Easter, Christmas, Epiphany, Ascension, Pentecost, and the Feast of John the Baptist.[147]

2) At a lower level of concentration were "proto-urban" sites like the "emporia" or "wics" of northern Europe. These were economically vibrant settlements on coasts or rivers.[148] Sometimes they grew on or near older Roman sites, as with Lundenwic. In other cases, they emerged beyond the Roman pale.[149] Comacchio and early Venice offer a southern equivalent: growing but youthful conurbations. Such centers were magnets for merchants and targets for raiders.[150] Their population density varied seasonally. One archaeologist imagines Dorestad's population oscillating between summer and winter "like a holiday resort."[151] In this, they were like eighteenth- and nineteenth-century New England whaling villages, with stark, predictable demographical cycles.[152]

Aside from London—an exception because of the city's wider significance as a religious, economic, and political site—emporia populations were in the low thousands. Dorestad may have numbered about 2,000 in the busy season; Hedeby about 1,500; Birka fewer still.[153] A topographical peculiarity of emporia was their physical sprawl compared to low populations.[154] Hamwic, to give a conspicuous example, did not have anywhere near the 18,000 inhabitants it could have accommodated physically; instead, its excavator guesses 2,000 or 3,000.[155] But at busy times of year, such towns sprang to life.

3) In addition, there were any number of smaller towns, whether old or new, with hundreds of inhabitants or more. By the tenth or eleventh century, some grew into significant population centers. Schofield and Steuer give the example of Hildesheim, where a new bishop's see met an important trading center.[156] New towns proliferate in the written and archaeological record after the year 1000, and there can be no comparing the modest growth of towns between c. 700 and c. 1000 to this later urban takeoff. But many cities of the high Middle Ages had their early medieval prehistory.

Mid-Sized Pools (Hundreds–Thousands): Palaces, New Episcopal Sees, Monasteries, Fortresses (4–7)

4) Extra-urban palaces, residences for rulers and their entourages, incorporated residential structures, chapels, and storage or production buildings in addition to the palace hall (*aula*).[157] While early medieval rulers maintained palaces in cities, especially in Italy, there was a Europe-wide tendency to develop royal palaces somewhat away from population centers.[158] Some, like the Frankish palace at Quierzy, were located off the old Roman road system.[159] Among the Franks, such sites were intentionally situated near good hunting grounds.[160] As with emporia, palaces were seasonally populous, swelling when rulers were present, emptying out otherwise.[161] Over time, however, palaces could nourish larger populations. The Carolingians and Ottonians invested in several sites that subsequently expanded: Aachen, Ingelheim, Duisburg, Frankfurt, Paderborn, Werla, Tilleda, Magdeburg, Regensburg, and Zürich.[162]

Palaces brought together numbers for many reasons. Einhard's *Translatio Marcellini et Petri* describes large crowds conducting business (*negotia*) in the town alongside the palace at Aachen.[163] Elites built residences around royal dwellings, spurring local economic development.[164] Non-elites came in large numbers for justice's sake. In a celebrated case of 861, twenty-three men, eighteen women, and at least twenty children from Mitry trekked to Charles the Bald's palace at Compiègne to defend their freedom; twenty-two of their neighbors also came to swear oaths against them.[165] Palaces were spatially designed to manipulate such crowds: halls, courtyards, chapels, balconies, and interior ins and outs. They were equipped with professionals who could attend to the complex logistics of temporary numbers. Even if Aachen could not measure up to the extraordinary Umayyad palace city built by Abd al-Rahman III outside of Córdoba, palace populations may have rivaled those of small to mid-sized towns or even small cities when rulers were present.

5) A feature of Christianization in the early medieval period was the foundation or refoundation of episcopal sees. Although these usually coincided with preexisting Roman settlements (e.g., Utrecht) or new royal palaces (e.g., Paderborn), the presence of a bishopric—a bishop, a city cathedral, an episcopal palace, a clergy, an episcopal retinue—was its own spur to agglomeration.[166] Early medieval England had a number of mobile sees whose bishops held authority over peoples rather than cities; by the 700s and 800s, these were settling down. Some episcopal complexes emerged as miniature cities in their own right. A good example is Salzburg, formerly a Roman *municipium*, which grew from the early eighth century as the seat of an important bishopric.

6) Large monasteries too functioned as virtual towns, and were closely integrated into local economies.[167] Monasteries had been a staple of Late

Antiquity in the East, and they expanded in the West across the early Middle Ages. With the rise of oblation, many monastic houses expanded into little cities of God.[168] As Hendrik Dey has observed, monasteries self-consciously adopted a quasi-urban armature.[169] Thanks to confraternity books, books of the dead, and monastic lists, we sometimes have a sense of the number of male or female members of these houses.[170] Gregory of Tours estimated that there were around two hundred nuns at Radegund's monastery upon her death in 587.[171] From the liturgical arrangements of seventh-century Remiremont, we can estimate a convent of about eighty-four nuns, relatively stable over time.[172] There were 114 monks at Jumièges in 828.[173] The rich monastery of Saint-Denis counted some 150 monks in the early ninth century.[174] The great house of Fulda had 603 monks in 825.[175]

The human weight of early medieval monasteries went beyond the number of active monks or nuns. Servants, dependents, visitors, and the attached "poor" added to the total. The "people" of a monastery's patron saint were counted as part of the wider community. When in 589–590 Radegund's monastery at Poitiers fell into a bitter schism after its founder's death, the rival factions of nuns commanded formidable entourages, large enough to terrorize Poitiers and rout an episcopal delegation.[176]

Furthermore, both predictable festivals and the unexpected arrival of new relics drew crowds to monasteries. As organizers of liturgical services, monasteries might incorporate crowds drawn from the wider community. Abbot Angilbert of Saint-Riquier recruited the local populace to ceremonies in Centula's sprawling complex and the surrounding area.[177] He may have even founded a new village called "Angilbertvillia" to safeguard his numbers.[178] The provisions drawn up for the monastery of Corbie similarly planned for non-monastic participation.[179] The famous Saint-Gall Plan shows laborers, dependents, craftspeople, and visitors as part of the ideal monastic family. With their relics, guesthouses for both the needy and the powerful, monasteries could accommodate vast numbers of pious visitors, the "happy crowds" (*turbae . . . hilares*) envisioned marching down the entrance path to the Saint-Gall Plan's church.[180]

Although for most of the year the total numbers at large monasteries like Fulda or San Vincenzo were probably outmatched by cities, towns, and emporia, at certain times—the translation or celebration of relics, the visit of an important personage, the calling in of dues or services—these cities of God marshaled some of the largest crowds in Europe. Moreover, monasteries were landowners whose dependents could number in the tens of thousands; similarly, their spiritual alliances could include tens of thousands of confraternal friends. It is unlikely that such numbers ever came together in one place at one time. But in monastic books, whether polyptychs or confraternity books, multitudes linked economically or spiritually to a great monastery were united on vellum.

7) A conspicuous development of high medieval Europe was *incastellamento*, the expansion of fortified rural sites. Pierre Toubert, who popularized the term, detected it in tenth- and eleventh-century Latium.[181] The process characterized European settlement from the end of our period into the eleventh century, culminating in the growth of castles around Europe.[182] Already by the ninth century, fortifications were gaining in importance as population centers, as they had in the hard years of the 400s and 500s. They are important in the Slavlands; fortified sites like Kolberg, Wollin, and Stettin on the Baltic Coast, Ostrów Lednicki, Gniezno, and Poznań in Poland, and Milkulčice, Stará Kouřim, and Pohansko in Greater Moravia may have rivaled western towns in size.[183] Like towns, fortresses could serve as population centers for hundreds or perhaps even thousands, and might accommodate even larger numbers in times of danger.

Smaller Pools (Hundreds): Markets, Sites of Production and Exchange (8–9)

8) Across Europe, markets (*mercata*) were established or licensed by elites, especially kings, in order to act as economic centers.[184] Sometimes they were located in established towns or cities, or at a short distance from a population center. Large annual markets, often pegged to saints' days, could not rival high and late medieval fairs in scale, but there were not insignificant. A charter of 709 describes "all of the merchants [*negutiatores*] from the Saxons and other peoples . . . coming to the market [*ad illo marcado*] upon the festival of Saint Dionysius," just outside of Paris in early October.[185] Such sites have been difficult to identify archaeologically, so it is hard to estimate their scale.[186] The largest markets, like this one at Saint-Denis, must have assembled hundreds, if not thousands. More local markets were probably a staple of peasant daily life in the early Middle Ages; one would guess they brought in dozens, but it is hard to say.

9) Extraction and production sites, near larger settlements, could also pool numbers. Examples include specialist salt-production sites with long prehistories (e.g., Bad Neuheim), pottery-protection sites, and ore mining sites, most famously the Rammelsberg ore deposits in the Harz.[187] Such places were not necessarily themselves sites of population agglomeration, but mass-labor needs could, as with the Rammelsberg deposits, spur the development of towns like Ottonian Goslar.

Rural Sites: Estates, Villages, Hamlets

Far and away, the commonest pool for gatherings consisted of rural settlements. The majority of early medieval Europeans—the often-cited figure of 90 percent is probably not far off—were farmers or pastoralists living in sparsely populated settings. They inhabited estates, villages, hamlets, and scattered homesteads. The densest rural settlements were nucleated villages centered on the manors of landowners, with a core area marked by workshops and residences.[188] The smallest were isolated farmsteads, where households were the units of economic life.[189] Attempts to extrapolate rural settlement sizes from written or archaeological evidence must be taken with a grain of salt. But cemeteries and polyptychs suggest that village populations in the low hundreds or dozens were typical.[190]

A revealing hint of sparse countrysides, and their social consequences, survives in a ninth-century bishop's reading of forged canon law. The Pseudo-Isidorian decretals had included a ruling by "Pope Silvester" that a "cardinal priest" could not be condemned without forty-four witnesses.[191] Archbishop Hincmar of Reims, who took this to refer to any priest (not just cardinal priests at Rome), pointed out that this made many priests effectively immune, "since there are priests among us who lack the number of male-parishioners [*parochianos*] holding manses and having wives and sons that this text requires as suitable witnesses [*testes idoneos*] for adjudicating a priest."[192] As Charles West has noted, budgeting for families, that might suggest parishes in the low hundreds.[193]

On the other hand, labor needs concentrated rural pools, a subject that will be addressed more in the next chapter. Gregory of Tours relates a story in which "around seventy" hired harvest workers were supplied with miraculous beer.[194] Lords tapped into wide labor networks using chains of dependency.[195] Thomas Kohl and Alexis Wilkin have discussed the mobility of peasants going from estate to estate for work.[196] The eighth-century *Lex Baiuvariorum* describes the duties of *coloni* or *servi* to the church, including physical repairs to haylofts, granaries, fences, and limekilns.[197] One law suggests that, for repairs, a "hundred persons" could be summoned "either to the city [*civitas*] or to the estate [*villa*], as necessity dictates."[198] Horizontal communal action within peasant communities also turned scattered settlements into larger masses.[199]

Dispute settlement and justice pooled rural communities too. The Frankish *mallus*, councils in regions like Brittany and northern Spain, episcopal and royal *placita*, and courts of visiting royal *missi* were nodes for peasant assembly.[200] In May 847, two representatives (*missi*) of the archbishop of Reims, Sigloard and Dodilo, considered a case at the *placitum publicum* of Courtisols pertaining to "hear-tell" (*sonus*) of five *servi* and two *ancillae* claiming to be free.

In response to the argument that their grandmothers had been unfree, the seven peasants publicly declared: "That is not the case, for we are supposed to be free by birth."[201] But then seven "very elderly" witnesses testified against them. Eight judgment finders (*scabini*) declared against the unfree peasants, who then publicly committed themselves to unfree status.[202] Among the signatories of this notice, in addition to Sigloardus and Dodilo, were twenty-four additional men. Finally, two more peasants were confirmed to servile status. At minimum, then, adjudicating the status of nine unfree peasants meant gathering at least fifty persons, probably more.

Logistical Consequences

We can draw a few conclusions about the challenges of forming gatherings from these levels of feeder populations. Pools for assembly were smaller than in the Roman past. The logistical thresholds to crowds of thousands and tens of thousands, as in the Roman entertainment complexes, were prohibitively high. Even bringing forty-four local free men together could be a challenge, as Hincmar suggested. But in many settings—whether outlier settlements like Rome, or sites of anticipated gathering like fields at harvest or courts of justice—logistical constraints could be overcome.

Crowds of many hundreds, perhaps infrequent globally, were not inconceivable. Given small pools and high transaction costs, they required preparation. Exceptions occasioned astonishment. For a ninth-century archbishop, a crowd of "three hundred, four hundred, or even more persons" unexpectedly assembled in a Dijon church was a cause for amazement, and a reason to suspect the presence of ringleaders.[203] On the other hand, demographic constraints on gathering should not be overstated. Populations in Europe were never so diminished in the period c. 500–1000 as to make crowds of hundreds or dozens an impossibility.

Sizes of Gatherings

How big were early medieval gatherings? The question is difficult to answer. Untrained observers regularly miscalculate crowd size today.[204] Indeed, the very concept of a "crowd" is cognitive shorthand for numbers too large to estimate.[205] Words like *turba, caterva, multitudo,* and *frequentia* appear with adjectives "countless" or "innumerable."[206] But there are times when early medieval authors provided concrete figures, and there are indirect ways of estimating gathering size. We will consider 1) medieval numerical reports, 2) plausible coefficients for stated figures, and 3) indirect sources such as architectural spaces.

Numbers Reported in Textual Sources

It is axiomatic that ancient and medieval figures cannot be taken at face value.[207] Medieval authors attentive to the symbolic significance of ancient texts tended to reuse biblical, classical, and patristic numbers.[208] Stock figures like six hundred (*sescenti* or *sexcenti*) or ten thousand (μυριάς) meant "very many."[209] So when a ninth-century annalist describes "more than six hundred" casualties as a part of a military expedition, it is hard to know whether this is a serious estimate or a topos.[210] For good reason, scholars are suspicious of the round numbers that fill early medieval sources.[211]

Inflation of figures was common.[212] Numbers for the distant past or faraway settings (or both) were especially large.[213] Frechulf's ninth-century history offered enormous figures for Biblical, Greek, and Roman history.[214] The ninth-century historian Agnellus of Ravenna reported that thirty thousand were killed in an earthquake in Cilicia in the sixth century (not necessarily an unbelievable claim).[215] Speaking of the present, Alcuin reported that Charlemagne's campaign against the Byzantines involved four thousand imperial dead and one thousand prisoners—figures on the edge of plausibility.[216] Frankish chroniclers reported that over ten thousand were killed in a Danish succession dispute in 812.[217]

Imaginary numbers could be gigantic. The outlandish figure of ten thousand times one hundred thousand (that is, ten billion) occurs repeatedly. This figure derives from the apocalyptic vision of Daniel 7:10 ("A swift stream of fire issued forth from before him; thousands of thousands ministered to him, and ten thousand times a hundred thousand stood before him; the judgment sat, and the books were opened").[218] The *Cosmographia* of Aethicus Ister, a late seventh- or early eighth-century book of wonders, explained that a battle between Alexander the Great and Arboges, chief of the Albanians, left ten billion dead after three days.[219] Such enormous figures—a bit like the English word "gazillion"—do not invalidate more credible estimates made by authors who use them.[220]

Less fantastical figures shaped expectations. The benchmarks for ecumenical councils were among the best-known gathering-sizes of early medieval Christendom. The 318 "holy fathers" at the council of Nicaea I (325), the 150 fathers at the council of Constantinople I (381), and the 630 fathers at the council of Chalcedon (451) were canonical figures, to the point that Nicaea was called "the council of the 318."[221] It is not clear whether these numbers reflected realities. The figure of 318 was first proposed by Athanasius in the fourth century, not long after the event; it likely owed something to the biblical 318 servants of Abraham (Genesis 14:14).[222] What matters is that these famous figures gave early medieval bishops a sense of the appropriate size of an ecumenical (a "world" as opposed to a "provincial") council.²²³ They were in Anastasius Bibliothecarius's mind when he or one of his scribes added a note to the hundred subscriptions to a session of the fourth "ecumenical" council at Constantinople (869–70): "Do not let the small number of subscribers scandalize you."²²⁴

Specific but not overlarge or stereotyped numbers merit attention. Amolo of Lyon's shocked report of three hundred to four hundred "or more" ecstatic visitors to illicit relics at Dijon has no obvious parallel.²²⁵ We cannot compare Amolo's number to a spatial analysis of the Carolingian church of St. Bénigne.²²⁶ But Amolo's shock suggests that a few hundred felt excessive for an urban church of the 840s. An even more precise figure appears in the ninth-century *Annals of Saint-Bertin*. A dune-flattening tsunami caused havoc on the Frisian coast in December 838, killing, Prudentius of Troyes reports, exactly 2,437 people. Prudentius notes that the figure was "most diligently acquired."²²⁷ But this refers to casualties over a large area, and not one particular site.

Armies: The Largest Gatherings in the Early Medieval World?

The largest physical gatherings in the early medieval West were probably armies, not so much in battle, but when mustered at the start of campaigns. We have occasional troop estimates and casualty figures, indirect archaeological evidence, and scattered sources for the logistics of troop-assembly and provisioning.²²⁸ But for all the famous battles and sieges of the early medieval world—Vouillé (507), Tertry (687), Toulouse (721), Tours/Poitiers (732), Roncevaux (778), the Avar campaigns (791, 796), Barcelona (801), Fontenoy (841), Paris (845), Bari (871), Andernach (876), Saucourt (881), Paris (885–86), Garigliano (915), Lechfeld (955), Stamford Bridge (1066), and Hastings (1066)—numbers are guesswork. Scholars disagree wildly about the size of the early medieval armies. Minimalists picture hundreds; maximalists imagine tens of thousands.²²⁹

Since Hans Delbrück, scholars have suspected that ancient and medieval authors exaggerated figures.²³⁰ Reported figures do not always agree. For the same battle between Franks and Saxons in 798, different chroniclers reported that 2,800, 2,901, and 4,000 Saxons perished.²³¹ In 881, the young Carolingian king of West Francia Louis III (r. 879–82) defeated a Viking force at Saucourt in Picardy.²³² The *Annals of Fulda* reports that 9,000 "horsemen" on the Viking side were slain, but admits that the "Northmen" recuperated, then ravaged to the north and west.²³³ Regino of Prüm, writing later, reported that Louis "laid low more than eight thousand enemies by the sword."²³⁴ No source indicates the size of Louis's army or his "lordly retinue" (*fronisc githigini*), as the *Ludwigslied* calls it.²³⁵ But taking the *Annals of Fulda* and Regino at face value would mean a clash of tens of thousands. Similarly, Abbo of Saint-Germain-des-Prés implied that a Viking army of 40,000 besieged a Frankish force of mere hundreds at Paris in 885–86.[236] Without the Muster Rolls that survive from later medieval Europe to corroborate such numbers, many have followed Delbrück in assuming annalistic inflation or error.[237]

But there is not much consensus as to what constitutes a reasonable alternative. For minimalists like Guy Halsall, early medieval armies were more warbands than armies.[238] In some settings, this is right. The late seventh- or early eighth-century Law Code of the West Saxon king Ine defined an "army" (*here*) as thirty-five armed men or more.[239] But later Continental armies may have been larger. In 1968, Karl Ferdinand Werner complained that it had become "customary" to cultivate "extraordinary mistrust against any claim for a somewhat larger number of troops."[240] By reverse engineering from population estimates (itself a dubious prospect), Werner arrived at a high notional "total" Frankish military manpower of 30,000 heavy cavalry ("Reiter") and 100,000 less heavily armed men for the period c. 800–840.[241] This is manpower potential only. The size of armies as physical gatherings—the number of troops and followers actually assembled in any given place and time—would have been smaller.[242]

Werner thought that a major Carolingian campaign like the one against the Avars in 791 involved 15,000–20,000 heavy cavalry marching with as many or more infantry and support, though he emphasized that such a force would have been "organized into several army columns."[243] Early medieval rulers, despite decentralized taxation and organization, achieved impressive feats of military assembly. At the upper limits of the possible, budgeting for retinues, camp-followers, and baggage trains, physical gatherings in the tens of thousands are conceivable. Yet there is reason to suppose that numbers of this size were rare. Frankish planners thought in terms of the *scara* (cf. modern German *Schar*), a "unit," "group," or "division" of variable size, but not thousands strong.[244]

Moreover, while early medieval authors valued size—as with Charlemagne's huge ironclad army seen by Desiderius from the ramparts of Pavia—the warriors of the age prided themselves on quality over quantity.[245] A snarky letter from Louis II to Basil I, penned by Anastasius Bibliothecarius in the wake of the combined Frankish-Byzantine siege of Bari in 871, accused the Byzantines of locust-like assaults on the Saracen stronghold. The less numerous Franks, unimpressed by their allies' insectoid numbers, took the citadel successfully.[246] The early medieval ideal of war centered on small cadres of heavily armed elites, not vast hordes.

But there were exceptions. In 782, Charlemagne was reported to have decapitated 4,500 Saxons at Verden, a mass-execution that would have necessitated hundreds if not thousands of Franks to carry out.[247] The springtime gatherings that doubled as annual assembly and campaign muster in the Frankish were probably, in the late eighth or early ninth century, the largest agglomerations in the West. Numerically such gatherings may have been smaller than the biggest Roman circus audiences, to say nothing of Roman armies. Whether they were smaller than contemporary Islamic and Byzantine armies is an open question.[248] But the army in its splendor—thousands or tens of thousands in fields and tents—shaped expectations about the upper range of possibility for gatherings.

Coefficients: Entourages and Retinues

Historians are most willing to accept early medieval figures when they appear as countable names in administrative documents (conciliar acts, *placita*, diplomas, and private charters). As we have seen, the placitum at Courtisols had at least fifty persons. An even more vivid example comes from the long-running territorial dispute between Arezzo and Siena over shrines that fell under Siena's political dominion but Arezzo's spiritual jurisdiction.[249] The dispute produced a famous placitum in 715, affirming a decision made the previous summer, in which seventy-seven witnesses swore before a Lombard notary called Gunteram that their spiritual lives fell under the jurisdiction of Saint Donatus's church at Arezzo. Aside from being terrifically vivid—"I am nearly a hundred years old," says a rural cleric named Godo, "and we have always been dioceses of Saint Donatus, and have always gotten consecration and chrism for the people from there"—the placitum gives a sense of the numbers involved in an early eighth-century summertime (June 5) appeals-hearing "in the royal court of Siena" (*in curte regia Senense*) involving rural participation.[250] The placitum allows us to picture the crowded hall where witnesses were interrogated in the presence of the four gospels, the lord's cross, and the chalice and paten.

How many people attended on this early summer day? The seventy-seven witnesses came from a mix of statuses, but even rural priests of lower status must have come with family, friends, or servants. Godo, the self-proclaimed centenarian, probably did not hobble up to Siena alone. Gunteram the notary would have arrived from Pavia with an entourage. The local *gastald* and his followers, the main parties, local officials, curious onlookers, and others must have rounded out these numbers. We should picture not seventy-seven people, but twice that or more. A month later in July, when fourteen subscribers signed the "judgment" *ad ecclesia Sancti Genesii in uico Uuallari*, including four bishops, the archpriest of Pisa, one unnamed individual, and eight priests, again the actual assembled crowd must have been larger.[251] But how does one go from a credible count to a reasonable inference about total numbers?

The placitum of 715 is unusual for its rich prosopographical detail, but we face the same challenge for thousands of similar documents with witness data from the early Middle Ages. We might know how many magnates attended an assembly, how many bishops, abbots, or priests participated in a council, or how many witnesses attested a transaction or court meeting, but the total size of the public gatherings behind these subtotals remains unknown. To arrive at plausible totals, we need plausible coefficients.

Rulers and elites had large retinues.[252] To judge by food and fodder needs, their numbers varied.[253] Scholars have concluded that early medieval kings traveled with as many as hundreds at a time.[254] Anecdotes support this. In Einhard's biography of Charlemagne, the emperor "invited not only his sons to the bath, but nobles and friends, and occasionally even a crowd [*turba*] of subordinates and bodyguards, so that sometimes a hundred men or more would be bathing together."[255]

But how often was "sometimes"? Retinue figures may only be mentioned because they were exceptional.[256] Contentious proceedings at the council of Savonnières in 862 led the drafter of the acts, probably Hincmar of Reims, to note the presence of "nearly two hundred advisers [*consiliarii*] of the three kings [Louis the German, Charles the Bald, and Lothar II], both bishops and abbots and laymen."[257] But this high number may reflect the unusual, tense circumstances of the meeting. Even then, it is hard to know how many servants or retainers, if any, accompanied these nearly two hundred "advisers."

We know most about the size of episcopal retinues.[258] This is because bishops' overlarge retinues burdened parishioners with mouths to feed.[259] A conciliar canon of the Seventh Council of Toledo (646) decreed that bishops visiting their dioceses should not "act as a burden on account of a multitude [*prae multitudine*]," and ordered them to set a retinue limit at "the number fifty" (a number of biblical significance).[260]

That Toledo number became a yardstick, even for nonepiscopal collectivities. It was likely in Charlemagne's head when he fixed the number of monks at one monastery at "no more than the number fifty."[261] The Council of Toulouse in 844, in regulating the supplies a bishop could exact from local presbyters, made reference to Toledo VII.[262] Hincmar of Reims cited Toledo VII in his treatise *Collectio de ecclesiis et capellis* (857–58), complaining that bishops in his time were traveling with huge, hungry entourages.[263] Despite the fifty-person limit prescribed at Toledo, wrote Hincmar, "we, for our part, go about our parishes with an assembled army [*cum hoste collecta*], and now to our priests we seem not so much preachers of God's word as exactors and impoverishers."[264]

One rare early medieval report of an abbot's retinue suggests that higher numbers were not impossible despite these regulations. Bede reports that more than eighty "Englishmen" were with Ceolfrith, abbot of Warmouth-Jarrow, when he died at Langres on September 25, 716, adding "many of the locals" were also present.²⁶⁵ Ceolfrith had been *en route* to Rome, bringing the famous *Codex Amiatinus* with him. After his death, his retinue split into three groups. One returned to Britain to inform the monks of Wearmouth-Jarrow of Ceolfrith's death, the next continued on to Rome, and the third stayed with the body.²⁶⁶ This case shows that the fifty-person limit was not fanciful.

The reduction of entourages was a tool of control and even humiliation. Charles West estimates that thirty to forty armed men had accompanied Hincmar of Laon to the Council of Douzy in 871, when the assembled bishops forced Hincmar to content himself with only "ten or a dozen" followers.²⁶⁷ Hincmar of Laon's entourage may have been on the high side, since the bishop (rightly) suspected he was heading into a trap. On the other hand, Janet Nelson has reasonably asked whether Hincmar's armed retinue was only unusual "in the sense of being unusually well documented."²⁶⁸

Entourages were particularly important for travel, and grew—as with Ceolfrith—in proportion to the distance journeyed. Less than twenty years after Douzy, Charles III ("the Fat") issued a charter that allotted the abbot of Corvey thirty "noble men" when he traveled in his capacity as *missus*, but "even more" if he had to travel outside of his "home country" (*patria*), due to "the massive invasion of barbarians."²⁶⁹ In 929, the bishop of Worcester, Cenwald, toured the monasteries of "Germania" on behalf of the English king Æthelstan.²⁷⁰ He reached St. Gallen just in time to celebrate the feast of the monastery's patron, Saint Gall.²⁷¹ A list of English names was added to the St. Gallen confraternity book (including the king, the archbishop of Canterbury, seven bishops, and two abbots back in England), and there are also twelve names that may have been men in Cenwald's party.²⁷² There may have been more with him still, given that Cenwald was traveling with enough treasure to disburse among "monasteries throughout Germania."²⁷³ On his 968 expedition to Constantinople, Liutprand brought twenty-five followers (*asseclae*), a figure that only covers his personal retainers.²⁷⁴

Hosts were required to prepare for the logistics of high-status visitors. The fact that Cenwald arrived at St. Gallen on Saint Gall's feast day itself may reflect courtesy on the English visitors' part. At Fulda in the ninth century, the abbot made special provisions for those times "when many people arrive at once, as for the mass of Saint Boniface," one of the most important local patrons.²⁷⁵ Visiting at predictable times, like major holidays or a local saint's feast, facilitated planning when a luminary's visit involved dozens of others. Conversely, Notker's late ninth-century *Life of Charlemagne* describes how unexpected royal visits inspired terror for hosts forced to scramble.²⁷⁶

Sometimes grandees traveled with smaller retinues. In her study of Merovingian episcopal entourages, Jamie Kreiner offers "at a guess" ten to twenty men as the norm, noting that successful assassination attempts coincided with insufficient numbers.[277] Traveling with small numbers could be a (risky) virtue. A senatorial aristocrat in a late seventh-century saint's life journeyed with only three *pueri*, while a ninth-century holy woman in Saxony went to vigils with one young male or female servant; this numerical abstemiousness was saintly.[278] Witness lists provide a sense of the numbers for traveling entourages of middling individuals below the level of bishops and counts. One Joseph who appears in a charter of Freising in 902–3 brought with him nine of "his (free) men" to act as witnesses, a small but respectable retinue.[279]

Carolingian attempts to fix daily rations for royal officials—similar to the Toledo VII decree—attest to entourage sizes at different social levels. The frequent repetition of such attempts shows that sizes of followings presented a persistent logistical challenge. A ninth-century Carolingian capitulary regulated the size of entourages of *missi* (traveling officials sent to conduct royal business) by fixing their daily rations on the basis of rank (*qualitas*).[280] These rations were clearly intended to supply retinues:

> Concerning the provisioning of our *missi*, what should be given and received by each one according to his rank: namely, to a bishop forty loaves of bread, three freshlings [suckling pigs], three measures of drink, one piglet, three chickens, fifteen eggs, four measures of fodder for the horses. To an abbot, a count, or to one of our vassals each should be given daily thirty loaves of bread, two freshlings, two measures of drink, one piglet, three chickens, fifteen eggs, and three measures of fodder for the horses. To one of our vassals [*ministerialis*], ten and seven loaves of bread, one freshling, one measure of drink, two chickens, ten eggs, and two measures of fodder for the horses.[281]

Michael McCormick has used this legislation to extrapolate rough figures for entourage sizes.[282] Building upon a ratio of one loaf per man, which prevailed in contemporary Carolingian monasteries, he arrived at expected ninth-century numerical limits for bishops (forty persons), abbots or counts (thirty persons), and vassals (seventeen persons).[283] These restrictions may not evince real limits to entourages so much as limits to the king's willingness to support them. Still, the extrapolated totals provide a yardstick—impressively high—that lets us construct projections from recorded numbers.

Extrapolations: The Example of Frankish Councils

Can we use our rough entourage-coefficients to reconstruct total gathering sizes from existing records? Unfortunately, numbers are infrequently reported for secular assemblies.[284] Moreover, there were differences in how political assemblies worked across post-Roman kingdoms.[285] For the Frankish world, we must make do with bland references to a few named individuals and "the bishops, dukes, counts, and faithful men present."[286] But as mentioned above, at Savonnières, just outside of Toul, in November 862, some two hundred *consiliarii* were present.[287] McCormick's extrapolation for entourages, based on the coefficients above, gives a total size of five thousand.[288]

If that is correct, Savonnières in 862 may have been one of the largest royal assemblies in the ninth-century West.[289] A few factors contributed to its size. First, three Carolingian kings assembled at once: Louis the German, Charles the Bald, and Lothar II. Second, the drafter, likely Hincmar of Reims, wished to emphasize the legitimacy of the pro-Charles proceedings. Other royal assemblies, even those involving multiple kings, brought together smaller numbers. At the treaty of Meersen (870), on Louis the German's initiative, each king was only to bring four bishops, ten "counsellors," and thirty "ministerial vassals."[290] So, Savonnières is an outlier. Moreover, we should distinguish, as Gerd Althoff insisted, between assemblies of a genuinely deliberative nature and those of a more celebratory tenor.[291] The former were considerably smaller than the latter.

For England from the 900s onward, we have better data. In royal diplomas, it became customary to provide hierarchically ordered witness lists. Since such charters were often produced on the occasion of large royal assemblies, such lists are vistas onto *witenagemot* size. A minimal attendance of around two hundred people with a large attendance of about six hundred or more is reasonable.[292] It should be emphasized that the English case is doubly anomalous, both because these assemblies played such a large role in the ideological ambitions of the West Saxon kings of the tenth and eleventh centuries, and because they are relatively late in our period.

But our best figures come from church councils. Following late Roman tradition, bishops and clerics in attendance subscribed their names to conciliar decrees, providing a baseline from which totals can be extrapolated.[293] We sometimes lack subscription figures for councils known to have been significant (e.g., Lyon in 516 and Valence in 528). But conciliar documents from the early Middle Ages often permit a head count of the most important participants. Table 2.3, drawn from sixth- to eighth-century Frankish councils (as assembled by Halfond), lists signatories and then two estimates for additional participants: one low (based on Kreiner's estimates for episcopal entourages) and one high (based on McCormick's coefficients).[294]

These coefficients allow some sense of the possible scope of early medieval church councils. Even a rather small council—with only four bishops—might have involved some 60–160 persons from episcopal retinues, while a large council like Paris in 614, with its seventy-six bishops, might have entailed

TABLE 2.3. Frankish Councils, 511–762, total number extrapolations

Date	Place	Signatories	Low Estimate	High Estimate
511	Orléans	32 bishops	480	1,280
517	Epaone	24 bishops, 1 presbyter	362	977
518 / 519	Lyon	11 bishops	165	440
524	Arles	14 bishops, 4 presbyters	218	628
527	Carpentras	16 bishops	240	640
529	Orange	14 bishops, 1 praetorian prefect, 7 *viri clarissimi*	229	709
529	Vaison	12 bishops	180	480
533	Marseille	15 bishops, 1 abbot, some laymen	235	680
533	Orléans	26 bishops, 5 presbyters	400	1,125
535	Clermont	15 bishops	225	600
538	Orléans	19 bishops, 7 presbyters	299	879
541	Orléans	42 bishops, 1 abbot, 10 presbyters	655	1,880
549	Orléans	50 bishops, 6 archdeacons, 3 deacons, 10 presbyters, 2 abbots	780	2,230
551	Eauze	8 bishops, 1 presbyter	122	337
551 / 552	Paris	27 bishops	405	1,080
554	Arles	11 bishops, 4 presbyters, 2 archdeacons, 2 deacons	181	576
556 × 573	Paris	15 bishops	225	600
567	Tours	9 bishops	135	360
567 × 570	Lyon	8 bishops, 5 presbyters, 1 deacon	132	422
573	Paris	32 bishops, 1 presbyter	482	1,297
577	Paris	45 bishops	675	1,800
571 × 583	Mâcon	21 bishops	315	840
583	Lyon	8 bishops	120	320
583 × 585	Valence	17 bishops	255	680
585	Mâcon	54 bishops, 12 others	822	2,280
585 × 605	Auxerre	1 bishop, 34 presbyters, 3 deacons, 7 abbots	124	879
589	unknown	10 bishops	150	400
589–90	Poitiers	4 bishops	60	160
614	Paris	76 bishops, 1 abbot	1,145	3,070

TABLE 2.3. (continued)

Date	Place	Signatories	Low Estimate	High Estimate
627	Clichy	40 bishops, 1 deacon, 1 abbot	607	1,647
636	Clichy	26 bishops	390	1,040
647 × 653	Chalon-sur-Saone	39 bishops, 5 abbots, 1 archdeacon	612	1,727
653	Paris	26 bishops	390	1,040
654	Clichy	15 bishops, 2 deacons, 8 *viri inlustri*, 1 mayor of the palace, others	255	850
662 × 675	Bordeaux (St Pierre de Granon)	16 bishops, 2 abbots, 1 dux	255	730
742	"Germania"	7 bishops	105	280
744	Soissons	23 bishops, unknown number of other ecclesiastics and optimates	350	970
757	Compiègne	21 bishops, 1 abbot, 1 deacon, 16 men of unknown status	322	887
762	Attigny	27 bishops, 17 abbots	490	1,590

Source: Figures drawn from Gregory Halfond, *Archaeology of Frankish Church Councils, AD 511–768* (Leiden, 2010), 223–64 (appendix), using numbers drawn from Karl Joseph von Hefele and H. Leclercq, *Histoire des conciles d'après les documents originaux*, 2nd ed., 8 vols. (Paris, 1907–10).

between a thousand and well over three thousand people. If we assume the Toledan figure of fifty persons per bishop instead of McCormick's capitulary-based forty, that number goes up to 3,800. Of course, councils as physical gatherings hardly involved participants' entourages. At a large council, such as Orléans in 549 or Chalon in 647–53, only some tiny portion of a bishop's retinue—or none at all—must have attended him in the actual proceedings. The rest might have spent the day attending to business or pleasure. The numbers are more useful in speaking to a horizon of possibilities.

Impressive as some of these numbers might have been, it is worth stressing that they do not compare with late Roman councils or high medieval ones at their grandest.[295] No early medieval Western council appears to have occurred on the scale of eleventh- and twelfth-century councils like the grand Council of

Piacenza convened by Urban II in 1095.[296] Even if we do not trust extravagant figures for that period—one chronicler claims that in addition to some two hundred bishops "nearly three thousand clerics and more than thirty thousand laymen are said to have been present" at Piacenza[297]—this synod and others in the "reform period" were much larger than those of our period.[298]

Spatial Estimates

Finally, one last—rough—means of estimating possible crowd size is through extrapolations from measurable spaces in which crowds assembled. By taking known areas of standing room in early medieval palace halls or churches, and multiplying by a plausible coefficient, we may be able to get a sense of some assembly figures that are not reported in writing. Ramsay MacMullen has used this method to estimate maximum possible capacities for late Roman churches.[299] The attempt has also been applied to the audiences of later medieval preachers. We can compare the huge numbers reported by sources to the available space in Italian *piazze*. Maria Giuseppina Muzzarelli has shown that our sources for the audiences of Bernardino da Siena and Bernardino da Feltre need not have been exaggerating when they reported tens of thousands of listeners.[300]

Such methods have been applied to early medieval spaces. Kazhdan and McCormick estimated possible crowd capacity in Constantinople's Hagia Sophia.[301] Building on an estimate of 2,867 square meters of "total usable space in the galleries" of Hagia Sophia in Constantinople, with a "generous square meter for each person," they arrive at a theoretical maximum capacity of around 2,900 persons.[302] The reckoning of a square meter per person is crude, as the authors acknowledge, and fails to account for the ritual necessity of empty space, but it provides a sense of possibilities. In a subsequent essay, McCormick extended this approach to Carolingian palaces.[303] Using the same calculation of 1 square meter per person, he provided rough guesses for the capacity of palace halls (*aulae*), suggesting they could have accommodated only hundreds: 748 square meters at Aachen, 310 square meters at Paderborn, 668 square meters at Ingelheim, and 323 square meters at Frankfurt.[304] McCormick muses whether it is "coincidental that the throne rooms appear to be smaller as one moves farther away from what were likely the more densely populated territories of the empire."[305]

The result is that interior audiences for royal palace gatherings probably only numbered in the hundreds. Open-air assemblies accommodated many more (estimating crowd capacity for outside spaces is a more difficult prospect). Still, numbers are not everything. Exclusivity and coziness could be virtues. Fewer but denser crowds can feel grander than bigger but more spread-out ones. Contrasts between open space (courtyard) and closed space (hall) were mobilized in collective ritual.[306]

Numbers and Crowds

During the early Middle Ages, European countrysides were thinner than they had been since perhaps the late Iron Age. Settlements diminished in density and number. The urban regime never wholly perished, particularly in Italy, Spain, and southern Gaul. But the kind of cities that had shaped ancient Roman crowds—settlements of tens of thousands or more with complex, specialized economies—were vanishingly rare by the seventh century. Theaters, entertainment buildings, and baths were reused for material or space.[307] Collective life adjusted to a new scale.

The demographic crisis was short-lived. Population recovery began almost as soon as mortality pressures were mitigated. But this growth took place in rural settings, whereas towns and cities caught up later in the 900s and 1000s. In such a regime, crowds, even at their largest, could not compare with the multitudes of Roman times. Yet the regular assembly of dozens and hundreds remained possible throughout the period, both during the acutest stages of demographic crisis (sixth–seventh centuries) and during the long recovery (eighth–tenth centuries). Given the right spaces, times, and institutional support, some gatherings—armies and assemblies—regularly convened thousands.

Scale change did not imply any one destiny. There is no political economy, mentality, or lifestyle bound to one level of concentration as opposed to another.[308] The next two chapters will explore the many new patterns of collective behavior that emerged amid demographic downscaling. Communities regularly overcame logistical constraints by favoring venues or occasions that facilitated assembly or by coordinating motivations for gatherings (e.g., economic and religious). If decline and disequilibrium altered the possibilities for assembly, early medieval communities adapted to this new ecology.

They also maintained a healthy imagination. Memorial books listing spiritual allies—like the list into which Cenwald's monks added their name in 929—were kept for the purposes of prayer. These contained thousands or even tens of thousands of names. By the 900s, the largest surviving early medieval example, the confraternity book at Reichenau, contained 38,232 names. That would have been more souls than inhabited contemporary Rome.[309] Early medieval demographic constraints on gathering were real, but they were meant to be broken, one way or another.

3

Peasants and Other Non-Elites

REPERTORY AND RESISTANCE

The Problem of Non-Elite Crowds

Twice in the ninth century, crowds of peasants took up arms against the Vikings. In 859, a "mixed rabble" (*vulgus promiscuum*) from between the Seine and the Loire banded together to fight the Danes on the Seine. They formed a *coniuratio* or "sworn-association." Although they fought bravely, they were "easily slain"—and not by the Danes, but by aristocrats hostile to their "incautiously formed" collective.[1] In 882, "an innumerable multitude" (*innumera multitudo*) "came together from the fields and villages into a single force" (*agmen*) to fight the Northmen near the monastery of Prüm. This time the Vikings got there first. The "ignoble rabble" (*ignobile vulgus*), we are told, was slaughtered "like brute beasts, not human beings."[2] These two cases are often cited to highlight the limits of peasant collective action in the early Middle Ages.[3]

Confrontational collective behavior was risky for early medieval non-elites.[4] In the wake of the scale change that characterized fifth- to seventh-century European demographic history, opportunities for popular self-assertion via collective behavior contracted. As the last chapter showed, gatherings were smaller and more predictable, and that made them more governable. Since the "crowd in history" has centered on protests, uprisings, or other Bakhtinian actions by which the socially marginalized seize power, it is tempting to suppose that numbers became a less effective weapon of the weak in this period. This chapter argues that this is not the full story.

Quotidian crowds, that is, "gatherings," remained essential for early medieval economic and social life. Agrarian collective labor, local councils, and churchgoing are hardly what Canetti had in mind when he spoke of "open crowds" (as opposed to the heroic bands of 859 and 882). Rather, these gatherings constitute the background noise of collective normalcy that Natalie Davis called "repertory": the routinized gatherings that spontaneous, atypical crowds are supposedly in dialogue with.[5] This chapter will argue that routinized gatherings were not only means for structuring daily life, with elite approval, but also venues of self-assertion and resistance.

It is true that elites were best situated to predict and stage gatherings. Crowds were more often a tool of surplus extraction or hierarchical celebration than of resistance. But that did not make crowds a strong tool of economic or social control. If the early Middle Ages was an age of the closed crowd, the crowd was a weak weapon of the strong. In a period of fragile governance, elites were vulnerable to nonparticipation and participation at cross purposes. Non-elites knew how to work around "closed crowds" to fulfil their own needs and wants. That, more than anything, helps to explain the gut-reaction of hostility to unexpected acts of nonaristocratic collective autonomy.

Peasants: Far from the Madding Crowd?

The vast majority of gatherings in the early Middle Ages were carried out by peasants living in rural contexts.[6] Only by the tenth or eleventh centuries did a new order of urbanism allow artisans and merchants in cities to play a larger role in the collective life of the West.[7] There is a myth that rural life is lacking in crowds, as Thomas Gray imagined in his "Elegy Written in a Country Churchyard":

> Far from the madding crowd's ignoble strife
> Their sober wishes never learn'd to stray;
> Along the cool sequester'd vale of life
> They kept the noiseless tenor of their way.[8]

Thomas Hardy's ironically named *Far from the Madding Crowd* provides a literary antidote to that misconception. Sheep run off a cliff in droves, laborers gather at hiring fairs, a crowd rushes to put out a fire, and banquets, acting troupes, and judicial dramas fill out the narrative.[9] Peasant life, Hardy reminds us, is full of crowds.

But what are "peasants"?[10] Here the term is used for agriculturalists and pastoralists at the lower end of the social hierarchy.[11] For Marxian anthropologists, "peasant" denotes rural cultivators whose surpluses are transferred to a dominant elite.[12] By the 800s, perhaps a majority of rural cultivators in Europe met that description. Here, unfree laborers and free folk without lords also count. The imperfect catchall "non-elite" will also be used, to cover both peasants and artisans, merchants, petty clergy, servants, and slaves who did not work the land. Non-elites could be free, unfree, or partially free by any number of legal, social, or economic definitions, many contested and negotiable.[13]

The sources for peasant collective life in early medieval Europe are not so vivid as Hardy's novel.[14] But there is enough information to sketch out commonalities. *Placita* and charters show peasant communities as they came together before judges or counts to resolve issues. Lists of tenants, properties, and dues in polyptychs provide details about gatherings relating to labor and surplus extraction. Archaeology offers clues to the lifeways behind ceramic sherds, loomweights, and pollen samples. Miracle stories in saints' lives and relic translation accounts, probably the best source of stories about rustic crowds, portray the dramas of rural life.[15] Renewed scholarly interest is shedding fresh light on early medieval peasant gatherings.[16] As the end of the chapter will explore, peasants did use gatherings for resistance. Usually, they were a means of getting by.

Agrarian Labors

Peasant gatherings were shaped by the risks and rewards of the agrarian cycle, which varied by ecology, labor regime, crops, livestock, and technology.[17] An ideal type can be sketched. Wintertime tasks included coppicing, tending to livestock, breaking fields, pruning, and making repairs. In spring, peasants oversaw lambing and calving, mended fences, sowed spring crops, replanted orchards or grafted, and fertilized. They milked and made cheese, dug ditches and built fences, and turned out animals from stalls into pastures. After Easter, they picked fruits, turned up fields sown the previous autumn, bred livestock, and planted gardens. In summer, they tended gardens, sheared sheep, and mowed hay. Late summer and autumn were harvest time. First came the winter crops: wheat, barley, flax, and (in the north) rye and spelt. Next, the spring: spelt, oats, barley, flax, and pulses. Harvest was earlier in the Mediterranean (June–July) than it was north of the Alps (August). Fruits and cash crops— grapes, olives, and chestnuts—were usually harvested later. In late fall, peasants set pigs to pannage so as to slaughter them in early winter, collected fish from weirs, and prepared for the challenges and festivities of the cold season. Some labors, especially for women, were year-round: milling grain or having it milled, caring for livestock, protecting crops, rearing children, cooking, milking, brewing, spinning, weaving, and making crafts.

When performed for subsistence, many if not most agrarian labors were the work of a single household, the Chayanovian unit of analysis of peasant economic life.[18] For instance, plowing was a task of high drudgery but low manpower. "Alas, alas, what labor it is!" cries the plowman in Ælfric's *Colloquy*, who has one boy to help him.[19] A team of two, leading oxen or horses, sufficed for most fields. Sowing too was accomplished by few hands: someone to broadcast seeds, someone (again often a younger person) to frighten off birds. Sometimes, however, peasants had to work in large numbers.

Harvest

Harvests of all kinds—grain, hay, grape, olive, chestnut—demanded urgent collective effort from both sexes, with complex divisions of labor on the front and back ends.[20] In early modern Europe, the rule for wheat harvests was that fifteen to twenty men were needed to reap the area plowed and sown by four sowers.[21] The reason was timing. Begin too soon, and unripe grain will go to waste in threshing. Begin too late, and overripe grain will fall to the ground, lost to the elements, the birds, and the gleaners. Begin after your neighbors, and they might intrude, accidentally or intentionally, into your fields.[22]

In cereal harvests (wheat, rye, barley, spelt), grain was reaped by sickle, generally by men, next to be bound and sheaved, usually by women. Sheaves had to be laid out to be dried by the sun or in drying ovens.[23] Dried grain must be properly stored, and eventually threshed and winnowed (often at a delay). After reaping, stalks—that is, straw—also had to be gathered, dried, and stored, for fodder, thatching, bedding, fuel, and crafts. All this took weeks. The more hands a family, community, or estate had at its disposal, the faster the risks of delay could be overcome. The poorest paid in time what they lacked in numbers.[24]

Dependent peasants—the majority—had to devote labor to their lords' fields as well as their own. At harvest, lords called in day-work, deployed unfree dependents, and hired or leased workers, a process rather murky for this period. In the last chapter, we saw how a sixth-century magnate hired "around seventy" reapers, a number that omits dependents and unfree labor.[25] Little is known about the factor markets for such workers: where they came from, how they were hired, what they did for the rest of the year.[26] It is likely that *mancipia* (chattel-slaves) owned by smallholders were leased out. On some estates, lords required dependents to supply them with slave-labor as a part of harvest services.[27]

Other day-workers may have been recruited from the poor folk sustained by alms and religious charity. A hint of this is provided by a Frankish "bishops' capitulary" issued during a late eighth-century famine, which stipulated that bishops, abbots, and abbesses were to take in four of the "hungry poor" (*pauperes famelici*) and feed them "until the time of harvests."[28] The timing may be less about food availability than labor availability. In harvest, the "hungry poor" could find day-work or pay back benefactors in labor.

An additional complication was posed by injunctions against work on Sundays and festival days.[29] One miracle story depicts a peasant couple doing carting work on a Sunday in harvest season (*dum tempore messis*), evidently on their own fields, only to face divine retribution in the form of a stalk of straw to the laboring man's right eye.[30] As Lisa Bailey has stressed, peasants and even clerics pushed against Sunday work restrictions.[31] Yet here was another way numbers mitigated against risk. Those without access to extra hands weighed the risk of loss against the risk of offending the Lord.

Non-Cereal Harvests

Cereal harvests were not the only ones to require pooling of energies. The hay harvest, the early summer mowing of meadow grasses for animal fodder, called for less labor than grain harvests. One could use scythes instead of sickles. But the work still had to be finished with haste. Rain spoils hay by leaching sugars and encouraging mold. So, one must make it while the sun shines, or risk the welfare of livestock whose milk, meat, manure, and pulling power made the difference between felicity and ruin. On certain estates of Prüm, dependents who supplied the abbey with two *mancipia* for the grain harvest were also obliged to do so for hay mowing.[32] This was a typical instance of kicking the labor problem down the chain. Getting two unfree laborers in the busiest time of the year was the peasants' problem, not the monastery's.

The same scramble for laborers affected cash crops. Grapes must be picked when ripe, sooner when these finicky crops are threatened by ailments, and must be crushed in good time. Olives grow rancid if not pressed soon after being harvested. If uncollected, chestnuts fall from the tree, rot, and attract pests.[33] So the harvest crush lasted from hay mowing in midsummer to late fruit harvests in autumn. Failed harvests at any stage were a calamity with snowballing consequences, since they forced farmers to consume seed set aside for next year's harvest, or fall into debt or dependency.[34]

This risk must have formed deep grooves in the way common people thought about gatherings. Conversely, successful harvests meant collective joy. They were a time to mingle with a broader than usual company, to gossip, to get news, to sing together, to make extra income, and to enjoy extra rations of food and drink. Debts and dues could be paid, families could be fed. For all the stress on armies, royal assemblies, and church councils in our sources, we should remember that annual harvests would have been the gatherings most charged with fear, hope, and excitement for early medieval people.

Labor in Common

Non-harvest activities also demanded group labor. Despite lordly efforts to limit horizontal organization among peasants—banning *coniurationes* (sworn-oaths), restricting *gilds* (communal associations)—it was impossible for peasants to manage the risks and rewards of agricultural life without banding together sometimes.[35] That is not to deny strife among neighbors. Charter evidence suggests that kinship bonds were the most reliable lines of coordination; village communities, no less than the imperial aristocracy, had their prickly politics.[36] But scholars such as Davies, Oexle, Wickham, Devroey, Naismith, West, Schroeder, and Kohl have argued that peasant communities coordinated to minimize risk and drudgery, maximize profit and pleasure, and resolve conflicts.[37]

Some rural labor was unperformable on the household scale. Peasants living along flood-prone rivers or low-lying coasts had to maintain dykes and spring into action to make repairs. Certain crops (e.g., wheat) were more labor-intensive than others (e.g., millet, spelt), so those who cultivated them needed larger numbers at summer's end. Salt pan operations were necessarily collaborative.[38] Fishing communities too must have worked collaboratively: behind marine remains in cesspits, one might imagine the singing fishermen of Vittorio De Seta's *Contadini del mare* (1955).[39] On a humbler scale, even riverine fish weirs required collective coordination.

Likewise, artisanal work was sometimes a matter of collective labor. As the previous chapter discussed, pottery and glass workshops, buildings for hand-milling (only ever gradually displaced by the water mill), and women's workshops devoted to weaving operations brought dozens of laborers together.[40] Larger operations are usually thought to imply vertical organization: a lord calling the shots. This is probably true in most cases, but the assumption that archaeological signs of economic scale or specialization always indicates ruling elites may transform a commonality into a rule.[41] Unless otherwise informed, we should leave open the possibility of horizontal organization.

Mobility

Gone are the days when scholars believed that early medieval peasants never set foot outside of their hamlets.[42] Non-elites regularly traveled to perform labor duties (see further below). They also traveled to visit shrines, seek justice, and enjoy the utility and pleasure of markets. But they rarely traveled alone. Bandits, enslavers, and beasts menaced the roads.

A vivid example of group travel as the "usual custom of rustics" comes from the tenth-century life of Saint Manuetus (*BHL* 5210) by Adso of Montier-en-Der. In Adso's admonitory tale, a "not small number of rustics" (*non parvo numero rustici*) travels from Bar-le-Duc in a kind of "flock" (*grege facto*) to cart food and other items to sell at Vic-sur-Seille in exchange for salt.[43] Their journey, probably a week's travel either way, held dangers, including a river crossing.

In Adso's story, the peasant cortege made the error of spurning the Feast of Saint Manuetus (September 3) on their return journey.[44] When the locals of

Gondreville on the Moselle expressed astonishment that the rustics "were sweating away at carting work" (*cur eo die rotalibus actibus insudantes*) on this rather obscure saint's feast day, the peasants replied that they did not hold Manuetus in reverence. The divine vengeance that followed was the point of the story: the peasants' oxen ran amok until the traveling peasants "publicly" confessed their guilt.[45] As Nicholas Schroeder argues, the story shows "two groups of locals"—the traveling peasants and the local devotees—"apparently acting autonomously, without direct involvement of aristocrats."[46]

Animal Crowds

Adso's use of animal crowds to paint a moral reminds us that some of the most conspicuous crowds of the peasant world were nonhuman. Multitudes of beasts outnumbered humans in the early medieval countryside by an unknown but considerable factor.[47] Domesticated animals furnished the largest gatherings regularly seen by early medieval eyes. The majority of early medieval farming was mixed, that is, a combination of agriculture and husbandry. Peasants reared cattle, pigs, sheep, and goats, and in some regions specialized herders led animals in droves. Every peasant household had its flock of poultry, as testified by lords' constant demand for eggs. Mass calamities among domesticated animals—diseases, freak storms, predators—were among the tragedies of agrarian life, no less serious than crop failures.[48] Herds that damaged farmers' fields were an enduring object of early medieval legislation.[49]

Wild animals too formed multitudes that inspired fascination or terror. Birds, insects, and rodents menaced sown or stored grain.[50] Swarms of locusts were one of the horrors of the early medieval countryside, closely monitored and given coverage in annals.[51] Unusual gatherings of animals—both fearsome creatures like wolves and less dangerous beasts like deer—called for ritual purification. One of the ostensible reasons for the fifth-century invention of pre-Ascension rogations (eventually known as the Minor Rogations) was the strange behavior of groups of wild animals in the city of Vienne, a fact long commemorated as this ritual gained in importance.[52] Or animals could evoke the lives of certain strata of society. Herding animals like deer held a close association with the aristocrats and kings who hunted them.[53]

If asked to envision multitudes, then, peasants may have thought of beasts. Surviving representations of animal crowds come mainly from elite sources, but it may be possible to glimpse the thought-worlds of non-elites through sermons or miracle tales designed for their consumption. As was true of the Bible, with its legion of demons sent into a herd of pigs (Mark 5:1–20, Matthew 8:28–34, Luke 8:26–39), animal crowds appear in exemplary miracle stories as foils or illuminations of human multitudes.[54] Groups of animals resist or act in pious obedience to a saint. Such animal crowds served, as in Adso's story, as narrative signs of divine will.[55] These signs were doubtless all the more meaningful to those who knew animal behavior intimately.

Horizontal and Vertical Coordination

Life in common was planned in common. The organization of peasant communities was kept humming by local meetings. Although we know most about the "vertical" or top-down relations that structured the labor and lives of early medieval peasants, scholarship has increasingly stressed the importance of "horizontal" relations managed in poorly documented village-level councils.[56]

Horizontal Coordination

Public life in peasant communities was regulated by local gatherings. Groups of witnesses verified pacts, sales, and family unions. Ad hoc processions moved through the fields to fend off crop failure. Village councils settled scores. Local posses went after thieves. As Bloch long ago noted, the presence of communal ovens, irrigation ditches, coppices, commons, and ordered fields implies collective coordination.[57] The small-scale peasant assemblies that managed this coordination took many forms and names, but they were ubiquitous in early medieval Europe.[58]

While comital or royal courts offered vertically organized venues for dispute settlement, field use, harvest timing, and pest control must have been hammered out in more local meetings. In Kentish law, a small-scale assembly called a *mæthl*, handled separately from the larger *thing*, has been plausibly described as a village gathering. Although the king was invested in the good order of the *mæthl* and punished those who disrupted it, he left it to its own devices.[59] Lombard law uses the verb *thingare* ("to give in a *thing*," "to confirm in a *thing*") to describe this public legitimation.[60] Wendy Davies used the charters of Redon to show how the peasants of early Brittany resorted to mini-assemblies to resolve social issues.[61] The tenth-century *conventiae* or *convenientiae* of northern Spain show similar examples of peasants resorting to autonomous decision-making in councils.[62]

In addition to deliberative meetings, there were the more durable self-help associations known as "gilds" (the "Genossenschaften" of nineteenth-century fame).[63] These lay collectives addressed issues such as charity for the poor, collective prayer, candle supply, and arrangements for funerals. But they also feasted, competed in pious generosity, and engaged in rowdy behavior.[64] We glimpse these associations almost exclusively through their critics. *Concilii* appear in Lombard laws prohibiting them.[65] *Coniurationes* (sworn associations) were condemned in Frankish capitularies, elided with illegal *conspirationes* (conspiracies).[66] Most of what we read about self-help associations is hostile.[67] But they remained popular. To be part of a *concilius*, a *coniuratio*, a *collecta*, or a *gild* was to participate in acts of oath-taking, deliberation, prayer, and celebration together.[68] Such gilds not only managed quotidian affairs but addressed wider communal threats. When authorities failed to stop criminals, Viking raiders, and "robberies" by royal officials, gilds took on the danger.[69]

Vertical Coordination: Collective Labor

For the reasons explored in the last chapter, vertical relations probably generated larger gatherings than horizontal ones (though perhaps horizontal motivations were more frequent). In agrarian labor, the number of workers was proportional to the involvement of the rich and powerful. This was not only because larger estates needed more workers. Lords (*seniores, domini*) extracted surplus primarily through collective labor.[70]

Lords mobilized peasants for an array of tenurial duties. These included *corvadas* ("corvées"), *araturas* ("plowings"), *dies* ("days"), *noctes* ("nights"), *carropera* ("carting work"), *manopera* ("hand work"), *angaria* ("long-distance hauling"), *caplim* ("wood cutting"), and *riga* ("piecework").[71] In the economic boom years of the twelfth century, such services were commuted to cash payments, which paid for more motivated workers than one's own heel-dragging dependents (until inflation rendered fixed payments insufficient). In our period, they were still physical labors. At fixed times, peasants assembled, sometimes over long distances, to perform them.[72]

Even solitary labors such as plowing might turn into crowds on lordly estates. A tenth-century saint's life describes how "crowds of cultivators" (*arantium turbae*), dragooned by an overstepping nobleman, beseeched Saint Maximin's aid at the place where the lord's own "multitude of plowmen" (*aratorum multitudo*) were taking lunch. A divine whirlwind taught the lord a lesson—to modern sensibilities a rather unfair one—by casting his farmers' oxen and plows into a valley.[73] Setting aside the moral, the story assumes familiarity with lordly labor agglomeration.

The same was true for crafts. Peasant women spun and wove at home, but at the female workshops known as *gynaecea*, they did so in groups. *Gynaecea* ranged in size from seven to fifty-five women or more.[74] For building repairs, as the last chapter discussed, the *Lex Baiuvariorum* envisioned fifty *coloni* or *servi*—and sometimes as many as a hundred—assembling on behalf of ecclesiastical lords.[75] The carting duties of great monasteries sent convoys of peasants across regional networks, transporting grain, wood, or wine.[76]

Early medieval observers grasped that any large crowd of toiling rustics implied the presence, as with the "multitude of plowmen" above, of a "noble and rich" organizer.[77]

So it is possible to contrast horizontal agglomeration of agrarian labor with that of lords. The former involved large gatherings at predictable times, like harvests, or during unpredictable crises. Lordly surplus extraction, by contrast, regularly assembled much larger gatherings.[78]

Agglomeration for labor was linked with status. Some work could only be done by the unfree. That meant that whole communities as well as individuals defended their freedom together. On July 1, 861, as the last chapter mentioned, twenty-three men, eighteen women, and an unspecified number of children, all peasants of Saint-Denis, traveled sixty kilometers from the *villa* of Mitry to the royal palace at Compiègne to complain against the monk Deodatus, who had demanded unfree labor of them (they lost the case to the oaths of twenty-two of their free neighbors, also present).[79] When mid-ninth-century lords in West Francia added marling duties to their dependents' hand-and-cart-work—that is, transporting mudstone to be used as a soil conditioner—royal authority had to step in to make peasants comply.[80] In early tenth-century Italy, peasants at Limonta by Lake Como asserted their freedom against the monastery of Sant'Ambrogio in Milan by challenging at court the monastery's efforts to make them work the lord's olive harvest, press the oil, and transport it to the monastery.[81]

Vertical Coordination: Rents, Fees, and Dues

While labor was the most obvious way lords extracted surplus through numbers, it should not be forgotten that rents and taxes were also paid in gatherings. Peasants were subject to a range of payments in kind or in coin, owed to more than one authority at once. Although the state taxation of the Romans decayed in the West, petty exactions sprouted like ferns on the old fiscal stump. There were rents for land, fees for the use of facilities, pastures, and forests, more or less obligatory gifts and alms, justice fees, army taxes, first-fruits, special levies, tithes, votive oblations, and hospitality dues—not to mention bribes. As often as possible, peasants paid these at the same time and place. A few stewards may have gone door to door, like the bedraggled tax collector in Carlo Levi's *Christ Stopped at Eboli*, but most probably insisted that peasants come to them. On a fixed date, they lined up with clucking chickens or bleating goats at the manor house to pay the steward, or carried oblations to church, or otherwise made their excuses.[82]

Our evidence for this is mostly indirect. Most surviving polyptychs, with their adumbrations of dues in cash and kind, do not specify deadlines. This custom of collecting dues on feast days—in the case of religious houses with dependents, a local saint's feast day—would become ubiquitous in high medieval Europe, but the custom is patchily attested before the 900s.[83] Still, there is reason to think it was common. At Weissenburg, Saint Martin's Day became, by the late 700s, the standard deadline for rents.[84] In many places, tithes were ritualized as part of the yearly liturgy.[85]

Royal Exactions

The state, if that term can be used of early medieval kingdoms, brought together non-elites in the course of governance. The exaction of public repairs to bridges and roads, the demands of hospice and foddering, and the raising of military levies all summoned crowds, usually by means of the same cascading sequence of middlemen that characterized lordly exaction.[86] Taxes—like the *hostilicium* in support of the army—were farmed out to subordinates. But big projects brought large groups together. Charlemagne's attempted canal between the Rhine and the Danube needed the labor of many hands.[87] According to the Revised Frankish Annals for 793, Charlemagne came to the Altmühl and the Rezat "with all his court [*comitatus*] and, having assembled a great multitude of men [*magna hominum multitudine congregata*], consumed the whole space of autumn" in his canal scheme.[88] While his project failed, the king made rural Bavaria a crowded place at harvest time—for none of the usual reasons.

More quotidian governance called peasants to assemble en masse. Comital or episcopal courts, like the *mallus* that met about once a month, provided an occasion for the settling of disputes by the assembly of witnesses. Traveling royal courts dwarfed these local ones. Some three score from the contested territory between Siena and Arezzo assembled—twice in two years—to testify before the *missus* or traveling judge of the Lombard king early in the 700s.[89] In circa 804, the Plea of Rižana brought together 172 *capitanei* representing the cities of Istria.[90] "Crowds upon crowds," bribes in hand, came before the king's *missi* as they traveled around southern Gaul, according to Theodulf of Orléans, who served in 798 / 799.[91] We have seen the large group at Compiègne in 861.

Oaths of fealty, one of the most important tools of early medieval kingship, were collected in public gatherings.[92] According to a Frankish formulary, counts were to arrange that "all of their *pagenses*"—the word, meaning "people of the county" (*pagus*), implies peasant involvement—were to "assemble [*congregare*] in fitting places [*loca congrua*] in cities, villages, and fortresses, so that, before the presence of our *missus*, the illustrious So-and-So, whom we have sent thither from our side for this purpose, they should promise and swear faith and fealty [*leudesamio*] to our glorious son and to ourselves by the shrines of the saints and their relics, which we have sent through the same individual."⁹³ In 789, in the wake of a major conspiracy, Charlemagne insisted that all men over twelve—"the whole generality of the people who come to assemblies [*placita*]"—swear an oath of fealty to him, as follows: "I, So-and-So, hereby promise to the party of my lord King Charles and his sons that I am faithful [*fidelis*] and that I will remain so for the days of my life without fraud or wicked design."⁹⁴ *Missi* were to make sure that these swearing-assemblies took place in proper order, that none evaded them, and that participation was carefully recorded.

Spirituality and Recreation

Gatherings helped non-elites balance what the dry language of peasant economics calls the utility of income against the disutility of labor.⁹⁵ In plain language, crowds were central to how peasants managed drudgery and risk, their own needs and demands upon them. But gatherings were not all labor and duty. They were also about sanctity and fun.

Peasant Collective Religion

Religion was vital to rural communities. Fear and risk mitigation played a role in peasant interest in the holy. Those who assembled at church or before the bones of the saints hoped to forestall troubles. Religious leaders encouraged attendance at churches by threatening divine miseries endured by shirkers. But there were positive inducements. The poorest could expect assistance from God's stewards on earth.⁹⁶ Church ceremonies were not all dour Lenten affairs. While there is no way to measure the percentage of wealth and time early medieval peasants devoted to festivities, rustic gifts to holy sites show that outlays were substantial.⁹⁷ When development economists Esther Duflo and Abhijit Banerjee studied family spending habits in Udaipur, India, they found that even the extremely poor devoted 14 percent of their budget to secular and religious festivals.⁹⁸

We are best informed about ceremonies early medieval peasants were told to attend. Non-elites were an indispensable part of the religious system. In liturgical books, the *populus* appear in vigils, masses, processions, and prayers.⁹⁹ Benedictions against crop failure, mildew, rust, and other country dangers show the Christian investment in agriculture.¹⁰⁰ The major festivals—Easter, Ascension, Pentecost, All Saints', Annunciation, Christmas, Saint Stephen's— were times of required presence, in theory if not in practice. Out of a welter of late antique "rogations" (rituals beseeching aid in times of need), two annual processions, the Minor and Greater Rogations, came to express "visions of the community" across Europe.[101] The feast of an important local saint vied with the greatest festivals of the temporal calendar. Relics, new and old, attracted crowds of peasant worshippers bearing donations.

Economically and ideologically, churches and shrines depended on regular crowds of non-elites. A range of gifts were expected by caretakers of holy sites. If properly advertised, new relics were a windfall.[102] The hagiographical sources suggest that church leaders wanted even the humblest to show up.[103] A Merovingian saint's life describes how one bishop founded a *xenodochium* with accommodations for twenty people, including a staff of doctors.[104] Many larger establishments had "matriculated" paupers who received disbursements at predictable times.[105] The monastery of Bobbio kept a list of six *xenodochia* that gave charity to poor people.[106] Twelve were fed each Kalends at the *xenodochium* in Piacenza; at a larger *xenodochium* in Pavia, the number was two hundred.[107] In return, beneficiaries might feel called upon to defend the honor of a local saint, as when a hubbub of Tours citizens—including "rustics"—rose up to defend the honor of Saint Martin early in the ninth century.[108]

There was competition for peasant feet on church pavement. Curators of relic cults promoted the virtues of saints fresh from Italy or the East, and warned commoners against neglecting them.[109] Ecclesiastical authorities reminded parishioners of the benefits of regular churchgoing, and threatened neglect with force. In the mid-ninth century, Bishop Amolo of Lyon addressed lay people who had been led astray from home parishes by untested new relics (or rather, by crowds of ecstatic worshippers). The parish church, admonished Amolo, was "where [each congregation] receives sacred baptism, where it experiences the body and blood of the Lord, where it has become accustomed to hear the celebration of mass, where it obtains from its own priest penance from wrongdoing, visitation in sickness, burial in death, where too it is commanded to offer its own tithes and first-fruits, where it rejoices to have its own sons admitted by the grace of baptism, where it regularly hears the word of God, and learns how to act and how not to act."[110] In exchange for these regular benefits, Amolo expected regular attendance and the timely payment of tithes and dues at "one's own church." Competing demands for physical presence meant that peasants, burdened by labor needs, also had split spiritual loyalties.

Popular Religion and "Superstition"

Peasants practiced forms of religiosity not in line with the visions promoted by authorities such as Amolo.[111] "Superstitions," as these practices were denigratingly called, entailed gatherings too. Our best evidence comes from the complaints of the authorities: the sermons of Caesarius of Arles, the eighth-century list of "superstitions and paganisms" known as the *Indiculus superstitionum et paganiarum*, missionary writings, capitularies, conciliar decrees, and the letters of bishops like Amolo and his acerbic predecessor Agobard.[112] Peasants built bonfires, marched in unauthorized processions, assembled before magicians, pseudo-saints, and pseudo-prophets, and shouted to the moon in eclipse.[113] In Amolo's case, crowds of hundreds—"especially women"—were flailing in the presence of suspicious "relics" brought to Saint Bénigne in Dijon, refusing the leave the church, and inspiring others to act similarly at Saulieu.[114] Bishops were quick to condemn such forms of spirituality, playing them up as rustic or female.[115] But texts such as the eleventh-century penitential of Burchard of Worms show that these behaviors outlived criticism.[116]

Tropes of "high" versus "low" Christianity or notions that peasant spirituality amounted to pagan recidivism must be taken with a grain of salt. In her study of the peasants Bodo and Ermentrude, Eileen Power pictured these ninth-century peasants whispering charms "hoary with age" as they went about their daily lives.[117] Doubtless, there were moments when humble folk acted in ways they knew would meet with the disapproval of a parish priest or bishop. But the line between licit and illicit collective religious behavior must have been blurry. After all, even priests numbered among the crowds that assembled before "pseudo-prophets" and "pseudo-saints."[118]

Moreover, you could only be in one place at a time. Peasants faced top-down pressure to attend services at parish churches, to seek out the latest relics, and to make pilgrimages. In the words of Thomas Kohl, they faced "incompatible expectations."[119] Differences between hucksters and hermits, pigs' bones and saints' thighs, or even hedge wizards and parish priests were more subjective than our sources allow. Peasants had agency in how they chose to interact with the holy, but the "freedom to make choices," as Kohl writes, "brought with it risks and dangers."[120] Moral suasion and physical coercion did not always guarantee that peasants honored God and his saints in what powerful people around them thought were the right ways or the right times.[121]

Festivals and Recreation

Seasonal festivities linked with agriculture, feasting and drinking parties, celebrations of family milestones, hazing rituals like the early modern *charivari*, and carnivalesque misrule surely played a role in the collective lives of early medieval peasants. Alas, the sources give only the slightest hints.[122] Priests and clerics were supposed to bow out of feasts and nuptial celebrations discretely before the "entertainers" (*thimelici*) arrived.[123] Hincmar of Reims warned priests in his diocese not to indulge in rustic revels. While priests were permitted to assemble to commemorate the honored dead on anniversaries, Hincmar warned them against drinking bouts, toasting to the saints or the dead, indulging in tall tales, jokes, and songs, watching bear baiting, permitting "masks of devils which are vulgarly called *talamascas*," or getting into brawls.[124] His list of proscribed behaviors hints at common collective recreations.

The regional diversity of festive practices in the later Middle Ages cautions against generalization.[125] But we know enough to suspect that raucous celebrations were a regular part of peasant life. When people are gathered together in a giddy state of mind, especially in rites of misrule, the chances for anomalous behavior are high. In the ninth century, it is not unusual to find collective rowdiness ascribed to celebratory drink.[126] Amolo made the obscure suggestion that flailing women of Dijon had something to do with "feasts and drinking parties"; the Lenten timing of these events—that is, close to what became Carnival—is suggestive.[127] The best we can do given the evidence is to remember, as Hardy said, that country life was never solitary or quiet.

Resistance

What about "crowds" in the traditional historiographical sense: acts of non-elite collective resistance pursuing what Tilly called "contentious politics"?[128] Marc Bloch asserted that "agrarian revolt is as natural to the seigneurial regime as strikes, let us say, are to large-scale capitalism."[129] This observation applies well to the later Middle Ages, particularly the fourteenth and fifteenth centuries, with their "plagues of insurrection."[130] But is it valid for the early Middle Ages? As we will see, unrest in towns or cities was a throughline of the whole period. For rural uprisings, the story is more complicated.

Unrest in Towns and Cities

Non-elite crowds of resistance most often appear in what remained of Europe's urban fabric. That should not be surprising in light of the previous chapter. Towns and cities remained the largest pools of assembly; urban politics were fractious. It should be stressed that such uprisings were far rarer than in Roman or later medieval times.[131] Also, it is not always possible to know when an urban crowd was "non-elite" in membership or motivation. But the possibility of being surrounded by a menacing crowd never fully vanished for early medieval elites venturing into cities and towns.

Italy, the most urbanized part of Latin Europe, saw the unruliest crowds.[132] The citizenry of Ravenna was known for targeting papal interlopers, foreigner elements, and unpopular archbishops.[133] Early in the eighth century, a massacre erupted from out of ritualized brawls between rival districts at Ravenna.

This was crowd violence in spite of authority, not against it; but its intensity has few transalpine parallels.[134] Crowd politics played a role in the murky dramas of early Venice and Naples.[135] Toward the end of our period, revolts with an alleged popular component are recorded for Cremona (852), Turin (897), Verona (968), and Milan (983).[136]

Rome, non-Muslim Europe's largest city, was the Latin West's hotspot for unruly crowds.[137] The Romans did not forget how to be Romans. In the sixth century, when Pope Vigilius (537–55) was arrested by imperial authorities, he suffered the jeers of a disgruntled populace. When the Romans saw his ship moving down the Tiber, explains the *Liber Pontificalis*, "a crowd [*populus*] began to throw stones, sticks, and cooking vessels after him, saying: 'Take your famine with you! Take your mortality with you! You treated the Romans badly, may you find bad things wherever you go!'"[138]

Crowds rose up on behalf of popes too. When a Byzantine official attempted to arrest Pope Sergius I (687–701), a "crowd of laymen" (*turba militiae*) defended the pope's honor, forcing the official to take shelter under Sergius's bed in the Lateran, while the pope calmed the multitude. Sergius persuaded them not to kill the official, but the would-be papal kidnapper was showered with insults.[139] Crowds were regularly implicated in papal succession disputes.[140] The debacle of 767–69—with its rival elections, street fights, and crowds from outside the city—is the most infamous example.[141] But even supposedly orderly elections involved if not riotous at least raucous collective behavior.[142] Still, it has been argued that early medieval Roman crowds were more "passive" than their ancient predecessors.[143] These were not the self-confident riots of Antiquity, combating slights to a moral economy, but acts of popular partisanship.

When an urban crowd targeted some powerful figure, there was frequently a hint of elite sponsorship. Between 776 and 780, Pope Hadrian I wrote to Charlemagne to inform him that inhabitants of Istria, inspired by "wicked Greeks," had "dug out the eyes" of their bishop Mauricius, when he had collected papal dues (*pensiones beati Petri*).[144] The details of the case are murky. This act of violence may have been spontaneous, but the mention of Greek involvement may speak to Byzantine state interests.

North of the Alps, towns were smaller and fewer, but they could still be unruly places. In recounting the feuds and rivalries of sixth-century Gallic *civitates*, Gregory of Tours highlights the role of crowds. Low-status crowds appear in disputes between rival claimants to the bishopric of Clermont, secular and ecclesiastical authorities at Marseille, and nuns battling for control of Radegund's monastery at Poitiers in 589–90.[145] On several occasions, Gregory describes urban tax revolts that look similar to Roman-style uprisings. In 548, the wealthy aristocrat Parthenius was lynched at Trier in what Gregory calls a "rising of the people" (*populi seditio*).[146] Parthenius had collected taxes for Theudebert I, who had just died, and now he faced the fury of the people, "because he had inflicted the taxes of the aforementioned king upon them" (Gregory also implied Parthenius's demise was divine punishment for an unavenged double murder).[147]

Parthenius's plan had been to seek refuge in one of Trier's churches. Gregory explains that two (unnamed) bishops hid him in a chest where vestments were stored. But the crowd (*populus*) entered the church and searched every corner until one man cried: "Hey, look at this chest, where no search has been made for our foe!" When Parthenius was found, the mob cheered (*plaudentes*), allegedly repeating the words of the Philistines when they seized Samson (Judges 16:23): "God has handed over our enemy into our hands."[148] Striking and spitting on him, the mob bound Parthenius's hands, dragged him to a column, and stoned him to death.

This vivid story—which would have taken place when Gregory was about ten—is typical of Gregory's outlook toward "sedition." He hints at his disapproval of the Philistine-like crowd, but the story ends by meditating upon Parthenius's wickedness. On March 1, 579, when Gregory was already bishop of Tours, there was another tax riot at Limoges, in which tax documents (*descriptiones*) were burned and King Chilperic's tax collector, the *referendarius* Mark, barely escaped with his life. Ferreolus, the local bishop, supposedly persuaded the crowd to spare the man.[149] The next year, according to Gregory, King Chilperic and Queen Fredegund voluntarily burned their tax books, for they interpreted the death of their son in a dysentery epidemic as divine retribution for the tears of the poor, the widows, and the orphans hurt by taxes.[150]

After the death of Chilperic in 584, the Parisian home of a *iudex* ("judge") named Audo was burned to the ground because he had presumed to tax "free" (*ingenui*) Franks during the former king's reign.[151] As with the case of Parthenius, this occurred in an urban context, after the death of a king. Gregory, who opposed royal taxation wherever he saw it, showed riots as rough justice against avarice. Neither the tax collectors nor the crowds were wholly in the right. The correct approach was shown by Gregory and his predecessors, who persuaded the agents of kings that Tours was immune from taxes, forestalling popular discontent.[152] The "riots" of 548, 579, and 584 were exceptional, though; Gregory reveals that the commoner response to ruinous taxation was to flee from an offending king's territory.[153]

Gregory's tax riots have few later parallels, but towns remained risky into the Carolingian period. In a poem about his work as a royal *missus* (less famous than the one about bribe-bearing multitudes), Theodulf of Orléans describes a misadventure at Limoges two centuries after Mark's close call. Theodulf had spent considerable time at Limoges with a large entourage. After nine days of hospitality from "a crowd [*turba*] of abbots, clergy, and others" (note the positive valence to the word *turba*), the "peaceable" town turned hostile. "A wine-sodden common-crowd" (*plebes madefacta Lyaeo*) would have killed the outsiders, Theodulf explained, had not two individuals, Ephraim and Mancio the priest, intervened to curb their "rage" (*furor*).[154] In 801, Theodulf felt the same sting indirectly, when his men sent to retrieve a criminal cleric from Saint-Martin at Tours were manhandled by crowds of drunk "rustics."[155] Here, as in other cases, it can be difficult to differentiate popular unrest from popular involvement in elite competition. Either way, urban numbers retained strategic advantage against the power of elites.

Peasant Uprisings

If urban unrest was uncommon but not unheard of in early medieval Europe, peasant uprisings were downright rare. This observation is not easy to quantify, since we are at the mercy of hostile sources. But since Chris Wickham has inventoried the few peasant revolts in this period (as well as over the next two centuries), his small harvest can be compared with catalogues of unrest for parallel settings (see Table 3.1).[156] There are many caveats here. The regional and temporal coverage varies; each author has a slightly different definition of subject (including urban and military as well as rural revolts); and later centuries are better documented than earlier ones. If one budgets for urban uprisings, the early Middle Ages would be a little rowdier, while the period c. 1000–1200 would be much rowdier. Likewise, Wickham's list excludes isolated acts of collective violence like the lynching of witches or suspected weather-wizards.[157] But despite its imperfections, the comparison shows that early medieval peasants did not usually resort to active mass resistance.

It is worth taking a closer look at the six "peasant revolts" in question. They consist of 1) a rural uprising of unfree persons (*mancipia*) outside of Naples in 592; 2) a "great contention" in which peasants encroached against monastery lands near Dijon in 664–65; 3) a revolt in the Asturias around 770; 4) a series of acts of resistance (779, 787, 822–24, 854, 872–73) carried out by peasants of Valle Trita in Abruzzo against the monastery of San Vincenzo al Volturno; 5) the *Stellinga* revolt in Saxony in the 840s; and 6) a Norman rising of *rustici* sometime around c. 997–1008.[158]

Six may be generous. The 592 *seditio*, documented by a letter of Gregory the Great, was more a case of servile flight than fight.[159] The case of the "people" (*homines*) of seventh-century Burgundy who carried out "violence" against the lands of the monastery of Saint-Bénigne in Dijon can be removed entirely.[160] This event is recounted in a charter that was either reworked or wholly forged in the eleventh century, and the monastic compilers were explicit that the

TABLE 3.1. Relative Frequency of Non-Elite Contentious Actions in Different Settings

	Roman Empire (31 BCE–235 CE)	Late Antiquity (300–600 CE)	Early Medieval Europe (600–1000)	High Medieval Europe (1000–1200)	Late Medieval Europe (1200–1425)	Early Modern France (1661–1789)
Total number of collective actions	241	108	6	9	1,000+	8,528
Rate	~1 per year	~1 every 3 years	1 every 67 years	1 every 22 years	~4 per year	~67 per year
Source	Pekáry, "Seditio" and Sünskes Thompson, *Aufstände und Protestaktionen*	Magalhães de Oliveira, "Late Antiquity"	Wickham, "Looking Forward"	Wickham, "Looking Forward"	Cohn, *Lust for Liberty*	Nicolas, *La rébellion française*

Source: Based on: Thomas Pekáry, "'Seditio': Unruhen und Revolten im römischen Reich von Augustus bis Commodus," *Ancient Society* 18 (1987): 133–50; Julia Sünskes Thompson, *Aufstände und Protestaktionen im Imperium Romanum: Die severischen Kaiser im Spannungsfeld innenpolitischer Konflikte* (Bonn, 1990); Júlio César Magalhães de Oliveira, "Late Antiquity: The Age of Crowds?," *Past & Present* 249 (2020): 3–52; Chris Wickham, "Looking Forward: Peasant Revolts in Europe, 600–1200," in *The Routledge History Handbook of Medieval Revolt*, ed. Justine Firnhaber-Baker and Dirk Schoenaers (London, 2017), 155–67; Samuel Kline Cohn, *Lust for Liberty: The Politics of Social Revolt in Medieval Europe, 1200–1425* (Cambridge, MA, 2008); Jean Nicolas, *La rébellion française: Mouvements populaires et conscience sociale, 1661–1789* (Paris, 2002).

"people" were "knights" (*milites*), not peasants.[161] One could exclude the Norman peasants' "revolt" for happening at "the beginning of a different political world," though there are reasons to see it as a legacy of the early Middle Ages.[162] Still, on closer examination, it hardly qualifies as a revolt.

The Asturian Revolt (c. 770)

Probably the clearest-cut case is the Asturian revolt, although the sources are late and laconic.[163] A family of chronicles written in the ninth century gives slightly different versions of what happened under the reign of King Aurelius (r. 768–74): "In his time, the slaves" (*servi*)—another version reads "freedmen" (*libertini*)—"took up arms against their own lords [*contra proprios dominos*], and rose up tyrannously, but overcome by the prince's industry, all of them were reduced to their original servitude" (*servitus*).[164] From this, we can say little about the causes, scale, or comportment of the revolt. It is possible that peasants—if this is the right term—trusted in the mountainous terrain of the Asturias, but that is an inference from geography.[165] It is noteworthy that they are said to have taken up arms. Elite allegations of peasant or slave "violence" or "aggression" were sometimes more like encroachments on disputed land or refusal to do labor, but this revolt seems the genuine article: armed mass resistance. The salient fact is the denouement: the rebellion's thorough suppression and the enslavement or re-enslavement of surviving protagonists.

Valle Trita (779–873)

The century-long affair at Valle Trita (779–873) is better documented, thanks to eight documents preserved in the Chronicle-Cartulary of San Vincenzo al Volturno.[166] In the mid-eighth century, the monastery of San Vincenzo had received from the Lombard king a grant of territory in the Valle Trita, about a hundred kilometers and a mountain-range away in Abruzzo. The monks believed they were entitled to rents and labor from the supposedly unfree peasants there. The locals insisted upon their freedom, cited documents of the Lombard dukes of Spoleto that safeguarded their independence, and refused to pay rents or carry out demanded services.

In fact, the Valle Trita affair is more a case of passive collective resistance than an active uprising. The monks' legal claim that the peasants had used violence— had "invaded" their land—was a rhetorical strategy. "We have invaded nothing, except for our own property," the peasants retorted.[167] Despite repudiation from the Carolingian authorities, who sided with the monks, the peasants were able to flee into the mountains when dues or services were sought of them, effectively nullifying legal decisions in favor of their would-be lords. The case was still unresolved in 881, when the monastery was sacked by an Arab army. Although the peasants did make their case before the law (unsuccessfully) nine times, and at least once may have manhandled monastic officials, ultimately their most successful strategy was this refusal to show up.

As Chris Wickham has argued, Valle Trita shows how "the collective action and the remoteness characteristic of marginal lands could hold off a powerful and determined monastery, even though the latter was backed up by all the state power that was available."[168] In several analogous cases, especially from Italy, peasants banded together, sometimes with artisans, notaries, and middling gentry, to resist lordly demands in a court of law, by passive resistance, or both.[169] It is likely that cases like these were common. Since most disputes of this kind are preserved in ecclesiastical archives, we are also less likely to possess evidence of cases that went in peasants' favor. But only in the fevered rhetoric of the monastery was this collective refusal a peasant revolt.

The Stellingas (841–42)

Which brings us to the Stellingas.[170] This famed rebellion against Frankish power in Saxony, which broke out in 841 and was suppressed by Louis the German in 842, is the best-known early medieval example of non-elites using the power of numbers against lords. It is unusually well documented, by early medieval standards, by four contemporary sources (all hostile): Nithard's *Histories*, the *Annals of Saint-Bertin*, the *Annals of Fulda*, and the *Annals of Xanten*.[171] It took place in a recently conquered and Christianized region, in the midst of Carolingian civil wars. We are told that the Saxons, with the encouragement of Emperor Lothar, rose up in revolt against "their lords."[172] The rebels called themselves "Stellingas," a point on which all four chronicles agreed, and, as Nithard wrote, "they lived in the old manner, by whatever law each person wished."[173]

The sources stress the involvement of non-elites. The *Annals of Saint-Bertin* noted that the Stellingas comprised "the more copious number among that people."[174] Nithard said they consisted primarily of *frilingi* (freemen) and *lazzi* (half-freemen), "whose multitude is infinite."[175] So great were their numbers that they "nearly drove their lords from the kingdom."[176] The *Annals of Xanten* put it more bluntly: "The power of the slaves [*servi*] greatly waxed against their own lords, and they usurped for themselves the name of Stellingas and carried out many irrational acts. And the nobles of that country were much assailed and humiliated [*valde afflicti et humiliati sunt*] by the slaves [*servi*]."[177] It is possible that the sources played up the non-elite nature of the rebellion, but it is certain the Stellingas included swathes of the rural peasantry.[178]

What exactly the Stellingas did is somewhat obscure. What, for instance, does it mean that the nobles of Saxony were "much assailed and humiliated"?

Or that lords were "nearly" (*poene*) driven out? The *Annals of Fulda* used the loaded term *conspiratio* to describe the revolt, implying an illegal sworn conspiracy, and both these annals and the *Annals of Saint-Bertin* insisted that there were specific "ringleaders" (*auctores*). Such language is redolent of Carolingian legislation against *conspirationes*, and casts the Stellingas as an illegal rebellion, a fact that would justify the actions that followed.[179] In another gesture of delegitimation, the sources implied that pagan recidivism lay behind the uprising. The Saxons were "more inclined to follow the rite of the pagans than the sacraments of the Christian faith."[180] But as Ingrid Rembold has carefully noted, this accusation of pagan motivation was always insinuated, never openly stated.[181]

The Stellingas were rapidly and cruelly put down. In the wake of an oppression marked by "terror," Louis the German decapitated 140, hanged fourteen from the gibbet, and "rendered innumerable others disabled [*debiles*] by removing their limbs"[182] As the *Annals of Xanten* put it with smug satisfaction, he "nobly crushed the Saxon slaves [*servi*], haughty in their pride, and restored them to their proper nature."[183] While the Stellingas' motives and even their precise actions were kept shrouded by the sources, their ultimate fate was celebrated.

The Stellinga Revolt has been interpreted many ways, from a tragic act of class warfare, to an assertion of ethnic identity, to a defense of the old gods.[184] Recently, a consensus has developed that the Stellingas emerged from regularly existing horizontal bonds among Saxon non-elites.[185] The name *stellingas* was Old Saxon for "comrades"; older scholarship tended to see this in a military light ("comrades in arms"), but now the term is thought to have denoted self-help institutions parallel to the gilds.[186] The idea is that the Stellingas, like E. P. Thompson's eighteenth-century rioters, saw themselves not as partisans for Old Saxony, but as defenders of menaced old norms.

On this view, it is possible the Stellingas did not even conceive of themselves as rebelling. They seem to have resorted to violence, but it is possible, based on the sources, that this consisted of threats, insults, and humiliation. None of our sources explicitly says that nobles were killed, nor is there a hint of pitched battles. In fact, the Stellingas may have felt they had the go-ahead of the senior Carolingian, Emperor Lothar I. The Stellingas look like a self-help association, such as the ones discussed above, but under extraordinary circumstances. As Rembold puts it, the "origins of the *Stellinga* are to be found not in revolt, but rather in the tradition of the early medieval guilds."[187]

The Norman Peasants' "Revolt" (c. 997–1008)

The same has been said of the so-called Norman "peasants' revolt" early in the reign of Richard II of Normandy (996–1026).[188] This affair was first recounted by William of Jumièges, writing about seven decades after the event. William tapped into the language of illicit self-governance that marked the Stellingas' hostile chroniclers two centuries earlier. His account is worth quoting in full:[189]

> Although he [Richard II] abounded in his powers of great wisdom, in the early days of his youth, it so happened that a certain seed-bed of pestilent discord [*quoddam pestiferi . . . seminarium discidii*] arose within the Norman duchy. For the rustics [*rustici*] across the diverse counties of the whole country of Normandy unanimously stirred up numerous mini-assemblies [*plurima agentes conuenticula*] and decided to live according to their own wishes [*iuxta suos libitus uiuere decernebant*], to the effect that that both with respect to woodland paths and riverine traffic, with no obstacle from earlier establishment of law [*status iuris*] stopping them, they planned to use their own rulings [*legibus uterentur suis*]. In order to make their decisions stick, two legates [*legati*] were elected from each gathering of the furious rabble [*cetus furentis uulgi*], who were to carry their decrees to be confirmed at the mid-province assembly [*qui decreta ad mediterraneum ferrent roboranda conuentum*]. When the duke learned of this, he at once sent against them Count Rodulf together with a multitude of soldiers [*cum militum multitudine*], in order to crush the peasant aggression [*agrestem comprimeret ferocitatem*] and to break up the rustic gathering [*rusticam dirimeret contionem*]. The latter, not delaying in carrying out these commands, instantly seized the legates with several others, had their hands and feet cut off, sending them back maimed [*inutiles*] to their own people, so that they would be checked from doing like things, and by their fates make them cautious [*cauti*] lest they suffer even worse. Having seen this, the rustics, putting aside their gatherings [*contionibus omissis*], went back to their plows.[190]

A later retelling of this story, by the twelfth-century vernacular poet Wace, cast this as open revolt.[191] In Wace's version, the peasants brag that each Norman knight would have to reckon with thirty or forty peasants (*trente u quarante païsanz*).[192] But as Bernard Gowers has pointed out, Wace concocted this from William's account, whose original story suggests yet another case of peasant self-help met with reflexive repression.[193]

The peasants' actions, according to Gowers, were akin to assertions of collective autonomy like those at Valle Trita. Their defiance of lordly privileges over wood and waterways was certainly risky, but it was not the puffed-up rebellion depicted by Wace. The Norman duchy's hyperbolic reaction to acts of self-help simply recast a series of orderly looking councils as "aggression." William of Jumièges's metamorphosis of "little councils" (*conventicula*) into a "furious rabble" complimented the violence of the lords. In this way, the Norman "peasants' revolt" is most typical of early medieval peasant revolts in that it was, once again, hardly a revolt at all.

Reasons for the Rarity of Non-Elite Collective Resistance

With the exception of the Asturian revolt (c. 770), most of the "peasant revolts" listed above merit the name with caveats. Likewise, apart from Gregory of Tours's tax "revolts" (548, 579, 584), documented cases of crowd unrest in towns and cities in the early medieval period were generally bound up with factional politics. Why were acts of genuine non-elite collective resistance so rare?

Partly, this was owing to the disadvantageous conditions of assembly discussed above. Anonymity, a protective feature of crowd resistance in many ages, was harder to achieve in the small, face-to-face societies of the early Middle Ages.[194] In an age when, in Eric Goldberg's words, "well-fed, disciplined, armored men with iron weapons" jealously guarded the monopoly on violence, peasants may have lacked the confidence in numbers that Wace anachronistically attributed to the Norman rustics.[195] There is a reason the Stellingas broke out in a borderland region at a time of civil war.[196]

Another cause may be the vehemence of elite reactions. Most premodern mass resistance by non-elites was essentially conservative and defensive. Before the French Revolution, it was rare for non-elites to demand the overthrow of the whole society. That is because participants, in E. P. Thompson's words, were "informed by the belief that they were defending traditional rights or customs," and could expect "some measure of licence afforded by the authorities."[197] If the Stellingas and the *conventicula* of the Norman peasants shared these expectations, they were horribly mistaken.

Ruling elites not only met direct uprisings with unhearing violence, but also persecuted collective behavior that was only indirectly threatening. The most chilling example is the case from 859 mentioned at the start of the chapter. To quote Prudentius:

> The Danes were devastating the regions beyond the Scheldt. A mixed rabble between the Seine and the Loire swore oaths among themselves, and bravely resisted the Danes on the Seine. But because their sworn-association [*coniuratio*] had been taken up incautiously [*incaute*], they were easily killed by our own more powerful people [*a potentioribus nostris*].[198]

This finale is so shocking that some have insisted the Latin must be corrupt.[199] But most historians agree with Janet Nelson: "The nobility saw their social control endangered; and that was a higher priority than defence against potential rival-exploiters of the peasantry," that is, the Vikings.[200]

What accounted for aristocratic trigger-happiness? Why did nobles respond so brutally not only to open resistance, as with the Asturian revolt and the Stellingas, but to more ambiguous cases, like the *coniuratio* of 859 and the Norman mini-assemblies? We might expect them to be caught flat-footed, given the scarcity of non-elite uprisings. But elite reactions in this period were far more decisively violent than in earlier and later societies more used to popular riots and revolts. Thompson ends his essay with the half-sympathetic words of an eighteenth-century sheriff about the mob's "courage, prudency, justice, and a consistency toward that which they profess to obtain."[201] The Romans, as we saw in chapter 1, also acknowledged the *populus'* right to rise up over high bread prices and subpar amenities.[202] This license is still visible early in our period. Gregory of Tours sympathized with the lynch mobs of 548, 579, and 584. In 592, in response to the rising of the *mancipia* outside of Naples, Pope Gregory I wondered if the slaves had a "just quarrel" with their masters.[203]

But by the ninth century, early medieval aristocrats refused to recognize the reasons for misrule.[204] Even a sympathetic text like the capitulary of Ver in 884, which lamented *rapina* against peasant communities, banned peasant gilds to combat it.[205] Partly, this may be because unexpected collective autonomy already endangered resource acquisition in this decentralized political economy. We have seen how much surplus extraction relied upon regular, predictable gatherings. As Valle Trita shows, "the marvelous inertia" of peasants was a formidable weapon when aimed against lordly interests.[206] By not showing up, peasants could avoid taxes and deprive lords of legitimacy, and there was only so much lords could do against organized passive resistance.[207] "Slantwise" resistance, that is, behavior that threatened elite authority incidentally or accidentally, could be just as ruinous.[208] In no sense did the rarity of non-elite collective uprisings before 1000 make the early Middle Ages an age of elite domination. Refusal to assemble, or "slantwise" assembly, was a weapon of the weak.

In fact, the central reason riots and revolts were rare may be quite simply that they were rare. People tend to see non-elite uprisings as universal phenomena, "spasmodic" or "natural" responses to suffering or oppression.[209] But if we have learned anything from crowd historians like Rudé, Thompson, and Davis, it is that direct collective action is as much subject to history as any institution. Riots or revolts have a well-documented mimetic or "contagious" quality; mathematicians studying riots in London have argued that the best predictor of a future riot is a previous riot.[210] As Thompson argued, the frequency of riots is central to their deterrence power.[211] Even if a riot ends in disaster for participants, a "social calamity" in County A might well convince authorities, farmers, dealers, and gentry in County B to find a happy medium between their economic wants and the "moral economy" of the crowd.[212] For these dynamics to function, non-elite unrest must be legible both as strategy and as threat.

In the early Middle Ages, this was no longer the case. Popular uprisings became so illegible that, as we will see in chapter 5, there was no specialized word for riots. By contrast, nonparticipation in the expected gatherings of daily life became a powerful form of passive resistance. So were orderly collective appeals to authority. We have seen how peasants from Mitry trudged to the palace court Compiègne in 861 in the hopes of a favorable judgment.²¹³ Our sources show peasants losing such legal disputes, but that may not tell the full story, as Chris Wickham has argued.²¹⁴ Ecclesiastical houses, our best source for early medieval dispute settlement documents, did not preserve the evidence of their own losses. Gatherings remained central to non-elite resistance, but in ways and forms not usually anticipated by crowd history.

Sporadic Collective Violence and Lordly Involvement

It should be acknowledged, however, that there is evidence for sporadic acts of rural collective violence (or disorder) below the level of revolt. In addition to brawls and illicit celebrations, groups of non-elites can be spotted banding together against what they saw as malefactors; sometimes, the line between malefactor and authority was thin, as with the late ninth-century *collectae* or *geldae* directed "against those who rob something."²¹⁵

In Italy, legal evidence for peasant group violence goes back to the 600s. Two laws (c. 279 and c. 280) from the mid-seventh-century *Edict of Rothari* of Lombard Italy envision violent gatherings of *rusticani* (unfree peasants specializing in field work).²¹⁶ The first, "On a council of rustics" (*De concilio rusticanorum*), describes an offensive action, in which "slaves" (*serui*) have formed a "band" or "council" (*concilius*) and "enter some village in an armed band in order to do mischief."²¹⁷ The second, "On a sedition of rustics" (*De rusticanorum seditionem* [*sic*]), pictures a defensive action, in which "slaves" (*serui*) band together (*se collegerint*) to resist a lord's effort to seize property, including human property, from "the house of his slave."²¹⁸

The laws pictured ringleaders. In the case of an offensive *concilius*, the instigator, presumed to be "a free man under the authority of our rule," was to lose his life or pay nine hundred *solidi* (half to the king, half to the victim), the standard composition for breach of the peace. Each participating "slave" was to pay a ruinous forty *solidi* (also split half and half). In the case of a defensive *seditio*, the presumed ringleader (*ille, qui in caput ex ipsis rusticis fuerit*) was either to be killed or to pay his own life-price in compensation, "whatever that may amount to" (multiple statuses are thus possible). All who "charged into that sedition to do mischief" were obliged to pay twelve *solidi*, a formidable if not catastrophic sum. If the lord or his representative were injured in the struggle, he was to be compensated at the going rate (three *solidi* per blow). Should any participating slave die, no compensation was owed, "because he who killed him did this to defend himself and recover his properties."²¹⁹

The two laws limited themselves to the acts of unfree, male agricultural workers (and their instigators).²²⁰ It is worth noting that the term *seditio* does not mean "uprising," but was used across Lombard laws for breaches of the peace (which all faced the same death-or-nine-hundred-*solidi* punishment). Other Lombard laws against *seditio* dealt with armed bands (*harschild*), with reference to feuds within the warrior class.[221] But *concilius* was used only for these peasant compacts. The idea that *rusticani* could band together in a just cause is not contemplated. That does not mean that Lombard society could not imagine a scenario in which unfree men were wronged. But in the eyes of the law, "slaves" were in the wrong as soon as they "banded together to do mischief."

Doubtless real-world scenarios were behind these laws. In the first, the idea seems to be of a free man using his unfree dependents for dirty work in a feud. In the second, the idea seems to be a scuffle in the course of lordly exaction. Both the aggressive *concilius* and the defensive *seditio* are imagined as being instigated by one individual, of higher social status (a "free man") in the first and of indeterminate status in the second.[222] Given the more stringent discipline meted out in the first law, it is reasonable to assume that King Rothari was more concerned with feuding nobles who marshaled unfree workers than with rustics who banded together to resist surplus extraction.

A revealing later law of King Liutprand (r. 712–44) reinforces this impression, while shedding light on the gender dynamics of rural brawls. In a law of 734, Liutprand wrote that "certain perfidious men crafty in their wickedness" had tried to circumvent Rothari's old laws by "causing their womenfolk [*mulieres suae*] to gather together, however many they had, both free and slave," and then send them against their enemies, whom the women assaulted "even more cruelly than men."[223] The malefactors did this because another law of Rothari's, concerning "a free woman rushing into a conflict [*scandalum*] in which men are disputing," had specified that the nine-hundred-*solidi* fine for breaking the peace would be waved when women were the protagonists, on the logic "that it is unworthy [*inhonestum*] for women to do such things."[224] Liutprand had to concede that collective attacks by women could not be classed as a *harschild* or a *concilius rusticanorum* "because these are things that men do, not women."[225] But to dissuade women from performing such attacks ("both for the sake of discipline and for the sake of compensation"), he laid down new deterrents. Not only would the women's husbands be responsible for whatever damage they caused, but those who participated would be entitled to no compensation if hurt or killed. Furthermore, local public officials were to arrange for the guilty women's subsequent humiliation: first shaving (*decaluare*) and then parading (*frustare*) them through neighboring villages (*per uicos uicinantes ipsius loci*). This would still insulate any ringleader from the nine-hundred-*solidi* charge for breaking the peace. Here, there is some foretaste of later crowd history, in which women took the lead in contentious actions for reasons of presumed legal leniency.[226]

These Lombard laws suggest a countryside more plagued by peasant collective violence than may seem the case from the record of revolts or riots. It is typical, however, that the laws dwell on ringleaders. The idea that behind every crowd is an instigator is an old trope, but there are two reasons it may have been valid. First, early medieval peasants banding together on their own initiative tended to proceed more warily, resorting to law or passive resistance in disputes with lords.[227] Second, as we have seen in the case of urban unrest, elites were best positioned to mobilize non-elite crowds for contentious purposes.

As the next chapter will discuss, this is clearest with religious elites, who incorporated rural populations into liturgical rituals, readying them for collective organization. In the complex liturgical and organizational operations devised by the Carolingian courtier-turned-abbot Angilbert of Saint-Riquier (d. 814), the *populus vulgaris*—the lay communities living in the vicinity—enjoyed a prominent role alongside the monks and boys' choirs on fixed feast days.[228] By regular mobilization, rural communities might be readied for more rowdy action. A well-documented case is the basilica of Saint Martin at Tours. Whenever Saint Martin's dignity was threatened, his "people" (*populus*) sprang to his defense. Sometimes, the zeal of the saint's defenders outstripped the interests of basilica leadership. When a "tumult" of locals, including "rustics," attacked Theodulf's men from Orléans early in the ninth century, Charlemagne was furious with the courtier-turned-abbot Alcuin, despite the latter's insistence that the crowd had acted spontaneously. Alcuin lost his case, but the crowd's collective anger temporarily prevented a bishop and an emperor from getting their way.[229]

Repertory and Resistance

Marc Bloch's dictum that non-elite revolt was inherent to the medieval political economy does not apply to the early Middle Ages.[230] Urban crowd violence directed at elites was not unheard of, "peasant revolts" occurred, and collective violence marred the countryside, but all of this was rarer. In part, this was due to the hopelessness of revolt, in part to disproportionate aristocratic responses. Coordination among peasants could end in terror, death, and mutilation, even when it hardly looked like direct resistance. In the face-to-face communities of early medieval rural Europe, group violence lacked the anonymity and scale that has made it a plausible weapon of the weak in other societies. Towns offered the safest venues for collective action, and most reports of tumults we have come from urban settings. But even there, the success rate was low, particularly after about the year 600. There still were outbursts of group violence. In Lombard Italy, unfree peasants took part in feuding and resisted lordly exaction enough to spark legislation. In periods of political chaos, such as the later ninth and early tenth centuries, rural gilds united to defend themselves, whether from Vikings or from their own lords.

But most of the time, there were better ways of using numbers. Coalitions of peasants went to law together. We usually see them losing, but this may be a quirk of evidentiary survival. Coordinated passive resistance—refusal to participate in the regular gatherings—had a good chance of success if the community could keep out of arm's reach, as Bloch was among the first to recognize.[231] Slantwise resistance, assembly in unexpected configurations, was another means of voting with one's feet. Peasants could use intra-elite competition to their advantage. Since hierarchical relations both economic and ideological relied so much on gatherings, refusal to gather in the expected ways at the expected times became, effectively, refusal to submit. In this way, gatherings remained—albeit in inverted form—a powerful tool of non-elite resistance.

Seeing crowds exclusively as a means of resistance misses the point. For early medieval peasants, crowds served many aims. Gatherings mitigated against risk in an agrarian system where few other remedies had the same power as sheer number. They were central to spirituality. They enabled small societies to achieve consensus or, failing that, to agree upon matters of justice. They were fun. It is precisely because crowds did so much that they remained, albeit in new ways, a powerful tool of resistance.

4

The Closed Crowd

ELITE VENUES AND OCCASIONS
FOR GATHERING

Predictability, Hierarchy, Unity

The last chapter focused on collective behavior among non-elites, both repertory and resistance.[1] This one turns to elite-run venues for gathering: liturgical rites, sermons, relic cults, courts, collective pastimes like hunting, church councils, and secular assemblies. Three factors characterized these gatherings organized by and for early medieval elites: predictability, hierarchy, and unity. Those happen to be the ideal type traits of the top-down gatherings Elias Canetti called "closed crowds."[2] Unlike boundary-defying "open" crowds, closed crowds are planned out and stage-managed. They do not level distinctions, but solidify and perpetuate them. Yet they aim for a unity of purpose or action reminiscent of more spontaneous crowds, and their power of legitimation derives from the same magic of numbers. This chapter explores the characteristics of the closed crowd in the early Middle Ages.

Canetti's schema is far from perfect. No gathering is truly "closed." As we will see in cases of intra-elite competition, supposedly ordered gatherings got out of hand. Cases of "ritual failure" were not uncommon.[3] Ritual gatherings could be manipulated or reframed by propagandists after the fact.[4] Top-down assemblies were not smooth sailing, as the Frankish emperor Louis the Pious (r. 814–40) discovered when he was unmade by the penitential councils that were supposed to restore his authority.[5] There were always opportunities for resistance, passive or discursive, to what James Scott has termed "the public transcript of the powerful."[6] But this chapter argues that the solemn assembly, despite the often unrealizable qualities of the hierarchy and unity it stood for, became something like the default gathering for elites in early medieval Europe.

Religious Gatherings

For Canetti, the quintessential "closed crowd" was the religious gathering.[7] Early medieval religiosity encompassed a bewildering variety of locally specific Christianities.[8] But most religious gatherings met at predictable times and followed set procedures, even if these varied from setting to setting. Some ceremonies, like the divine offices of monks and nuns, took place largely outside of public view, among a select class of professional worshippers (though their prayers were felt to have society-wide influence).[9] Wealthy aristocrats had private chapels, religious staff, and liturgical apparatus.[10] But Sunday services and major ceremonies—at least theoretically—served the whole community, the *populus* or plebs.[11] Mass processions, as John Romano has explained, staged public unity at known times.[12] Relics drew vast numbers wherever they were installed, and the feasts of the saints involved were dates in the calendar when crowds of worshippers could be expected.

There were many venues for religious assemblies. Churches stand out, but pious crowds gathered in all sorts of natural and built environments. Meeting points of fluvial or land routes were favored for mass gatherings. The insular missionary Paulinus catechized and baptized thousands at the confluence of two rivers.[13] Rogationtide processions beat the bounds of fields.[14] In towns, processions took place on the streets, and liturgies made use of the monumental spaces of post-Roman cities.[15] The long porticoes of a rural monastery could be used to frame a communal procession.[16] Across these settings, seasonality and procedure served—not always successfully, as we saw in the last chapter—to harness the power of crowds for the sake of Christian order. What follows is only a partial overview. Above all, attention will be given to the ways in which sacred space reinforced hierarchy and celebrated consensus.

Churchgoing: Aspirations and Limitations

Many types of church dotted the early medieval landscape, from humble wooden structures to vast stone-built cathedral complexes.[17] There is uncertainty as to how regularly people attended church services. Late antique churches had never been intended to house more than a thin slice of local populations.[18] Unexpectedly large audiences took preachers by surprise. Augustine complained about having to reread a Gospel passage "because yesterday there was a great crowd, crushed even in the passages, and rather restless, which did not give my voice a chance; for my voice is such that it will only carry in a great silence."[19] The wish to expand and regularize lay churchgoing, especially on Sundays and festivals, was an aspirational drumbeat of early medieval legislation.[20] But normative efforts to increase the regularity and quality of church attendance persisted up to the time of the Fourth Lateran Council (1215). Realistic early medieval churchmen grasped that most laypeople might not take communion more than three times a year (at Christmas, Epiphany, and Easter).[21] Then again, they may have come to "hear mass" more frequently than they partook of the Eucharist.

Furthermore, local identity was bound up with central churches even when people visited them infrequently. We have seen the importance of the basilica of Saint Donatus in Arezzo to the seventy-seven witnesses at the 715 placitum in Siena.[22] These humble folk, who lived in Siena's secular jurisdiction and received pastoral care at local shrines, identified themselves with the cathedral at Arezzo. Saint Donatus was where their local churches and shrines received chrism, and where their priests had been ordained and performed the *manu mea* (the confirmation of their duties with their "own hand"). It is conceivable that some of these witnesses and their families had only visited the church in Arezzo once or twice, presumably on some grand occasion, or never. Still, a memory or idea of this space of assembly defined their religious identity.

Carolingian rulers in the eighth and ninth centuries made efforts to ensure that their subjects sought and received pastoral care at churches, taking their place and paying their tithes in a society conceived as one great *ecclesia*.[23] Authorities devoted efforts to improving church rituals too. The competence and saintliness of priests, the correctness of texts and rituals, were all critical in ensuring the continued support of God.[24] Only in the ninth century did parish churches become the (normative) focal point of religious life.[25] The gradual development of a parish system in Europe took centuries, and at no point in the early Middle Ages did it function perfectly. There was always something aspirational in efforts to center religious charisma on people's "own priests" and "own parish churches" where they received sacraments.[26] But when such ceremonies worked, they were powerful motors of communal feeling.

As in Late Antiquity, church crowds were reliably biggest on festival days, at Christmas, Epiphany, Easter, Pentecost, and the feast days of locally important saints.[27] The extraordinary flavor of collective worship on red letter days can be gleaned from a passage in Angilbert of Saint-Riquier's late eighth-century *Institutio de diversitate officiorum*. On Easter and Christmas, lay members of the congregation were expected not just to "hear" mass but take communion alongside the monastic brothers in the great monastic church of the Holy Savior. The rituals involved played up both hierarchical separateness and spiritual communion:

> I have ordained that on the most holy day of Easter and on the Nativity of the Lord [Christmas], the brothers [the monks of Saint-Riquier] and all others who are standing in the church of the Holy Savior to hear mass are

to partake of communion in that same church. For while the brothers and the rest of the clerics take communion from the priest who sang mass on that day, let there be two other priests with two deacons and two subdeacons, one of whom should give communion to the men, the other to the women in the same church, so that the clergy and the people [*clerus et populus*], taking communion together [*simul communicati*], will be able to hear the blessing and the ending of the mass on equal terms [*pariter*]. When this is finished, let them depart together [*simul egrediantur*], praising God and blessing the Lord. Once that is done, let the aforementioned two priests stay behind, one of them at the one door and the other at the other, from whom the boys [*pueri*], coming down from the ambulatories, will take communion. After all this has been done, let the one descend from the one site, the other from the other, together with their ministers, and standing at the last step, let them at last give communion to those who did not have a chance to take communion at the other aforementioned places.[28]

Hierarchical differentiation and unity are equally important here. Clerics and monks take communion from the celebrant while the two priests with their numerically matched subordinates minister in separate lines to men and women. But all leave the church together. Separated by status, gender, and function, the *clerus et populus* is nevertheless united in one church by one ritual. Here is the early medieval closed crowd in a nutshell.

Ecclesiastical elites had some leeway in shaping opportunities for gatherings of this kind. A new relic brought with it a new festival day. In the last chapter, we saw how church charities disbursed largess to the poor at predictable and presumably well-advertised dates.[29] Popes are known to have coordinated their celebrations with times of more-than-usual pilgrimage.[30] The seasonality of religious crowds, therefore, was partly fixed by a shared Christian liturgy, partly controllable. There were known times when crowds could be relied on, and it was at these moments that public acts calling for differentiated but united crowds—the collection of dues, the baptism of children, the election of public figures, the celebration of ordinations—were performed.[31]

Sermons

While churches were primarily sites of liturgical rituals, sacraments, and acts of almsgiving, they were also where classical oratory lived on in the form of sermons.[32] Preaching would become a major crowd phenomenon in later medieval Europe.[33] The massive audiences in fields and piazzas that proliferated from the twelfth century onward were not typical of early medieval practice.[34] Nevertheless, preaching to lay audiences turns out to have been more important than previously believed. Historians once dismissed the early medieval experience of preaching as restrictive and small-scale: largely a question of ecclesiastics reading soulless homilies to one another from ancient homiliaries.[35] As recently as 1991, one scholar characterized the period between c. 500 and c. 1200 as "an inhospitable landscape to the historian of preaching."[36] But more recent work on the large body of sermons and homilies composed or copied in the early Middle Ages, particularly with a focus on manuscript transmission, has led to a reassessment.[37] The old view that early medieval preachers spoke to closed-off audiences of monks and clerics is being abandoned.

James McCune, Maximilian Diesenberger, and others have highlighted the genuine concern early medieval authorities seem to have had with giving good sermons to mixed crowds.[38] Who actually constituted these audiences is not always clear. Despite Gregory the Great's admonition to would-be preachers to know their audiences, sermons are often frustratingly sparse on details.[39] Doubtless many were indeed performed for a restricted audience of religious specialists.[40] But the existence of a few fragments of vernacular sermons alongside persistent legislative demands for vernacular preaching show that lay people consumed sermons frequently enough—perhaps more often than they took communion.[41] This reiterates the importance of crowds in a largely nonliterate population that relied on the spoken word for mass communication.[42]

Church Space: Differentiation and Unity

New early medieval churches were, on the whole, smaller than their late antique counterparts.[43] That said, the Christian built environment was the feature of Roman urbanism that survived most completely into the early medieval period. Italy especially boasted numerous late antique basilicas that could accommodate thousands.[44] But interiors even in the grandest early medieval churches were not open spaces. Today, visitors experience basilicas like Santa Sabina (c. 417–32) and Santa Maria Maggiore (c. 420–40) in Rome as open expanses. In the early Middle Ages, all churches from the smallest to the greatest were subdivided in ways that reinforced the hierarchical divisions so important to religious rituals.

Franz Bauer has termed this "liturgical fragmentation."[45] Cloisters, sacristies, crypts, and narthexes had separate functions in the liturgy.[46] A sharp separation of church interiors, using obstructing chancels as well as curtains, columns, and other structures, enabled the kind of sacred division of labor churchmen dreamed of. One pope at Rome redesigned his seat in Santa Maria Maggiore to prevent the sound of crowds of women from intruding on his and the priests' aural space.[47] As Carol Heitz has shown, the adumbrated liturgy described by Angilbert was assisted by the complex architecture of the westwork of Holy Savior at Saint-Riquier.[48] Not just that. Church artwork provided cosmic models for the differentiation-within-unity on the ground. In Pope John VII's (r. 705–7) Santa Maria Antiqua, the minute subdivisions of the building were reflected in the apocalyptic art of the church. A great triumphal fresco depicts crowds, in hierarchical order, beneath a vision of God.[49] The apocalyptic scene would have mirrored the bodies assembled in the church below.

A century later, Paschal I (r. 817–24), the pope who redesigned Santa Maria Maggiore to avoid the sound of female crowds, initiated a campaign of church building.[50] One of his earliest achievements was Santa Prassede, the storehouse for a huge collection of relics that the pope translated from the catacombs into the city.[51] Art historians have noted that Santa Prassede's mosaics eternalize this 817 translation.[52] The mosaics depict highly differentiated heavenly crowds. The Lamb of God occupies a central position, surrounded by the seven candle-stands of Revelation 1:12, together with divine figures and the pope himself. The twenty-four elders of Revelation 4:4 stand below to the left and right, arrayed in their white robes. The important saints are led into the heavenly Jerusalem at the highest section of the triumphal or outer mosaic. Martyrs with palm fronds, excluded from the innermost apse mosaic, are placed lower down and further out on the triumphal mosaic. These serried, ordered ranks, visually aligned, heads-in-a-row (or "isocephalic"), represented the cosmic version of differentiated unity. Yet we should remember that this muscular messaging was partly defensive. In transferring saints (and the pilgrims and money they attracted) from the catacombs, Paschal initiated a "reversal of tradition and interruption of a long-standing pattern of worship in Rome."[53] Hence the need for spatial divisions and art stressing the divine virtue of keeping to one's proper place.

Church entrances were also specialized sites for assembly. Old Saint Peter's in Rome had an oratory "of Saint Petronilla," which seems to have served as a point of entry for high-ranking Franks.[54] As we have seen in the previous chapter, Merovingian and Carolingian churches were supposed to keep *matricula*, lists of the poor whose needs they provided for; these indigents hung about the narthex.[55] The predictable presence of poor folk and *debiles* at church entrances facilitated acts of generosity.[56] In the *Passio Praeiecti*, a sick man makes an arduous journey to the shrine of the saint. By giving to a crowd of poor people (*turba pauperum*) at the shrine, the man earns his cure.[57] An east Frankish noble woman sent money to Dorestad because she heard there were "multitudes" of poor at the town's churches.[58] Over time, a symbiotic relationship developed between the poor or disabled, ecclesiastical authorities, and elite benefactors, not unlike that which had united the Roman plebs, state, and elites. But churches, not entertainment buildings, were the new stage.

Church Space: Awe and Instruction

As sites of gathering, the power of churches to generate awe arose in part from their alterity. They were often made of a different fabric from the rest of early medieval settlements: stone or brick as opposed to wood or daub. They looked, felt, sounded, and smelled different. The distinct flavor of their light, through high windows or hundreds of lit candles, was unique in the early medieval world.[59] The scent of incense or cut flowers mirrored the holy odor of sanctity.[60] Grand frescoes and mosaics, rare textiles between partitions, the blocked-off altar with relics below, beneath an apse showing the awful multitudes of the Final Judgment: these features explain why churches were such effective sites of agreement, asylum, and mass ritual. Gregory of Tours, who developed his own major building program, vividly recalled the great fifth-century church of his hometown at Clermont: 150 (Roman) feet long, sixty feet wide, and fifty feet tall, with forty-two windows, seventy columns, and eight doors.[61] As Catherine Hailstone has sensitively explored, Gregory knew this grand building was designed to inspire *terror Dei*, "the fear of God" in its observers, that is, the beginning of wisdom (Proverbs 9:10).[62]

The hulking giants of Late Antiquity (the fourth and fifth centuries saw a frenzy of urban church construction across the West) would have been all the more impressive for the downward demographic scaling around them. If MacMullen is correct, most late antique cities were only able to accommodate a minority of their populations in available church spaces, in some cases only 5–10 percent.[63] But after demographic thinning, that percentage would have improved considerably. In early medieval Rome, it would have been possible to accommodate the entire population of the seventh- to ninth-century city into the fifteen or so largest of its hundreds of churches.[64] Rome was a city of pilgrims, so its inhabitants were, in fact, supplemented by streams of visitors, but even then it remained a city of potentially underpopulated sacred spaces.[65] Small crowds in huge spaces can experience effects no less profound than large crowds in small ones.

These effects show why churches served as venues for many kinds of public business. As Marc Bloch noted, the church was the site par excellence of non-elite consensus building.[66] Churches often acted as venues for councils. The preamble to a Carolingian council held at Friuli in 796 / 797 opens with a depiction of a "full house," with all the relevant sub-gatherings in their place: a "large, harmonious crowd" (*non modica... consentanea turba*) of holy men within the church and a "throng of the common folk pressing at the door."[67] This spatially enabled communal validity was critical in representing conciliar decisions as universal decisions.

This suggests that religious closed crowds were not just about assembling the largest possible numbers, but about delivering meaningful messages to and through numbers. The complex physical articulation of early medieval churches put crowds in their places: male and female, ordained and lay, high and low, rich and poor.[68] They thereby reinforced the social distinctions that mattered most to elites. This may be one reason the Carolingians, with their especially knee-jerk reactions to collective autonomy, put so much energy into parish-level churchgoing.[69] Their reform efforts were pious, but they had material imperatives too: strengthening the indirect chains of dependence and obedience upon which early medieval governance depended.

In exchange for the genuine spiritual, sacramental, and material benefits they offered, early medieval churches took the bodies of the faithful and molded them into ideals of collective order.[70] In this, they replaced the theaters, amphitheaters, and circuses as the most ambitious "crowd containers" of the early medieval West.[71] Early medieval rulers who saw their polities as great *ecclesiae* were invested in the good condition of the individual churches that made up the whole.[72] That explains why misbehavior in churches was treated with such agitation. Amolo of Lyon, in dealing with the crowds of flailing women in Dijon, not only advised his suffragan to reinforce his flock's attendance at their own churches, but told him to beat those who refused to leave.[73]

Monasteries and Nunneries

Monasteries—whether male, female, or mixed—constitute a special case in the sacred topography of early medieval gatherings. Although monasteries were designed as spaces of exclusion from secular life, they were frequently associated with crowds, as we have seen in the case of Angilbert's Saint-Riquier. Many, such as San Vincenzo al Volturno in Italy or Fulda in Hesse, were attached to settlements of considerable size.[74] In principle, houses of worship consisted of gatherings of religious men or women who devoted their lives to asceticism and prayer. In practice, it was more complicated.

A community's renown manifested itself in throngs of pious members. A sign of one ninth-century abbess's sanctity was the massive influx of noble daughters who, "taking up the holy veil, chose a monastic life."[75] A hagiographical topos linked the foundation of daughter monasteries with the overcrowding of parent houses. Monastic founders were said to assemble (*coadunare*) "crowds" or "throngs" of religious into new communities.[76] As chapter 2 explained, great monasteries vied with small towns in size. The 603 monks of Fulda in c. 825 would have been an impressive sight assembled together.[77] Furthermore, servants and slaves, beneficiaries of *matricula*, the needful sick and *debiles*, beggars or opportunists at the gates, and visitors of all sorts swelled the numbers of any given house.[78] Space was partitioned to emphasize distinctions between such groups. But many classes participated in the spiritual life of a monastery.

Nunneries merit particular consideration, as the women within them were meant to be especially excluded from lay society.[79] A nunnery's worth as a center of prayer depended on its members' purity.[80] But by necessity nuns were regularly in contact with the lay world and the world of men. Masculine crowds of protectors, workers, and hangers-on surrounded them, and the priests that ministered to their spiritual needs were also male.[81] During the nuns' revolt at Poitiers of 589–90 (more of a power struggle over Radegund's monastery than a revolt), dozens of male ruffians fought it out on either side.[82] In emphasizing this point, the historian Gregory of Tours drew unkind attention to the polluting effect of male presence in a female sacred space, but he knew that this volatile mixture was unavoidable—including in a female monastery at Tours.[83]

Accusations of improper intercourse with the lay world by nuns could generate trouble, but this could be neutralized by the right collective performance. In a ninth-century story about an eighth-century miracle, a drowned infant was discovered near the nunnery of Tauberbischofsheim near Mainz, whose abbess, the redoubtable West Saxon noblewoman Leoba, responded with a dramatic crowd ritual.[84] According to Leoba's hagiographer Rudolf of Fulda, the child had been abandoned by a certain poor, disabled woman (*quaedam paupercula debilitate contracta*) who begged alms while lying on the ground in front of the monastery's gate. But a local woman, believing that the drowned infant was the exposed lovechild of one of the nuns, raised a hubbub, crying: "O what a chaste congregation, O what a glorious lifestyle of virgins, who while veiled give birth to children, and perform the office of mothers and priests alike, since they baptize the ones they birth!" The village's "whole populace [*plebs tota*], of every age and sex" assembled at these disgruntled shouts and "ran in one mass as if to a spectacle" (*quasi ad spectaculum uno agmine cucurrit*).[85]

Abbess Leoba, hearing the "tumult" (*tumultus*), but confident of her nuns' purity, took action. First, in the relative privacy of the oratory, she commanded her nuns to chant the entire psalter from start to finish while holding out their arms in the shape of the cross (*extensis in crucis modum brachiis*). Next, the nuns were to process in public around the monastery three times, at Terce (late morning), Sext (noon), and Nones (midafternoon), singing litanies and carrying a cross aloft.[86] After the third procession, the "whole people" (*cunctus populus, plebs omnis*) were assembled in the nuns' church, where Leoba stood at the altar in front of the very cross the nuns had carried in the procession. Tears flowing from her eyes, she lifted her arms to heaven and cried out: "Lord Jesus Christ, king of virgins, lover of integrity, unconquered God, show your power [*virtus*] and free us from this infamy [*infamia*], for the reproaches of the reproachful against you have fallen upon us!" At once, the poor woman confessed the truth, the crowd (*plebs*) raised up a huge cry (*clamor*), and the might (*potentia*) of Leoba and Christ was proclaimed "in common by all with one voice" (*in commune ab omnibus uno ore*).[87] In this way, the discipline of closed crowds overcame the "tumult" of a disgruntled local populace.

Early medieval monasteries were crowded by dramas of this sort because they catered to public needs. In the story above, the trouble originated from a poor woman's need to beg for alms in a public place—the nunnery entrance—where she could expect to receive them. As much as some writers grumbled that the benefits of perpetual prayer would be interrupted by some *vulgus promiscuum*, generally one monastic foot in the secular water was seen as natural.[88] In rural areas, monasteries took responsibility for the pastoral care of communities, and were essential in bringing institutional Christianity to newly converted regions.[89] Early in the period, nunneries fulfilled this role too, as Gisela Muschiol and Felice Lifshitz have shown.[90] Monasteries planned for guests. A provision in the *Supplex Libellus* drawn up for the monastery of Fulda by Ratger in 812 accounted for extra numbers during Saint Boniface's feast day (June 5).[91] On the famous ninth-century Saint-Gall Plan, the front gate of an idealized monastery bore the caption: "Here the whole crowd, coming in, has its entrance!" The path leading up to the gate carries a poem about "rejoicing throngs."[92] Architecture attests to the spaces set aside by early medieval monasteries for nonmembers.[93] A council at Soissons in 853 sent out *missi* to guarantee that monasteries were ready to receive the poor (*pauperes*) with sufficient supplies and lodgings.[94]

Monks and nuns—together with secular canons—were crowd specialists in another way too. As members of networks of prayer, they tapped into an invisible "community of the living and the dead."[95] Martyrologies and litanies brought together crowds of saints in the space of monastic churches.[96] With 534 saints' names, the Lorsch Rotulus (Stadt- und Universitätsbibliothek, Frankfurt am Main, MS. Barth. 179), a massive Rogationtide litany on a parchment scroll measuring eight feet long, is among the largest.[97] Astrid Krüger has argued that this scroll was designed for Louis the German (d. 876) by the abbey of Lorsch during the 860s.[98] Eric Goldberg has further posited that it should be associated with Rogation Sunday of 868, which fell upon May 23, in the middle of a large synod at Worms, when Louis drafted a charter in favor of the monks, asking them for their prayers in exchange.[99] For Goldberg, the monks spectacularly obliged by invoking "the army of heaven to the defense of [Louis the German's] kingship and dynasty as he had requested."[100]

Another monastic virtual crowd appears in the *libri memoriales*, books in which names of spiritual brothers and sisters, living and dead, are listed for commemoration and prayer.[101] The largest of these contained more souls than any surviving polyptych, and possibly more than inhabited any contemporary city. The *libri memoriales* had origins in physical gatherings. At the royal palace of Attigny in 762, forty-four abbots and bishops assembled to form an *amicitia* or "friendship pact" where they promised to pray for one another in perpetuity; a second prayer-league met at Dingolfing in Bavaria in 770. These formed the basis of what became the Reichenau Confraternity Book, though the version we have was not compiled until around 823 or 824.[102]

In its ninety-nine parchment folios, the Reichenau Confraternity Book ultimately counted 38,232 co-brothers and co-sisters.[103] The Confraternity Book of St Peter's, Salzburg, compiled in 784, had a respectable 7,614 names.[104] The early ninth-century Pfäfers *Liber Viventium* consisted of 4,644 names added to a beautiful gospel-book, with the names in arches as if in canon-tables.[105] The St. Gall *Liber memorialis* is actually two different books, one compiled before 817 and the other around 870. Together they contain 14,932 names (from forty-eight religious houses).[106] The Remiremont *Liber memorialis* contained 10,631 names. Its entries go back to the foundation of the nunnery in the seventh century, but names continued to be added into the ninth century.[107] The book of San Salvatore and Santa Giulia in Brescia contained a total of 7,002 names.[108] The Corvey *Liber vitae* lists 2,642 names.[109] A humbler list in Cividale consisted of 1,600 names added to a Gospel-book.[110] Finally, the Durham *Liber Vitae* belonged to the peripatetic monastic community of Saint Cuthbert (chased by Vikings from Lindisfarne to Chester-le-Street to Durham), and by the ninth century contained over 3,000 names.[111] In considering monastic crowds, we must reckon these ink-and-parchment multitudes as part of the power of numbers that early medieval monasteries wielded.

The Cult of Relics

The early Middle Ages saw a great exodus of dead saints to new churches, and a concurrent rash of relic translations (*translationes*).[112] Relics had the power to attract large crowds.[113] As sources of succor, health, intercession, and dispute-settlement, they were a central destination for early medieval pilgrims.[114] The cult of relics was deeply implicated with public order and the stability of kingdoms.[115] Crowds sought the aid of saints, and the presence of crowds in turn testified to the validity of relics, and revealed the approval of the holy men and women whose earthly remnants they were.[116] For their earthly stewards, the crowds were a source of legitimacy and donations. Translation narratives and miracle stories about relics typically had two goals: first, to promote a cult of relics; second, to dispel any doubts about their veracity. Both were achieved by recounting miracles involving crowds—preferably crowds from all walks of life—drawn to piety by the relics' wonder-working powers.[117]

Hedwig Röckelein has argued that crowds functioned almost like an early medieval public sphere in the conceptualization of relic cults. Röckelein stresses the irenic function of this "Öffentlichkeit," the collective agreement of public facts about the earthly presence of sanctity.[118] But the publicity of crowds also played a role in intra-elite competition. Einhard, Charlemagne's courtier, wrote a famous account of his translation of the relics of two saints, Marcellinus and Petrus, from Rome to Frankland in 830 or 831, a text chockablock with multitudes.[119] Einhard was defending his claims to these relics against those of a rival, Hilduin of Saint-Denis—after all, in material terms these were bones and dust stolen from a Roman tomb in dark of night—so crowds served a crucial probative aim. In some cases, a crowd witnesses a miracle, as when a slave woman is healed before many witnesses. Frequently a miracle is enacted upon a crowd, as when a crowd of sick are healed en masse. Sometimes, the miracle is the crowd itself, as when Einhard describes "a very dense and large crowd" suddenly drawn to the relics as *quid miraculi*, "a kind of miracle."[120]

Einhard's dispute with Hilduin shows that relics on their own were not always sufficient. They had to be accompanied by propaganda campaigns, a mix of blandishment and threat to the right ears. Moreover, as Einhard's story also made clear, the relics had to be placed in reasonably accessible places. Sites of regular assembly included mills, mints, courts, villas, and markets. Einhard had initially situated the relics in a new-built church in Michelstadt in the Odenwald. Petrus and Marcellinus made clear via a dream that they wished to be moved from this wooded and mountainous place to what is now called Seligenstadt ("saints' town"), but then called Obermühlheim, "the upper milling site."[121] It was a wise choice: from an isolated site in the woods, Einhard moved the relics to a much-frequented center of economic activity on the Main River. Even the lure of sanctity sometimes needed practical aid in drawing numbers.

Gatherings in "Public" Life

The early Middle Ages is famous for its religious gatherings, but routinized gatherings were important to economic and political life. We saw in the last chapter that gatherings structured agrarian labor and surplus extraction. For elites, life in public was lived in gatherings. Status was conveyed by the crowds one marshaled or joined. Land grants, sales and purchases, manumissions, dispute settlements, legislation, and political successions were confirmed by the power of numbers.[122] Some numbers counted more than others. Witnesses had to be free and in good standing (social or legal infamy could invalidate potential witnesses). Episcopal and comital voices mattered more than those of lower orders. A social fact promulgated in a properly run *thing*, placitum, or assembly could not be established by any old crowd. Even in assemblies, the quorum had a more confirmatory role, while the king's councilors played a more deliberative one.[123]

If gatherings produced a "public sphere" in the early Middle Ages, therefore, it was not the wide-open space of debate in Habermasian theory, but a more circumscribed space of deliberation, contestation, and agreement.[124] Still, as with Habermas's *Öffentlichkeit*, the "elitist-early-medieval public sphere" (as Leidulf Melve has termed it) generated poles of facticity beyond the control of the highest authorities.[125] Gatherings legitimized ruling elites, but they could force the hands of kings. In this section, a partial accounting is offered of types and venues of gathering that structured elite identity, especially heading into the Carolingian period as this elite public sphere came to be characterized by a culture of frequent solemn assemblies.

Entourages

As we saw in chapter 2, social and political legitimacy was closely related to one's ability to marshal numbers. This was nothing new. Horace wrote that great men in Rome vied to appear in public with the biggest "crowd" of clients (*turba clientium*).[126] The ninth-century scribes who preserved the first-century BCE satirist would not have been surprised to read this.[127] Nothing expressed high status like a ring of satellites.[128] Public solitude was unthinkable. A Lombard queen was embarrassed to arrive at the baths with a smaller entourage than a noblewoman.[129] Popes were required to maintain a permanent entourage of at least two priests and three deacons at all times.[130] Not just kings and bishops, but all nobles wished to be surrounded by impressive entourages. As Michael McCormick has written, "no Carolingian grandee traveled alone."[131]

Our knowledge of the makeup of lordly entourages is not detailed. On a few occasions, court documents give us names, as with "the men" of the Joseph discussed in chapter 2 who served as his witnesses at Freising early in the tenth century: Abraham, Prozilo, Petto, Seman, Tribagos, a second Abraham, Pretimir, Prozila, Joseph.[132] These men probably were not the only people with Joseph as he attended to his business at Freising. But we know nothing of his servants and attendants. Entourages were themselves hierarchical, though this is not always made clear by laconic sources. Most commonly written sources take their logistics and personnel for granted, using phrases like *sui* ("his people") with little additional information.[133] Detailed accountings of entourage sizes tended to be exceptional and signs of trouble or at least dispute.[134]

As with peasants who traveled in groups, elites relied on entourages not just for standing, but for security. Travel was dangerous for persons of high rank too.[135] Feuds made solitude deadly.[136] The seventh-century *Vita Leudegarii*, composed sometime after 692 by a monk of Saint-Symphorian at Autun, describes how the secular lord Ebroin plotted to murder Saint Leudegar after their mutual escape from Luxeuil. Ebroin, Leudegar, and Genesius, the bishop of Lyon, all had retinues of various sizes, and the hagiographer mused that Ebroin was prevented from attacking his old enemy Leudegar by Genesius because of "the strong war-band [*manus valida*] with which he had come."[137] A bishop's dedication to peace did not always extend to his bodyguard.[138] Early medieval sources are full of assassinations, like that of Fulk of Reims, which occurred when the archbishop's retinue was too small to fend off his foes.[139] Medieval exegetes know from the Gospel of Luke that Judas could only put his betrayal into effect when Jesus Christ was alone, "crowdless" (*sine turbis*).[140]

It is worth remembering that there were good reasons to *be* in an entourage as well as to have one. Members of retinues, as we have seen, were fed and sheltered. Coteries may have been one of a few venues for social mobility in a world not replete with them. They were a source of safety in numbers. Amalarius, a ninth-century intellectual and exegete, in a convoluted metaphor, imagined a man being captured and brought to Constantinople as a slave "on account of my carelessness" (*propter meam incuriam*).[141] *Incuria*, in this hypothetical case, may well have been solitude.[142] There were protective benefits of being a member of an entourage.

Elections

Among the public rituals that demanded the presence of crowds, elections were among the most fraught.[143] Early medieval elections—of kings, bishops, abbots, and abbesses—were not democratic in any modern sense, though their association of public good with public approbation was typical of "democracy" as it later developed in the Middle Ages.[144] Instead, early medieval elections consisted of ritual acclamations by specific stakeholders, usually topped off by performative approbation by as large a crowd as possible.[145] Sources insist upon the importance of such crowds.[146] The assembled nobles, churchmen, and "people" who affirmed the election of an early medieval king or bishop—or, by contrast, the hired ruffians of a false leader[147]—are such a consistent feature of election narratives that they can seem like wallpaper. But the public sphere such groups embodied was felt to be essential.

We see this when elites failed to take the proper steps to stage-manage consensus. To return to the *Vita Leudegarii* above, when the Merovingian king Chlothar III died in 673, the mayor of the Neustrian palace Ebroin quickly appointed Chlothar's brother Theuderic III. We read that Ebroin failed to call an assembly of magnates to discuss the succession.[148] Because of this, Ebroin's foes were able to accuse him of seizing power illegitimately.[149] Only when Ebroin used force to assemble a "crowd" (*populus*) was he able to convince "everybody" (*cuncti*) that Chlothar III was truly Childeric's son.[150] Making a "fact" a "fact" meant exacting the proper acknowledgment from the proper groups in the right order. That included the "fact" of a king's legitimacy.

Elections, like other liturgical rites, had some protections against ritual failure. *Ordines*—that is, written procedures describing the liturgy step by step—mitigated against unexpected behavior.[151] Christina Pössel has noted that ritual solemnity might have prevented those with doubts from expressing them in the middle of a ceremony.[152] As with assemblies, a "discussion" and planning stage preceded any election (in part, this was what had been lacking in Ebroin's case).[153] But one often suspects the unanimity of acclamatory crowds in the sources was a historiographical fiction covering up dissention and discord.[154] The *Liber Pontificalis*, which cheerily acknowledged the unanimous nature of papal elections, also noted that a fraught campaign between "two parties" was the "usual" practice at the death of a pope.[155] This series of papal biographies was in large part designed to translate the messy realities of papal election into "One Will, One Voice, and Equal Love."[156] The best we can say is that early medieval elites felt that mass approbation was necessary in the transfer of authority, and took pains to stage performances of popular consensus.

Courts and Palaces as Gathering Sites

We have seen how court sites—royal, missal, comital—drew non-elite crowds for the sake of justice. The obligation to serve the populace was taken seriously. Kings took the time to arrange for mass judgement. "It so happened that a certain count of the Frankish people called Dotto was sitting, with a not-trifling multitude of Franks gathered around, to resolve legal cases," reports an eighth-century saint's life, "as was enjoined to him" (*ut erat illi iniunctum*).[157] *Missi* and counts were repeatedly warned not to neglect juridical duties.[158] To the obligation of justice was added that of munificence. A royal hall (*sala regalis*) at Annappes was equipped with a balcony (*solarium*) for the distribution of largess to the poor.[159] Despite genuine concessions to crowds of non-elites, however, early medieval courts primarily catered to elite needs—and pastimes.[160]

That was especially true at royal palaces. As we saw in chapter 2, royal palaces tended to be located away from urban sites, often on the edge of or surrounded by forest, where the hunting was good.[161] Kings contrived to spend the late fall and winter seasons there for that reason. The hunt, as Eric Goldberg has explored, was a crowd sport with a crowd's reward; success there proclaimed one's nobility to a crowd of peers.[162] Hunting was followed by banqueting, even if the more scrupulous Carolingian kings purported to favor more austere dining practices.[163] About other elite pastimes we know less. Ball games may have continued; they were being practiced in Late Antiquity.[164]

For rulers, populous courts were an essential ornament of power. "In the multitude of people is the dignity of the king: and in the small number of the people the dishonor of the prince," as Proverbs proclaimed.[165] Hincmar speaks of "that multitude," which "must always be present in the palace."[166] Palaces, like churches, were spaces designed to inscribe ideals of hierarchy onto the bodies assembled there.[167] Royal assistants were in a position—by their presence—to choose when and where numbers would swell. A palace neglected during Christmas, Easter, or Pentecost was a lonely place. By contrast, as we have seen in chapter 2, repeated ceremonial use, as at Aachen, could transform a palace into a stable settlement.

From the perspective of courtiers, "closeness to the king" (*Königsnähe*) was an essential resource, and the crowdedness of courts was both a means and an impediment to this end.[168] It was probably not easy to get close to Charlemagne when he was bathing with a "hundred or more" men in the springs at Aachen.[169] On the other hand, the larger the crowd—think of the hundreds that could have been accommodated in the *aulae* of Carolingian palaces—the more impressive close proximity became. Intellectual pursuits involved numbers too. Learning may not seem a quintessential crowd activity, but poetry was consumed orally in front of crowds.[170] Probably early medieval letters, outgoing as well as incoming, were also read aloud before audiences at court.[171]

The palaces of ecclesiastical magnates deserve special focus. In some ways, their crowd dynamics worked as in secular palaces or courts, in other ways they were more like monasteries.[172] Bishops were expected to hold their palaces open to the poor and needy, all the more important at times of public humility such as Maundy Thursday.[173] As Jamie Kreiner has shown, hagiography and law united to persuade bishops that the open doors for the poor were part of their duty. Long resistance hints that some bishops saw their métier differently.[174] In one celebrated church council, bishops were warned not to keep guard dogs: "The habitation of a bishop ought to be guarded by hymns, not barks, by good works, not poisonous bites."[175] An episode in a saint's life adds color to this decree. Young Saint Praeiectus miraculously avoided the attacks of a wicked deacon's guard dogs, even as the dogs attacked others in search of aid.[176]

Commerce and Crowds

Commerce was a markedly seasonal crowd phenomenon.[177] Although this was not an age famous for its commerce, trade and communications picked up in Europe from the seventh century onward.[178] At no point from the sixth century to the eleventh did seas, waterways, or roads go untraveled. But the velocity of early medieval trade was lower than before or after (or in the Eastern Mediterranean). Paradoxically, lower levels of trade may have meant that trading parties were all the more sizeable. The seventh-century chronicle of Fredegar describes a huge coterie assembled by "Samo, surnamed Winedos" when he set out to trade with the Slavs in 623 / 624.[179] Given unfavorable economies of scale, this hedging with numbers made good sense.

As we saw in chapter two, coastal settlements, built along trade networks but connected to local economies, blossomed when trade winds below.[180] At their seasonal peaks, they drew merchants, elites, and enterprising beggars. Dorestad could become a *villa non modica*, "no small village," which made it an attractive target for Vikings.[181] Outside of specialized settlements like Dorestad, smaller markets (*mercata, nundinae*) were a seasonal draw, as we have seen. Peasants going to larger markets also did so in the service of landlords, who demanded transport duties at times of buying and selling.[182] In theory, early medieval markets were highly regulated. But repeat legislation restricting markets suggests that they were not always as predictable as authorities desired.[183]

Like the fairs of Champagne in the high Middle Ages, the greatest fairs occurred on an annual basis.[184] Perhaps the most famous example from the early Middle Ages was the fair celebrating the feast day of Saint Denis.[185] October 9 marked the saint's feast day, when sacred and secular rituals coincided with a wine-harvest fair. At Saint-Denis, kings built a palace to conduct royal ceremonies, while secular and church leaders built ever-larger basilicas, culminating in Suger's great Gothic church.[186] Fueling it all was the harvest and the fair, where fun could be had and information could be shared. At Saint-Denis, it is easy to see how ideological and material factors coalesced. The Seine valley was densely populated, politically important, serviced by rivers and roads, and in the middle of several regional economies with different comparative advantages. The ideological significance of Saint Denis was high and the saint's martyrdom came at the tail end of harvest season. It is little wonder the fair was packed even by the 700s.[187]

Armies

We have seen that armies were among the largest gatherings of the early medieval period.[188] As specialized assemblages designed for battle, it is odd to think of armies as "closed crowds." But they often functioned as such. A well-organized army, assembled at the start of a campaigning season, would have been a marvel of ordered agglomeration matched in few other contexts. Military gatherings were hierarchical by nature. They were predictably seasonal, apt to be largest in the summer just before setting out to war. Furthermore, they attracted large penumbras of camp followers, religious professionals, lay officials, and merchants.[189] Under the right circumstances, armies, like courts, were collective microcosms of society as a whole, which is why so much public business occurred before their eyes.

But armies can be unruly or rebellious. Battle is chaotic. Rout is among the purest forms of uncontrolled collective behavior.[190] Moreover, the damage done, even in one's own country, by troops trying to feed themselves could be terrible.[191] The decentralized organization of early medieval forces undermined top-down efforts to smooth over the dangers of fighters on the move. Especially over the course of the ninth century, Frankish authorities became concerned with robberies (*rapina*) carried out not by brigands or Vikings, but by soldiers and their provisioners using royal authority to justify their actions. Hincmar of Reims prepared a formal admonition to be read aloud to the king's troops and officials by the priests of his archdiocese.[192] As we saw in the last chapter, peasants formed gilds to resist unruly royal troops or officials.[193]

Hence, armies were an avatar of closed crowds and open ones alike. This may be one reason, as the next chapter explores, that terms for armies, in Latin and vernacular languages, were used to describe all sorts of "crowds," not just military ones. To early medieval communities, they reflected collective behavior both at its best and at its worst.

Intra-Elite Competition and Conflict: The Case of Tours

This chapter has focused on how formal gatherings served elite aims. Yet elite aims were not uniform or uncontentious. Royal and imperial claims were challenged by internal and external rivals.[194] The powerful squabbled for status and resources. Resentments among classes and between peasant groups implicated elites, as we saw in the previous chapter. As arbiters of legitimacy and sources of power, gatherings played an important role in all this early medieval competition, as has emerged from a major research program on the subject led by Régine Le Jan and Geneviève Bührer-Thierry.[195]

In all the forms and venues of gathering discussed above, competition was a factor. Rival arbiters of spiritual authority competed for bodies. Feuds consisted of brawls between armed entourages. While the delivery of justice, the celebration of authority, and the exchange of resources were matters of collective gathering, the question of whose justice, whose authority, and whose resources should prevail were decided in and by crowds. Factional conflicts over elections—particularly episcopal elections—manifested themselves as rival crowds.[196] Above all, armies were designed to win struggles by force of numbers. Since crowds tended to be seen as buttresses of legitimate authority, this meant that they were effective tools of contention. In what follows, a single, well-known case of elite competition—from early ninth-century Carolingian Francia—will be explored in terms of the role of crowds.

The Tumult at Tours, 801 / 802

In 801 / 802, a dispute broke out between two former courtiers of Charlemagne's court, the learned Goth Bishop Theodulf of Orléans and the learned Englishman Alcuin, abbot of Saint Martin's at Tours. The event comes down to us through a dossier of letters linked with Alcuin.[197] Having already had some poetic clashes at court, Theodulf and Alcuin now entered a more serious dispute.[198] A cleric convicted of crimes at Orléans had fled the 115 kilometers southwest to seek asylum at Saint Martin's, Tours (together with a small entourage of supporters). Alcuin claims that the man confessed his sins, begged for reconciliation, and appealed to the emperor. When a small group of unarmed men came from Orléans to Tours to retrieve the fugitive, whispered reports of an "ambush" on their way made them second-guess their plans.[199]

Now a much larger group of Orléans men arrived, armed this time.[200] With the help of Joseph, the bishop of Tours, eight of them entered Saint Martin's on a Sunday to seize the cleric, who was prostrating himself at the altar.[201] The monks of Saint Martin's responded angrily, one of the cleric's entourage (his *homo*) raised a hue, and a "tumult" (*tumultus*) broke out.[202] This last word, *tumultus*, which Alcuin repeatedly used in his apologetic letter to the emperor, was a term of art from Roman law for a breach of the peace.[203] As we will see in the next chapter, it largely supplanted *turba* as the word of choice for a "rabble." Large numbers of townsfolk, including "rustics," now assembled to defend their saint. Amid the "huge clamor and gathering of people, especially of the poor" (*clamor ingens et concursus populi, maxime pauperum*), the men of Orléans felt their danger—towns, as the last chapter pointed out, remained one of the places it was still possible for elites to run into trouble of this kind. Alcuin writes that his monks protected Theodulf's men, and sent the people out of the basilica.[204]

Alcuin professed his and his monks' innocence. The crowds that endangered Theodulf's men, argued Alcuin, had acted on their own initiative. Samuel Collins has ably explored Alcuin's patristically influenced (i.e., old-fashioned) depiction of the crowd here as uncontrollable.[205] The tumult consisted of an "unlearned crowd" (*indoctum vulgus*) such as one might find in Augustine and Jerome.[206] Alcuin claimed that the rowdiest members of the crowds were "peasants in their cups" (*rusticos inter pocula*).[207] At the same time, Alcuin hoped his readers would be put in mind of Gregory of Tours, whose *Histories* and *Miracles* are full of crowds defending justice.[208] He shared Gregory's conviction, discussed in the previous chapter, that crowd violence could be both wrong in itself and justifiable. For Theodulf's men to crash into Saint Martin's Basilica on a Sunday was like lobbing a grenade into a nuclear reactor. To his former students, Alcuin wrote, "There was suddenly a crowd [*concursus*] consisting of beggars coming from all parts of the city in order to defend their defender."[209] To Charlemagne, he added, "One thing common to everyone everywhere is to take it poorly when one's own saints are dishonored."[210]

Alcuin knew the weakness of his position. Two bishops, Joseph of Tours (a metropolitan) and Theodulf of Orléans, had been defied. But Alcuin hoped to find justification by differentiating among the various collectivities in the affair. Theodulf's initial party was foolish and timid to suspect an ambush. Theodulf never should have sent an armed crowd to carry out the interests of justice. His men crashed through a sanctuary with high disrespect. Alcuin's most defensible gathering was that of his monks, whose anger at the disrespect to their sanctuary was understandable, but whose crowd-control and rescue of Theodulf's men was laudable. To anyone familiar with the awesome power of Saint Martin, and his vengeance against those who insulted him, Alcuin hoped that it would seem that the Orléans men were lucky to escape with their lives. Alcuin framed the *tumultus* of drunken rustics as God's rough justice, while the crowd of his own self-controlled monks stood for God's mercy.

Charlemagne was having none of it. The emperor thundered back with a furious written command to release the fugitive at once.[211] All Alcuin's subtle divisions of moral labor were waved aside in what Rob Meens has called Charlemagne's "formal legal line."[212] The emperor hinted ominously that the Tours congregation's irregularity ("sometimes you seem to be saying they are monks, sometimes canons, sometimes neither") was the root of the problem.[213] In part, this was politics. Bishops tended to win out over abbots and, at this point in time, Theodulf enjoyed more *Königsnähe* than Alcuin. But there is also a sign of the shift in mentalities discussed in the last chapter, as Roman license gave way to zero-tolerance for non-elite contentious action. The emperor's letter is reminiscent of one that E. P. Thompson quotes at the end of his essay on the moral economy of eighteenth-century crowds. A millennium after these events at Tours, the Duke of Portland wrote angrily of the "bounden duty to suppress and punish" rioters to the Town Clerk at Oxford, who had expressed the old paternalistic sympathies for the just reasons of the lawbreakers.[214] Urban crowds had the power to allow an abbot to defy the higher authority of a bishop temporarily, but in the early Middle Ages such a victory was destined to be short-lived.

The Solemn Assembly

Across sacred and secular gatherings, we can identify an early medieval ideal type: the solemn assembly. As we have seen, formalized assemblies were among the most important and regular gatherings of early medieval political and religious life.[215] Assemblies governed all levels of society, from the *mallus* assemblies that met every six weeks to grand imperial musters.[216] The assembly's legitimacy as a site of deliberation and command owed to the porous boundary between religious and secular meetings.[217] As Jürgen Hannig has emphasized, ideals about collective consensus were always religiously charged.[218] Rule-bound, hierarchical deliberative rallies established themselves as the main tool of early medieval governance and social order.[219] Confronted with one of the various Latin or vernacular words for "crowd," an early medieval elite may well have thought first of a solemn assembly.

Assembly politics are particularly associated with the Franks under the Carolingians. As Chris Wickham has argued, assembly practices varied, sometimes considerably, from one post-Roman kingdom to another. While the Franks and the English both respected the importance of assemblies as engines of consensus, Visigothic and Lombard rulers were more inclined to treat them as rubber stamps.[220] Still, this caveat should not be taken too far. Lombard assemblies had a representative quality just like Frankish ones. The assembly (*thing*) of judges and *fideles* stood for the whole people/army, and this gave legitimacy to decisions publicized (*thingare*) there.[221] Certainly there were regional variations, but there was no community big or small in the early medieval West that did not make use of formal public gatherings.

Royal assemblies gave to kings "the aura of empire and hegemonic rule."[222] Ritual performances there took place before witnesses arrayed in hierarchical order.[223] Of course, there is reason to doubt how fully early medieval rulers controlled assemblies.[224] We see this in acts of public penance that backfired. Louis the Pious came to rue the series of penitential assemblies he permitted among his bishops in 829, which led to his public penance in 833.[225] Assemblies could be marred by ritual failure too. At an assembly at Frankfurt in 873, Louis the German's son Charles III ("the Fat") stopped the proceedings to proclaim his desire to abandon the secular world, stripping off his secular garb and crying, "Woe! Woe!" Contemporaries thought he was possessed.[226] Simon MacLean has explained this event as a penitential performance gone awry and played up by a hostile chronicler.[227] Charles was hoping to use the assembly as a stage for a public performance of contrition for betraying his father, but his ritual act failed to convince its audience. Edward Coleman has suggested that Italian assemblies of the tenth or eleventh centuries became messier and less irenic than their early medieval counterparts.[228] It is equally possible that sources of those earlier centuries preferred to suppress tensions.

The Logic of Assemblies

Assemblies claimed the form of legitimacy associated with all gatherings of Christians acting in concert: authoritative consensus.[229] The biblical motivation for this was Christ's promise in the Gospel of Matthew: "For where there are two or three gathered together in my name, there am I in the midst of them" (*ubi enim sunt duo vel tres congregati in nomine meo ibi sum in medio eorum*).[230] This logion was quoted in the liturgical acta of early medieval councils.[231] Pope Leo I (r. 440–61) had declared, "I feel that, where so many saints are gathered, the very angels are among us."[232] Because secular assemblies tended to share so much with religious ones, the logic of divine approbation spilled into the institution as a whole.

This power of public acclamations had its pernicious side, as Avitus of Vienne (d. c. 518) noted to King Gundobad in his treatise against Eutychianism. Eutyches's heresy had been quiet, Avitus reported, until a "practice of church in great cities" in the East, mass supplications to God at the beginning of the mass, led the populace (*plebs*) to give a supplicatory acclamation (*clamor*) to God whose wording allowed the Eutychian schism to break out.[233] The result was not only doctrinal confusion, but a "waxing storm of seditions" (*crescente seditionum procella*).[234] The same doctrinal schism also prompted Boethius to mull over the false sense of unanimity and certainty produced by mass acclamation. Boethius had been present when Eutyches's doctrines were condemned, in a series of acclamations, at a council at Rome. Boethius did not feel that the unsubtle medium of the acclamation grasped the doctrinal subtleties at play, and although he agreed Eutyches was wrong, he came to this conclusion only after much rumination.[235]

Nevertheless, the idea that numbers mattered in showing divine consensus proved influential despite doubting voices. In the ninth and tenth centuries, Photios, the patriarch of Constantinople (r. 858–67, 877–86), was widely attacked for allegedly doctoring or adding subscribers' names to his conciliar acta; the point was that, in reality, he lacked the requisite numbers.[236] Hermann Sieben argued that the early church developed a concept of conciliar legitimacy stressing quantitative (if not universal) consensus as opposed to the specialized consensus of the patriarchs.[237] Hannig in turn showed how this ideal was gradually secularized in Frankish assemblies.[238]

But did enormous gatherings of churchmen and aristocrats really come to collective decisions in the early Middle Ages? As with the elections discussed above, it is a stretch to describe assembly politics as "democratic" in any modern sense. In a famous article, Thomas Bisson went so far as to argue that early medieval "plenary assembles" were "celebrations of hierarchical order and majesty," rather than truly deliberative bodies like later medieval parliaments.[239]

Bisson's argument has received push-back from early medievalists, who note that assemblies had practical uses and genuine fault lines. The airing of grievances, the performance of diplomacy, conflict resolution, war planning, and the dissemination of information were among the non-celebratory functions of early medieval assembly culture.[240] Assemblies' location near campaign-sites made them genuinely helpful in war planning. They mustered troops and provided a critical venue for delivering orders.[241] They were also important as tools of control. Missing one was tantamount to treason.[242] On the other hand, Bisson's theory is not entirely off-base. As Gerd Althoff and Wilfried Hartmann have both explored, the "deliberations" of great assemblies appear to have been settled in smaller gatherings beforehand, or redirected in the medieval equivalent of "coffee pauses" that characterized councils that could stretch for days.[243]

Sites of Assembly

Where did assemblies take place? Church councils usually took place in the large, monumental churches. The spatial effects of liturgical fragmentation described above amply served the hierarchical nature of conciliar meetings. Secular assemblies sometimes also took place in churches, though when indoors they also took places in the grand *aulae* of royal palaces. Royal halls, like churches, had their equivalent of liturgical fragmentation. The drawback of indoor venues was lack of space. The particularly large gathering at Savonnières in 862, discussed in chapter 2, took place in a *casa* that Hincmar describes as completely packed by the end of the proceedings.[244]

Therefore, many assemblies, particularly in a military context, must have taken place at least partly outdoors. Gregory of Tours seems to have envisioned the early Frankish Marchfield as an open-air event.[245] There may be some archaeological evidence for such meeting spaces. John Baker and Stuart Brookes have singled out what they call "hanging promontories" as a common meeting spot for large insular assemblies.[246] By this, they mean open fields that slope downward, such that a speaker at a focal point on the higher elevation would dominate the attention of those lower down. Hanging promontories, identified by the toponymic and archaeological evidence, may well have been used by English kings for their outdoor assemblies.

There were also some purpose-built assembly structures. In the Northumbrian kingdom, the seventh-century *villa regia* at Yeavering (with a great hall, several smaller buildings, a cemetery, and a "Great Enclosure" thought to be a field for cattle) also included a giant wooden theater (the "cuneus").[247] This takes the shape of a quarter of a theater, consisting of a tiered array of stands focused toward a stage, and accommodating first 150 and then later 300 people.[248] It has been argued that this cuneus may have served for assemblies.[249] Interestingly, this settlement had been inhabited since the Neolithic period, and the early medieval buildings are aligned between an ancient stone circle, a hedge, and a manmade barrow.[250] As Robin Fleming suggests, "It seems that the Northumbrian kings had co-opted and emended a highly wrought ritual landscape and then used it as a theatrical backdrop for newly invented ritual practices of their own."[251]

Information Exchange

Whether via deliberation or celebration, one of the crucial functions of the solemn assembly was the management of information. Crowds have always been important for communications. Announcements to crowds were, quite simply, the most efficient way of spreading information in the premodern world. The Roman world possessed *praecones*, men often of lower-status origin who acted as public heralds.[252] Later medieval societies had town criers to spread news in public.[253] In the early Middle Ages, giving the word was "a delicate and sometimes dangerous task" that had to be kept in the hands of bishops and counts.[254] Assemblies provided the safest and most effective occasions for "newsgathering and the exchange of information."[255]

Here we may highlight a contrast to Roman practice. Romans made more use of monumental written dissemination.[256] This too was a kind of interaction with the crowd, and probably texts like the *Res Gestae* of Augustus or the Price Edict of Diocletian would have been read aloud when first publicly displayed.[257] Early medieval elites occasionally disseminated ideologically significant information using the written word in this fashion, particularly when the target audience involved clerics.[258] But generally speaking, ideological dissemination was oral in the early medieval world.

In terms of propaganda, this meant that Roman emperors could depend more than their early medieval successors on spontaneous passive gatherings, such as were likely to pass by urban spaces where inscriptions were set up. They always combined such displays with oral performances—the Roman city was full of speakers addressing multitudes—but higher rates of literacy and denser populations gave them a mechanism of communication absent in the post-Roman West. The early medieval *modus operandi* was different: to cultivate sites of predictable density and reach audiences through oral means. That is no small part of the assembly's importance in early medieval Europe.

Ramifications of the Closed Crowd

Three distinct patterns marked the early medieval elite crowd regime. First, gatherings tended to be logistically viable only in certain spaces on a seasonal basis.[259] Only in these contexts were transaction costs for gatherings suitably lowered. Such times included harvest time, which coincided with important feast days; the late autumn hunting season, when the sounds of dogs and trumpets filled the forests; the winter-to-spring ritual cycle, which involved some of the larger more intensive Christian rituals; and military campaign season, which coincided with major secular assemblies. Such seasonal patterns gave gathering predictable grooves. Kings knew when to start planning for the logistics of their armies. Abbots and abbesses knew when to expect a rush of pilgrims. Merchants and beggars knew when and where to seek out profit.

Second, built environments for assembly tended to encourage gatherings in which groups of people were physically divided into representative units. Divisions between clerics and non-clerics, men and women, high status and low status, rich and poor could be embodied in spaces—churches, palaces—that emphasized the proper place of each group. In this way, sites of assembly were inherently hierarchical. These venues were generally within elite control, but that did not prevent rival elites from competing over crowds with rival centers of agglomeration.

Third, unity and consensus became the expected—if not always the achieved—behavior of gatherings, while the rural and urban "tumults" that are the usual subject of "crowd history" became more of a fringe phenomenon. By their nature, riots and uprisings are effective through repetition. As we saw in the previous chapter, one of E. P. Thompson's most trenchant observations about the eighteenth-century crowd is that the efficacy of riots as a deterrent lies in their legibility as a threat, a legibility made by frequency.[260] Early medieval riots were close to being illegible. Their appearance on the scene drew dramatic, almost allergic, responses, as with the tumult at Tours. Nonparticipation in expected gatherings by non-elites was a far more effective tool of resistance.[261] As for elites, their acts of resistance too relied on formal venues of army and assembly, as with the humbling of Louis the Pious at the Field of Lies in 833.

Assemblies that proceeded "properly," "as the custom is," "solemnly" (*rite, ut mos est, solemniter*, etc.) dominated the elite-driven narrative of social reality that James Scott called the "public transcript."[262] The predictability, hierarchy, and consensus of such gatherings gave them their public legitimacy.[263] Church councils and royal assemblies represent the pinnacle of this ideal. But no less important were local assemblies and peasant councils. Solemn assemblies might be said to adhere to Elias Canetti's definition of the "closed crowd": defined by hierarchical boundaries and by repeatability over time.[264] Even if Canetti's concepts do not mesh perfectly with the patterns we have seen, they clarify a shift at the heart of the early medieval crowd regime. When Seneca set out to write a moral epistle on the subject of the *turba*, the "crowd," the form of gathering that presented itself to his mind was the gladiatorial spectacle.[265] By the ninth century, the *turba* could present itself to the mind of a bishop—with his share of crowd troubles—as an angelic assembly.[266]

Such ideals were perhaps only skin deep. The realities of assembly politics were more unpredictable and contentious than our sources prefer to let on. Moreover, this regime did not last. Spontaneous crowding reemerged in frequency and salience as cities and rural nucleated settlements expanded around

1000. Revolts, mass heresies, the peace of God, and eventually the "People's Crusade" all signal the arrival of a new regime of crowds—one more recognizable to traditional historiography.[267] These new forms were reflected in the revival of negative crowd discourse in the eleventh and twelfth centuries.[268] By the twelfth century, the first stirrings of a more deliberative political assembly challenged (while building on) the old model, with wide ramifications.[269] Yet early medieval experiments with assemblies also had lasting impact, particularly in associating gathering with notions of representation, consensus, and legitimacy.[270] The next two chapters will explore how perceptions developed from practices, starting with the words for gatherings themselves. Was Seneca's *turba*, with its connotations of danger, moral contagion, and violence, the same semantic entity as the ninth-century *turba*, with its connotations of uniformity, assembly, and counsel?

5

Words

Semantic History

The preceding chapters examined physical gatherings subject to demographic, logistical, economic, and political constraints. The next two examine the crowd of the imagination. In language and thought, crowds are protean. Their numbers can swell beyond the power of words. They oscillate between active and passive roles. They can represent abstract classes or principles, or stand for nothing at all. This makes the crowd of mentalities hard to pin down. To move from what it was possible to do with gatherings to what it was possible to say about them is to shift from solid ground to shifting sand.

Herbert Grundmann once described the history of words as a seismograph for the history of mentalities.[1] The aim of this chapter is to investigate the semantic field of collective behavior in early medieval European texts.[2] It highlights three trends across the evidence. First, the Greco-Roman world's richly calibrated and specialized vocabulary of collectivity gave way to a much less differentiated one. Second, early medieval crowd language was disproportionately shaped by biblical and patristic usage. Both of these trends began in Late Antiquity and also marked Byzantine Greek. A third trend, the loss of negative connotations, set the early medieval West apart. A discourse of rabbles, mobs, and seditions gave way, with significant exceptions, to one in which "crowds" were orderly and legitimizing by default.

These three trends—loss of differentiation, Christianization, and lopsided positive valence—characterize the surviving language of crowds in the post-Roman West. Still, a gap remains between the written evidence, dominated if not monopolized by elite, male, ecclesiastical perspectives, and the inner worlds of early medieval people. The chasm separating the monk writing in Latin and the peasant thinking in Romance or Old High German can never truly be bridged. But there is reason to suppose that patterns in learned texts mirror, however darkly, wider mentalities. This chapter offers a survey of crowd terms as they appear in the written word. Then it examines the three trends above using representative Latin words: *populus*, *contio*, and *turba*.

Crowds across Languages

The Classical Latin Legacy

The bulk of our evidence for the crowd vocabulary of Western Europe, c. 500–1000, comes from Latin, that "half-living father tongue."[3] Latin bequeathed a treasury of words for collectivities to the post-Roman West.[4] There were collective nouns (*turba, caterva, multitudo, populus, vulgus, frequentia, occursus, concursus, agmen, conventio, copia, contio, congressus, circulus, adunatio, coetus, gens, manus, grex, acervus, massa*); abstract collective terms (*collegium, communitas, confraternitas, consortium, corpus, ecclesia, societas, universitas*); specific nouns for conspiracy, unrest, or disorder (*coniuratio, seditio, tumultus, rixa*); nouns or substantives meaning "the poor" used as shorthand for crowds (*inopes, pauperes, plebs*); nouns for kin or ethnic groups that could be collective (*familia, gens, natio*); simple nouns that could be pluralized (e.g., *homines, viri, mulieres, personae, pueri, pullae, servi, milites*); ethnic substantives (e.g., *Romani, Franci, Gothi*); plural nouns with civic or institutional significance (*cives, comitium, concilium, curia, senatus, schola, comitatus*); military collectivities (*phalanx, cohors, turma, legio, ala, exercitus*); substantive adjectives (*cuncti, omnes, plurimi, multi, tanti*); verbs of assembly or collective action (e.g., *accumulare, adunare, ciere, congregare, stipare, frequentare, turbari, contionari*); adjectives (*numerosus, innumerabilis, copiosus, coadunatus, densus, celeber, frequens*); and adverbs like *una* ("all together") and *catervatim* ("in crowds"). Finally, new terms arose in late Latin, like the noun *populositas* ("multitude," "crowd"), the adjective *densatim* ("densely"), or the Germanic loanwords *drungus* ("military crowd"), *hansa* ("hanse"), and *gilda* ("guild").[5]

There are two generalities worth flagging about the ancient language of crowds. First, formal Classical Latin distinguished between definitions and valences of crowd terms. There were more concrete words, like *turba, frequentia, caterva*, or *coetus*, more abstract ones, like *populus, vulgus*, or *gens*, and words like *multitudo* ("a great quantity") somewhere in between.[6] Some words, like *contio* or *senatus*, had technical definitions. Others were more polysemic. *Populus* ("people") was used of any group of people, but also had a constitutional sense (the community of Roman citizens). *Turba* meant "riot" in law, but could be used of any "crowd." The narrative heft of collectivity terms came from their power to link physical gatherings with abstract notions of community, identity, or principle. But there is usually no confusion as to whether *populus* is meant concretely or abstractly, or whether *turba* is meant legally or colloquially. That would change.

Second, Classical Latin crowd terms were persistently—and disparagingly—bound up with non-elite status, as if crowds were vulgar and lowly by nature.[7] As Vergil wrote, "seditiousness [*seditio*] often arises in a large crowd [*populus*], and the ignoble mob [*ignobile uulgus*] rages at heart, and now they throw torches and stones, for madness supplies their arms."[8] Vergil's word *vulgus* (archaic *volgus*) was the one-word expression of this equivalency, but many collective nouns—*turba, populus, plebs, multitudo, frequentia*—had "vulgar" connotations.[9] Even when they were not seditious, crowds might be despicable, as in Horace's line: *odi profanum vulgus et arceo*, "I hate and shun the profane mob [*vulgus*]."[10] The Roman link between masses and "the" masses is all too familiar. But it is not universal. It is conspicuously absent, as we will see, from the Germanic vocabulary of gatherings. It would weaken in early medieval Latin too.

Protoromance

Latin changed in more fundamental ways.[11] Regional dialects and lower social registers existed from the early days of empire.[12] "Vulgar" or nonliterary Latin shaped the Latin of the Vetus Latina and Vulgate translations of the Bible, influencing the Christian sociolect known as *sermo humilis* or "humble talk."[13] From the fifth and sixth centuries, Latin-derived vernaculars, known to scholars as "protoromance," emerged out of spoken Latin. By the 700s and 800s, medieval writers acknowledged a division between Latin proper (*latina lingua*) and the "Romance tongue" (*romana lingua*).[14]

In a sense, medieval writers created that difference. "'Latin,' as we have known it for the last thousand years," argued Roger Wright, "is an invention of the Carolingian Renaissance."[15] He meant that strict orthography, artificial pronunciation, and grammar rules imposed by early medieval grammarians widened the gap between the learned and spoken languages. This can worry scholars of mentalities. The literary historian Erich Auerbach doubted whether the polished Suetonian Latin of an Einhard (as opposed to the unruly prose of a Gregory of Tours) truly expressed early medieval life.[16] Is it possible that Latin sources, aping classical texts, failed to reflect contemporary perceptions?

Auerbach's fears were overstated. First, as Michel Banniard has argued, Latin users could expect their language to be comprehensible orally by "Romance" speakers.[17] Second, men and women who entered young into religious life—and there were more of these than ever under the Carolingian empire—read, heard, and spoke Latin from early in their lives.[18] The same was true of educated lay elites, male and female. To them, Latin was not "dead."[19] Third, interaction between Latin and vernaculars, Romance, Germanic, and Celtic, continued throughout our period.[20] Vernacular trends followed Latin ones, and *vice versa*. The reorientation of meaning and valence that this chapter explores shows how much Latin responded to the expressive needs of its users.

One would like to know what a conversation about crowds in early medieval Northern Spain, Southern Gaul, or Italy sounded like. Sadly, there are not many surviving texts discussing crowds in Protoromance before c. 1000.[21] We know *populus* was on its way to *popolo* (Italian), *peuple* (French), *poble* (Catalan), *pueblo* (Spanish), *povo* (Portuguese), and *popór* (Romanian), as we see in a Trier inscription reading *pupulo* for *populus*.[22] In the Strasbourg Oaths (842), Louis the German spoke "Romance" (*romana lingua*) when he said, "pro christian poblo."[23] Likewise, *pleb(e)s*, which came to mean a Christian "parish," was heading toward *pieve* (Italian), *tšeive* (Genoese), *piove* (Venetian), and *plaif* (Occitan), as a seventh-century inscription with *pleui* for *plebe* attests.[24]

Other common words for crowds in Romance vernaculars—*foule* in Old French, *folla* in Italian, and *fola* in Provençal[25]—must have emerged in spoken language in our period, but are not attested until later.[26] *Foule*, *folla*, and *fola* derive from late Latin *fullare*, "to full (cloth)," from *fullo*, the "fuller," who cleans and thickens cloth by pounding it underfoot.[27] Like the English words "crowd," "throng," "press," and "crush," the term refers to the experience of pressure in a mass of people.[28] It would be interesting to know when this vivid metaphor came into use: sometime, presumably, between Late Antiquity and the early Middle Ages. But the word's origins are lost. So too with a common Old French / Provençal term for a "multitude," the fixed phrase *gran gent* ("many people").[29]

The Germanic Legacy: General Considerations

We are better off with another group of vernaculars, the Germanic languages: Gothic, Lombardic, Old Frisian, Old Low Franconian (Frankish), Old High German, Old Saxon, Old English, and Old Norse.[30] These languages shared a group of cognate terms for gatherings, many of them political or military. A famous example is the assembly-term "thing" (*thing, þing, ding, geþing*, etc.).[31] Originally *thing* referred to a deliberative gathering. It came to mean the place or time at which such an assembly was held, the discussions held there, or a decision promulgated there.[32] English "thing" and German "Ding" originally denoted the "subject matter" of public deliberation: the legacy of an early medieval ontology in which reality was a function of collective consensus. In the early Middle Ages, *thing* was used of sermons and church councils.[33] *Thinghûs* ("thing-house") meant "council" (*concilium*), "court" (*curia*), "consistory" (*consistorium*), and even "theater."[34] *Thingâri* ("one who performs a *thing*") came to mean a "speaker," "litigant," or "preacher."[35] In Lombard Italy, *thing* (or *thinx*) gave rise to a Latin noun (*thingatio*) and a verb (*thingare*) denoting public legitimation generally, and the manumission of unfree persons specifically.[36]

It is tempting to translate Germanic crowd words using primitivizing language: *menigî, folc, githigini, druhta, heri,* and *þing* as "band," "folk," "warband," "following," "host," and "Thing," rather than with all-purpose terms like "crowd," "people," "troop," "retinue," "army," and "assembly." But Germanic languages were not repositories of primitivism. They originated in the small worlds of the Iron Age, and lacked autochthonous terms for the urban crowds of the ancient Mediterranean world, but by Late Antiquity the "barbarians" were sufficiently acquainted with Roman life that old words had new uses. A multilingual Goth of Theoderic's day—to say nothing of Theoderic himself, who spent his youth in Constantinople—probably pictured the same roaring circus crowd whether one said *turba* or *managei*, just as a learned Frank of Charlemagne's time would have called the same hunting band a *turba* or a *menigî*.

Gothic and Lombardic

The East Germanic languages spoken early in our period (Gothic, Vandalic, Burgundian) are poorly attested, with the exception of Gothic, thanks to a biblical translation traditionally ascribed to Ulfilas (fourth century). Bible translations always shed light on a language's crowd vocabulary given the prevalence of crowds in the New Testament. In the Gothic Bible, the usual word for crowd, Greek ὄχλος (or λαός) is translated *managei*. This was the Gothic iteration of the commonest neutral Germanic term for "gathering," a cognate of English "many" and German "Menge."[37] One also finds the term *hiuhma* ("multitude") where the Greek has πλῆθος, from a root referring to "accumulation."[38] In addition, words like *thiud* ("people"), *iumjo* ("crowd, people"), *hansa* ("band"), and *harjis* ("army") graced name-elements (e.g., Theoderic, Eumeric: "king of the people").[39] In Late Antiquity, Gothic had been a lingua franca among the barbarians. This did not last. In Italy, its use petered out after the seventh century.[40] There is practically no evidence for it in Visigothic Spain.[41]

The West Germanic language of the Lombards, who migrated from the Middle Danube into Italy in the late sixth century, left some mark on Italian (e.g., *guancia*, "cheek," from **wangja*).[42] But Lombardic only survives as a pile of linguistic ruins. Words for "people" (*fulc, *þeuðo*) and "army" (**harja*) survive in name-elements.[43] The main exception is the word *thing* ("assembly"), which, as we have seen, entered legal Latin. For the most part, however, Latin drowned out the Germanic tongues in Italy, as it would with Gothic in Spain and Frankish in Gaul.

Old High German and Old Saxon

Our richest Continental evidence for Germanic crowd terms comes from Old High German. This is the scholarly designation for a bundle of mutually comprehensible West Germanic dialects as they appear in written sources from about the eighth to the eleventh century. Latin writers called it the *theudisca lingua*.[44]

Old High German enjoys an abundant early medieval corpus, including glosses, biblical translations, epic poems, and standalone texts.[45] The commonest term for gathering was *menigî* or *managî* ("crowd," "multitude"), cognate to Gothic *managei*, often glossed with Latin *turba* or *multitudo*.[46] *Folk, liuti,* and *thiota* ("people"), usually glossed by Latin *populus*, did double duty for "peoples" and "crowds." The adjective *al* ("all") was used like *omnis, universus, cunctus,* or *multus* in Latin to reinforce the size or unanimity of gatherings.[47] Military terms included *heri* ("army") and *scara* ("warband," "military unit," cf. German "Schar").[48] *Gelt* ("guild," "association") and *hansa* ("band," "gathering"), both originally all-purpose terms, acquired specific socioeconomic meanings.[49] Several words existed for entourages and retinues.[50] Their etymologies hint at the features of lordly followings: *fuora* (from "journey, march"), *ginôzscaf* (a "community of those enjoying something together"), *râtgebo* ("counselors"), and *githigini* ("troop of soldiers").

The smaller corpus of Old Saxon (eighth–twelfth centuries), the oldest attested form of Low German, is rich in crowd words thanks to the ninth-century *Heliand* ("Savior"), a Gospel paraphrase composed after the conversion of the Saxons by the Franks. The *Heliand* describes the "disciples" as a *iungaron managa*, literally a "crowd of young men," pictured as an entourage of "earls" (*erlos*) and "thanes" (*thanen*). The multitudes who hear Christ's miracles are *folc* ("folk," "people") or *liudi managa* ("crowds of people").[51] While some have played up this language—the disciples as "warrior-companions" or a "warrior-company"—literary Old Saxon is best understood as a compromise between old and new thought-worlds.[52]

Old English

Old English also preserves a large corpus of crowd words.[53] Some Old English crowd words, like *lēode* and *folc* ("people") closely mirrored their Continental cognates. There were the requisite terms for retinues (*folgaþ, dryht, hōs*) and many terms for deliberative assemblies: *geþing* ("thing," "assembly"), *here-meðel* ("army assembly"), *gemot* ("meeting"), and *witanagemot* ("meeting of the wise men").[54] The smaller sort of assembly, the local gatherings where peasants may have sorted out common obligations with minimal royal involvement, went by the name *mæthl* in the Kentish laws.[55]

Old English also had a rich vocabulary of crowd words related to the physicalities of accumulation, pressure, and density: (*ge-*)*gaderung* ("gathering"), *gelac* ("tumult"), *gemang*/*gemong* ("mingling"), *cruþ* or *gecrod* ("crowd"), *geþrang* / *geþring* / *geþryl* ("throng") or *folcgeprang* ("throng of people"), *heáp* ("troop"), *swearm* ("swarm"), *þring* ("press"), and *worn* ("multitude").[56] Germanic collectivity terms sometimes come off as less multifarious and vivid than Greco-Roman ones. Old English is an exception.

Old Norse

Old Norse, the catchall for North Germanic languages spoken in Scandinavia and Iceland, enjoys a large but late medieval corpus. Old Norse shares with other Germanic languages an abundance of political and military gathering terms, alongside a poverty of terms for riots or rabbles. *Mengi* ("crowd") had the same function as its more southerly cognates.[57] The prefix *fjǫl-* ("many," cf. German "viel")—as in *fjǫlði* ("a multitude") and *fjǫlmenni* ("many men")—had a similar multiplying function as the Old High German *al*.[58] *Fólk*, *þjóð*, and *lýðr* corresponded to Germanic cognates for "people"; *fylgð* or *fylgja* ("following"), tended to denote an entourage.[59] As in other Germanic languages, the polysemic *herr* ("army") was used of armed gatherings, but also of generic crowds.[60]

The Old Norse *þing* stands out as a term for an assembly institution prominent in texts, toponyms, runic inscriptions, and excavations.[61] The Alþingi (the "All-Thing") of Iceland, supposedly founded in 930 at the "Thing-Fields" (Þingvellir) not far from modern Reykjavík, is (by its own reckoning) the oldest still-running parliament. "Things" were not really democratic institutions, but they were expressions of the importance of gatherings in Scandinavian public life.

Germanic Generalities

Across the Germanic cases, a few patterns can be highlighted. There was a division of labor, halfheartedly upheld, between the more concrete *menegī* and the more abstract *folk* / *liuti* / *thiota*. Germanic words for "retinues" and "assemblies" reflect the variety and importance of these phenomena. Some Latin collectivity words (*comitatus*, *conventus*) seem to have acquired new meanings under their influence. But the most noteworthy feature of the Germanic vocabulary of crowds is a pair of absences. The first is a lack of terms for non-elite crowds (like *vulgus* and *turba*). The second is a loss—but nothing like a total loss—of negative valences. There were no obvious words for "riot," "rabble," or "mob," though by the Carolingian period, terms like Old High German *fâra* ("ambush") and *heimstrît* ("homeland strife") were used as equivalents for Latin *seditio* ("sedition") or *tumultus* ("unrest").[62] These concepts—"sedition" and "tumult"—retained their strong negative tenor. Yet, arguably, this goes to show that *seditio* and *tumultus* had changed quite as much as *fâra* and *heimstrît*; the "rebellion" and "strife" of nobles was as pressing a concern as the infrequent "revolt" or "unrest" of popular crowds.[63]

Celtic Languages

Celtic speakers occupied Ireland, parts of the British Isles, and Brittany. From the 600s, Old Irish-speaking monks were sprinkled across Europe.[64] The Old Irish word *drong*, cognate with "throng," did basic service for "gathering."[65] Irish also borrowed the word *popul* directly from Latin *populus* and *torb* from Latin *turba*.[66] Old Irish *slóg/slúag* (the ultimate origin of the English noun "slew") could be used of a "people" or "crowd"; its corresponding Brittonic form was *llu*, cognate with Old High German *liuti*, Old Saxon *liudi*, and Old English *lēode*.[67] *Slóg/slúag* primarily appears as a military term ("troop," "army"). We find it (in the form *sluag*) as a gloss for the Latin *agmen* ("troop," "column," "crowd") in the mid ninth-century Old Irish Priscian glosses.[68] It has a vivid appearance in the *Táin Bó Cúailnge*, the Irish epic (with early medieval oral origins). The seer Feidelm warns Queen Medb that Cú Chulainn will destroy her army. Medb asks, "Feidelm prophetess, how do you see our host [*slúag*]?" Feidelm replies that Cú Chulainn "will lay low your entire army [*slúag*]. He will slaughter you in dense crowds [*for tiugára*, lit. "in dense-slaughter"]. Ye will leave with him a thousand severed heads."[69] It is an interesting reflection of what counted as epic numbers in early medieval Ireland.

Slavic Languages

Old Church Slavonic, a learned language, sheds light on the crowd words used in Slavic languages at the eastern edge of the West by Carantanians, Slovenes, Moravians, Poles, and Bulgars. Key words include *narodъ* ("people," "crowd"), *ljudъ* ("people," "folk"), *mъnožьstvo* ("multitude"), *tlъpa* ("crowd," "throng"; cf. Czech *tlupa* and Polish *tłum*), and *voi* ("troops," "army").[70] These Slavic crowd words had much in common with their Indo-European cousins, with a basic division of labor between abstractions for "people," a more concrete "crowd" term, and military gatherings.

Hebrew

Jewish populations in early medieval Europe used Hebrew for liturgical purposes. Palestinian and Babylonian *responsa*, the written Talmud, and commentaries on the Talmud appeared in the East from the seventh to the ninth century.[71] In the ninth century, the Babylonian sage Amram Gaon wrote a prayer book for the Jews of Spain.[72] But the first explosion of Hebrew in non-Islamic Europe began in the eleventh century, the age of Joseph Tov-Elem (c. 980–1050), Schlomo Yitzchaki, known as Rashi (c. 1040–1105), and the narrative and poetic memorials of the First Crusade massacres.[73] Before that, there are hints only.[74] The Hebrew crowd language of Western Jews must remain speculative.[75] The Old Testament bequeathed a rich crowd vocabulary: *hamon* ("a sound," "murmur"), *edah* ("congregation," "assembly"), *rigmah* ("heap"), *regesh* ("throng," "rabble"), *qahal* ("assembly"), *gedud* ("troop").[76] But we do not know if these terms underwent similar semantic transformations as their Latin equivalents.

Greek

Greek, the language of the Byzantine East, possessed a vocabulary of crowd words rivaling or outmatching Latin for variety and nuance. For centuries, Latin and Greek collectivity language had intermingled. Greek, like Latin, had seen shifts in the language of crowds, visible in the *koine* of the Greek New Testament.[77] Thanks to biblical use, words like *ochlos* or *plethos* lost some of their Attic differentiation and negativity, as will be discussed further below. But in general—with the caveat that the question deserves more study—the Greek language of crowds changed less drastically in our period than the Latin. In Byzantium, the crowd's Janus-faced duality endured. Although older scholarship occasionally argued for an eleventh-century "return of the crowd" comparable to the one proposed for Europe by Moore, Beck and Kaldellis have convincingly argued for the continuity of Roman notions about popular sovereignty and urban crowds.[78]

That matters for two reasons. First, there were two conduits through which Greek representational patterns could enter a western consciousness. Westerners maintained contact with Greek-speakers throughout our period, and Greek continued to be used in parts of the West (especially Italy). A revelatory saint's life set in sixth-century Sicily and Rome—full of unruly crowds—was written in Greek for ninth-century Greek-speaking monks at Rome.[79] Its Greek kept alive a vivid, unruly crowd. Furthermore, intellectual engagement with Greek, superficial as it was, influenced esoteric Latin usage.[80] Second, for the historian, Greek is a good control case. While Christianity exerted similar pressure on the Greek vocabulary of crowds as in Latin, in other respects, such as the preservation of urban associations and negative valences, it offers a contrast.

Arabic

Arabic, the dominant language of the former southern and southeastern provinces of the Roman world, possessed a richly articulated language of collectivity, shaped by the usage of the Qur'an and the Hadith.[81] Among key words are *jamāʿa* ("gathering," "assembly"), *lafīf* (a word denoting winding or coiling), *sawād* ("masses," "common people"), and *ḍāgaṭa* (a word, like "crowd" itself, suggesting pressure). Technical distinctions and valences enabled a complex discourse of legitimate and illegitimate crowds, making the Arabic crowd discourse more akin to that of Roman than of early medieval Latin.[82]

There were some contact zones between Arabic and the Latin West. After 711, the largest was the Iberian Peninsula, where in the ninth century Paul Alvar bitterly complained that young Christians preferred the poetic Arabic to Latin.[83] Some Arabic influence can be detected in the Romance vocabulary of crowds. For instance, Spanish *alcavela* ("crowd," "herd") comes from Arabic *al-qabīlah* ("tribe").[84] Arabic was also spoken in Sicily (conquered in 827) and, from the mid-ninth century onward, the central and southern portions of Italy. So prevalent were Muslim slave dealers in central Italy that a late ninth-century Frankish emperor complained "that Naples seems to have turned into Palermo or Africa."[85] The Arabic vocabulary of crowds in this period is worthy of further attention, but for the purposes of this book, what stands out is its greater division of labor in terminology.

Other Language Traditions

Other vernaculars were spoken in the early medieval West and the wider Mediterranean world. The language(s) of the Danubian empire of the Avars (sixth–early eighth century) remains uncertain.[86] The crowd vocabulary of Basque and, from the tenth-century onward, Hungarian can be riskily reconstructed from later usage. We know more about Coptic, Ethiopic, Syriac, Middle and Early New Persian, Armenian, and Georgian.[87] A comparative analysis of collective terms across these linguistic contexts in the post-Roman period would be desirable, but that falls beyond the scope of this study.

Blurring Distinctions: *Populus*

In the early seventh century, Isidore of Seville penned a dictionary of nuances, the *De differentiis verborum*. Here the Iberian bishop contrasted words of similar meaning, but with telling "differences" (*differentiae*), for instance, "king" versus "tyrant." One was: "The difference between a multitude [*multitudo*] and a crowd [*turba*]." As Isidore explained, "A multitude is made by numbers, a crowd is established by space. For a few people can make up a crowd [*turba*] in narrow confines."[88] When Isidore wrote it down, this *differentia* was already being lost.[89]

Across crowd words, semantic barriers blurred or disappeared in the early Middle Ages. Abstract and concrete terms oscillated. Physically specific words (like *agmen,* "file," implying a procession-like crowd) tended to be used more freely.⁹⁰ The once abstract *gens* was used of "groups of people."⁹¹ Adjectival circumlocutions, such as *cuncti, multi,* and *plurimi,* took on broad abstract signification.⁹² Technical terms, especially from the political and military spheres (*legio, cohors, caterva, manus*), became catchalls for "many." The "differences" between collectivity words of all stripes—not just between "multitudes" and "crowds"—were disappearing.

Interchangeability of Crowd Words

The interchangeability of collectivity words is one of the most striking features of early medieval crowd language. Words with the most disparate ancient nuances were treated as synonyms. *Turba, multitudo, populus,* and the like shimmer in and out of physicality, abstraction, specificity, and generality.⁹³ In the Germanic languages, *menegî, folc,* and *liut* and their cognates lacked the firm semantic borders of modern German *Menge, Volk,* and *Leute.* There was blurring between physical gatherings and the wider groups they represented.

In a sense, the paradigm for this was the word *populus,* the most polysemic of all classical Latin collectivity words. Its entry in the *Thesaurus Linguae Latinae* by Marijke Ottink runs to twenty-three columns.⁹⁴ Its primary ancient meaning was a "multitude of people."⁹⁵ But *populus* covered the gamut of collectivity. In its older, stricter sense, it meant a "community of fellow-citizens," such as the *populus Romanus.* As a term of law and politics, it designated the "common citizenry" as opposed to the senate, magistracy, or imperial college. The habits, thoughts, emotions, and prerogatives of the *populus* denoted "publicity." At the same time, the term could denote any group: plebeians most often, but also magistrates, senators, knights, relatives, soldiers, a clientele, a collegium, or a religious group. It could be used of the living or the dead, of a crowd at the games, an audience for a speaker, a conceptual collectivity, all the people of one time or setting, or the human race in general. Finally, *populus* could be extended to nonhumans, whether animals, gods, and angels, or things. *Populus* was the all-rounder of Latin crowd words.

In the early Middle Ages, many crowd words followed classical *populus* in its polysemic use. This can be jarring for those with classical expectations. Perhaps this was not a big step for a word like *multitudo.*⁹⁶ But words like *caterva* and *turba,* markedly physical terms in classical Latin, now regularly functioned to mean a "collectivity" or a "whole" in the broadest of senses. In the prologue of a life of Saint Bertin (*BHL* 1290), composed most likely at the end of the ninth or beginning of the tenth century, an anonymous author explains that Christ's twelve apostles were "selected from the mass [*turba*] of the whole human race."⁹⁷

This blurring of distinctions predates the early Middle Ages. In Late Antiquity, it was a feature of nonliterary Latin and Greek.[98] This can be seen in the homey language of the New Testament, so influential to medieval usage.[99] The word λαός (*laos*), usually translated to *populus* in Latin, was one of several words used to describe Jesus's witness crowds. The Bible uses it synonymously with ὄχλος (*ochlos*)—Latin *turba*—and πλῆθος (*plethos*)—Latin *multitudo*.[100] This was why Isidore felt that *turba* and *multitudo* required a *differentia* in the first place; just as late Latin writers often failed to preserve the negative connotation of *tyrannus* as opposed to *rex*, they had lost track of the "differences" between one crowd word and another. There was a preference for umbrella terms over technical ones. This semantic indeterminacy allowed authors to make claims about factions, groups, communities, and peoples on the basis of the behavior of particular crowds.[101]

Pluralization, Pleonasm

Other losses of "difference" marked the early medieval vocabulary of crowds. Distinctions between singular and plural—*turba* and *turbae*, *plebs* and *plebes*, *populus* and *populi*, *multitudo* and *multitudines*—vanished. Pluralization for style's sake or meter's sake had always been a poetical or rhetorical prerogative, but by Late Antiquity crowd words were pluralized with meaning unaffected.[102] This was visible in Greek as well as in Latin, where *demos* and *demoi* (often used to denote "circus factions") were bound up in undifferentiated ways.[103]

Another striking feature of early medieval crowd language is reduplication: "a multitude of people," "crowds of folk." Such phrases may have originated to reduce semantic imprecision. In Classical Latin *multitudo populi* ("multitude of the people") specified a multitude consisting of plebeians.[104] But the Vulgate New Testament regularly uses *multitudo populi* to translate the Greek τὸ πλῆθος τοῦ λαοῦ, a mere pleonasm.[105] *Multitudo populi* also appears four times in the Vulgate Old Testament.[106] The Bible has many similar phrases, some of them calques (e.g., *turbae populorum* in Vulgate Genesis 28:3).[107] Ubiquitous in early medieval texts, pleonasms like *multitudo populi* or *turba populorum* are just longwinded ways of saying "crowd."[108]

Loss of Non-Elite Specification

A more meaningful change was the loss of associations between crowds and non-elites. When Gregory of Tours borrowed Vergil's lines about the seditious crowd to describe a sixth-century scrum, he envisioned a clash of warriors, not a city riot.[109] *Vulgus*, *plebs*, *turba*, and *populus* were still used of non-elite gatherings, and there was still a sense that this made them bad news. But there were two changes. First, the *vulgus* moved to the countryside. Peasants (*rustici*), not city- or town-dwellers, became the default non-elite crowd. Second, peasant crowds were not said to reach for firebrands and rocks like urban rioters. Instead, peasants were subjected to their own slurs—gullibility, superstition, unseriousness, stupidity—that sullied crowds associated with them.[110]

Populus still gave off a "plebeian" whiff.[111] In his *Moralia in Job*, Gregory I explained that the early church preached without letters, because *populos non sermo, sed causa suaderet* ("common crowds would not be swayed by the word, but by the thing").[112] Old French *peuple* meant "the (lowly) people" as well as "a crowd."[113] From *populus*'s vernacular descendant (Italian *popolo*), Byzantine Greek developed a term for the lower classes (πόπολον, πόπουλον, πόπολο, πόπουλο).[114] The adjective *popularis* usually denoted non-elite status.[115] But as early as the fifth century, *populus* as any "community" was drowning out *populus* as "the humble."[116] Often, it meant some whole Christian community.[117] Other times, it denoted a "discrete group," such as a monastic community or an aristocratic entourage.[118] Likewise, *multitudo* once smacked of commonness.[119] Now authors clarified when this was the case.[120] Even *plebs* (Classical Latin *plēbēs*), whose primary ancient meaning was "common folk," was used as a synonym for *populus* in its new all-purpose garb.[121] If *plebs* had a technical meaning, it was now a Christian one, as we saw above: a "parish" (e.g., Italian *pieve*). Across terms, to avoid confusion, it became necessary to specify "rustic," "peasant," or "poor" involvement in discussing non-elite gatherings.[122]

Only *vulgus*, and its derivatives, retained a primarily non-elite flavor.[123] *Vulgus* is, not coincidentally, the most consistently negative crowd word in early medieval Latin, together with *seditio* and *tumultus*.[124] But there were exceptions, thanks to biblical precedent.[125] In Old High German, *vulgus* was treated as an equivalent to the neutral *folc*.[126] The mid-eighth-century *Regula canonicorum* of Chrodegang of Metz insists that every *vulgus* should come to concord in the name of God (*omne vulgus pro nomine Dei consensit*).[127] He meant that all "communities" should turn to God, not all commoners. Even *vulgus* could be just another equivalent to the broad *populus* that was now the lodestar of all crowd words.

The Dangers of Indeterminacy

A failure to recognize this can lead to misunderstanding. A case in point is an episode in Paul the Deacon's *Liber de episcopis Mettensibus*.[128] Saint Peter, based in Rome, sends disciples to many regions. Clement he sends to Metz, because *copiosis populorum turbis abundaret*.[129] Damien Kempf, the text's capable and sensitive editor, translates: "[Metz] abounded in numerous uproars of its peoples."[130] But the *turbae* here are not "uproars," nor should plural *populi* be taken literally. Paul simply means that Metz was "crowded," "populous," and so required an apostle. Loss of distinction between physical and abstract collectivity, the unmeaningful plural, and pleonasm led this intelligent reader astray.

Indeterminacy could pose a problem for early medieval writers too. There was no easy way to denote a "mob," a "rabble," or a "riot." While some Carolingian authors—for instance, Alcuin and Agobard—tried to excavate ancient uses against unruly crowds, most did not.[131] If early medieval authors opposed some particular collective behavior, whether because it served the interests of their enemies or because it exerted some economic or ideological toll, they resorted to a traffic jam of words, piled one against the other in an attempt to achieve specificity.

The Uses of Indeterminacy

On the other hand, indeterminacy was useful in narrative.[132] Perceptions or assertions about leadership, community, identity, agency, and virtue could be articulated through descriptions of crowds. Statements about the latter became claims about the former. A manuscript illustration offers a visual representation. The donor page of the Raganaldus Sacramentary (Autun, Bibliothèque municipale, MS 19bis, fol. 173v), produced at Tours in the 840s or 850s for the abbot of Marmoutier, shows a scene in which Raganaldus blesses a small crowd. Raganaldus is identified by name on the left, where he stands at the base of his seat. Crozier in hand, the abbot reads from a book held aloft by a deacon, while blessing twelve bowing figures in hierarchical order. A caption reads, "He blesses the *populus*" (*Hic benedic[at] populu[m]*).[133] Here *populus* expresses many identities: a crowd, a Christian community, Raganaldus's people.

Christianization: *Contio*

Christianization marked early medieval crowd language.[134] *Populus*, as we have seen, joined *multitudo* and *turba* as words for pious crowds of witnesses. *Plebs* was used for "parish."[135] *Congregatio*, once a catchall for any "coming together" of people, meant a "congregation" of Christians, monks, or clerics.[136] Pagan collective rituals—*processio, rogatio, pompa*, and the like—were claimed for Christian equivalents. *Ecclesia*, originally "assembly" in Greek, was the polysemic word for "church."[137]

Contio, etymologically an abbreviated form of *couentio*, a "coming together" (*con + venire*), underwent a sea change.[138] In the Roman Republic, the *contio* was an assembly at which citizens heard information: before a major trial, legislation in the *comitia*, or electioneering.[139] By the early Middle Ages, it had a radically different meaning: a Christian congregation or sermon.

Contio *from the City of Man to the City of God*

The Republican *contio* was definitionally circumscribed.[140] "A *contio* signifies a gathering, but only one which has been convened by a magistrate or a public priest through a herald," explained Pompeius Festus.[141] *Contiones* met in public settings, most commonly an urban forum, but also the Campus Martius.[142] Once upon a time, this constitutional gathering had had mostly positive connotations.[143] But amid the "worse than civil wars" of the first century BCE, *contiones* were more press-gangs than orderly assemblies.[144] Already in Cicero's time one could speak of "rebellious" or "seditious" *contiones*.[145]

Under the principate, *contio* came to be used of any crowd assembled to hear a speaker. Armies listening to generals, citizens listening to politicians, and rebels listening to agitators could all be *contiones*.[146] Hence *contio* came to mean "speech" as well as the crowd that attended one.[147] This encouraged negative valences. The word's derivatives all have nasty undertones. *Contionari*, the verb, "to *contio*-nize," meant "to harangue."[148] A person who "contionizes" is a *contionator*, "an agitator, a demagogue." The adjective *contionalis*, "contional," meant "addicted to harangues or political rallies."[149]

At the same time, defunct constitutional phrases, like *contionem dare*, "to grant an opportunity of addressing a meeting," were relegated to the history books.[150] *In contionem escendere* originally meant "to rise up to give a *contio*," but the second-century author Aulus Gellius understood it literally—"to climb up onto a *contio*"—and imagined the *contio* as a raised rostrum for harangues.[151] By his day, a speechifier at a banquet might be said to "give a *contio*." Around 200 CE, Tertullian includes *contiones* among other "pomps of the devil" that Christians must avoid.[152]

Later, the *contio* was converted. Across the fourth and fifth centuries, *contio* became a synonym for "sermon" or "congregation," while the *contionator* became a "preacher" or a "pastor." This took time. In the fifth century, Jerome still used *contionari* to describe Herod in his translation of Acts, when the wicked king gives a speech that so angers God that he lives for only two more biblical verses.[153] But a century and a half later a Christian poet could praise a contemporary of Jerome as a *nobilis adstructor, facundus contionator*, a "dignified teacher, eloquent preacher."[154]

By the early seventh century, the *contio* had been definitively won over for the City of God.[155] Isidore of Seville's primary definition of *contionator* was "a comforter, a preacher."[156] He explained that "Ecclesiastes," the biblical nickname for the older, wiser Solomon, is best translated by a word that once meant a demagogue: "We call him *Contionator* in Latin since his admonishment is not specifically directed to one person, as in Proverbs, but to everyone generally, as if to the whole *contio* and church."[157]

The Early Medieval Contio

"Congregation" or "sermon" became the primary early medieval meanings of the term *contio*. The word's derivatives became warm and fuzzy.[158] Rather of Verona speaks of "contional eloquence" when talking about a good sermon.[159] The verb *contionari*, "to contionize," lost its dark connotations, and now meant "to preach, to give a homily."[160] In Old High German, *contio* and *contionator* were treated as synonyms for *thing* and *thingâri* in their homiletic sense (*Thingâri* was the Old High German name for "Ecclesiastes").[161] When it did not function as a Christian term of art, *contio* simply became another in the vast trove of mostly sunny crowd synonyms. Royal or military assemblies were called *contio*.[162] In Italy, the placitum or judicial assembly was called *contio*.[163]

The term lost its physicality. The Roman *contio* had been concrete: an audience for a speech in an urban setting. The early medieval *contio* was a mystic body. By the end of the eleventh century, an abbot "and the *contio* committed to him" could send their best wishes to an emperor.[164] It took a while for the word to enter church hymns, but by the tenth century, *contio* was a ready term for choirs of the faithful. A typical hymn for All Saints' Day speaks of "the sacred *concio* of angels."[165]

Contio was destined for another shift in valence. This seems to have begun with eleventh-century concerns about popular heresy.[166] If a preacher was a *contionator* and his audience was a *contio*, it was also possible for heresiarchs to be *contionatores* addressing *contiones*.[167] Hence *contio* regained its imperial-era ambiguity in the high Middle Ages. Here it was not alone. A twelfth-century poet sang of a *turba furens, gens dissona, concio discors*, "a raging mob, a strident brood, a warring *concio*," a return to ochlophobia that would mark the rest of the Middle Ages.[168]

Contio: *Antiquarian Exception*

Just as Isidore had articulated a vestigial "difference" between *multitudo* and *turba*, so too the learned knew about *contio*'s ancient meanings. We only possess the Republican definition of *contio* thanks to the eighth-century author Paul the Deacon, who preserved a second-century epitome (S. Pompeius Festus) of a lost first-century work on the signification of words (M. Verrius Flaccus).[169] Paul recorded this ancient meaning even as he sang of Saint Benedict's *contio sacra*.[170]

Isidore and Paul were not the only learned writers of the early Middle Ages aware that many crowd words had been used differently in the past. The learned knew the old military meanings of *legio, cohors,* and *caterva,* even as they used these words indiscriminately for "gatherings."[171] They knew what a "bacchanal" was, but they still used the term generically for a celebrating crowd.[172]

In fact, a whole genre perpetuated ancient meanings: the gloss tradition.[173] Some gloss collections, like the eighth-century Abba-Ababus glossary, provided only one definition of *contio*: a "coming together of people" (*conventus populi*).[174] But the *Liber Glossarum* lists several meanings of the word.[175] These include early medieval uses such as a "council," a "gathering of the people," a "a multitude of people, thus 'contional' speech," and "a congregation of people or a speech to the people." Yet alongside these "modern" meanings (by eighth-century standards) was the imperial-era *contemptio* ("disorder"). The Roman past was not wholly forgotten.

Erosion of Negative Connotations: *Turba*

The most distinctive transformation in the language of crowds was a creeping loss of negative connotations, replaced by a neutral to positive default. Unlike the blurring of meanings and Christianization, which also marked Byzantine Greek, this trend set the early medieval West apart, diachronically and synchronically. It can be tracked across several Latin terms associated with collective behavior (e.g., *populus, plebs, caterva, contio, vulgus*).[176] It is visible across the vernacular language of crowds. But the most striking instance is the fate of the word *turba*.

Turba *in Classical Latin*

In Classical Latin, *turba* bore stark negative connotations.[177] The word's Greek etymology (*turbē*) suggests violent physical activity: turmoil, disruption, commotion.[178] Its relatives—*turbo, turbare, turbidus, turbator*—all remained solidly negative into the early Middle Ages. *Turba* implied a physical gathering, often a mixed or promiscuous crowd. It was the main word for an unruly mob or rabble in its physical manifestation (*vulgus* being the abstract equivalent).[179] When Seneca in the first century CE warned Lucilius to avoid the contagious conversation of the "crowd," *turba* was the word he used.[180] As an abstraction, it meant "unrest," or "a state of disorder."[181]

Roman law gave the *turba* an even more fixed definition. The law made a numerical distinction between a *turba*, a "riot" or "mob," and *rixa*, a mere "brawl."[182] Instigators of *turbae*—similar to a *tumultus* or a *seditio*—were punished more harshly. The early third-century jurist Ulpian opined that a *rixa* was a matter of a few antagonists, but that a *turba* was the "agitation and assembly of a multitude of people," involving at least "ten to fifteen men," and certainly not just "three or four."[183]

At the same time, it would be wrong to characterize classical *turba* as an exclusively "negative" term. Patrizia Arena has emphasized *turba*'s polysemy and polyvalence.[184] It is true that the plural genitives that tended to accompany *turba* most often involved subaltern groups: plebs, clients, women, circus spectators, lowly classes, and slaves.[185] But there were tongue-in-cheek uses with a more positive slant. Romans might refer to a *turba* when speaking of family or some other tight-knit group, just as modern English-speakers might talk of the "clan" or the "gang."[186]

Moreover, neutral or positive uses of *turba* are regularly encountered. The *turba* was not exclusively linked to ideas of sedition or to lowly social status; as early as the first century, the word was a synonym for *multitudo* or *populus*. According to Arena, *turba* came to designate "the assembly of the whole civic body in one and in the presence of the emperor in the most diverse occasions."[187] This was true of crowds who received largess or who greeted the emperor on solemn occasions. In a fourth-century panegyric for Emperor Theodosius, Pacatus Drepanius spoke of "the crowd (*turba*) of your beneficiaries," even though he also used the term to deplore "impious crowds" (*impiae . . . turbae*) of rebels and to lament a piteous "crowd of exiles" (*exulum turbam*).[188]

Turba *in the Latin of Ammianus Marcellinus*

It helps to examine *turba*'s use in a single late antique author. Ammianus Marcellinus composed his *Res Gestae* at the end of the fourth century while Jerome was working on his translation of the Bible into Latin. Ammianus, "a former soldier and a Greek" (*miles quondam et Graecus*), wrote for a conservative senatorial audience at fourth-century Rome, known for its stubborn resistance to Christianity.[189] His use of *turba* stands as a representation of late antique Latin without Christian intermixture.[190]

For Ammianus, *turba* is nearly everywhere a negative force. Its first appearance describes the plebeian mob of Rome, who squander their days and nights in idle pleasure.[191] It could also be piteous: Ammianus speaks of a *turba flebilis* ("lamentable crowd") exiled from the city of Nisibis.[192] But usually *turbae* are "riots." They are the "commotions" for which wicked soldiers are "always eager."[193] One troublemaker, an "unquiet man," is "constantly addicted to his lust for *turbae*."[194] A foreign prince stirs up *turbarum difficultates* ("troubles involving crowds").[195] Ammianus denounces "agitators" in a way that envisions the *turba* as a mob whipped into action by a malign individual. One evildoer is a "blazing riot-inciter" (*igneus turbarum incentor*), another is a "most bitter agitator of riots" (*turbarum acerrimus concitor*), while a third is a "frightful stirrer-up of riots" (*metuendo ... incensore turbarum*). A disaffected soldier hopes that he and his companions will not be taken for mere "riot agitators" (*turbarum ... concitores*). Bad actors "stir up" (*ciere*) *turbae*, but envy is "the most bitter agitator of riots" (*turbarum acerrima concitatrix*); those who "author" *turbae* must be handed over for punishment; and foreign rulers are often "worker of disturbances [*turbae*]."[196]

Ammianus sometimes uses *turba* as an abstract designation for "commotion," "disorder," or "troubles" (perhaps thinking of his native language's τύρβη). A prefect leaves camp on the pretense of getting supplies, but really to escape the *turba* prevailing there.[197] Emperor Julian's father dies in the "strife" (*turba*) between would-be emperors.[198] The Romans cut a deal with the Persians to avoid *turbae* ("conflict").[199] Captives seized "at the start of a period of unrest" (*primis turbarum exordiis*) are to be returned.[200] The young emperor Gratian goes across the Rhine to "crush ... a wretched people devoted to causing trouble" (*delere ... malefidam et turbarum avidam gentem*).[201]

Sometimes Ammianus uses the term *turba* in a more physical sense to describe enemy troops, with a disparaging tone. A savage army of barbarians deserves the appellation *turbae* because it "scurries about."[202] Describing the slavish habits of the Persians, Ammianus explains that Persian foot-soldiers, poorly armed, go into battle in a "throng" (*turba*) "as if in perpetual servitude."[203] In one battlefield scene dead Persians lie in crowds (*turbae*) on the ground.[204] A young Theodosius proves his mettle by crushing *turbae* of onrushing foes.[205] Ammianus never applies *turba* in this physical sense to the Roman army, unless to decry a state of rebellion. When Ammianus uses the term to describe soldiers in battle, they are always barbarians.

Once Ammianus uses the term in a neutral or positive light. When Julian takes the city of Sirmium, on a collision path with his uncle Constantius II, a local crowd (*turba*) of soldiers and "all sorts" acclaims him.[206] But shortly after this passage, Julian learns that Constantius has died and is "overjoyed" to have escaped the "commotions of wartime worries" (*bellicarum sollicitudinum turbas*).[207] Elsewhere, the same emperor resists a "gaggle" (*turba*) denouncing a civil servant.[208] Thus, out of twenty-seven instances in the surviving works of this fourth-century historian, all but one are negative in valence.

The Christianized Turba in Late Antiquity

Ammianus's usage is representative of late antique pagan writing.[209] But *turba* was thrust into a more positive light for late antique Christians. The earliest Vetus Latina Bibles used *turba* for Greek ὄχλος.[210] The narrative function of crowds in the New Testament is complex, but most often they play the role of a witness to sacred drama: neither positive nor negative per se, but legitimizing and probative.[211] Biblical usage—itself influenced by everyday speech—passed through the bloodstream of Christian letters, down the arteries of hagiography, homilies, exegesis, and liturgy to the capillaries of sacred historiography and poetry.

Late antique Christian authors with formal training, such as Augustine and Jerome, showed bifurcation in their use of *turba*. Augustine threw the term at heretical enemies or unruly mobs, and lamented the addictive *turba* of the games, but he also used *turba* in positive terms when discussing Christians.[212] Jerome was capable of using the term traditionally, but chose to follow the Vetus in its use of *turba* for Christ's witnesses and beneficiaries, and devoted exegetical attention to these New Testament *turbae*.[213] On a lower linguistic register, negative connotations are harder to find. Egeria, a rich Christian woman who traveled to the Holy Land in 381–84, used *turba* to describe crowds of worshippers.[214] The hint of disorder still associated with *turba* in Augustine and Jerome is absent in her travel account. But this was also the case with highfalutin Christian poetry. The late fourth-century writer Victricius of Rouen consistently used the term *turba* to describe crowds of saints.[215] Gregory the Great used the word to describe a "crowd of thoughts" (*cogitationum turba*).[216]

In the fifth and sixth centuries, the word's positive sense was widely extended to secular crowds. Sidonius (d. 489) insults the *rustica turba*, but he also praises the *pia turba senatus* ("the pious crowd of the senate").[217] Cassiodorus (d. 585) in his *Variae* hopes that the "genius of your Liberty will look upon the grateful crowd [*turba*] of the senate."[218] He speaks of a "crowd of learned men" (*turba doctorum*).[219] In a famous letter to the *cancellarius* Vitalianus, Cassiodorus praised the *turbae* of Rome. The occasion is a demand to send pork and beef that Lucania and Bruttium owed, respectively, to the capital. This affords Cassiodorus an opportunity to compliment Rome's numbers:

> For how could she be small in number, she who came to possess the government of the universe! For the gigantic expanse of the walls, the gaping capacity of spectacle buildings, the mighty amplitude of the baths, and that great quantity of water mills, which was purposely established for the food supply, all attest to her crowds [*turbae*] of citizens.[220]

For Cassiodorus, in stark contrast with Ammianus a century and a half earlier, *turbae* were an ornament that honored a state. It is poignant that Cassiodorus, in his praise of Rome's crowds, protests too much. Rome in the 530s, when Cassiodorus wrote this letter, was shrinking, though it had not yet diminished to its most catastrophic lows. Rome's huge walls, numerous circuses, theaters, and amphitheaters, great baths, and water mills now testified less to its size than to numbers lost. Cassiodorus's letter shows how mightily civic officials strove to maintain numbers for glory's sake.[221] The *turba* remained an ornament to civic pride even as the city declined in numbers.[222]

The Early Medieval Turba

With little to hold its semantic field intact, and good reasons to favor its biblical appearance, writers from the late sixth to tenth centuries used *turba* as an equivalent for any other crowd term. Its older use as a term for unruly crowds was carried by the more specialized disorder-word *tumultus*.[223] A seventh-century hagiographer is typical in describing a *religiosa ac felix turba* ("a religious and happy crowd"), elaborating with other crowd words: *multitudo, viri, congeries*.[224] *Turba* designated the "large crowds" that received an important individual at the gates of a city.[225] It denoted a saint's "friends" all assembled.[226] Laypersons at church services were a *turba*.[227] There were *turbae* of monks, nuns, priests, and virgins.[228] A pious procession was a "copious crowd" (*turba*).[229] A ninth-century plan of an ideal monastery, the Saint-Gall Plan, shows the front gate open to *omnibus turbis*, "all crowds."[230] In the same plan, above the cloister we read: *Hinc pia consilium pertractet turba salubre*, "Through here let healthful counsel be debated by the pious crowd [*pia ... turba*]."[231] The word Seneca used to denigrate the "mob" of the amphitheater became a term for monks in their secret, sacred spaces.[232]

Hagiographical sources preferred *turba* for the "witness crowds" that observed and legitimized miracles.[233] The relics of Helianus were welcomed to their new home in Benevento by the city's "whole crowd" (*omnis turba*), to the light of candles and lamps amid a haze of incense.[234] When the bodies of Regnobertus and Zeno were translated, they were met by a "numerous crowd of people" (*plurima turba populi*) and accompanied by a "great crowd" (*multa turba*) as they went.[235] The positive glow of these crowds is expressed by a series of joyous exclamations: "What a great array [*ordo*] of monks was present there! What a numerous crowd [*turba*] of canons! For the whole multitude of the people [*omnis multitudo populi*] had assembled there from the neighboring provinces."[236] They even merited a miracle: their gathering site was spared a recent inundation.[237]

The liturgy embraced *turba* with special abandon. The Exultet, as it appears in the eighth-century Gellone sacramentary, is typical when it describes the rejoicing of an angelic crowd of the heavens: "exultet iam angelica turba caelorum."[238] There is little difference, semantically, between this angelic host and the "multitude [*multitudo*] of angels" that praises God elsewhere in the same collection.[239] Such angelic crowds are everywhere in liturgical texts.[240] A hymn of perhaps the ninth century, *De uno Pontifice*, describes the *praesul* as chosen by the "holy crowd [*turba*] of clergy and people."[241]

Nor were good *turbae* unique to religious texts. Formularies and charters too describe communities of monks as *turbae*.[242] The phrase *turba plurima monachorum* ("a numerous crowd of monks") is repeated across Merovingian formulary-books to describe any community of monks to which an individual might donate or sell properties.[243] The same expression can be found in a forgery of a Merovingian charter and in two genuine Carolingian royal charters by Pippin and Charlemagne.[244] The word is conspicuously absent in the *Annales Regni Francorum*, which prefers *multitudo* and *populus* for crowds (good as well as bad); but other influential histories deploy it. In a famous passage of Einhard's *Vita Karoli*, the ninth-century courtier describes how Charlemagne took baths with his assembled entourage at Aachen: "He invited not only his sons to the bath, but nobles and friends, and sometimes even a crowd [*turba*] of subordinates and bodyguards, so that often a hundred men or more would be bathing together."[245]

Bad Turbae *in the Early Middle Ages*

Turba did not lose all its negative potential. Something about the word remained vaguely ominous. In Anastasius Bibliothecarius's ninth-century translation of the passion of Saint Demetrius, Archbishop Eusebius of Thessaloniki sees himself in a dream in the city's theater with a "crowd of attendants" (*turba famulorum*).[246] These crowds, in an "obscene place," seem to foreshadow a "multitude of barbarians" that threaten the city.[247] There are also examples in which a *turba* is downright wicked. A seventh-century Spanish hymn for Lent describes Judas giving over his master to the crowds (*turbae*).[248] Another praises the archangel Michael for "crushing dark and demonic crowds" (*turbae*).[249] Hilduin of Saint-Denis, in his prose *vita* of saint Denis (*BHL* 2175) juxtaposes the *multitudo fidelium* that dies with Denis (and the *multitudo coelestis exercitus* that assists in his posthumous and headless march from Montmartre to what would become Saint-Denis) with *turbae infidelium*. It is into the midst of this "pagan rabble" that Larcia, a woman who had accused Denis but who repented upon seeing him carry his own head, threw herself, crying that she was a Christian.[250] A demonic *turba* is cast away in a ninth-century saint's life.[251] In another, a villainous character "in the likeness of Judas" arrives "close-packed by a wicked *turba*."[252] A "seditious rabble" (*seditiosum vulgus*), made "beastlike" by mad rage, attacks Saint Wandrille (*BHL* 8805): it is twice described as a *turba*.[253]

Carolingian elites sometimes used the term *turba* to denigrate superstitious or unpredictable crowds. The "crowd of amazed and astonished people" that drew the condemnation of a ninth-century archbishop for its credulity was a *turba*.²⁵⁴ But it is worth noting that what made such *turbae* bad was carefully adumbrated: superstition, the involvement of women, or rusticity (or all of the above).²⁵⁵ A host of negative modifiers—"dark," "demonic," "pagan," "faithless," "beastlike," "impious," and so on—was recruited to clarify which *turbae* were up to no good. Negativity was not built into the word itself, as with Ammianus. Bad *turbae* shared space with good *turbae*. The passion of Saint Saturninus of Cagliari (*BHL* 7491), an early medieval text, according to its most recent editor, imagines the saint being murdered "by one from out of the crowd" (*ab uno de turba*) in response to his profession of faith.²⁵⁶ But this "crowds of sinners" (*turbae sceleratorum*) is contrasted with a "crowd of believers" (*turba fidelium*) that "expanded day by day" thanks to the saint.²⁵⁷

There still was a narrative need for bad crowds, as the next chapter will discuss in greater detail, but *turba* was no longer the most obvious word for them. A bad crowd might just as equally appear as a *multitudo*, a *populus*, a *vulgus*, a *cohors*, a *contio*.²⁵⁸ The Royal Frankish Annals had a penchant for *multitudo* as the designation for pagan crowds.²⁵⁹ Metrical and stylistic considerations, more than a word's historical suitability, drove usage. When one ninth-century hymn concludes with an assault on "foul mobs" (*taetrae turbae*), *turba* was chosen to alliterate with *timor*, *tremor*, *taetras*, and *terreat*.²⁶⁰ This is not so different from a poem about bald men (*calvi*) that uses *caterva* for "crowd" because every word in the poem must begin with the letter C.²⁶¹

Turba would regain its stormy connotations in the high and later Middle Ages. As contentious non-elite crowds returned to daily life, artisans in town and city entered upon the political stage, and Roman law regained its place, *turba* came to be the word of choice for "riot" or "rabble."²⁶² Nevertheless, its early medieval holiday had interesting consequences. In some contexts, the word kept a warm glow for centuries. When *turba* came into Old Irish (*torb*), it just meant "crowd," without strong positive or negative associations.²⁶³ The late medieval French institution of the *enquête par turbe* or "inquiry by the crowd" preserved the probative importance of the crowd.²⁶⁴ Above all, hymns and other religious texts sang of sacred *turbae* all the way to the end of the Middle Ages.²⁶⁵

Crowd Words Transformed

Loss of differentiation, Christianization, and diminishment of negative valances marked the crowd vocabulary of the early Middle Ages. There are risks in assuming that written evidence, marked by the conventions of the learned, accurately reflected the mindset of most people. But the patterns are consistent enough, across languages and genres, that we can have some confidence in their representativeness. Collective terms were linked ever more closely with notions of unity, consensus, and legitimacy, ever less with disorder, unrest, and vulgarity. When bad crowds needed to be depicted, negative modifiers and bad associations were highlighted for clarity.

What drove this change? In part, this was a cultural transformation long in the making. Already in Late Antiquity popular language eschewed formal "differences" between crowd words. Christian uses gradually overwhelmed classical ones. The neutral or positive crowds of the Gospels replaced riotous mobs as the default subject of words like *populus*, *multitudo*, and *turba*. Both these trends have parallels in Byzantine Greek. Only the attenuation of negative connotations was a more western peculiarity, and even this had roots in the popular language of the Roman past.

But these three trends predominated after c. 500 due to the demographic and socioeconomic transformations explored in previous chapters. Representation did not escape the new materiality of gathering. Now that gatherings were more predictable, it stands to reason that a less differentiated and more positive representational regime of crowds would thrive in the written word. As we have seen, early medieval communities were still capable of assembling large numbers, but in hierarchical and controlled settings: in assemblies, councils, fairs, and liturgical celebrations.

Words thus prove an effective seismograph of the cultural resilience and material rupture that made up the early medieval crowd regime. The *populus* ceased to be a Roman civic concept, but remained the quintessential term for the assembled community. Preaching replaced public oratory, but the *contio* lived on as long as speech acts before crowds retained their power. As urban riots became a thing of the past, once-marginal uses of the word *turba* came to the fore. The next chapter will explore the patterns of representation that accompanied these changes of meaning, as well as what happened when crowds continued to be unpredictable.

6

Representations

Patterns of Representation

A circle of rapt onlookers, a throng of faithful supporters, a multitude drawn to a place of sanctity: the reader of early medieval texts encounters these stock crowds over and over.[1] Across genres, crowds of witnesses and pious actors, influenced by Christian models, validated events, individuals, or objects.[2] As for the fickle, vulgar, and violent crowds of classical literature, they grew rarer, but never vanished. The present chapter argues that this representational pattern reveals a discursive shift: in early medieval Europe, crowds became disproportionately associated with legitimacy.

There are three caveats to this thesis. First, the early medieval association of crowds with legitimation was not new; it existed in classical and early Christian sources. But the positive now overshadowed the negative. Second, bad crowds were not gone. Far from it. Crowds of non-Christian outsiders, partisan foes, and superstitious rustics were regularly denigrated. But it now took discursive effort, in a world with no proper concept of "riot," to dislodge undesirable gatherings from their default acceptability. Third, more theoretically, representational patterns, as with the semantic patterns examined in the last chapter, reflect mentalities imperfectly. Some genres—hagiography stands out—had more interest in legitimizing crowds than others. As with any attempt to derive perceptions from written texts, we are on firm ground only in speaking of elites and their spokespersons. But there is often reason to believe that elite representations reflected wider patterns of belief and thought.[3]

In discussing recurring images or narratives about crowds, this chapter borrows two concepts from literary studies: "topos" and "type scene." It was through tropes and anecdotes, rather than explicit statements, that early medieval authors expressed their ideas about crowds. There is no early medieval Le Bon, no Seneca issuing declaratory statements about the *turba*. One must read early medieval attitudes toward collective behavior between the lines.

But, through topoi, this can be done. This chapter first explores the classical, biblical, and patristic models for crowd depictions. Next, it describes the key qualities of crowds across early medieval texts: representativeness, number, density, agency, and unity. Crowd consensus, especially when cast as sincere and spontaneous, was confirmatory. Hence early medieval discourse framed the crowd as legitimizing. "Bad" crowds still appeared: foreigners, persecutors, competitors, non-elites carrying out resistance, and rustics performing "superstition." But in the absence of topoi of delegitimization specific to crowds, early medieval authors recruited from xenophobic, misogynistic, and anti-rustic stereotypes. These originally temporizing strategies had enduring consequences after negative ideas about crowds returned.

Topoi, Type Scenes, and Their Sources

"The Latin literature of the Middle Ages," wrote Paul Lehmann, "is full of borrowings and imitations." Ideas, phrases, and scenes are repeated "ad nauseam."[4] But clichés can be informative.[5] The term "topos" ("commonplace") was popularized by Ernst Robert Curtius, who applied it to stock characters (e.g., the *puer senex*, the young man with an old soul), recurring sentiments (e.g., "all must die," "all praise him"), and authorial poses (e.g., the topos of modesty) ubiquitous in medieval literature.[6] A "type scene," according to Joaquín Martínez Pizarro, is a topos in narrative form. For Pizarro, early medieval authors, unlike editorializing classical writers, made arguments and drew morals performatively through "scenes."[7] "Type" scenes—the prophet admonishing the king, the death-bed scene, the miraculous healing—acted as arguments-by-anecdote.[8]

The idea that "topoi" or "type scenes" reflect the mentality of an age has drawn criticism.[9] Such clichés had ancient pedigrees. The crowd that witnesses a miracle, the crowd that speaks in unison, the crowd healed by a saint, the crowd that demands the election of a reluctant future abbot or bishop, or the crowd that rushes to miracle-working relics reveal conventionality as well as conviction.[10] In hagiography and poetry, genres marked by high levels of borrowing, there is a danger of zombie imagery.[11] But early medieval writers used inherited imagery selectively, with telling alterations.

Classical Models

Classical literature provided early medieval writers with models for topoi and type scenes of crowds. Roman texts generally showed crowds as emotional and swayable, though not necessarily evil.[12] As we have seen, histories, panegyrics, and poems depicted crowds as accoutrements to legitimate (male) leadership. Vergil's *Aeneid* was as much about "crowds and the man" as about "arms and the man." "Father Aeneas" modeled elite male comportment by achieving a self-mastery that enabled him to master the crowd.[13] The image of the singular figure overcoming the crowd fascinated early medieval imaginations, but the gendered specificity of this Roman virtue diminished. Vergil's lone male hero standing firm before a crowd (*Aen.* 1.148–49) was extended to female saints.[14] The "great throng" of attendants "that pressed round" Dido as a sign of her royal dignity was repurposed for men.[15] Crowds remained an important mark of status, and imperturbability before the crowd was sublimated as a Christian virtue.[16]

Other ancient topoi became less current. The idea that crowds tended to misrule or sedition, so central to Greco-Roman discourse, diminished.[17] The Cataline-like evil genius who controlled the crowd, in an inversion of Vergil's heroic man, largely vanished, though this figure would return in the eleventh century.[18] There were early medieval depictions of lynch mobs.[19] But fear of sedition was differently constructed. Rebellion and conspiracy were the result of sworn plots (*coniurationes*), not spontaneous outpourings. If anything, public gatherings—assemblies, mass oaths of loyalty—were the solution, not the spur, to threats upon order.[20]

Biblical Models

The Bible was the most important source of crowd representations for early medieval authors.[21] The "innumerable multitude" of the Old Testament could legitimize or delegitimize.[22] God promised Abraham that his seed would be without number, like the stars in the sky and the sand on the shores of the sea.[23] But the countless Midianites and Amalekites were "like locusts in their multitude."[24] Other Old Testament crowd scenes, such as Moses handing down the law or the numbering of the tribes, influenced early medieval representations of assemblies.[25] The Psalms are full of intermingled references to multitudes, crowds, and peoples.[26] Crowds played a role in prophetic topoi of desolation.[27] The Acts of the Apostles provided models for good crowds (the thousands converted: Acts 2:41, Acts 4:4; the multitudes that must come together: Acts 21:22) and bad ones (cf. Stephen's death in Acts 7 and the silversmiths of Ephesus in Acts 19:23–41).[28] The apocalyptic multitudes of the Book of Revelation were among the most commonly depicted gatherings in early medieval art.[29]

But it was the Gospels that provided the essential pattern for early medieval authors. Jesus Christ taught, preached, performed miracles, and suffered in front of crowds.[30] "Many crowds" (*turbae multae*) followed him (Matthew 4:25) during his earthly mission in the Holy Land.[31] We have already seen how these representations altered the meaning and valence of collectivity words. Whereas the Roman hero had to master the crowd, Christ ministered to it:

> In those days again, when there was great multitude and they had nothing to eat; calling his disciples together, he saith to them: I have compassion on the multitude, for behold they have now been with me three days and have nothing to eat. And if I shall send them away fasting to their home, they will faint in the way: for some of them came from afar off. (Mark 8:1–3)[32]

Miserere super turba, "to have compassion for the crowd," became a hagiographic imperative.[33]

At the same time, the New Testament implied that crowds possessed insights into truth. When the ninth-century exegete Christian of Stavelot read Matthew 9:33 ("And after the devil was cast out, the dumb man spoke, and the multitudes wondered, saying, 'never was the like seen in Israel'"), he drew a lesson about the wisdom of crowds. "Crowds [*turbae*], which seem less learned, were always wondering at the teaching of the Lord," he wrote. "But the Pharisees and the Sadducees were denigrating it, or turned into a wicked faction on account of envy, because they suffered on account of the Lord's teaching, whereas Christ was believed to be both holier and wiser by the crowds [*a turbis*]."[34] The pious multitudes of the New Testament were also arbiters of truth.[35]

Late Antique Christian Models

Christian poets like Juvencus, Victricius, Proba, Prudentius, and Sedulius also provided models for the Christianized crowd.[36] Prudentius's *Peristephanon*, a much-read hagiographical anthology, is full of biblical crowds in Vergilian guise.[37] Late antique saints' lives were brimming with multitudes. A few hagiographic works, like martyrs' acts, were limited to dialogues between saints and persecutors.[38] But most saints' lives, sooner or later, involved crowds.[39] The mass healing or mass conversion, the flight from the crowd, and the miracle before the crowd were topoi consolidated in foundational late antique hagiographical texts, like Evagrius's translation of Athanasius's *Life of Anthony* (BHL 609), the Latin *Verba seniorum* (BHL 6527), Sulpicius Severus's *Life of Saint Martin* (BHL 5610), the anonymous *Acts of Saint Sylvester* (BHL 7725–43), and the *Dialogues* of Gregory the Great.[40]

The crowds of late antique hagiography were not always noble or good. Setting aside crowds of persecutors, well-meaning crowds could be ambivalently portrayed, as with the flight-from-the-crowd topos, in which a saint, motivated by modesty or asceticism, fled the adulation of the many.[41] Such crowds were not bad *per se*—the participants being motivated by faith—but they nevertheless tested and tempted. The saint had to resist the vain glory of adulation while obeying the precepts of charity.

This tension is carried to extremes in Jerome's *Life of Hilarion* (BHL 3879), a curious life written around 390.[42] As a fourth-century youth, Hilarion spurned circus, arena, and theater for the "assembly of the church," and ultimately chose a solitary life.[43] When he sought out Anthony of Egypt, he was perplexed to find the saint besieged by hordes of needy people: "He thought it strange to endure, out in the desert, the crowds of the cities."[44] After Hilarion set up his own hermitage near Gaza, he saw the same thing firsthand. Needy crowds flocked to him. His cures attracted ever larger numbers. A monastery grew up around him. He fled these crowds for Egypt but they followed him, so he went to Libya, then Sicily, then Cyprus, ever beset by multitudes. In Cyprus, one of his last acts was to cure a crowd of two hundred men and women with brusque alacrity, "as if lashing out to avenge himself."[45] Most early medieval hagiographers lacked Jerome's playful awareness of the ethical paradoxes of the crowd, but they agreed that crowds buzzed with moral risk; their positive valence was never straightforward.

Early Medieval Models

Early medieval sources also copied one another. Poets copied poets, chronicles were built upon older historiography, saints' lives were rife with pious plagiarism, and charters reiterated boilerplate. Among poets, Venantius Fortunatus (d. early seventh century) and Aldhelm of Malmesbury (d. 709) stood out.[46] The former combined the legitimizing crowd of Roman panegyric with the crowd topoi of Christian hagiography, while the latter offered a model for the indiscriminate mixing and matching of crowd terms. In historiography, patterns of depiction in the *Annales Regni Francorum* and Einhard's *Life of Charlemagne* retained currency for subsequent historians.[47] In hagiography, the genre of *translatio*—accounts of the transfer of a saint's earthly remains—was prone to recycled crowd scenes.[48] This is understandable given the importance of crowds in demonstrating the legitimacy of relics, particularly after a pious theft.[49] Crowd topoi in Einhard's *Translatio Marcellini et Petri* (BHL 5233) were copied nearly verbatim by Adrevald's *Miracula Benedicti* (BHL 1123–24), the mid-ninth-century *Historia Translationis Helenae* (BHL 3773), and the late ninth-century *Translatio Vincentii* (BHL 8644–8646) of Aimoin.[50] In charters, phrases emphasizing the presence of many witnesses—such as "with many people standing by" (*multis adstantibus*)—were so ubiquitous that is it easy to overlook them.[51] The endless recycling of such tropes across genres consolidated patterns of representation.

Qualities of the Crowd in Early Medieval Discourse

There were differences by author, time, region, and genre in the qualities of the crowd. Sixth-century sources often had one foot in the old Roman representational regime, while those of the eighth or ninth century spoke from the perspective of a more rural world. The *Liber Pontificalis*, written in fractious, bustling Rome, kept alive the urban rabbles conspicuously lacking in northern chronicles, where bad crowds tended to be "great multitudes" of enemy pagans. In general, hagiography, poetry, and liturgy depicted crowds more often and positively than historiography and epistolography. But there were common threads in how crowds were depicted in European texts, c. 500–1000.

Representativeness and Judgment

The primary narrative function of crowds was representative and moral. Crowds stood for something. A crowd reflected the qualities of a focal point. By its presence and comportment, it illuminated the rectitude, sanctity, or wickedness of a person, place, or thing. Alternatively, it might represent an identity or idea. A crowd of Franks stood for Frankishness; a crowd of women, femaleness; a crowd of peasants, rusticity; a crowd of pagans, paganism, and so on. The blurred lines between physical and abstract collectivity words, seen in the last chapter, strengthened this representational logic.

Moral judgments or statements about ethnicity, status, age, and gender were thus expressed via depictions of crowds. The unity of Christian peoples was shown by the unanimity of Christian crowds. The dangerousness of Saxons, Northmen, Saracens, or Magyars—or conversely the glory of their conversion—was embodied by numbers. The poor, that all-important class in Christian theology, appeared textually as crowds.[52] So did other groups: "nobles" (*proceres, senatus, nobiles, maiores*), monks, clerics, nuns, youths, and lay women.[53] The separateness of crowds of women reveals perspectives about gender and public order.[54] Women were theoretically restricted from participating in "general councils and public gatherings," though this seems the clerical ideal rather than the reality.[55] Authors depicted proper social order using representative crowds in hierarchical array, each in its proper place.[56] Conversely, a crowd could be cast in a positive or negative light by highlighting some participants as opposed to others. The presence of monks might elevate a mixed crowd. Authors eager to discredit collective behavior on the edge of the acceptable emphasized rustic or female involvement.[57]

Nonhumans, as we saw in chapter three, could also act as representative crowds. Aside from crowds of angels and demons—clear representations of good or evil—animal crowds served as conduits of moral truth. The "horn-bearing crowd" (*cornigera turba*) of deer laid low by aristocratic hunters revealed the prowess of a king and his companions.[58] A common hagiographical topos was the desert site inhabited only by crowds of animals; these inhuman multitudes were a foil to future human masses destined to assemble at the site after its sanctification.[59]

Number and Density

Insofar as a crowd reflected the good or bad qualities of some focal point or entity, number and density amplified those qualities. The bigger and denser the crowd, the more legitimate, holy, dangerous, or wicked its focal point. Number appears to have been the more important of these two properties in the early Middle Ages. In the post-Roman demographic regime, it was the rarer quality. Size-related adjectives ("many," "large," "great," "not small," "copious," "numerous," "uncountable") often appear alongside crowd words. Of the thirteen uses of the word *multitudo* in the *Annales Regni Francorum* (with a mix of subjects and valences) all but one are called "immense," "huge," "infinite," or the like, and that one exception goes on to speak of a "great number from out of the multitude."[60]

In modern crowd theory, density shares equal billing with number, because it is thought to be central to the crowd's emergent effects.[61] The "dense" crowd was less prominent in early medieval discourse than the "large" crowd. As much as Isidore of Seville tried to police the "difference" between the density-oriented "crowd" (*turba*) and the number-oriented "multitude" (*multitudo*), few authors took him up on this distinction.[62] But density remained a discursive amplifier. One hagiographical topos was the crowd so thick it blocked movement. Einhard revels in the dense crowds that assembled at his home in Aachen when news miraculously spread of his relics' arrival; that proved their veracity.[63]

Sometimes, number or density underscored legitimacy by making the crowd an obstacle to be overcome. In a scene derived from the New Testament (e.g., Matthew 9:20–22, Mark 5:25–34, Luke 8:43–48), a crowd in the *Translatio Sancti Viti* prevented a woman carrying a lame child from getting to the altar. She had to push herself into the throng (*ingerens se in medium populi*) as a sign of her faith.[64] Numbers justified the expansion or build-up of shrines or monasteries, as we will see below. The idea was enduring too. In the twelfth century, Suger's justification for the rebuilding of Saint-Denis explicitly rested on the uncomfortable crowdedness of the church during festival season.[65]

Finally, number and density were critical in the representation of military might. Warfare was partly a numbers game, and armies were among the largest gatherings of the early medieval West.[66] Writers boasted of their own side's numerous and dense multitudes of soldiers. In his poem *In honorem Hludowici Caesaris*, Ermold, writing in the late 820s about the siege of Barcelona in 800 / 801, paints a scene of endless Frankish forces closing in on the city: "Crowds [*catervae*] assemble from all sides, in the manner of the Franks, / and surround the walls of the city in a dense crown [*densa corona*]." For the poet, the military multitude constitutes an *agmen pulcrum*, a "beautiful crowd."[67] The same language is found in Notker's late ninth-century depiction of Charlemagne's attack on Pavia: as each wave of Charlemagne's army comes into view, the Lombard king asks his Frankish interlocutor whether Charlemagne himself has arrived, but only after an endless parade of densely packed troops does he see the ironclad king of the Franks.[68] On the other hand, as will be discussed below, it was just as common to inflate the number or density of enemy forces, to denigrate the locust-like inhumanity of the other and to highlight one's own prowess.

Agency

Occasionally, crowds were granted narrative agency. In the seventh-century *Passio Prisci et sociorum*, set in the third century, a crowd led by Saint Priscus speaks in dialogue with a Roman official, Alexander.[69] The "immense multitude" (*immensa multitudo*) talks like a single character in one voice.[70] The crowd's sobriquet varies as it responds to Alexander's angry questions: "the most sacred multitude" (*sanctissima multitudo*), "the holy men" (*sancti viri, viri sancti*), "the Christian congregation" (*congeries christiana*), and the "religious and happy crowd" (*religiosa ac felix turba*).[71] The exchange concludes with Alexander asking the crowd if it is ready to die for its faith. The crowd, in unison, tells the Roman to do what he must.[72] Jamie Kreiner has argued that such depictions of unanimous crowds "showed the processes of social solidarity in motion."[73] They promoted Christianity as a force for cohesion whose symbol was the unity of the crowd. This solidified the crowd's role as means of representation.

But the crowd's narrative role was more commonly passive. Crowds usually served as witnesses to speech or action.[74] Some other individual, not the crowd per se, is typically at the heart of the action. Even the passage just mentioned ends with Priscus, the saint, at the head of the crowd. The Roman official, exasperated, asks Priscus: "Do you also agree with them?" Priscus stands firm: "Just as we worship one God, so let us all unanimously hasten to be killed on his behalf" (*Sicut unum Deum colimus, ita et pro eo omnes unanimiter interfici festinamus*).[75] Alexander obliges, kills Priscus, and puts the multitude to death; it is the saint's agency that concludes the drama. After its active speaking role, the crowd's final act is passive. It is similar with other collective cults, such as

Saint Maurice and the Ten Thousand Martyrs, or Cassius, Victorinus, and Antholianus and the "sacred legion" that died with them; individuals act while the crowd follows.[76]

Crowd agency, or lack thereof, can be an important plot point. In one late eighth-century saint's life, the passion of Saint Salvius (*BHL* 7472), a large crowd (*multitudo populi*) tries and fails to move the saint's body from its resting place to its new home in the church of Saint-Martin at Valenciennes. Only when the crowd steps away (*ablata vero multitudine*) at the bishops' command are two oxen able to move the body to its new resting place.[77] Crowds confirm the will of God, but it is not their place to identify that will. The crowd's proper role was generally that of obedient follower—a confirmer or amplifier of truth—not an actor and initiator.

Unity and Universality

Unity, as an expression of spontaneous or unforced consensus, gave the crowd this confirmatory or amplifying authority. Even in the monarchical societies of the early medieval West, consensus remained an important source of political and spiritual legitimation.[78] This was not only true of the accession of kings, the election of clerics, and the translation of relics, but of all "public" acts. Land deals, manumissions, marriages, gifts, and dispute settlements were meant to be witnessed by "all." Ninth-century canon law forgers declared that episcopal translations, normally prohibited, were authorized if they had the approval of the whole local populace.[79] A united crowd represented the will of the whole community. Hence words such as "all" or "everyone" (*omnes, cuncti, universi*) were used interchangeably with words for crowds.[80] In a world with no voting booths or opinion polls, claims about collective will implied collective performances.

A powerful way to express collective unity was to emphasize that crowds in unison were heterogeneous in makeup. A "promiscuous" crowd of all statuses, genders, and ages was all the more impressive for sharing one voice and one will.[81] When a saint brings relics to a town, "the whole city rejoices," and the hagiographer specifies that "every sex, all ages, every rank, every status ran toward the vision of this great father, exulting."[82] Modoin's eclogue for Charlemagne calls Aachen the "new Rome" because "everyone will be here, every sex and age."[83] "An accumulation of crowds was packed together," reports the author of one ninth-century translation account approvingly, before specifying that both common people (*vulgus*) and aristocrats (*nobiles*), "all in common," were praising God with "one voice."[84] A sermon from the end of the ninth century dwells on the many groups that together praise the name of God: monks, clerics, priests, women, children, young men, and old men.[85] In the *Life of Gaugeric*, the saint's rogation brings in "all members of the populace" (*cuncti populi*).[86] The tenth-century hagiographer Baltherus of Säckingen describes how Saint Fridolin's reputation for mercy and healing miracles attracted an "innumerable crowd of people of either sex."[87] When "all ages, all classes, and both sexes" acted together, this affirmed the deed in question.[88]

Election accounts insist that all voiced support for the king, bishop, or abbot.[89] The topos of universal acclamation is taken to extremes in the *Liber Pontificalis*, with paradoxical results. One ninth-century papal life insists that all Romans desired Hadrian II (r. 867–72) as pope from the depths of their marrows: "All the fellow citizens of the city of Rome, as well as those who happened to be outside of the city, both poor and rich, both the clerical order and the whole mass of the people, namely, of every age, profession, and sex [...] wanted Hadrian," adding that no one in the city did not desire him as pope, that is, "except for anyone who wanted either himself or his choice to be promoted instead."[90] Universal demand afforded the chosen individual the opportunity to resist the call humbly, while also offering an excuse to acquiesce to popular pressure. Unanimous assent became an indispensable topos for those taking on official power, just as it was for promulgating a decision or promoting a holy cult.[91]

This ethos was among the most important representational legacies of the early medieval crowd. Louis Hamilton has shown how accounts of Italian church dedications in the eleventh century insisted on the presence of large crowds—specifically, large, mixed, and unexpected ones. A common phrase, "the crowd rushes forth" (*turba concurrit*) linked eleventh-century reformers with liturgical tradition.[92] Hamilton argues that church dedications were "among the religious and communal activities that fostered the development of the commune," because liturgical documents from the late tenth century to the twelfth insisted upon broad participation across the social spectrum.[93] What began as an early medieval idyll became a high medieval political and ritual necessity.[94]

Crowds and Sanctity

Crowds Drawn to Saints

The result of the nexus of representativeness and unity was the idea that crowds were drawn to, and thus testified to, holy power. Often this power was embodied by an individual saint, living or dead. Bede describes how a "crowd" (*caterua*) of students was drawn to Saints Theodore and Hadrian at the school of Canterbury in the late seventh century.[95] In some cases, rumor was acknowledged as the earthly mechanism of crowd assembly before relics.[96] In other cases, the assembly of the crowd was linked with a miracle.[97] In one saint's life, a girl falls into a well, and the hagiographer emphasizes the number and the variety of the crowds that observed her miraculous rescue.[98] Interaction with the crowd became a defining feature of sainthood. As a (possibly tenth-century) *vita* (BHL 2455) summarizes the virtues of Eleutherius of Tournai, "What more should be said? For many [*multi*] believed through him; many [*multi*] were baptized by him; many [*multi*] were killed in Christ's name together with this same martyr."[99]

The fact that a crowd could itself be miraculous was explicitly acknowledged by Einhard in his *Translatio Marcellini et Petri* (BHL 5233). In recounting a large crowd at Aachen drawn from their daily business to a procession of his relics by a sweet scent, Einhard begins by declaring that he must not "pass over in silence" "something of a miracle."[100] The appearance of an unexpected assembly proves that the fragments of bone, dust, and fabric Einhard's men had stolen by night from a faraway Roman catacomb were not mere stuff, but holy relics: living, willing agents of their own "translation" to Aachen. Einhard's case is instructive for two reasons. First, it shows the importance of spontaneity or unexpectedness as a legitimizing feature of crowd unity. Although stewards of relics made every effort to attract crowds—Einhard himself ultimately moved the shrine for Marcellinus and Petrus from a less to a more populous site—they downplayed their own efforts in written texts. Second, Einhard's crowd stories reveal the stakes of attracting crowds for a relic cult. Einhard wrote his *Translatio* to prove the veracity of the relics for which he was the earthly steward. The need to demonstrate their authenticity was caused by the counterclaim of Saint-Denis to possess the relics. Thus, crowds resolved matters of cultic competition.[101] As a result, a series of type scenes about crowds and saints characterizes early medieval hagiography.

Crowds at Saints' Funerals

The funerals of saints were depicted as crowded events.[102] An early example from the late fifth or early sixth century pictures the whole *civitas* of Orange reacting to the death of Saint Verus of Orange "with the collective lament of all."[103] In a seventh-century life, a "whole multitude of monks" arrives to grieve over the saint's demise.[104] The large number of individuals present is part of what allows a queenly saint in an eighth-century text to be buried "with full honor and great reverence."[105] In a saint's life revised early in the ninth century, the crowd (*turba*) buries a saint "in accordance with custom."[106] These examples could be extended.[107] In all these cases, saints are defined by their crowds and multitudes. The reputation (*fama*) of the saint or that saint's deeds may be mentioned as the catalyst, particularly after the saint's death.[108]

Crowds and Monastic Foundations

Holy sites themselves drew in multitudes, and justified the construction of monasteries or shrines. One type scene involving crowds was the foundation of a monastery or church as a result of multitudes.[109] A new monastery must be founded when an old one grows too large for the people its reputation attracts.[110] This type scene was a frequent justification for new foundations, especially in Columbanian lives.[111] It is used of both male and female monasteries.[112] New houses were often instituted not only because they existed on sites where miracles were being performed, but specifically because these miracles were drawing large numbers.[113]

This topos served two important discursive functions. First, the conceit that "crowds made them do it" assuaged anxieties about the worldly ambitions of monastic founders. Initiators of religious houses, whether pious aristocrats or serial founders like Columbanus, could not be guilty of self-aggrandizement if their actions were forced by human numbers. Second, by stressing links between monastic foundations and local crowds, hagiographers smoothed over real-world tensions between religious houses and the populations around them. As the story of the accusations against the nuns of Tauberbischofsheim in chapter 4 makes clear, locals were not always as enthusiastic about monastic neighbors as pious texts let on.

Processions and the Community

Crowds were indispensable to liturgical rituals. The most obvious example is the procession.[114] Rogational processions, widespread from Late Antiquity, consisted of mobilizing local populations in a shared expression of communal penance.[115] Some of these rituals, like an annual procession from Clermont to the body of Saint Julian at Brioude instituted in the sixth century, took days and involved large distances, here sixty-five kilometers.[116] They were felt to be the proper response to divine punishments meted out on whole communities for their sins, like plagues, invasions, fires, earthquakes, or floods.

Processions were also an important part of legitimizing relic cults. In the *Vita Arnulfi* (BHL 692), the saint leaves the city for a rogation procession with crosses and a mixed crowd (*cum crucibus adque promiscuo populi genere*).[117] The *Translatio Viti martyris* (BHL 8718–19) depicts the deposition of the relics of Vitus at the monastery of Rebais. Abbot Warin processes with the relics of Vitus from Saint-Denis to the abbey of Rebais "bringing with him an abundant crowd [*turba*] both of his own monks and of other men" (*habens secum turbam copiosam tam suorum monachorum quam aliorum virorum*), a journey of some seventy kilometers. Abbot Hilduin "with his monks" and the "whole crowd which had come to the festival day" (*omnis populus, qui ad diem festum convenerat*), all proceeded together to the monastery of Rebais, where Warin deposited the relics.[118] At each stage, multitudes of monks, canons, men, and women thronged the bier carrying the relics.[119] Thus—in a ritual that evoked Christ's crowd-strewn entry into Jerusalem—all parties to the translation were made witnesses to its divine approval.

The Crowd as Witness

Across early medieval narratives, then, crowds repeatedly functioned as what we might term a "witness crowd." A witness crowd observes an individual or event within a narrative, provokes or reacts to what it sees, but is peripheral to the main action of the text.[120] At their most inconspicuous, such crowds are relegated to an ablative absolute aside ("with crowds watching"), as in one late eighth- or early ninth-century saint's life in which a saint walking on water is seen "by watching crowds of heathens" (*aspicientibus gentilium turbis*).[121] Witness crowds intensify or illuminate drama.[122] They frequently act as a mirror and guide for the audience.[123] Despite, perhaps because of, their ubiquity, they have not attracted the attention one might expect from students of early medieval topoi.[124]

Witnesses to Propriety

Often the focal point of a witness crowd is a heroic protagonist. Christ's interactions with the crowd set the pattern here.[125] Many early medieval sources possess shadows of these biblical crowds.[126] They act as witness crowds that observe miracles and sacred words: throngs coming to see saints and relics; assemblies assenting to political decisions; groups performing approbatory rituals in liturgy; and opposing sides in legal disputes staking their claims. The crowd may be depicted as more or less aligned with the positive or negative valence of what its members observe. Such crowds go from being witnessing crowds, defined by their largely passive role in the narrative, to a more active crowd: persecuting or persecuted, participating, reacting emotionally or verbally (e.g., crying, "amen").[127] A crowd may be part of a vision: a group among whose ranks a saint appears, for instance.[128]

Witnesses to Evil

Another kind of witness crowd observes wicked behavior. Early medieval narrators sometimes avoid describing the crowd's disapprobation. Instead, they point to a distinction by using contrasting descriptors of the crowd and the individual or event confronted with it. In one ninth-century set of miracles, the translation of Saint Genesius, a "crowd of faithful heading to the ceremony of the mass" meets a blasphemer who has visited the relics "without due devotion, as it later turned out, and without pure faith."[129] In this story, a crowd (*caterva*) of faithful people going to mass asks "a certain man of the plebeian rabble" (*quidam vir ex plebeio conventu*) what miracles the saint's relics have accomplished. The man blasphemously responds that the only miracle the relics have inspired is that "some woman, by a hidden power of her womb, brazenly let forth a noise."[130] Not long after, this man is struck, falls off his horse and breaks his arm, and only the relics he had insulted can (partly) heal his resulting torpor. As a continued chastisement, he is left partly weakened.

The crowd in this little drama provokes the man's behavior, by asking him what sign (*signum*) the relics had been accomplishing. But it is also peripheral. Its members are not depicted reacting to the man's blasphemy, and they mainly serve as spark and contrast to the wicked rustic. Their candid faith contrasts with the "wayward devotion and impure faith" with which the blasphemer visited the relics in the first place.[131] They display a narratively useful passive agency: in seeking out the saint, they come across the real focus of the exemplum.[132] Despite this marginal narrative role, the crowd's presence made sure that the right moral lessons were conveyed.

Witnesses and Truth

Witness crowds functioned to lend credence. One reason that crowds were so prominent in translation accounts was that these were often concerned with competing truth claims.[133] As we saw, Einhard's *Translatio*, with its dozens of crowd scenes, was in part a polemic against a rival staking a claim to the same set of relics. The *Translatio Genesii* used crowd scenes to dispel doubt (*dubietas, ambiguitas*), evidently quite real, about the validity of the relics at the center of the account. The hagiographer (writing in the 820s or 830s in Reichenau) depicts crowds as witnesses to retributive or healing miracles, and often explicitly concludes anecdotes with phrases such as "who could doubt . . . ?"[134] A hagiographical text written in the middle of the ninth century under the auspices of Hincmar of Reims describes how the veracity of Saint Helen's relics was proven before a large assembly (*conventus*) of the church of Reims.[135]

There were telling exceptions, when the crowd—most often the *vulgus*—stood for foolish belief rather than wisdom. In the early ninth-century *Annales Mettenses priores*, the Merovingian king Theuderic III was said to "trust more in the multitude of an innumerable people than in the counsels of prudence" in opposing Pippin II.[136] The effort to link a common crowd with folly was occasionally a tool in the arsenal of delegitimation. But the inverse was more common.

Witness crowds allowed authors to clarify value judgments about the behavior of individuals or the moral or political status of events described.[137] If texts are, as Buc has argued, "forces in the practice of power," then the topos of the witness crowd acted to bolster the authority of textual assertions.[138] In a case that will be explored shortly, when Germanus of Auxerre and Lupus of Troyes come to Britain to (in Bede's understanding) refute the Pelagian heresy, their arrival attracts "huge crowds from all directions" and news about them spreads across the island.[139] Germanus and Lupus are right because they are orthodox, but the crowds serve as critical witnesses to the truth of their doctrine.

The literary witness crowd had real world parallels. Proof in cases of injury depended on not just the testimony of witnesses, but their presence supporting a defendant's innocence or an accuser's just complaint.[140] The *narrationes* of early medieval charters also tend to stress overcoming *dubietas* or *ambiguitas* by means of the legitimizing presence of witnesses.[141] The truth-validating crowd was not merely literary. It informed the way that early medieval consumers of texts understood how collective behavior should function and what it meant.

Witnesses and Legitimation

Early medieval dispute resolution—justice—was articulated in terms of judgments before crowds.[142] In hagiography, competition scenes include martyrs disputing with their persecutors, missionary saints disputing with pagans, and Catholic saints prevailing against the heretics. A clear example emerges in the first book of Bede's eighth-century *Historia Ecclesiastica gentis Anglorum*.[143] In Bede's account of Germanus of Auxerre's and Lupus of Troyes's arrival on the shores of Britain to combat the heresy of Pelagianism, the Catholic bishops' opponents approach the holy men with a multitude of followers, which attracts further crowds of men, women, and children. Making specious arguments, and giving a good show in their finery, the corrupted Pelagians attempt to persuade the crowd. But they are refuted by the "waves of eloquence" poured upon them by the bishops of Gaul. Then Germanus, with recourse to a bag of relics around his neck, heals the sick daughter of a "tribune," and both forms of her blindness—the physical and the spiritual—are replaced by light.

Bede is keen to stress that this occurred in the sight of "all."[144] In a subsequent scene, the Pelagian heresy arises again and Germanus returns. A local leader, Elafius, hastens to the bishop with his ill son, bringing a crowd of local people. Again, Germanus heals the young child "in the presence of all," and having duly impressed the crowd, Germanus proceeds to give them a sermon that ensures the survival of Catholic faith there for a long time to come.[145] The witness crowds in Bede's miracle competition, even when acting implicitly as judges, stand at the periphery. They are neither the active subject nor the passive object of the main action.[146]

Yet witness crowds can easily achieve greater prominence in narrative. In other hagiographical texts, crowds serve both as witness and beneficiary of saints' wonder-working. Crowds of converts both witness and react to narrative heroes.[147] In such cases, the crowd is the object of the central action; as a whole, it hears the sermon, receives the miracle, or even responds verbally.[148] This is seen in crowds healed en masse by saints. A seventh-century story tells of how the prayers of Saint Honoratus and the intercession of Saint Genesius rescued a crowd from a collapsing bridge.[149] Conversely, a topos of the modest miracle worker meant that saints might be depicted as trying to avoid the ostentation of working wonders in front of crowds.[150]

Frequently, the line between a witness crowd and a crowd receiving the benefits of a miracle worker is crossed. In the late sixth- or early seventh-century *Life of Saint Amator of Auxerre*, the bishop of Auxerre miraculously resurrects a child who is brought to him by a lamenting crowd. The hagiographer emphasizes the crowded nature of the scene: "A crowd [*turba*] of sick ran forth in droves [*catervatim*], and prostrated themselves before the vestibule of the prelate."[151] Not only does Amator heal the child, but he also cures the whole crowd from "numerous afflictions." The villain Germanus, playing the role of Saul, brings a crowd with him to kill the current bishop of Auxerre for attacking a sacred tree. In order to overcome the "assembly of Christians," he gathers together his own "crowd" (*turba*) to oppose the Christian one.[152] This bad crowd ends up as a witness to good deeds, however, and is converted.

The effect of such representations of witness crowds was to consolidate the crowd's discursive relationship with legitimacy. Saintliness was proven, miracles were verified, rituals were confirmed, and, conversely, crimes were aired in public because these things happened in the crowd's view. In this way, crowds in texts served as models and mirrors for the gatherings that filled early medieval public life.

Bad Crowds

The default crowd in early medieval discourse was orderly and ordering. This chimes with what we have seen of early medieval gatherings, which were more predictable and controllable by elites, less prone to non-elite spontaneity.[153] Bluntly put, early medieval elites were not much threatened by crowds, so their literary spokesmen had fewer reasons to depict *turbae* and *multitudines* as threatening. But not all gatherings were so congenial, and exceptions caused a discursive quandary. If the crowd was a bulwark of public order, how were early medieval writers to describe the illegitimacy of a dangerous crowd?

There were four areas where negative representation was most needed. First, the biblical trope of locust-like "numberlessness" was used of hostile outsiders, especially non-Christians (but not exclusively). Second, clichés about furious, deindividuating mobs kept some currency, particularly in hagiography, though they lost their dread. Third, in a context of intra-elite competition, negative topoi about paid followers or conspiratorial plots had more use than stereotypes about crowd madness. Fourth, crowds of non-elites still posed a threat—albeit a dimmer one than before. The few instances of outright collective resistance by peasants in the early Middle Ages were fiercely condemned in writing. Far more often, though, non-elite crowds were chastised because they crossed a finer line of propriety. In cases of passive or "slantwise" collective resistance, early medieval writers called in discursive mercenaries (folly, femininity, superstition) to condemn crowds on the edge of acceptability.[154]

The Multiplying Gaze

One durably negative topos, common across historical settings, was the "innumerable multitude" of barbarian or infidel others. Countlessness could be a positive quality, but unbounded nature was potentially dehumanizing as well. Herds of beasts, swarms of insects, rushing waters, and engulfing flames were anything but humane. Early medieval Christians portrayed "Saxons," "Northmen," "Magyars," and "Saracens" as numberless, likening them to these avatars of hostile nature. In annals and chronicles, the pejorative multiplying gaze is probably the commonest negative crowd topos. Nor was it unique to the West. When an Umayyad ambassador visited the Slavs, he was sure they were the most numerous people on earth; that was not meant as a compliment.[155]

The multiplying gaze was best suited to a military context. While propagandists did inflate numbers on their own side, the inverse was more often the case. Delbrück established as a principle of military history that sources exaggerate enemy numbers.[156] Defeated foes in early medieval annals had to consist of "countless multitudes."[157] The numberlessness of one's enemies reflected one's own courage or prowess. When the bold count Boniface led an impromptu attack in North Africa "between Utica and Carthage" in 828 with a small band of men, he met local resistance from what the *Royal Frankish Annals* calls an "unnumbered multitude of local inhabitants suddenly assembled together" (*innumera incolarum multitudo subito congregata*).[158] When Boniface's men acquitted themselves, "this fact struck the Africans with great fear," and allowed the annalist to elevate a raid into a glorious victory.[159]

Numbers played a similar role in a tense exchange between the Frankish emperor Louis II of Italy (r. 855–75) and the Byzantine emperor Basil I (r. 867–86) after their successful joint siege of the Muslim enclave of Bari in February 871. A letter from Louis, ghost-written by Anastasius Bibliothecarius, responds to a now-lost Byzantine missive, in which Basil I had accused the Franks of contributing minimally to victory. Basil had argued that the more numerous Byzantine soldiers had done the bulk of the fighting, while the smaller number of Franks had stood back "looking on" and even "eating" luncheon, only entering the fray at the last moment. Louis replied by likening the Byzantines to the Midianites and Amalekites of the Old Testament, who were "like locusts for multitude" (Judges 7:12):

> As for your people, they looked just like swarming-insects [*bruchi*] for their multitude [*prae multitudine*], and gave their first attack just like locusts [*locustae*]. This is because they gave all their effort in the first push, and then, overcome by their own cowardliness, they were at once broken, and in the fashion of locusts no sooner had they jumped forward, than they immediately fell back, as if exhausted by the work of flying. In that sense, true, they were not "looking on," nor "eating," but they were not waging war either, at least not in any way that might show signs of victory. Rather, they scuttled back with automatic and secretive motion, and retreated unhelpfully, having taken several captives, and against the Christians' interests, back to their own places.[160]

In the end, Louis II insisted, it was the less numerous but more disciplined Franks who took Bari "with divine assistance." "And why should you marvel at their paucity, if they were few in number but still managed to accomplish much good?" Louis added pointedly that his smaller armies had already laid low "a numberless multitude of Saracens" (*innumerata multitudo Sarracenorum*).[161]

Numberlessness was ambivalent. Of some ninety-one occurrences of the phrase "innumerable multitude" (*multitudo innumerabilis*) in a database of Latin sources from the sixth century to the tenth, about 43 percent describe impious or dangerous crowds. Of these last, about half were non-Christian others: Saxons, Saracens, Jews. Some 16 percent were used neutrally of armies, nonhuman crowds, or populations, and 41 percent describe holy or pious multitudes.[162] For all the slurs against the inhuman numbers of barbarians, power and divine approval also abided in crowd size. Thietmar of Merseberg relates a telling story from the early eleventh century. After a Saracen army had been rebuffed by papal forces, the "king of the Saracens" threateningly sent the pope a sack of chestnuts, to show how many men he intended to send against the Christians. Pope Benedict VIII (r. 1012–24) responded by sending back a bag of millet, warning that the Saracens would meet "as many armored men or more" as there was grain in the bag.[163] The multiplying gaze could be an insult, but sometimes it was a boast.

The Madding Crowd

The rage-mad mob, which targets an individual, place, or group with contagious violence, is among the more durable negative topoi of collective behavior.[164] It is the bane of social scientists, who have questioned its empirical veracity.[165] But the stereotype of the irrational crowd is age-old. Aside from innumerable classical examples (see chapter 1), the stoning of the Protomartyr Stephen (Acts 7:54–8:2) and the attempt of the silversmiths of Ephesus to persecute the Christians (Acts 19:23–41) provided influential biblical models of collective fury.

The madding crowd was less frequent in early medieval texts, but it was not absent. At the end of the sixth century, Gregory of Tours, with quiet approval, depicted furious mobs murdering or attempting to murder tax collectors.[166] In the ninth century, Agobard of Lyon described a crowd of deluded rustics that had attacked a man the people believed had fallen from an air ship from "Magonia."[167] Northerners enjoyed playing up the savagery of Italian factional crowds. When Pope Leo III (r. 795–816) was ambushed by his aristocratic enemies in 799 or Pope John VIII (r. 872–82) was hammered to death by his foes, they professed to be scandalized by the mobs that had committed these acts of spiritual parricide.[168]

The madding crowd appeared most commonly in saints' lives, particularly those set in the Roman past or in a missionary context.[169] The backdrop was usually an act of persecution—or persecution averted, when the crowd was turned. An example comes from the *Life of Desiderius of Vienne* (BHL 2148), composed by the Visigothic king Sisebut (r. 612–21). This life of a recently martyred bishop (d. 607) was also a polemic against a branch of the Merovingian dynasty that had sparred with the bishop of Vienne. In the end, Desiderius is stoned to death by a crowd set upon him by King Theuderic II (d. 613) and the king's grandmother Brunhild (d. 613):

> So he spoke, and behold! At once a packed, raving crowd [*caterua*] of madmen advanced, men ruinous and vile in aspect, whose face was pitiless, eyes savage, mien despicable, motion horrid; and they were wicked of mind, in habits depraved, in speech lying, in words obscene, outwardly swollen, inwardly empty, loathsome left and right, poor in good deeds, rich in evil ones, guilty of crimes, enemies of God, friends indeed of the age-old devil, utterly bent on death.[170]

The crowd that stoned Desiderius displays the classic pathologies of the persecuting mob. Raging with criminal emotion, it rushes to accomplish the worst possible deed: the killing of a saint. Its individual participants are indistinct. The monstrous entity, somewhere between plurality and singularity, careens to its members' collective spiritual doom. To be sure, Sisebut's *vita* contained the requisite witness crowds too, in greater number.[171] But the "raving crowd of madmen" plays a decisive role in the polemics of the life: only wicked rulers, like Theuderic and Brunhild, could have set such a crowd upon a saint.[172]

The topos of the persecuting crowd made accusations of crowd madness a potent slur. Nevertheless, the deindividuating, irrational crowd was handled with somewhat less reverence by early medieval authors than had once been the case. In Augustine's Alypius vignette in the *Confessions*, arguably the most famous crowd scene in early Christian literature, the power of the madding crowd had no earthly equal.[173] By contrast, in early medieval representations, the madding crowd was a bit player, ineffectual in the end. An instructive example comes from one of the best-studied early medieval crowd episodes, a famous ninth-century account of an eighth-century massacre at Ravenna.[174]

In his mid-ninth-century history of the archbishops of Ravenna, Agnellus tells a story about a crowd incident early in the 700s. There was a longstanding ritual of the people of Ravenna, allegedly still in practice at the time of writing. On Sundays and the Feast of Peter and Paul, all the different neighborhoods of Ravenna carried out mock battles, not unlike the fight games of high medieval Italian cities. In these brawls, citizens went "wild and mad" (*delirati et insani*), losing reason and letting violence get out of hand.[175] One year, during the archbishopric of Damian (r. 692–708), the inhabitants of one quarter, the Tegurienses, had been on a winning streak that led to several actual deaths; their rivals, the Posturulenses, began to fear for their own survival. "Inspired by the devil," the Posturulenses premeditated the cold-blooded mass murder of the Tegurienses, inviting the men of that district into their homes on the pretext of breaking bread, only to murder them one by one and hide their bodies.[176] As the relatives of the missing citizens lamented, Archbishop Damian commanded the whole city to perform a three-day liturgical procession, reminiscent of Gregory the Great's septiform litany against plague in 590. United in action but divided into distinct troops marching "separately" (*separatim*) "at a stone's throw from one another," the whole people did penance in a microcosm of social order.[177] Damian's well-organized ritual miraculously disclosed the bodies of the victims and restored peace.[178]

The significance of this story has been debated.[179] But most scholars agree that Agnellus meant to draw an important moral about crowds. For Joaquín Martínez Pizarro, among the passage's best interpreters, Agnellus "sets side by side two kinds of solidarity and collective action: the factional spirit of the Posturulenses, which allows them to eliminate their enemies, and the mourning of the entire city under the leadership of the archbishop, which allows them to discover the truth and find the hidden bodies." Pizarro speculated that for Agnellus "the crowd is protean and morally neutral, equally amenable to good and to evil," leaving Christian ritual as the "most powerful weapon" to combat the "unplanned, uncontrolled character of crowd behaviour."[180] Channeling Canetti, Pizarro argued that ordered rituals, like Damian's litany, offer "a weakened, watered-down equivalent of the crowd experience, and by so doing rob the crowd of its distinctive irrationality and power." Here the "open" crowd is harnessed by a "closed" crowd.

This is an elegant reading, but it is possible to see things otherwise. Agnellus's story is not about a stage-managed collective ritual overcoming spontaneous collective violence, but about one stage-managed collective act overcoming another. True, spontaneity plays a role. The ludic brawl gets out of control; a spontaneous outpouring of grief inspires Damian to initiate his litany.[181] But the driving dichotomy is between a carefully planned mass-murder and a carefully planned procession. Canetti's distinction between "open" and "closed" crowds is secondary to the deeper distinctions in Agnellus's tale of dueling organized collectivities: factional versus universal, secret versus open, secular versus ecclesiastical, unjust versus just. In Agnellus's schema, the crowd of murderers is certainly "mad," but in its organization it is just as closed as Damian's citywide collectivities.

The Staged Crowd

As sources of power, resources, and legitimacy for elites, gatherings were most discursively charged in contexts of intra-elite competition.[182] In cases of factional squabble, feud, or aristocratic rebellion, where opposing parties might have the same power to organize gatherings, polemics were needed to separate chaff from wheat. Sometimes writers dredged up topoi about madding crowds, as with Sisebut, or played up the violence of crowds. But the best way to delegitimize a crowd was with an accusation of disingenuity. This had been an old Roman trick.[183] Crowd legitimacy, as we have seen, was rooted in spontaneous unanimity. If an organizer had arranged a feigned collective consensus, this deprived the crowd of mystic virtue.

As Philippe Buc has explored, this was where ritual-in-text became important.[184] "Our" crowds showed the will of the people; "theirs" were the work of conspiratorial stage-management. Gregory of Tours accepted the legitimizing authority of crowd acclamations (*laudes*, *voces*) in several instances.[185] But when Cato the Priest (d. 571), pretender to the bishopric of Clermont, wished to reject a conciliatory offer to renounce his claim to Clermont and become bishop of Tours, Gregory insisted that he had stage-managed a "crowd of paupers" (*multitudo pauperum*) to beg him not to depart.[186] Cato, "having assembled the throng of paupers" (*adunata pauperum caterva*), instructed them to raise a clamor (*clamor*) in his favor: "Why are you abandoning your sons, good father, whom you reared up until now? Who will refresh us with food and drink, if you depart? We ask that you not leave us, we whom you once supported."[187] According to Gregory, the usurper turned to the clergy, saying, "You see you, beloved brothers, how this multitude of the poor [*haec multitudo pauperum*] loves me; I cannot leave them and go with you."[188] Years later, when Gregory himself was bishop of Tours, King Chilperic threatened him with the prospect of staged acclamations of disapproval: "I shall call together the people [*populus*] of Tours and I shall say to them: 'level the slogan [*voceferamini*] against Gregory that he is unjust and gives justice to no human being.'"[189] In reality, all crowd acclamations involved coordination and planning. But Gregory dwelt on such logistics only when he wanted to cast aspersions.

In the factional disputes that fill the pages of the *Liber Pontificalis*, descriptions of unanimous crowds electing legitimate popes are matched by recriminations against the crowds of their rivals. The *Liber Pontificalis* entry for Stephen III (r. 768–72) had to reckon with an unruly election involving three "elected" candidates: Constantine, Philip, and Stephen. The anonymous author undermined the legitimacy of Stephen's rivals by drawing attention to the makeup and numerical insufficiency of their supporters. Constantine was put in power by his brother Toto, duke of Nepi, and their two other brothers, "who gathered both from Nepi itself and other cities of Tuscia a multitude of soldiery [*multitudo exercitus*]" and "a crowd of rustics [*caterva rusticorum*]."[190] He had numbers, but not Romans. Philip, the candidate of Waldipert, received acclamations from "a few [*aliquanti*] Romans" and "a few [*aliquanti*] of the primates of the church and the nobles of the militia."[191] These were the right constituencies, but Waldipert had failed to assemble enough of them. Only Stephen managed to win universal acclaim from the right people: "All the priests and the pinnacle of the clergy and the nobles of the militia and the whole army and the good citizens and a crowd of all the people of Rome, from the greatest to the smallest."[192] One doubts that the actual difference between these three crowds would have been as obvious as the *Liber Pontificalis* pretended.

As we have seen above, most gatherings of a political or religious nature in the early medieval West had to be unspontaneous. The demographic and logistical realities of the period hindered truly spontaneous collective performances. Probably no papal candidate could fill the great public spaces of Rome—the forums, the Lateran, Santa Maria Maggiore, and Saint Peter's—without bringing in supporters from the countryside or the *scholae*. Before Einhard emphasized the miraculous spontaneity of the crowds that gathered before his relics in writing, he guaranteed their physical presence by processing the relics through populated regions and storing them in a busy mill town renamed "Saint City." Early medieval elites knew perfectly well that organization, funds, and planning were necessary for assembling crowds. But this only placed greater value on the fiction of spontaneity and made accusations of stage-management all the more wounding.

Arguably the most important discursive function of the tumultuous crowd was not to condemn its activities, but to obfuscate them. Crowds in discourse were, above all, a tool of plausible deniability. They invoked a vague, imprecise agency, sometimes even implied to be God's will through the blunt instrument of the many. In blaming acts on the crowd, writers cleared themselves or their favorites from responsibility. The *Liber Pontificalis* often wept crocodile tears over crowds that accomplished some nasty but useful task—like the blinding of a rival—in a pope's interest but certainly not at his command.[193] Alcuin professed to be unsuspecting of the "gathering and tumult" that assailed the men of Orléans in Tours one wild Sunday in 801.[194] If the readers of his letters were not persuaded by his implication that these incensed townsfolk were, like the mobs in Gregory of Tours's *Histories* and *Miracles,* God's instruments, he could at least repose in the relative safety of declaring himself and his monks innocent of their crimes.

Non-Elite Collective Resistance

Livy had written that "the nature of the multitude" (meaning "the masses") "is that it either serves in humility or dominates in pride."[195] This once-prominent topos—the rebellious popular crowd—in which the common folk used numbers to "dominate" their proper masters, lost its sway. That marked a difference from old Roman discourse as well as contemporary Byzantine and Islamic discourse, where lynched officials, defaced statues, damaged buildings, and deposed rulers attested to a healthy, living concern for non-elite collective resistance.

Exceptions were treated with vehement disapproval. As we have seen, there were a handful of non-elite collective risings in the early medieval West: an eighth-century peasant revolt in the Asturias, the Stellinga revolts in Saxony in the 840s, and a scattering of urban uprisings—sometimes hard to distinguish from factional disputes—against Italian bishops in the 800s and 900s. Cases of outright non-elite mass resistance were met with outrage: they were "rebellions of slaves," the work of the devil, and motivated by perfidy.[196]

That vehemence is telling. E. P. Thompson argued that part of the eighteenth-century "moral economy of the crowd" was a widespread conviction that the common people were sometimes entitled, when injustice went unanswered, to revolt or riot. The idea that "the men and women in the crowd were informed by the belief that they were defending traditional rights or customs" was "supported by the wider consensus of the community" and even "endorsed" by authorities.[197] Thompson ended his famous essay with a quote from a sheriff who acknowledged the "courage, prudence, justice" and "consistency" of the mobs in 1766.[198] Similar license, or understanding, was granted to non-elite crowds in settings proximate in geography and time to the early medieval West. As we have seen, the Roman world made space for the crowd's moral sentiments; this sensibility lived on in the Byzantine world. Paul Cobb has shown that Arabic writers did not disapprove of mob action when rulers were unjust.[199] In the later medieval West, chroniclers recorded John Ball's dictum—"when Adam delved and Eve span, who was then a gentleman?"—with a mixture of horror and sympathy.[200] But early medieval elites reacted to the few open peasant riots like the heartless Duke of Portland in Thompson's essay, who responded—with an inflexibility that shocked magistrates—to crowds of laborers who saw themselves not as law-breakers, but as citizens justified in "fixing" the price of foodstuffs.[201]

As chapter 3 explored, peasant collective autonomy of all kinds was treated with suspicion. Capitulary legislation against "guilds" has been read as a criticism of any horizontal collective organization.[202] In the drastic case from 859, when a "mixed crowd" of Frankish peasants swore oaths to defend the Seine against the Vikings, only to be killed by their own lords, the annalist conceded that the peasants had, after all, acted "incautiously."[203] As much as early medieval sources pretended to locate political and religious legitimacy in the spontaneous unity of mixed crowds, their sympathy for actual non-elite collective autonomy was limited. On the other hand, peasants were entitled to justice in a collective setting. They were supposed to take their disputes to court. Charlemagne sought to provide venues for common people to achieve justice.[204] Peasants were entitled to gather, but their gatherings were to be carefully and predictably circumscribed.

Responses to "Slantwise Resistance"

If few non-elite gatherings threatened elite power openly in the early Middle Age, many did so indirectly. Socioeconomic domination and religious order relied on repeated physical gatherings.[205] People were encouraged to assemble at courts and shrines, gifts in hand, and warned not to shirk the regular gatherings of orderly society. But if crowds assembled in the wrong place, at the wrong time, or in the wrong way, there were two risks. First, unregulated gatherings disrupted the flow of resources and legitimacy upon which order depended. Second, they weakened the authority of legitimate gatherings.

The most salient early medieval examples have to do with what the sources call "superstition." This was the term for rustic behaviors that were felt to of-fend Christian truth.[206] Crowds drawn to false preachers or dubious relics were set aside for special opprobrium. For Gregory of Tours, a self-declared Christ of Bourges who assembled vast droves of men and women before his death was proof of the impending end of the world.[207] In the 700s, a certain Aldebert claimed that he was an apostle who spoke with angels, selling his own hair and fingernails as relics, and won over a "multitude of simple people." The churchman Boniface found him a lamentable, if useful, foil to his own efforts to assemble Christians into a more perfect union.[208] Early in the ninth century, Bishop Agobard of Lyon (r. 816–34, 837–40) wrote of common folk who credited the duke of Benevento with spreading a cattle-killing dust across the north, leading them to lynch the duke's supposed agents. Agobard gave advice to the bishop of Uzès when crowds moved by "unreasoning fear" brought gifts to flailing individuals. Agobard's successor Amolo (r. 841–52) wrote a lengthy letter to a suffragan ordering him to put down wild gatherings of people "and women especially" who were flailing in front of untested relics at Saint Bénigne in Dijon and other sites in the region.[209]

An especially famous case from 847 is the Thiota affair.[210] Thiota was a "pseudo-prophetess" from Alemania who "disturbed" (*turbaverat*) the region around Constance by preaching the end of the world and other holy secrets. "For this reason," reported the *Annals of Fulda*, "many of the common folk of either sex, prompted by fear, came to her and offered her gifts and commended themselves to her prayers; and, what is worse, men of holy orders followed her as if she were a teacher sent from heaven, in so doing casting aside church teachings." Thiota was dragged before a synod of bishops, flogged publicly until she confessed "that a certain priest had fed her these [prophecies] and that she had said these things for the sake of gain."[211] A similar affair took place twenty years later, when two priests from Saxony, dressed as monks, lured crowds to their side: "A great multitude of the local people flowed to them, both rich and even poor, bringing diverse gifts." Once again, episcopal intervention put an end to these gift-bearing multitudes.[212]

What "disturbed" elites so much about these events was not their outlandishness but their similarity to approved gatherings.[213] Crowds were encouraged to seek out new relics and bring them gifts. People were supposed to perform penance en masse. "Satan transforms himself into an angel of light" (2 Corinthians 11:14), warned Amolo to his suffragan in the case of the flailing women, and what made these crowds so dangerous was their apparent validity.[214] Anthropologists of the US-Mexican border have called this dynamic "slantwise resistance": when individuals mean only to get by, but when ruling elites see their behavior as threatening authority.[215] In written propaganda, early medieval authorities used four tools of delegitimation against this kind of indirect threat. First, they highlighted the rusticity or superstitiousness of the crowd. Second, they emphasized that fear motivated gatherings. Third, they emphasized female involvement. Fourth, they targeted the giving of gifts.

All these things, on their own, could be licit in crowds. Non-elites were supposed to participate in gatherings. The fear of God was the beginning of wisdom. Women were strongly encouraged to participate in the cult of relics—if not to give sermons like Thiota. Without the gifts, dues, taxes, and tithes paid in gatherings across contexts, early medieval society would have fallen apart. As with accusations of staging, these methods of delegitimating crowds were hypocritical. But they show how the written word neutralized threats posed by collective behavior. They were, in a sense, discursive mercenaries. The crowd no longer bore the stigma of the Roman-era mob. Polemics against rustics, the illegitimacy of unreasoning fear, misogyny, and criticism of filthy lucre were discursive tools for wrenching crowds out of their default respectability. In the long run, some of these negative traits attached themselves permanently to the crowd as concept. In particular, the linkage between misogyny and bad crowds was to have a long afterlife.

Epilogue: Into the Eleventh Century

The first part of this chapter argued that the commonplaces that typified the literary representation of the early medieval crowd reinforced links between crowds and legitimacy. Particularly during the Carolingian period, the predominance of what Canetti termed a "closed" or controlled crowd permitted this representational regime to flourish.[216] Yet if the Carolingian era really was a golden age for the "closed crowd," this rested on more than the thinness of populations and the power of ideology, or even on the crafty might of the written word. When crowds assembled in the wrong place or at the wrong time, elites turned to new polemics, emphasizing the rustic or female qualities of dangerous crowds. They sometimes went further. "If some should happen to appear more obstinate in a case of this nature, it seems to us they should be compelled, coerced by very harsh blows, to confess the truth," Amolo wrote.[217] Even then, repeated patterns of good crowds informed the victims of such blows what the "truth" was.

By the early eleventh century, however, the demographic regime that had prevailed for a half-millennium was changing. Some of these changes must have been underfoot by the tenth century, as Marc Bloch suspected long ago.[218] Demographic growth in the aggregate seems now to have begun as early as plague's ravages ebbed. But the single most significant demographic change of this period was the "décollage urbain," the takeoff of larger towns and cities.[219] Towns and cities with a markedly "urban" character were agglomerating both in the North Sea trade zone and in the Mediterranean after

1000.²²⁰ In light of this development, Moore's "appearance of the crowd" on the eleventh-century "public stage," which also meant the return of a much more ambivalent if not negative portrayal of the crowd, is not surprising.²²¹ Spectacular new collective forms exploded onto the scene: the great fairs of Champagne, the heretical gatherings at Orléans and Arras that terrified bishops in France, the mass armed pilgrimages that came to be known as Crusades, and the huge outdoor sermons that inspired them.²²² It was in the first decades of the eleventh century that the initial signs appeared of a violent new mass persecution of the Jews of Western Europe.²²³

All of this coincided with a change in representational patterns. To be sure, certain elements of the early medieval depiction of crowds remained intact. Hagiography long continued to depict witness crowds on the model of the New Testament's masses.²²⁴ An early sign of change, however, may be the proliferation of concerns about unregulated military bands or gangs in clerical historians of the tenth century.²²⁵ The rémois historians of tenth-century France, Flodoard and Richer, tell gruesome stories about private entourages conducting illicit feuds.²²⁶ Seditious or violent crowds appear in saints' lives with greater frequency.²²⁷ By the high Middle Ages, the motif of the riotous crowd storming a palace became a staple of courtly literature.²²⁸

There is one other sign of changing attitudes to crowds around the end of the tenth and the beginning of the eleventh century: a new interest in solitude. Solitude had long been considered a spiritual virtue, and the twelfth century especially saw new expressions of virtuosic solitude.²²⁹ Perhaps this had something to do with the dangers that urban life posed for those under religious vows. The late eleventh-century preacher and hermit Rainald of the Melinais feared for the moral safety of urban monks, who might be drawn into sin by the sounds of urban crowds—particularly the songs or chatter of women.²³⁰ Rainald himself ended his life as a solitary.²³¹

The practice of solitary mass, in which priests performed the sacrament of the Eucharist by themselves, meant that the liturgical crowd of participants could be excluded even from the central collective rite of the Christian church. Eleventh- and twelfth-century commentators had to make sense of the plural language in the liturgy of the mass, as priests performed this popular new practice of solitary masses in larger numbers.²³² A line in Hrotsvit's drama *Pafnutius* speaks to the growing importance of sacred solitude as early as the tenth century. Pafnutius is on his way to see Thaïs, the famous prostitute, when he encounters a small group of *iuvenes* or "youths." They mistrustfully exchange information, and the young men show Thaïs's residence to Pafnutius. "If you'd like, we could come along with you," they tell him. "I'd prefer to go alone," he replies.²³³ Pafnutius's response probably provoked a smile ("as you please," respond the *iuvenes*), but it is also programmatic in the drama. Hrotsvit's play is about a man of solitude rescuing a woman bound to the crowd (in this case, a crowd of men) by bringing her into a long eremitical solitude, a pious inversion of usual comic narratives derived from Terence.[234] There was an easy road from solitude-as-noble-spiritual-virtue to solitude-as-object-of-aesthetic-interest.

Yet both spiritual and aesthetic solitude must have been shaped by the changes in collective life that accompanied demographic expansion from the tenth century into the eleventh century. Might the praise of solitude in eleventh- and twelfth-century poetry reflect the new, sometimes frightening forms of gathering that emerged after the year 1000? In language that builds on the Song of Songs, one of the most beautiful poems from the Cambridge Songs (in fact, probably compiled in the Rhineland sometime in the tenth century) depicts the voice of a woman delighting in lonely woods. There were perhaps always early medieval women and men who "fled the crowd," but this sentiment was the harbinger of a new age:[235]

Ego fui sola in silua
et dilexi loca secreta
fugique frequentius turbam
atque plebis cateruam.[236]

I have been alone in the forest
And I have loved hidden places
And often have I fled the crowd.
And the throng of the people.

Conclusion

The Crowd in the Early Middle Ages

For nearly a half millennium after the year 500, the crowd was a scarce resource in Europe. Only after centuries of jagged demographic recovery did the European crowd assume a form more familiar to modern historiography. By the eleventh century, crowds as vehicles for popular expression again proliferated, in Moore's words, "on the stage of public events."[1] The century ended with one of the most astounding mass movements in world history. Europeans in their thousands—if not, as the Byzantine princess Anna Komnene believed, migrating all at once like locusts in a single body—trekked to the Holy Land on the armed mass pilgrimage that would later be called the First Crusade.[2]

Crowds did not disappear between the Fall of Rome and the march on Jerusalem. The crowd, despite demographic decline and a concomitant breakdown in the spontaneity of gatherings, remained a force in the economic, social, and cultural life of the early Middle Ages. After the end of Roman rule in the West, physical gatherings formed less readily, but collective behavior and its representations regulated labor, rituals, and institutions. The agrarian economy gave structure to a regular calendar of gatherings for field work, harvesting, day labor, and building projects. Church spaces allowed bishops and abbots to inscribe visions of order and hierarchy onto pious gatherings. Religious councils invoked the legitimacy of orderly numbers to justify decisions. Politics remained an affair of mass acclamations and solemn assemblies, even if rulers now had to be sure to schedule these rituals at opportune times and places. Gatherings were as essential as they had ever been.

But there were changes in how crowds worked and were perceived. Ancient Latin words for all kinds of collectivities (*turba, caterva, contio, multitudo, populus, vulgus*) still populated early medieval chronicles, saints' lives, law books, poems, and liturgical texts, but their meanings altered. New "crowds" emerged, many of them invisible and abstract. Abbots eager to reinforce networks of prayers and resources commissioned virtual crowds in name-lists of spiritual brothers and sisters. Artists decorated walls and manuscripts with isocephalic multitudes. Litanies in church and in outdoor processions filled sacred spaces with crowds of saints and angels. A striking reflection of the period is the fact that, by the tenth century, after decades of additions, the confraternity book of Reichenau contained a human multitude—38,232 names—more populous than any Western Christian city.[3]

This book has proceeded under the assumption that it is possible to speak historically of an early medieval crowd regime. This is not to deny the diversity of the early medieval crowd. "The crowd" in the intentionally broad sense adopted by this book stands for a bewildering variety of gatherings, real and imagined, from disorderly brawling to hierarchical assembly. The survival of urbanism in southern Europe—however attenuated—meant that the crowd remained a more turbulent force in places like Italy, Southern Gaul, and Spain than in the transalpine North. Assemblies worked in different ways from community to community.[4] Moreover, there were significant changes over time. The most important was the shift from a sixth- to eighth-century decentralized regime of agrarian exploitation to a more intensive one in the Carolingian and post-Carolingian periods.[5] This hardened elite attitudes toward horizontal collaboration, to the point that by the ninth century elites more readily expressed hostility toward non-elite gatherings. That did not equal the vehement ochlophobia of eleventh- and twelfth-century writers, but it was a step on the road to the crowd culture of the high Middle Ages.

Despite synchronic and diachronic diversity, however, it is possible to sketch an ideal type encompassing the economic, sociopolitical, and discursive matrix of gatherings in post-Roman Europe. Not only did a combination of demographic thinning and Roman legacy prevail across the West, but there was a surprising degree of cultural cohesion. Connectivity was weaker than it had been in Roman times, but trade, war, diplomacy, and Christian culture united Western Europe—all the more so after 800. Elites, traders, pilgrims, religious authorities, and ambassadors experienced both the seasonal assemblies of the north and the urban crowds of the south.

Crowds in early medieval Europe exhibited three key characteristics. First, they posed logistical challenges. Second, they were seen as inherently legitimizing. Third, negative associations about them withered, though they did not vanish. Urban violence remained a feature of cities like Rome, Ravenna, Milan, and Naples, even if this could not compare to the urban turmoil of the later Middle Ages.[6] But collective behavior and its representation in this half millennium were different from what came before and after. Between Christian values and new physical realities, elites abandoned old prejudices against mobs. This was a distinctive chapter of crowd history.

The preceding pages examined the early medieval crowd's distinctiveness on several levels. The size, density, and carrying capacities of crowds in the early medieval West were reduced. Early medieval gatherings depended on temporary agglomerations of populations, and so became less spontaneous and more seasonally dependent. That does not mean there were fewer crowds, or that crowds ceased to play a role in socioeconomic push and pull. In the countryside, gatherings remained essential to labor, risk management, and spirituality. By refusing to participate in resource-extracting or celebratory crowds, peasants voted with their feet against secular and ecclesiastical lords. Late antique urban crowd spaces (circuses, theaters, baths, colonnades) gave way to new gathering sites in a mix of enclosed and open-air spaces, such as assemblies (from village gatherings to church councils), hunts, war-bands and armies, and political ceremonies. Although Roman entertainment venues lost their importance, early medieval people still had regular, seasonal venues to shape expectations for how gatherings ought to function.

The result was the shift in the meaning of collectivity in early medieval Latin and vernacular sources. Technical and connotative distinctions in ancient words for crowds became attenuated. Influenced by the Latin Bible and early Christian texts, writers tended to imagine the crowd as a witnessing phenomenon or even a kind of miracle. Crowds conformed to clichés and type scenes of witness or affirmation repeated in saints' lives, histories, liturgy, and poetry. The default crowd was now positive and legitimizing. The *turba*, the *populus*, the *multitudo*, and the *caterva* all conjured up ordered, hierarchical assemblies. Not only in political and religious ritual, but also in visual culture, the early medieval crowd enjoyed default prestige. Of course, elites did not always find crowds so congenial in reality. But now, when crowds were "bad," they had to be marked with *other* symbols of illicitness: rusticity, foreignness, femininity. The crowd itself was no longer a byword for danger and disorder on its own. Crowds could still be sullied discursively, and often had to be, but this sullying had to come from the outside.

The early medieval crowd was both a scarce resource and a tool of social control. In some respects, the early Middle Ages was an age of "closed" and not of "open" crowds, in Canetti's terminology.[7] Organization prevailed over spontaneity. This does not mean that crowds never arose spontaneously or served the interests of social dissolution. The risk of both intra-elite conflict and nonelite resistance kept the crowd dangerous. Elites exercised vigilance against crowds that did not conform to their visions of hierarchical order. Yet it was disruption of collective order, rather than outright collective resistance, that became the most effective and feared weapon of dissent. Precisely because the crowd was inherently a weapon of the strong, it became vulnerable to nonparticipation, participation against the grain, and discursive second-guessing.

This crowd regime emerged not only because of material factors tending to circumscribe spontaneous assembly—demographic decline, the weakening of urbanism, logistical decentralization—but also because the early Middle Ages refused to let go of the Roman past. Visigothic, Lombard, Frankish, and Insular elites remained bound up with the Roman world and its logic. Ancient associations between mass acclamation and authority, combined with "Germanic" ones about collective legitimacy, meant that the crowd never lost its social utility in mediating conflict or promoting one's power. Engagement with Christian tradition led early medieval people to see the crowd all the more as a manifestation of divinely approved authority.

Ramifications

Three wider conclusions can be drawn from these findings. First, the history of crowds illuminates the early Middle Ages (c. 500–1000) as a coherent period of European history. Second, it offers a fuller picture of the subsequent history of collective behavior in the European Middle Ages. Third, it challenges some of the guiding assumptions of crowd studies in history and in other social scientific fields.

The Early Middle Ages

For crowds as for other phenomena, the early Middle Ages had one foot in antiquity and one foot in a new world. By approaching "the crowd" both as a physical phenomenon (the "gathering") and as subject of discourse, I have tried to emphasize that a focus on either continuity or collapse obscures this period's significance in European history. The early medieval crowd regime emerged precisely where material change met cultural tenacity.[8] Its distinctness was a result of that clash of fire and ice.

The history of demography, central to the present study, is the most important case in point. This book has argued that demography mattered in the making of the early Middle Ages. The thinning out of European populations at the beginning of the early medieval period underpinned the shift in crowd culture. Unfortunately, demographic decline is easily associated with immiseration and civilizational decay, or, alternately, with the supposed benefits of smaller, face-to-face populations.[9] Such crypto-normative concerns are misleading. Population decline ushered in new economic and cultural game rules, but it did not make for a better or worse society.

In particular, the fate of cities shaped the new social role of crowds. This pushes against some efforts to dethrone the city in framing the early Middle Ages. Two decades ago, Peregrine Horden and Nicholas Purcell argued that scholars of Mediterranean history should disown cities as "a particularly helpful category."[10] For them "the town" and "the city" were so intrinsically part of ecological history that it made no sense to separate urbanism from environmental history.[11] More recently, Bonnie Effros has called for historians to "abandon scholarly attachment to the elegant vision of urban life and trade as a measure of premodern civilization."[12] There are good reasons to dethrone the city (and its luxuries) from our grand narratives, but for the story at the heart of this book, the loss of cities made a difference. True, the majority of the premodern European population—before, during, and after the early Middle Ages-—inhabited the countryside.[13] True, urbanism endured and took on new forms.[14] But the shrinking of cities, c. 500–1000, clarifies to a considerable degree why crowds worked so differently.

At the same time, that history only makes sense with respect to Roman continuities. From the perspective of the very *longue durée*, the population of western Europe had not reached its "nadir" in the seventh century, even on the most "catastrophist" reading of post-Roman demographic decline. Instead, in terms of the density of urban settlement, conditions in the western Mediterranean and northwestern Europe were probably close to what they had been in the centuries before the Roman period.[15] The difference was that rulers and cultural brokers within these societies were bound up with the Roman world. The significance accorded to the crowd by the New Testament—originally Greek texts produced by Jews of the Levant—became the prism through which even British kings viewed the crowd. The isocephalic crowds of early medieval art built on ancient and late antique precursors. The *adventus* in its episcopal and royal forms drew directly on the late imperial entry. The very language of crowds in the written records—the treasury of Latin words that underwent semantic transformation—was a Roman inheritance. This early medieval engagement with the "resources of the past" meant that rupture was never complete.[16] It is this mix of material transformation and cultural atavism that makes the early Middle Ages the early Middle Ages.

The Later Middle Ages

The collective forms developed in this period lived on into the later Middle Ages. Moore had good reason to signal the eleventh century as a moment of change in the history of crowds.[17] With correspondingly larger towns and cities, and social tensions related to economic disruption and political change, the age of the closed crowd was fated to end. The crowd took on a new shape in a society more accustomed to crowds as vehicles for popular expression and discontent.[18] Yet alongside new high medieval forms of mass gathering—public preaching, crusades, urban ceremonial, factional brawls—and the robust return of negative topoi, early medieval attitudes about crowds lived on, sometimes transformed, just as Roman ones had lived on into the early Middle Ages. As James Norrie has recently explored, that included slantwise uses of collective repertory as a tool of popular self-expression.[19]

The early medieval ceremonial assembly—that "centerpiece" of early medieval politics—set the stage for high medieval parliaments.[20] Notions of representationality in law and politics had their origin in the liturgical and political collective fictions of the Carolingian period.[21] The inquiry "by crowd" became a feature of late medieval French procedural law.[22] In scholastic philosophy, Aristotelian commentators debated the nature of the multitude in ways that built upon the early medieval equivalency between crowds and communities.[23] In saints' lives, hymns, litanies, and many other texts, noble and pious *turbae* were just as ubiquitous as ever.[24] The "good crowd" of the later Middle Ages was often that of the early Middle Ages. Early medieval visions of throngs of angels and saints lived on in later art and literature. In the *Paradiso*, when Dante is overwhelmed by the beauty of celestial crowds, Beatrice tells him he should have expected these orderly throngs. "Non sai tu che tu se' in cielo?" she asks him. "Don't you understand that you're in Heaven?"[25] By the fourteenth century, it was self-evident that Heaven contained throngs of angels arrayed in hierarchical splendor.

The Crowd as Historical Subject

Finally, what can crowds in the early Middle Ages tell us about crowds as a historical subject? The crowd has attracted enormous scholarly and popular interest. We encounter crowds constantly, in history, in the news, on the street, and in our virtual lives. They are implicated in riots, revolutions, protests, elections, and inaugurations, but they are also involved in routine phenomena like shopping, work, and entertainment. Despite their protean forms, however, crowds are often treated as timeless and transhistorical. They are thought to possess mysterious powers to render the normal strange, to alter the psychology of participants, and, above all, to give voice to the voiceless.[26]

The topsy-turvy history of the early medieval crowd offers a reminder that crowds, like other phenomena, are historically contingent. Popular crowd resistance, all too easily naturalized as a transhistorical tool of resistance, emerges in our story as a human institution bounded by demography, political economy, and space. Yet while the early medieval period saw a lower number of riots or peasant revolts, non-elites were able to use nonparticipation or slantwise participation in gatherings as tools of resistance. In other words, the crowd remained a weapon of the weak, but any definition of "the crowd" that limits itself to active, resistant gatherings would overlook that dynamic.

Studying radical differences in how collective behaviors were organized twelve centuries ago may help us refine our own pressing questions about the subject. Are crowds emergent physical phenomena or figures of discourse? Are they a source of agency for the powerless or a force that strips individuals of their freedom? If crowds "flood their subjects with affect," as Victor Turner argued, is this for good or for ill?[27] Should we see them as tools of liberty and emancipation, or as weapons for dictators and demagogues?[28] Can we hold them accountable for their actions?[29]

Anthropologist Mary Douglas once spoke of the "spiky, verbal hedges that arbitrarily insulate one set of human experiences . . . from another."[30] The early medieval history of collective behaviors helps us interrogate our own spiky intuitions about what collective behavior is and should be, both as a historical subject and a present concern. Crowds in the early Middle Ages functioned as they did in no other moment of European history, thanks to a combination of new material possibilities for assembly and an ancient legacy of assumptions about gatherings. Alongside a reminder of the radical contingency of our ideas of collectivity, this subject offers lessons about how societies manage change when demographic and economic realities do not keep time with the course of culture, religion, and politics.

NOTES

Introduction

1. R. Meneghini and R. Santangeli Valenzani, *Roma nell'Altomedioevo: Topografia e urbanistica della città dal V al X secolo* (Rome, 2004), 21–8 (Roman population); K. Hopkins and M. Beard, *The Colosseum* (London, 2005), 112 (Colosseum capacity).

2. For the crowd's "reappearance" after 1000: R. I. Moore, "Family, Community and Cult on the Eve of the Gregorian Reform," *Transactions of the Royal Historical Society*, 6th ser., 30 (1980): 49–69, at 49; R. I. Moore, "The Weight of Opinion: Religion and the People of Europe From the Tenth to the Twelfth Century," in *Making Early Medieval Societies: Conflict and Belonging in the Latin West, 300–1200*, ed. K. Cooper and C. Leyser (Cambridge, 2016), 202–19, at 214–16; G. Dickson, "Medieval Christian Crowds and the Origins of Crowd Psychology," *Revue d'histoire ecclésiastique* 95 (2000): 54–75, at 58–59; G. Constable, *The Reformation of the Twelfth Century* (Cambridge, 1996), 301; Charles W. Connell, *Popular Opinion in the Middle Ages: Channeling Public Ideas and Attitudes* (Berlin, 2016), 62–72.

3. Epilogue: Bryan Ward-Perkins, *From Classical Antiquity to the Middle Ages* (Oxford, 1984), 116–18. Preface: Moore, "Family, Community and Cult," 49; compare Moore, "Weight of Opinion," 208–10. Romedio Schmitz-Esser, "Bestrafung des Leichnams zur Purifizierung der Christenheit? Der Ursprung der Verbrennungsstrafe an Häretikern und Hexen im Früh- und Hochmittelalter und sein Verhältnis zum Reliquienkult," *Frühmittelalterliche Studien* 44 (2010): 227–63, at 235–39, makes a similar observation.

4. Harvesters: Gregory of Tours, *Liber in gloria confessorum*, c. 1, ed. Bruno Krusch, MGH SRG 1.2, revised ed. (Hanover, 1969), 298–99. Port: Annemarieke Willemsen, "Dorestad, a Medieval Metropolis," in *From One Sea to Another: Trading Places in the European and Mediterranean Early Middle Ages*, ed. Sauro Gelichi and Richard Hodges (Turnhout, 2012), 65–80, at 70. Populace and count: Gregory of Tours, *Historiae*, 6.8, ed. B. Krusch and W. Levison, MGH SRM 1.1 (Hanover, 1951), 278. Bishop and child: Stephen of Auxerre [fl. late sixth century], *Vita S. Amatoris Ep. Autissiodorensis* (BHL 356), c. 22, AASS Mai 1.1.57A. Abbess and nuns: Rudolf of Fulda [ninth century], *Vita Leobae abbatissae Biscofesheimensis* (BHL 4845), c. 12, ed. Georg Waitz, MGH SS 15.1 (Hanover, 1887), 126–27. Assembly: Hincmar of Reims [ninth century], *De ordine palatii*, c. 6, ed. T. Gross and R. Schieffer, MGH Font. iur. Germ. 3, 2nd ed. (Hanover, 1980), 82–90. Hunt: *Karolus Magnus et Leo Papa* [late eighth century], lines 159–64, ed. H. Beumann, F. Brunhölzl, and W. Winkelmann, *Karolus Magnus et Leo Papa: Ein paderborner Epos vom Jahre 799* (Paderborn, 1966), 70. Bath: Einhard, *Vita Karoli* [ninth century], ed. O. Holder-Egger, MGH SRG 25 (Munich, 1911), 27. Prayer in church: Jean Deshusses, ed., *Missa sanctae Mariae*, in *Le sacramentaire grégorien: Ses principales formes d'après les plus anciens manuscrits*, 2nd ed. (Fribourg, 1988), vol. 2, no. 10, 45. Relics: Amolo of Lyon, *Epistolae*, Ep. 1, ed. Ernst Dümmler, MGH Epp 5, 363–68. Rival candidates: *Vita Hadriani II*, LP 2, no. 108, c. 14, 176. Papal acclamations: AH 27, no. 184, 260. Angels and saints: AH 7, no. 118, 132. Cf. B. Krusch and W. Levison, eds., *Vita Sadalbergae abbatissae Laudunensis* (BHL 7463), c. 14, MGH SRM 5 (Hanover, 1910), 58, for an

"angelic crowd" (*angelica turba*). "Multitudes, multitudes": Joel 3:14, ed. Weber-Gryson, 1387. For a mid-ninth-century exegesis of this passage, see Haimo of Halberstadt, *In Joel prophetam*, c. 3, PL 117, col. 106.

5. Shane Bobrycki, "The Flailing Women of Dijon: Crowds in Ninth-Century Europe," *Past & Present* 240 (2018): 3–46, at 7–8.

6. The literature is vast. For a representative (Anglophone) sample: Ervand Abrahamian, "The Crowd in Iranian Politics 1905–1953," *Past & Present* 41 (1968): 184–210; Ervand Abrahamian, "The Crowd in the Persian Revolution," *Iranian Studies* 2 (1969): 128–50; Thomas Africa, "Urban Violence in Imperial Rome," *Journal of Interdisciplinary History* 2 (1971): 3–21; Shimon Applebaum, "The Zealots: The Case for Revaluation," *The Journal of Roman Studies* 61 (1971): 155–70; Herbert Atherton, "The 'Mob' in Eighteenth-Century English Caricature," *Eighteenth-Century Studies* 12 (1978): 47–58; Margaret Aston, "Corpus Christi and Corpus Regni: Heresy and the Peasants' Revolt," *Past & Present* 143 (1994): 3–47; William Beik, "The Violence of the French Crowd from Charivari to Revolution," *Past & Present* 197 (2007): 75–110; Alastair Bellany, "The Murder of John Lambe: Crowd Violence, Court Scandal and Popular Politics in Early Seventeenth-Century England," *Past & Present* 200 (2008): 37–76; David Blackbourn, *Marpingen: Apparitions of the Virgin Mary in a Nineteenth-Century German Village* (New York, 1994); Nicholas Brooks, "The Organization and Achievements of the Peasants of Kent and Essex in 1381," in *Studies in Medieval History Presented to R.H.C. Davis*, ed. H. Mayr-Harting and R. I. Moore (London, 1985), 247–70; Peter Brunt, "The Roman Mob," *Past & Present* 35 (1966): 3–27; Juan Cole, "Of Crowds and Empires: Afro-Asian Riots and European Expansion, 1857–1882," *Comparative Studies in Society and History* 31 (1989): 106–33; Juan Cole, *Colonialism and Revolution in the Middle East* (Princeton, NJ, 1993); Edward Countryman, "The Problem of the Early American Crowd," *Journal of American Studies* 7 (1973): 77–90; Robert C. Davis, *The War of the Fists: Popular Culture and Public Violence in Late Renaissance Venice* (Oxford, 1994); Amina Elbendary, *Crowds and Sultans: Urban Protest in Late Medieval Egypt and Syria* (Cairo, 2015); Manfred Gailus, "Food Riots in Germany in the Late 1840s," *Past & Present* 145 (1994): 157–93; Myra Glenn, "It's a Riot! Mob Violence in Antebellum America," *Reviews in American History* 27 (1999): 210–17; Ruth Harris, "Possession on the Borders: The 'Mal De Morzine' in Nineteenth-Century France," *The Journal of Modern History* 69 (1997): 451–78; Mark Harrison, "The Ordering of the Urban Environment: Time, Work and the Occurrence of Crowds 1790–1835," *Past & Present* 110 (1986): 134–68; Benjamin Heller, "The 'Mene Peuple' and the Polite Spectator: The Individual in the Crowd at Eighteenth-Century London Fairs," *Past & Present* 208 (2010): 131–57; Steve Hindle, "Imagining Insurrection in Seventeenth- Century England: Representations of the Midland Rising of 1607," *History Workshop Journal* 66 (2008): 21–61; Cemal Kafadar, "Janissaries and Other Riffraff of Ottoman Istanbul: Rebels without a Cause?," in *Identity and Identity Formation in the Ottoman World: A Volume of Essays in Honor of Norman Itzkowitz*, ed. Baki Tezcan and Karl K. Barbir, 113–34 (Madison, WI, 2007); Christian D. Liddy, "Urban Enclosure Riots: Risings of the Commons in English Towns, 1480–1525," *Past & Present* 226 (2015): 41–77; Colin Lucas, "The Crowd and Politics Between 'Ancien Regime' and Revolution in France," *The Journal of Modern History* 60 (1988): 421–57; Pauline Maier, "Popular Uprisings and Civil Authority in Eighteenth-Century America," *The William and Mary Quarterly*, 3rd ser., 27 (1970): 3–35; Mischa Meier, "Die Inszenierung einer Katastrophe: Justinian und der Nika-Aufstand," *Zeitschrift für Papyrologie und Epigraphik* 117 (2003): 273–300; M. Meyers, "Feminizing Fascist Men: Crowd Psychology, Gender, and Sexuality in French Antifascism, 1929–1945," *French Historical Studies* 29 (2006): 109–42; Philip D. Morgan, "Conspiracy Scares," *The William and Mary Quarterly*, 3rd ser., 59 (2002): 159–66; Rosemary Morris, "The Powerful and the Poor in Tenth-Century Byzantium: Law and Reality," *Past & Present* 73 (1976): 3–27; J. B. Peires, "'Soft' Believers and 'Hard' Unbelievers in the Xhosa Cattle-Killing," *The Journal of African History* 27 (1986): 443–61; Christine Poggi, "'Folla / Follia': Futurism and the Crowd," *Critical*

Inquiry 28 (2002): 709–48; Donald Richter, "The Role of Mob Riot in Victorian Elections, 1865–1885," *Victorian Studies* 15 (1971): 19–28; George Rudé, "English Rural and Urban Disturbances on the Eve of the First Reform Bill, 1830–1831," *Past & Present* 37 (1967): 87–102; William Sachse, "The Mob and the Revolution of 1688," *The Journal of British Studies* 4 (1964): 23–40; Jan Marco Sawilla, "On Histories, Revolutions, and the Masses: Visions of Asymmetry and Symmetry in German Social Sciences," in *Asymmetrical Concepts after Reinhart Koselleck: Historical Semantics and Beyond*, ed. Kay Junge and Kirill Postoutenko (Bielefeld, 2011), 165–96; Buchanan Sharp, "The Food Riots of 1347 and the Medieval Moral Economy," in *Moral Economy and Popular Protest: Crowds, Conflicts and Authority*, ed. Adrian Randall and Andrew Charlesworth (New York, 2000), 33–54; Brent D. Shaw, "Bandits in the Roman Empire," *Past & Present* 105 (1984): 3–52; Gregory Shaya, "The Flâneur, the Badaud, and the Making of a Mass Public in France, Circa 1860–1910," *The American Historical Review* 109 (2004): 41–77; Robert Shoemaker, "The London 'Mob' in the Early Eighteenth Century," *The Journal of British Studies* 26 (1987): 273–304; Geoffrey Sumi, "Power and Ritual: The Crowd at Clodius' Funeral," *Historia: Zeitschrift für alte Geschichte* 46 (1997): 80–102; Caroline Sumpter, "The Cheap Press and the 'Reading Crowd,'" *Media History* 12 (2006): 233–52; E. A. Thompson, "Peasant Revolts in Late Roman Gaul and Spain," *Past & Present* 2 (1952): 11–23; Charles Tilly, "Major Forms of Collective Action in Western Europe 1500–1975," *Theory and Society* 3 (1976): 365–75; Charles Tilly, *Social Movements, 1768–2004* (Boulder, CO, 2004); Alexandra Walsham, "'The Fatall Vesper': Providentialism and Anti-Popery in Late Jacobean London," *Past & Present* 144 (1994): 36–87; Dale Williams, "Morals, Markets and the English Crowd in 1766," *Past & Present* 104 (1984): 56–73; Gordon Wood, "A Note on Mobs in the American Revolution," *The William and Mary Quarterly*, 3rd ser., 23 (1966): 635–42; Madeline Zilfi, "The Kadizadelis: Discordant Revivalism in Seventeenth-Century Istanbul," *Journal of Near Eastern Studies* 45 (1986): 251–69. See also the essays in J. Schnapp and M. Tiews, eds., *Crowds* (Stanford, 2006), and those collected in Michael T. Davis, ed, *Crowd Actions in Britain and France from the Middle Ages to the Modern World* (London, 2015).

7. The *Oxford English Dictionary* lists the following meanings: (1) "1a. A large number of persons gathered so closely together as to press upon or impede each other; a throng, a dense multitude"; "1b. spec. A mass of spectators; an audience"; "1c. A collection of actors playing the part of a crowd; freq. attrib."; (2, *trans.*) "2a. A large number (of persons) contemplated in the mass"; "2b. The people who throng the streets and populous centres; the masses; the multitude"; "2c. orig. U.S. A company; 'set', 'lot'. colloq."; "2d. colloq. A military unit"; "2 e. Colloq. phr. to pass (muster) in a crowd, not to fall so short of the standard as to be noticed; not to be conspicuously below the average (freq. with the implication of mediocrity)"; (3, *trans.* and *fig.*) "3a. A great number of things crowded together, either in fact or in contemplation; a large collection, multitude"; "3b. Naut. crowd of sail: an unusual number of sails hoisted for the sake of speed; a press of sail"; along with compounds (some now more or less out of use) such as the nouns: "crowd-control"; "crowd-mind"; "crowd-morality"; "crowd-panic"; "crowd-pleaser"; "crowd-poison" and "crowd-poisoning"; "crowd-psychology"; "crowd-suggestion"; the adjectives: "crowd-drawing"; "crowd-pleasing"; "crowd-pulling"; and expressions with the definite article *the* ("the crowd"): "a. The direction or option favoured by common opinion; the prevailing view in a group, or in society in general; the majority. Freq. in to follow the crowd, to go with (also against) the crowd, and similar phrases"; "b. In phrases expressing distinction or difference from the general run of people or things, esp. in a particular category, as to stand out from the crowd, to set (a person) apart from the crowd, etc. Usually with positive connotations."

8. *Oxford English Dictionary*, s.v. "crowd, n.3" (definition 1a).
9. Elias Canetti, *Masse und Macht* (Düsseldorf, 1978), 12–14.
10. Prominent examples include Charles MacKay, Cesare Lombroso, Scipio Sighele, Gabriel Le Bon, Gabriel Tarde, Wilfred Trotter, Sigmund Freud, and William McDougall. For a useful

survey, see Michael Gamper, *Masse lesen, Masse schreiben: Eine Diskurs- und Imaginationsgeschichte der Menschenmenge, 1765–1930* (Munich, 2007).

11. Gustave Le Bon, *La psychologie des foules* (Paris, 1894). There is a large literature on Le Bon and his place in nineteenth-century crowd theory. See Robert A. Nye, *The Origins of Crowd Psychology: Gustave Le Bon and the Crisis of Mass Democracy in the Third Republic* (London, 1975); Jaap van Ginneken, *Crowds, Psychology, and Politics, 1871–1899* (Cambridge, UK, 1992); Benoît Marpeau, *Gustave Le Bon: Parcours d'un intellectuel 1841–1931* (Paris, 2000); Jean-François Phelizon, *Relire la psychologie des foules de Gustave Le Bon* (Paris, 2011). Le Bon's influences include Sigmund Freud, *Massenpsychologie und Ich-Analyse* (Vienna, 1921).

12. Le Bon, *Psychologie des foules*, 18: "Mille individus accidentellement réunis sur une place publique sans aucun but déterminé, ne constituent nullement une foule au point de vue psychologique."

13. Le Bon's main (unacknowledged) influence was Scipio Sighele, *La folla delinquente* (Torino, 1891). The second French edition of Sighele's study (the first came out in 1892) opens with a preface drily accusing Le Bon of using but not citing his book: Scipio Sighele, *La foule criminelle, essai de psychologie collective* (Paris, 1901), i. The publisher F. Alcan published several theoretical works on the crowd, including Le Bon, Sighele, and Gabriel Tarde, *L'opinion et la foule* (Paris, 1901).

14. Yvon Thiec, "Gustave Le Bon, prophète de l'irrationalisme de masse," *Revue française de sociologie* 22 (1981): 409–28, at 421–37.

15. Mikhail Bakhtin, *Rabelais and His World*, trans. Hélène Iswolsky (Bloomington, IN, 1984), 5–7.

16. Émile Durkheim, *Les formes élémentaires de la vie religieuse*, 4th ed. (Paris, 1960 [1912]), 308: "Une fois les individus assemblés il se dégage de leur rapprochement une sorte d'électricité qui les transporte vite à un degré extraordinaire d'exaltation."

17. As was noticed by Mary Douglas, *Purity and Danger: An Analysis of Concept of Pollution and Taboo* (London, 2004 [1966]), 25.

18. Arnold van Gennep, *Les rites de passage* (Paris, 1909).

19. Victor Turner, *The Ritual Process: Structure and Anti-Structure* (London, 1969), 132, quote at 128. If "structure" is the social forest of meaning, "communitas" in its "leveling" and "stripping" effects is pure connectedness. Society for Turner is a never-ending process of dialectic between structure (order) and communitas (freedom).

20. See Marvin Harris, "History and Significance of the EMIC / ETIC Distinction," *Annual Review of Anthropology* 5 (1976): 329–50. These names derive from the linguistic distinction phon*emic* / phon*etic*.

21. Emma Cohen et al., "Rowers' High: Behavioural Synchrony Is Correlated with Elevated Pain Thresholds," *Biology Letters* (2009), 1–3, with literature at 2. See also, for heart rate, Dimitris Xygalatas et al., "Quantifying Collective Effervescence: Heart-Rate Dynamics at a Fire-Walking Ritual," *Communicative and Integrative Biology* 4 (2011): 735–38.

22. See the website of the Couzin Lab, an influential research team: https://www.ab.mpg.de /couzin.

23. Adorno also smelled something "phony" in totalitarian crowds: Theodor W. Adorno, "Freudian Theory and the Pattern of Fascist Propaganda," in T. W. Adorno, *Gesammelte Schriften*, vol. 8, *Soziologische Schriften* 1, ed. R. Tiedemann (Frankfurt-am-Main, 1972), 408–33, esp. 430–33.

24. For an extensive overview see: Reinhard Koselleck et al., "Volk, Nation, Nationalismus, Masse," *Geschichtliche Grundbegriffe: Historisches Lexikon zur politisch-sozialen Sprache in Deutschland*, ed. Otto Brunner, Werner Conze, and Reinhart Koselleck (Stuttgart, 1992), vol. 7, 141–431.

25. I borrow "discourse history" from Gamper's subtitle to *Masse lesen, Masse schreiben*. Although "discourse" is indeed "one of the most loosely used terms of our time," it is a useful

shorthand for certain phenomena of mentality history, as Martin Jay, *Downcast Eyes: The Denigration of Vision in Twentieth-Century French Thought* (Berkeley, 1993), 15–16, has helpfully defined it: "Despite . . . contrary and shifting usages, discourse remains the best term to denote the level on which the object of this inquiry is located, that being a corpus of more or less loosely interwoven arguments, metaphors, assertions, and prejudices that cohere more associatively than logically in any strict sense."

26. E. Auerbach, *Mimesis: The Representation of Reality in Western Literature*, trans. W. R. Trask (Princeton, NJ, 1953); E. Auerbach, *Literary Language and Its Public in Late Latin Antiquity and in the Middle Ages*, trans. R. Manheim (New York, 1965).

27. Auerbach, *Literary Language*, 12. For Erich Auerbach's own account of his historicism, see his "Vico and Aesthetic Historism," *The Journal of Aesthetics and Art Criticism* 8 (1949): 110–18.

28. Auerbach, *Mimesis*, 57–60, esp. 60.

29. E.g., Rhiannon Ash, *Ordering Anarchy: Armies and Leaders in Tacitus' Histories* (Ann Arbor, MI, 1999); William D. Barry, "Aristocrats, Orators, and the 'Mob': Dio Chrysostom and the World of the Alexandrians," *Historia* 42 (1993): 82–103; Anthony John Woodman, "Mutiny and Madness: Tacitus *Annals* 1.16–49," *Arethusa* 39 (2006): 303–29.

30. For the logistics of the preachers' crowd, see the essays in Peter Van Moos, ed., *Zwischen Babel und Pfingsten: Sprachdifferenzen und Gesprächsverständigung in der Vormoderne (8.–16. Jahrhundert)* (Berlin, 2008); for one of the most important thirteenth-century preachers, see Antonio Rigon, *Dal libro alla folla: Antonio di Padova e il francescanesimo medioevale* (Rome, 2002); on Dante, see Jonathan Usher, "'Più di mille': Crowd Control in the *Commedia*," in *Word and Drama in Dante: Essays on the Divina Commedia*, ed. John C. Barnes and Jennifer Petrie (Dublin, 1993), 55–71; for a famous late medieval visionary, see Arnold Sanders, "Illiterate Memory and Spiritual Experience: Margery Kempe, the Liturgy, and the 'Woman in the Crowd,'" in *Mindful Spirit in Late Medieval Literature: Essays in Honor of Elizabeth D. Kirk*, ed. B. Wheeler (New York, 2006), 237–48; see too Neil Cartlidge, "The Battle of Shrovetide: Carnival Against Lent as a Leitmotif in Late Medieval Culture," *Viator* 35 (2004): 517–42.

31. Alexander Murray, *Reason and Society in the Middle Ages* (Oxford, 1985), 234–57.

32. Dickson, "Medieval Christian Crowds," 70–74; see also 68–70, for earlier images of bad preachers mesmerizing the crowd. See also Carla Casagrande, "*Sermo Affectuosus*: Passions et éloquence chrétienne," in *Zwischen Babel und Pfingsten: Sprachdifferenzen und Gesprächsverständigung in der Vormoderne (8.–16. Jahrhundert)*, ed. Peter Van Moos (Berlin, 2008), 519–32, at 530–31, for Bacon's critique of preachers who manipulated the crowd.

33. Sara Lipton, *Dark Mirror: The Medieval Origins of Anti-Jewish Iconography* (New York, 2014), 240–81.

34. Joaquín Martínez Pizarro, "Crowds and Power in the *Liber Pontificalis Ecclesiae Ravennatis*," in *The Community, the Family and the Saint: Patterns of Power in Early Medieval Europe*, ed. J. Hill and M. Swann (Turnhout, 1998), 265–83, esp. 271; Hugh Magennis, "Crowd Control? Depictions of the Many in Anglo-Saxon Literature, with Particular Reference to the Old English Legend of the Seven Sleepers," *English Studies* 93 (2012): 119–37.

35. Georges Lefebvre, "Foules révolutionnaires," in G. Lefebvre, *Études sur la Révolution française* (Paris, 1963 [1934]), 371–92.

36. George Rudé, *The Crowd in History: A Study of Popular Disturbances in France and England, 1730–1848*, revised edition (London, 1981 [1964]), 3. On George Rudé, see Nicholas Rogers, "George Rudé (1910–1993)," *Labour* 33 (1994): 9–11. For Rudé's definition put to work, see George Rudé, "English Rural and Urban Disturbances on the Eve of the First Reform Bill, 1830–1831," *Past & Present* 37 (1967): 87–102; George Rudé, "Protest and Punishment in Nineteenth-Century Britain," *Albion: A Quarterly Journal Concerned with British Studies* 5 (1973): 1–23. See also George Rudé, *The Crowd in the French Revolution* (Oxford, 1959).

37. Rudé, *The Crowd in History*, 8–9.

38. Rudé, *The Crowd in History*, 4.

39. Rudé, *The Crowd in History*, 4.

40. As early as 1901, Gabriel Tarde criticized Le Bon for failing to distinguish between face-to-face crowds and virtual publics: Tarde, *L'opinion et la foule*, 11. Twentieth-century American sociologists—Robert Park, Herbert Blumer, and Neil Smelser—produced cathedrals of taxonomy to avoid imprecision. R. E. Park and Herbert Blumer were the founding fathers of the American approach to crowd sociology. See the useful overview by Herbert Blumer, "Collective Behavior," *Review of Sociology: Analysis of a Decade*, ed. J. B. Gittler (New York, 1957): 127–58. For other representative essays, see Herbert G. Blumer, "Social Psychology," in *Man and Society: A Substantive Introduction to the Social Sciences*, ed. Emerson P. Schmidt (New York, 1937), 144–98; Herbert Blumer, "Social Problems as Collective Behavior," *Social Problems* 18 (1971): 298–306. Part of Blumer's contribution was to place analysis of the crowd within the context of other social questions: e.g., Herbert Blumer, "Fashion: From Class Differentiation to Collective Selection," *The Sociological Quarterly* 10 (1969): 275–91; Herbert Blumer, "Public Opinion and Public Opinion Polling," *American Sociological Review* 13 (1948): 542–49. For a positive retrospective of Blumer's contribution, see Clark McPhail, "Blumer's Theory of Collective Behavior: The Development of a Non-Symbolic Interaction Explanation," *The Sociological Quarterly* 30 (1989): 401–23. Rudé makes most use of the American sociologist Neil J. Smelser, *Theory of Collective Behavior* (New York, 1962), who tacked a somewhat different approach. David Schweingruber and Ronald Wohlstein, "The Madding Crowd Goes to School: Myths about Crowds in Introductory Sociology Textbooks," *Teaching Sociology* 33 (2005): 136–53, laments the continued survival of "myths about crowds" despite decades of work.

41. *Past & Present* has traditionally been a leading journal for publications on the history of crowds: E. Abrahamian, "The Crowd in Iranian Politics 1905–1953," *Past & Present* 41 (1968): 184–210; Margaret Aston, "Corpus Christi and Corpus Regni: Heresy and the Peasants' Revolt," *Past & Present* 143 (1994): 3–47; William Beik, "The Violence of the French Crowd from Charivari to Revolution," *Past & Present* 197 (2007): 75–110; Alastair Bellany, "The Murder of John Lambe," *Past & Present* 200 (2008): 37–76; P. A. Brunt, "The Roman Mob," *Past & Present* 35 (1966): 3–27; Manfred Gailus, "Food Riots in Germany in the Late 1840s," *Past & Present* 145 (1994): 157–93; Benjamin Heller, "The 'Mene Peuple' and the Polite Spectator," *Past & Present* 208 (2010): 131–57; Rosemary Morris, "The Powerful and the Poor in Tenth-Century Byzantium," *Past & Present* 73 (1976): 3–27; George Rudé, "English Rural and Urban Disturbances on the Eve of the First Reform Bill, 1830–1831," *Past & Present* 37 (1967): 87–102; Brent D. Shaw, "Bandits in the Roman Empire," *Past & Present* 105 (1984): 3–52; E. A. Thompson, "Peasant Revolts in Late Roman Gaul and Spain," *Past & Present* 2 (1952): 11–23; Alexandra Walsham, "'The Fatall Vesper': Providentialism and Anti-Popery in Late Jacobean London," *Past & Present* 144 (1994): 36–87; Dale Edward Williams, "Morals, Markets and the English Crowd in 1766," *Past & Present* 114 (1987): 200–213. See Moore, "Family, Community and Cult on the Eve of the Gregorian Reform," esp. 50–51; but see also his *The Origins of European Dissent* (New York, 1985). The kind of sources amenable to "bottom-up" social history (especially wage figures) do not emerge in adequate numbers until the fourteenth and fifteenth centuries, for which there is a large literature on peasant and laboring crowds. See especially Christopher Dyer, Peter Coss, and Chris Wickham, eds., *Rodney Hilton's Middle Ages: An Exploration of Historical Themes* (Oxford, 2007). See also, among many others, Peter Arnade, "Crowds, Banners, and the Marketplace: Symbols of Defiance and Defeat During the Ghent War of 1452–1453," *Journal of Medieval and Renaissance Studies* 24 (1994): 471–97; Manuel Sánchez Martínez, "Les revoltes pageses a l'Europa baixmedieval," *L'Avenç* 93 (1986): 22–30; Christine Jéhanno, "L'émeute' du 11 juillet 1497 à l'hôtel-Dieu de Paris: Un récit de violences," in *Violences souveraines au Moyen Âge: Travaux d'une école historique*, ed. F. Foronda, C. Barralis, and B. Sère, 67–77 (Paris, 2010); and Aston, "Corpus Christi and Corpus Regni."

42. E. Hobsbawm, *Labouring Men: Studies in the History of Labour* (New York, 1965); E. Hobsbawm, *Primitive Rebels* (Manchester, 1959); E. Hobsbawm and G. Rudé, *Captain Swing* (London, 1969).

43. Natalie Davis, "The Rites of Violence: Religious Riot in Sixteenth-Century France," *Past & Present* 59 (1973): 53 n. 6, n. 7, n. 8.

44. E. P. Thompson, "The Moral Economy of the English Crowd in the Eighteenth Century," *Past & Present* 50 (1971): 76–136; see also E. P. Thompson, *The Making of the English Working Class* (New York, 1964), 62–78 (on the "mob"); Davis, "Rites of Violence," 51–91. For a subsequent critique of Thompson's "moral economy" as "a less than satisfactory historical explanation," see Dale Williams, "Morals, Markets and the English Crowd in 1766," *Past & Present* 104 (1984): 56–73, at 73. See also the critical comment of Janine Estèbe, "The Rites of Violence: Religious Riot in Sixteenth-Century France; A Comment," *Past & Present* 67 (1975): 127–30, which provoked a response by Natalie Davis, "The Rites of Violence: Religious Riot in Sixteenth-Century France; A Rejoinder," *Past & Present* 67 (1975): 131–35. For critical examination of both essays, see Suzanne Desan, "Crowds, Community, and Ritual in the Work of E. P. Thompson and Natalie Davis," in *The New Cultural History*, ed. Lynn Hunt, 47–71 (Berkeley, 1975). Another helpful reassessment, by John Bohstedt, "The Moral Economy and the Discipline of Historical Context," *Journal of Social History* 26 (1992): 265–84, notes the risks in Thompson's approach of overgeneralizing about the dynamics of food riots despite considerable variation from context to context: "I am suggesting that an alternative heuristic might now try to make progress from *explaining* the variations rather than the unifying themes of conflict. Instead of focussing on common moral *motivations* of food rioters, we might now analyze their *actions* as adaptive responses to the changing political and economic contexts that affected their livelihoods" (284).

45. Thompson, "Moral Economy," 78.

46. Davis, "Rites of Violence," 53, 81–85.

47. Thompson, "Moral Economy," 107–15; Davis, "Rites of Violence," 55–65; Natalie Z. Davis, "The Reasons of Misrule: Youth Groups and Charivaris in Sixteenth-Century France," *Past & Present* 50 (1971): 41–75.

48. Davis, "Rites of Violence," 52: "By religious riot, I mean, as a preliminary definition, any violent action, with words or weapons, undertaken against religious targets by people who are not acting *officially and formally* as agents of political and ecclesiastical authority."

49. Desan, "Crowds, Community, and Ritual," 68–70, notes that the casting of crowd violence as ritual may come after the fact: they may be "endowed only tenuously with ritual legitimacy through a violent and polemical struggle" (68).

50. Desan, "Crowds, Community, and Ritual."

51. Moore, "Family, Community and Cult on the Eve of the Gregorian Reform," 49.

52. Rodney Hilton, *Bond Men Made Free: Medieval Peasant Movements and the English Rising of 1381* (London, 1973), 63–95; Chris Wickham, *Framing the Early Middle Ages: Europe and the Mediterranean, 400–800* (Oxford, 2005), 140–42, 578–88; Chris Wickham, "Looking Forward: Peasant Revolts in Europe, 600–1200," in *The Routledge History Handbook of Medieval Revolt*, ed. Justine Firnhaber-Baker and Dirk Schoenaers (London, 2017), 155–67; Eric Goldberg, "Popular Revolt, Dynastic Politics, and Aristocratic Factionalism in the Early Middle Ages: The Saxon Stellinga Reconsidered," *Speculum* 70 (1995): 467–501, at 500; Ingrid Rembold, *Conquest and Christianization: Saxony and the Carolingian World, 772–888* (Cambridge, UK, 2018), 85–140; Bernard Gowers, "996 and All That: the Norman Peasants' Revolt Reconsidered," *Early Medieval Europe* 21 (2013): 71–98, esp. 97–98.

53. Thomas S. Brown, "Urban Violence in Early Medieval Italy: The Cases of Rome and Ravenna," in *Violence and Society in the Early Medieval West*, ed. Guy Halsall (Woodbridge, UK, 1998), 76–89; Judith Herrin, "Urban Riot or Civic Ritual? The Crowd in Early Medieval

Ravenna," in *Raum und Performanz: Rituale in Residenzen von der Antike bis 1815*, ed. D. Boschung, K.-J. Hölkeskamp, and C. Sode, 219–40 (Stuttgart, 2015); Veronica West-Harling, *Rome, Ravenna and Venice, 750–1000: Byzantine Heritage, Imperial Present, and the Construction of City Identity* (Oxford, 2020).

54. Moore, "Weight of Opinion," 211 (skeptically building on Dominique Barthélemy); see also Bobrycki, "Flailing Women," 41.

55. Clark McPhail, *Myth of the Madding Crowd* (New York, 1991), 177. For a more complicated taxonomy of what the authors term "elementary forms of collective action" (EFCA), see David S. Schweingruber and Clark McPhail, "A Method for Systematically Observing and Recording Collective Action," *Sociological Methods and Research* 27 (1999): 451–98; and Clark McPhail, "Gatherings as Patchworks," *Social Psychology Quarterly* 71 (2008): 1–5. Cf. Clark McPhail and Ronald T Wohlstein, "Individual and Collective Behaviors within Gatherings, Demonstrations, and Riots," *Annual Review of Sociology* 9 (1983): 579–600.

56. Clark McPhail, "Crowd Behavior," in *The Blackwell Encyclopedia of Sociology*, ed. George Ritzer (Malden, 2007), vol. 2, 880–84, at 880: "Over the past two decades sociologists working at different levels of analysis have adopted 'the gathering' as a more neutral and useful concept for referring to a temporary collection of at least two persons in a common location in space and time without regard to their actions or motives." See also the "deliberately vague" (5) use of "aggregazione" as set out by Elio Lo Cascio, "Introduzione," in *Forme di aggregazione nel mondo romano*, ed. Elio Lo Cascio and Giovanna D. Merola (Bari, 2007), 5–10, at 5–6.

57. Jeremy Duquesnay Adams, *The Populus of Augustine and Jerome: A Study in the Patristic Sense of Community* (New Haven, CT, 1971).

58. For an excellent recent study, see Cécile Voyer, "La parole d'autorité et sa sacralisation par l'écrit: Les représentations d'assemblées dans quelques images du haut Moyen Âge," *Cahiers de civilization médiévale* 250–51 (2020): 151–62.

59. Moreover, such historicist determinism, as Habermas noted, is implicitly judgmental without justifying its grounds for judgment: Jürgen Habermas, *Philosophical Discourse of Modernity: Twelve Lectures*, trans. Frederick G. Lawrence (Cambridge, MA, 1990), 275–77.

60. Eric Goldberg, "Popular Revolt, Dynastic Politics, and Aristocratic Factionalism in the Early Middle Ages: the Saxon Stellinga Reconsidered," *Speculum* 70 (1995): 467–501, at 468; Wickham, *Framing*, 347–51, 578–88. See also in chapter 3, at pp. 78–89 below.

61. Literary crowds: Martínez Pizarro, "Crowds and Power in the *Liber Pontificalis Ecclesiae Ravennatis*"; Magennis, "Crowd Control?"; urban violence: Thomas S. Brown, "Urban Violence in Early Medieval Italy: The Cases of Rome and Ravenna," in *Violence and Society in the Early Medieval West*, ed. Guy Halsall (Woodbridge, 1998), 76–89; Judith Herrin, "Urban Riot or Civic Ritual? The Crowd in Early Medieval Ravenna," in *Raum und Performanz: Rituale in Residenzen von der Antike bis 1815*, ed. D. Boschung, K.-J. Hölkeskamp, and C. Sode (Stuttgart, 2015), 219–40.

62. Susanna Elm, "Captive Crowds: Pilgrims and Martyrs," in *Crowds*, ed. J. T. Schnapp and M. Tiews (Stanford, 2006), 133–48, largely bypasses the early Middle Ages. For pilgrim crowds, see Diana Webb, *Medieval European Pilgrimage, c. 700–c. 1500* (New York, 2002); Adrian R. Bell and Richard S. Dale, "The Medieval Pilgrimage Business," *Enterprise and Society* 12 (2011): 601–27.

63. See the volumes in the Collection Haut Moyen Âge: J.-P. Devroey et al., eds., *Les élites et la richesse durant le haut Moyen Âge* (Turnhout, 2010); P. Depreux et al., eds., *Les élites et leurs espaces* (Turnhout, 2007); F. Bougard, R. Le Jan, R. McKitterick, eds., *La Culture du haut Moyen Âge: Une question d'élites?* (Turnhout, 2009); Régine Le Jan, ed., *La royauté et les élites dans l'Europe carolingienne (début IXe siècle aux environs de 920)* (Villeneuve d'Ascq, 1998).

64. J. Nelson, *Politics and Ritual in Early Medieval Europe* (London, 1986); Gerd Althoff, *Spielregeln der Politik im Mittelalter* (Darmstadt, 1997). On assembly culture, see Timothy Reuter, "Assembly Politics in Western Europe," in *Medieval Polities and Modern Mentalities*, ed. J.

Nelson (Cambridge, UK, 2006), 193–216; Thomas Bisson, "Celebration and Persuasion: Reflections on the Cultural Evolution of Medieval Consultation," *Legislative Studies Quarterly* 7 (1982): 181–204; and John R. Maddicott, *The Origins of the English Parliament, 924–1327* (Oxford, 2010), which traces the medieval English parliament to the large assemblies of the tenth-century West Saxon king Æthelstan. See also P. S. Barnwell and Marco Mostert, eds., *Political Assemblies in the Earlier Middle Ages* (Turnhout, 2003). For the representation of assembly crowds, see Voyer, "La parole d'autorité."

65. Verena Epp and Christoph Meyer, ed., *Recht und Konsens im frühen Mittelalter* (Ostfildern, 2017); Philippe Depreux and Steffen Patzold, eds., *Versammlungen im Frühmittelalter* (Berlin, 2023).

66. On legal effectiveness, see Hermann Nehlsen, "Aktualität und Effektivität der ältesten germanischen Rechtsaufzeichnungen," in *Recht und Schrift im Mittelalter*, ed. P. Classen (Sigmaringen, 1977), 449–502; for an approach focusing not on normative laws but on the records of dispute settlement, see the essays in Wendy Davies and Paul Fouracre, eds., *The Settlement of Disputes in Early Medieval Europe* (Cambridge, UK, 1992). François Louis Ganshof, "La preuve dans le droit franc," in *La Preuve*, vol. 2, *Moyen Âge et Temps Modernes* (Paris, 1965), 71–98.

67. The point may be extended beyond representative assemblies. See, e.g., Walter Ullmann, "Public Welfare and Social Legislation in the Early Medieval Councils," in W. Ullmann, *The Church and the Law in the Earlier Middle Ages* (London, 1975), 1–39, at 1, contending that "some of the great merits of modern welfare institutions and modern social legislative measures have their definite and demonstrable roots, not in antiquity, not in the high Middle Ages, not in the nineteenth century, but roughly speaking in the Frankish Age."

68. Bobrycki, "Flailing Women," 5, 31, 45. For the concept of "slantwise" action, see Howard Campbell and Josiah Heyman, "Slantwise: Beyond Domination and Resistance on the Border," *Journal of Contemporary Ethnography* 36 (2007): 3–30, esp. 3–5, intended as a riposte to anthropological or sociological models focused on dominance / resistance. Campbell and Heyman examine behaviors that pertain to dominance and resistance, but that may be understood by participants in those terms, as a counter to anthropologists who force "accidental defiance, avoidance, and similar phenomena into resistance, a category best reserved for actions and meanings that actors themselves understand to be defiant" (4).

69. Bryan Ward-Perkins, "Continuitists, Catastrophists, and the Towns of Post-Roman Northern Italy," *Papers of the British School at Rome* 65 (1997): 157–76.

Chapter 1. The Roman Legacy

1. Jennifer R. Davis and Michael McCormick, eds., *The Long Morning of Medieval Europe: New Directions in Early Medieval Studies* (Aldershot, UK, 2008).

2. Jonathan Conant, *Staying Roman: Conquest and Identity in Africa and the Mediterranean, 439–700* (Cambridge, UK, 2012).

3. J. W. Hanson, *An Urban Geography of the Roman World, 100 BC to AD 300* (Oxford, 2016), 193–791, catalogues 1,388 urban settlements (see 18–24 for definition). The total number was probably higher. See Alan Bowman and Andrew Wilson, eds., *Settlement, Urbanization, and Population* (Oxford, 2011).

4. For a useful introduction, see K. M. Coleman, "'The Contagion of the Throng': Absorbing Violence in the Roman world," *Hermathena* 164 (1998): 65–88; see also her "General Introduction" to Martial, *M. Valerii Martialis liber spectaculorum*, ed. K. M. Coleman (Oxford, 2006), esp. lxv–lxxx. The classic on gladiators remains Georges Ville, *La gladiature en Occident des origines à la mort de Domitien* (Rome, 1981). For synthetic entries on Roman spectacle, see K. M. Coleman, "Spectacle," in *Oxford Handbook of Roman Studies*, ed. A. Barchiesi and W. Scheidel (Oxford: Oxford University Press, 2010), 651–70; K. M. Coleman, "Public entertainments," in *Oxford*

Handbook of Social Relations in the Roman World, ed. M. Peachin (Oxford, 2011), 335–57. The frequent appearance of gladiatorial decorations in private homes provides a striking reflection of how quotidian gladiatorial violence was in Roman Antiquity: Shelby Brown, "Death as Decoration: Scenes From the Arena on Roman Domestic Mosaics," in *Pornography and Representation in Greece and Rome*, ed. Amy Richlin (Oxford, 1992), 180–211, at 184, noting that crowds (and the *editor* who paid for their entertainment) are rarely depicted in private mosaics, "so the viewer of the scene replaces the crowd at ringside." For theaters, see Frank Sear, *Roman Theatres: An Architectural Study* (Oxford, 2006).

5. Paul Veyne, *Le pain et le cirque: Sociologie historique d'un pluralisme politique* (Paris, 1976). See also Peter Garnsey, "The Generosity of Veyne," *The Journal of Roman Studies* 81 (1991): 164–68, and Arjan Zuiderhoek, "The Ambiguity of Munificence," *Zeitschrift für alte Geschichte* 56 (2007): 196–213, for how "legitimation and reinforcement of social bonds" and "the expression of discontent" were "two sides of the same coin" in euergetic rituals (213). For processions, see Friederike Fless, "Römische Prozessionen," in *Thesaurus Cultus et Rituum Antiquorum* (Los Angeles, 2004), vol. 1, 33–58.

6. Baths: Fikret Yegül, *Baths and Bathing in Classical Antiquity* (Cambridge, MA, 1992); for public toilets, see Ann Olga Koloski-Ostrow, *The Archaeology of Sanitation in Roman Italy* (Chapel Hill, NC, 2015).

7. Christopher Jones, "Interrupted Funerals," *Proceedings of the American Philosophical Society* 143 (1999): 588–600.

8. Acclamations: Theodor Klauser, "Akklamation," on *Reallexikon für Antike und Christentum*, ed. Franz Joseph Dölger et al. (Stuttgart, 1950), vol. 1, col. 216–33. Riots: Gregory Aldrete, "Riots," in *The Cambridge Companion to Ancient Rome*, ed. Paul Erdkamp (Cambridge, UK, 2013), 425–40; Thomas Pekáry, "Seditio: Unruhen und Revolten im römischen Reich von Augustus bis Commodus," *Ancient Society* 18 (1987): 133–50; Julia Sünskes Thompson, *Aufstände und Protestaktionen im Imperium Romanum: Die severischen Kaiser im Spannungsfeld innenpolitischer Konflikte* (Bonn, 1990); Benjamin Kelly, "Riot Control and Imperial Ideology in the Roman Empire," *Phoenix* 61 (2007): 150–76; Cameron Grey and Anneliese Parkin, "Controlling the Urban Mob: The *colonatus perpetuus* of C.Th. 14.18.1," *Phoenix* 57 (2003): 284–99; Wilfried Nippel, "Aufruhr und Polizei in der späten römischen Republik und in der frühen Kaiserzeit," *Humanistische Bildung* 6 (1983): 85–118; Wilfried Nippel, "Policing Rome," *The Journal of Roman Studies* 74 (1984): 20–29.

9. For the debate about the significance of the Late Republican *contio*, see Fergus Millar, *The Crowd in Rome in the Late Republic* (Ann Arbor, MI, 1998); Karl-Joachim Hölkeskamp, "The Roman Republic: Government of the People, by the People, for the People?," *Scripta Classica Israelica* 19 (2000): 203–23; R. Morstein-Marx, *Mass Oratory and Political Power in the Late Roman Republic* (Cambridge, UK, 2004); F. Pina Polo, "Procedures and Functions of Civil and Military Contiones in Rome," *Klio* 77 (1995): 203–16; F. Pina Polo, *Contra Arma Verbis: Der Redner vor dem Volk in der später römischen Republik*, trans. E. Liess (Stuttgart, 1996); James Tan, "Contiones in the Age of Cicero," *Classical Antiquity* 27 (2008): 163–201; and the collected essays in M. Jehne, ed., *Demokratie in Rom? Die Rolle des Volkes in der Politik der römischen Republik* (Stuttgart, 1995). Both Gregory S. Aldrete, *Gestures and Acclamations in Ancient Rome* (Baltimore, 1999) and Michael McCormick, *Eternal Victory: Triumphal Rulership in Late Antiquity, Byzantium, and the Early Medieval West* (Cambridge, UK, 1986), discuss the role of the crowd in later imperial politics. For the continued importance of the people in Byzantine imperial politics, see Anthony Kaldellis, *The Byzantine Republic: People and Power in New Rome* (Cambridge, MA, 2015).

10. Luke Lavan, *Public Space in the Late Antique City*, 2 vols. (Leiden, 2021).

11. Brent D. Shaw, *Bringing in the Sheaves: Economy and Metaphor in the Roman World* (Toronto, 2013); Paul Erdkamp, *The Grain Market in the Roman Empire: A Social, Political and*

Economic Study (Cambridge, UK, 2005); Kyle Harper, *Slavery in the Late Roman World, AD 275–425* (Cambridge, UK, 2011); Michael Decker, *Tilling the Hateful Earth: Agricultural Production and Trade in the Late Antique East* (Oxford, 2009); Cam Grey, *Constructing Communities in the Late Roman Countryside* (Cambridge, UK, 2011); Robert Knapp, *Invisible Romans* (Cambridge, MA, 2014); Kim Bowes, ed., *The Roman Peasant Project 2009–2014: Excavating the Roman Rural Poor*, 2 vols. (Philadelphia, 2021).

12. For circus collapse, see J. Humphrey, *Roman Circuses: Arenas for Chariot Racing* (London, 1986), 115. See Tacitus, *Annales*, 4.62–64, ed. H. Heubner, *P. Cornelii Taciti libri qui supersunt*, ed. H. Heubner, vol. 1, *Ab excessu divi Augusti* (Stuttgart, 1983), 168–69, for the collapse of a wooden amphitheater at Fidenae in 27 CE. See Guy Chamberland, "A Gladiatorial Show Produced *in sordidam mercedem* (Tacitus *Ann.* 4.62)," *Phoenix* 61 (2007): 136–49. This is a typically Roman use of the *topos* of crowd disaster in the context of the games to say something deeper about the sickness of the state: compare Cassius Dio, *Roman History*, 79.25–26, ed. U. P. Boissevain, *Cassii Dionis Cocceiani Historiarum romanarum quae supersunt* (Berlin, 1901), vol. 3, 431–32, where the Colosseum is damaged by lighting in 217 CE during the Vulcania, portending terrible things. Mary Beard et al., *Religions of Rome* (Cambridge, UK, 1998), vol. 1, 263.

13. John Bodel, "From Columbaria to Catacombs: Collective Burial in Pagan and Christian Rome," in *Commemorating the Dead: Texts and Artifacts in Context; Studies of Roman, Jewish and Christian Burials*, ed. L. Brink and D. Green (Berlin, 2008), 177–242.

14. Graeber and Wengrow, *The Dawn of Everything: A New History of Humanity* (New York, 2021), 288–97.

15. Walter Scheidel, "Demographie," in *Handbuch: Antike Wirtschaft*, ed. Sitta von Reden and Kai Ruffing (Berlin, 2023), 209–226, at 221.

16. Theodor Mommsen, *Römisches Staatsrecht*, 3rd ed., 3 vols. (Darmstadt, 1971 [1887]), vol. 2, 1133. Compare Kaldellis, *Byzantine Republic*, 89–117.

17. For a useful overview, see "Volk, Nation, Nationalismus, Masse," in *Geschichtliche Grundbegriffe: Historisches Lexikon zur politisch-sozialen Sprache in Deutschland*, ed. O. Brunner, W. Conze, and R. Koselleck (Stuttgart, 1992), vol. 7, 141–431, at 151–71 (Fritz Gschnitzer: "II. Altertum").

18. See Bertrand Lançon, "Les forms d'assemblée dans l'Empire romain tardif en Occident (IVe–Ve siècles)," in *Versammlungen im Frühmittelalter*, ed. Philippe Depreux and Steffen Patzold (Berlin, 2023), 37–52.

19. Kaldellis, *Byzantine Republic*, xvi; explored at length in Anthony Kaldellis, *Romanland: Ethnicity and Empire in Byzantium* (Cambridge, MA, 2019).

20. Lily Ross Taylor, *Roman Voting Assemblies: From the Hannibalic War to the Dictatorship of Caesar* (Ann Arbor, MI, 1966).

21. Dan-El Padilla Peralta, *Divine Institutions: Religions and Community in the Middle Roman Republic* (Princeton, NJ, 2020), 2 (and 141–50), argues that the Middle Republic (c. 400–200 BCE) "vaulted itself into a new kind of statehood" using number-hungry temple rituals (festivals, pilgrimages).

22. Robert Morstein-Marx, *Mass Oratory and Political Power in the Late Roman Republic* (Cambridge, UK, 2004). For an outside-in view of trials, emphasizing the importance of strict procedure, see Clifford Ando, "Performing Justice in Republican Empire," in *Legal Engagement: The Reception of Roman Law and Tribunals by Jews and Other Inhabitants of the Empire*, ed. Katell Berthelot et al. (Rome, 2021), 69–85.

23. *TLL* 4:986, s.v. "corona" (III.A).

24. Cicero, *Brutus*, 290, ed. E. Malcovati, *M. Tulli Ciceronis scripta quae manserunt omnia* (Leipzig, 1970), vol. 4, 89: "Volo hoc oratori contingat, ut cum auditum sit eum esse dicturum, locus in subselliis occupetur, compleatur tribunal, gratiosi scribae sint in dando et cedendo loco, corona multiplex, iudex erectus; cum surgat is qui dicturus sit, significetur a corona

silentium, deinde crebrae adsensiones, multae admirationes; risus, cum velit, cum velit, fletus: ut, qui haec procul videat, etiam si quid agatur nesciat, at placere tamen et in scaena esse Roscium intellegat."

25. Hermann Dessau, ed., *Senatus consultum de Bacchanalibus* [186 BCE], in *Inscriptiones Latinae Selectae* (Berlin, 1892), vol. 1, no. 18, 5–6; Livy, *Ab urbe condita*, 39.8–18, ed. John Briscoe, *Titi Livi Ab Vrbe Condita Libri XXXVI–XL* (Leipzig, 2012), 617–34.

26. Aldrete, "Riots," 431–33.

27. *Dig.* 47.8.4.3.

28. Veyne, *Le pain et le cirque*; Peter Brunt, "The Roman Mob," *Past & Present* 35 (1966): 3–27, at 27.

29. Lewis Mumford, *The City in History* (San Diego, 1961), 84.

30. McCormick, *Eternal Victory*, 389.

31. Cassius Dio, *Roman History*, 68.15.1. This is usually assumed to have taken place in 108–9 CE.

32. Klauser, "Akklamation," col. 216: "Unter Akklamationen versteht man die oft rhythmisch formulierten u. sprechchorartig vorgetragenen Zurufe, mit denen eine Volksmenge Beifall, Lob u. Glückwunsch, oder Tadel, Verwünschung u. Forderung zum Ausdruck bringt." Compare Erik Peterson, *Heis Theos: Epigraphische, formgeschichtliche und religionsgeschichtliche Untersuchungen zur antiken Ein-Gott-Akklamation* (Würzburg, 2012 [1920]), 141–45.

33. Clifford Ando, *Imperial Ideology and Provincial Loyalty in the Roman Empire* (Berkeley, 2000), 200.

34. Aldrete, "Riots," 439; Catherine Virlouvet, *Famines et émeutes à Rome des origins de la République à la mort de Néron* (Rome, 1985), 39–80.

35. Aldrete, "Riots," 427.

36. Cassiodorus, *Variae* 6.18.2, ed. Andrea Giardina, Giovanni Alberto Cecconi, and Ignazio Tantillo, *Flavio Magno Aurelio Cassiodoro Senatore, Varie*, 6 vols. (Rome, 2008–), vol. 3, 34, with helpful commentary at 161–63.

37. E. P. Thompson, "The Moral Economy of the English Crowd in the Eighteenth Century," *Past & Present* 50 (1971): 76–136, at 78. As an example of this official recognition, see Symmachus, *Relationes*, no. 6, ed. Otto Seeck, MGH AA 6.1 (Berlin, 1883), 285.

38. *Historia Augusta* 33.1–3. For these celebrations, see Christian Körner, *Philippus Arabs: Ein Soldatenkaiser in der Tradition des antoninisch-severischen Prinzipats* (Berlin, 2002), 248–59.

39. A.H.M. Jones, *The Later Roman Empire*, 2 vols. (London, 1964 [reprint Baltimore, 1986]); Timothy D. Barnes, *The New Empire of Diocletian and Constantine* (Cambridge, MA, 1982).

40. Ramsay MacMullen, *Changes in the Roman Empire: Essays in the Ordinary* (Princeton, NJ, 1990), 250–76; Peter Brown, *Power and Persuasion in Late Antiquity: Towards a Christian Empire* (Madison, WI, 1992), esp. 71–117; Neil McLynn, "Christian Controversy and Violence in the Fourth Century," *Kodai* 3 (1992): 15–44, for a partial critique of MacMullen's argument.

41. Júlio César Magalhães de Oliveira, "Late Antiquity: The Age of Crowds?," *Past & Present* 249 (2020): 3–52.

42. Oliveira, "Late Antiquity," 4.

43. Thomas N. Sizgorich, *Violence and Belief in Late Antiquity: Militant Devotion in Christianity and Islam* (Philadelphia, 2008); Peter Van Nuffelen, "'A Wise Madness': A Virtue-Based Model for Crowd Behaviour in Late Antiquity," in *Reconceiving Religious Conflict: New Views from the Formative Centuries of Christianity*, ed. Wendy Mayer and Chris De Wet (London, 2018), 234–58; Harold A. Drake, *Constantine and the Bishops: The Politics of Intolerance* (Baltimore, 2000); Michael Gaddis, *There Is No Crime for Those Who Have Christ: Religious Violence in the Christian Roman Empire* (Berkeley, 2005); Leslie Dossey, *Peasant and Empire in Christian North Africa* (Berkeley, 2010); Polymnia Athanassiadi, *Vers la pensée unique: La montée de l'intolérance dans l'Antiquité tardive* (Paris, 2010); Johannes Hahn, *Gewalt und religiöser Konflikt: Studien zu*

den Auseinandersetzungen zwischen Christen, Heiden und Juden im Osten des Römischen Reiches (von Konstantin bis Theodosius II) (Leipzig, 2004); Carlos Galvão-Sobrinho, *Doctrine and Power: Theological Controversy and Christian Leadership in the Later Roman Empire* (Berkeley, 2013); Erika Manders and Daniëlle Slootjes, eds., *Leadership, Ideology and Crowds in the Roman Empire of the Fourth Century AD* (Stuttgart, 2019).

44. Pekáry, "Seditio"; Sünskes Thompson, *Aufstände*.

45. Oliveira, "Late Antiquity," 6.

46. Oliveira, "Late Antiquity," 13, 42. But see Giovanni Alberto Cecconi, "Crisi e trasformazioni del governo municipale in Occidente fra IV e VI secolo," in *Die Stadt in der Spätantike: Niedergang oder Wandel?*, ed. Jens-Uwe Krause and Christian Witschel (Stuttgart, 2006), 285–318, at 311.

47. Van Nuffelen, "'A Wise Madness,'" esp. 234–35.

48. Hans-Ulrich Wiemer, "Akklamationen im spätrömischen Reich: Zur Typologie und Funktion eines Kommunikationsrituals," *Archiv für Kulturgeschichte* 86 (2004): 27–73.

49. *Gesta Senatus*, ed. Theodor Mommsen, *Theodosiani libri XVI*, 4th ed., 3 vols. (Zürich, 1971), vol. 2.2, 2–3: "Adclamatum est: Augusti Augustorum, maximi Augustorum. Dictum VIII. . . . Ut vivere delectet Augustos nostros semper. Dictum XXII. . . . Haec sunt vota senatus, haec sunt vota populi Romani. Dictum X. . . . Liberis cariores, parentibus cariores. Dictum XVI. . . . Dispositioni vestrae gratias agimus. Dictum XXIII."

50. Ramsay MacMullen, *Voting About God in Early Church Councils* (New Haven, CT, 2006), 17; Wiemer, "Akklamationen," 29–35; Lançon, "Les forms d'assemblée," 39.

51. Rene Pfeilschifter, *Der Kaiser und Konstantinopel: Kommunikation und Konfliktaustrag in einer spätantiken Metropole* (Berlin, 2013), 179–210 ("Akzeptanzgruppen"), building on Egon Flaig, *Den Kaiser herausfordern: Die Usurpation im Römischen Reich*, 2nd ed. (Frankfurt, 2019 [1992]), 39–74, and see also 227–30, for the logic of the *consensus omnium*.

52. MacMullen, *Voting About God*, 13.

53. McCormick, *Eternal Victory*, 131–230.

54. Daniëlle Slootjes, "Crowd Behavior in Late Antique Rome," in *Pagans and Christians in Late Antique Rome: Conflict, Competition, and Coexistence in the Fourth Century*, ed. Michele Renee Salzman, Marianne Sághy, and Rita Lizzi Testa (Cambridge, UK, 2016), 178–94, at 187–92. On the crowd in late antique Christianity, see Peter Brown, *Society and the Holy in Late Antiquity* (Berkeley, 1982), 17–19 (cure of the possessed), 112–15 (the holy man) and Brown, *Power and Persuasion*, 148. Violent Christian crowds of Late Antiquity have received special attention: see the essays in Werner Riess and Garrett G. Fagan, eds., *The Topography of Violence in the Greco-Roman World* (Ann Arbor, MI, 2016); Clifford Ando, "Religion and Violence in Late Roman North Africa," *Journal of Late Antiquity* 6 (2013): 197–202 (on a special issue in that volume); Remo Cacitti, *Furiosa Turba: I fondamenti religiosi dell'eversione sociale, della dissidenza politica e della contestazione ecclesiale dei Circoncellioni d'Africa* (Milan, 2006); Brent D. Shaw, *Sacred Violence: African Christians and Sectarian Hatred in the Age of Augustine* (Cambridge, UK, 2011); Dossey, *Peasant and Empire in Christian North Africa*; Edward J. Watts, *Riot in Alexandria: Tradition and Group Dynamics in Late Antique Pagan and Christian Communities* (Berkeley, 2010); Gaddis, *There Is No Crime for Those Who Have Christ*; Júlio César Magalhães de Oliveira, "Le 'pouvoir du peuple': Une émeute à Hippone au début du Ve siècle connue par le Sermon 302 de Saint Augustin pour la Fête de Saint Laurent," *Antiquité Tardive* 12 (2004): 309–24; Júlio César Magalhães de Oliveira, "'Vt maiores pagani non sint!': Pouvoir, iconoclasme et action populaire à Carthage au début du Ve siècle (Saint Augustin, Sermons 24, 279 et Morin 1)," *Antiquité Tardive* 14 (2006): 245–62; Michael Kulikowski, "Fronto, the Bishops, and the Crowd: Episcopal Justice and Communal Violence in Fifth-Century Tarraconensis," *Early Medieval Europe* 11 (2002): 295–320; Timothy Gregory, "Urban Violence in Late Antiquity," in *Aspects of Graeco-Roman Urbanism: Essays on the Classical City*, ed. Ronald T. Marchese (Oxford, 1983),

137–61; Timothy Gregory, *Vox Populi: Popular Opinion and Violence in the Religious Controversies of the Fifth Century A.D.* (Columbus, OH, 1979).

55. Classically Peter Brown, "The Rise and Function of the Holy Man in Late Antiquity," *Journal of Roman Studies* 61 (1971): 80–101; see Ramsay MacMullen, "The Place of the Holy Man in the Later Roman Empire," *Harvard Theological Review* 112 (2019): 1–32, for a critical reassessment.

56. Brown, *Power and Persuasion*, 148.

57. Ammianus 27.14.

58. Peter Brown, *Through the Eye of a Needle: Wealth, the Fall of Rome, and the Making of Christianity in the West, 350–550 AD* (Princeton, NJ, 2012), 125–26.

59. Watts, *Riot in Alexandria*.

60. Oliveira, "Late Antiquity," 48.

61. Ando, "Religion and Violence," 202.

62. MacMullen, *Voting About God*, 7.

63. Michael Whitby, "An Unholy Crew? Bishops Behaving Badly at Church Councils," in *Chalcedon in Context: Church Councils, 400–700*, ed. Richard Price and Mary Whitby (Liverpool, 2009), 178–96; Slootjes, "Crowd Behavior," 188–89.

64. XI Toledo (675), c. 1, ed. Alberigo et al., 406 (Mansi, vol. 11, 137).

65. Michael McCormick, *Origins of the European Economy* (Cambridge, UK, 2001), 115–19; Chris Wickham, *Framing the Early Middle Ages* (Oxford, 2005), 33–50.

66. Examples such as the *gairethinx*, the "spear-gathering," which officialized public acts in Lombard Italy (the Lombard-inflected Latin verb *thingare* meant "to publicize"), had affinities with Roman military rituals (like the elevation of a new emperor upon a shield), but they can also be seen as a departure from Roman practice.

67. *Oxford Dictionary of Byzantium*, s.v. "Hippodromes," vol. 2, 394–95.

68. Nancy Shatzman Steinhardt, *Chinese Imperial City Planning* (Honolulu, 1990), 67–68.

69. Humphrey, *Roman Circuses*, 126. Some estimate a larger capacity of up to 200,000.

70. Richard Duncan-Jones, *Structure and Scale in the Roman Economy* (Cambridge, UK, 1990), 159–73; Hanson, *Urban Geography*; Simon Esmonde Cleary, *The Roman West, AD 200–500: An Archaeological Study* (Cambridge, UK, 2013); Ray Laurence, Simon Esmonde Cleary, and Gareth Sears, *The City in the Roman West, c. 250 BC–c. AD 250* (Cambridge, UK, 2011).

71. Brown, *Through the Eye of a Needle*, 118.

72. Jones, *Later Roman Empire*, 1021.

73. Daniele Manacorda, ed., *Crypta Balbi: Archeologia e storia di un paesaggio urbano* (Milan, 2001); *Archeologia urbana a Roma: Il progetto della Crypta Balbi*, 5 vols. (Florence, 1982–1990).

74. Hendrick W. Dey, *The Afterlife of the Roman City: Architecture and Ceremony in Late Antiquity and the Early Middle Ages* (Cambridge, UK, 2015), 3, 119.

75. John Matthews, *Empire of the Romans: From Julius Caesar to Justinian; Six Hundred Years of Peace and War* (Hoboken, NJ, 2021), 73.

76. Janet DeLaine, *The Baths of Caracalla: A Study in the Design, Construction, and Economics of Large-Scale Building Projects in Imperial Rome* (Portsmouth, RI, 1997), 184.

77. Hendrik Dey, *The Aurelian Wall and the Refashioning of Imperial Rome, A.D. 271–855* (Cambridge, UK, 2011), 97–98.

78. Bowes, ed., *Roman Peasant Project*, vol. 2, 462–69.

79. Shaw, *Bringing in the Sheaves*, 19–20.

80. For smallholding versus *latifundia*, see Duncan-Jones, *Structure and Scale*, 121–42, esp. 127–29, with the essays collected in *Du latifundium au latifondo: Un héritage de Rome, une création médiévale ou moderne?* (Paris, 1995).

81. Georges Dumézil, *Fêtes romaines d'été et d'automne, suivi de dix questions romaines* (Paris, 1975), 59–107.
82. Dio Chrysostom, *Or.* 7; Erdkamp, *Grain Market*, 55–58.
83. Carlo Levi, *Cristo si è fermato a Eboli* (Torino, 1947), 1. That is, the peasants were so isolated from the world that the Gospel had never gotten past the last train stop before their province, a statement whose inherent self-contradiction never seemed to dawn on the otherwise sensitive Levi. One of the peasants had lived for a time in America.
84. Peter F. Bang, *The Roman Bazaar: A Comparative Study of Trade and Markets in a Tributary Empire* (Cambridge, UK, 2008); Morris Silver, "Historical Otherness, the Roman Bazaar, and Primitivism: P. F. Bang on the Roman Economy," *Journal of Roman Archaeology* 22 (2009): 421–43.
85. Cf. Jack Tannous, *The Making of the Medieval Middle East: Religion, Society, and Simple Believers* (Princeton, NJ, 2018), 40.
86. Georg Wissowa, *Religion und Kultus der Römer*, 2nd ed. (Munich, 1912), 199–200.
87. Shaw, *Bringing in the Sheaves*.
88. Paul Erdkamp, ed., *A Companion to the Roman Army* (Malden, MA, 2007).
89. Jones, *Later Roman Empire*, 679–86, calculating 600,000 from the *Notitia dignitatum* (683), while stressing that this is a "paper figure."
90. Robin Fleming, *The Material Fall of Roman Britain, 300–525 CE* (Philadelphia, 2021), 10–33, for the "world the *annona* made."
91. Nicholas Horsfall, "The Cultural Horizons of the 'Plebs Romana,'" *Memoirs of the American Academy in Rome* 41 (1996): 101–19; Pierre Cagniart, "The Philosopher and the Gladiator," *The Classical World* 93 (2000): 607–18.
92. Patrizia Arena, *Feste e rituali a Roma: Il principe incontra il popolo nel Circo Massimo* (Bari, 2010), 53–102; Jacob Latham, *Performance, Memory, and Processions in Ancient Rome: The Pompa Circensis from the Republic to Late Antiquity* (Cambridge, UK, 2016).
93. Juvenal, *Satire* 10.81.
94. *Codex Theodosianus* 14.15, ed. T. Mommsen and P. Meyer, *Theodosiani libri XVI cum constitutionibus Sirmondianis et Leges novellae ad Theodosianum pertinentes*, 3rd ed. (Berlin, 1954) (*panis fiscalis*).
95. Theodoret, *Historia Ecclesiastica* 5.26; Thomas Wiedemann, "Das Ende der römischen Gladiatorenspiele," *Nikephoros* 8 (1995): 145–59.
96. Garrett Fagan, *The Lure of the Arena: Social Psychology and the Crowd at the Roman Games* (Cambridge, UK, 2011), 202–9, at 209.
97. A first-century BCE law allowed betting on sporting events that showcased *virtus*, masculine virtue—otherwise games of chance (*alea*) were supposedly forbidden, and claims arising from them were not actionable: Adolf Berger, *Encyclopedic Dictionary of Roman Law* (Philadelphia, 1953), 549 (the *lex Cornelia de aleatoribus*, dated to 81 BCE).
98. Tertullian, *De spectaculis* 15: "Nemo denique in spectaculo ineundo prius cogitat nisi videri et videre."
99. As Cicero noted of himself with palpable false modesty: Cicero, *Ad Atticum* (4.15), 90.6: "Redii Romam Fontei causa a.d. VII Id. Quint. veni spectatum, primum magno et aequabili plausu—sed hoc ne curaris, ego ineptus qui scripserim."
100. Arena, *Feste e rituali*, 103–45, esp. 123–25.
101. Alan Cameron, *Circus Factions: Blues and Greens at Rome and Byzantium* (Oxford, 1976).
102. Coleman, "'The Contagion of the Throng,'" 76–78.
103. Michael McCormick, "Emperor and Court," in *The Cambridge Ancient History*, vol. 14, *Late Antiquity: Empire and Successors, A.D. 425–600*, ed. A. Cameron, B. Ward-Perkins, and M. Whitby (Cambridge, UK, 2000), 135–63, at 159.
104. Cameron, *Circus Factions*, 173–75.

105. Brown, *Through the Eye of a Needle*, 339–58.
106. Symmachus, *Epistolae*, 2.78, ed. Jean Pierre Callu, *Symmaque, Lettres* (Paris, 1972), vol. 1, 204: "auidus ciuicae gratiae."
107. Boethius, *De consolatione philosophiae*, book 2, Prosa 3, c. 8: "Si quis rerum mortalium fructus ullum beatitudinis pondus habet, poteritne illius memoria lucis quantalibet ingruentium malorum mole deleri cum duos pariter consules liberos tuos domo prouehi sub frequentia patrum sub plebis alacritate uidisti, cum eisdem in curia curules insidentibus tu regiae laudis orator ingenii gloriam facundiaeque meruisti, cum in circo duorum medius consulum circumfusae multitudinis exspectationem triumphali largitione satiasti?"
108. Philo Judaeus, *De praemiis et poenis* (3).20, ed. L. Cohn, in *Philonis Alexandrini opera quae supersunt* (Berlin, 1962 [1906]), vol. 5, 340: "ὅ τι γὰρ ἄτακτον, ἄκοσμον, πλημμελές, ὑπαίτιον, τοῦτο ὄχλος ἐστί . . ."
109. Vergil, *Aeneid* 1.148–53, in *P. Vergilius Maro, Aeneis*, ed. Gian Biagio Conte (Berlin, 2011), 6. This simile of a "man" (*vir*) calming a riotous crowd is used to describe Neptune as he calms the waves.
110. Seneca, *Epistulae morales* 7.2–3, ed. L. D. Reynolds, *L. Annaei Senecae ad Lucilium Epistulae Morales* (Oxford, 1965), vol. 1, 12: "Nihil vero tam damnosum bonis moribus quam in aliquo spectaculo desidere. Tunc enim per voluptatem facilius vitia subrepunt. [. . .] Avarior redeo, ambitiosior, luxuriosior, immo vero crudelior et inhumanior, quia inter homines fui."
111. Knapp, *Invisible Romans*, 274.
112. E. Auerbach, *Mimesis: The Representation of Reality in Western Literature*, trans. W. R. Trask (Princeton, NJ, 1953), 37 (discussing Tacitus's analysis of a revolt).
113. Tacitus, *Annales* 14.20.1–5, ed. H. Heubner (Stuttgart, 1983), 319; Zosimos, *New History*, 1.6.1, ed. F. Paschoud, *Histoire nouvelle* (Paris, 1971). Alan Cameron, "The Date of Zosimus' *New History*," *Philologus* 113 (1969): 106–10, dates the first book of Zosimos's history to between 501 and 502, when such dances were prohibited. Concern about pantomimes was not unique to Constantinople. Cassiodorus, *Variae* 1.20, 1.32, ed. Å. J. Fridh, CCSL 96 (Turnhout, 1958), 28–29, 38–39, complains about pantomimes or spectacles being linked with squabbles and sedition at Rome. (I did not have the opportunity to consult Giardina et al., *Varie*, vol. 1, containing books 1 and 2.) See also Cameron, *Circus Factions*, 227.
114. Cassiodorus, *Variae*, 1.27.4, ed. Fridh, 35: "Mores autem graues in spectaculis quis requirat? ad circum nesciunt conuenire Catones." Compare to the criticism of circus spectacle at Cassiodorus, *Variae* 3.51.3, ed. Giardina et al., *Varie*, vol. 2, 64: "Spectaculum expellens grauissimos mores, inuitans leuissimas contentiones, euacuator honestatis, fons irriguus iurgiorum, quod uetustas quidem habuit sacrum, sed contentiosa posteritas fecit esse ludibrium" (with commentary at 294–95).
115. Cassiodorus, *Variae*, 1.27, ed. Fridh, 35: "Sed ne forsitan magnificos uiros loquacitas popularis offenderit, praesumptionis huius habenda discretio est."
116. *Excessus* was the word for "leave-taking," whence its figurative meaning: a "departure" from self-mastery: *TLL*, s.v. "excessus" (Leumann), vol. 2, 1228–30.
117. Cassiodorus, *Variae* 1.27.5, ed. Fridh, 35: "Quicquid illic a gaudenti populo dicitur, iniuria non putatur. Locus est qui defendit excessum. Quorum garrulitas si patienter accipitur, ipsos quoque principes ornare monstratur." See Valérie Fauvinet-Ranson, *Decor civitatis, decor Italiae: Monuments, travaux publics et spectacles au VIe siècle d'après les Variae de Cassiodore* (Bari, 2006), 309–11.
118. *Codex Theodosianus*, 16.2.31, ed. Mommsen and Meyer, 845.
119. Coleman, "'The Contagion of the Throng,'" 77. The games could reflect the moral qualities of a public figure in other ways. Cassius Dio, *Roman History*, 72.29, ed. Boissevain, vol. 3, 269, underscores Marcus Aurelius's mercy by emphasizing that he patronized gladiatorial bouts with blunted weapons. See Michael Carter, "Gladiatorial Combat with 'Sharp' Weapons (Τοῖς Ὀξέσι Σιδήροις)," *Zeitschrift für Papyrologie und Epigraphik* 155 (2006): 161–75, esp. 170–72.

120. Ammianus 22.7.2.

121. Seneca, *Ep.* 7.2–3, ed. Reynolds, vol. 1, 12: "Nihil vero tam damnosum bonis moribus quam in aliquo spectaculo desidere. Tunc enim per voluptatem facilius vitia subrepunt."

122. Augustine, *Confessiones*, 6.8.13, ed. M. Skutella and L. Verheijen, CCSL 27 (Turnhout, 1981): "ille clausis foribus oculorum interdixit animo ne in tanta mala procederet. atque utinam et aures obturavisset! nam quodam pugnae casu, cum clamor ingens totius populi vehementer eum pulsasset, curiositate victus et quasi paratus, quidquid illud esset, etiam visum contemnere et vincere, aperuit oculos. et percussus est graviore vulnere in anima quam ille in corpore quem cernere concupivit, ceciditque miserabilius quam ille quo cadente factus est clamor. qui per eius aures intravit et reseravit eius lumina, ut esset qua feriretur et deiceretur audax adhuc potius quam fortis animus, et eo infirmior quo de se praesumpserat [cf. Judith 6.15], qui debuit de te. ut enim vidit illum sanguinem, immanitatem simul ebibit et non se avertit, sed fixit aspectum et hauriebat furias et nesciebat, et delectabatur scelere certaminis et cruenta voluptate inebriabatur. et non erat iam ille qui venerat sed unus de turba ad quam venerat, et verus eorum socius a quibus adductus erat." See Franz-Frieder Lühr, "Zur Darstellung und Bewertung von Massenreaktionen in der lateinischen Literatur," *Hermes* 107 (1979): 92–114, at 111–14; Gottfried Mader, "Blocked Eyes and Ears: The Eloquent Gestures at Augustine, *Conf.*, VI, 8, 13," *L'Antiquité classique* 69 (2000): 217–20; Daniel Slyke, "The Devil and His Pomps in Fifth-Century Carthage: Renouncing *Spectacula* with Spectacular Imagery," *Dumbarton Oaks Papers* 59 (2005): 53–72.

123. Isidore, *Et.*, 18.59.1: "Proinde nihil esse debet Christiano cum Circensi insania, cum inpudicitia theatri, cum amphitheatri crudelitate, cum atrocitate arenae, cum luxuria ludi."

124. Jonathan Arnold, *Theoderic, the Goths, and the Restoration of the Roman Empire* (Cambridge, UK, 2014), 212–24. Alan Cameron, *Porphyrius the Charioteer* (Oxford, 1973), 230, stresses that a special horror was reserved for the *venatio*. For the *Variae*'s historical reliability, see Shane Bjornlie, *Politics and Tradition between Rome, Ravenna and Constantinople: A Study of Cassiodorus and the Variae, 527–554* (Cambridge, UK, 2013), esp. 19–26; Shane Bjornlie, "The Rhetoric of *Varietas* and Epistolary Encyclopedism in the *Variae* of Cassiodorus," in *Shifting Genres in Late Antiquity*, ed. Geoffrey Greatrex, Hugh Elton, and Lucas McMahon (Farnham, UK, 2015), 289–303.

125. Gregory of Tours, *Hist.*, 5.17, ed. Krusch and Levison, 216: "Quod ille dispiciens, apud Sessionas atque Parisius circus aedificare praecepit, eosque populis spectaculum praebens." Dey, *The Afterlife of the Roman City*, 167–68. What is meant by *spectacula* is not clear; Gregory uses this term in reference to "proper" circus spectacles at Constantinople (*Hist.* 5.30, 235), but also in a more all-encompassing sense for impressive sites: Gregory of Tours, *Liber de miraculis Andreae apostoli* [*BHL* 430], 1.2.23, ed. B. Krusch, MGH SRM 1.2 (Hanover, 1885), 389: "Sed postmodum in nomine Iesu Christi resuscitavit puerum, et omnis civitas cucurrit ad hoc spectaculum." The story is not meant to be flattering to Chilperic, who may have been trying to win over the local Latin-speaking populace in a moment of civil strife. Chilperic's patronage of the old forms of collective behavior contrasts with Guntram's defense of pious collective institutions (*Hist.* 9.21, 441).

126. In 507, Chilperic's grandfather Clovis I had distributed gold and silver to crowds along the Roman road leading to the church of the city of Tours: Gregory of Tours, *Hist.*, 2.37–38, ed. Krusch and Levison, 88–89: "Tunc ascenso equite, aurum argentumque in itinere illo, quod inter portam atrii et eclesiam civitatis est, praesentibus populis manu propria spargens, voluntate benignissima erogavit, et ab ea die tamquam consul aut augustus est vocitatus." Michael McCormick, "Clovis at Tours: Byzantine Public Ritual and the Origins of Medieval Ruler Symbolism," in *Das Reich und die Barbaren*, ed. Evangelos Chrysos and Andreas Schwarcz (Vienna, 1989), 155–80.

127. Alan Cameron, *The Last Pagans of Rome* (Oxford, 2011), 787–92, esp. 791: "First, Christians would not help seeing pagan festivals as an evil counterpart to the festivals of the church. Second, simply because they drew the crowds. No festival of the church could hope to generate

the excitement of a major festival day in theatre, amphitheatre, or circus, excitement that the church could not control." Compare Brown, *Through the Eye of a Needle*, 353–58, for the "war of giving" (355) between church and civic authorities; Peter Brown, *The Ransom of the Soul: Afterlife and Wealth in Early Western Christianity* (Cambridge, MA, 2015), 83–91.

128. Coleman, "'The Contagion of the Throng,'" 79: "Their disappearance seems to have been brought about by economic pressure rather than by a change of heart accompanying the Christianization of the Empire"; Ignazio Tantillo, "I munera in età tardoantica," in *Aurea Roma: Dalla città pagana alla città cristiana*, ed. Serena Ensoli and Eugenio La Rocca (Rome, 2000), 120–25; Cameron, *Circus Factions*, 297–308; Jones, *The Later Roman Empire*, 1016.

129. Bryan Ward-Perkins, *From Classical Antiquity to the Middle Ages: Urban Public Building in Northern and Central Italy, AD 300–850* (Oxford, 1984), 92–118. For the trade in animals, see David Bomgardner, "The Trade in Wild Beasts for Roman Spectacles: A Green Perspective," *Anthropozoologica* 16 (1992): 161–66.

130. Carlrichard Brühl, *Palatium und Civitas: Studien zur Profantopographie spätantiker Civitates vom 3. bis 13. Jahrhundert*, 2 vols. (Cologne, 1975–90), vol. 1, 6–33, 53–72, 83–90; vol. 2, 41–62. Amiens's amphitheater, close to the city center, was incorporated into the walls: E. M. Wightman, *Gallia Belgica* (London, 1985), 232.

131. Brühl, *Palatium und Civitas*, vol. 1, 100–106 (Tours), 240–41 (Arles); Ward-Perkins, *From Classical Antiquity to the Middle Ages*, 92–118. Wightman, *Gallia Belgica*, 229–33, 293; Kim Bowes and Afrim Hoti, "An Amphitheatre and Its Afterlives: Survey and Excavation in the Durres Amphitheatre," *Journal of Roman Archaeology* 16 (2003): 380–94, at 388. For an exemplary study, see Hélène Noizet, *La fabrique de la ville: Espaces et sociétés à Tours (IXe–XIIIe siècle)* (Paris, 2007).

132. Jules Formigé, "L'amphithéâtre d'Arles," *Revue archéologique* 2 (1964): 113–63, at 140.

133. Julian of Toledo, *Historia Wambae regis*, c. 18, ed. W. Levison, CCSL 115 (Turnhout, 1976), 234: "At ubi feroces nostrorum animos sustinere non possunt, intra arenas, quae ualidiori muro, antiquioribus aedificiis cingebantur, se muniendos includunt." Cf. André Dupont, *Les cités de la Narbonnaise première depuis les invasions germaniques jusqu'à l'apparition du Consulat* (Nîmes, 1942), 229.

134. *Gesta Treverorum*, c. 20, ed. G. Waitz, MGH SS 8 (Hanover, 1848), 157: "in harena civitatis, id est in amphiteatro, quam munierant." For Trier, see Brühl, *Palatium und Civitas*, vol. 2, 63–88.

135. Alessandro Delfino and Claudia Minniti, "Un butto della prima metà dell'XI secolo presso piazza del Colosseo," *Bullettino della Commissione archeologica comunale di Roma* 109 (2008): 161–73. For animal remains, see Michael MacKinnon, "Supplying Exotic Animals for the Roman Amphitheatre Games: New Reconstructions Combining Archaeological, Ancient Textual, Historical and Ethnographic Data," *Mouseion* 6 (2006): 137–61, and Jacopo De Grossi Mazzorin and Claudia Minniti, "The Impact of Trade on Animal Exploitation in Rome During the Roman Period: The Evidence from Zooarchaeological Analysis," *Journal of Archaeological Science: Reports* 47 (2023): 1–7, at 5. See also the reports in Giulia Facchin, Rea Rossella, and Riccardo Santangeli Valenzani, eds., *Anfiteatro Flavio: Transformazioni e riusi* (Milan, 2018).

136. Paul the Deacon, *Historia Langobardorum* 4.30, ed. L. Bethmann and G. Waitz, MGH SRL 1 (Hanover, 1878), 127: "Igitur sequenti aestate mense Iulio levatus est Adaloaldus rex super Langobardos apud Mediolanum in circo, in praesentia patris sui Agilulfi regis, adstantibus legatis Teudeperti regis Francorum, et disponsata est eidem regio puero filia regis Teudeperti, et firmata est pax perpetua cum Francis." See Reinhard Schneider, *Königswahl und Königserhehung im Frühmittelalter: Untersuchungen zur Herrschaftsnachfolge bei den Langobarden und Merowingern* (Stuttgart, 1972), 33–35.

137. *Vita Theodori*, ed. T. Mommsen, MGH Gesta Pontif. Rom. 1, 179: "ad exemplum multorum." Ward-Perkins, *From Classical Antiquity to the Middle Ages*, 117.

138. *Vita Stephani III*, c. 14, *LP* 1, 472: "Postmodum vero quidam iniqui Campanini qui hic Roma advenerant, adortati ab aliis nequioribus se et impiissimis, eundem Gracilem ex ipsa custodia abstollentes et quasi eum in monasterio deportantes, dum Colosseo advenissent, illic eius oculos eruerunt, etiam et linguam abstulerunt."

139. Ward-Perkins, *From Classical Antiquity to the Middle Ages*, 116–18.

140. For the Colosseum's sixth-century history, see Silvia Orlandi, "Il Colosseo nel V secolo," in *The Transformations of Vrbs Roma in Late Antiquity*, ed. W. V. Harris (Portsmouth, RI, 1999), 249–63.

141. Agnellus, *Liber pontificalis ecclesiae Rauennensis*, c. 2, ed. Otto Holder-Egger, MGH SRL 1 (Hanover, 1878), 149: "Templum Apollinis, quod ante portam quae uocatur Aurea, iuxta amphitheatrum, suis orationibus demoliuit [*sc.* Saint Apollinaris]"; c. 129, ed. Holder-Egger, 305: "Ab amphitheatro, quod fuit priscis temporibus iuxta portam quae uocatur Aurea, usque ad iam dictam posterulam factus est quasi crepitus et sonitus ingens, et eleuatus est fumus quasi nebula, et hians terra omnes mortuos quos infra se clausos habuit, quos Posterulenses demoliti sunt, cum nimio foetore in suo sinu ostendit." For the second passage, without reference to the amphitheater, see Joaquín Martínez Pizarro, "Crowds and Power in the *Liber Pontificalis Ecclesiae Ravennatis*," in *The Community, the Family and the Saint: Patterns of Power in Early Medieval Europe*, ed. J. Hill and M. Swann (Turnhout, 1998), 265–83; Joaquín Martínez Pizarro, *Writing Ravenna: The Liber Pontificalis of Andreas Agnellus* (Ann Arbor, MI, 1995), 146–48.

142. Giorgio Vespignani, "Il circo di Ravenna *regia civitas* (secc. V–X)," in *Ravenna: Da capitale imperiale a capitale esarcale* (Spoleto, 2005), vol. 2, 1133–42; Deborah Deliyannis, *Ravenna in Late Antiquity* (Cambridge, UK, 2010), 59–60; Humphrey, *Roman Circuses*, 632–33.

143. E.g., Benedict of Aniane, *Corcordia regularum*, c. 25, ed. P. Bonnerue, CCCM 168A (Turnhout, 1999), 199: "Diligenter, quaeso, fratres, adtendite et cognoscite, quia in nobismetipsis habemus amphitheatrum spiritale, et illam quam silua barbara in spectaculis fingunt, cotidie patimur in ambitu cordis nostri." See Joseph Szöfférffy, *Concise History of Medieval Latin Hymnody* (Leiden, 1985), 16; Geneviève Bührer-Thierry, "Qui sont les athlètes de dieu? La performance sportive par l'ascèse et la prédication," in *Agôn: La compétition, Ve–XIIe siècle*, ed. F. Bougard, R. Le Jan, and T. Lienhard (Turnhout, 2012), 293–310, esp. 296–98.

144. Michael McCormick and Alexander Kazhdan, "Chariot Races," in *The Oxford Dictionary of Byzantium*, ed. A. Kazhdan (Oxford, 1991), vol. 1, 412; Gilbert Dagron, *L'hippodrome de Constantinople: Jeux, peuple et politique* (Paris, 2011), 119–26.

145. Alain Ducellier, "Jeux et sports à Byzance," *Les dossiers de l'archéologie* 45 (1980): 83–87, at 87; see also Lynn Jones and Henry Maguire, "A Description of the Jousts of Manuel I Komnenos," *Byzantine and Modern Greek Studies* 26 (2002): 104–48.

146. A. A. Vasiliev, "The Monument of Porphyrius in the Hippodrome at Constantinople," *Dumbarton Oaks Papers* 4 (1948): 29–49, at 29: "In the course of history the Hippodrome became not only the place for races and entertainments but also the scene of many important and some tragic events in Byzantine history." The most important sources for early Byzantine ceremonial are found in the tenth-century collections by Constantine VII Porphyrogenitos, *De administrando imperio*, ed. Gyula Moravcsiks, trans. R.J.H. Jenkins, revised ed. (Washington, DC, 1985); and Constantine VII Porphyrogenitus, *De ceremoniis*, ed. Gilbert Dagron and Bernard Flusin, *Le livre des cérémonies*, 5 vols., Corpus fontium historiae Byzantinae 52 (Paris, 2020).

147. Rodolphe Guilland, "Études sur l'Hippodrome de Byzance (VI)," *Byzantinoslavica* 27 (1968): 289–307, esp. 302–5, for public displays of punishment and humiliation up to the twelfth century.

148. J. B. Bury, "The Nika Riot," *The Journal of Hellenic Studies* 17 (1897): 92–119, is still valuable in reconstructing events. See also Geoffrey Greatrex, "The Nika Riot: A Reappraisal," *The Journal of Hellenic Studies* 117 (1997): 60–86; Mischa Meier, "Die Inszenierung einer Katastrophe: Justinian und der Nika-Aufstand," *Zeitschrift für Papyrologie und Epigraphik* 117 (2003):

273–300. For the prevalence of riots centered on the hippodrome in this period, see Cyril Mango, *Le développement urbain de Constantinople (IVe–VIIe siècles)* (Paris, 1985), 51–52. For broad streets and other public spaces, see Albrecht Berger, "Streets and Public Spaces in Constantinople," *Dumbarton Oaks Papers* 54 (2000): 161–72.
149. McCormick, *Eternal Victory*, 73.

Chapter 2. Numbers

1. Administration: John Matthews, *Western Aristocracies and Imperial Court, A.D. 364–425* (Oxford, 1975), esp. 319–25; Chris Wickham, "The Other Transition: From the Ancient World to Feudalism," *Past & Present* 103 (1984): 3–36; Alexander Demandt, *Die Spätantike: Römische Geschichte von Diocletian bis Justinian, 284–565 n. Chr.*, revised ed. (Munich, 2007), 204–16; A.H.M. Jones, *The Later Roman Empire, 284–602: A Social, Economic, and Administrative Survey*, 2 vols. (Baltimore, 1986 [1964]), esp. 182–92, 199–202, 240–48. Kingdoms: Jones, *Later Roman Empire*, 245–65; Roger Collins, "The Western Kingdoms," in *The Cambridge Ancient History*, vol. 14, 112–34; Chris Wickham, *Framing the Early Middle Ages* (Oxford, 2005), 80–124. Peoples: Guy Halsall, *Barbarian Migrations and the Roman West* (Cambridge, UK, 2007), 488–94; Walter Pohl, "Konfliktverlauf und Konfliktbewältigung: Römer und Barbaren im frühen Mittelalter," *Frühmittelalterliche Studien* 26 (1992): 165–207. Religion: Jones, *Later Roman Empire*, 873–937; Pierre Chuvin, *Chronique des derniers païens: La disparition du paganisme dans l'empire romain, du règne de Constantin à celui de Justinien*, 2nd ed. (Paris, 1991), 21–152; Peter Brown, *The Rise of Western Christendom*, revised ed. (Malden, MA, 2013), 54–92; Christopher Jones, *Between Pagan and Christian* (Cambridge, MA, 2014), esp. 107–25. Economy: Michael McCormick, *Origins of the European Economy* (Cambridge, UK, 2001), 25–119, with summary at 115–19; Wickham, *Framing*, 708–20; Jairus Banaji, "Late Antiquity to the Early Middle Ages: What Kind of Transition?," *Historical Materialism* 19 (2011): 109–44. East and West: Jones, *Later Roman Empire*, 1027–31; Fergus Millar, *A Greek Roman Empire: Power and Belief under Theodosius II (408–450)* (Berkeley, 2006); Wickham, "The Other Transition," 33–36. Demography is discussed below, along with environmental drivers, but for the latter, see Kyle Harper, "The Environmental Fall of the Roman Empire," *Daedalus* 145 (2016): 6–15; and Kyle Harper, *The Fate of Rome: Climate, Disease, and the End of an Empire* (Princeton, NJ, 2017), 249–59; and critical response by Kristina Sessa, "The New Environmental Fall of Rome: A Methodological Consideration," *Journal of Late Antiquity* 12 (2019): 211–55.

2. Peter Brown, *The World of Late Antiquity, AD 150–750* (New York, 1989 [1971]), remains a reference point for scholars emphasizing continuities between the ancient and medieval worlds. See the classic assessment by Andrea Giardina, "Esplosione di tardoantico," *Studi Storici* 40 (1999): 157–80. Political ceremony: Sabine MacCormack, *Art and Ceremony in Late Antiquity* (Berkeley, 1981); Michael McCormick, *Eternal Victory: Triumphal Rulership in Late Antiquity, Byzantium and the Early Medieval West* (Cambridge, UK, 1986), 260–387; Francis Oakley, *Empty Bottles of Gentilism: Kingship and the Divine in Late Antiquity and the Early Middle Ages* (New Haven, CT, 2010), 67–78, 143–57. Funeral cutoms: Michel Kazanski and Patrick Périn, "Le tombeau de Childéric: Un tumulus oriental?," *Travaux et mémoires* 15 (2005): 287–98; Bonnie Effros, *Caring for Body and Soul: Burial and Afterlife in the Merovingian World* (University Park, PA, 2002). Romanness as inspiration: Helmut Reimitz, *History, Frankish Identity and the Framing of Western Ethnicity, 550–850* (Cambridge, UK, 2015), 1–24; Rosamond McKitterick, *History and Memory in the Carolingian World* (Cambridge, UK, 2004), 84–119; and the essays in Walter Pohl, Clemens Gantner, Cinzia Grifoni, and Marianne Pollheimer-Mohaupt, eds., *Transformations of Romanness: Early Medieval Regions and Identities* (Berlin, 2018). Law: Stefan Esders, *Römische Rechtstradition und merowingisches Königtum* (Göttingen, 1997).

3. Hendrick Dey, *The Afterlife of the Roman City: Architecture and Ceremony in Late Antiquity and the Early Middle Ages* (Cambridge, UK, 2015), 250–51.

4. March Bloch, *Feudal Society*, trans. L. A. Manyon (London, 1965), 60–1; Henri Pirenne, *A History of Europe: From the Invasions to the Sixteenth Century*, trans. B. Miall (New York, 1955), vol. 1, 75. Compare Renée Doehaerd, *Le haut Moyen Âge occidental: Économies et sociétés* (Paris, 1971), 136; Georges Duby, *Guerriers et paysans: VIIe–XIIe siècle, premier essor de l'économie européenne* (Paris, 1973), 19–21; David Herlihy, "Demography," in *Dictionary of the Middle Ages*, ed. J. R. Strayer (New York, 1982), vol. 4, 136–48, at 139; Kathryn L. Reyerson, "Urbanism, Western European," in *Dictionary of the Middle Ages* (New York, 1989), vol. 12, 311–20, at 311.

5. Josiah Russell, *Late Ancient and Medieval Population*, Transactions of the American Philosophical Society, n.s., 48 (Philadelphia, 1958), 88.

6. General: McCormick, *Origins*, 10–11, 30–41, 115, 752–52; Wickham, *Framing*, 547–50, 591–692, 830. France: Michel Rouche, "Le haut Moyen Âge," in *Histoire des populations de l'Europe*, ed. Jean-Pierre Bardet and Jacques Dupâquier (Paris, 1997), vol. 1, 133–67; Irene Barbiera, Maria Castiglioni, and Gianpiero Dalla Zuanna, "Demography, Peasantry, and Family in Early Medieval Provence, 813–814," *Population* 77 (2022): 249–74, at 251–52. Italy: Irene Barbiera and Gianpiero Dalla Zuanna, "Le dinamiche della popolazione nell'Italia medievale: Nuovi riscontri su documenti e reperti archeologici," *Archeologia Medievale* 34 (2007): 19–42; Irene Barbiera and Gianpiero Dalla Zuanna, "Population Dynamics in Italy in the Middle Ages: New Insights From Archaeological Findings," *Population and Development Review* 35 (2009): 367–89; Elio Lo Cascio and Paolo Malanima, "Cycles and Stability: Italian Population Before the Demographic Transition (225 B.C.—A.D. 1900)," *Rivista di storia economica* 21 (2005): 5–40; Fabio Giovannini, *Natalità, mortalità e demografia dell'Italia medievale sulla base di dati archeologici* (Oxford, 2001); Fabio Giovannini, "Archeologia e demografia dell'Italia medievale," *Popolazione e Storia* 2 (2002): 63–81; Neil Christie, *From Constantine to Charlemagne: An Archaeology of Italy AD 300–800* (Aldershot, UK, 2006), 249–62; Pierre Toubert, *Dalla terra ai castelli: Paesaggio, agricoltura e poteri nell'Italia medievale* (Turin, 1995), 128–32; Paolo Squatriti, "Barbarizing the Bel Paese: Environmental History in Ostrogothic Italy," in *A Companion to Ostrogothic Italy*, ed. Jonathan Arnold, Shane Bjornlie, and Kristina Sessa (Leiden, 2016), 390–423. Germany: Dietrich Lohrmann, "La croissance agricole en Allemagne au haut moyen âge," in *La croissance agricole du Haut Moyen Age: Chronologie, modalités, géographie* (Auch, 1990), 103–15, at 115; LA III, 292. Northern Europe: Jean-Pierre Devroey, *Économie rurale et société dans l'Europe franque (VIe-IXe siècles)*, vol. 1, *Fondements, matériels, échanges, et lien social* (Brussels, 2003), 41–77; Helena Hamerow, *Early Medieval Settlements: The Archaeology of Rural Communities in Northwest Europe* (Oxford, 2002), 88–89, 106–14, 139–40; Jean-Pierre Devroey and Anne Nissen Jaubert, "Family, Income and Labour Around the North Sea, 500–1000," in *Making a Living: Family, Income and Labour*, ed. Eric Vanhaute, Isabelle Devos, and Thijs Lambrecht (Turnhout, 2011), 1–40, at 7–24; Jean-Pierre Devroey and Anne Nissen, "Early Middle Ages, 500–1000," in *Struggling with the Environment: Land Use and Productivity*, ed. Erik Thoen, Tim Soens, and Annie Antoine (Turnhout, 2015), 11–68, at 19–21.

7. Gregory the Great, *Homily on Ezechiel*, 2.6.22, ed. C. Morel, *Homélies sur Ezéchiel: texte latin, introduction, traduction et notes*, SC 360 (Paris, 1990), vol. 2, 312–15 (on Ezekiel 24): "Destructae urbes, euersa sunt castra, depopulati agri, in solitudinem terra redacta est. Nullus in agris incola, pene nullus in urbibus habitator remansit . . . Ipsa autem quae aliquando mundi domina esse videbatur qualis remanserit Roma conspicimus. Immensis doloribus multipliciter attrita, desolatione civium, impressione hostium, frequentia ruinarum." See Biagio Saitta, "Crisi demografica e ordinamento ecclesiastico nell'Italia di Gregorio Magno," *Quaderni catanesi di studi antichi e medievali* 3 (2004): 62–108.

8. Luigi Gallo, "Popolosità e scarsità di popolazione: Contributo allo studio di un *Topos*," *Annali della scuola normale superiore di Pisa: Classe di lettere e filosofia* 10 (1980): 1233–70.

9. Robert Fossier, *Polyptyques et censiers*, Typologie des Sources 28 (Turnhout, 1978), 64–65; Charles-Edmond Perrin, "Observations sur le manse: Dans la région parisienne au début du

IXe siècle," in *Annales d'histoire sociale: Hommages à Marc Bloch II* (Paris, 1945), 39–52; Yoshiki Morimoto, "État et perpectives des recherches sur les polyptyques carolingiens," *Annales de l'Est* 5 (1998): 99–149; Britta Lützow, "Studien zum Reimser *Polyptychum Sancti Remigii*," *Francia* 7 (1979): 19–99; Jean-Pierre Devroey, "Les méthodes d'analyse démographique des polyptyques du Haut Moyen Âge," *Acta Historica Bruxellensia* 4 (1981): 71–88; Jean-Pierre Devroey, "Problèmes de critique autour du polyptyque de l'abbaye de Saint-Germain-des-Prés," in *La Neustrie: Les pays au nord de la Loire de 650 à 850*, ed. H. Atsma (Sigmaringen, 1989), 441–63; Monique Zerner-Chardavoine, "Enfants et jeunes au IXe siècle: La démographie du polyptyque de Marseille 813–814," *Provence Historique* 31 (1988): 355–77; Monique Zerner, "La population de Villeneuve-Saint-Georges et de Nogent-sur-Marne au IXe siècle d'après le polyptique de Saint-Germain-des-Près," in *L'Histoire dans ses variantes* (Nice, 1979), 17–24; J. Bessmerny, "Les structures de la famille paysanne dans les villages de la Francia au IXe siècle: Analyse anthroponymique du polyptyque de l'abbaye de Saint-Germain-des-Prés," *Le Moyen Âge* 90 (1984): 165–93. For a wide ranging critique, see L. R. Ménager, "Considérations sociologiques sur la démographie des grands domaines ecclésiastiques carolingiens," in *Études d'histoire du droit canonique dédiées à Gabriel Le Brase* (Paris, 1965), vol. 2, 1317–35. Most recently: Barbiera, Castiglioni, and Dalla Zuanna, "Demography, Peasantry, and Family."

10. Dieter Hägermann, Konrad Elmshäuser, and Andreas Hedwig, eds., *Das Polyptychon von Saint-Germain-des-Prés: Studienausgabe* (Cologne, 1993). Older editions retain value due to their commentary: Benjamin Guérard, ed., *Polyptyque de l'Abbé Irminon ou dénombrement des manses, des serfs et des revenus de l'abbaye de Saint-Germain-des-Prés*, 2 vols. (Paris, 1844); Auguste Longnon, ed., *Polyptyque de l'abbaye de Saint-Germain-des-Prés*, 2 vols. (Paris, 1886–95).

11. See Gregory of Tours, *Hist.* 5.28, ed. Krusch and Levison, 233–34, for parallel burning of tax *descriptiones* in sixth-century Gaul. See Jean-Pierre Devroey, "Élaboration et usage des polyptyques: Quelques éléments de réflexion à partir de l'exemple des descriptions de l'Église de Marseille (VIIIe–IXe siècles)," in *Akkulturation: Probleme einer germanisch-romanischen Kultursynthese in Spätantike und frühem Mittelalter*, ed. Claudia Giefers et al. (Berlin, 2004), 436–72, at 443–44, for seven polyptychs known to have been compiled for Marseille between c. 740 and c. 900, of which only two (813–14 and 835) survive.

12. Fossier, *Polyptyques et censiers*, for a useful overview. Apart from Saint-Germain-des-Prés (cited above), polyptychs include Prüm: Ingo Schwab, ed., *Das Prümer Urbar* (Düsseldorf, 1983); Saint-Bertin (Saint-Omer): François-Louis Ganshof, ed., *Le polyptyque de l'abbaye de Saint-Bertin (844–859)* (Paris, 1975); Reims: Jean-Pierre Devroey, ed., *Le polyptyque et les listes de cens de l'abbaye de Saint-Remi de Reims (IXe–XIe siècles)* (Reims, 1984); Lobbes: Jean-Pierre Devroey, ed., *Le polyptyque et les listes de biens de l'abbaye Saint-Pierre de Lobbes (IXe–XIe siècles)* (Brussels, 1986); Marseille: Benjamin Guérard, ed., *Descriptio Mancipiorum Ecclesiae Massiliensis* (Polyptych of St Victor, Marseille, 813–814), *Cartulaire de l'Abbaye de Saint-Victor de Marseille*, 2 vols. (Paris, 1857), vol. 2, 633–56; St. Bavo's, Ghent: Adriaan Verhulst, "Das Besitzverzeichnis der Genter Sankt-Bavo-Abtei von ca. 800 (Clm 6333): Ein Beitrag zur Geschichte und Kritik der karolingischen Urbarialaufzeichnungen," *Frühmittelalterliche Studien* 5 (1971): 193–234, at 232–34; Weissenburg (Wissembourg): Christophe Dette, ed., *Liber possessionum Wizenburgensis* (Mainz, 1987); Montiérender: Claus-Dieter Droste, ed., *Das Polyptichon von Montierender* (Trier, 1988); Saint Maur-des-Fossés: Dieter Hägermann and Andreas Hedwig, eds., *Das Polyptychon und die Notitia de Areis von Saint-Maur-des-Fossés: Analyse und Edition*, Beihefte der Francia 23 (Sigmaringen, 1990); Lucca: Paolo Tomei, "Un nuovo 'polittico' lucchese del IX secolo: Il Breve de Multis Pensionibus," *Studi Medievali*, 3rd ser., 53 (2012): 567–602.

13. Pierre Toubert, "Le moment carolingien (VIIe–Xe siècle)," in *Histoire de la Famille*, ed. André Burguière et al. (Paris, 1986), vol. 1, 333–59, 336. Jean-Pierre Devroey, *Puissants et misérables: Système social et monde paysan dans l'Europe des Francs (VIe–IXe siècle)* (Brussels, 2006), 377–81.

14. Zerner-Chardavoine, "Enfants et jeunes"; Barbiera, Castiglioni, and Dalla Zuanna, "Demography, Peasantry, and Family."

15. Emily Coleman, "L'infanticide dans le Haut Moyen Age," *Annales: Histoire, Sciences Sociales* 29 (1974): 315–35. For criticism, see Jean-Pierre Devroey, "A propos d'un article récent: L'utilisation du polyptyque d'Irminon en démographie," *Revue belge de philologie et d'histoire* 55 (1977): 509–14.

16. Ferdinand Lot, "Conjectures démographiques sur la France au IXe siècle," in *Recueil des travaux historiques de Ferdinand Lot* (Geneva, 1973 [1921]), vol. 3, 465–521.

17. Wickham, *Framing*, 546–48.

18. Devroey and Nissen Jaubert "Family, Income and Labour," 16.

19. For an overview of methods, see Frank Nikulka, *Archäologische Demographie: Methoden, Daten und Bevölkerung der europäischen Bronze- und Eisenzeiten* (Leiden, 2016). See also the essays in Pilar Diarte-Blasco and Neil Christie, eds., *Interpreting Transformations of People and Landscapes in Late Antiquity and the Early Middle Ages: Archaeological Approaches and Issues* (Oxford, 2018); Luc Buchet, Claudine Dauphin, and Isabelle Séguy, eds., *La paléodémographie: Mémoire d'os, mémoire d'hommes* (Antibes, 2006); Jean-Pierre Bocquet-Appel, ed., *La paléodémographie: 99,99% de l'histoire démographique des hommes* (Paris, 2008).

20. M. Fulford and M. Allen, "Introduction: Population and the Dynamics of Change in Roman South-Eastern England," in *Agriculture and Industry in South-Eastern Roman Britain*, ed. D. Bird (Oxford, 2017), 1–14, at 5–13.

21. Joachim Henning, et al., "Reccopolis Revealed: The First Geomagnetic Mapping of the Early Medieval Visigothic Royal Town," *Antiquity* 93 (2019): 735–51.

22. Kim Bowes, "Beyond Pirenne's Shadow? Late Antique San Vincenzo Reconsidered," in *Between Text and Territory: Survey and Excavations in the Terra of San Vincenzo Al Volturno*, ed. Kim Bowes, Karen Francis, and Richard Hodges (London, 2006), 287–305, at 303.

23. McCormick, *Origins*, 31–32; Wickham, *Framing*, 495. For a case study, see Kirsty E. Squires, "Populating the Pots: The Demography of the Early Anglo-Saxon Cemeteries at Elsham and Cleatham, North Lincolnshire," *Archaeological Journal* 169 (2014): 312–42.

24. Devroey and Nissen Jaubert "Family, Income and Labour," 10–15; Frederic Cheyette, "The Disappearance of the Ancient Landscape and the Climatic Anomaly of the Early Middle Ages: A Question to Be Pursued," *Early Medieval Europe* 16 (2008): 127–65. The classic study using cemetery findings is Peter Donat and H. Ullrich, "Einwohnerzahl und Siedlungsgrösse der Merowingerzeit: Ein methodischer Beitrag zur demographischen Rekonstruktion frühgeschichtlicher Bevölkerungen," *Zeitschrift für Archäologie* 5 (1971): 234–65. For the theoretical relationship between simplification of technology and depopulation, see Ester Boserup, *The Conditions of Agricultural Growth: The Economics of Agrarian Change under Population Pressure* (London, 1965), 62–63, and Ester Boserup, *Population and Technological Change: A Study of Long-Term Trends* (Chicago, 1981).

25. Cheyette, "Disappearance," 131–44; Riccardo Francovich, "The Beginnings of Hilltop Villages in Early Medieval Tuscany," in *The Long Morning of Medieval Europe: New Directions in Early Medieval Studies*, ed. Jennifer R. Davis and Michael McCormick (Aldershot, UK, 2008), 55–82.

26. Giuseppe Muci, "Dinamiche insediative e demografiche nelle Puglia meridionale in età Medievale," in *Storia e archeologia globale dei paesaggi rurali in Italia fra Tardoantico e Medioevo*, ed. Giuliano Volpe (Bari, 2018), 291–95

27. Wickham, *Framing*, 312, 507–9, 548; Robin Fleming, *The Material Fall of Roman Britain, 300–525 CE* (Philadelphia, 2021), 15–16.

28. Devroey and Nissen, "Early Middle Ages," 28–29. For Italy, by contrast, see Barbiera and Dalla Zuanna, "Population Dynamics," 368; Lo Cascio and Malanima, "Cycles and Stability," 12–13.

29. See Christopher Loveluck, *Northwest Europe in the Early Middle Ages* (Cambridge, UK, 2013).

30. Donat and Ullrich, "Einwohnerzahl" (but see LA III, 285); Didier Paillard, Luc Buchet, and Armelle Alduc-Le Bagousse, "Nombre d'inhumés, nombre d'habitants: Estimations archéologiques et anthropologiques," in *La paléodémographie: Mémoire d'os, mémoire d'hommes*, ed. Luc Buchet, Claudine Dauphin, and Isabelle Séguy (Antibes, 2006), 209–24; Irene Barbiera, "Buried Together, Buried Alone: Christian Commemoration and Kinship in the Early Middle Ages," *Early Medieval Europe* 23 (2015): 385–409.

31. Barbiera and Dalla Zuanna, "Population Dynamics," 378–79; Francovich, "The Beginnings of Hilltop Villages," 56–57.

32. Richard Steckel, Clark Larsen, Charlotte Roberts, and Joerg Baten, *The Backbone of Europe: Health, Diet, Work and Violence over Two Millennia* (Cambridge, UK, 2018); Nikulka, *Archäologische Demographie*; see also Adrien Bayard, Vanessa Bayard-Maret, and Gabriel Cordeiro, "Vers une archéologie des crises alimentaires?," *Mélanges de l'Ecole française de Rome: Moyen Âge* 131 (2019). For the later period, see Maryanne Kowaleski, "Medieval People in Town and Country: New Perspectives from Demography and Bioarchaeology," *Speculum* 89 (2014): 573–600.

33. Irene Barbiera, Maria Castiglioni, and Gianpiero Dalla Zuanna, "A Synthetic Measure of Mortality Using Skeletal Data from Ancient Cemeteries: The d Index," *Demographic Research* 38 (2018): 2053–72.

34. One promising area of focus is the genetic investigation of "effective population" (N_e) that is, not total population size but a notional breeding population accounting for observed genetic drift. For examples of what can be done with N_e reconstructions, see Daniel M. Fernandes et al., "A Genetic History of the Pre-Contact Caribbean," *Nature* 590 (2021): 103–10, and Dirk Seidensticker et al., "Population Collapse in Congo Rainforest from 400 CE Urges Reassessment of the Bantu Expansion," *Sciences Advances* 7 (2021): 1–13, at 5–6.

35. Harper, *Fate of Rome*, 65–118, 136–45; Colin Elliott, *Pox Romana: The Plague That Shook the Roman World* (Princeton, NJ, 2024). Arthur E. R. Boak, *Manpower Shortage and the Fall of the Roman Empire in the West* (Ann Arbor, MI, 1955), for a discussion based on written sources, but see the riposte by Charles Whittaker, "Agri deserti," in *Studies in Roman Property*, ed. Moses Finley (Cambridge, UK, 1976), 137–65.

36. Bruce W. Frier, "Demography," in *Cambridge Ancient History*, vol. 11, *The High Empire, A.D. 70–192*, ed. A. K. Bowman, P. Garnsey, and D. Rathbone (Cambridge, UK, 2000), 787–816, at 814–15; Walter Scheidel, "Demography," in *The Cambridge Economic History of the Greco-Roman World*, ed. Walter Scheidel, Ian Morris, and Richard Saller (Cambridge, UK, 2007): 38–86, at 47. But see also Walter Scheidel, "Demographie," in *Handbuch: Antike Wirtschaft*, ed. Sitta von Reden and Kai Ruffing (Berlin, 2023), 209–26, at 222–23, for uncertainty.

37. For rejuvenation of eastern cities, see Noel Lenski, *Constantine and the Cities: Imperial Authority and Civic Politics* (Philadelphia, 2016), 131–49.

38. Walter Goffart, *Barbarians and Romans, A.D. 418–584: The Techniques of Accommodation* (Princeton, NJ, 1980), 4–5, 231–34; Halsall, *Barbarian Migrations*, 424–25. To acknowledge low numbers is not to deny impact. Peter Heather, *Empires and Barbarians: The Fall of Rome and the Birth of Europe* (Oxford, 2010), who sees migration as a "major theme of the first millennium" (578), acknowledges the small scale of the numbers involved (154, 175, 424). See further Peter Heather, "The Creation of the Visigoths," in *The Visigoths from the Migration Period to the Seventh Century: An Ethnographic Perspective*, ed. Peter Heather (Woodbridge, UK, 1999), 43–92, at 52–55.

39. This was the view of Russell, *Late Ancient and Medieval Population*, 37; Josiah Russell, "That Earlier Plague," *Demography* 5 (1968): 174–84, at 174, 180. For a judicious discussion, see Bryan Ward-Perkins, "Land, Labour and Settlement," in *The Cambridge Ancient History*, vol. 14, *Late Antiquity: Empire and Successors, A.D. 425–600*, ed. Averil Cameron, Bryan Ward-Perkins, and Michael Whitby (Cambridge, UK, 2000), 315–45, at 320–27.

40. Ulf Büntgen et al., "Cooling and Societal Change during the Late Antique Little Ice Age from 536 to around 660 AD," *Nature Geoscience* 9 (2016): 231–36; Peter N. Peregrine, "Climate and Social Change at the Start of the Late Antique Little Ice Age," *Holocene* 30 (2020): 1643–48; Ulf Büntgen et al., "Global Wood Anatomical Perspective on the Onset of the Late Antique Little Ice Age (LALIA) in the mid-6th Century CE," *Science Bulletin* 67 (2022); 2336–44; Pierre Toubert, "Fluctuations climatiques et désastres démographiques au Moyen Âge," in *Colloque: Vie et climat d'Hésiode à Montesquieu*, ed. Jacques Jouanna, Christian Robin, and Michel Zink, Cahiers de la Villa Kérylos 29 (Paris, 2018), 385–402; Harper, *Fate of Rome*, 160–98. The theory of cooling climate with averse agrarian effects precedes the recent scientific characterization of the LALIA by Büntgen et al.: See Cheyette, "Disappearance," 155–65; Jean-Pierre Devroey, "Catastrophe, crise et changement social: À propos des paradigmes d'interprétation du développement médiéval (500–1100)," in *Vers une anthropologie des catastrophes: Actes des 9e journées anthropologiques de Valbonne*, ed. Luc Buchet and Isabelle Séguy (Antibes, 2008), 67–89.

41. The literature is vast. Recent publications provide bibliographical orientation: Kyle Harper, "The First Plague Pandemic in Italy: The Written Evidence," *Speculum* 98 (2023): 369–420; Peter Sarris, "New Approaches to the 'Plague of Justinian,'" *Past & Present* 254 (2022): 315–46; Michael McCormick, "Gregory of Tours on Sixth-Century Plague and Other Epidemics," *Speculum* 96 (2021): 38–96; John Mulhall, "Confronting Pandemic in Late Antiquity: The Medical Response to the Justinianic Plague," *Journal of Late Antiquity* 14 (2021): 498–528. Lester Little, ed., *Plague and the End of Antiquity: The Pandemic of 541–750* (Cambridge, UK, 2007), remains a landmark, though the field has advanced. On demographic impacts, see Harper, *Fate of Rome*, 199–245, with 304–15; Mischa Meier, "The 'Justinianic Plague': The Economic Consequences of the Pandemic in the Eastern Roman Empire and Its Cultural and Religious Effects," *Early Medieval Europe* 24 (2016): 267–92, at 270–82; and McCormick, *Origins*, 40–41, 113–14, 783. For the "minimalist" riposte, see below. The most important recent scientific contribution is Marcel Keller et al., "Ancient *Yersinia pestis* Genomes from across Western Europe Reveal Early Diversification during the First Pandemic (541–750)," *PNAS* (2019): 1–10 (with valuable Supplementary Information). It summarizes the earlier aDNA research. Plague's long-term demographic impact was a function of its high case-mortality (50–60 percent) and of the disease's tendency to recur at intervals, striking replacement generations (Harper, *Fate of Rome*, 244–45). Known, dated outbreaks after 541–44 include: 558, 561–62, 565, 571, 573–74, 576, 582–84, 586, 588, 590–91, 592, 597–98, 599–600, 609, 619, 626–28, 638–39, 663–66, 670–71, 672–73, 680, 684–87, 687–89, 689–90, 693, 698–700, 704–6, 707–9, 713, 714–15, 718–19, 725–26, 729, 732–35, 743–50, 766. See Keller et al., "Ancient *Yersinia pestis* Genomes," figure 1, with Supplementary Information, 18–23; Harper, *Fate of Rome*, 304–15, a plague catalogue improving upon Dionysios Stathakopoulos, *Famine and Pestilence in the Late Roman and Early Byzantine Empire* (Birmingham, 2004).

42. Chris Wickham, *Early Medieval Italy* (Ann Arbor, MI, 1989), 26–27; Harper, *Fate of Rome*, 84–88.

43. For other diseases, human and animal, see McCormick, "Gregory," 49–60; Peregrine Horden, "Public Health, Hospitals, and Charity," in *The Oxford Handbook of the Merovingian World*, ed. Bonnie Effros and Isabel Moreira (Oxford, 2020), 299–319; Kyle Harper, "Invisible Environmental History: Infectious Disease in Late Antiquity," in *Environment and Society in the Long Late Antiquity*, ed. Adam Izdebski and Michael Mulryan (Leiden, 2019), 298–313, esp. 307–10; Timothy Newfield, "Malaria and Malaria-like Disease in the Early Middle Ages," *Early Medieval Europe* 25 (2017): 251–300; Timothy Newfield, "Human–Bovine Plagues in the Early Middle Ages," *Journal of Interdisciplinary History* 46 (2015): 1–38. For the reaction to epidemics, see Thomas Wozniak, *Naturereignisse im frühen Mittelalter: Das Zeugnis der Geschichtsschreibung vom 6. bis 11. Jahrhundert* (Berlin, 2020), 630–62.

44. E.g., Adam Izdebski et al., "L'émergence d'une histoire environnementale interdisciplinaire: Une approche conjointe de l'Holocène tardif," *Annales* 77 (2022): 11–58; Hendrik Dey and

Paolo Squatriti, "Late Antique 'Natural' Disasters: *De te fabula narratur?*," *Antiquité Tardive* 29 (2021): 69–80; the essays in Adam Izdebski and Michael Mulryan, eds., *Environment and Society in the Long Late Antiquity* (Leiden, 2019); Sessa, "New Environmental Fall of Rome"; Paolo Squatriti, "The Floods of 589 and Climate Change at the Beginning of the Middle Ages: An Italian Microhistory," *Speculum* 85 (2010): 799–826.

45. Amartya Sen, "Ingredients of Famine Analysis: Availability and Entitlements," *The Quarterly Journal of Economics* 96 (1981): 433–64, esp. 459–62.

46. For the argument that the impact of plague was "inconsequential," see Merle Eisenberg and Lee Mordechai, "The Justinianic Plague and Global Pandemics: The Making of the Plague Concept," *American Historical Review* 125 (2020): 1632–67; Lee Mordechai et al., "The Justinianic Plague: An Inconsequential Pandemic?," *PNAS* 116 (2019): 1–9; Lee Mordechai and Merle Eisenberg, "Rejecting Catastrophe: The Case of the Justinianic Plague," *Past & Present* 244 (2019): 3–50. While there are reasons to be skeptical of this "minimalist" case, the model of asymmetric impacts is credible. See Philippe Leveau, "Le destin de l'Empire romain dans le temps long de l'environnement (note critique)," *Annales* 77 (2022): 61–83; McCormick, "Gregory," 95. Asymmetric impact was central in the Second Pandemic: Guido Alfani, "Plague in Seventeenth-Century Europe and the Decline of Italy: An Epidemiological Hypothesis," *European Review of Economic History* 17 (2013): 408–30; Adam Izdebski et al., "Palaeoecological Data Indicates Land-Use Changes across Europe Linked to Spatial Heterogeneity in Mortality during the Black Death Pandemic," *Nature Ecology and Evolution* 6 (2022): 297–306.

47. For the complex mutual interaction of climate change and epidemic burden, see Timothy Newfield, "Mysterious and Mortiferous Clouds: The Climate Cooling and Disease Burden of Late Antiquity," in *Environment and Society in the Long Late Antiquity*, ed. Adam Izdebski and Michael Mulryan (Leiden, 2019), 271–97.

48. Chris Wickham, *Framing*, 535–50, esp. 547–50; cited as alternative to plague-driven decline by Mordechai and Eisenberg, "Rejecting Catastrophe," 6.

49. Wickham, *Framing*, 550.

50. Wickham follows the reasoning of Marshall Sahlins, *Stone Age Economics* (New York, 1972), esp. 1–37 ("The Original Affluent Society"), about hunter-gatherers. For a critique of Sahlins, see David Graeber and David Wengrow, *The Dawn of Everything: A New History of Humanity* (New York, 2021), 135–40. If long-term decline was the result of persistent peasant sub-replacement fertility, early medieval Europe would be nearly unique in world history: Massimo Livi-Bacci, "What We Can and Cannot Learn from the History of World Population," *Population Studies* 69 (2015): 21–28, at 24–25.

51. Skeletal ratios suggesting high mortality in fifth- and sixth-century Italy: Barbiera, Castiglioni, and Dalla Zuanna, "The d Index"; Barbiera and Della Zuana, "Population Dynamics," 378–79. Genetic diversity of plague genomes: Keller et al., "Ancient *Yersinia pestis* Genomes," 7. Immunological adaptations: Yong Hwan Park, et al., "Ancient Familial Mediterranean Fever Mutations in Human Pyrin and Resistance to Yersinia Pestis," *Nature Immunology* 21 (2020): 856–67, at 859 (figure 1d), 863, 865.

52. John of Naples, *Gesta episcoporum neapolitanorum*, c. 42, ed. Georg Waitz, MGH SRL 1 (Hanover, 1878), 425, reports that "a great plague raged in Naples, which is called by the physicians inguinal" (*tanta desaevit clades in Neapoli, quae a medicis inguinaria vocatur*). John wrote around 900 but used older sources. Michael McCormick, "Toward a Molecular History of the Justinianic Plague," in *Plague and the End of Antiquity*, ed. Little, 290–312, at 292 n. 7, argued that John misdated this event to 766, and suggests 747 as the proper date. Harper, "First Plague Pandemic in Italy," 415–16, makes the case for 766.

53. That is not to say this period did not see environmental crises. See Jean-Pierre Devroey, *La nature et le roi: Environnement, pouvoir et société à l'âge de Charlemagne (740–820)* (Paris,

2019); John Haldon et al., "History Meets Palaeoscience: Consilience and Collaboration in Studying Past Societal Responses to Environmental Change," *PNAS* 115 (2018): 1–9, at 3–4.

54. Medieval Quiet Period: Raymond S. Bradley, Heinz Wanner, and Henry F. Diaz, "The Medieval Quiet Period," *The Holocene* 26 (2016): 990–93, at 990. For the MCA, fundamental studies include M. E. Mann, R. S. Bradley and M. K. Hughes, "Global-Scale Temperature Patterns and Climate Forcing over the Past Six Centuries," *Nature* 392 (1998): 779–87; A. Moberg et al., "Highly Variable Northern Hemisphere Temperatures Reconstructed from Low- and High-Resolution Proxy Data," *Nature* 433 (2005): 613–17; M. E. Mann, et al. "Global Signatures and Dynamical Origins of the Little Ice Age and Medieval Climate Anomaly," *Science* 326 (2009): 1256–60; Elena Xoplaxi, et al., "Medieval Climate Anomaly," *PAGES News* 19, no. 1 (2011); S. Lüning, et al., "The Medieval Climate Anomaly in the Mediterranean Region," *Paleoceanography and Paleoclimatology* 34 (2019): 1569–1670; Jesper Björklund et al., "Fennoscandian Tree-Ring Anatomy Shows a Warmer Modern than Medieval Climate," *Nature* 620 (2023): 97–103. For early stirrings of the anomaly in the late 800s, see Heather Clifford, et al., "A 2000 Year Saharan Dust Event Proxy Record from an Ice Core in the European Alps," *Journal of Geophysical Research: Atmospheres* 124 (2019): 12882–900.

55. But see Nicolas Schroeder, "Observations about Climate, Farming, and Peasant Societies in Carolingian Europe," *The Journal of European Economic History* 48 (2019): 189–210.

56. For the older view of early medieval technological and agricultural stagnation giving way to high medieval efflorescence, see Lynn White, Jr., *Medieval Technology and Social Change* (Oxford, 1962), 39–78; Duby, *Guerriers et paysans*. For the presence of metal tools, better crop yields, and early land-reclamation, see Joachim Henning, "Revolution or Relapse? Technology, Agriculture and Early Medieval Archaeology in Germanic Central Europe," in *The Langobards before the Frankish Conquest: An Ethnographic Perspective*, ed. Giorgio Ausenda, Paolo Delogu, and Chris Wickham (Woodbridge, UK, 2009), 149–73; Jonathan Jarrett, "Outgrowing the Dark Ages: Agrarian Productivity in Carolingian Europe Re-Evaluated," *The Agricultural History Review* 67 (2019): 1–28; Thomas Kohl, *Lokale Gesellschaften: Formen der Gemeinschaft in Bayern vom 8. bis zum 10. Jahrhundert* (Ostfildern, 2010), 361–65.

57. Devroey, *Économie rurale*, 64–65, shows an increase in the average number of Frankish queens' children surviving childhood (3.4 in the 600s, 3.5 in the 700s, 4 in the 800s, 4.3 in the 900s). But that may be a function of mortality, not fertility, and hardly reflects society as a whole. For peasant fertility, see Barbiera, Castiglioni, and Dalla Zuanna, "Demography, Peasantry, and Family," 260–61.

58. A minority of scholars doubt significant post-Roman depopulation: Bernard Bachrach, "Continuity in Late Antique Gaul: A Demographic and Economic Perspective," in *Comparative Perspectives on History and Historians: Essays in Memory of Bryce Lyon (1920–2007)*, ed. David Nicholas, Bernard Bachrach, and James M. Murray (Kalamazoo, MI, 2012), 27–50; Bernard Bachrach, "Plague, Population, and Economy in Merovingian Gaul," *Journal of the Australian Early Medieval Association* 3 (2007): 29–57; Bernard Bachrach, "Some Observations on the Plague in the *Regnum Francorum*," in *Auctoritas: Mélanges offerts à Olivier Guillot*, ed. G. Constable and M. Rouche (Paris, 2006), 157–66; Bernard Bachrach, *Charlemagne's Early Campaigns (768–777): A Diplomatic and Military Analysis* (Leiden, 2013), 9–17; Dick Harrison, "Plague, Settlement and Structural Change at the Dawn of the Middle Ages," *Scandia* 59 (1993): 15–48. Before them, a similar skepticism was defended by Alfons Dopsch, *Wirtschaftliche und soziale Grundlagen der europäischen Kulturentwicklung: Aus der Zeit von Caesar bis auf Karl den Grossen*, 2nd ed. (Vienna, 1923), vol. 1, esp. 330–31.

59. Nikola Koepke and Joerg Baten, "The Biological Standard of Living in Europe during the Last Two Millennia," *European Review of Economic History* 9 (2005): 61–95. Steckel et al., *Backbone*, adds nuance to the picture. For an extended version of this argument, see Fabio

Giovannini, *Natalità, mortalità e demografia dell'Italia medievale sulla base dei dati archeologici* (Oxford, 2001).

60. F. Irsigler et al., "Bevölkerung," in *Lexikon des Mittelalters* (Munich, 1977–99), vol. 2, cols. 10–21, at col. 14 (by Josiah Russell).

61. Jean-Noël Biraben, "Essai sur l'évolution du nombre des hommes," *Population* 34 (1979): 13–25, at 16 (table 2); adopted with due warnings by Devroey and Nissen, "Family, Income and Labour," 9.

62. Paul Bairoch, *Cities and Economic Development from the Dawn of History to the Present*, trans. Christopher Braider (Chicago, 1988 [1985]), 118.

63. Wickham, *Framing*, 674–75.

64. Devroey and Nissen "Family, Income and Labour," 8–15.

65. Barbiera, Castiglioni, Dalla Zuanna, "Demography, Peasantry, and Family," 249. See also the contributions to Steckel et al., *Backbone*, for interregional differences.

66. Lo Cascio and Malanima, "Cycles and Stability," 12–13; Barbiera and Dalla Zuanna, "Population Dynamics," esp. 378–79. For the extent of Italian urbanization in Antiquity, see Neville Morley, *Metropolis and Hinterland: The City of Rome and the Italian Economy, 200 BC–AD 200* (Cambridge, UK, 1996), 182.

67. Riccardo Francovich, "The Beginnings of Hilltop Villages," 65; Riccardo Francovich, "The Hinterlands of Early Medieval Towns: The Transformation of the Countryside in Tuscany," in *Post-Roman Towns, Trade and Settlement in Europe and Byzantium*, ed. J. Henning (Berlin, 2007), vol. 1, 135–52, at 135–36. For another case, Bryan Ward-Perkins, "Luni—The Decline and Abandonment of a Roman Town," *Papers in Italian Archaeology* 1 (1978): 313–21.

68. Lo Cascio and Malanima, "Cycles and Stability"; Richard Hodges and David Whitehouse, *Mahomet, Charlemagne et les origines de l'Europe*, trans. Cécile Morrisson with Jacques Lefort and Jean-Pierre Sodini (Paris, 1996), 45.

69. Francovich, "The Beginnings of Hilltop Villages."

70. Robust church-building continued in Apulia: Gioia Bertelli et al., "La Puglia tra tardo antico e altomedioevo," in *Arte in Puglia dal Medioevo al Settecento*, ed. Francesco Abbate (Bari, 2010), 31–45, at 32–35. Sicily, which enjoyed humid climatic conditions between about 450 to 750, shows mixed signs of demographic growth as well: Laura Sadori et al., "Climate, Environment and Society in Southern Italy During the Last 2000 Years: A Review of the Environmental, Historical and Archaeological Evidence," *Quaternary Science Reviews* 136 (2016): 173–88.

71. Christie, *From Constantine to Charlemagne*, 183–280, 412–28.

72. Caroline Goodson, *Cultivating the City in Early Medieval Italy* (Cambridge, UK, 2021), 1–31.

73. Goodson, *Cultivating*, 222–37. Paola Galetti, *Uomini e case nel Medioevo tra Occidente e Oriente* (Rome, 2001), 109–14; Bryan Ward Perkins, *From Classical Antiquity to the Middle Ages: Urban Public Building in Northern and Central Italy, AD 300–850* (Oxford, 1984), v; J.H.W.G. Liebeschuetz, *Decline and Fall of the Roman City* (Oxford, 2001), 94–95.

74. Paul Arthur, *Naples: From Roman Town to City-State; An Archaeological Perspective* (London, 2002); Veronica West-Harling, *Rome, Ravenna and Venice, 750–1000: Byzantine Heritage, Imperial Presence, and the Construction of City Identity* (Oxford, 2020); Ross Balzaretti, *Dark Age Liguria: Regional Identity and Local Power, c. 400–1020* (London, 2013).

75. Roberto Meneghini and Riccardo Santangeli Valenzani, *Roma nell'Altomedioevo: Topografia e urbanistica della città dal V al X secolo* (Rome, 2004); Roberto Santangeli Valenzani, ed., *Roma altomedievale: Paesaggio urbano, società e cultura (secoli V–X)* (Rome, 2023). For the political and social history, see Paolo Brezzi, *Roma e l'impero medioevale, 774–1252* (Bologna, 1947); Chris Wickham, *Medieval Rome: Stability and Crisis of a City, 900–1150* (Oxford, 2015). For the fabric of the city, see Robert Coates-Stephens, "Dark Age Architecture in Rome," *Papers of the British School at Rome* 65 (1997): 177–232; Robert Coates-Stephens, "Housing in Early

Medieval Rome, 500–1000 AD," *Papers of the British School at Rome* 64 (1996): 239–59; Robert Coates-Stephens, "The Walls and Aqueducts of Rome in the Early Middle Ages, A.D. 500–1000," *The Journal of Roman Studies* 88 (1998): 166–78.

76. Paolo Squatriti, *Landscape and Change in Early Medieval Italy: Chestnuts, Economy, and Culture* (Cambridge, UK, 2013), 68–69; Meneghini and Santangeli Valenzani, *Roma*, 213–15.

77. Meneghini and Santangeli Valenzani, *Roma*, 21–28. The frequently cited number thirty thousand probably derives its authority from Richard Krautheimer, *Rome: Profile of a City, 312–1308* (Princeton, NJ, 2000), 65; Jean-Claude Maire Vigueur, *L'autre Rome: Une histoire des Romains à l'époque des communes, XIIe–XIVe siècle* (Paris, 2010), 36, notes that this number is commonly advanced without explanation. See the cautious new analysis: Roberto Meneghini and Roberto Santangeli Valenzani, "Vivere e morire a Roma," in *Roma altomedievale*, ed. Santangeli Valenzani, 205–29, at 205–8. They note (207) that at the start of the sixth century, the population was probably around 50,000–60,000, a postclassical high point; the wars and epidemics of the sixth century lowered it, but it is hard to say by how much or how lastingly.

78. Russell Meiggs, *Roman Ostia*, 2nd ed. (Oxford, 1973), 532–34, estimates a population of Ostia at its height at c. 50,000–60,000.

79. Chris Wickham, "'The Romans According to Their Malign Custom': Rome in Italy in the Late Ninth and Tenth Centuries," in *Early Medieval Rome and the Christian West: Essays in Honour of Donald A. Bullough*, ed. Donald A. Bullough and Julia M. H. Smith (Leiden, 2000), 151–68.

80. Michael Kulikowski, *Late Roman Spain and Its Cities* (Baltimore, 2004), 192; for plague's possible impact, see Henry Gruber, "Eastern Mediterranean Fine Ware Imports to the Iberian Peninsula, 300–700 CE, and the Economic Impact of the Justinianic Pandemic," *Journal of Late Antiquity* (forthcoming).

81. Michael Kulikowski, "Plague in Spanish Late Antiquity," in *Plague and the End of Antiquity*, ed. Little, 150–70, at 154. For debates about the demographic impact of the Islamic invasion on Iberian populations, see María de los Ángeles Utrero Agudo, "Late-Antique and Early Medieval Hispanic Churches and the Archaeology of Architecture: Revisions and Reinterpretation of Constructions, Chronologies and Contexts," *Medieval Archaeology* 54 (2010): 1–33, at 4–5, for an older model stressing disruption, and 5–9, for a new model arguing against a depopulated "no-man's land."

82. Kulikowski, *Late Roman Spain*, 287–88.

83. Liebeschuetz, *Decline and Fall of the Roman City*, 89–94. But see Enrique Ariño Gil, "Modelos de poblamiento rural en la provincia de Salamanca (España) entre la Antigüedad y la Alta Edad Media," *Zephyrus* 59 (2006): 317–37.

84. Joachim Henning et al., "Reccopolis Revealed: The First Geomagnetic Mapping of the Early Medieval Visigothic Royal Town," *Antiquity* 93 (2019): 735–51. See also Isabel Velázquez and Gisela Ripoll, "Recopolis: *Vrbs Relicta*? An Historico-Archaeological Debate," in *Vrbes Extinctae: Archaeologies of Abandoned Classical Towns*, ed. Neil Christie and Andrea Augenti (Farnham, UK, 2012), 145–75, esp. 153–58. For the foundation story, see John of Biclar, *Chronicon*, c. 50, ed. C. Cardelle de Hartmann, CCSL, 173A (Turnhout, 2001), 70; Isidore of Seville, *Historia Gothorum*, ed. Theodor Mommsen, MGH AA 11 (Berlin, 1894), 288.

85. Dey, *The Afterlife of the Roman City*, 140–60. The capacity of the circus is estimated at fifteen thousand.

86. They included Zaragoza, Tarragona, Gerona, Barcelona, Lérida, Valencia, Braga, Narbonne, Seville, Huesca, Egara, and Mérida. José Vives, *Concilios visigóticos e hispano-romanos*, España Cristiana 1 (Barcelona, 1963), ix. For the councils, see especially Stocking, *Bishops, Councils, and Consensus in the Visigothic Kingdom, 589–633* (Ann Arbor, MI, 2000).

87. Roger Collins, *Early Medieval Spain: Unity in Diversity, 400–1000* (New York, 1983), 263–66.

88. John Schofield and Heiko Steuer, "Urban Settlement," in *The Archaeology of Medieval Europe*, ed. J. Graham-Campbell with M. Valor (Aarhus, 2007), vol. 1, 111–53, at 122.

89. For older population estimates, see Leopoldo Torres Balbás, *Ciudades hispanomusulmanas*, 2nd ed., 2 vols. (Madrid, 1985). Hugh Kennedy, *Muslim Spain and Portugal: A Political History of Al-Andalus* (London, 1996), 107, is more circumspect. For Córdoba, see Marc Boone, "Medieval Europe," in *The Oxford Handbook of Cities in World History*, ed. Peter Clark (Oxford, 2013), 221–39, at 222 (100,000 to 200,000). Manuel Acién Almansa and Antonio Vallejo Triano, "Urbanismo y estado islámico: De Corduba a Qurtuba—Madinat al Zahrah," in *Genèse de la ville islamique en al-Andalus et au Maghreb occidental*, ed. Cressier and M. García Arenal (Madrid, 1998), 107–36, cast some doubt on this figure.

90. Michel Reddé, "Le développement économique des campagnes romaines dans le nord de la Gaule et l'île de Bretagne: Des approches renouvelées," *Annales* 77 (2022): 105–45, at 128–30. Estimates based on written evidence place the first-century BCE population of the Three Gauls (Aquitania, Belgica, and Lugdunensis) at about 7.5 million, with the Romanized Gallia Narbonensis accounting for another two million: Julius Beloch, *Die Bevölkerung der Griechische-Römischen Welt* (Leipzig, 1886), 460, with 448–60; Julius Beloch, "Die Bevölkerung Galliens zur Zeit Caesars," *Rheinisches Museum für Philologie* 54 (1899): 414–45, at 443. Beloch's figures are largely based on Julius Caesar's commentaries. Beloch thought the imperial-era population of Gaul grew to 10–12 million, whereas Camille Jullian, *Histoire de la Gaule* (Paris, 1908–26), vol. 2, 3–8, thought it climbed as high as 20–30 million.

91. For an evocation of population decline from the second century to the fourth century in northern Gaul, see E. M. Wightman, *Gallia Belgica* (London, 1985), 243: "An inhabitant of second-century Belgica who had awakened from a magic sleep two centuries later would have found the rural scene much altered ... The overall impression of a lower density of people would be unavoidable, though more obvious in some areas than others." See also Russell, *Late Ancient and Medieval Population*, 84; Dey, *The Afterlife of the Roman City*, 250.

92. Ausonius, *Mosella*, lines 455–56, in *The Works of Ausonius*, ed. R.P.H. Green (Oxford, 1991), 129, for city walls transformed to granaries. For fifth-century decline, Russell, *Late Ancient and Medieval Population*, 85; Rouche, "Le haut Moyen Âge," 147–49.

93. Gregory of Tours, *Hist.* 4.31, ed. Krusch and Levison, 165; McCormick, "Gregory," 95.

94. By 1200, when Paris was Europe's largest city, its population is thought to have been around 200,000: Herlihy, "Demography," 141.

95. Simon T. Loseby, "Marseille and the Pirenne Thesis, II: 'Ville Morte,'" in *The Long Eighth Century*, ed. Inge Lyse Hansen and Chris Wickham (Leiden, 2000), 167–93.

96. LA III, 268; Adriaan Verhulst, *The Carolingian Economy* (Cambridge, UK, 2002), 23–28. For a more pessimistic view, see Timothy Newfield, "The Contours, Frequency and Causation of Subsistence Crises in Carolingian Europe (750–950 CE)," in *Crisis alimentarias en la Edad Media: Modelos, Explicaciones y Representaciones*, ed. Pere Benito i Monclús (Lleida, 2013), 117–172, at 170; compare Schroeder, "Observations," 189–90. See also Reinhard Schneider, *Das Frankenreich*, 4th ed. (Munich, 2001), 134–37, esp. 134, for the difficulties of estimating population.

97. Joëlle Burnouf, "Towns and Rivers, River Towns: Environmental Archaeology and the Archaeological Evaluation of Urban Activities and Trade," in *Post-Roman Towns, Trade and Settlement in Europe and Byzantium*, ed. J Henning (Berlin, 2007), vol. 1, 165–80, at 116–17.

98. G. M. Schwarz, "Village Populations According to the Polyptyque of the Abbey of St Bertin," *Journal of Medieval History* 11 (1985): 31–41, with lower estimates than Hans van Werveke, "De bevolkingsdichtheid in de IXe eeuw: Poging tot schatting," in *Miscellanea Mediaevalia* (Ghent, 1968), 283–90. For lower Rhineland figures in the Merovingian period, see, e.g., LA III, 290 (table 27), 291–92.

99. See Hans-Werner Goetz, "Palaiseau: Zur Struktur und Bevölkerung eines frühmittelalterlichen Dorfes in der Grundherrschaft des Klosters Saint-Germain-des-Pres," in *Kleine Welten:*

Ländliche Gesellschaften im Karolingerreich, ed. Thomas Kohl, Steffen Patzold, Bernhard Zeller (Ostfildern, 2019), 205–34.

100. Guy Halsall, *Settlement and Social Organization: The Merovingian Region of Metz* (Cambridge, UK, 1995), 198, based on extrapolations from cemetery numbers.

101. In the third and fourth centuries CE, two developments in late Iron Age settlements are usually seen as signs of growth: the appearance of enclosed farmsteads with subdivided longhouses and the expansion of divisions within longhouses: Heiko Steuer, *Frühgeschichtliche Sozialstrukturen in Mitteleuropa: Eine Analyse der Auswertungsmethoden des archäologischen Quellenmaterials* (Göttingen, 1982), 167–81, 277–81; Hamerow, *Early Medieval Settlements*, 88–89. See also Heiko Steuer, "Besiedlungsdichte, Bevölkerungsgrößen und Heeresstärken während der älteren römischen Kaiserzeit in der Germania Magna," *Abhandlungen der Akademie der Wissenschaften in Göttingen, Philologisch-Historische Klasse* 279 (2007): 337–62, esp. 340–41, for undulating Germanic population cycles just beyond the Roman borders.

102. Peter Schmid, "Ländliche Siedlungen der vorrömischen Eisenzeit bis Völkerwanderungszeit im niedersächsischen Küstengebiet," *Offa* 39 (1982): 73–96, at 92; Hamerow, *Early Medieval Settlements*, 89, 106–13.

103. For a tentative argument for depopulation based on concentration of inhumations in a smaller number of sites during the late Roman period, see Michael Gebühr, "Angulus desertus?," in *46. Internationales Sachsensymposion "Die Wanderung der Angeln nach England" im Archäologischen Landesmuseum der Christian-Albrechts-Universität, Schloß Gottorf, Schleswig*, ed. Hans-Jürgen Häßler et al. (Oldenburg, 1998), 43–85, at 55; Hamerow, *Early Medieval Settlements*, 109–12. For the written evidence, see Jordanes, *Getica* IV.25, ed. Theodor Mommsen, MGH AA (Berlin, 1882), 60. For the defense of *Scandza* over *Scandia* as Jordanes's preferred term, see Peter Van Nuffelen and Lieve Van Hoof, trans., *Jordanes, Romana and Getica* (Liverpool, 2023), 225 n. 38.

104. Hamerow, *Early Medieval Settlements*, 112–13; Herbert Jankuhn, "Die frühmittelalterlichen Seehandelsplätze im Nord- und Ostseeraum," in *Studien zu den Anfängen des europäischen Städtewesens* (Sigmaringen, 1976 [1958]), 451–98.

105. Daniel Nösler and Steffen Wolters, "Kontinuität und Wandel: Zur Frage der spätvölkerwanderungszeitlichen Siedlungslücke im Elbe-Weser-Dreieck," in *Dunkle Jahrhunderte in Mitteleuropa? Tagungsbeiträge der Arbeitsgemeinschaft Spätantike und Frühmittelalter*, ed. O. Heinrich-Tamaska, N. Krohn, and S. Ristow (Hamburg, 2009), 367–88, at 371. For later population growth in Saxony, see Karlheinz Blaschke, "Menge und Gliederung in der Bevölkerungsentwicklung Sachsens: Eine Langzeitbeobachtung vom 10. bis zum 20. Jahrhundert," in *Struktur und Dimension: Festschrift für Karl Heinrich Kaufhold zum 65. Geburtstag*, ed. Hans-Jürgen Gebhard (Stuttgart, 1997), 223–41, at 230. But there are exceptions. A study of one longhouse site on the Saxon coast suggested an enduring continuity of habitation from antiquity to the modern period: Erwin Strahl, "Archaeology on the North Sea Coast of Lower Saxony: Recent Research," in *The Rising Tide: Archaeology and Coastal Landscapes*, ed. Alan Aberg and Carenza Lewis (Oxford, 2000), 17–21.

106. For settlements in the region of Drenthe (northeastern Netherlands), see J.A.J. Vervloet, "Early Medieval Settlements on the Sandy Soils of the Netherlands, with Special Attention to the Developments on the Drenthe Plateau," *Geografiska Annaler, Series B: Human Geography* 70 (1988): 187–96.

107. Evelien van Dijk et al., "Climatic and Societal Impacts in Scandinavia Following the 536 and 540 CE Volcanic Double Event," *Climate of the Past* 19 (2023): 357–98. Ole Benedictow, "Demographic Conditions," in *The Cambridge History of Scandinavia*, vol. 1, *Prehistory to 1520*, ed. Knut Helle (Cambridge, UK, 2003), 237–49, at 248, puts the population of eleventh-century Norway at about 185,000. For the possibility that Scandinavian growth may have owed to the Medieval Climate Anomaly, see T. Douglas Price, *Ancient Scandinavia: An Archaeological History from the First Humans to the Vikings* (Oxford, 2015), 384–85.

108. Anders Winroth, *The Age of the Vikings* (Princeton, NJ, 2014), 51–52, criticizes the overpopulation thesis as a "cliché that has no basis in fact." For armies, see Shane McLeod, *The Beginning of Scandinavian Settlement in England: The Viking 'Great Army' and Early Settlers, c. 865–900* (Turnhout, 2014).

109. Benedictow, "Demographic Conditions," 237, estimating their populations at "3,000–5,000 inhabitants." For Ribe, see Claus Feveile, "Ribe: Emporium and Town in the 8th and 9th Centuries," in *Dorestad in an International Framework: New Research on Centres of Trade and Coinage in Carolingian Times*, ed. Annemarieke Willemsen and Hanneke Kik (Turnhout, 2010), 143–48. For another excavated site, Stavnsager, see Reno Fiedel, Karen H. Nielsen, and Christopher Loveluck, "From Hamlet, to Central Place, to Manor: Social Transformation of the Settlement at Stavnsager, Eastern Jutland, and Its Networks, AD 400–1100," in *Transformations in North-Western Europe (AD 300–1000)*, ed. Titus A.S.M. Panhuysen and Babette Ludowici (Stuttgart, 2011), 161–76.

110. Bede, *HE* 1.14, ed. Lapidge, vol. 1, 158–62.

111. The jury is still out on the insular impact of plague. Phylogenetic evidence shows that it struck Britain very early in the First Pandemic: Keller et al. "Ancient *Yersinia pestis* genomes," 3; Peter Sarris, "New Approaches to the 'Plague of Justinian,'" *Past & Present* 254 (2022): 315–46, at 315.

112. Pam Crabtree, *Early Medieval Britain: The Rebirth of Towns in the Post-Roman West* (Cambridge, UK, 2018), 23–24.

113. Crabtree, *Early Medieval Britain*, 86–137.

114. Wendy Davies, "Economic Change in Early Medieval Ireland: The Case for Growth," in *L'Irlanda e gli Irlandesi nell'alto Medioevo* (Spoleto, 2010), 111–33; Christopher Loveluck and Aidan O'Sullivan, "Travel, Transport and Communication to and from Ireland, c. 400–1100: An Archaeological Perspective," in *The Irish in Early Medieval Europe: Identity, Culture and Religion*, ed. Roy Flechner and Sven Meeder (New York, 2016), 19–37, at 20.

115. Gordon Malcolm and David Bowsher with Robert Cowie, *Middle Saxon London: Excavations at the Royal Opera House, 1989–99* (London, 2003), 192–93; Derek J. Keene, "London from the Post-Roman Period to 1300," in *The Cambridge Urban History of Britain*, vol. 1, *600–1540*, ed. D. M. Palliser (Cambridge, UK, 2000), 187–216, at 188, suggested a figure of 5,000 to 10,000 people. Derek J. Keene, "London 600–1200," in *Europäische Städte im Mittelalter*, ed. Ferdinand Opll and Christoph Sonnlechner (Innsbruck, 2010), 95–118, at 97, offers "a population in excess of 5,000 persons." This latter estimate is accepted by Schofield and Steuer, "Urban Settlement," 114, 121.

116. Crabtree, *Early Medieval Britain*, 126, for estimates ranging between 6,000 and 13,700.

117. Crabtree, *Early Medieval Britain*, 160–66 (York), 166–68 (Dublin).

118. Helena Hamerow, *Rural Settlements and Society in Anglo-Saxon England* (Oxford, 2012).

119. McCormick, *Origins*, 11; Petr Meduna and Eva Černá, "Settlement Structure of the Early Middle Ages in Northwest Bohemia," *Antiquity* 65 (1991): 388–95, at 390; Petr Meduna and Eva Černá, "Die Entwicklung der frühmittelalterlichen Siedlungsstruktur im Peptipsy-Becken auf Grund der Ergebnisse der systematischen Landesaufnahme," *Veröffentlichungen des Museums für Ur- und Frühgeschichte Potsdam* 25 (1991): 135–40; Jan Klápště, "Studies of Structural Change in Medieval Settlement in Bohemia," *Antiquity* 65 (1991): 396–405, at 396.

120. Johan Callmer, "Urbanisation in Northern and Eastern Europe," in *Post-Roman Towns*, ed. Henning, vol. 1, 233–70, at 254–55.

121. Jirí Macháček, "Disputes Over Great Moravia: Chiefdom or State? The Morava or the Tisza River?," *Early Medieval Europe* 17 (2009): 248–67, at 254–56.

122. Andrzej Buko, *The Archaeology of Early Medieval Poland: Discoveries, Hypotheses, Interpretations* (Leiden, 2008), 219.

123. Tadeusz Kowalski, ed., *Relacja Ibrahim Ibn Jakuba z podróży do krajów słowiańskich* (Kraków, 1946).

124. Gunita Zariņa, "The Main Trends in the Palaeodemography of the 7th–18th Century Population of Latvia," *Anthropologischer Anzeiger* 64 (2006): 189–202, at 199–200. For Wolin, see Elisabeth Anna Krüger, "Wolin—ein slawisch-wikingischer Seehandelsplatz an der polnischen Ostsee," in *Transformationen und Umbrüche des 12./13. Jahrhunderts*, ed. Felix Biermann et al. (Langenweissbach, 2012), 131–38.

125. John Haldon et al., "The Climate and Environment of Byzantine Anatolia: Integrating Science, History and Archaeology," *Journal of Interdisciplinary History* 45 (2014): 113–61.

126. Prosperity: Wickham, *Framing*, 27–28. Decline: Guy Bar-Oz et al., "Ancient Trash Mounds Unravel Urban Collapse a Century Before the end of Byzantine Hegemony in the Southern Levant," *PNAS* 116 (2019): 8239–48; Nimrod Marom et al., "Zooarchaeology of the Social and Economic Upheavals in the Late Antique-Early Islamic Sequence of the Negev Desert," *Scientific Reports* 9 (2019): 6702; Michael McCormick, "Radiocarbon Dating the End of Urban Services in a Late Roman Town," *PNAS* 116 (2019): 8096–98.

127. For Byzantium, see John Haldon, *The Empire That Would Not Die: The Paradox of Eastern Roman Survival, 640–740* (Cambridge, MA, 2016).

128. Hugh Kennedy, "From Polis to Madina: Urban Change in Late Antique and Early Islamic Syria," *Past & Present* 106 (1985): 3–27; reinforced by the archaeological survey of Gideon Avni, *The Byzantine-Islamic Transition in Palestine: An Archaeological Approach* (Oxford, 2014), 40–106. For an early attempt to estimate the population size of the Arab empire, see Charles Issawi, "The Area and Population of the Arab Empire: An Essay in Speculation," in *The Islamic Middle East, 700–1900: Studies in Economic and Social History*, ed. A. L. Udovitch (Princeton, NJ, 1981), 375–96.

129. *Vita Basilii imperatoris* (Theophanes Continuatus, book 5), c. 74, ed. Ihor Ševčenko, *Chronographiae quae Theophanis Continuati nomine fertur: Liber quo Vita Basilii Imperatoris amplectitur*, Corpus Fontium Historiae Byzantinae 42 (Berlin, 2011), 256.

130. Martin Millett, *The Romanisation of Britain: An Essay in Archaeological Interpretation* (Cambridge, UK, 1992), 181–86; LA III, 266–92.

131. McCormick, "Gregory," 78 n. 205.

132. Barbiera and Dalla Zuanna, "Population Dynamics," 380.

133. For now, see Nikulka, *Archäologische Demographie*.

134. Gary Warrick, *A Population History of the Huron-Petun, A.D. 500–1650* (Cambridge, UK, 2008).

135. Schofield and Steuer, "Urban Settlement," 136–44. They work from Martin Biddle, "Towns," in *The Archaeology of Anglo-Saxon England*, ed. D. M. Wilson (Cambridge, UK, 1976), 99–150, at 100, listing twelve criteria with which to analyze urbanism: defenses, street planning, markets, mint, legal status, role as a central place, large and dense population, diverse economic base, houses, social differentiation, religious organization, and judicial centralization. Compare Edith Ennen, *Die europäische Stadt des Mittelalters*, 4th ed. (Göttingen, 1987); and David Nicholas, "The Urban Typologies of Henri Pirenne and Max Weber: Was There a 'Medieval' City?," in *Comparative Perspectives on History and Historians: Essays in Memory of Bryce Lyon (1920–2007)*, ed. David Nicholas, Bernard S. Bachrach, and James M. Murray (Kalamazoo, MI, 2012), 75–96; Galetti, *Uomini e case*, 114–15. For the utility of this kind of "ideal type" analysis, see Wickham, *Framing*, 592, who builds on Biddle's typology (with important updates and caveats at 592–96). See also (albeit for a later period) the concept of a "quasi-city" by Giorgio Chittolini, "'Quasi-città': Borghi e terre in area lombarda nel tardo medioevo," *Società e storia* 47 (1990): 3–26.

136. See Frank G. Hirschmann, *Die Anfänge des Städtewesens in Mitteleuropa: Die Bischofssitze des Reiches bis ins 12. Jahrhundert*, 3 vols. (Stuttgart, 2011–12).

137. Paul the Deacon, *Liber de episcopis Mettensibus*, ed. and trans. Damien Kempf, Dallas Medieval Texts and Translations 19 (Paris, 2013), 48.

138. Adriaan Verhulst, *The Rise of Cities in North-West Europe* (Cambridge, UK, 1999), 2–3; Alain Vanderhoeven, "Changing Urban Topography in Late Roman and Early Medieval Tongeren," in *Transformations in North-Western Europe, AD 300–1000*, ed. Titus A.S.M. Panhuysen and Babette Ludowici (Stuttgart, 2011), 128–38; Alain Vanderhoeven, "Die römische Stadt Tongeren," in *Römisches Aachen: Archäologisch-historische Aspekte zu Aachen und der Euregio*, ed. Raban von Haehling and Andreas Schaub (Regensburg, 2013), 387–411.

139. Schofield and Steuer, "Urban Settlement," 136; Dey, *The Afterlife of the Roman City*, 127–40; Liebeschuetz, *Decline and Fall of the Roman City*, 74–103; Manfred Groten, "Die mittelalterliche Stadt als Erbin der antiken *civitas*," in *Gründungsmythen Europas im Mittelalter*, ed. M. Bernsen, M. Becher, and E. Brüggen (Bonn, 2013), 21–33, at 23–24, for the shifting meaning of *civitas*.

140. Volker Bierbrauer, "Die Kontinuität städtischen Lebens in Oberitalien aus archäologischer Sicht (5.-7. / 8. Jahrhundert)," in *Die Stadt in Oberitalien und in den nordwestlichen Provinzen des Römischen Reiches: Deutsch-italienisches Kolloquium im Italienischen Kulturinstitut Köln*, ed. Werner Eck and Hartmut Galsterer (Mainz, 1991), 263–86; Hartmut Wolff, "Die Kontinuität städtischen Lebens in den nördlichen Grenzprovinzen des römischen Reiches und das Ende der Antike," in *Die Stadt in Oberitalien und in den nordwestlichen Provinzen des Römischen Reiches*, ed. Eck and Galsterer, 287–318. For the illuminating case of the city of Trier and environs, see Lukas Clemens, "Trier im Umbruch - die Stadt während des 5. bis 9. Jahrhunderts n. Chr.," in *Ein Traum von Rom: Stadtleben im römischen Deutschland* (Darmstadt, 2014), 328–35.

141. For some Merovingian-era estimates, see LA III, 289–90: Cologne (5,000), Trier (2,500), Aachen, Bonn, Deutz, Jülich, Gellep, Koblenz, Mainz, Zülpich, and Xanten (each approximately 300–900).

142. Gregory of Tours, *Hist.* 8.33, ed. Krusch and Levison, 401–3; *Hist.* 9.21–9.22, 441–42. Gregory's language in discussing fire at Paris and plague at Marseille intentionally mirrors Revelation 18 on the Fall of Babylon.

143. Dey, *The Afterlife of the Roman City*, esp. 244–51. Compare Liebeschuetz, *The Decline and Fall of the Roman City*, 1–25, conceding much functional if not material continuity.

144. Carlrichard Brühl, *Palatium und Civitas: Studien zur Profantopographie spätantiker Civitates vom 3. bis 13. Jahrhundert*, 2 vols. (Cologne, 1975–90), vol. 2, 41–62.

145. *Breve de inquisitione* (715), ed. Luigi Schiaparelli, *Codice Diplomatico Longobardo* 1 (Rome, 1929), no. 19, 61–77. See pp. 55–56 below.

146. Liebeschuetz, *Decline and Fall of the Roman City*, 85.

147. *Council of Agde* (506), canon 21, CCSL 148, 189–226.

148. Lucie Malbos, *Les ports des mers nordiques à l'époque viking (VIIe-Xe siècle)* (Turnhout, 2017); Loveluck, *Northwest Europe*, 178–212; Schofield and Steuer, "Urban Settlement," 136–38. On the fate of the *wics*, see R. A. Hall, "The Decline of the Wic?," in *Towns in Decline, AD 100–1600*, ed. T. R. Slater (Aldershot, 2000), 120–36; Hodges and Whitehouse, *Mahomet, Charlemagne et les origines de l'Europe*, 83–103, with revisions at 171–72. For some classic sites, see, e.g., A. Morton, ed., *Excavations at Hamwic I* (London, 1992) and P. Andrews, ed., *Excavations at Hamwic II* (York, 1997); David Hill et al., "The Definition of the Early Medieval Site of Quentovic," *Antiquity* 66 (1992): 965–69; Herbert Jankuhn, *Haithabu: Ein Handelsplatz der Wikingerzeit*, revised ed. (Neuminster, 1986). For London as an *emporium*, see Bede, *HE*, 2.3.1, ed. Lapidge, vol. 1, 298–300.

149. See also Georges Despy, "Villes et campagnes aux IXe et Xe siècles: l'exemple du pays mosan," in *Anfänge des Städtewesens an Schelde, Maas und Rhein bis zum Jahre 1000*, ed. Adriaan Verhulst (Cologne, 1996), 299–322, for towns on the Meuse that originated in Roman times but gained importance as mints and centers of trade in the Merovingian and Carolingian period.

See also Adriaan Verhulst, "The Origins and Early Development of Medieval Towns in Northern Europe," *The Economic History Review*, n.s., 47 (1994): 362–73.

150. *AB*, s.a. 863, ed. Grat et al., 95–96: "Dani mense ianuario per Rhenum uersus Coloniam nauigio ascendunt, et depopulato emporio quod Dorestatus dicitur, sed et uillam non modicam ad quam Frisii confugerant, occisis multis Frisiorum negotiatoribus et capta non modica populi multitudine, usque ad quandam insulam secus castellum Novesium perueniunt." Jan van Doesburg, "*Villa non modica*? Some Thoughts on the Interpretation of a Large Early Medieval Earthwork near Dorestad," in *Dorestad in an International Framework: New Research on Centres of Trade and Coinage in Carolingian Times*, ed. Annemarieke Willemsen and Hanneke Kik (Turnhout, 2010), 51–58, esp. 56.

151. Annemarieke Willemsen, "Dorestad, a Medieval Metropolis," in *From One Sea to Another: Trading Places in the European and Mediterranean Early Middle Ages*, ed. Sauro Gelichi and Richard Hodges (Turnhout, 2012), 65–80, at 70. For the estimate of "a few thousand people," see Annemarieke Willemsen, *Dorestad: Een wereldstad in de middeleeuwen* (Zutphen, 2009), 7.

152. Lisa Norling, *Captain Ahab Had a Wife: New England Women and the Whalefishery, 1720–1870* (Chapel Hill, NC, 2000), 128. Compare Loveluck, *Northwest Europe*, 210.

153. David M. Nicholas, *The Growth of the Medieval City: From Late Antiquity to the Early Fourteenth Century* (London, 1997), 40–41; Helen Clarke and Björn Ambrosiani, *Towns in the Viking Age* (Leicester, 1991), 157.

154. Schofield and Steuer, "Urban Settlement," 136–38.

155. Phil Andrews, ed., *Excavations at Hamwic*, vol. 2, *Excavations at Six Dials* (York, 1997), 253.

156. Schofield and Steuer, "Urban Settlement," 142.

157. Schofield and Steuer, "Urban Settlement," 138–39.

158. David Rollason, *The Power of Place: Rulers and Their Palaces, Landscapes, Cities, and Holy Places* (Princeton, NJ, 2016), 151.

159. Josiane Barbier, "Quierzy (Aisne): Résidence pippinide et palais carolingien," in *Palais médiévaux (France-Belgique): 25 ans d'archéologie*, ed. Annie Renoux (Le Mans, 1994), 85–86. For spatial and political aspects of the palace system, see Simon MacLean, "Palaces, Itineraries and Political Order in the Post-Carolingian Kingdoms," in *Diverging Paths? The Shapes of Power and Institutions in Medieval Christendom and Islam*, ed. John G. H. Hudson and Ana María Rodríguez López (Leiden, 2014), 291–320.

160. Eric J. Goldberg, *In the Manner of the Franks: Hunting, Kingship, and Masculinity in Early Medieval Europe* (Philadelphia, 2020), 93.

161. Stuart Airlie, "The Palace of Memory: The Carolingian Court as Political Centre," in *Courts and Regions in Medieval Europe*, ed. Sarah Rees Jones, Richard Marks, A. J. Minnis (Rochester, NY, 2000), 1–20, discussing Compiègne at 14: "As a centre for gatherings of the Carolingian élite, Compiègne was a theatre that played to a large audience, and theatre is the appropriate term." See also May Vieillard-Troïekouroff, "La chapelle du palais de Charles le Chauve à Compiègne," *Cahiers Archéologiques* 21 (1971): 89–108; Sebastian Ristow, "Aachen und Köln, Ingelheim und Mainz—Residenz und Stadt: Siedlungsentwicklung zwischen Spätantike und Frühmittelalter," *Hortus Artium Medievalium* 20 (2014): 85–97.

162. Donald Bullough, "*Aula Renovata*: The Carolingian Court Before the Aachen Palace," *Proceedings of the British Academy* 71 (1985): 267–301. For archaeological findings at Aachen, see U. Heckner and E.-M. Beckmann, eds., *Die karolingische Pfalzkapelle in Aachen: Material, Bautechnick, Restaurierung* (Worms, 2012); H. Müller, C. M. Bayer, and M. Kerner, eds., *Die Aachener Marienkirche: Aspekte ihrer Archäologie und frühen Geschichte* (Regensburg, 2014); T. R. Kraus, ed., *Aachen von den Anfängen bis zur Gegenwart*, vol. 2, *Karolinger–Ottonen–Salier, 765–1137* (Aachen, 2013).

163. E.g., Einhard, *Translatio Marcellini et Petri* (BHL 5233), 2.4, ed. G. Waitz, MGH SS 15.1 (Hanover, 1887), 247.

164. Einhard, *Translatio Marcellini et Petri*, 2.3, ed. Waitz, 246, describes his own residence adorned with what he calls "an oratory of unremarkable workmanship"; Uwe Lobbedey, "Carolingian Royal Palaces: The State of Research From an Architectural Historian's Viewpoint," in *Court Culture in the Early Middle Ages: The Proceedings of the First Alcuin Conference*, ed. Catherine Cubitt (Turnhout, 2003), 129–54, at 130–31, for possible archaeological evidence of an episcopal residence at Aachen. It would be interesting to know if this role shifted as Aachen went from being a de facto residence in Charlemagne's time to a primarily ritual site for major ceremonies (coronation, Easter) in the Ottonian period: Thomas Zotz, "Die Pfalz Aachen als Versammlungsort," in *Versammlungen im Frühmittelalter*, ed. Philippe Depreux and Steffen Patzold (Berlin, 2023) 193–214.

165. Georges Tessier et al., eds., *Recueil des actes de Charles II le Chauve, roi de France (840–877)*, 3 vols. (Paris, 1943–55), vol. 2, no. 228, 7–9. For the reckoning of a minimum of sixty-one, based on ten women who came *cum infantibus suis*, see Janet Nelson, "Dispute Settlement in Carolingian West Francia," reprinted in Janet Nelson, *The Frankish World, 750–900* (London, 1996), 51–74, at 57. See below at p. 73.

166. Bernard Bachrach, "Fifth-Century Metz: Late Roman Christian *Urbs* or Ghost Town?," *Antiquité Tardive* 10 (2002): 363–81, in speaking of *civitates* sometimes does not distinguish between the *civitates* so-called because they are episcopal seats and large settlements. See, e.g., Boone, "Medieval Europe," 221–22, for cities that were large but lacked bishops until the end of the Middle Ages.

167. Schofield and Steuer, "Urban Settlement," 139.

168. Mayke de Jong, *In Samuel's Image: Child Oblation in the Early Medieval West* (Leiden, 1996), 56–99; John Boswell, "*Expositio* and *Oblatio*: The Abandonment of Children and the Ancient and Medieval Family," *The American Historical Review* 89 (1984): 10–33.

169. Dey, *The Afterlife of the Roman City*, 221–33; Federico Marazzi, *Le città dei monaci: Storia degli spazi che avvicinano a Dio* (Milan, 2015).

170. Ursmer Berlière, "Le nombre des moines dans les anciens monastères," *Revue bénédictine* 41 (1929): 231–61; Ursmer Berlière, "Le nombre des moines dans les anciens monastères (suite et fin)," *Revue bénédictine* 42 (1930): 19–42; Ian Wood, "Entrusting Western Europe to the Church, 400–750," *Transactions of the Royal Historical Society* 23 (2013): 37–73.

171. Gregory of Tours, *Liber in gloria confessorum*, c. 104, ed. Bruno Krusch, *Gregorii Turonensis opera*, vol. 2, *Miracula et opera minora*, MGH SRM 1.2 (Hanover, 1885), 814; Friedrich Prinz, *Frühes Mönchtum im Frankenreich: Kultur und Gesellschaft in Gallien, den Rheinlanden und Bayern am Beispiel der monastischen Entwicklung (4. bis 8. Jahrhundert)*, 2nd ed. (Darmstadt, 1988), 158.

172. Eduard Hlawitschka, "Beobachtungen und Überlegungen zur Konventsstärke im Nonnenkloster Remiremont während des 7.–9. Jahrhunderts," in *Secundum Regulam Vivere: Festschrift Für P. Norbert Backmund O. Praem*, ed. Gert Melville (Windberg, 1978), 31–39, at 32–33.

173. Berlière, "Le nombre des moines dans les anciens monastères."

174. Michel Félibien, *Histoire de l'abbaye royal de Saint-Denys en France* (Paris, 1706), 79.

175. Karl Schmid, "Mönchslisten und Klosterkonvent von Fulda zur Zeit der Karolinger," in *Die Klostergemeinschaft von Fulda im früheren Mittelalter*, ed. K. Schmid, 3 vols. (Munich, 1976–78), vol. 2, 571–639.

176. Gregory of Tours, *Hist.* 9.39–43, 10.15–17, 20, 22, ed. Krusch and Levison, 460–75, 501–9, 513, 514. For this affair, see Georg Scheibelreiter, "Königstöchter im Kloster: Radegund (gest. 587) und der Nonnenaufstand von Poitiers (589)," *Mitteilungen des Instituts für Österreichische Geschichtsforschung* 87 (1979), 1–37; Martina Hartmann, "*Reginae sumus*: Merowingische Königstöchter und die Frauenklöster im 6. Jahrhundert," *Mitteilungen des Instituts für Österreichische*

Geschichtsforschung 113 (2005): 1–19; E. T. Dailey, *Queens, Consorts, Concubines: Gregory of Tours and Women of the Merovingian Elite* (Leiden, 2015), 64–79.

177. Angilbert of Saint-Riquier, *Institutio de diversitate officiorum*, c. 9, ed. K. Hallinger, M. Wegener, and H. Frank, CCM 1 (Siegburg, 1963), 296. See Edmund Bishop, "Angilbert's Ritual Order for Saint-Riquier," in E. Bishop, *Liturgica Historica: Papers on the Liturgy and Religious Life of the Western Church* (Oxford, 1918), 314–32.

178. Angilbert of Saint-Riquier, *Institutio de diversitate officiorum*, c. 9, ed. K. Hallinger, M. Wegener, and H. Frank, CCM 1 (Siegburg, 1963), 296 (providing one procession with a cross), 299 (as a stop on a large regional procession). See Carol Heitz, "Architecture et liturgie en France de l'époque carolingienne à l'an Mil," *Hortus Artium Medievalium* 1 (1995): 57–73, at 58–59. Cf. the discussion in Dey, *The Afterlife of the Roman City*, 226–28; Honoré Bernard, "Saint-Riquier: L'abbaye carolingienne d'Angilbert," in *Saint-Riquier: Une grande abbaye bénédictine*, ed. Aline Magnien (Paris, 2009), 55–82. Friedrich Möbius, "Die 'Ecclesia Maior' von Centula (790–799): Wanderliturgie im höfischen Kontext," *Kritische Berichte* 11 (1983): 42–58, esp. 48–50, for the relationship between Angilbert's new liturgy and the politics of the Carolingian court.

179. Adalhard, *Statuta*, ed. J. Semmler, CCM 1 (Siegburg, 1963), 365–418.

180. W. Horn and E. Born, *The Plan of St. Gall: A Study of the Architecture and Economy of and Life in a Paradigmatic Carolingian Monastery*, 3 vols. (Berkeley, 1979), vol. 1, 128.

181. Pierre Toubert, *Les structures du Latium médiéval: Le Latium méridional et la Sabine du IXe siècle à la fin du XIIe siècle*, 2 vols. (Rome, 1973).

182. Schofield and Steuer, "Urban Settlement," 139–40; Hermann Vetters, "Von der spätantiken zur frühmittelalterlichen Festungsbaukunst," in *Ordinamenti militari in Occidente nell'alto medioevo* (Spoleto, 1968), 929–60. For a fortress that developed into an early medieval episcopal residence, see Ralph Röber, "Von der spätrömischen Festung zum frühmittelalterlichen Bischofssitz: Konstanz am Bodensee," in *Kontinuität und Diskontinuität im archäologischen Befund*, ed. Matthias Untermann (Paderborn, 2006), 13–18.

183. For Pohansko see Jirí Macháček, *The Rise of Medieval Towns and States in East Central Europe: Early Medieval Centres as Social and Economic Systems* (Leiden, 2010), esp. 433–35; and Jirí Macháček, *Pohansko bei Breclav: Ein frühmittelalterliches Zentrum als sozialwirtschaftliches System* (Bonn, 2007).

184. Cf. the Edict of Pîtres (864), c. 19, ed. Boretius, MGH Capit. 2, no. 273, 317–18; cf. Schofield and Steuer, "Urban Settlement," 142–44.

185. Placitum of Childebert III (709), ed. Theo Kölzer, MGH DD Merov 1, no. 156, 389–90.

186. For an attempt to reconstruct systems of markets in early medieval northern Italy using the written sources, see Aldo Settia, "'Per Foros Italiae': Le aree extraurbane fra Alpi e Appennini," in *Mercati e mercanti nell'alto medioevo: L'area euroasiatica e l'area mediterranea* (Spoleto, 1993), 187–233, esp. 191–201 (seasonality), 201–12 (space). Metal-rich finds outside of known settlements are sometimes interpreted as possible market sites: Tim Pestell and Katharina Ulmschneider, eds., *Markets in Early Medieval Europe: Trading and Productive Sites, 650–850* (Macclesfield, 2003).

187. Friedrich-Albert Linke, "Archaeological Survey of Monuments of Early Mining and Smelting in the Harz Mountains," in *Aspects of Mining and Smelting in the Upper Harz Mountains (up to the 13th / 14th century)*, ed. Christiane Segers-Glocke and Harald Witthöft (St. Katharinen, 2000), 30–52; Erich Herzog, *Die ottonische Stadt: Die Anfänge der mittelalterlichen Stadtbaukunst in Deutschland* (Berlin, 1964), 71–77. For the impact of the Rammelsberg mine on coin production, see Rory Naismith, "The Social Significance of Monetization in the Early Middle Ages," *Past & Present* 223 (2014): 3–39, at 14.

188. Schofield and Steuer, "Urban Settlement," 139. For rural settlement in transalpine Europe, see Loveluck, *Northwest Europe*, 33–56; for Italy, see Christie, *From Constantine to Charlemagne*, 401–96.

189. Hamerow, *Early Medieval Settlements*, 52: "The individual household appears to have been the basic unit of agricultural production in northwest Europe from the Roman Iron Age to the Carolingian / Viking periods. The economic importance and, to some degree, independence of the household is underscored by the fact that in most cases each lay within its own enclosure and had its own storage facilities."

190. Cemeteries: LA III, 287–289 (with table 26), use cemetery data to extrapolate Merovingian-era (c. 565–670 / 80) population bounds ranging from 4 at the lowest to 151 at the highest, with a mean around 50. Polyptychs: Konrad Elmshäuder and Andreas Hedwig, *Studien zum Polyptychon von Saint-Germain-des-Prés* (Cologne, 1993); Zerner-Chardavoine, "Enfants et jeunes," 378–81 (Annexes); M. Vleeschouwers-Van Melkebeek, "Demografische problemen in verband met de polyptiek van Sint-Bertijns," in *Demografische evoluties en gedragspatronen van de 9de tot de 20ste eeuw in de Nederlanden* (Ghent, 1977), 239–45.

191. *Ex synodalibus gestis Silvestri*, c. 2, ed. Paul Hinschius, *Decretales Pseudo-Isidorianae* (Leipzig, 1863), 449: "Presbiter autem cardinalis nisi quadraginta quatuor testibus non dampnabitur."

192. Hincmar of Reims, *De presbiteris criminosis*, c. 24, ed. Gerhard Schmitz, MGH Studien und Texte, 34 (Hannover, 2004), 95: "Sunt enim apud nos presbiteri, qui tot parrochianos non habent, qui mansa teneant et uxores ac filios habeant, quot testes idoneos ad comprobandum presbiterum sermo ille requirit."

193. Charles West, *Reframing the Feudal Revolution: Political and Social Transformation between Marne and Moselle, c. 800–c. 1100* (Cambridge, UK, 2013), 35.

194. Gregory of Tours, *Liber in gloria confessorum*, c. 1, ed. Bruno Krusch, MGH SRG 1.2, revised ed. (Hanover, 1969), 299: "iam operariis in segite collocatis circiter septuaginta"; Brent D. Shaw, *Bringing in the Sheaves: Economy and Metaphor in the Roman World* (Toronto, 2013), 83–84.

195. Jean-Pierre Devroey, "Un monastère dans l'économie d'échanges: Les services de transport à l'abbaye Saint-Germain-des-Prés au IXe siècle," *Annales: Histoire, Sciences Sociales* 39 (1984): 570–89.

196. Thomas Kohl, "Peasants' Landholdings and Movement in the Frankish East (8th–9th Centuries)," *Journal of European Economic History* 48 (2019): 147–65; Alexis Wilkin, "Preserving Stability in a Changing World: Free and Unfree Labour, Peasant Mobility and Agency on Manorial Estates between the Loire and the Rhine," *The Journal of European Economic History* 48 (2019): 167–87.

197. *Lex Baiuvariorum*, 1.13, ed. E. von Schwind, MGH LL nat. Germ. 5.2 (Hanover, 1926), 288; and K. Bayerle, ed., *Lex Baiuvariorum: Lichtdruckwiedergabe der Ingolstädter Handschrift des bayerischen Volksrechts mit Transkription, Textnoten, Übersetzung, Einführung, Literaturübersicht und Glossar* (Munich, 1926), 46. For this law, see Theodore John Rivers, "Seigneurial Obligations and 'Lex Baiuvariorum' I,13," *Traditio* 31 (1975): 336–43; Theodore John Rivers, "The Manorial System in the Light of 'Lex Baiuvarium,' I,13," *Frühmittelalterliche Studien* 25 (1991): 89–95. For an overview of the dating issues, see Harald Siems, "Lex Baiuvariorum," RGA^2 18 (Berlin, 2001), 305–15.

198. *Lex Baiuvariorum*, 1.13: "Casas dominicas stabilire, fenile, granicam vel tuninum recuperando pedituras rationabiles accipiant et quando necesse fuerit, omnino conponant; calcefurnum, ubi prope fuerit, ligna aut petras L homines faciant, ubi longe fuerit, centum homines debeant expetiri et ad civitatem vel ad villam, ubi necesse fuerit, ipsam calcem trahant." For the reception of this text, see Raymund Kottje, "Die Lex Baiuvariorum—das Recht der Baiern," in *Überlieferung und Geltung normativer Texte des frühen und hohen Mittelalters*, ed. Hubert Mordek (Sigmaringen, 1986), 9–23.

199. Rory Naismith, "Gilds, States and Societies in the Early Middle Ages," *Early Medieval Europe* 28 (2020): 627–62.

200. For the *mallus*, see Francis N. Estey, "The Meaning of *Placitum* and *Mallum* in the Capitularies," *Speculum* 22 (1947): 435–39. See also the essays in S. Barnwell and Marco Mostert, eds., *Political Assemblies in the Earlier Middle Ages* (Turnhout, 2003), 61–72; and Philippe Depreux and Steffen Patzold, eds., *Versammlungen im Frühmittelalter* (Berlin, 2023).

201. The notice, preserved in the polyptych of Saint-Remi of Reims, was separately edited by Jean-Pierre Devroey, "Libres et non-libres sur les terres de Saint-Remi de Reims: La notice judiciare de Courtisols (13 Mai 847) et le Polyptyque d'Hincmar," *Journal des Savants* (2006): 65–103, at 102–3, quote at 102 ("Non est ita, quoniam ex natiuitate ingenui esse debemus"). The seven individuals were "Grimoldus, Warmherus, Leuthadus, Ostroldus, Adelardus, Iuoia, Hildiardis filia" (102). For what we know of them, see Devroey's table at 86–87.

202. For a masterful overview of the scholarship on the *scabini*, see Alice Hicklin, "The *scabini* in Historiographical Perspective," *History Compass* 18 (2020): e12624.

203. Amolo, *Ep.* 1, c. 2, ed. Dümmler, 364: "trecente sive quadringente aut eo amplius personae." See Shane Bobrycki, "The Flailing Women of Dijon: Crowds in Ninth-Century Europe," *Past & Present* 240 (2018): 3–46, at 23; Charles West, "Unauthorised Miracles in Mid-Ninth-Century Dijon and the Carolingian Church Reforms," *Journal of Medieval History* 36 (2010): 295–311.

204. Ray Watson and Paul Yip, "How Many Were There When It Mattered? Estimating the Sizes of Crowds," *Significance* 8 (2011): 104–7, at 105; David Landy, Noah Silbert, and Aleah Goldin, "Estimating Large Numbers," *Cognitive Science* 37 (2013): 775–99; David Miller, *Introduction to Collective Behavior and Collective Action*, 3rd ed. (Long Grove, IL, 2013), 72. The best methods of crowd counting today involve strict protocols: Raul Yip, Ray Watson, et al., "Estimation of the Number of People in a Demonstration," *Australian & New Zealand Journal of Statistics* 52 (2010): 17–26.

205. Robin Dunbar, *Grooming, Gossip, and the Evolution of Language* (Cambridge, MA, 1996), 55–79, for the (controversial) theory that human neocortices are designed to map relationships within small social groups only (about 150 individuals).

206. Erich Auerbach, *Mimesis: The Representation of Reality in Western Literature*, trans. W. R. Trask (Princeton, NJ, 1953), 50–76, esp. 52–53.

207. Cf. Bloch, *Feudal Society*, 74–75.

208. See, e.g., Isidore of Seville, *Mysticorum expositiones sacramentorum seu Quaestiones in Uetus Testamentum*, c. 7.19, PL 83, col. 232: "A senario autem numero et sexaginta commemorantur, et sexcenta, et sex millia, et sexaginta millia, et sexcenta millia, et sexcenties, et quidquid deinceps in majoribus summis per eumdem articulum numeri in infinita incrementa consurgit."

209. For more, see Regine Sonntag, *Studien zur Bewertung von Zahlenangaben in der Geschichtsschreibung des früheren Mittelalters: Die Decem Libri Historiarum Gregors von Tours und die Chronica Reginos von Prüm* (Kallmünz, 1987).

210. *AX*, s.a. 845, ed. von Simson, 14: "Alia pars eorum Galliam petierunt, ibique ceciderunt ex eis plus quam sexcenti viri." See also Bede, *Vita beatorum abbatum Benedicti, Ceolfridi, Eosterwini, Sigfridi et Hwaetberti (BHL* 8968), c. 17, ed. and trans. Christopher Grocock and I. N. Wood, in *The Lives of the Abbots of Wearmouth and Jarrow* (Oxford, 2013), 382: "Ascendunt et diacones aecclesiae cereas ardentes et crucem ferentes auream, transiit flumen, adorat crucem, ascendit equum, et abiit, relictis in monasteriis suis fratribus numero ferme sexcentorum."

211. Gregory of Tours, *Hist.* 4.31, ed. Krusch and Levison, 165, speaks of three hundred dead in one church on one day amid the plague outbreak of 571 at Clermont. Saint Eligius saved captives in groups, allegedly of twenty, thirty, or even forty at a time (*simul*): Audoenus, *Vita Eligii Noviomagensis* (*BHL* 2474–76), c. 10, ed. B. Krusch, MGH SRM 4 (Hanover, 1902), 677: "interdum etiam usque ad viginti et triginta seu et quinquaginta numero simul a captivitate redimebat."

212. Schneider, *Frankenreich*, 134, writes of "unbrauchbare Zahlenangaben."

213. For instance, Gregory of Tours, *Hist.* 10.4, ed. Krusch and Levison, 487, describes a Frankish ambassador to Constantinople waylaid by a mob at Carthage of some 2,000–3,000 persons.

214. Frechulf of Lisieux, *Historiarum libri XII*, part 1: 3.2, 3.18, 4.6; part 2: 1.13, 1.15, ed. M. I. Allen, in *Frechulfi Lexoviensis episcopi opera omnia*, CCCM 169 (Turnhout, 2002), 160, 201, 207, 463, 466.

215. Agnellus of Ravenna, *Liber pontificalis ecclesiae Ravennatis*, c. 78, ed. Otto Holder-Egger, MGH SRL 1 (Hanover, 1878), 246.

216. Alcuin, *Ep.* 7, ed. Ernst Dümmler, MGH Epp. 4 (Berlin, 1895), 32: "Greci vero tertio anno cum classe venerunt in Italiam; et, a ducibus regis praefati victi, fugerunt ad naves. Quattuor milia ex illis occisi et mille captive feruntur." See Joanna Story, *Carolingian Connections: Anglo-Saxon England and Carolingian Francia, c. 750–870* (Aldershot, UK, 2003), 93–94.

217. *ARF*, s.a. 812: 10,940 men, with one manuscript reading XDCCCXL; *AF*, s.a. 812: 10,840 men; cf. Sigurd Abel and Bernhard Simson, *Jahrbücher des fränkischen Reiches unter Karl dem Großen*, vol. 2, *789–814* (Leipzig, 1883), 479 n. 3.

218. Daniel 7:10, ed. Weber-Gryson, 1359: "fluvius igneus rapidusque egrediebatur a facie eius milia milium ministrabant ei et decies milies centena milia adsistebant ei iudicium sedit et libri aperti sunt."

219. Aethicus Ister, *Cosmographia*, c. 64, ed. M. Herrin, *The Cosmography of Aethicus Ister: Edition, Translation, and Commentary* (Turnhout, 2011), 140. See also Herrin's commentary on 237 n. 209.

220. Thus, we should not discount Procopius's estimations of military figures or plague deaths in the *Wars* because in the *Secret History* he says that the biblical "ten thousand ten thousands of ten thousand" perished under Justinian I's misrule (Procopius, *Secret History* 18).

221. Norman Tanner, *The Councils of the Church: A Short History* (New York, 2001), 14–15, for the role of the Chalcedonian Definition in developing the concept of an "ecumenical council." Council of Chalcedon (451), ed. G. Alberigo et al., in *Conciliorum oecumenicorum generaliumque decreta* (Turnhout, 2006), vol. 1, 134: "Symbolum trecentorum decem et octo patrum qui in Nicaea. Et idem centum quinquaginta sanctorum patrum qui Constantinopolim congregati sunt." The number of 630 for Chalcedon derives from the report in the Council of Constantinople II (553), ed. Alberigo, 169: "quae a sexcentis triginta Calchedone congregatis definita sunt." In early medieval canon law collections, these numbers usually appear in the rubrics for councils. See, e.g., Munich, Clm 14008 (late ninth century), fol. 32r, before the list of subscribers to Nicaea I (325) the heading: "Et subscripserunt trecenti decem et octo qui in eodem concilio conuenerunt." See also Paris, BnF, lat. 4762 (saec. IX², France), f. 45r, for the Chalcedonian figure.

222. Michel Aubineau, "Les 318 serviteurs d'Abraham (Gen., XIV, 14) et le nombre des pères au Concile de Nicée (325)," *Revue d'histoire ecclésiastique* 61 (1966): 5–43; Enzo Lucchesi, "318 ou 319 pères de Nicée?," *Analecta Bollandiana* 102 (1984): 394–96. As an example, Frechulf of Lisieux, *Historiarum libri XII*, part 2, 5.27, ed. Allen, 723.

223. Concilium Suessionense (744), c. 1, MGH Conc. 2.1, 34: "In primitus constituimus fide catholica, quam constituerunt CCCXVIII episcopi in Nicaeno concilio, ut denuntiaretur per universa regione nostra, et iudicias canonicas aliorum sanctorum quae constituerunt in synodis suis; quomodo lex Dei et ecclesiastica regula recuperetur, quae in diebus priorum principum dissipata corruit." See Walter Brandmüller, "'*Traditio Scripturae Interpres*': The Teaching of the Councils on the Right Interpretation of Scripture Up to the Council of Trent," *The Catholic Historical Review* 73 (1987): 523–40, at 535, for the Carolingian councils' "conscious integration into tradition."

224. BAV Vat. lat. 4965, fol. 140v; repeated in the copy, Vat. lat. 5749, fol. 118r; Claudio Leonardi, "Anastasio Bibliotecario e l'ottavo concilio ecumenico," *Studi Medievali*, 3rd ser., 8 (1967):

59–192, at 182: "Non te scandalizet subscribentium paucitas, quia dum Photius diu tyranidem exercuisset et pene omnes a piis decessoribus suis sacratos deposuisset et in loca eorum fautores suos tantummodo provexisset, quorum nullus in hac synodo est receptus, isti soli ex priorum patriarcharum consecratione superstites sunt inventi. Verum quotquot sub Nicolaeo et Hadriano summis pontificibus episcopi fuerunt, huius synodi sensui consenserunt. Licet hęc paucitas illi gregi pro sui iustitia comparetur cui Dominus dicit: 'Nolite timere pusillus grex' et cetera."

225. Amolo, *Ep.* 1, c. 2, ed. Dümmler, 364: "trecente sive quadringente aut eo amplius personae."

226. The church was, in the next generation, renovated and enlarged by Isaac of Langres. C. Sapin, *La Bourgogne préromane: Construction, décor et fonction des édifices religieux* (Paris, 1986), 75–79.

227. *AB*, s.a. 839 (recte: 838), ed. Grat et al., 28: "Praeterea die septimo Kalendas Ianuarii, die videlicet passionis beati Stephani protomartyris, tanta inundatio contra morem maritimorum aestuum per totam paene Frisiam occupavit, ut aggeribus arenarum illic copiosis, quos dunos vocitant, fere coaequaretur, et omnia quaecumque involverat, tam homines quam animalia caetera et domos, absumpserit; quorum numerus diligentissime conprehensus duorum milium quadringentorum triginta septem relatus est." Daniël A. Gerrets, *Op de grens van land en water: Dynamiek van landschap en samenleving in Frisia gedurende de Romeinse tijd en de Volksverhuizingstijd* (PhD diss., University of Groningen, 2010), 41.

228. Stefan Esders, "Die 'Capitula de expeditione Corsicana' Lothars I. vom Februar 825: Überlieferung, historischer Kontext, Textrekonstruktion und Rechtsinhalt," *Quellen und Forschungen aus italienischen Archiven und Bibliotheken* 98 (2018): 91–144.

229. Guy Halsall, *Warfare and Society in the Barbarian West, 450–900* (London, 2003), 119–33, for small warbands of hundreds; Bernard Bachrach, *Early Carolingian Warfare: Prelude to Empire* (Philadelphia, 2001), 51–83, estimating that Charlemagne had an army of 100,000 "effectives." Eric Goldberg, *Struggle for Empire: Kingship and Conflict under Louis the German, 817–876* (Ithaca, 2006), 124–26, ably surveys the "two main schools" of thought ("big" and "small"). See also the lucid discussion in Ingrid Rembold, *Conquest and Christianization: Saxony and the Carolingian World, 772–888* (Cambridge, UK, 2017), 49–53.

230. Hans Delbrück, *Geschichte der Kriegskunst im Rahmen der politischen Geschichte, 3. Teil: Das Mittelalter* (Berlin, 1907).

231. *Annales Laureshamenses*, s.a. 798, ed. Georg H. Pertz, MGH SS 1, 37 (*duo milia 901*); *ARF*, s.a. 798, ed. Kurze, 104 (*quattuor milia*); *ARF* (revised), s.a. 798, ed. Kurze, 105 (*quattuor milia*); *Chronicon Moissiacense*, s.a. 798, ed. Pertz, MGH SS 1, 303 (*duo milia 800*). See Rembold, *Conquest and Christianization*, 52.

232. For this battle and the Old High German poem celebrating it, see Elisabeth Berg, "Das Ludwigslied und die Schlacht bei Saucourt," *Rheinische Vierteljahrsblätter* 29 (1964): 175–99.

233. *Annales Fuldenses*, s.a. 881, 96: "Nepos [Louis III] vero illius cum Nordmannis dimicans nobiliter triumphavit; nam novem milia equitum ex eis occidisse perhibetur. At illi instaurato exercitu et amplificato numero equitum plurima loca in regione regis nostri vastaverunt."

234. Regino of Prüm, *Chronicon*, s.a. 883, MGH SRG 50, 120: "in quo certamine, ut ferunt, plusquam octo milia adversariorum gladio prostravit."

235. *Ludwigslied*, line 5.

236. Abbo of Saint-Germain-des-Prés, *Bella Parisiacae Urbis*, ed. Paul von Winterfeld, MGH Poetae 4 (Berlin, 1899), 78–121.

237. See Bernard Bachrach, "Early Medieval Military Demography: Some Observations on the Methods of Hans Delbrück," in *The Circle of War in the Middle Ages: Essays on Medieval Military and Naval History*, ed. Donald J. Kagay and L. J. Andrew Villalon (Woodbridge, UK, 1999), 3–20.

238. Guy Halsall, *Warfare and Society in the Barbarian West, 450–900* (London, 2003), 119–33.

239. Code of Ine 13:1, ed. and trans. F. L. Attenborough, *The Laws of the Earliest English Kings* (Cambridge, UK, 1922), 40–41: "Ðeofas we hatað oð VII men; from VII hloð oð XXXV; siððan bið here." Attenborough's translation of *here* is "raid" (but it could be "army"): "We use the term 'thieves' if the number of men does not exceed seven, 'band of marauders' for a number between seven and thirty-five. Anything beyond this is a 'raid.'"

240. Karl Ferdinand Werner, "Heeresorganisation und Kriegführung im deutschen Königreich des 10. und 11. Jahrhunderts," in K. F. Werner, *Structures politiques du monde franc (VIe-XIIe siècles): Études sur les origines de la France et de l'Allemagne* (London, 1979 [1968]), 791–843, at 813–32, here 813.

241. Werner, "Heeresorganisation," 821. This is followed by Bachrach, *Early Carolingian Warfare*, 58, and Bachrach, *Charlemagne's Early Campaigns*, 78–79, and he favors higher estimates for other settings: Bernard Bachrach, "The Hun Army at the Battle of Chalons (451): An Essay in Military Demography," in *Ethnogenese und Überlieferung: Angewandte Methoden der Frühmittelalterforschung*, ed. Karl Brunner and Brigitte Merta (Vienna, 1994), 59–67; Bernard Bachrach, "Magyar-Ottonian Warfare: À Propos a New Minimalist Interpretation," *Francia* 27 (2000): 211–30.

242. Werner, "Heeresorganisation," 821, noting that "Selbstverständlich wurden solche Massen nie vereinigt—sie standen nicht nur über das ganze, riesige Reich verteilt ..."

243. Werner, "Heeresorganisation," 821: "Für eine Operation grossen Stils, etwa gegen die Avaren mit konzentrischem Angriff von Baiern und von Italien her dürften immerhin 15–20,000 Reiter (in *mehrere* Heersäulen gegliedert!) und entsprechendes Fuss- und Begleitvolk aufgeboten worden sein."

244. Bachrach, *Early Carolingian Warfare*, 80–82.

245. For Charlemagne's iron-covered host, see Notker the Stammerer, *Gesta Karoli Magni imperatoris*, 2.17, ed. Hans F. Haefele, *Notker der Stammler: Taten Kaiser Karls des Großen*, MGH SRG N. S. 12 (Berlin, 1959), 83–84. The plot of the *Waltharius* is that one warrior fends off a whole army at a narrow pass: Karl Strecker, ed., *Waltharius*, MGH Poetae 6.1 (Weimar, 1951), 24–83.

246. Louis II (dict. Anastasius Bibliothecarius), *Epistola ad Basilium I. imperatorem* (871), ed. Walter Henze, MGH Epp 7 (Berlin, 1928), 385–94, at 391. Interestingly, Byzantine sources remembered their forces as few in number: *Vita Basilii* (Theophanes Continuatus, book 5), c. 55, ed. Ševčenko, 198–200.

247. *ARF*, s.a. 782, ed. Kurze, 62. See Rembold, *Conquest and Christianization*, 49–53, for scholarly disagreement about the plausibility of the massacre.

248. Compare Hugh Kennedy, *The Armies of the Caliphs: Military and Society in the Early Islamic State* (New York, 2001), 98, who places overall 'Abbasid capacity around 100,000, but notes that individual army size was smaller, in the thousands or tens of thousands.

249. *Breve de inquisitione* (715), ed. Luigi Schiaparelli, *Codice Diplomatico Longobardo* 1 (Rome, 1929), no. 19, 61–77. See Jean Pierre Delumeau, *Arezzo: Espace et sociétés, 715–1230: Recherches sur Arezzo et son contado du VIIIe au début du XIIIe siècle*, 2 vols. (Rome, 1996), vol. 1, 475–87; Wickham, *Framing*, 392–93, 546; Stefano Gasparri, "Il regno longobardo in Italia: Struttura e funzionamento di uno stato altomedievale," in *Langobardia*, ed. Stefano Gasparri and Paolo Cammarosano (Udine, 2007 [1990]), 237–305, at 241–24; Mario Bezzini, *Controversia territoriale tra i vescovi di Siena ed Arezzo dal VII al XIII secolo* (Siena, 2015).

250. *Breve de inquisitione* [20 June, 715, Siena], ed. Schiaparelli, 61 (*in curte regia*), 68 (Godo).

251. *Iudicatum* (715), ed. Schiaparelli, *Codice Diplomatico Longobardo*, no. 20, 84.

252. Walter Schlesinger, "Herrschaft und Gefolgschaft in der germanisch-deutschen Verfassungsgeschichte," in *Herrschaft und Staat im Mittelalter*, ed. Hellmut Kämpf (Darmstadt, 1964 [1953]), 135–90; D. H. Green, *The Carolingian Lord: Semantic Studies on Four Old High German Words: Balder, Frô, Truhtin, Hêrro* (Cambridge, UK, 1965), 115–215, 270–401.

253. Carlrichard Brühl, *Fodrum, Gistum, Servitium Regis: Studien zu den wirtschaftlichen Grundlagen des Königtums im Frankenreich und in den fränkischen Nachfolgestaaten Deutschland, Frankreich und Italien vom 6 bis zur Mitte des 14 Jahrhunderts* (Cologne, 1968), 168–71; John Bernhardt, *Itinerant Kingship and Royal Monasteries in Early Medieval Germany, c. 936–1075* (Cambridge, UK, 1993), 58; Rosamond McKitterick, *Charlemagne: The Formation of a European Identity* (Cambridge, UK, 2008), 179.

254. Eckhard Müller-Mertens, *Die Reichsstruktur im Spiegel der Herrschaftspraxis Ottos des Grossen* (Berlin, 1980), 108.

255. Einhard, *Vita Karoli*, c. 22, ed. O Holder-Egger, MGH SRG 25 (Munich, 1911), 27: "Et non solum filios ad balneum, verum optimates et amicos, aliquando etiam satellitum et custodum corporis turbam invitavit, ita ut nonnumquam centum vel eo amplius homines una lavarentur." See Janet L. Nelson, "Was Charlemagne's Court a Courtly Society?," in *Court Culture in the Early Middle Ages: The Proceedings of the First Alcuin Conference*, ed. Catherine Cubitt (Turnhout, 2003), 39–57, at 40–41, 56.

256. Stuart Airlie, "Talking Heads: Assemblies in Early Medieval Germany," in *Political Assemblies in the Earlier Middle Ages*, ed. S. Barnwell and Marco Mostert (Turnhout, 2003), 29–46, at 38–39.

257. Hludowici, Karoli et Hlotharii II, *Conventus apud Saponarias* [November 3, 862], ed. A. Boretius, MGH Capit. 2 (Hanover, 1897), no. 243, 165: "Quoniam istas, quae praecedunt, adnuntiationes Hludowicus et Hlotharius cum illorum sequacibus, postquam coram omnibus, qui adfuerunt, trium regum consiliariis fere ducentis, tam episcopis quam abbatibus et laicis, relectas penitus reiecerunt, ne populo legerentur, ut causa Hlotharii penitus taceretur, hanc, quae sequitur adnuntiationem, domnus Karolus istis ipsis verbis iam vesperi adnuntiavit apud Sablonarias, anno incarnationis dominicae DCCCLXII, indictione XI, III. Nonas Novembris, in ipsa casa, ubi relectae sunt praecedentes adnuntiationes, in quam pauci alii intraverunt, quam qui antea fuerunt, quoniam fere plena de ipsis erat."

258. Jamie Kreiner, "About the Bishop: The Episcopal Entourage and the Economy of Government in post-Roman Gaul," *Speculum* 86 (2011): 321–60.

259. Cf. Council of Braga II (572), c. 2, ed. José Vives, *Concilios visigóticos e hispano-romanos*, España Cristiana 1 (Barcelona, 1963), 81–82.

260. Council of Toledo VII (646), c. 4, ed. Vives, 254–55: "Quum vero episcopus dioecesem visitat, nulli prae multitudine onerosus existat nec multum quinquagenarium numerum evectionis excedat, aut amplius quam una die per unamquamque basilicam remorandi licentiam habeat." The phrasing of "the number fifty" (*quinquagenarius numerus*) taps into biblical language. Rulers of "fifties" (*quinquagenarii*) appear in several places in the Old Testament (Ex. 18:21, 18:25; Deut. 1:15; 2 Kings 1:9–14).

261. Diplomata Karolinorum, Diplomata Caroli Magni, MGH DD Kar. 1, D. 58, 86: "Interea etiam constituimus, ut numerus fratrum ultra quinquagenarium numerum ab aliquo eorum abbate ullo unquam tempore non augeatur."

262. Council of Toulouse (844), c. 2, ed. Wilfried Hartmann, MGH Conc. 3 (Hanover, 1984), 20: "Ut unum modium frumenti et unum modium hordei atque unum modium vini cum mensura, quae publica et probata ac generalis seu legitima per civitatem et pagum atque vicinitatem habetur, episcopi a presbyteris accipiant, et frischingam sex valentem denarios aut sex pro ea denarios et non amplius exigant; et si haec non accipiunt, accipiant, si volunt, pro his omnibus duos solidos in denariis, sicut in Toletano et Bracharense consensu episcopi considerasse dicuntur." Cf. the Council of Pavia (845 / 50), c. 15, ed. Hartmann, 214. Both built upon the earlier Council of Braga II (572), c. 2, ed. Vives, 81–82.

263. Hincmar of Reims, *Collectio de ecclesiis et capellis*, c. 2, 3, ed. M. Stratmann, *Hinkmar von Reims: Collectio de ecclesiis et capellis*, MGH Font. iur. Germ. 14 (Hanover, 1990), 111, 120–21. Ambros M. Gietl, "Hincmars Collectio de ecclesiis et capellis: Eine Studie zur Geschichte des

Kirchenrechts," *Historisches Jahrbuch* 15 (1894): 556–73, at 565, noted that the ending of this phrase did not match the version in the Hispana. As Stratmann notes (111 n. 256), Hincmar quotes instead from the Dacheriana, Form B II, c. 73, ed. Luc d'Achery, *Spicilegium, sive, Collectio veterum aliquot scriptorum qui in Galliae bibliothecis delituerant*, revised ed. (Farnham, UK, 1967 [1723]), vol 1, 540.

264. Hincmar of Reims, *Collectio de ecclesiis et capellis*, c. 3, ed. Stratmann, 121: "Nos autem cum hoste collecta parrochias circuimus et non iam tantum praedicatores verbi dei, quantum exactores et exhauritores oblationum fidelium presbiteris commissarum videmur . . ."

265. Bede, *Vita beatorum abbatum Benedicti, Ceolfridi, Eosterwini, Sigfridi et Hwaetberti* (*BHL* 8968), c. 21, ed. C. Plummer, *Venerabilis Bedae opera historica* (Oxford, 1896), vol. 1, 385; reedited in Christopher Grocock and I. N. Wood, ed. and trans., *The Lives of the Abbots of Wearmouth and Jarrow* (Oxford, 2013), 70: "Perueniens namque Lingonas circa horam diei tertiam decima ipsius diei hora migrauit ad Dominum, et crastino in ecclesia beatorum Geminorum martyrum honorifice sepultus est, non solum Anglis genere qui plusquam octoginta numero in eius fuerant comitatu, sed et illius loci accolis pro retardato tam reuerendi senis desiderio, in lacrimas luctusque solutis."

266. Bede, *Vita abbatum* (*BHL* 8968), c. 21, ed. Plummer, 385–86; cf. *Vita Ceolfridi* (*BHL* 1727), c. 37–38, ed. C. Plummer, *Venerabilis Bedae opera historica* (Oxford, 1896), vol. 1, 402–3; Grocock and Wood, ed. and trans., *Lives of the Abbots of Wearmouth and Jarrow*, 116–18.

267. Council of Douzy (a. 871), ed. W. Hartmann, MGH Conc. 4, 507; Charles West, "Lordship in Ninth-Century Francia: The Case of Bishop Hincmar of Laon and His Followers," *Past & Present* 226 (2015): 3–40, at 10.

268. Janet L. Nelson, "The Church's Military Service in the Ninth Century: A Contemporary Comparative View?," in J. L. Nelson, *Politics and Ritual in Early Medieval Europe* (London, 1986), 117–32, at 125–26. For the political background, Peter R. McKeon, *Hincmar of Laon and Carolingian Politics* (Urbana, 1978), 132–55; Wilfried Hartmann, *Die Synoden der Karolingerzeit im Frankenreich und in Italien* (Paderborn, 1989), 325–27.

269. MGH DD Karl, no. 158, 257: "Nam propter immensam barbarorum infestationem necesse habemus cum universo populo nobis divinitus commisso ecclaesiae Christi defensioni insistere et ob hoc non omnes submemorati loci dominio consistentes a profectionibus in hostem inmunes relinquere possumus, sed quoniam eiusdem loci abbates missaticum regium peragere soliti erant, concedimus eis, ut triginta homines nobiles ab aliis profectionibus secum immunes habeant et, si extra patriam est legatio peragenda, plures nobiles ad hoc opus paratos teneant, reliqui vero cum suo populo in hostem proficiscantur, et hoc quandiu tanta bellorum pericula imminent."

270. Simon Keynes, "King Athelstan's Books," in *Learning and Literature in Anglo-Saxon England: Studies Presented to Peter Clemoes on the Occasion of His Sixty-Fifth Birthday*, ed. Michael Lapidge and Helmut Gneuss (Cambridge, UK, 1985), 143–201, at 198–201.

271. St. Gallen, Stiftsbibliothek 915, 5; ed. Piper, *Liber Confraternitatum Sancti Galli, Augiensis, Fabariensis*, MGH Necr. Suppl. (Berlin, 1884).

272. Keynes, "King Athelstan's Books," 200.

273. *Liber Confraternitatum Sancti Galli*, ed. Piper, 136–37.

274. Liutprand, *Relatio de legatione Constantinopolitana*, c. 34, ed., Chiesa, CCCM 156 (Turnhout, 1998), 193; Michael McCormick, "Diplomacy and the Carolingian Encounter with Byzantium Down to the Accession of Charles the Bald," in *Eriugena: East and West: Papers of the Eighth International Colloquium of the Society for the Promotion of Eriugenian Studies, Chicago and Notre Dame, 18–20 October 1991*, ed. Bernard McGinn and Willemien Otten, 15–48 (Notre Dame, 1994), 25–27; cf. McCormick, *Origins*, 162; Andrew Gillett, *Envoys and Political Communication in the Late Antique West, 411–533* (Cambridge, UK, 2003), 256 (envoys exposed to crowds), 260 (envoy attacked by crowds).

275. Ratger, *Supplex libellus monachorum Fuldensium Carolo imperatori porrectus*, c. 14, ed. J. Semmler, CCM 1 (Siegburg, 1963), 325: "Quod hospitalitas antiqua non obliviscatur, sed omnibus hospitibus congruus honor et omnis humanitas exhibeatur. Quando autem plures simul advenerint, ut in missa sancti Bonifatii, consolatione undique facta ab his qui cellas provident omnibus refectio praebeatur." See Josef Semmler, "Studien zum *Supplex Libellus* und zur anianischen Reform in Fulda," *Zeitschrift für Kirchengeschichte* 69 (1958): 268–97, at 282–83; Peter Willmes, *Der Herrscher-Adventus im Kloster des Frühmittelalters* (Munich, 1976), 117–18.

276. E.g., Notker, *Gesta Karoli*, c. 6–9, ed. Haefele, 53–65.

277. Kreiner, "About the Bishop," at 341 n. 85.

278. Bobolenus, *Vita S. Germani abbatis Grandivallensis* (BHL 3467), c. 4, ed. B. Krusch MGH SRM 5 (Hanover, 1910), 34; *Vitae Liutbirgae inclusae* (BHL 4936), c. 11, ed. Ottokar Menzel, MGH Deutsche Mittelalter 3 (Leipzig, 1937), 17.

279. Theodor Bitterauf, ed., *Die Traditionen des Hochstifts Freising*, 2 vols. (Munich, 1905), vol. 1, n. 1037, 782. Members of Joseph's entourage of lower social status would not have been summoned as witnesses.

280. For the institution of the royal *missi*, see esp. Karl Ferdinand Werner, "*Missus— Marchio—Comes*: Entre l'administration centrale et l'administration locale de l'empire carolingien," in *Histoire comparée de l'administration (IVe–XVIIIe siècles)*, ed. Karl Ferdinand Werner and Werner Paravicini (Munich, 1980), 191–239.

281. Capitulare missorum (no. 141), c. 29, ed. A. Boretius, MGH Capit. 1 (Hanover, 1883), 291: "De dispensa missorum nostrorum, qualiter unicuique iuxta suam qualitatem dandum vel accipiendum sit: videlicet episcopo panes quadraginta, friskingas tres, de potu modii tres, porcellus unus, pulli tres, ova quindecim, annona ad caballos modii quatuor. Abbati, comiti atque ministeriali nostro unicuique dentur cottidie panes triginta, friskingas duas, de potu modii duo, porcellum unum, pulli tres, ova quindecim, annona ad caballos modii tres. Vassallo nostro panes decem et septem, friskinga una, porcellus unus, de potu modius unus, pulli duo, ova decem, annona ad caballos modii duo." This legislation made its way into the widely disseminated capitulary collection of Ansegis of Sens: *Capitularia regum Francorum*, ed. G. Schmitz, *Die Kapitulariensammlung des Ansegis*, MGH Capit. N. S. 1 (Hanover, 1996), 659. For *friskinga*, "suckling pig," see Ruth Schmidt-Wiegand, "Stammesrecht und Volkssprache in karolingischer Zeit," in *Aspekte der Nationenbildung im Mittelalter: Ergebnisse der Marbuger Rundgespräche 1972–1975*, ed. Helmut Beumann and Werner Schröder (Sigmaringen, 1978), 171–203, at 180. For pork finds on Carolingian sites, see Hamerow, *Early Medieval Settlements*, 134; Frédéric Chantinne et al., ed. *L'archéologie en Wallonie: Le Premier Moyen Âge* (Namur, 2014), 47–49 (up to 80 percent at Carolingian royal sites in the Low Countries); and above all Jamie Kreiner, *Legions of Pigs in the Early Medieval West* (New Haven, CT, 2021). Providing bread was a major part of being a lord, as the English word "lord" ("loaf-protector") attests; cf. Dáibhí Ó Cróinín, *Early Medieval Ireland, 400–1200* (London, 1995), 94–95, for the contemporary Irish ideal of bread-bestowing kings.

282. McCormick, "Diplomacy and the Carolingian Encounter with Byzantium," 26–27; cf. McCormick, *Origins*, 162, 665.

283. McCormick, "Diplomacy and the Carolingian Encounter," 27, 44 n. 55; McCormick, *Origins*, 162; Michel Rouche, "La faim à l'époque carolingienne: Essai sur quelques types de rations alimentaires," *Revue historique* 250 (1973): 295–320, at 308–9.

284. See, for a helpful overview, S. Barnwell, "Political Assemblies: Introduction," in *Political Assemblies in the Earlier Middle Ages*, ed. Barnwell and Mostert, 1–10.

285. Chris Wickham, "Consensus and Assemblies in the Romano-Germanic Kingdoms: A Comparative Approach," in *Recht und Konsens im frühen Mittelalter*, ed. Verena Epp and Christoph Meyer (Ostfildern, 2017), 389–424.

286. Reuter, "Assembly Politics in Western Europe," 193–216.

287. Hludowici, Karoli et Hlotharii II, Conventus apud Saponarias [November 3, 862], ed. A. Boretius, MGH Capit. 2 (Hanover, 1897), no. 243, 165. On this council, see Robert Parisot, *Le royaume de Lorraine sous les Carolingiens (843–923)* (Paris, 1898), 203–10; Joseph Calmette, *La diplomatie carolingienne; du traité de Verdun à la mort de Charles le Chauve (843–877)* (Paris, 1901), 81–86.

288. McCormick, *Origins*, 665.

289. See Brühl, *Fodrum, Gistum, Servitium Regis*, 70–72.

290. *AB*, s.a. 870, ed. Grat et al., 171. Janet Nelson, *Charles the Bald* (London, 1992), 224–25: "The numbers were similar to those responsible for the peace of Verdun in 843: in other words, a representative group of the elite in the kingdoms concerned."

291. Gerd Althoff, "Colloquium Familiare—Colloquium Secretum—Colloquium Publicum: Beratung im politischen Leben des früheren Mittelalters," in G. Althoff, *Spielregeln der Politik im Mittelalter: Kommunikation in Frieden und Fehde* (Darmstadt, 1997), 157–84.

292. Levi Roach, *Kingship and Consent in Anglo-Saxon England, 871–978: Assemblies and the State in the Early Middle Ages* (Cambridge, UK, 2013), 42–43, at 43. See also Sören Kaschke, "Politische Versammlungen im angelsächsischen England," in *Versammlungen im Frühmittelalter*, ed. Philippe Depreux and Steffen Patzold (Berlin, 2023), 103–15.

293. In two important articles, Evangelos Chrysos showed the basic distinction between early church councils that influenced the structure of later conciliar procedure: Evangelos K. Chrysos, "Konzilsakten und Konzilsprotokolle vom 4. bis 7. Jahrhundert," *Annuarium Historiae Conciliorum* 15 (1983): 30–40; Evangelos K. Chrysos, "Konzilspräsident und Konzilsvorstand: Zur Frage des Vorsitzes in den Konzilien der byzantinischen Reichskirche," *Annuarium Historiae Conciliorum* 11 (1979): 1–17. For Merovingian councils, see J. Champagne and Romuald Szramkiewicz, "Recherches sur les conciles des temps mérovingiens," *Revue historique de droit français et étranger* 49 (1971): 5–49.

294. Figures drawn from Gregory Halfond, *Archaeology of Frankish Church Councils, AD 511–768* (Leiden, 2010), 223–64; with reference to Karl Joseph von Hefele and H. Leclercq, *Histoire des conciles d'après les documents originaux*, 2nd ed., 8 vols. (Paris, 1907–10). The low estimate assumes an episcopal entourage of fifteen, an abbatial or high-elite entourage of five, and other entourages at two; unknowns are counted singly. The high estimate assumes an episcopal entourage of forty, an abbatial or high-elite entourage of thirty, and other entourages at seventeen; unknowns are given entourages of ten. An unknown number of laymen is pegged at five (plus entourages).

295. In the Latin version of the Chalcedonian Definition of 451, G. Alberigo et al., ed., *Conciliorum oecumenicorum generaliumque decreta* (Turnhout, 2006), vol. 1, 134: "Symbolum trecentorum decem et octo patrum qui in Nicaea. Et idem centum quinquaginta sanctorum patrum qui Constantinopolim congregati sunt."

296. Robert Somerville, *Pope Urban II's Council of Piacenza, March 1–7, 1095* (Oxford, 2011), 8–11; Georg Gresser, *Die Synoden und Konzilien in der Zeit des Reformpapstuums in Deutschland und Italien von Leo IX. bis Calixt II., 1049–1123* (Paderborn, 2006), 293–98.

297. Bernold of Constance, *Chronicon*, s.a. 1095, ed. I. Robinson, *Die Chroniken Bertholds von Reichenau und Bernolds von Konstanz 1054–1100*, MGH SRG N.S. 14 (Hanover, 2003), 521.

298. Gresser, *Die Synoden und Konzilien*.

299. Ramsay MacMullen, *The Second Church: Popular Christianity, A.D. 300–400* (Atlanta, 2009), 117–41, taking into account internal obstructions.

300. Maria Giuseppina Muzzarelli, *Pescatori di uomini: Predicatori e piazze alla fine del Medioevo* (Bologna, 2005), 161. Bernardino Guslino, *La vita del beato Bernardino da Feltre*, ed. Ippolita Checcoli (Bologna, 2008), provides several lists of audience numbers.

301. Alexander Kazhdan and Michael McCormick, "The Social World of the Byzantine Court," in *Byzantine Court Culture From 829 to 1204*, ed. Henry Maguire (Washington, DC, 1997), 167–97, at 175–76.

302. Kazhdan and McCormick, "The Social World of the Byzantine Court," 175.

303. Michael McCormick, "From One Center of Power to Another: Comparing Byzantine and Carolingian Ambassadors," in *Deutsche Königspfalzen: Beitrag zu ihrer historischen und archäologischen Erforschung*, vol. 8, *Places of Power—Orte der Herrschaft—Lieux du Pouvoir*, ed. Caspar Ehlers (Göttingen, 2007), 45–72, at 50–51.

304. McCormick, "From One Center of Power to Another," 51 n. 18: "Only the roughest of approximations." For Ingelheim's growing use in the ninth-century, see H. Grewe, "Die Königspfalz zu Ingelheim am Rhein," in *799: Kunst und Kultur der Karolingerzeit: Karl der Große und Papst Leo III in Paderborn*, ed. C. Stiegemann and M. Wemhoff (Mainz, 1999), 142–51; Uwe Lobbedey, "Carolingian Royal Palaces: The State of Research from an Architectural Historian's Viewpoint," in *Court Culture in the Early Middle Ages: The Proceedings of the First Alcuin Conference*, ed. Catherine Cubitt (Turnhout, 2003), 129–54, at 141.

305. McCormick, "From One Center of Power to Another," 51 n. 18.

306. Airlie, "Talking Heads," 39–40.

307. For the illuminating parallel case of the reuse of elite spaces on the Palatine Hill of Rome, see Andrea Augenti, *Il Palatino nel Medioevo: Archeologia e Topografia (Secoli VI-XIII)* (Rome, 1996), summarized helpfully in Andrea Augenti, "Continuity and Discontinuity of a Seat of Power: The Palatine Hill From the Fifth to the Tenth Century," in *Early Medieval Rome and the Christian West: Essays in Honour of Donald A. Bullough*, ed. Julia M. H. Smith (Leiden, 2000), 1–17. For a recent consideration of the end of Roman baths, see Jordan Pickett, "A Social Explanation for the Disappearance of Roman Thermae," *Journal of Late Antiquity* 14 (2021): 375–414.

308. Graeber and Wengrow, *Dawn of Everything*, 277–78.

309. J. Autenrieth, Dieter Geuenich, and Karl Schmid, eds., *Das Verbrüderungbuch der Abtei Reichenau*, MGH Libri Memoriales Et Necrologia, N.S. I (Hanover, 1979), xlii (Dieter Geuenich, "Die Namen des Verbrüderungsbuches").

Chapter 3. Peasants and Other Non-Elites: Repertory and Resistance

1. *AB*, s.a. 859, ed. Grat et al., 80. For the quote, see below.

2. Regino of Prüm, *Chronicon*, s. a. 882, ed. Friedrich Kurze, MGH SRG 50 (Hanover, 1890), 118: "Arduennam percurrentes Prumiam monasterium ingrediuntur ipso die epiphaniae Domini, ubi triduo commorantes omnem in circuitu regionem depopulati sunt. In quo loco innumera multitudo peditum ex agris et villis in unum agmen conglobata eos quasi pugnatura adgreditur. Sed Nortmanni cernentes ignobile vulgus non tantum inerme, quantum disciplina militari nudatum, super eos cum clamore irruunt tantaque caede prosternunt, ut bruta animalia, non homines mactari viderentur. His itaque patratis, honerati preda ad castra redeunt. Illis discedentibus ignis, qui in diversis habitaculis accensus remanserat, cum nullus esset, qui eum extingueret, monasterium consumpsit."

3. Chris Wickham, *Framing the Early Middle Ages: Europe and the Mediterranean, 400–800* (Oxford, 2005), 581, 585; and Eric Goldberg, "Popular Revolt, Dynastic Politics, and Aristocratic Factionalism in the Early Middle Ages: The Saxon Stellinga Reconsidered," *Speculum* 70 (1995): 467–501, at 500. See also Ryan Lavelle, *Places of Contested Power: Conflict and Rebellion in England and France, 830–1150* (Woodbridge, UK, 2020), 64–65; Rory Naismith, "Gilds, States and Societies in the Early Middle Ages," *Early Medieval Europe* 28 (2020): 627–62, at 636, 641; Shane Bobrycki, "The Flailing Women of Dijon: Crowds in Ninth-Century Europe," *Past & Present* 240 (2018): 3–46, at 42; Otto Gerhard Oexle, "Conjuratio und Gilden im frühen Mittelalter: Ein Beitrag der sozialen Kontinuität zwischen Antike und Mittelalter," in Otto Gerhard Oexle, *Die Wirklichkeit und das Wissen: Mittelalterforschung - Historische Kulturwissenschaft - Geschichte und Theorie der historischen Erkenntnis*, ed. Andrea von Hülsen-Esch, Bernhard Jussen, and Frank Rexroth (Göttingen, 2011), 496–568, at 498–99.

4. Goldberg, "Popular Revolt," 500–501.

5. Elias Canetti, *Masse und Macht* (Düsseldorf, 1978), 12–14; Natalie Davis, "The Rites of Violence: Religious Riot in Sixteenth-Century France," *Past & Present* 59 (1973): 51–91, at 53, 81–85.

6. See pp. 50–51 above. See also Christopher Loveluck, *Northwest Europe in the Early Middle Ages* (Cambridge, UK, 2013), 33–56 (smaller communities), 57–75 (larger communities); and Edith Ennen, *Frühgeschichte der europäischen Stadt* (Bonn, 1981), 84–121.

7. For the eleventh- and twelfth-century development of new coastal centers, see Loveluck, *Northwest Europe in the Early Middle Ages*, 352–60. For other forms of evidence for eleventh-century demographic growth, see L. Genicot, "Sur les témoignages d'accroissement de la population en occident du XIe au XIIIe siècle," *Cahiers d'histoire mondiale* 1 (1953): 446–62; cf. Florian Mazel, *Féodalités, 888–1180* (Paris, 2010), 387–88. For demographic growth in twelfth-century Italy around Verona, see Gian Maria Varanini and Fabio Saggioro, "Ricerche sul paesaggio e sull'insediamento d'età medievale in area veronese," in *Dalla curtis alla pieve fra archeologia e storia: Territori a confronto: L'Oltrepò pavese e la pianura veronese*, ed. Silvia Lusuardi Siena (Mantua, 2008), 101–60, at 116 and 127 (figure 11).

8. Thomas Gray, "Elegy Written in a Country Churchyard" (1751), lines 73–76, in A. M. Van Dyke, ed., *Gray's Elegy in a Country Churchyard and Other Selections* (New York, 1910), 23–24.

9. Thomas Hardy, *Far from the Madding Crowd*, ed. Robert Schweik (New York, 1986 [1874]).

10. A variety of Latin words, covering social, juridical, and functional statuses, were used: *rustici* or *rusticae, agricolae, accolae, coloni* or *colonae, laeti* or *laetae* (or *liti*), *mancipia, servi, ancillae, inquilini, incolae, pagenses, famuli* or *famulae, ingenui, liberti, colliberti, pauperes*, or simply *homines* and *mulieres*. For three terms, see Gerhard Köbler, "'Bauer' (*agricola, colonus, rusticus*) im Frühmittelalter," in *Wort und Begriff Bauer*, ed. Reinhard Wenskus, Herbert Jankuhn, and Klaus Grinda (Göttingen, 1975), 230–245.

11. Compare Wickham, *Framing*, 386: "A settled cultivator (or, more rarely, a pastoralist) cultivating largely for subsistence, who does at least some agricultural work personally, and who controls his or her labour on the land." See also Kim Bowes, ed., *The Roman Peasant Project 2009–2014: Excavating the Roman Rural Poor*, 2 vols. (Philadelphia, 2020), vol. 1, 3–4.

12. Eric R. Wolf, *Peasants* (Englewood Cliffs, NJ, 1966), 3–4. See also Frank Ellis, *Peasant Economics: Farm Households and Agrarian Development*, 2nd ed. (Cambridge, UK, 1993), 2–3.

13. Alice Rio, *Slavery After Rome, 500–1100* (Oxford, 2017); Jean-Pierre Devroey, *Puissants et misérables: Système social et monde paysan dans l'Europe des Francs (VIe-IXe siècles)* (Brussels, 2006).

14. See Wickham, *Framing*, 383–85.

15. Matthew Innes and Charles West, "Saints and Demons in the Carolingian Countryside," in *Kleine Welten: Ländliche Gesellschaften im Karolingerreich*, ed. Thomas Kohl, Steffen Patzold, and Bernhard Zeller (Ostfildern, 2019), 67–99.

16. Among others, see Kohl, Patzold, and Zeller, eds., *Kleine Welten*; Bernhard Zeller et al., *Neighbours and Strangers: Local Societies in Early Medieval Europe* (Manchester, 2020); Wendy Davies, *Small Worlds: The Village Community in Early Medieval Brittany* (Berkeley, 1988); Thomas Kohl, "Peasants' Landholdings and Movement in the Frankish East (8th–9th Centuries)," *Journal of European Economic History* 48 (2019): 147–65; Thomas Kohl, "Peasant Agency and the Supernatural," *Studia Historica: Historia Medieval* 38 (2020): 97–116; Richard Hodges, "The Primitivism of the Early Medieval Peasant in Italy?," in *Social Inequality in Early Medieval Empire: Local Societies and Beyond*, ed. Juan Antonio Quirós Castillo (Turnhout, 2020), 165–74; and the series of essays published as "Beyond the Manorial Economy: Peasant Labour and Mobility in Carolingian and Post-Carolingian Europe," special issue, *The Journal of European Economic History* 48 (2019); Alain Dierkens, Nicolas Schroeder, and Alexis Wilkin, eds., *Penser la paysannerie médiévale, un défi impossible? Recueil d'études offert à Jean-Pierre Devroey* (Paris, 2017). For the later period, see Constance Bouchard, *Negotiation and Resistance: Peasant Agency in High Medieval France* (Ithaca, NY, 2022).

17. As stressed by Peter Fowler, *Farming in the First Millennium: British Agriculture between Julius Caesar and William the Conqueror* (Cambridge, UK, 2002).

18. A. V. Chayanov, *The Theory of Peasant Economy*, ed. Teodor Shanin, trans. Christel Lane (Madison, WI, 1986).

19. Ælfric, *Colloquy*, line 34, ed. G. N. Garmonsway, *Ælfric's Colloquy* (London, 1939), 21: "Hiʒ! Hiʒ! micel ʒedeorf ys hyt. *O! O! magnus labor.*"

20. See Jean Meuvret, *Le problème des subsistances à l'époque Louis XIV: La production des céréales dans la France du XVIIe et du XVIIIe siècle*, 2 vols. (Paris, 1977), vol. 1, 174–76; Brent D. Shaw, *Bringing in the Sheaves: Economy and Metaphor in the Roman World* (Toronto, 2013), 11–12, with table 1.3 ("Elements of the harvesting labour process").

21. G. W. Grantham, "Divisions of Labour: Agricultural Productivity and Occupational Specialization in Pre-Industrial France," *Economic History Review* 46 (1993): 478–502, at 484. This was for a farm of one hundred hectares on a three-course rotation, where thirty hectares at a time were devoted to wheat.

22. Jan Zadoks, *Crop Protection in Medieval Agriculture: Studies in Pre-Modern Organic Agriculture* (Leiden, 2013), 72–73. Barley needed to be reaped with special alacrity, since the heads shattered when they fell: Shaw, *Bringing in the Sheaves*, 24.

23. For the labor involved, see Gregory of Tours, *Hist.* 4.34, ed. Krusch and Levison, 167.

24. Zeller et al., *Neighbours and Strangers*, 90.

25. Gregory of Tours, *Liber in gloria confessorum* 1, ed. Krusch, MGH SRM 1.2, 298–99.

26. Polyptychs suggest the presence of classes of individuals without land but with payment requirements who may have earned their keep by hiring out their labor: Konrad Elmshäuder and Andreas Hedwig, *Studien zum Polyptychon von Saint-Germain-des-Prés* (Cologne, 1993), 71–72.

27. Two *mancipia*: Ingo Schwab, ed., *Das Prümer Urbar*, c. 114 (Düsseldorf, 1983), 252.

28. *Capitulare Episcoporum* (780?), ed. Boretius, MGH Capit 1, no. 21, 52: "Episcopi et abbates atque abbatissae pauperes famelicos quatuor pro isto inter se instituto nutrire debent usque tempore messium; et qui tantum non possunt, iuxta quod possibilitas est, aut tres aut duos aut unum." See also Hubert Mordek, "Karls des Großen zweites Kapitular von Herstal und die Hungersnot der Jahre 778/779," *Deutsches Archiv* 61 (2005): 1–52, at 50–52.

29. E.g., *Admonitio Generalis*, c. 81, ed. Boretius, MGH Capit 1, 22.

30. *Miracula Remacli*, col. 697. See Ellen Arnold, *Negotiating the Landscape: Environment and Monastic Identity in the Medieval Ardennes* (Philadelphia, 2013), 141–42; Zeller et al., *Neighbours and Strangers*, 90.

31. Lisa Bailey, *The Religious Worlds of the Laity in Late Antique Gaul* (London, 2017), 128–32.

32. Schwab, ed., *Prümer Urbar*, c. 114, 252.

33. Paolo Squatriti, *Landscape and Change in Early Medieval Italy: Chestnuts, Economy, and Culture* (Cambridge, UK, 2013), 47.

34. R. W. Fogel, "Second Thoughts on the European Escape from Hunger: Famines, Chronic Malnutrition, and Mortality Rates," in *Nutrition and Poverty*, ed. S. R. Osmani (Oxford, 1992), 243–86, at 261.

35. Charles West, *Reframing the Feudal Revolution: Political and Social Transformation between Marne and Moselle, c. 800–c. 1100* (Cambridge, UK, 2013), 65; Nicolas Schroeder, "Peasant Initiative and Monastic Estate Management in 10th Century Lotharingia," *Studia Historica, Historia Medieval* 38 (2020): 75–95, at 80.

36. Wickham, *Framing*, 390–91.

37. Davies, *Small Worlds*; Oexle, "Conjuratio und Gilden"; Wickham, *Framing*, 519–88; Devroey, *Puissants et misérables*; Naismith, "Gilds"; West, *Reframing the Feudal Revolution*; Schroeder, "Peasant Initiative"; Nicolas Schroeder, *Les hommes et la terre de saint Remacle: Histoire*

sociale et économique de l'abbaye de Stavelot-Malmedy, VIIe-XIVe siècle (Brussels, 2015); Thomas Kohl, *Lokale Gesellschaften: Formen der Gemeinschaft in Bayern vom 8. bis zum 10. Jahrhundert* (Ostfildern, 2010).

38. For the later period, see Jean-Claude Hocquet, "Culture du sel, société et habitat des sauniers sur les rivages adriatiques," in *Le paysan et la mer: Ruralités littorales et maritimes en Europe au Moyen Âge et à l'époque moderne*, ed. Jean-Luc Sarrazin and Thierry Sauzeau (Toulouse, 2020), 127–147.

39. Also for the later period, see Jacques Boucard, "Les 'paysans de la mer' sur l'île de Ré et l'exploitation des écluses à poissons," in *Le paysan et la mer*, ed. Sarrazin and Sauzeau, 67–86.

40. Edith Ennen, *Frauen im Mittelalter* (Munich, 1994), 89; Valerie Garver, *Women and Aristocratic Culture in the Carolingian World* (Ithaca, NY, 2009), 259.

41. David Graeber and David Wengrow, *The Dawn of Everything: A New History of Humanity* (London, 2021), esp. 276–327, 359–440, contend that scale cannot be correlated with the presence of elites (i.e., the existence of social hierarchy).

42. Alexis Wilkin, "Preserving Stability in a Changing World: Free and Unfree Labour, Peasant Mobility and Agency on Manorial Estates between the Loire and the Rhine," *The Journal of European Economic History* 48 (2019): 167–87.

43. Adso of Montier-en-Der, *Vita Mansueti* (BHL 5210), c. 24, ed. Monique Goullet, *Adsonis Dervensis Opera hagiographica*, CCCM 198 (Turnhout, 2003), 159–60, quote at 159: "quidam barrinsium partium non paruo numero rustici grege facto, sumptis uehiculis et redarum copiis, uicos expetierant salinarum, datisque in coemptionem rerum uenalium conuectationibus, ad sua redire cupientes, salis comertia referebant . . ." For analysis, Schroeder, "Peasant Initiative," 80–81.

44. Adso of Montier-en-Der, *Vita Mansueti* (BHL 5210), c. 24, ed. Goullet, 159 (*ut moris est rusticorum*).

45. Adso of Montier-en-Der, *Vita Mansueti* (BHL 5210), c. 24, ed. Goullet, 159–60.

46. Schroeder, "Peasant Initiative," 80–81, at 81.

47. For an overview, see Sándor Bökönyi, "The Development of Stockbreeding and Herding in Medieval Europe," in *Agriculture in the Middle Ages: Technology, Practice, and Representation*, ed. Del Sweeney (Philadelphia, 1995), 41–61; for pigs especially, Jamie Kreiner, *Legions of Pigs in the Early Medieval West* (New Haven, CT, 2021).

48. Thomas Wozniak, *Naturereignisse im frühen Mittelalter: Das Zeugnis der Geschichtsschreibung vom 6. bis 11. Jahrhundert* (Berlin, 2020), 668–87.

49. Kreiner, *Legions of Pigs*, 40–41.

50. Zadoks, *Crop Protection*, 81–120.

51. E.g., Gregory of Tours, *Hist.* 4.20, 6.33, 6.44, ed. Krusch and Levison, 153, 304, 316; *Annales Lausannenses*, s.a. 868, ed. Holder-Egger, MGH SS 24, 779; Folcwin, *Gesta Abbatum S. Bertini Sithiensium*, 74 (874), ed. Holder-Egger, MGH SS 13, 621. See Wozniak, *Naturereignisse*, 549–80.

52. Nathan J. Ristuccia, *Christianization and Commonwealth in Early Medieval Europe: A Ritual Interpretation* (Oxford, 2018), 46, 57.

53. Eric J. Goldberg, *In the Manner of the Franks: Hunting, Kingship, and Masculinity in Early Medieval Europe* (Philadelphia, 2020), 134, for environmental pressure on deer.

54. Kreiner, *Legions of Pigs*, 182–95, for the evolution of the legion story.

55. Oxen: Adso of Montier-en-Der, *Vita Mansueti* (BHL 5210), c. 24, ed. Goullet, 159–60. Fish: *Vita Bertini* I (BHL 763), c. 21, ed. W. Levison, MGH SRM 5 (Hanover, 1910), 768. Wild beasts: Jonas of Bobbio, *Vita Columbani abbatis discipulorumque* (BHL 1898), 1.10, ed. B. Krusch, MGH SRG 37 (1905), 169.

56. Philippe Depreux and Steffen Patzold, "Einleitung," in *Versammlungen im Frühmittelalter*, ed. Philippe Depreux and Steffen Patzold (Berlin, 2023), 1–18, at 6.

57. Marc Bloch, *French Rural History: An Essay on Its Basic Characteristics*, trans. Janet Sondheimer (London, 1996 [1931]), 11, 40–47, 55, 58, 61.

58. See Janet Nelson, "Peers in the Early Middle Ages," reprinted in Janet Nelson, *Courts, Elites, and Gendered Power in the Early Middle Ages* (Aldershot, UK, 2007), 27–46, at 30–40.

59. Tom Lambert, *Law and Order in Anglo-Saxon England* (Oxford, 2017), 44–47; Aliki Pantos, "'In medle oðð̄e an þinge': The Old English Vocabulary of Assembly," in *Assembly Places and Practices in Medieval Europe*, ed. Aliki Pantos and Sarah Semple (Dublin, 2004), 181–204, at 182–84.

60. *Edictus Rothari*, c. 156, 157, 168, 170, 171, 172, 173, 176, 222, 224, 360, 367; *Liutprandi Leges*, c. 9, 55, 77, 140; *Ahistulfi Leges*, c. 11, 12, ed. Franz Beyerle, *Leges Langobardorum, 643–866*, 2nd ed. (Witzenhausen, 1962), 40–41, 44, 45, 46; 103, 124, 135, 169–70; 198–99, 199–200.

61. Davies, *Small Worlds*, 134–60.

62. Adam Kosto, *Making Agreements in Medieval Catalonia: Power, Order, and the Written Word, 1000–1200* (Cambridge, UK, 2007), 26–77.

63. Naismith, "Gilds"; Oexle, "Conjuratio und Gilden." For the older approach: Otto von Gierke, *Die Genossenschaftstheorie und die deutsche Rechtsprechung* (Berlin, 1887).

64. Hincmar of Reims, *First Capitulary*, c. 16, MGH Capit. Episc. 2 (Hannover, 1995), 43.

65. See below, pp. 89–91.

66. *Synodus Franconofurtensis* (794), ed. Boretius, MGH Capit 1, no., c. 31, 77; *Capitulare Missorum in Theodonis Villa Datum Secundum, Generale*, ed. Boretius, MGH Capit 1, no. 44, c. 10, 124.

67. Naismith, "Gilds," 649.

68. Naismith, "Gilds," 629–30.

69. Capitulary of Ver (884), c. 14, MGH Capit. 2, 375. See Eric Goldberg, "Vikings, Vassals, Villagers, and the Capitulary of Ver (884)," in *Living in a Carolingian World*, ed. Valerie Garver and Noah Blan (forthcoming).

70. This dependency took a bewildering array of forms: Rio, *Slavery*, 248: "The early middle ages were the Burgess Shale of the history of unfreedom in Europe: an explosion of different and inventive experiments, followed by severe subsequent selection."

71. Werner Rösener, *Peasants in the Middle Ages*, trans. Alexander Stützer (Urbana, IL, 1992), 11–21; Ludolf Kuchenbuch, *Bäuerliche Gesellschaft und Klosterherrschaft im 9. Jahrhundert: Studien zur Sozialstruktur d. Familia d. Abtei Prüm* (Wiesbaden, 1978), 118–95; Rio, *Slavery*, 189–91.

72. For the large distances sometimes involved, Kohl, "Peasants' Landholdings and Movement," 158.

73. *Miracula Sancti Maximini* (BHL 5826), AASS 29 May, vol. 7, col. 29; Zeller et al., *Neighbours and Strangers*, 89.

74. Dieter Hägermann and Helmuth Schneider, *Landbau und Handwerk: 750 v. Chr. bis 1000 n. Chr.* (Berlin, 1991), 488.

75. *Lex Baiuvariorum*, 1.13, ed. E. von Schwind, MGH LL nat. Germ. 5.2 (Hanover, 1926), 288–89; and also K. Bayerle, ed., *Lex Baiuvariorum: Lichtdruckwiedergabe der Ingolstädter Handschrift des bayerischen Volksrechts mit Transkription, Textnoten, Übersetzung, Einführung, Literaturübersicht und Glossar* (Munich, 1926), 46.

76. Jean-Pierre Devroey, "Un monastère dans l'économie d'échanges: Les services de transport à l'abbaye Saint-Germain-des-Prés au IXe siècle," *Annales: Histoire, Sciences Sociales* 39 (1984): 570–89.

77. *Miracula Sancti Maximini*, col. 29.

78. Zeller et al., *Neighbours and Strangers*, 89: "When collective agricultural work does appear in the evidence . . . it is usually in the context of obligations owed to landlords."

79. Georges Tessier et al., eds., *Recueil des actes de Charles II le Chauve, roi de France (840–877)*, 3 vols. (Paris, 1943–55), vol. 2, no. 228, 7–9. See Janet Nelson, "Dispute Settlement in Carolingian

West Francia," reprinted in Janet Nelson, *The Frankish World, 750–900* (London, 1996), 51–74, at 57–59; Rio, *Slavery*, 196–97, 203, 205.

80. Edict of Pîtres [June 25, 864], c. 29, ed. Boretius, MGH Capit. 2, no. 273, 323.

81. Cesare Manaresi, ed., *I placiti del 'Regnum Italiae'*, vol. 1, (a. 776–945) (Rome, 1955), no. 117, 431–36, at 434; Andrea Castagnetti, "Dominico e massaricio a Limonta nei secoli IX e X," *Rivista di storia dell'agricoltura* 8 (1968): 3–20; Wickham, *Framing*, 582.

82. Dmitri Starostine, "... *In Die Festivitatis*: Gift-Giving, Power and the Calendar in the Carolingian Kingdoms," *Early Medieval Europe* 14 (2006): 465–86, esp. 478–79.

83. Starostine, "... *In Die Festivitatis*," 469–70; Hans Martin Schaller, "Der heilige Tag als Termin mittelalterlicher Staatsakte," *Deutsches Archiv* 30 (1974): 1–24.

84. Karl Glöckner and L. Anton Doll, eds., *Traditiones Wizenburgenses: Die Urkunden des Klosters Weissenburg, 661–864* (Darmstadt, 1979), no. 77 (*ad festivitatem sancti Martini*); also nos. 83, 99, 101; Starostine, "... *In Die Festivitatis*," 475–77.

85. Giles Constable, *Monastic Tithes from Their Origins to the Twelfth Century* (Cambridge, UK, 1964), 19–31.

86. Janet Nelson, *King and Emperor: A New Life of Charlemagne* (London, 2019), 267.

87. Paolo Squatriti, "Digging Ditches in Early Medieval Europe," *Past & Present* 176 (2002): 11–65. Christoph Zielhofer et al., "Charlemagne's Summit Canal: An Early Medieval Hydro-Engineering Project for Passing the Central European Watershed," *PLOS ONE* 9 (2014): e108194.

88. *ARF*, s.a. 793, ed. Kurze, 93–94, at 94: "cum omni comitatu suo ad locum venit ac magna hominum multitudine congregata totum autumni tempus in eo opera consumpsit."

89. See above at p. 46.

90. Plea of Rižana (804), ed. Anamari Petranović and Anneliese Margetić, "Il Placito del Risano," *Atti, Centro Di Ricerche Storiche—Rovigno* 14 (1983): 55–70, at 56; also edited in Manaresi, ed. *Placiti*, no. 17, 50.

91. *Contra iudices*, line 153, ed. Ernst Dümmler, MGH Poetae 1 (Berlin, 1881), 498.

92. Nelson, *King and Emperor*, 267; Matthias Becher, *Eid und Herrschaft: Untersuchungen zum Herrscherethos Karls des Grossen* (Sigmaringen, 1993).

93. Formulary of Marculf 1.40, MGH Formulae, 68: "Ille rex ille comis. Dum et nos una cum consensu procerum nostrorum in regno nostro illo glorioso filio nostro illo regnare precipemus, adeo iubemus, ut omnes paginsis vestros, tam Francos, Romanos vel reliqua natione degentibus, bannire et locis congruis per civitates, vicos et castella congregare faciatis, quatenus presente misso nostro, industris vero illo, quem ex nostro latere illuc pro hoc direximus, fidelitatem precelso filio nostro vel nobis et leudesamio per loca sanctorum vel pignora, quas illuc per eodem direximus, dibeant promittere et coniurare." Becher, *Eid und Herrschaft*, 79–85, 122–23, 195–201.

94. MGH Capit 1, no. 25, c. 18, 63: "Sic promitto ego ille partibus domini mei Caroli regis et filiorum eius, quia fidelis sum et ero diebus vitae meae sine fraude et malo ingenio"; MGH Capit. 1, no. 25, 66–67 (c. 4, 67: "cunctas generalitas populi, tam puerilitate annorum XII quamque de senili, qui ad placita venissent"); see Nelson, *King and Emperor*, 264–67.

95. Ellis, *Peasant Economics*, 109.

96. Michael Moore, *A Sacred Kingdom: Bishops and the Rise of Frankish Kingship, 300–850* (Washington, DC, 2011), 194–202; Kohl, "Peasant Agency," 103.

97. Matthew Innes, *State and Society in the Early Middle Ages: The Middle Rhine Valley, 400–1000* (Cambridge, UK, 2000), 159–62.

98. Abhijit V. Banerjee and Esther Duflo, *Poor Economics: A Radical Rethinking of the Way to Fight Global Poverty* (New York, 2011), 37: "In Udaipur, India, where almost no one has a television, the extremely poor spend 14 percent of their budget on festivals (which includes both lay and religious occasions)."

99. E.g., *Liber Sacramentorum Gellonensis*, ed. A. Dumas and Jean Deshusses, CCSL 159A (Turnhout, 1981), rubric 72, 87, 96, 125, 144, 160, 229, 252, 264, 289, 294, 300, 362, 372, 377, 382, 387, 394, 415, 420, 425, 431, 436, 442, 448, 473, 478, 483, 489, 494, 519, 570, 581, 626, 631, 640, etc.; Jean Deshusses, ed., *Le Sacramentaire grégorien: Ses principales formes d'après les plus anciens manuscrits, édition comparative*, 2nd ed., 3 vols. (Fribourg, 1988), vol. 2, no. 9, 44; no. 10, 45. See also Els Rose, "'Plebs Sancta Ideo Meminere Debet': The Role of the People in the Early Medieval Liturgy of Mass," in *Das Christentum im frühen Europa: Diskurse, Tendenzen, Entscheidungen* (Berlin, 2019), 459–76.

100. Zadoks, *Crop Protection*, 126.

101. Ristuccia, *Christianization and Commonwealth*, 175.

102. Innes, *State and Society*, 18–19, 29–30.

103. Kohl, "Peasant Agency," 103–5.

104. *Passio Praeiecti episcopi et martyris Averni* (BHL 6915–16), c. 16, ed. Krusch, 235, with doctors to heal twenty sick people at once.

105. Franz Irsigler, "Matriculae, xenodochia, hospitalia und Leprosenhäuser im Frühmittelalter," in Franz Irsigler, *Spätlese: Aufsätze aus den ersten beiden Jahrzehnten des 21. Jahrhunderts: Festgabe für Franz Irsigler zum 80. Geburtstag*, ed. Michael Embach et al. (Trier, 2021 [2008]), 73–87; Michel Rouche, "La matricule des pauvres: Evolution d'une institution de charité du Bas Empire jusqu'à la fin du Haut Moyen Age," in *Études sur l'histoire de la pauvreté (Moyen Age—XVIe siècle)*, ed. Michel Mollat, 2 vols. (Paris, 1974), vol. 1, 83–110.

106. *Abbreviatio de rebus monasterii Bobiensis*, c. 42–47, Ludo M Hartmann, ed., "Adbreviatio de rebus monasterii Bobiensis," *Bolletino storico-bibliografico subalpino* 8 (1903): 393–404, at 402–3.

107. *Adbreviatio de rebus monasterii Bobiensis*, c. 45, 47, ed. Hartmann, 402, 403.

108. Alcuin, *Ep*. 249, ed. Ernst Dümmler, MGH Epp 4, 401–4.

109. Bobrycki, "Flailing Women," 26.

110. Amolo, *Ep*. 1, c. 7, ed. Dümmler, 366. Translation from Bobrycki, "Flailing Women," 36.

111. Raoul Manselli, *La religion populaire au Moyen Âge: Problèmes de méthode et d'histoire* (Montreal, 1975); Oronzo Giordano, *Religiosità popolare nell'alto medioevo* (Bari, 1979); Jean-Claude Schmitt, "Les 'superstitions,'" in *Histoire de la France religieuse*, ed. J. Le Goff and R. Remond, vol. 1, *Des dieux de la Gaule à la papauté d'Avignon* (Paris, 1988); Aron Gurevich, *Medieval Popular Culture: Problems of Belief and Perception*, trans. János M. Bak and Paul A. Hollingsworth (Cambridge, UK, 1990); Jack Tannous, *The Making of the Medieval Middle East: Religion, Society, and Simple Believers* (Princeton, NJ, 2018).

112. Bobrycki, "Flailing Women," 16 n. 19.

113. Dieter Harmening, *Superstitio: Überlieferungs- und theoriegeschichtliche Untersuchungen zur kirchlich- theologischen Aberglaubensliteratur des Mittelalters* (Berlin, 1979); Bernadette Filotas, *Pagan Survivals, Superstitions, and Popular Cultures in Early Medieval Pastoral Literature* (Toronto, 2005); Valerie J. Flint, *The Rise of Magic in Early Medieval Europe* (Oxford, 1991).

114. Amolo of Lyon, *Epistolae*, Ep. 1, ed. Dümmler, 363–68. For Saulieu, see Bobrycki, "Flailing Women," 23, 26.

115. Bobrycki, "Flailing Women," 16. See below, chapter 6.

116. Cyrille Vogel, "Pratiques superstitieuses au début du XIe siècle d'après le 'Corrector sive medicus' de Burchard, évêque de Worms (965–1025)," in *Études de civilisation médiévale (IXe–XIIe siècles): Mélanges offerts à Edmond-René Labande* (Poitiers, 1974), 751–61.

117. Eileen Power, *Medieval People*, 10th ed. (London, 1986 [1924]), 27–29.

118. E.g., *Annales Fuldenses*, s.a. 847, ed. F. Kurze, 36–37.

119. Kohl, "Peasant Agency," 105.

120. Kohl, "Peasant Agency," 113.

121. Bobrycki, "Flailing Women," 45–46.

122. Christian of Stavelot, *Expositio super Librum generationis*, ed. R.B.C. Huygens, CCCM 224 (Turnhout, 2008), 284, for the throwaway line that Basques and Spaniards like dancing at *convivia* while Franks prefer not to.

123. Council of Mainz (AD 852), c. 23, ed. W. Hartmann, MGH Conc. 3 (Hanover, 1984), 252: "Quod non oportet sacerdotes aut clericos quibuscumque spectaculis in caenis aut in nuptiis interesse, sed antequam thimelici ingrediantur, exsurgere eos convenit atque inde decedere."

124. Hincmar of Reims, *First Capitulary*, c. 14, MGH Capit. Episc. 2, 41–42.

125. Festive behavior has historically been implicated in non-elite crowd resistance: Emmanuel Le Roy Ladurie, *Le carnaval de Romans: De la chandeleur au mercredi des cendres 1579–1580* (Paris, 1979).

126. Alcuin, *Ep.* 249, ed. Ernst Dümmler, MGH Epp 2, 403; Theodulf of Orléans, *Carm.* no. 48 ("Itinerarium"), ed. Ernst Dümmler, MGH Poetae 2, 549 (*plebes madefacta Lyaeo*); Hincmar of Reims, *First Capitulary*, c. 16, MGH Capit. Episc. 2 (Hannover, 1995), 43.

127. Amolo, *Ep.* 1, c. 7, ed. Dümmler, 366–67; Bobrycki, "Failing Women," 29.

128. Charles Tilly and Sidney Tarrow, *Contentious Politics*, 2nd ed. (Oxford, 2015).

129. Bloch, *French Rural History*, 170. For East German Marxian approaches, see Siegfried Epperlein, *Herrschaft und Volk im karolingischen Imperium: Studien über soziale Konflikte und dogmatisch-politische Kontroversen im fränkischen Reich* (Berlin, 1969), and Wolfgang Eggert, "Rebelliones servorum: Bewaffnete Klassenkämpfe im Früh- und frühen Hochmittelalter und ihre Darstellung in zeitgenössischen erzählenden Quellen," *Zeitschrift für Geschichtswissenschaft* 23 (1975): 1147–1264.

130. Michel Mollat and Philippe Wolff, *Ongles bleus, Jacques et Ciompi: Les révolutions populaires en Europe aux 14e et 15e siècles* (Paris, 1970); Peter Bierbrauer, "Bäuerliche Revolte im Alten Reich: Ein Forschungsbericht," in *Aufruhr und Empörung? Studien zum bäuerlichen Widerstand im Alten Reich*, ed. Peter Blickle (Munich, 1980), 1–68; William H. TeBrake, *A Plague of Insurrection: Popular Politics and Peasant Revolt in Flanders, 1323–1328* (Philadelphia, 1993); Jan Dumolyn and Jelle Haemers, "Patterns of Urban Rebellion in Medieval Flanders," *Journal of Medieval History* 31 (2005): 369–93; Samuel Kline Cohn, *Lust for Liberty: The Politics of Social Revolt in Medieval Europe, 1200–1425* (Cambridge, MA, 2008); Justine Firnhaber-Baker, "Introduction: Medieval Revolt in Context," in *The Routledge History Handbook of Medieval Revolt*, ed. Justine Firnhaber-Baker and Dirk Schoenaers (London, 2017), 1–15; Justine Firnhaber-Baker, *The Jacquerie of 1358: A French Peasants' Revolt* (Oxford, 2021), for an exemplary study.

131. See the overview in Cohn, *Lust for Liberty*, 1–24, and the essays in Firnhaber-Baker and Schoenaers, eds., *Routledge History Handbook of Medieval Revolt*.

132. Thomas S. Brown, "Urban Violence in Early Medieval Italy: The Cases of Rome and Ravenna," in *Violence and Society in the Early Medieval West*, ed. Guy Halsall (Rochester, NY, 1998), 76–89; Joaquín Martínez Pizarro, "Crowds and Power in the *Liber Pontificalis Ecclesiae Ravennatis*," in *The Community, the Family and the Saint: Patterns of Power in Early Medieval Europe*, ed. J. Hill and M. Swann (Turnhout, 1998), 265–83; Judith Herrin, "Urban Riot or Civic Ritual? The Crowd in Early Medieval Ravenna," in *Raum und Performanz: Rituale in Residenzen von der Antike bis 1815*, ed. Dietrich Boschung, Karl-Joachim Hölkeskamp, and Claudia Sode (Stuttgart, 2015), 219–40; Veronica West-Harling, *Rome, Ravenna, and Venice, 750–1000. Byzantine Heritage, Imperial Present, and the Construction of City Identity* (Oxford, 2020).

133. West-Harling, *Rome, Ravenna, and Venice*, 462.

134. See below at pp. 162–63.

135. Venice: Stefano Gasparri, "Venezia fra l'Italia bizantina e il regno italico: La civitas e l'assemblea," in *Venezia: Itinerari per la storia della città*, ed. Stefano Gasparri, Giovanni Levi, and Pierandrea Moro (Bologna, 1997), 61–82; West-Harling, *Rome, Ravenna, and Venice*, 461–62. Naples: Brown, "Urban Violence," 78.

136. Brown, "Urban Violence," 77; Chris Wickham, *Early Medieval Italy* (Ann Arbor, MI, 1989), 190–91.

137. West-Harling, *Rome, Ravenna, and Venice*, 460–61.

138. *Vita Vigilii*, c. 4, *LP* 1, 297: "Videntes Romani quod movisset navis in qua sedebat Vigilius, tunc coepit populus iactare post eum lapides, fustes, caccabos, et dicere: 'Famis tua tecum! mortalitas tua tecum! Male fecisti Romanis, male invenias ubi vadis.'"

139. *Vita Sergii I*, c. 8–9, *LP* 1, 373–74.

140. Contested elections occurred in 686, 687, 767–68, 824, 844, 855, 903, 974, 997, and 1012.

141. *Vita Stephani III*, *LP* 1, 468–80; Stefano Gasparri, *Desiderio* (Rome, 2019), 123–32.

142. For an insulting slogan that was written and said: *Vita Hadriani II*, c. 14, *LP* 2, 176.

143. Brown, "Urban Violence," 82.

144. *Codex Carolinus*, no. 63, ed. W. Gundlach, MGH Epp 3 (Berlin, 1892), 590. Hadrian cannily framed this as a matter of loyalty, not taxes: Erich Caspar, *Pippin und die römische Kirche: Kritische Untersuchungen zum fränkisch-päpstlichen Bunde im 8. Jahrhundert* (Berlin, 1914), 120.

145. Clermont: Gregory of Tours, *Hist.* 4.11, ed. Krusch and Levison, 141–42. Marseille: Gregory of Tours, *Hist.* 6.11, ed. Krusch and Levison, 280–82. Poitiers: Gregory of Tours, *Hist.* 9.39–43, 10.15–17, 20, 22, ed. Krusch and Levison, 460–75, 501–9, 513, 514.

146. Gregory of Tours, *Hist.* 3.36, ed. Krusch and Levison, 131–32; *PLRE* 2, 833–34 (Parthenius 3). See Allen Jones, *Death and Afterlife in the Pages of Gregory of Tours: Religion and Society in Late Antique Gaul* (Amsterdam, 2020), 179–80, for discussion of Gregory's interests in this passage.

147. Gregory of Tours, *Hist.* 3.36, ed. Krusch and Levison, 131.

148. Gregory of Tours, *Hist.* 3.36, ed. Krusch and Levison, 132. In the original biblical context, the "god" in question is Dagon and the enemy is Samson, reflecting Gregory's hostile attitude not only toward Parthenius but also to the crowd that lynched him.

149. Gregory of Tours, *Hist.* 5.28, ed. Krusch and Levison, 234.

150. Gregory of Tours, *Hist.* 5.34, ed. Krusch and Levison, 239–40.

151. Gregory of Tours, *Hist.* 7.15, ed. Krusch and Levison, 336–37.

152. Gregory of Tours, *Hist.* 9.30, ed. Krusch and Levison, 448–49. See also *Hist.* 4.2, ed. Krusch and Levison, 136, for Gregory's predecessor Iniuriosus.

153. Gregory of Tours, *Hist.* 5.28, ed. Krusch and Levison, 233–34.

154. Theodulf of Orléans, *Carm.* no. 48 ("Itinerarium"), ed. Dümmler, 549. My thanks to Laurent Jégou for bringing this passage to my attention.

155. Alcuin, *Ep.* no. 245–249, ed. Ernst Dümmler, MGH Epp 4 (Berlin, 1895), 393–404; Samuel Collins, *The Carolingian Debate over Sacred Space* (New York, 2012), 91–120.

156. Chris Wickham, "Looking Forward: Peasant Revolts in Europe, 600–1200," in *Routledge History Handbook of Medieval Revolt*, ed. Firnhaber-Baker and Schoenaers, 155–67; building on Chris Wickham, "Space and Society in Early Medieval Peasant Conflicts," in *Uomo e spazio nell'alto Medioevo* (Spoleto, 2003), 551–86. The other sources in the table are: Thomas Pekáry, "Seditio: Unruhen und Revolten im römischen Reich von Augustus bis Commodus," *Ancient Society* 18 (1987): 133–50; Julia Sünskes Thompson, *Aufstände und Protestaktionen im Imperium Romanum: Die severischen Kaiser im Spannungsfeld innenpolitischer Konflikte* (Bonn, 1990); Júlio César Magalhães de Oliveira, "Late Antiquity: The Age of Crowds?," *Past & Present* 249 (2020): 3–52; Cohn, *Lust for Liberty*; Jean Nicolas, *La rébellion française: Mouvements populaires et conscience sociale, 1661–1789* (Paris, 2002).

157. See Jean-Pierre Devroey, "La poudre du duc Grimoald: Une affaire criminelle au début du IXe siècle," *Revue belge de philologie et d'histoire* 96 (2018): 349–63.

158. For the dating, see Bernard Gowers, "996 and All That: The Norman Peasants' Revolt Reconsidered," *Early Medieval Europe* 21 (2013): 71–98, at 82–83.

159. Gregory the Great, *Registrum*, 3.1, ed. Ewald, 158–59.

160. MGH D Merov 103, ed. Kölzer, 267–68; Werner Bergmann, "Untersuchungen zu den Gerichtsurkunden der Merowingerzeit," *Archiv für Diplomatik, Schriftgeschichte, Siel- und Wappenkunde* 22 (1976): 1–186, at 157–58. For the fullest elaboration of Wickham's theory, see Wickham, "Space and Society," 552–54, 559, 564, 583.

161. Forgery: Theo Kölzer, *Merowingerstudien II* (Hanover, 1999), 93–94; Kölzer, MGH D Merov 1, 266. Manuscript context: Dijon, Bibliothèque municipale, MS 591 (348), fol. 69v–70r (no. 21), ed. Georges Chevrier, Maurice Chaume, and Robert Folz, *Chartes et documents de Saint-Bénigne de Dijon: Prieurés et dépendances des origines à 1300*, 2 vols. (Dijon, 1943–86), vol. 1, 50–52 (no. 14). See E. Bougaud and Joseph Garnier, eds., *Chronique de l'abbaye de Saint-Bénigne de Dijon, suivie de la chronique de Saint-Pierre de Bèze publiées d'après les textes originaux* (Dijon, 1875), 29–30, 41–42, 61–62, for the corresponding treatment in the chronicle (Dijon, BM, MS 591 [348], fol. 9v–10r, 13r, and 20r). At 61–62, the monastic compilers of the chronicle describe the antagonists as *milites*.

162. Wickham, "Looking Forward," 160: "The Norman rising of c. 1000 takes us to the beginning of a different political world."

163. Collected in Juan Gil Fernández, José Moralejo, and Juan Ruiz de la Peña, *Crónicas asturianas* (Oviedo, 1985), 136–37 ("Ad Sebastianum"), 174 ("Chronica Albendensia").

164. *Ad Sebastianum*, c. 17, ed. Gil Fernández et al., 137: "Post Froilanis interitum consubrinus eius Aurelius filius Froilani fratris Adefonsi successit in regnum. Cuius tempore libertini contra proprios dominos arma sumentes tyrannice surrexerunt, sed principis industria superati in seruitutem pristinam sunt omnes redacti." *Chronica Albendensia*, c. 5, ed. Gil Fernández et al., 174: "Eo regnante serbi dominis suis contradicentes eius industria captis in pristina sunt serbitute redacti."

165. Wickham, *Framing*, 584.

166. *Chronicon Vulturnense del Monaco Giovanni*, ed. Vincenzo Federici (Rome, 1938), vol. 3, nos. 23–26, 55, 71–72, 157, 180; Manaresi, ed., *Placiti*, nos. 4, 8–10; no. 72, 261–65; no. 58, 205–8.

167. Manaresi, no. 4, 9: "Nichil invasimus, nisi nostra substantia."

168. Wickham, *Framing*, 583.

169. Wickham, *Framing*, 582.

170. See esp. Ingrid Rembold, *Conquest and Christianization: Saxony and the Carolingian World, 772–888* (Cambridge, UK, 2017), 85–140; Goldberg, "Popular Revolt."

171. Nithard, *Historiae* 4.2, 4.4, 4.6, ed. Philipe Lauer, revised by Sophie Glansdorff, *Histoire des fils de Louis le Pieux* (Paris, 2012), 130–34, 142, 152–54; [Prudentius of Troyes], *AB*, s.a. 841, 842, ed. Grat, 38–40, 42–43; *AF*, s.a. 842, ed. Kurze, 33–34; *AX*, s.a. 841, ed. von Simson, 12.

172. Maria Schäpers, *Lothar I. (795–855) und das Frankenreich* (Cologne, 2018), 411–14.

173. Nithard, *Hist.* 4.2, ed. Lauer and Glansdorff, 132.

174. *AB*, s.a. 841, ed. Grat, 38–39: "quorum multiplicior numerus in eorum gente habetur."

175. Nithard, *Hist.* 4.2, ed. Lauer and Glansdorff, 132: "etiam in Saxoniam misit [Lothar] frilingis lazzibusque, quorum infinita multitudo est . . ."

176. Nithard, *Hist.* 4.2, ed. Lauer and Glansdorff, 132: "Qua supra modum cupidi nomen novum sibi, id est Stellinga, imposuerunt et in unum conglobati dominis e regno poene pulsis more antiquo qua quisque volebat lege vivebat."

177. *AX*, s.a. 841, 12: "Eodem anno per totam Saxoniam potestas servorum valde excreverat super dominos suos, et nomen sibi usurpaverunt Stellingas et multa inrationabilia conmiserunt. Et nobiles illius patriae a servis valde afflicti et humiliati sunt."

178. This is often taken at face value, but Caspar Ehlers, "Frühmittelalter: Voraussetzungen und prägende Faktoren der wirtschaftlich-sozialen Entwicklung (8. bis 11. Jahrhundert)," in *Die Wirtschafts- und Sozialgeschichte des braunschweigischen Landes: Mittelalter*, ed. Claudia Märtl et al. (Hildesheim, 2008), 27–233, at 184, makes the case that the Stellingas were not from the very lowest classes.

179. Goldberg, "Popular Revolt," 481–82.
180. *AB*, s.a. 841, ed. Grat, 39.
181. Rembold, *Conquest and Christianization*, 109–14.
182. *AB*, s.a. 842, ed. Grat, 42–43.
183. *AX*, s.a. 842, 13: "servos Saxonum superbe elatos nobiliter afflixit [sc. Louis the German] et ad propriam naturam restituit."
184. Goldberg, "Popular Revolt," 468–70, offers a good summary of older perspectives.
185. Rembold, *Conquest and Christianization*, 100.
186. Norbert Wagner, "Der Name der Stellinga," *Beiträge zur Namenforschung*, N.S. 15 (1980): 128–33, at 133; Naismith, "Gilds," 637–38.
187. Rembold, *Conquest and Christianization*, 107.
188. Gowers, "996 and All That." Compare the perspective of Mathieu Arnoux, "Classe agricole, pouvoir seigneurial et autorité ducale: L'évolution de la Normandie féodale d'après le témoignage des chroniqueurs (Xe-XIIe siècles)," *Le Moyen Âge* 98 (1992): 35–60.
189. William of Jumièges, *Gesta Normannorum Ducum* 5.2, *The Gesta Normannorum Ducum of William of Jumièges, Orderic Vitalis and Robert of Torigni*, ed. Elisabeth van Houts, 2 vols. (Oxford, 1992), vol. 2, 8.
190. William of Jumièges, *Gesta Normannorum Ducum* 5.2, ed. van Houts, 8. Here I have departed somewhat from van Houts's translation (9).
191. Wace, *Roman de Rou*, 3.815–958, *Le Roman de Rou de Wace*, ed. A. J. Holden, 3 vols. (Paris, 1970). For literary context, see Hannah Weaver, "A 'Geste' for the King: Wace's Epic Experiment in the *Roman de Rou*," *Viator* 46 (2015): 41–60.
192. Wace, *Roman de Rou*, 3.875–77. See Gowers, "996 and All That," 76–79.
193. Gowers, "996 and All That," 88–89.
194. James C. Scott, *Domination and the Arts of Resistance* (New Haven, CT, 1990), 140–52.
195. Goldberg, "Popular Revolt," 500; Goldberg adds (500–501) that similar dynamics prevailed later.
196. Goldberg, "Popular Revolt," 493.
197. E. P. Thompson, "The Moral Economy of the English Crowd in the Eighteenth Century," *Past & Present* 50 (1971): 76–136, at 78.
198. *AB*, s.a. 859, ed. Grat et al., 80: "Dani loca ultra Scaldem populantur. Vulgus promiscuum inter Sequanam et Ligerim inter se coniurans, aduersus Danos in Sequana consistentes fortiter resistit. Sed quia incaute sumpta est eorum coniuratio, a potentioribus nostris facile interficiuntur."
199. Johann Christoph Krause, *Geschichte der wichtigsten Begebenheiten des heutigen Europa* (Halle, 1791), vol. 3, 223 n. "p" (Krause's notes are alphabetical): "a potentioribus *nostris* facile interficiuntur . . . ist falsch und muß heißen nostri. Es wär zu abscheulich, wenn es nostris hiesse, d. h. das der fr. Adel selbst die Bauern unterdrückt habe." Later on, a group of Francophone historians endorsed this suggestion: C. Dehaisnes, *Les Annales de Saint-Bertin et de Saint-Vaast, suivies de fragments d'une chronique inédite* (Paris, 1871), 98 n. 1; Numa Denis Fustel de Coulanges, *Histoire des institutions politiques de l'ancienne France*, vol. 6, *Les transformations de la royauté pendant l'époque carolingienne*, ed. Camille Jullian (Paris, 1892), 679 n. 1; Jules Lair, *Les Normands dans l'île d'Oscelle, 855 à 861* (Paris, 1897), 13; Ferdinand Lot, "La grande invasion normande de 856-862," *Bibliothèque de l'École des Chartes* 49 (1908): 5–62, at 32 n. 2. The standard edition of the *Annals of Saint-Bertin* agrees with Lot's interpretation, but does not accept his emendation, ingeniously but most improbably seeing *nostris* as an ablative of comparison: Grat et al., *AB*, 80, n. 1: "Sur les interprétations diverses de ce passage, voir F. Lot . . . qui propose de corriger *nostris* en *nostri*, correction qui aurait l'avantage de fournir un sujet au verbe *interficiuntur*; cependant, la correction ne s'impose pas; nous avons ici un comparatif suivi de l'ablatif, *a potentioribus nostris*, 'par de plus puissants que les nôtres.'"

200. Janet Nelson, *Charles the Bald* (London, 1992), 194. Many have drawn this conclusion, going back not only to Ernst Dümmler, *Geschichte des ostfränkischen Reiches*, 2nd ed., 3 vols (Leipzig, 1887), vol. 1, 447, but before him to Heinrich Luden, *Geschichte des teutschen Volkes* (Gotha, 1831), vol. 6, 518–19. Among many, see Wickham, *Framing*, 580–81 ("any autonomous peasant action was . . . regarded as illegitimate by aristocrats, and thus dangerous, even if at present aimed at the enemies of the kingdom"), 585 ("peasant initiatives were, even if not directed against lords, more dangerous than rearguard reactions"). Paul Fouracre, *Eternal Light and Early Concerns: Belief and the Shaping of Medieval Society* (Manchester, 2021), 117, with 147 n. 43; Ryan Lavelle, *Places of Contested Power: Conflict and Rebellion in England and France, 830–1150* (Woodbridge, UK, 2020), 64–65; Naismith, "Gilds," 636, 641; Bobrycki, "Flailing Women," 42; Rachel Stone, *Morality and Masculinity in the Carolingian Empire* (Cambridge, UK, 2011), 88; Marios Costambeys, Matthew Innes, and Simon MacLean, *The Carolingian World* (Cambridge, UK, 2011), 249–50; Oexle, "Conjuratio und Gilden," 498–99; Claire Taylor, "The Year 1000 and Those Who Labored," in *The Year 1000: Religious and Social Response to the Turning of the First Millennium*, ed. M. Frassetto (New York, 2002), 187–236, at 197; Epperlein, *Herrschaft und Volk*, 29; Eggert, "Rebelliones servorum," 1152.

201. Thompson, "Moral Economy," 136.

202. Gregory Aldrete, "Riots," in *The Cambridge Companion to Ancient Rome*, ed. Paul Erdkamp (Cambridge, 2013), 425–40, at 439.

203. Gregory the Great, *Registrum*, 3.1, ed. Ewald, 159: "Et si iustam contra dominos suos querellam habuerint, cum congrua ordinatione de ecclesiis exire necesse est" (the *mancipia* had perched themselves in church and refused to leave); Wickham, *Framing*, 582.

204. Wickham, *Framing*, 580–81.

205. Capitulary of Ver (884), c. 14, ed. MGH Capit. 2, no. 287, 375; Goldberg, "Vikings, Vassals, Villagers."

206. Marc Bloch, "Avènement et conquêtes du moulin à eau," *Annales d'histoire économique et sociale* 7 (1935): 538–63, at 556 ("leur merveilleuse inertie").

207. James McCune, "The Preacher's Audience, c. 800–c. 950," in *Sermo Doctorum: Compilers, Preachers and Their Audiences in the Early Middle Ages*, ed. Maximilian Diesenberger, Yitzhak Hen, and Marianne Pollheimer (Turnhout, 2013), 283–338, at 293; Chris Wickham, "Gossip and Resistance among the Medieval Peasantry," *Past & Present* 160 (1998): 3–24, esp. 18–19, analyzes peasant "gossip" (as it is described in our sources) in terms of Scott's resistance.

208. Bobrycki, "Flailing Women," 43–44.

209. Thompson, "Moral Economy," 76–77, with reference to Max Beloff, *Public Order and Popular Disturbances, 1660–1714* (Oxford, 1928). For revolts as "natural," see Bloch, *French Rural History*, 170.

210. Toby Davies et al., "A Mathematical Model of the London Riots and Their Policing," *Scientific Reports* 3 (2013): 1–9, at 3. See also Adam Kucharski, *The Rules of Contagion: Why Things Spread—And Why They Stop* (New York, 2020), 136–38.

211. Thompson, "Moral Economy," 120–26.

212. Thompson, "Moral Economy," 126.

213. Wickham, *Framing*, 578–82.

214. Wickham, *Framing*, 578–79.

215. Capitulary of Ver (884), c. 14, ed. MGH Capit. 2, no. 287, 375.

216. *Edictus Rothari*, c. 279–280, *Leges Langobardorum, 643–866*, ed. Franz Beyerle, 2nd ed. (Witzenhausen, 1962), 73. For *servi rusticani*, see Rio, *Slavery*, 152–53.

217. *Edictus Rothari*, c. 279, ed. Beyerle, 73.

218. *Edictus Rothari*, c. 280, ed. Beyerle, 73.

219. *Edictus Rothari*, c. 279–80, ed. Beyerle, 73.

220. Rio, *Slavery*, 152–53.
221. *Edictus Rothari*, c. 19; *Liutprandi Leges*, c. 35, 134, 141, ed. Beyerle, 21, 119, 170–71.
222. *Edictus Rothari*, c. 279–80, ed. Beyerle, 73.
223. *Liutprandi Leges*, c. 141, ed. Beyerle, 170–71. Ross Balzaretti, "'These Are Things That Men Do, Not Women': The Social Regulation of Female Violence in Langobard Italy," in *Violence and Society in the Early Medieval West*, ed. Guy Halsall (Woodbridge, UK, 1998), 175–92.
224. *Edictus Rothari*, c. 378, ed. Beyerle, 91.
225. *Liutprandi Leges*, c. 141, ed. Beyerle, 170–71.
226. See John Walter, *Crowds and Popular Politics in Early Modern England* (Manchester, 2006), 40–41.
227. Wickham, *Framing*, 574, 581.
228. Angilbert, *Institutio* c. 6, ed. Hallinger, 294 (Palm Sunday); c. 7, 295 (Good Friday, where the phrase *populus uulgaris* is used); c. 8, 296 (Easter); c. 9, 296, 297, 299 (rogations); c. 14, 301 (festival of Saint Riquier).
229. Alcuin, *Ep.* 249, ed. Ernst Dümmler, MGH Epp 4, 401–4. See Rob Meens, "Sanctuary, Penance, and Dispute Settlement under Charlemagne: The Conflict between Alcuin and Theodulf of Orléans over a Sinful Cleric," *Speculum* 82 (2007): 277–300.
230. Bloch, *French Rural History*, 170.
231. Bloch, "Avènement," 556.

Chapter 4. The Closed Crowd: Elite Venues and Occasions for Gathering

1. For "repertory," see Natalie Davis, "The Rites of Violence: Religious Riot in Sixteenth-Century France," *Past & Present* 59 (1973): 51–91, at 53, and above pp. 8–9.
2. Elias Canetti, *Masse und Macht* (Düsseldorf, 1978), 12–14.
3. Nathan J. Ristuccia, *Christianization and Commonwealth in Early Medieval Europe: A Ritual Interpretation* (Oxford, 2018), 21–22, 136–37.
4. Philippe Buc, *The Dangers of Ritual: Between Early Medieval Texts and Social Scientific Theory* (Princeton, NJ, 2001). For responses to Buc's arguments on the historiographical misuse of polemic, see Janet Nelson, review of *The Dangers of Ritual*, by Philippe Buc, *Speculum* 78 (2003): 847–51; Geoffrey Koziol, "The Dangers of Polemic: Is Ritual Still an Interesting Topic of Historical Study?," *Early Medieval Europe* 11 (2002): 367–88; Philippe Buc, "The Monster and the Critics: A Ritual Reply," *Early Medieval Europe* 15 (2007): 441–52; Christina Pössel, "The Magic of Early Medieval Ritual," *Early Medieval Europe* 17 (2009): 111–25.
5. Mayke de Jong, *The Penitential State: Authority and Atonement in the Age of Louis the Pious, 814–840* (Cambridge, UK, 2009); Courtney Booker, *Past Convictions: The Penance of Louis the Pious and the Decline of the Carolingians* (Philadelphia, 2012).
6. James Scott, *Weapons of the Weak: Everyday Forms of Peasant Resistance* (New Haven, CT, 1987), 288.
7. Canetti, *Masse und Macht*, 22–24.
8. For overviews see the essays in Thomas Noble and Julia Smith, eds., *The Cambridge History of Christianity*, vol. 3, *Early Medieval Christianities, c 600–c. 1100* (Cambridge, UK, 2008); Arnold Angenendt, *Geschichte der Religiosität im Mittelalter* (Darmstadt, 1997).
9. For the public ramifications of this worship, see Mayke De Jong, "*Ecclesia* and the Early Medieval Polity," in *Staat im frühen Mittelalter*, ed. Stuart Airlie, Walter Pohl, and Helmut Reimitz (Vienna, 2006), 113–32; Mayke de Jong, "Carolingian Monasticism: The Power of Prayer," in *The New Cambridge Medieval History*, vol. 2, *c. 700–c. 900*, ed. Rosamond McKitterick (Cambridge, UK, 1995), 622–653.
10. Julia Smith, "Religion and Lay Society," in *New Cambridge Medieval History*, ed. McKitterick, vol. 2, 654–78, at 664–65.

11. Smith, "Religion and Lay Society," 661; Els Rose, "'Plebs Sancta Ideo Meminere Debet': The Role of the People in the Early Medieval Liturgy of Mass," in *Das Christentum im frühen Europa: Diskurse, Tendenzen, Entscheidungen* (Berlin, 2019), 459–76, at 467.

12. John Romano, *Liturgy and Society in Early Medieval Rome* (Farnham, 2014), 109–40, on the "staging" of public unity.

13. Bede, *HE* 2.14.2, ed. Lapidge, vol. 1, 370.

14. Nathan J. Ristuccia, *Christianization and Commonwealth in Early Medieval Europe: A Ritual Interpretation* (Oxford, 2018).

15. Romano, *Liturgy and Society in Early Medieval Rome*, 25–74.

16. Angilbert of Saint-Riquier, *Institutio de diversitate officiorum*, c. 9, ed. K. Hallinger, M. Wegener, and H. Frank, CCM 1 (Siegburg, 1963), 296. See Carol Heitz, "Architecture et liturgie en France de l'époque carolingienne à l'an Mil," *Hortus Artium Medievalium* 1 (1995): 57–73, at 58–59; Hendrick Dey, *The Afterlife of the Roman City: Architecture and Ceremony in Late Antiquity and the Early Middle Ages* (Cambridge, UK, 2015), 226–28.

17. See, e.g., Jose Sánchez-Pardo and Michael Shapland, eds., *Churches and Social Power in Early Medieval Europe: Integrating Archaeological and Historical Approaches* (Turnhout, 2015).

18. Ramsay MacMullen, "The Preacher's Audience (AD 350–400)," *The Journal of Theological Studies* 40 (1989): 503–11; Ramsay MacMullen, *The Second Church: Popular Christianity, A.D. 300–400* (Atlanta, 2009); Peter Brown, *Through the Eye of a Needle: Wealth, the Fall of Rome, and the Making of Christianity in the West, 350–550 AD* (Princeton, NJ, 2012), 339–58.

19. Augustine, *Sermo* 68.1, ed. G. Morin, *Sancti Augustini Sermones post Maurinos reperti* (Rome, 1930), 356: "istam sancti euangelii lectionem etiam hesterno dominico die, sicut meministis, audiuimus: sed hodie ut legeretur nos uoluimus, propterea quia heri multitudo constipata etiam angustiis aliquanto inquietas uoci nostrae non dabat facilitatem; quoniam non est talis ut sufficiat nisi magno silentio."

20. E.g., Council of Paris (829), c. 50 ("De observatione diei dominici"), MGH Conc 2.2, 643–44; Wilfried Hartmann, *Die Synoden der Karolingerzeit im Frankenreich und in Italien* (Paderborn, 1989), 433–35. See Smith, "Religion and Lay Society," 660–65, and for the earlier period, Lisa Bailey, *The Religious Worlds of the Laity in Late Antique Gaul* (London, 2017).

21. Smith, "Religion and Lay Society," 663.

22. *Breve de inquisitione* (715), ed. Luigi Schiaparelli, *Codice Diplomatico Longobardo* 1 (Rome, 1929), no. 19, 61–77. See above, pp. 46, 55–56.

23. Rosamond McKitterick, *The Frankish Church and the Carolingian Reforms, 789–895* (London, 1977), esp. 80–154; Owen Phelan, *The Formation of Christian Europe: The Carolingians, Baptism, and the Imperium Christianum* (Oxford, 2014), 1, for links between regular liturgical celebration and empire building, with the baptism as the "most basic organizing principle" of Carolingian society. For the rise of tithes, see Giles Constable, *Monastic Tithes from Their Origins to the Twelfth Century* (Cambridge, UK, 1964), 9–56; John Eldevik, *Episcopal Power and Ecclesiastical Reform in the German Empire: Tithes, Lordship and Community, 950–1150* (Cambridge, UK, 2012), 34–61; Steffen Patzold, "Tithes in the Long 10th Century: The Example of the Dioceses of Freising and Mâcon," *Frühmittelalterliche Studien* 57 (2023): 295–314.

24. See Arnold Angenendt, "*Donationes pro anima*: Gift and Countergift in the Early Medieval Liturgy," in *The Long Morning of Medieval Europe: New Directions in Early Medieval Studies*, ed. J. Davis and M. McCormick (Aldershot, UK, 2008), 131–54; Carine van Rhijn, *Shepherds of the Lord: Priests and Episcopal Statutes in the Carolingian Period* (Turnhout, 2007); Steffen Patzold, *Presbyter: Moral, Mobilität, und die Kirchenorganisation im Karolingerreich* (Stuttgart, 2020).

25. At the conciliar level, see, e.g., Council of Mainz (813), c. 34, 36, ed. A. Werminghoff, MGH Conc. 2.1 (Hanover, 1906), 269–70 (focusing on the enforcement of fasting). See Dominique Iogna-Prat, *La maison Dieu: Une histoire monumentale de l'Église au moyen-âge, 800–1200* (Paris, 2006); Dominique Iogna-Prat, "Penser l'église, penser la société après le Pseudo-Denys

l'Aréopagite," in *Hiérarchie et stratification sociale dans l'Occident médiéval (400–1100)*, ed. François Bougard, Dominique Iogna-Prat, and Régine Le Jan (Turnhout, 2008), 55–81.

26. Amolo, *Ep.* 1, c. 7, ed. Dümmler, 366; Charles West, "Unauthorised Miracles in Mid-Ninth-Century Dijon and the Carolingian Church Reforms," *Journal of Medieval History* 36 (2010): 295–311.

27. MacMullen, "Preacher's Audience," 506–7; Smith, "Religion and Lay Society," 661; Phelan, *Formation*, 71. In the literary imagination, such ceremonies, with their large audiences, were a natural venue for miracles. In the *Vita Amandi altera* (*BHL* 335), c. 15, AASS Feb. 1.6.855D, an infant being baptized utters the word "Amen." On this *vita*, see Charles Mériaux, *Gallia irradiata: Saints et sanctuaires dans le nord de la Gaule du haut Moyen Âge* (Stuttgart, 2006), 347.

28. Angilbert of Saint-Riquier, *Institutio*, c. 8, ed. Hallinger et al, 295–96. Heitz, "Architecture et liturgie," 58–59; Susan Rabe, *Faith, Art, and Politics at Saint-Riquier: The Symbolic Vision of Angilbert* (Philadelphia, 1995), 19–20; Smith, "Religion and Lay Society," 661.

29. See above, pp. 75–76.

30. In the 830s, pope Gregory IV celebrated All Saints' Day on November 1, which Thomas F. X. Noble, "The Reception of Visitors in Early Medieval Rome," in *Discovery and Distinction in the Early Middle Ages: Studies in Honor of John J. Contreni*, ed. Cullen J. Chandler and Steven A. Stofferahn (Kalamazoo, MI, 2013), 205–17, at 217, calls "a good example of the kinds of hints we have about the presence of pilgrims in Rome and papal solicitude for them." See also Hendrik Dey, "*Diaconiae, Xenodochia, Hospitalia* and Monasteries: 'Social Security' and the Meaning of Monasticism in Early Medieval Rome," *Early Medieval Europe* 16 (2008): 398–422; Riccardo Santangeli Valenzani, "Pellegrini, senatori e papi: Gli xenodochia a Roma tra il V e il IX secolo," *Rivista dell'istituto nazionale d'archeologia e storia dell'arte* 19 / 20 (1997): 203–26; Riccardo Santangeli Valenzani, "Hosting Foreigners in Early Medieval Rome: From *Xenodochia* To *Scholae Peregrinorum*," in *England and Rome in the Early Middle Ages: Pilgrimage, Art, and Politics*, ed. Francesca Tinti (Turnhout, 2014), 69–88.

31. Michael Sierck, *Festtag und Politik: Studien zur Tagewahl karolingischer Herrscher* (Cologne, 1995), 177–97; Hans-Werner Goetz, "Der kirchliche Festtag im frühmittelalterlichen Alltag," in *Feste und Feiern im Mittelalter*, ed. D. Altenburg, J. Jarnut, and H.-H. Steinhoff (Sigmaringen, 1991), 53–62.

32. Beverly M. Kienzle and René Nöel, eds., *The Sermon*, Typologie des Sources 81–83 (Turnhout, 2000). See also Beverly M. Kienzle, "Medieval Sermons and Their Performance: Theory and Record," in *Preacher, Sermon, and Audience in the Middle Ages*, ed. C. Muessig (Leiden, 2002), 89–124.

33. Jean Longère, *La prédication médiévale* (Paris, 1983); Maria Giuseppina Muzzarelli, *Pescatori di uomini: Predicatori e piazze alle fine del Medioevo* (Bologna, 2005).

34. Even in the large cities during Late Antiquity, huge sermons were limited to major festivities, and the normal crowd for a late Roman sermon was probably a small gathering of upper-class hearers. See André Mandouze, *Saint Augustin: L'aventure de la raison et de la grâce* (Paris, 1968), 591–653; Brown, *Through the Eye of a Needle*, 339–58; MacMullen, "Preacher's Audience," 510.

35. Rudolf Cruel, *Geschichte der deutschen Predigt im Mittelalter* (Detmold, 1879), 1; Anton Linsenmayer, *Geschichte der Predigt in Deutschland von Karl dem Grossen bis zum Ausgange des vierzehnten Jahrhunderts* (Frankfurt, 1969), 6. For the homiliaries, see Aimé G. Martimort, *Les Lectures liturgiques et leurs livres*, Typologie des Sources 64 (Turnhout, 1992); Réginald Grégoire, *Homéliaires liturgiques médiévaux: Analyse de manuscrits* (Spoleto, 1980); Henri Barré, *Les homéliaires carolingiens de l'école d'Auxerre* (Vatican City, 1962).

36. R. Emmet McLaughlin, "The World Eclipsed? Preaching in the Early Middle Ages," *Traditio* 46 (1991): 77–122, at 77.

37. See above all Maximilian Diesenberger, *Predigt und Politik im frühmittelalterlichen Bayern: Arn von Salzburg, Karl der Große und die Salzburger Sermones-Sammlung* (Berlin, 2015), 18–20, 35–48, for the ambitions of sermon collections. See also James McCune, "Rethinking the Pseudo-Eligius Sermon Collection," *Early Medieval Europe* 16 (2008): 445–76, arguing for a ninth-century date and a mixed audience for this sermon collection; Thomas Hall, "The Early Medieval Sermon," in *The Sermon*, ed. Kienzle and Noël, 204–69; Thomas Leslie Amos, "Early Medieval Sermons and Their Audience," in *De l'homélie au sermon: Histoire de la prédication médiévale*, ed. J. Hamesse and X. Hermand (Louvain-la-Neuve, 1993), 1–14; Maximilian Diesenberger, "Introduction: Compilers, Preachers, and Their Audiences in the Early Medieval West," in *Sermo Doctorum: Compilers, Preachers and Their Audiences in the Early Middle Ages*, ed. Maximilian Diesenberger, Yitzhak Hen and Marianne Pollheimer (Turnhout, 2013), 1–24.

38. James McCune, "The Preacher's Audience, c. 800—c. 950," in *Sermo Doctorum: Compilers, Preachers and Their Audiences in the Early Middle Ages*, ed. Maximilian Diesenberger, Yitzhak Hen, and Marianne Pollheimer (Turnhout, 2013), 283–338. McCune builds on Thomas L. Amos, "The Origin and Nature of the Carolingian Sermon" (PhD diss., Michigan State University, 1983). For Old English texts, see Milton Gatch, *Preaching and Theology in Anglo-Saxon England* (Toronto, 1977).

39. Gregory the Great, *Homily on Ezechiel*, 1.11.12, ed. C. Morel, *Homélies sur Ezéchiel: Texte latin, introduction, traduction et notes*, SC 327 (Paris, 1986), vol. 1, 464: "Pensare etenim doctor debet quid loquatur, cui loquatur, quando loquatur, qualiter loquatur, et quantum loquatur." See, for an attempt to reconstruct audience from text, Maximilian Diesenberger, "How Collections Shape the Texts: Rewriting and Rearranging Passions in Carolingian Bavaria," in *Livrets, collections et textes: Études de la tradition hagiographique latine*, ed. Martin Heinzelmann (Ostfildern, 2006), 195–224.

40. Diesenberger, *Predigt und Politik*, 4.

41. Theodulf of Orléans, *Capitulare ad presbyteros Parochiae suae*, c. 28, ed. Peter Brommer, MGH Capit. Episc. 1 (Hanover, 1984), 125–26; cf. McKitterick, *Frankish Church*, 190; Guy de Poerck, "Le sermon bilingue sur Jonas du ms. Valenciennes 521 (475)," *Romanica Gandensia* 4 (1955): 31–66; David Ganz, "The Old French Sermon on Jonah: The Nature of the Text," in *Sermo Doctorum: Compilers, Preachers and Their Audiences in the Early Middle Ages*, ed. Maximilian Diesenberger, Yitzhak Hen, and Marianne Pollheimer (Turnhout, 2013), 427–39; Rob Meens, "A Preaching Bishop: Atto of Vercelli and His Sermon Collection," in *Sermo Doctorum*, ed. Diesenberger et al, 263–82.

42. Michael Richter, *The Oral Tradition in the Early Middle Ages*, Typologie des Sources 71 (Turnhout, 1994).

43. Bryan Ward-Perkins, *The Fall of Rome and the End of Civilization* (Oxford, 2005), 149–50, with figure 7.5 (149), though even if new early medieval churches in Italy and Spain became smaller, many of the older, grand basilicas not only continued to be used, but continued to be restored and built up. Cf. MacMullen, *Second Church*, 117–41.

44. See Richard Krautheimer, *Corpus basilicarum christianarum Romae: The Early Christian Basilicas of Rome (IV–IX cent.)* (Vatican City, 1937–77); Richard Krautheimer, "The Constantinian Basilica," *Dumbarton Oaks Papers* 21 (1967): 115–40; and the estimates in MacMullen, *Second Church*, 117–41, accounting for obstructive features like columns, chancels, etc., esp. 136–40: St. John Lateran (less than 2,500; compared to Krautheimer's 3,000); Old Saint Peter's (less than 3,000; compared to Krautheimer's 4,000); S. Paolo fuori le Mura (c. 500); Sant'Agnese fuori le Mura (less than 3,750).

45. Franz Alto Bauer, "La frammentazione liturgica nella chiesa romana del primo medioevo," *Rivista di archeologia cristiana* 75 (1999): 385–446; Cécile Treffort, "Espace ecclésial et paysage mémoriel (IXe–XIIIe siècle)," in *Espace ecclésial et liturgie au Moyen Âge*, ed. Anne Baud (Lyon, 2010), 239–52.

46. E.g., Caroline Goodson, "La cripta anulare di San Vincenzo Maggiore nel contesto dell'architettura di epoca carolingia," in *Monasteri in Europa Occidentale (Secoli VIII–XI): Topografia e Strutture*, ed. Flavia De Rubeis and Federico Marazzi (Rome, 2008), 425–42.

47. *Vita Paschalis*, c. 30, ed. Duchesne, *Liber Pontificalis*, vol. 2, 60; Caroline Goodson, *The Rome of Pope Paschal I: Papal Power, Urban Renovation, Church Rebuilding and Relic Translation, 817–824* (Cambridge, UK, 2010), 123.

48. Heitz, "Architecture et liturgie," 58–59.

49. John Osborne, *Rome in the Eighth Century: A History in Art* (Cambridge, UK, 2020), 22–66, 95–136.

50. Goodson, *The Rome of Pope Paschal I*, 197–256.

51. A large inscription inside the church lists the names of the saints translated into the city, but the original position is lost: Goodson, *Rome of Pope Paschal I*, 5.

52. Marchita Mauck, "The Mosaic of the Triumphal Arch of S. Prassede: A Liturgical Interpretation," *Speculum* 62 (1987): 813–28, at 827: "In a stunning tour de force, Paschal incorporated the splendid *translatio* in 817 that was part of the dedication of his church into the timeless heavenly liturgy." See also Judson Emerick, "Focusing on the Celebrant: The Column Display Inside Santa Prassede," *Mededelingen van het Nederlands Instituut te Rome* 59 (2000): 129–59.

53. Goodson, *Rome of Pope Paschal I*, 235.

54. Joanna Story, "The Carolingians and the Oratory of Saint Peter the Shepherd," in *Old Saint Peter's, Rome*, ed. R. McKitterick, J. Osborne, C. M. Richardson, and J. Story (Cambridge, UK, 2013), 257–73, at 269. See also Anna Maria Voci, "'Petronilla auxiliatrix regis Francorum': Anno 757: Sulla 'memoria' del re dei Franchi presso San Pietro," *Bullettino dell'Istituto storico italiano per il medio evo* 99 (1993): 1–28.

55. E.g., Gregory of Tours, *Liber de passione et virtutibus Iuliani martyris* (BHL 4541), c. 38, ed. B. Krusch, MGH SRM 1.2 (Hanover, 1885), 130. Michel Rouche, "La matricule des pauvres: Évolution d'une institution de charité du Bas Empire jusqu'à la fin du Haut Moyen Âge," in *Études sur l'histoire de la pauvreté (Moyen Âge—XVIe siècle)*, ed. Michel Mollat (Paris, 1974), 83–110. The poor of Saint Martin's at Tours lynched one Claudius who insulted the saint in Gregory of Tours, *Hist.*, 7.29, ed. Krusch and Levison, 346–49, and these poor folk are tentatively identified as the *matricularii* by Simon Loseby, "Gregory's Cities: Urban Functions in Sixth-Century Gaul," in *Franks and Alamanni in the Merovingian Period: An Ethnographic Perspective*, ed. Ian Wood (Woodbridge, UK, 1998), 239–84, at 257–58.

56. Hans-Werner Goetz, "*Debilis*: Vorstellungen von menschlicher Gebrechlichkeit im frühen Mittelalter," in *Homo debilis: Behinderte—Kranke—Versehrte in der Gesellschaft des Mittelalters*, ed. Cordula Nolte (Korb, 2009), 21–56.

57. *Passio Praeiecti episcopi et martyris Averni* (BHL 6915–16), c. 35, ed. B. Krusch, MGH SRM 5 (Hanover, 1910), 245. Cf. Aigradus of Fontenelle, *Vita Ansberti* (BHL 520a / 523), c. 16, ed. Wilhelm Levison, MGH SRM 5 (Hanover, 1910), 629. The outside spaces of churches could be fragmented spatially as well. Sixteenth-century images of Old Saint-Peter's during the 1575 Jubilee give an idea of how the space was parceled out in front of the entrance: Franz Ehrle, ed., *Piante e vedute di Roma e del Vaticano dal 1300 al 1676*, Studi e documenti per la storia del Palazzo apostolico vaticano 1 (Vatican City, 1956), table 31; see also Giovanni Antonio Dosio, *Roma antica e i disegni di architettura agli Uffizi*, ed. Franco Borsi et al. (Rome, 1976), figure 139, 136. I am grateful to Jo Story for bringing these early modern images to my attention.

58. Rimbert, *Vita Anskarii* (BHL 544–5), c. 20, ed. G. Waitz, MGH SRG 55 (Hanover, 1884), 45: "Ibi sunt ecclesiae plurimae et sacerdotes ac clerici, ibi indigentium multitudo."

59. Paul Fouracre, *Eternal Light and Early Concerns: Belief and the Shaping of Medieval Society* (Manchester, 2021).

60. Martin Roch, *L'intelligence d'un sens: Odeurs miraculeuses et odorat dans l'Occident du haut Moyen Âge (Ve–VIIIe siècles)* (Turnhout, 2009).

61. Gregory of Tours, *Hist.* 2.16, ed. Krusch and Levison, 64.

62. Gregory of Tours, *Hist.* 2.16, ed. Krusch and Levison, 64, See the excellent discussion by Catherine Rose Hailstone, "Atmospheric Architecture: Gregory of Tours's Use of the Fear of God in Tours Cathedral and the Basilica of St Martin," *Early Medieval Europe* 30 (2022): 325–49. For Gregory's building projects, see John Merrington, "The Building Projects and the *Histories* of Gregory of Tours," *Early Medieval Europe* (2022): 159–84.

63. MacMullen, *Second Church*, 95–114.

64. Romano, *Liturgy and Society in Early Medieval Rome*, 55.

65. A testament to Rome's draw for early medieval visitors is a ninth-century manuscript containing inscriptions from the city: Gerold Walser, ed., *Die Einsiedler Inschriftensammlung und der Pilgerführer durch Rom: Codex Einsidlensis 326: Facsimile, Umschrift, Übersetzung und Kommentar* (Stuttgart, 1987); Franz Alto Bauer, "Das Bild der Stadt Rom in karolingischer Zeit: Der Anonymus Einsidlensis," *Römische Quartalschrift für christliche Altertumskunde und Kirchengeschichte* 92 (1997): 190–229; Riccardo Santangeli Valenzani, "Le più antiche guide romane e l'itinerario di Einsiedeln," in *Romei e Giubilei: Il pellegrinaggio medievale a San Pietro (350–1350)*, ed. Mario D'Onofrio (Milan, 1999), 195–98.

66. Marc Bloch, *French Rural History: An Essay on Its Basic Characteristics*, trans. Janet Sondheimer (London, 1996 [1931]), 170.

67. Council of Friuli (796 or 797), ed. A. Werminghoff, MGH Conc. 2.1 (Hanover, 1906), 179: "Igitur resedentibus cunctis ex more in sedilibus praeparatis, adsistente vero circumquaque non modica fratrum consentanea turba in ecclesia beate semperque virginis Dei genetricis Mariae, immolato namque Deo primum in ara cordis sacrificio laudis et orationis hostia in altare pectoris caritatis igne concremata, post apostolicam et evangelicam lectionem imnisque spiritalibus salubriter praelibatis necdum valvis puplicis reseratius patefactis, persistente nimirum pro foribus vulgi glomerata caterva, per secretioris ianue aditum vocante archidiacono intromissus est ad brevem sacerdotalis sub silentio venerabilis quoetus."

68. For the possibility that this was not resented, see Michael McCormick, "The Imperial Edge: Italo-Byzantine Identity, Movement, and Integration, A.D. 650–950," in *Studies on the Internal Diaspora of the Byzantine Empire*, ed. H. Ahrweiler and A. Laiou (Washington, DC, 1998), 17–52, at 47–51, discussing ex-Byzantine subjects of Rižana objecting to their new Carolingian overlords for failing to maintain order of precedence.

69. François-Louis Ganshof, "Charlemagne's Use of the Oath," in F.-L. Ganshof, *The Carolingians and the Frankish Monarchy: Studies in Carolingian History*, trans. J. Sondheimer (London, 1971), 111–24, 112–13.

70. Charles Bonnet, "Éléments de topographie chrétienne à Genève (Suisse)," *Gallia* 63 (2006): 111–15, at 114, revealing a physical transformation of the episcopal complex at Geneva that responded to the evolution of the liturgy. For the earlier period, see Anne Marie Yasin, *Saints and Church Spaces in the Late Antique Mediterranean: Architecture, Cult, and Community* (Cambridge, UK, 2009), 210–39.

71. For the entertainment building as microcosm of empire, see Rossella Rea, "Le antiche raffigurazione dell'Anfiteatro," in *Anfiteatro Flavio: Immagine, testimonianze, spettacoli*, ed. M. Conforto et al. (Rome, 1988), 23–46, at 32–33.

72. Rutger Kramer, *Rethinking Authority in the Carolingian Empire: Ideals and Expectations during the Reign of Louis the Pious (813–828)* (Amsterdam, 2019); Mayke De Jong, "Ecclesia and the Early Medieval Polity," in *Staat im frühen Mittelalter*, ed. Stuart Airlie, Walter Pohl, and Helmut Reimitz (Vienna, 2006), 113–32.

73. West, "Unauthorised Miracles."

74. Richard Hodges, *Light in the Dark Ages: The Rise and Fall of San Vincenzo al Volturno* (Ithaca, NY, 1997); Richard Hodges, Sheila Gibson, and John Mitchell, "The Making of a Monastic City: The Architecture of San Vincenzo Al Volturno in the Ninth Century," *Papers of the British School at Rome* 65 (1997): 233–86.

75. Rudolf of Fulda, *Vita Leobae* (*BHL* 4845), c. 16, ed. Georg Waitz, MGH SS 15.1 (Hanover, 1887), 129.

76. Ardo, *Vita Benedicti abbatis Anianensis* (*BHL* 1096), c. 24, ed. G. Waitz, MGH SS 15.1 (Hanover, 1887), 209: "non parvam monachorum turbam coadunarunt" (composed c. 822–23); corrections to this text are printed by L. H. Lucassen, "À propos d'un texte de la vie de saint Benoît d'Aniane par Ardon," *Archivum Latinitatis Medii Aevi* 4 (1928): 78–79. On Ardo, see Wattenbach-Levison-Löwe, fasc. 3 (Weimar, 1957), 338–39. See also the likely eighth-century *Vita Agili abbatis Resbacensis* (*BHL* 148), AASS Aug. 6.30.586D–E.

77. Karl Schmid, "Mönchslisten und Klosterkonvent von Fulda zur Zeit der Karolinger," in *Die Klostergemeinschaft von Fulda im früheren Mittelalter*, ed. K. Schmid, 3 vols. (Munich, 1976–78), vol. 2, 571–639.

78. See pp. 47–49 above. See also Ian Wood, "Entrusting Western Europe to the Church, 400–750," *Transactions of the Royal Historical Society* 23 (2013): 37–73, at 67–69.

79. Suzanne Fonay Wemple, *Women in Frankish Society: Marriage and the Cloister, 500 to 900* (Philadelphia, 1981), 127–88; Gisela Muschiol, *Famula Dei: Zur Liturgie in merowingischen Frauenklöstern* (Münster, 1994); Felice Lifshitz, *Religious Women in Early Carolingian Francia: A Study of Manuscript Transmission and Monastic Culture* (New York, 2014); Bruce Venarde, *Women's Monasticism and Medieval Society: Nunneries in France and England, 890–1215* (Ithaca, NY, 1997); Steven Vanderputten, *Dark Age Nunneries: The Ambiguous Identity of Female Monasticism, 800–1050* (Ithaca, NY, 2018).

80. Jane Tibbetts Schulenburg, *Forgetful of Their Sex: Female Sanctity and Society, ca. 500–1100* (Chicago, 2001), 59–125.

81. Fiona Griffiths, *Nuns' Priests' Tales: Men and Salvation in Medieval Women's Monastic Life* (Philadelphia, 2018).

82. Gregory of Tours *Hist.* 9.40, 466; *Hist.* 10.15, 501.

83. At Tours, the parallel drama at the monastery of Ingitrudis (involving her daughter Berthegundis) included similar elements: Gregory of Tours, *Hist.* 9.33, ed. Krusch and Levison, 451–54; *Hist.* 10.12, ed. Krusch and Levison, 495 (Berthegundis's goons prepare "seditions"). See E. T. Dailey, *Queens, Consorts, Concubines: Gregory of Tours and Women of the Merovingian Elite* (Leiden, 2015), 57; Martina Hartmann, "*Reginae sumus*: Merowingische Königstöchter und die Frauenklöster im 6. Jahrhundert," *Mitteilungen des Instituts für Österreichische Geschichtsforschung* 113 (2005): 1–19, esp. 14–16.

84. Rudolf of Fulda, *Vita Leobae*, c. 12, ed. Waitz, 126–27. See Lisa Bitel, *Women in Early Medieval Europe, 400–1100* (Cambridge, UK, 2002), 143–44. Schulenberg, *Forgetful of Their Sex*, 492 n. 172, notes that part of the trouble was that the child's body had polluted the water of a pond used by the locals for a mill.

85. Rudolf of Fulda, *Vita Leobae*, c. 12, ed. Waitz, 127.

86. Rudolf of Fulda, *Vita Leobae*, c. 12, ed. Waitz, 126–27.

87. Rudolf of Fulda, *Vita Leobae*, c. 12, ed. Waitz, 127.

88. Albrecht Diem, "Who is Allowed to Pray for the King? Saint-Maurice d'Agaune and the Creation of a Burgundian Identity," in *Post-Roman Transitions: Christian and Barbarian Identities in the Early Medieval West*, ed. Walter Pohl and Gerda Heydemann (Turnhout, 2013), 47–88, at 52–55. Diem stresses (55–63) a multiplicity of views: attacks on "promiscuous" crowding seem to have gone against a "moral economy" of the crowd about the relationship between monasteries and wider population. See also Barbara Rosenwein, "One Site, Many Meanings: Saint-Maurice

d'Agaune as a Place of Power in the Early Middle Ages," in *Topographies of Power in the Early Middle Ages: The Transformation of the Roman World*, ed. Mayke De Jong and Frans Theuws with Carine Van Rhijn (Leiden, 2001), 271–90; Barbara Rosenwein, "Perennial Prayer at Agaune," in *Monks and Nuns, Saints and Outcasts: Religion in Medieval Society: Essays in Honor of Lester K. Little*, ed. Sharon Farmer and Barbara Rosenwein (Ithaca, NY, 2000), 37–56.

89. Giles Constable, "Monasteries, Rural Churches and the *Cura Animarum* in the Early Middle Ages," in *Cristianizzazione ed organizzazione ecclesiastica delle campagne nell'alto Medioevo*, Settimana 28 (Spoleto, 1982), 349–95. For England, see Alan Thacker, "Monks, Preaching and Pastoral Care in Early Anglo-Saxon England," in *Pastoral Care Before the Parish*, ed. John Blair and Richard Sharpe (Leicester, 1992), 137–70.

90. Muschiol, *Famula Dei*; Lifshitz, *Religious Women in Early Carolingian Francia*.

91. Ratger, *Supplex libellus monachorum Fuldensium Carolo imperatori porrectus*, c. 14, ed. J. Semmler, CCM 1 (Siegburg, 1963), 325; Peter Willmes, *Der Herrscher-Adventus im Kloster des Frühmittelalters* (Munich, 1976), 117–18.

92. W. Horn and E. Born, *The Plan of St. Gall: A Study of the Architecture and Economy of, and Life in a Paradigmatic Carolingian Monastery*, 3 vols. (Berkeley, 1979), vol. 1, 128. A digital facsimile of the Saint Gall Plan can be consulted online at: http://www.stgallplan.org/en/.

93. Matthias Untermann, "Kirchenfamilien, Grossklöster, Cellae: Schweizer Klöster im karolingischen Umfeld," in *Die Zeit Karls des Grossen in der Schweiz*, ed. Markus Riek, Jürg Goll, Georges Descœudres (Zürich, 2013), 48–56, at 49. This space for guests, however, was also the result of the close relationship between monasteries and secular rulers.

94. Council of Soissons (853), c. 1, ed. W. Hartmann, MGH Conc. 3 (Hanover, 1984), 284–85.

95. Karl Schmid and Joachim Wollasch, "Die Gemeinschaft der Lebenden und Verstorbenen in Zeugnissen des Mittelalters," *Frühmittelalterliche Studien* 1 (1967): 365–405.

96. Martyrologies: Usuard, *Martyrologium, Le martyrologe d'Usuard: Texte et commentaire*, ed. Jacques Dubois, Subsidia hagiographica 40 (Brussels, 1965). See also Felice Lifshitz, *The Name of the Saint: The Martyrology of Jerome and Access to the Sacred in Francia, 627–827* (Notre Dame, 2006). Litanies: Astrid Krüger, *Litanei-Handschriften der Karolingerzeit*, MGH Hilfsmittel 24 (Hanover, 2007).

97. Krüger, *Litanei-Handschriften*, 296–306. For a facsimile, see Katharina Bierbrauer, *Der Lorscher Rotulus: Vollständige Faksimile-Ausgabe im Originalformat des Lorscher Rotulus: Stadt- und Universitätsbibliothek Frankfurt am Main, Ms. Barth. 179* (Graz, 1994).

98. Astrid Krüger, "*Sancte Nazari ora pro nobis*: Ludwig der Deutsche und der Lorscher Rotulus," in *Ludwig der Deutsche und seine Zeit*, ed. W. Hartmann (Darmstadt, 2004), 184–202, esp. 200–202.

99. D Louis the German, no. 126, ed. P. Kehr, *Die Urkunden Ludwigs des Deutschen*, MGH DKar Germ. 1 (Berlin, 1934), 176–77; Eric Goldberg, *Struggle for Empire: Kingship and Conflict under Louis the German, 817–876* (Ithaca, NY, 2006), 291–92.

100. Goldberg, *Struggle for Empire*, 292. Louis the German asked the monks to pray for him and his family in perpetuity in exchange for properties in Gochsheim (Kreichgau): "ut eos [sc. the monks] pro nostra coniugis ac carissimae prolis nostrę salute nec non pro remedio animarum antecessorum nostrorum domini clementiam delectabilius exorare delectet" (D Louis the German, no. 126. Kehr, 176–77).

101. Régine Le Jan, "*Nomina viventium, nomina defunctorum*: Les interactions entre vivants et morts dans les *libri memoriales* carolingiens," in *Les vivants et les morts dans les sociétés médiévales* (Paris, 2018), 121–34; and the essays in Dieter Geuenich and Uwe Ludwig, *Libri vitae: Gebetsgedenken in der Gesellschaft des Frühen Mittelalters* (Cologne, 2015). See also Régine Le Jan, "Mémoire et politique: Les rois d'Italie dans les *libri memoriales* de Salzbourg, Saint-Gall, Pfäfers et Reichenau (fin VIIIe-début IXe siècle)," in *I Longobardi a Venezia: Scritti per Stefano

Gasparri, ed. Irene Barbiera, Francesco Borri, and Annamaria Pazienza (Turnhout, 2020), 139–53; Dieter Geuenich, "Der *Liber Viventium Fabariensis* als Zeugnis pragmatischer Schriftlichkeit im frühmittelalterlichen Churrätien," in *Schrift, Schriftgebrauch und Textorten im frühmittelalterlichen Churrätien*, ed. H. Eisenhut, K. Fuchs, M. H. Graf, H. Steiner (Basel, 2008), 65–77; Andrea Decker-Heuer, *Studien zur Memorialüberlieferung im Frühmittelalterlichen Paris* (Sigmaringen, 1998); Otto Gerhard Oexle, *Forschungen zu monastischen und geistlichen Gemeinschaften im westfränkischen Bereich: Bestandteil des Quellenwerkes Societas et Fraternitas* (Munich, 1978); Andrea Decker-Heuer, *Studien zur Memorialüberlieferung im Frühmittelalterlichen Paris* (Sigmaringen, 1998). For France, Jean-Loup Lemaître, *Répertoire des documents nécrologiques français*, 2 vols. (Paris, 1980), brings together three thousand entries for the Middle Ages.

102. Karl Schmid and Otto Gerhard Oexle, "Voraussetzungen und Wirkung des Gebetsbundes von Attigny," *Francia* 2 (1974): 71–122.

103. Zürich, Zentralbibliothek, MS Rh. Hist. 27, ed. J. Autenrieth, Dieter Geuenich, and Karl Schmid, *Das Verbrüderungsbuch der Abtei Reichenau*, MGH Libri mem. N.S. I (Hanover, 1979); see Karl Schmid, "Zum Quellenwert der Verbrüderungsbücher von St. Gallen und Reichenau," *Deutsches Archiv* 41 (1985): 345–89.

104. Salzburg, Stiftsarchiv St. Peter, MS A 1, ed. S. Herzberg-Fränkel, MGH Necr. 2 (Berlin, 1904), 3–64. On this confraternity book and its organization of names, see Rosamond McKitterick, "Geschichte und Gedächtnis im frühmittelalterlichen Bayern: Virgil, Arn und der Liber Vitae von St. Peter zu Salzburg," in *Erzbischof Arn von Salzburg*, ed. Meta Niederkorn-Bruck and Anton Scharer (Munich, 2004), 68–80.

105. St. Gall, Stiftsarchiv, Fonds Pfäfers, MS 1, ed. A. Bruckner, H. R. Sennhauser, and F. Perret, *Liber Viventium Fabariensis I: Faksimile-Edition* (Basel, 1975); P. Piper, ed., *Libri Confraternitatum Sancti Galli, Augiensis, Fabariensis*, MGH Necr. Suppl. (Berlin, 1884).

106. St. Gall, Stiftsarchiv, Class. I. Cist. C3, MS B 55, ed. M. Borgolte, D. Geuenich, and K. Schmid, *Subsidia Sangallensia* (St. Gall, 1986), vol. 1, 13–284.

107. Rome, Biblioteca Angelica, MS 10, ed. E. Hlawitschka, K. Schmid, and G. Tellenbach, *Liber memorialis von Remiremont*, MGH Libri mem. 1 (Munich, 1981).

108. Brescia, Biblioteca civica Queriniana, MS G VI. 7, ed. D. Geuenich, U. Ludwig, et al., *Der Memorial- und Liturgiecodex von San Salvatore / Santa Giulia in Brescia*, MGH Libri mem. N.S. 4 (Hanover, 2000). This is thought to have been compiled in 865, perhaps when Emperor Louis II visited Brescia.

109. Münster, Staatsarchiv, MS Misc. I 133, ed. K. Schmid and J. Wollasch, *Der Liber Vitae der Abtei Corvey* (Wiesbaden, 1983). Many were added later.

110. Cividale, Museo Archeologico Nazionale, CXXXVIII; Dieter Geuenich, "A Survey of the Early Medieval Confraternity Books on the Continent," in *The Durham Liber Vitae and Its Context*, ed. David Rollason et al. (Rochester, NY, 2004), 141–47, at 142.

111. London, British Library, MS Cotton Domitian VII, with ninth-century levels at fols. 15–45, 47. See the preface to Rollason et al., eds., *The Durham Liber Vitae and Its Context*, xi.

112. Francesco Veronese, *Reliquie in movimento: Politiche della mobilità e rappresentazioni agiografiche in epoca carolingia (VIII–X secolo)* (Rome, 2023); Heinrich Fichtenau, "Zum Reliquienwesen des früheren Mittelalters," in H. Fichtenau, *Beiträge zur Mediävistik: Ausgewählte Aufsätze* (Stuttgart, 1975), vol. 1, 108–44; Patrick Geary, *Furta Sacra: Thefts of Relics in the Central Middle Ages*, revised ed. (Princeton, NJ, 1990), 28–43. For earlier on, see Sean Lafferty, "Ad Sanctitatem Mortuorum: Tomb Raiders, Body Snatchers and Relic Hunters in Late Antiquity," *Early Medieval Europe* 22 (2014): 249–79.

113. *Annales Mettenses priores* (s.a. 690), ed. B. von Simson, MGH SRG 10 (Hanover, 1905), 12: "Quorum maxima turba ad beati Quintini martiris limina, nonnulli ad Perronam Scottorum monasterium, in quo beatus Furseus corpore requiescit, confugium fecerunt." On these annals, see Irene Haselbach, *Aufstieg und Herrschaft der Karolinger in der Darstellung der sogenannten*

Annales Mettenses priores: Ein Beitrag zur Geschichte der politischen Ideen im Reich Karls des Großen (Lübeck, 1970), 25–40.

114. Diana Webb, *Medieval European Pilgrimage, c. 700–c. 1500* (New York, 2002).

115. Edina Bozoky, "Les reliques, le Prince et le bien public," in *Le Prince, son peuple et le bien commun: De l'Antiquité tardive à la fin du Moyen Âge*, ed Hervé Oudart, Jean-Michel Picard, and Joëlle Quaghebeur (Rennes, 2013), 203–15, at 204–5; Julia M. H. Smith, "Rulers and Relics c.750–c.950: Treasure on Earth, Treasure in Heaven," supplement 5, *Past & Present* 206 (2010): 73–96.

116. Hedwig Röckelein, *Reliquientranslationen nach Sachsen im 9. Jahrhundert: Über Kommunikation, Mobilität und Öffentlichkeit im Frühmittelalter* (Stuttgart, 2002), 359–70.

117. E.g., *Vita Audoeni altera* (BHL 751–52), 5.43, AASS Aug 4.24.819B: "Convocato igitur agmine plurimorum monachorum, omnique ecclesia, seu populo ipsius urbis, totiusque provinciæ, totam noctem cum laudibus & hymnis duxit pervigilem." This set of texts, circulating in eleventh-century legendaries, probably represents epitomes of earlier, ninth-century lives: Felice Lifshitz, *The Norman Conquest of Pious Neustria: Historiographic Discourse and Saintly Relics, 684–1090* (Toronto, 1995), 87–88.

118. Röckelein, *Reliquientranslationen*, 359–70.

119. Einhard, *Translatio Marcellini et Petri* (BHL 5233), ed. G. Waitz, MGH SS 15.1 (1887). For this influential text, see Veronese, *Reliquie in movimento*, 116–32; Martin Heinzelmann, *Translationsberichte und andere Quellen des Reliquienkultes*, Typologie des Sources 33 (Turnhout, 1979), esp. 52–62, 94–125. For other *translationes*: Veronese, *Reliquie in movimento*; Giorgia Vocino, "Le traslazioni di reliquie in età carolingia (fine VIII–IX secolo): Uno studio comparativo," in *Del visibile credere: Pellegrinaggi, santuari, miracoli, reliquie*, ed. Davide Scotto (Florence, 2011), 193–240; Henryk Fros, "Liste des translations et inventions de l'époque carolingienne," *Analecta Bollandiana* 104 (1986): 427–29.

120. Einhard, *Translatio Petri et Marcellini*, 2.4, 247. The phrase *quid miraculi* lacks any diminutive effect: e.g., Eucherius of Lyon, *Passio Acaunensium martyrum* (BHL 5737–40), c. 16, ed. B Krusch, MGH SRM 3 (Hanover, 1896), 38; *Vita Genovefae* (redactio C) (BHL 3336), c. 20, ed. K. Künstle, *Vita Sanctae Genovefae virginis Parisiorum patronae* (Leipzig, 1910), 11.

121. Maurits Gysseling, *Toponymisch woordenboek van België, Nederland, Luxemburg, Noord-Frankrijk en West-Duitsland (vóór 1226)*, 2 vols. (Brussel, 1960), vol. 1, 721–22 ("Mühlheim": "Germ. *mulīn* 'Mühle' + *haima*- n. 'Wohnung.' "), vol. 2, 753–54: ("Ober" becomes *superior* in the Latin). In this case, "upper" refers to the town's position on the Main relative to a second Mühlheim, now called Mühlheim am Main, approximately 18 km downriver. This is attested in medieval sources as *Mulinheim inferior*. The area was well inhabited. Cf. Einhard, *Ep.* no. 9, ed. K. Hampe, MGH Epp. 5 (Berlin, 1899), 113: "Nam, sicut audivimus, de illa annona sive ad farinam sive ad bracem faciendam, quam ad Mulinheim mittere debuisti, nihil misisti; nec aliud aliquid nisi triginta porcos et illos ipsos non bonos, sed mediocres, et tres modios de legumine; de cetero nihhil [sic]." Michelstadt in the Odenwald is about forty-five kilometers south of Seligenstadt and eighteen kilometers southwest into the woods of the (current) position of the Main.

122. See the classic essays in Wendy Davies and Paul Fouracre, eds., *The Settlement of Disputes in Early Medieval Europe* (Cambridge, UK, 1986) and the follow-up volume, Wendy Davies and Paul Fouracre, eds., *The Languages of Gift in the Early Middle Ages* (Cambridge, UK, 2010).

123. Gerd Althoff, "Colloquium Familiare—Colloquium Secretum—Colloquium Publicum: Beratung im politischen Leben des früheren Mittelalters," in G. Althoff, *Spielregeln der Politik im Mittelalter: Kommunikation in Frieden und Fehde* (Darmstadt, 1997), 157–84.

124. Leidulf Melve, *Inventing the Public Sphere: The Public Debate During the Investiture Contest (c. 1030–1122)* (Leiden, 2007), esp. 3–22. Although Habermas's model presumes a shift from medieval to early modern realities, it has become attractive for historians exploring medieval debates over public facts and public goods. See, e.g., Patrick Boucheron, "Espace public et lieux

publics: Approches en histoire urbaine," in *L'espace public au Moyen Âge: Débats autour de Jürgen Habermas*, ed. Patrick Boucheron and Nicolas Offenstadt (Paris, 2011), 99–117; Nicolas Offenstadt, "Le Moyen Âge de Jürgen Habermas: Enquête sur une réception allemande," in *L'espace public*, ed. Boucheron and Offenstadt, 77–98. For the original argument, see Jürgen Habermas, *Strukturwandel der Öffentlichkeit: Untersuchungen zu einer Kategorie der bürgerlichen Gesellschaft*, 5th ed. (Berlin, 1971 [1962]); and Jürgen Habermas, *Ein neuer Strukturwandel der Öffentlichkeit und die deliberative Politik* (Berlin, 2022).

125. A central part of Habermas's argument is the role eighteenth-century literary societies, coffeehouses, and salons played in opening up an alternative to statist proclamations for discourse on public affairs. The public sphere of the early Middle Ages was far less open-ended, but general assemblies allowed for elite leeway in shaping the public script. For an "elitist-early-medieval public sphere" supposedly supplanted by a "semi-elitist" one in the eleventh century, see Melve, *Inventing the Public Sphere*, 173.

126. Horace, *Carm.* 3.1, lines 9–16 (at line 13), ed. D. R. Shackleton Bailey, *Q. Horati Flacci Opera* (Stuttgart, 1995), 67.

127. E.g., Berne, Burgerbibliothek, MS 363 (s. IX^2); Vatican City, BAV, Reg. lat. 1703 (s. IX$^{2/4}$); Leiden, Bibliotheek der Rijksuniversiteit, BPL 28 (s. IX).

128. See conversely, how the former Queen Emma (through her ghostwriter Gerbert of Aurillac) complains of her fallen status in a letter of 988 by complaining that she no longer has an entourage to accompany her during travel: Gerbert of Aurillac, *Ep.*, no. 147, ed. Pierre Riché and Jean-Pierre Callu, *Gerbert d'Aurillac: Correspondance* (Paris, 2008), 360: "Ego illa He[mma] quondam Francorum regina, quae tot millibus imperavi, nunc nec vernaculos comites habeo, quibus saltem stipata conventus adeam tanti ducis Henr[ici], nec desiderabili praesentia vestra [the recipient is an unknown cleric] frui licet causa captandae salutis atque consilii."

129. Procopius, *Gothic Wars*, 2.3.1, ed. Jacob Haury, revised Gerhard Wirth, *Procopii Caesariensis opera omnia* (Leipzig, 1962). See Paolo Squatriti, *Water and Society in Early Medieval Italy, AD 400–1000* (Cambridge, UK, 1998), 50–51, for the baths as a place to "flaunt one's status" with crowds of followers even into the seventh century.

130. Kristina Sessa, *The Formation of Papal Authority in Late Antique Italy: Roman Bishops and the Domestic Sphere* (Cambridge, UK, 2013), 194.

131. Michael McCormick, *Origins of the European Economy* (Cambridge, UK, 2001), 665.

132. Theodor Bitterauf, ed., *Die Traditionen des Hochstifts Freising*, 2 vols. (Munich, 1905), vol. 1, n. 1037, 782, after listing nine *testes per aures tracti* adds, "Istique homines sui istius traditionis testes fuerunt: Abraham. Prozilo. Petto. Seman. Tribagos. Alter Abraham. Pretimir. Prozila. Joseph." For this list, including its Slavic names, see Geneviève Bührer-Thierry, *Evêques et pouvoir dans le royaume de Germanie: Les Eglises de Bavière et de Souabe, 876–973* (Paris, 1997), 130. See above, p. 58.

133. Jamie Kreiner, "About the Bishop: The Episcopal Entourage and the Economy of Government in Post-Roman Gaul," *Speculum* 86 (2011): 321–60.

134. See above, p. 57.

135. A late ninth-century miracle collection describes a pilgrim murdered on his way to the body of a saint: Wolfhardus of Herrieden, *Miracula Waldburgis Monheimensia* (BHL 8765), 2.6.a–b, ed. A. Bauch, *Ein bayerisches Mirakelbuch aus der Karolingerzeit: Die Monheimer Walpurgis-Wunder des Priesters Wolfhard* (Regensburg, 1979), 222–26.

136. Irene Barbiera, "Remembering the Warriors: Weapon Burials and Tombstones Between Antiquity and the Early Middle Ages in Northern Italy," in *Post-Roman Transitions: Christian and Barbarian Identities in the Early Medieval West*, ed. Walter Pohl and Gerda Heydemann (Turnhout, 2013), 407–35.

137. *Passio Leudegarii episcopi et martyris Augustodunensis* I (BHL 4849b), c. 17, ed. Krusch and Levison, 298–99.

138. Kreiner, "About the Bishop," 341.

139. Flodoard, *Historia Remensis ecclesiae*, 4.10, ed. M. Stratmann, MGH SS 36 (Hanover, 1998), 402: "dum paucis admodum comitatus regis peteret alloquium."

140. Luke 22:6: "et quaerebat oportunitatem ut traderet illum sine turbis." A few Carolingian exegetes make a point of bringing in this passage of Luke to explain Matthew 26:16 ("et exinde quaerebat oportunitatem ut eum traderet"): Christian of Stavelot, *Expositio in euangelium Matthaei*, c. 26, ed. R.B.C. Huygens, CCCM 224 (Turnhout, 2008), 475; Hrabanus Maurus, *Expositio in Matthaeum*, book 8, ed. B. Löfstedt, CCCM 174A (Turnhout, 2000), 685.

141. Amalarius, *Liber officialis*, 1.38.8, ed. J. M. Hanssens, *Amalarii opera liturgica omnia*, Studi e Testi 139 (Vatican City, 1948), vol. 2, 184: "Verbi gratia, fui catecuminus Constantinopoli captus; quaesivit me dominus meus misericors et piissimus, invenit me captivum, occidit illum qui me rapuit propter meam incuriam, et me reddidit libertati, ut reverterer ad patriam meam." In the passage, Amalarius speaks in the first person but he is referring to a hypothetical character. See Shane Bobrycki, "A Hypothetical Slave in Constantinople: Amalarius's Liber Officialis and the Mediterranean Slave Trade," *Haskins Society Journal* 26 (2014): 47–67.

142. Bobrycki, "Hypothetical Slave," 60–61.

143. For royal inauguration rituals, see Janet L. Nelson, "Inauguration Rituals," in Janet Nelson, *Politics and Ritual in Early Medieval Europe* (London, 1986), 283–307; Janet L. Nelson, "National Synods, Kingship as Office, and Royal Anointing: An Early Medieval Syndrome," in Janet Nelson, *Politics and Ritual in Early Medieval Europe* (London, 1986), 239–57; Janet L. Nelson, "Symbols in Context: Rulers' Inauguration Rituals in Byzantium and the West in the Early Middle Ages," in Nelson, *Politics and Ritual in Early Medieval Europe*, 259–81.

144. See Kenneth Pennington and David Napolitano, eds., *A Cultural History of Democracy in the Medieval Age* (London, 2022); Jacques Dalarun, *To Govern Is to Serve: An Essay on Medieval Democracy*, trans. Sean Field (Ithaca, 2023) [French edition, 2012].

145. See the account of Valentine's election. *Vita Valentini*, c. 5–8, *LP* 2, 72. Philip Daileader, "One Will, One Voice, and Equal Love: Papal Elections and the 'Liber Pontificalis' in the Early Middle Ages," *Archivum Historiae Pontificiae* 31 (1993): 11–31.

146. E.g., for a typical topos of unanimity in "a great and mighty crowd of the city," see the ninth-century *Vita Chrodegangi ep. Mettensis* (*BHL* 1781), c. 15, ed. G. H. Pertz, MGH SS 10 (Hanover, 1852), 560: "Se vero unanimes in praesule eligendo conclamant, nec unum restitisse dicunt in tanta ac tali turba civitatis, qui electioni generali alicuius controversiae machinamentis resistere conaretur."

147. Buc, *Dangers of Ritual*, 102–3.

148. *Passio Leudegarii episcopi et martyris Augustodunensis* I (*BHL* 4849b), c. 5, ed. B. Krusch and W. Levison, MGH SRM 5 (Hanover, 1910), 287–89. For the authorship and dating, see Joseph-Claude Poulin, "Saint Léger d'Autun et ses premiers biographes (fin VIIe—milieu IXe siècle)," *Bulletin de la société des antiquaires de l'Ouest et des musées de Poitiers*, 4th ser., 14 (1978): 167–200.

149. *Passio Leudegarii*, c. 5, ed. Krusch and Levison, 287–89: "Sed cum Ebroinus eius fratrem germanum nomen Theodericum, convocatis obtimatis, cum solemniter, ut mos est, debuisset sublimare in regnum, superbiae spiritu tumidus eos noluit deinde convocare. Ideo magis coeperunt metuere, eo quod regem, quem ad gloriam patriae publicae debuerat sublimare, dum post se eum retineret pro nomine, cui malum cupierat audenter valeret inferre."

150. *Passio Leudegarii*, c. 19, ed. Krusch and Levison, 301: "Qua de re multum colligerunt hostiliter populum, eo quod veresimile videbatur esse cunctorum."

151. E.g., the requirement to act *per ordinem* from rite to rite is consistently emphasized in conciliar *ordines*: Ordo 2, c. 10, ed. H. Schneider, *Die Konzilsordines des Früh- und Hochmittelalters*, MGH Ordines 1 (Hanover, 1996), 182; Ordo 2C, c. 12, ed. Schneider, 197; Ordo 3, c. 20, ed. Schneider, 214; Ordo 5, c. 13, 18, ed. Schneider, 253, 255. See also Schneider's detailed introduction (1–122, esp. 4–11).

152. Pössel, "Magic of Early Medieval Ritual," 123: "For the duration of the performance, the ritualized frame can create the illusion of consensus and harmony, and make disagreement and subversion costly."

153. Althoff, "Colloquium Familiare—Colloquium Secretum—Colloquium Publicum."

154. Buc, *The Dangers of Ritual*, 1–12, 88–122.

155. *Vita Hadriani II*, c. 4, *LP* 2, 174.

156. Daileader, "One Will, One Voice, and Equal Love."

157. *Vita Amandi episcopi* I (*BHL* 332), c. 14, ed. B. Krusch, MGH SRM 5 (Hanover, 1910), 438: "Agebat namque, quod comes quidam ex genere Francorum cognomine Dotto, congregata non minima multitudine Francorum, ut erat illi iniunctum, ad dirimendas resederat actiones."

158. Jennifer Davis, "A Pattern for Power: Charlemagne's Delegation of Judicial Responsibilities," in *The Long Morning of Medieval Europe: New Directions in Early Medieval Studies*, ed. Jennifer Davis and Michael McCormick (Aldershot, UK, 2008), 235–46, at 239–40.

159. *Brevium exempla*, c. 25, ed. A. Boretius, MGH Capit. 1 (Hanover, 1883), 254: "et desuper solarium ad dispensandum."

160. Uwe Lobbedey, "Carolingian Royal Palaces: The State of Research From an Architectural Historian's Viewpoint," in *Court Culture in the Early Middle Ages: The Proceedings of the First Alcuin Conference*, ed. Catherine Cubitt (Turnhout, 2003), 129–54. For surveys of medieval palaces in the German lands, see *Die Deutschen Königspfalzen: Repertorium der Pfalzen, Königshöfe und übrigen Aufenthaltsorte der Könige im deutschen Reich des Mittelalters*, ed. T. Zotz (Göttingen, 1983–2004).

161. Karl Bosl, "Pfalzen und Forsten," in *Deutsche Königspfalzen: Beiträge zu ihrer historischen und archäologischen Erforschung* (Göttingen, 1963), vol. 1, 1–29, esp. 23–25. For archaeology at Aachen, see U. Heckner and E.-M. Beckmann, eds., *Die karolingische Pfalzkapelle in Aachen: Material, Bautechnick, Restaurierung* (Worms, 2012); H. Müller, C. M. Bayer, and M. Kerner, eds., *Die Aachener Marienkirche: Aspekte ihrer Archäologie und frühen Geschichte* (Regensburg, 2014); T. R. Kraus, ed., *Aachen von den Anfängen bis zur Gegenwart*, vol. 2, *Karolinger–Ottonen–Salier 765–1137* (Aachen, 2013).

162. H. Beumann, F. Brunhölzl, and W. Winkelmann, eds., *Karolus Magnus et Leo Papa: Ein paderborner Epos vom Jahre 799* (Paderborn, 1966), line 152, 369; Eric J. Goldberg, *In the Manner of the Franks: Hunting, Kingship, and Masculinity in Early Medieval Europe* (Philadelphia, 2020). For the notion that the hunt stood in for war, see Eric J. Goldberg, "Louis the Pious and the Hunt," *Speculum* 88 (2013): 613–43, esp. 624.

163. Matthew Innes, "'He Never Even Allowed His White Teeth to Be Bared in Laughter': The Politics of Humour in the Carolingian Renaissance," in *Humour, History and Politics in Late Antiquity and the Early Middle Ages*, ed. Guy Halsall (Cambridge, UK, 2002), 131–56, at 138–39.

164. Sidonius Apollinaris, *Ep.* 2.2, *Sidoine Apollinaire*, ed. André Loyen, vols. 2–3, *Lettres* (Paris, 1970), vol. 2, 5, describes playing "balls," *pilae*, on a green shaded by trees. See François Bougard, "Des jeux du cirque au tournois: Que reste-t-il de la compétition antique au haut Moyen Âge," in *Agôn: La Compétition, Ve–XIIe siècle*, ed. F. Bougard, R. Le Jan, and T. Lienhard (Turnhout, 2012), 5–42. Perhaps there were military exercises. Nithard describes "games for military exercise" (*ludi causa exercitii*) in which armies mock-fought: Nithard, *Historiae*, 3.6, ed. Lauer, revised Sophie Glansdorff, *Histoire des fils de Louis le Pieux* (Paris, 2012), 120–22 (*Ludos . . . causa exercitii*). See also Dominique Barthélemy, "Les origines du tournoi chevaleresque," in *Agôn: La compétition, Ve–XIIe siècle*, ed. F. Bougard, R. Le Jan, and T. Lienhard (Turnhout, 2012), 111–30.

165. Prov. 14:28: "in multitudine populi dignitas regis et in paucitate plebis ignominia principis."

166. Hincmar of Reims, *De ordine palatii*, c. 27, ed. Thomas Gross and Rudolf Schieffer, MGH Font. iur. Germ. 3, 2nd ed. (Hanover, 1980), 526: "illa multitudo quae in palatio semper esse debet."

167. Régine Le Jan, "Les cérémonies carolingiennes: Symbolique de l'ordre, dynamique de la compétition," in *Le corti nell'alto medioevo* (Spoleto, 2015), 167–94, at 180. See also Philippe Depreux, "Hiérarchie et ordre au sein du palais: L'accès au prince," in *Hiérarchie et stratification sociale dans l'Occident médiéval (400–1100)*, ed. François Bougard, Dominique Iogna-Prat, and Régine Le Jan (Turnhout, 2008), 305–23.

168. Simon MacLean, *Kingship and Politics in the Late Ninth Century: Charles the Fat and the End of the Carolingian Empire* (Cambridge, UK, 2003), 64–75.

169. Einhard, *Vita Karoli*, c. 22, ed. O Holder-Egger, MGH SRG 25 (Munich, 1911), 27.

170. Danuta Shanzer, "Capturing Merovingian Courts: A Literary Perspective," in *Le corti nell'alto Medioevo*, 2 vols., Settimane 62 (Spoleto, 2015), vol. 2, 667–700.

171. E.g., *AB*, s.a. 868, ed. Grat et al., 143.

172. Maureen Miller, *The Bishop's Palace: Architecture and Authority in Medieval Italy* (Ithaca, NY, 2000), 54–85.

173. For an eighth-century hagiographic depiction of how a *turba pauperum* might gather before the gates (*prae foribus*) of a saint, see *Vita Ansberti* (BHL 520), c. 16, ed. W. Levison, MGH SRM 5 (Hanover, 1910), 629. According to a fifth-century papal letter, bishops were expected to spend a full quarter of their revenues on the poor: Simplicius, *Epistola* 1, ed. A. Thiel, *Epistolae Romanorum pontificum* (Brunsberg, 1868), vol. 1, 175–77. How often they met this standard of institutional charity is another question.

174. Jamie Kreiner, *The Social Life of Hagiography in the Merovingian Kingdom* (Cambridge, UK, 2014), 189–229.

175. Council of Mâcon (AD 585), c. 13, ed. C. de Clercq, *Concilia Galliae a 511–695*, CCSL 148A (Turnhout, 1963), 245: "Propterea tractatis omnibus, quae diuine uel humane iuris fuerunt, et finem usque perducta putauimus congruum esse de canibus etiam uel accipitribus aliqua statuere. Volumus igitur, quod episcopalis domus, quae ad hoc deo fauente instituta est, ut sine personarum acceptione omnes in hospitalitate recipiat, canes non habeat, ne forte hii, qui in ea miserarium suarum leuamen habere confidant, dum infestorum canum morsibus laniantur, detrimentum uersa uice suorum susteneant corporum. Custodienda est igitur episcopalis habitatio hymnis, non latratibus, operibus bonis, non morsibus uenenosis. Vbi igitur dei est assiduitas cantilenae, monstrum est et dedecoris nota canes ibi uel accipitres habitare." In an age without antibiotics, the description of dogs' bites as "venomous" may not be just rhetorical.

176. *Passio Praeiecti episcopi et martyris Averni* (BHL 6915–16), c. 3, ed. Krusch, 227.

177. Michael McCormick, "Movements and Markets in the First Millennium: Information, Containers, and Shipwrecks," in *Trade and Markets in Byzantium*, ed. Cécile Morrisson (Washington, DC, 2012), 51–98, at 53. We know more about the archaeology of physical markets in the East than the West: Luke Lavan, "From *Polis* to *Emporion*? Retail and Regulation in the Late Antique City," in *Trade and Markets in Byzantium*, ed. Cécile Morrisson (Washington, DC, 2012), 33–77.

178. McCormick, *Origins*, 639–69.

179. Fredegar, *Chronicon* 4.48, ed. Bruno Krusch, MGH SRM 2, 144.

180. Frans Theuws, "River-Based Trade Centres in Early Medieval Northwestern Europe: Some 'Reactionary' Thoughts," in *From One Sea to Another: Trading Places in the European and Mediterranean Early Middle Ages*, ed. Sauro Gelichi and Richard Hodges (Turnhout, 2012), 25–46, esp. 40–44; Annemarieke Willemsen, "Dorestad, a Medieval Metropolis," in *From One Sea to Another: Trading Places in the European and Mediterranean Early Middle Ages*, ed. Sauro Gelichi and Richard Hodges (Turnhout, 2012), 65–80; H. Tiefenbach, "Dorestad," *RGA*² 6 (Berlin, 1986), 59–82; McCormick, *Origins*, 653–54; W. A. van Es, Wietske Prummel, and W.J.H. Verwers, *Excavations at Dorestad*, 3 vols. (Amersfoort, 1980–2009). See above, chapter 2.

181. *AB*, s.a. 863: "Dani mense Ianuario per Rhenum versus Coloniam navigio ascendunt, et depopulato emporio quod Dorestatus dicitur, sed et villam non modicam, ad quam Frisii

confugerant, occisis multis Frisiorum negotiatoribus, et capta non modica populi multitudine, usque ad quandam insulam secus castellum Novesium perveniunt." Jan van Doesburg, "*Villa non modica*? Some Thoughts on the Interpretation of a Large Early Medieval Earthwork near Dorestad," in *Dorestad in an International Framework: New Research on Centres of Trade and Coinage in Carolingian Times*, ed. Annemarieke Willemsen and Hanneke Kik (Turnhout, 2010), 51–58, esp. 56.

182. Jean-Pierre Devroey, "Un monastère dans l'économie d'échanges: Les services de transport à l'abbaye de Saint-Germain-des-Prés au IXe siècle," *Annales: Histoire, Sciences Sociales* 39 (1984): 570–89.

183. Edict of Pîtres (864), c. 19, ed. A. Boretius, MGH Capit. 2 (Hanover, 1897), no. 273, 317–18.

184. For an overview of the history of the fairs of Champagne, Franz Irsigler and Winfried Reichert, "Les foires de Champagne," in *Foires, marchés annuels et développement urbain en Europe*, ed. F. Irsigler and M. Pauly (Trier, 2007), 89–105.

185. McCormick, *Origins*, 647–53; Levillain, "Études sur l'abbaye de Saint-Denis," *Bibliothèque de l'école des chartes* 91 (1930): 5–65, at 7–9; see also Devroey, "Un monastère dans l'économie d'échanges," 578–79.

186. See Werner Jacobsen, "Saint-Denis in neuem Licht: Konsequenzen der neuentdeckten Baubeschreibung aus dem Jahre 799," *Kunstchronik* 36 (1983): 301–8. For the period leading up to Suger's abbacy, see Rolf Grosse, *Saint-Denis zwischen Adel und König: Die Zeit vor Suger (1053–1122)*, Beihefte der Francia 57 (Stuttgart, 2002).

187. Placitum of Childebert III (709), ed. Theo Kölzer, MGH DD Merov 1, no. 156, 389–90.

188. See above, pp. 53–55. Their large size is zealously defended by Bernard Bachrach, *Early Carolingian Warfare: Prelude to Empire* (Philadelphia, 2001); Bernard Bachrach, *Charlemagne's Early Campaigns (768–777): A Diplomatic and Military Analysis* (Leiden, 2013).

189. McCormick, *Origins*, 665–68.

190. Bernard Bachrach, "Armies as Mobs in the Early Middle Ages," in *Mobs: An Interdisciplinary Inquiry*, ed. Nancy Van Deusen and Leonard Michael Koff (Leiden, 2012), 63–78.

191. Gregory of Tours, *Hist.* 6.31, ed. Krusch and Levison, 299–300, where the armies of Chilperic ravage (*multum vastantes*) the regions they travel through, including Tours, in 583; see also *Hist.* 10.3, 483–84.

192. Hincmar of Reims, *Ep.* 125–26, MGH Epp 8.1, 60–65; Elisabeth Magnou-Nortier, "The Enemies of the Peace: Reflections on a Vocabulary, 500–1100," in *The Peace of God: Social Violence and Religious Response in France Around the Year 1000*, ed. Thomas Head and Richard Landes (Ithaca, NY, 1992), 58–79, at 75; Geoffrey Koziol, "Pragmatic Sanctions? The Peace of God and Its Carolingian Antecedents," in *Visions of Medieval History in North America and Europe: Studies on Cultural Identity and Power*, ed. Courtney Booker, Hans Hummer and Dana Polanichka (Turnhout, 2022), 257–86, 259–73; Eric Goldberg, "Vikings, Vassals, Villagers, and the Capitulary of Ver (884)," in *Living in a Carolingian World*, ed. Valerie Garver and Noah Blan (forthcoming); Shane Bobrycki, "The Carolingian *Cocio*: On the Vocabulary of the Early Medieval Petty Merchant," *Early Medieval Europe* 32 (2024): 57–81.

193. See pp. 71–72.

194. Rosamond McKitterick, *Perceptions of the Past in the Early Middle Ages* (Notre Dame, 2006), 69–89; Karl Brunner, *Oppositionelle Gruppen im Karolingerreich* (Vienna, 1979).

195. On intra-elite competition, a group of collected essays has considerably advanced the discussion: Sylvie Joye and Régine Le Jan, eds., *Genre et compétition dans les sociétés occidentales du haut Moyen Âge, IVe-XIe siècle* (Turnhout, 2018); Régine Le Jan, Geneviève Bührer-Thierry, and Stefano Gasparri, eds., *Coopétition: Rivaliser, coopérer dans les sociétés du haut Moyen Âge*

(*500–1100*) (Turnhout, 2018); Geneviève Bührer-Thierry, Régine Le Jan, and Vito Loré, eds., *Acquérir, prélever, contrôler: Les ressources en compétition (400–1100)* (Turnhout, 2017); Philippe Depreux, François Bougard, and Régine Le Jan, eds., *Compétition et sacré au haut Moyen Âge: Entre médiation et exclusion* (Turnhout, 2015); François Bougard, Régine Le Jan, and Thomas Lienhard, eds., *Agon: La compétition, Ve–XIIe siècle* (Turnhout, 2012).

196. Veronica West-Harling, *Rome, Ravenna, and Venice, 750–1000: Byzantine Heritage, Imperial Present, and the Construction of City Identity* (Oxford, 2020), 454–63.

197. Alcuin, *Ep.* nos. 245–49, ed. Ernst Dümmler, MGH Epp 4 (Berlin, 1895), 393–404. See Samuel Collins, *The Carolingian Debate over Sacred Space* (New York, 2012), 91–120; Warren Brown, *Violence in Medieval Europe* (London, 2010), 82–84; Rob Meens, "Sanctuary, Penance, and Dispute Settlement under Charlemagne: The Conflict Between Alcuin and Theodulf of Orléans over a Sinful Cleric," *Speculum* 82 (2007): 277–300; Hélène Noizet, "Alcuin contre Théodulphe: Un conflit producteur de norms," *Annales de Bretagne* 111 (2004): 113–29; Liutpold Wallach, *Alcuin and Charlemagne: Studies in Carolingian History and Literature* (Ithaca, NY, 1959), 99–140. I wish to express my gratitude toward the participants at the conference "Communautés éphémères de pratiques et d'expériences au premier Moyen Âge: Études de cas et réflexions méthodologiques," at the Université du Québec à Montréal (September 30, 2022), for their helpful discussion of this case.

198. Peter Godman, *Poets and Emperors: Frankish Politics and Carolingian Poetry* (Oxford, 1987), 68–70.

199. Alcuin, *Ep.* 245, ed. Dümmler, 393.

200. Alcuin, *Ep.* 245, 249, ed. Dümmler, 393–94, 402–3.

201. Alcuin, *Ep.* 245, 249, ed. Dümmler, 394, 403.

202. Alcuin, *Ep.* no. 249, ed. Dümmler, 402–3.

203. Adolf Berger, *Encyclopedic Dictionary of Roman Law* (Philadelphia, 1953), 746.

204. Alcuin, *Ep.* no. 246, ed. Dümmler, 398.

205. Collins, *Sacred Space*, 91–120. As Karl Pivec, "Stil- und Sprachentwicklung in mittellateinischen Briefen vom 8.–12. Jahrhundert," in *Hans Hirsch dargebracht als Festgabe zu seinem 60. Geburtstag von seinen Kollegen, Mitarbeitern und Schülern*, MIÖG Ergänzungsband 14 (Vienna, 1939) 33–51, at 42, showed, Alcuin's style was fundamentally modeled on biblical and late antique Christian Latin, with judicious borrowings from the pagan classics.

206. Collins, *Sacred Space*, 117.

207. Alcuin, *Ep.* no. 249, ed. Dümmler, 403: "Fortassis et ille miser hortatus est ad mansionem suam rusticos venientes inter pocula, ut defenderent ecclesiam sancti Martini, ne violenter raperetur ab ea."

208. Collins, *Sacred Space*, 117–19, 121–22.

209. Alcuin, *Ep.* no. 245, ed. Dümmler, 294.

210. Alcuin, *Ep.* no. 249, ed. Dümmler, 403: "Illud etiam commune est omnibus ubique quod moleste ferant suos dehonorare sanctos."

211. Alcuin, *Ep.* 247 (Charlemagne to Alcuin), ed. Dümmler, 399–401.

212. Meens, "Sanctuary, Penance, and Dispute Settlement," 298.

213. Alcuin, *Ep.* 247 (Charlemagne to Alcuin), ed. Dümmler, 400.

214. E. P. Thompson, "The Moral Economy of the English Crowd in the Eighteenth Century," *Past & Present* 50 (1971): 76–136, at 129–31.

215. Timothy Reuter, "Assembly Politics in Western Europe," in *Medieval Polities and Modern Mentalities*, ed. J. Nelson (Cambridge, UK, 2006), 193–216, at 198; Wilfried Hartmann, "Eliten auf Synoden, besonders in der Karolingerzeit," *Théorie et pratiques des élites au haut Moyen Âge*, ed. François Bougard, Hans-Werner Goetz, and Régine Le Jan (Turnhout, 2011), 351–72, for the synods. See also Philippe Depreux and Steffen Patzold, eds., *Versammlungen im Frühmittelalter* (Berlin, 2023).

216. Ruth Schmidt-Wiegand, "Mallus," *RGA*² 19 (Berlin, 2001), 191–92. See also Ruth Schmidt-Wiegand, "Rechtsvorstellungen bei den Franken und Alemannen," in *Die Franken und die Alemannen bis zur 'Schlacht bei Zülpich' (496/97)*, ed. Dieter Geuenich (Berlin, 1998), 545–55, at 548–49, for the *thunginus*.

217. Reuter, "Assembly Politics," 201; Thomas Bauer, "Kontinuität und Wandel synodaler Praxis nach der Reichsteilung von Verdun: Versuch einer Typisierung und Einordnung der karolingischen Synoden und *concilia mixta* von 843 bis 870," *Annuarium Historiae Conciliorum* 23 (1991): 11–116, is valuable on so-called "mixed councils" that combined both secular and ecclesiastical elements.

218. Jürgen Hannig, *Consensus Fidelium: Frühfeudale Interpretationen des Verhältnisses von Königtum und Adel am Beispiel des Frankenreiches* (Stuttgart, 1982), esp. 3–41, 64–79; Janet L. Nelson, "How Carolingians Created Consensus," in *Le monde Carolingien: Bilan, perspectives, champs de recherches*, ed. Wojciech Fałkowski and Yves Sassier (Turnhout, 2009), 67–81; Steffen Patzold, "*Consensus—Concordia—Unitas*: Überlegungen zu einem politisch-religiösen Ideal der Karolingerzeit," in *Exemplaris Imago: Ideale in Mittelalter und Früher Neuzeit*, ed. Nikolaus Staubach (Frankfurt, 2012), 31–56, at 44–46. For the older perspective, see Erich Seyfarth, *Fränkische Reichsversammlungen unter Karl dem Großen und Ludwig dem Frommen* (Leipzig, 1910), 1–10.

219. Seyfarth, *Fränkische Reichsversammlungen*, remains foundational.

220. Chris Wickham, "Consensus and Assemblies in the Romano-Germanic Kingdoms: A Comparative Approach," in *Recht und Konsens im frühen Mittelalter*, ed. Verena Epp and Christoph Meyer (Ostfildern, 2017), 389–424.

221. Paolo Delogu, "Lombard and Carolingian Italy," in *New Cambridge Medieval History*, vol. 2, *c. 700–c. 900*, ed. Rosamond McKitterick (Cambridge, UK, 1995), 290–319, at 290. Delogu goes on to contend that the Lombard practice of "promulgation in front of an assembly" ceased to be important in the "basis of legislative authority" after the Carolingian conquest (307).

222. Levi Roach, *Kingship and Consent in Anglo-Saxon England, 871–978: Assemblies and the State in the Early Middle Ages* (Cambridge, UK, 2013), 233.

223. Pössel, "Magic of Early Medieval Ritual," 124: "The practicality of managing public interactions between powerful people required (and still today requires) some markers, and interactions before crowds needed visual clues for those too far away to hear."

224. Buc, *The Dangers of Ritual*, 131–32, 140–41; Leidulf Melve, "Assembly Politics and the 'Rules-of-the-Game' (ca. 650–1150)," *Viator* 41 (2010): 69–90, at 89.

225. For Louis the Pious's penance in 833, see de Jong, *Penitential State*, 245–49; with ramifications in Stuart Airlie, *Making and Unmaking the Carolingians, 751–888* (London, 2020), 121–72.

226. *AB*, s.a. 862, ed. Grat et al., 93.

227. Simon MacLean, "Ritual, Misunderstanding, and the Contest for Meaning: Representations of the Disrupted Royal Assembly at Frankfurt (873)," in *Representations of Power in Medieval Germany, 800–1500*, ed. Björn Weiler and Simon MacLean (Turnhout, 2006), 97–119; Goldberg, *Struggle for Empire*, 314–17.

228. Edward Coleman, "Representative Assemblies in Communal Italy," in *Political Assemblies in the Earlier Middle Ages*, ed. Paul S. Barnwell and Marco Mostert (Turnhout, 2003), 193–210. Melve, "Assembly Politics," 79, uses these "dialogic" Italian assemblies to support his "staged" thesis of assemblies.

229. For the dynamics in early Gallic councils, see especially Bruno Dumézil, "Consultations épiscopales et délibérations conciliaires dans la Gaule du VIe siècle," in *Consulter, délibérer, décider: Donner son avis au Moyen Âge*, ed. Martine Charageat and Corinne Leveleux-Teixeira (Toulouse, 2010), 61–75.

230. Matthew 18:20, ed. Weber-Gryson, 1554.

231. Ordo 12, *Ordines de celebrando concilio*, ed. H. Schneider, MGH Ordines, 398; Council of Frankfurt (794), ed. A. Werminghoff, MGH Conc. 2.1 (Hanover, 1906), 143; Council of Trier (927 / 28), c. 3, *Concilia aevi Saxonici a. 916–960*, ed. Ernst-Dieter Hehl and Horst Fuhrmann, MGH Conc. 6.1 (Hanover, 1987), 79. Cf. Benedict of Aniane, *Concordia regularum*, c. 25, ed. Bonnerue, CCCM 168A (Turnhout, 1999), 198: "Nam qui dixit: Vbi sunt duo uel tres congregati, quomodo probabitur congregatus, qui a semetipso cogitatione et uagatione dispersus est?"

232. Leo I, *Tractatus septem et nonaginta*, 2.2, *Sancti Leonis Magni romani pontificis tractatus septem et nonaginta*, ed. A. Chavasse, CCSL 138 (Turnhout, 1973): "Cumque hanc uenerabilium consacerdotum meorum splendidissimam frequentiam uideo, angelicum nobis in tot sanctis sentio interesse conuentum."

233. Avitus of Vienne, *Contra Eutychianam haeresim*, 2.3, ed. R. Peiper, *Alcimi Ecdicii Aviti Viennensis Episcopi opera quae supersunt*, MGH AA 6.2 (Berlin, 1883), 22–23. Charlotte Roueché, "Acclamations in the Later Roman Empire: New Evidence from Aphrodisias," *The Journal of Roman Studies* 74 (1984): 181–99, at 181–88, provides an overview of the late Roman practice of acclamations. For later Byzantine metrical acclamations, see Paul Maas, "Metrische Akklamationen der Byzantiner," *Byzantinische Zeitschrift* 21 (1912): 28–51.

234. Avitus, *Contra Eutychianam haeresim*, 2.3, ed. Peiper, 23.

235. Boethius, *Contra Eutychen et Nestorium*, praef., *Boethius, De consolatione philosophiae, Opuscula theologica*, ed. Claudio Moreschini (Munich, 2000), 207–8: "Meditabar igitur dehinc omnes animo quaestiones nec eglutiebam quod acceperam, sed frequentis consilii iteratione ruminabam."

236. Anastasius, *Epistolae sive praefationes*, no 5, ed. Ernst Perels and Gerhard Laehr, MGH Epp. 7 (Berlin, 1928), 406; *Vita Hadriani II*, c. 31, ed. L. Duchesne, *Le Liber pontificalis*, vol. 2, 179: "Inde est quod subscriptionum istius videntur diversi caracteres, et quidam eorum acutiori penna, quidam grossa, nonnulli vero, decrepitum simulantes, grossiori, membranam inquinantes, describunt; ut videlicet fraude presentium simplicitati absentium illudatur, et illud credat facilius universitas esse verissimum quod dissimilibus litteris fecerit falsitas esse diversum. At vos ilico subscriptionum dissimilitudinem, librum reserantes videbitis; fraudem vero, nisi Constantinopolim miseritis, minime cognoscetis"; Nicetas David, *The Life of Patriarch Ignatius* (BHG 817), c. 56–57, ed. A. Smithies with J. M. Duffy, Corpus Fontium Historiae Byzantinae 51 (Washington, DC, 2013), 82–84.

237. Hermann-Josef Sieben, *Die Konzilsidee der alten Kirche* (Paderborn, 1979), esp. 307–14; Hermann-Josef Sieben, *Die Konzilsidee des lateinischen Mittelalters (847–1378)* (Paderborn, 1984). See also Andreas Weckwerth, *Ablauf, Organisation und Selbstverständnis westlicher antiker Synoden im Spiegel ihrer Akten* (Münster, 2010).

238. Hannig, *Consensus Fidelium*, 152–63. See also Roger Reynolds, "Rites and Signs of Conciliar Decisions in the Early Middle Ages," in R. Reynolds, *Clerics in the Early Middle Ages: Hierarchy and Image* (Aldershot, UK, 1999), 207–49; see also pp. 151–52 below.

239. Thomas Bisson, "Celebration and Persuasion: Reflections on the Cultural Evolution of Medieval Consultation," *Legislative Studies Quarterly* 7 (1982): 181–204, at 183; compare Thomas Bisson, "The Military Origins of Medieval Representation," *The American Historical Review* 71 (1966): 1199–1218.

240. Reuter, "Assembly Politics," 206: "Of course, to point to elements of staging and of ritualized or symbolised collective behaviour is not necessarily to deny the existence of more *ad hoc* and less structured elements, and hence ways of 'reading' these gatherings which legitimately treat the layer of staging and symbolic action as transparent and go through and beyond it."

241. Karl Ferdinand Werner, "*Missus—Marchio—Comes*: Entre l'administration centrale et l'administration locale de l'empire carolingien," in *Histoire comparée de l'administration (IVe–XVIIIe siècles)*, ed. Karl Ferdinand Werner and Werner Paravicini (Munich, 1980), 191–239, at 194–95.

242. *Capitulare Missorum* (819), c. 28, ed. A. Boretius, MGH Capit. 1 (Hanover, 1883), no. 141, 291: "Ut omnis episcopus, abbas et comes, excepta infirmitate vel nostra iussione, nullam excusationem habeat, quin ad placitum missorum nostrorum veniat aut talem vicarium suum mittat, qui in omni causa pro illo rationem reddere possit"; Lupus of Ferrières, *Ep.* 67 (24 June, 847), *Loup de Ferrières: Correspondance*, ed. L. Levillain (Paris, 1927), vol. 1, 246–48. Cf. Jean-Pierre Devroey, *Puissants et misérables: Système social et monde paysan dans l'Europe des Francs (VIe–IXe siècle)* (Brussels, 2006), 74.

243. Althoff, "Colloquium Familiare—Colloquium Secretum—Colloquium Publicum"; Wilfried Hartmann, "Gespräche in der 'Kaffeepause'—Am Rande des Konzils von Attigny 870," *Annuarium Historiae Conciliorum* 27 (1996): 137–45.

244. Hludowici, Karoli et Hlotharii II, *Conventus apud Saponarias* (November 3, 862), ed. A. Boretius, MGH Capit. 2 (Hanover, 1897), no. 243, 165: "in ipsa casa [...] in quam pauci alii intraverunt, quam qui antea fuerunt, quoniam fere plena de ipsis erat." For the full quote, see p. 221, n. 257.

245. Gregory of Tours, *Hist.* 2.27, ed. Krusch and Levison, 72–73.

246. John Baker and Stuart Brookes, "Monumentalising the Political Landscape: A Special Class of Anglo-Saxon Assembly Site," *The Antiquaries Journal* 93 (2013): 147–62. On Shetland, see Joris Coolen and Natascha Mehler, *Excavations and Surveys at the Law Ting Holm, Tingwall, Shetland: An Iron Age Settlement and Medieval Assembly Site* (Oxford, 2014), 126–28, for ceremonial use that seems to end with the Picts. For a Scandinavian comparison, see Alexandra Sanmark, "Administrative Organisation and State Formation: A Case Study of Assembly Sites in Södermanland, Sweden," *Medieval Archaeology* 53 (2009): 205–41, showing how topographical assembly features often combine with environment-shaping. For instance, Kjula, a Thing site in Österrekarne is well documented as a meeting place for assemblies. A large mound provided the requisite lines of sight and sound, and in the eleventh century, a rune-stone was established at the base of the mound (211–14).

247. Brian Hope-Taylor, *Yeavering: An Anglo-British Centre of Early Northumbria* (London, 1977), 119–22, 241–44, for the "cuneus" (or "Building E"). For more recent historical contextualization, see Colm O'Brien, "Yeavering and Bernician Kingship: A Review of Debate on the Hybrid Culture Thesis," in *Early Medieval Northumbria: Kingdoms and Communities, 450–1100*, ed. D. Petts and S. Turner (Turnhout, 2011), 207–20; Ian Wood, "An Historical Context for Hope-Taylor's Yeavering," in *Yeavering: People, Power and Place*, ed. Paul Frodsham and Colm O'Brien (Stroud, 2005), 185–88; Paul S. Barnwell, "Anglian Yeavering: A Continental Perspective," in *Yeavering: People, Power and Place*, ed. Paul Frodsham and Colm O'Brien (Stroud, 2005), 174–84; Simon Keynes, "Church Councils, Royal Assemblies, and Anglo-Saxon Royal Diplomas," in *Kingship, Legislation and Power in Anglo-Saxon England*, ed. Gale Owen-Crocker and Brian Schneider (Woodbridge, UK, 2013), 17–184, at 30.

248. Hope-Taylor, *Yeavering*, 161.

249. Roach, *Kingship and Consent*, 43; Stéphane Lebecq, "Imma, Yeavering, Beowulf: Remarques sur la formation d'une culture aulique dans l'Angleterre du VIIe siècle," in *La culture du haut Moyen Âge: Une question d'élites?*, ed. François Bougard, Régine Le Jan, and Rosamond McKitterick (Turnhout, 2009), 239–55, at 247. Bede, *HE* 2.14.2, ed. Lapidge, vol. 1, 370, describes this site as a *villa regia* called "ad Gefrin," where the famous debate about Christianization may have happened.

250. See the historical overview in Hope-Taylor, *Yeavering*, 276–324.

251. Robin Fleming, *Britain after Rome: The Fall and Rise, 400–1070* (London, 2010), 102. Cf. Clare Lees and Gillian Overing, "Anglo-Saxon Horizons: Places of the Mind in the Northumbrian Landscape," in *A Place to Believe In: Locating Medieval Landscapes*, ed. C. Lees and G. Overing (University Park, PA, 2006), 1–26, at 13–15.

252. Theodor Mommsen, *Römisches Staatsrecht* (Leipzig, 1871–88), v. 1, 191–209; Sarah Bond, *Trade and Taboo: Disreputable Professions in the Roman Mediterranean* (Ann Arbor, MI, 2016), 21–58.

253. Nicolas Offenstadt, *En place publique: Jean de Gascogne, crieur au XVe siècle* (Paris, 2013).

254. Marianne Pollheimer, "Hrabanus Maurus—The Compiler, the Preacher, and His Audience," in *Sermo Doctorum: Compilers, Preachers and Their Audiences in the Early Middle Ages*, ed. Maximilian Diesenberger, Yitzhak Hen, and Marianne Pollheimer (Turnhout, 2013), 203–28, at 218–19.

255. Rosamond McKitterick, *Charlemagne: The Formation of a European Identity* (Cambridge, UK, 2008), 222, with further discussion at 222–24.

256. Ramsay MacMullen, "The Epigraphic Habit in the Roman Empire," *The American Journal of Philology* 103 (1982): 233–46, esp. 245–46.

257. Paul Zanker, *Augustus und die Macht der Bilder*, 2nd ed. (Munich, 1990); Cf. David Potter, *Constantine the Emperor* (Oxford, 2012), 88.

258. Joanna Story et al., "Charlemagne's Black Marble: The Origin of the Epitaph of Pope Hadrian I," *Papers of the British School at Rome* 73 (2005): 157–90.

259. Cf. Sierck, *Festtag und Politik*.

260. Thompson, "Moral Economy," 120.

261. Devroey, *Puissants et misérables*, 192–98; Scott, *Weapons of the Weak*, 289–303.

262. Christina Pössel, "Symbolic Communication and the Negotiation of Power at Carolingian Regnal Assemblies, 814–840" (PhD diss., University of Cambridge, 2004), 226–32, 237–38.

263. Not unlike "WUNC" (worthiness, unity, numbers, commitment), the four legitimizing elements of modern social movement according to Charles Tilly, *Social Movements, 1768–2004* (Boulder, CO, 2004), 3–4.

264. Canetti, *Masse und Macht*, 12–14. I do not mean to sign on to all of Canetti's claims about the nature of open and closed crowds, but merely intend to build upon his fundamental distinction between spontaneous and planned crowds. For Canetti's place in crowd theory, see J. S. McClelland, *The Crowd and the Mob from Plato to Canetti* (London, 1989), 293–326.

265. Seneca, *Ep.* 7, ed. Reynolds, vol. 1, 11–14.

266. Theodulf of Orléans, *Carm.* 2.234–35, ed. Ernst Dümmler, MGH Poetae 1 (Berlin, 1881), 457: "Praemia luciflui promittunt ardua regni, / Quo chorus angelicus, quo pia turba patrum est."

267. R. I. Moore, "Family, Community and Cult on the Eve of the Gregorian Reform," *Transactions of the Royal Historical Society*, 6th ser., 30 (1980): 49–69, at 49: "One of the most obvious novelties of the eleventh century is the appearance of the crowd on the stage of public events." Gary Dickson, "Medieval Christian Crowds and the Origins of Crowd Psychology," *Revue d'histoire ecclésiastique* 95, no. 1 (2000): 54–75, at 58–59, for a turning point around the year 1000; Giles Constable, *The Reformation of the Twelfth Century* (Cambridge, UK, 1996), 301; expressed carefully but convincingly: James Norrie, "Rites of Resistance: Urban Liturgy and the Crowd in the Patarine Revolt of Milan, c. 1057–75," *The English Historical Review* 137 (2022): 1575–1605.

268. E.g., *Carmina ad schisma Alexandrinum pertinentia*, 1.51–52, ed. H. Boehmer, MGH LdL 3 (Hanover, 1897), 550: "Qui turbas turbet, qui ius abiuret, iniquos / Approbet, electos exprobet, iste fuit." See Dickson, "Medieval Christian Crowds and the Origins of Crowd Psychology," 58–74; Alexander Murray, *Reason and Society in the Middle Ages* (Oxford, 1985), 234–57.

269. Thomas Bisson, *Crisis of the Twelfth Century: Power, Lordship, and the Origins of European Government* (Princeton, NJ, 2009), 507–9; John Maddicott, *The Origins of the English Parliament, 924–1327* (Oxford, 2010), 376–80.

270. Louis I. Hamilton, *A Sacred City: Consecrating Churches and Reforming Society in Eleventh-Century Italy* (Manchester, 2010), 56–88, for liturgical crowds in eleventh-century Italy (and notes of skepticism about their novelty at 360); Norrie, "Rites of Resistance," 1604–5, shows how this association with legitimacy was weaponized.

Chapter 5. Words

1. Herbert Grundmann, "Literatus–Illiteratus: Der Wandel einer Bildungsnorm vom Altertum zum Mittelalter," *Archiv für Kulturgeschichte* 40 (1958): 1–65, at 3.

2. "Semantic field" characterizes a network of related terms and phrases that may refer to individually variable ideas under one conceptual umbrella (a riot, an audience, a spiritual network, etc.). The concept was popularized by Jost Trier, *Der deutsche Wortschatz im Sinnbezirk des Verstandes: Die Geschichte eines sprachlichen Feldes* (Heidelberg, 1931), vol. 1, 1. See Werner Zillig, "Wörter, Felder und Wortfelder: Ein Essay über eine sprachwissenschaftliche Metapher," in *Jost Trier: Leben—Werk—Wirkung*, ed. W. Zillig (Münster, 1994), 129–203; see also D. H. Green, *The Carolingian Lord* (Cambridge, UK, 1965), xiii.

3. Jan Ziolkowski, "The Obscenities of Old Women: Vetularity and Vernacularity," in *Obscenity: Social Control and Artistic Creation in the European Middle Ages*, ed. Jan Ziolkowski (Leiden, 1998), 73–89, at 74. Ziolkowski borrows the phrase from the twelfth-century author Nigel of Canterbury, *The Passion of St. Lawrence: Epigrams and Marginal Poems*, ed. and trans. Jan Ziolkowski (Leiden, 1994), 10.

4. Pierre Michaud-Quantin, *Universitas: Expressions du mouvement communautaire dans le moyen-âge latin* (Paris, 1970); Hermann Menge, "Heer, Schar, Haufe," in *Lateinische Synonymik*, ed. O. Schönberger, 6th revised ed. (Heidelberg, 1977), 95–96.

5. *TLL* 10.1: 2712, s.v. "populōsitās"; cf. Henri Goelzer, "Remarques lexicographiques sur le latin de saint Avit, évêque de Vienne (1)," *Archivum Latinitatis Medii Aevi* 3 (1927): 173–95, at 192. MLW 3.1, 323–24, s.v. "densatim"; *TLL* 5.1: 2071, s.v. "drungus"; MLW 4.3, col. 943, s.v. "hansa" (cf. Stotz 3§30.7); MLW 4.2, col. 706, s.v. "gilda" (cf. Stotz 3§30.6).

6. *TLL* 8: 1600–1603, s.v. "multitudo" (Geralt Ustrnul).

7. See Catherine Virlouvet, *Famines et émeutes à Rome des origins de la République à la mort de Néron* (Rome, 1985), 56–57 (table 3), for crowd terms used as shorthand for "riots": the "people" (*populus*), the "plebs" (*plebs*), "everyone" (*omnes*), a "multitude" (*multitudo*), a "crowd" (*turba*), the "poor" (*inopes*).

8. See above, pp. 27–28. Vergil, *Aen.* 1.148–50: "ac ueluti magno in populo cum saepe coorta est / seditio saeuitque animis ignobile uulgus, / iamque faces et saxa uolant, furor arma ministrat."

9. *OLD*, vol. 2, 2339, s.v. "uulgus" (1–2); *OLD*, vol. 2, 2193, s.v. "turba" (1–2); *TLL* 10.1: 2727, s.v. "populus" (I.D.3); *TLL* 10.1: 2386, s.v. "plebes" (II.A.1.a); *TLL* 8:1600–1601, s.v. "multitudo" (I.A.1.a.α); *TLL* 6.1: 1305, s.v. "frequentia" (1d).

10. Horace, *Carmina* 3.1, ed. D. R. Shackleton Bailey, 3rd ed. (Leipzig, 1995).

11. The fundamental resource is Peter Stotz, *Handbuch zur lateinischen Sprache des Mittelalters*, 5 vols., Handbuch der Altertumswissenschaft 2.5 (Munich, 1996–2004). For valuable introductions, see also Veikko Väänänen, *Introduction au latin vulgaire*, 3rd ed. (Paris, 1981); Dag Norberg, *Manuel pratique de latin médiéval* (Paris, 1968).

12. Roger Wright, *A Sociophilological Study of Late Latin* (Turnhout, 2002), 1–68; J. N. Adams, *The Regional Diversification of Latin, 200 BC—AD 600* (Cambridge, UK, 2007); and J. N. Adams, *Social Variation and the Latin Language* (Cambridge, UK, 2013), are important synthetic reassessments.

13. Erich Auerbach, *Literary Language and Its Public in Late Antiquity and in the Middle Ages*, trans. Ralph Manheim (Princeton, NJ, 1965), 27–66. Some of Auerbach's nuances are lost in translation, so I will occasionally refer to the German original: Erich Auerbach, *Literatursprache und Publikum in der lateinischen Spätantike und im Mittelalter* (Bern, 1958).

14. E.g., Council of Tours (813), c. 17, ed. A. Werminghoff, MGH Conc 2.1 (Hanover, 1906), 288: "Et ut easdem omelias quisque aperte transferre studeat in rusticam Romanam linguam aut Thiotiscam, quo facilius cuncti possint intellegere quae dicuntur"; Council of Mainz (847),

c. 2, ed. W. Hartmann, MGH Conc 3 (Hanover, 1984), 164; Additamenta ad capitularia Regum Franciae Orientalis, c. 248, ed. A. Boretius and V. Krause, MGH Capit. 2 (Hanover, 1897), 176. Nithard, *Historiae*, 3.5, ed. Philippe Lauer, revised Sophie Glansdorff, *Nithard, Histoire des fils de Louis le Pieux* (Paris, 2012), 112–16: ". . . Lodhuvicus romana, Karolus vero teudisca lingua, juraverunt"; "Ac sic, ante sacramentum, circumfusam plebem, alter teudisca, alter romana lingua alloquuti sunt"; ". . . Karolus haec eadem verba romana lingua perorasset . . ."; "Sacramentum autem quod utrorumque populus, quique propria lingua, testatus est, romana lingua sic se habet . . ."

15. Roger Wright, *Late Latin and Early Romance in Spain and Carolingian France* (Liverpool, 1982), ix.

16. Auerbach, *Literatursprache und Publikum*, 86: "Mit suetonischem Latein konnte man Worte des Lebens der karolingischen Welt nicht wiedergeben" (Auerbach, *Literary Language and Its Public*, 118).

17. Michel Banniard, *Viva voce: Communication écrite et communication orale du IVe au IXe siècle en occident latin* (Paris, 1992); Wright, *Sociophilological Study*, 10; Rosamond McKitterick, *Carolingians and the Written Word* (Cambridge, UK, 1989), 1–22.

18. For the spread of child oblation in the Carolingian period, see Mayke de Jong, *In Samuel's Image: Child Oblation in the Early Medieval West* (Leiden, 1996), 56–99.

19. McKitterick, *The Carolingians and the Written Word*.

20. Michael McCormick, *Five Hundred Unknown Glosses from the Palatine Virgil: The Vatican Library, MS. Pal. lat. 1631* (Rome, 1992); Cinzia Grifoni, "Reading the Catholic Epistles: Glossing Practices in Early Medieval Wissembourg," in *The Annotated Book in the Early Middle Ages: Practices of Reading and Writing*, ed. Mariken Teeuwen and Irene van Renswoude (Turnhout, 2018), 705–42.

21. No crowds appear in the *Sequence of Saint Eulalia* (c. 880).

22. Meyer-Lübke, 6654, s.v. "populus"; *Recueil des inscriptions chrétiennes de la Gaule antérieures à la Renaissance carolingienne*, vol. 1, *Première Belgique*, ed. Nancy Gauthier (Paris, 1975) no. 135, 352 (dated to between the fifth and early seventh century).

23. Nithard, *Historiae*, 3.5, ed. Lauer, revised Glansdorff, 114. For remarks on the language, see Wright, *Late Latin*, 122–31.

24. *TLL* 10.1: 2379, s.v. "plebes" (lines 62–71). *Recueil des inscriptions chrétiennes de la Gaule antérieures à la Renaissance carolingienne*, vol. 8, *Aquitaine première*, ed. Françoise Prévot (Paris, 1997), no. 25, 140 (Clermont, seventh century). Note that the orthography is preserved by a copyist; the original inscription does not survive.

25. For **fulla*, see W. Meyer-Lübke, *Romanisches etymologisches Wörterbuch* (Heidelberg, 1911), 265. Meyer-Lübke also lists Provençal *fola*; G. Körting, *Lateinisch-romanisches Wörterbuch*, 3rd ed. (Paderborn, 1907), 460; Walter von Wartburg et al., *Französisches etymologisches Wörterbuch: Eine darstellung des galloromanischen Sprachschatzes*, vol. 3 (Bonn, 1922–2003), s.v. "fullare" (III), 848–49; Salvatore Battaglia et al., *Grande dizionario della lingua Italiana*, vol. 4, *Fio–graul* (Torino 2004), 111 (for *folla*).

26. Stotz, *Handbuch* 5§24.7 (vol. 2, 55). See also John B. Hill, "'Foule,' 'Folla': French / Italian" (Mini-Essay 9A) in *Crowds*, ed. J. T. Schnapp and M. Tiews (Stanford, 2006), 216–18.

27. Meyer-Lübke, *Romanisches etymologisches Wörterbuch*, 265; *TLL* 6.1, 1523, s.v. "1. fullo."

28. The English word "crowd" derives from the Old English *crúdan*, to press, crush, or push. *OED*, s.v. "crowd." "Throng" derives from an Old English word, *geþrang*, referring to pressure. *OED*, s.v. "throng."

29. Frede Jensen, *Old French and Comparative Gallo-Romance Syntax* (Tübingen, 1990), 47 (c. 99). See variations such as the *grant bruit de gent* that follows Yder in Chrétien de Troyes, *Erec et Enide*, line 789, *Chrétien de Troyes: Romans*, ed. Jean-Marie Fritz (Paris, 1994), 85.

30. Jay H. Jasanoff, "Germanic (le germanique)," in *Langues indo-européennes*, ed. F. Bader (Paris, 1994), 251–80; Orrin W. Robinson, *Old English and Its Closest Relatives: A Survey of the Earliest Germanic Languages* (Stanford, 1992). For a vivid sense of how vernaculars were used, see Robert Gallagher et al., *The Languages of Early Medieval Charters: Latin, Germanic Vernaculars, and the Written Word* (Leiden, 2020). For the Romance / Germanic linguistic border, see Frauke Stein, "Frühmittelalterliche Bevölkerungsverhältnisse im Saar-Mosel-Raum: Voraussetzungen der Ausbildung der deutsch-französischen Sprachgrenze?," in *Grenzen und Grenzregionen—Frontières et régions frontalières—Borders and Border Regions*, ed. W. Haubrichs and R. Schneider (Saarbrücken, 1994), 69–98, esp. 87.

31. *AWB*, s.v. "thing"; Elisabeth Karg-Gasterstädt, "Althochdeutsch thing—neuhochdeutsch Ding: Die Geschichte eines Wortes," *Berichte über die Verhandlungen der Sächsischen Akademie der Wissenschaften: Philologisch-Historische Klasse* 104 (1958): 3–31.

32. Nithard, *Hist.* 3.5, MGH SRG 44, 36: "indi mit Ludheren in nohheiniu thing ne gegango, zhe minan uuillon imo ce scadhen uuerhen."

33. *AWB*, s.v. "thing."

34. *AWB*, s.v. "thinghûs."

35. *AWB*, s.v. "thingâri."

36. Franz Beyerle, ed., *Leges Langobardorum, 643–866*, 2nd ed. (Witzenhausen, 1962), 226.

37. Wilhelm Streitberg, ed., *Die gotische Bibel*, 2nd ed. (Heidelberg, 1919), 172–73 (Mark 3:20): *ochlos*; 158–59 (Luke 19:48): *laos*.

38. Streitberg, ed., *Die gotische Bibel*, 84–85 (Luke 1:10).

39. Ferdinand Wrede, *Über die Sprache der Ostgoten in Italien* (Strassburg, 1891), 51–57.

40. Wrede, *Über die Sprache der Ostgoten*, 37–42, for the testimonies.

41. Roger Collins, *Visigothic Spain, 409–711* (Malden, MA, 2004), 242; Hermann Reichert, "Die Bildungsweise der frühen germanischen Personennamen," in *Linguistica et Philologica: Gedenkschrift für Björn Collinger (1894–1983)*, ed. Otto Gschwantler, Károly Rédei, and Hermann Reichert (Vienna, 1984), 355–68.

42. For the onomastic evidence, see Nicoletta Francovich Onesti, *Vestigia longobarde in Italia (568–774): Lessico e antroponimia* (Rome, 1999).

43. Francovich Onesti, *Vestigia*, 84–86 (*fulc*), 216–18 (**þeuðo*), 200–201 (**harja*).

44. E.g., Alcuin, *Ep.* 3, ed. Ernst Dümmler, MGH Epp 4, 28; *Annales Laurissenses* MGH SS 1, 172; *ARF*, s.a. 788, ed. Kurze, 80; MGH Capit 1, 205; MGH Capit. 2, 171.

45. Elmar Seebold et al., *Chronologisches Wörterbuch des deutschen Wortschatzes: Der Wortschatz des 8. Jahrhunderts (und früherer Quellen)* (Berlin, 2001). Texts in OHG include Otfrid of Weissemburg's *Evangelienbuch*, the Heliand, hymns (like the *Georgslied*, the Murbach Hymns), epic poetry (Muspilli, Ludwigslied, Hildebrandslied), Biblical translations (Mondsee Fragments), Notker, translations (OHG Isidore, Regula Benedicti, Tatian, etc.), and glosses.

46. *AWB*, s.v. "menigî(n)." Alternative spellings include *manaki, meniki, menighi*, etc.

47. *AWB*, s.v. "al."

48. Rudolf Schützeichel, *Althochdeutsches Wörterbuch*, 7th ed. (Berlin, 2012), 109, 217

49. Stotz 3§30.6–7.

50. Green, *Carolingian Lord*, 115–215, for a lucid discussion of the language of the "comitatus" in Old High German and Old Saxon, including discussion of key words (*triuwa, trôst, huldi, milti*, and *êra*, plus *ginâda*).

51. Heliand, Fitt 34, in *Heliand und Genesis*, ed. Otto Behaghel, 10th ed. (Tübingen, 1996 [1882]): miracle of the five loaves and two fishes.

52. Ronald Murphy, *The Saxon Savior: The Germanic Transformation of the Gospel in the Ninth-Century Heliand* (Oxford, 1989).

53. For an overview of key genres, see Robinson, *Old English and Its Closest Relatives*, 143–48.

54. See Aliki Pantos, "'In medle oððe an þinge': The Old English Vocabulary of Assembly," in *Assembly Places and Practices in Medieval Europe*, ed. Aliki Pantos and Sarah Semple (Oxford, 2002), 181–204.

55. Tom Lambert, *Law and Order in Anglo-Saxon England* (Oxford, 2017), 44–45.

56. These terms are drawn from the 3,047 texts that comprise Angus Cameron, Ashley Crandell Amos, Antonette diPaolo Healey et al., eds., *Dictionary of Old English: A to I* online (Toronto, 2018), https://tapor.library.utoronto.ca/doe/.

57. Jan de Vries, *Altnordisches etymologisches Wörterbuch*, 2nd ed. (Leiden, 1977), 384, s.v. "mengi."

58. de Vries, *Altnordisches etymologisches Wörterbuch*, 125, s.v. "fǫl 2."

59. de Vries, *Altnordisches etymologisches Wörterbuch*, 137, s.v. "folk"; 613, s.v. "þjóð"; 369, s.v. "lýðr"; 147, s.v. "fylgð"; 144–48, s.v. "fylgja 1."

60. de Vries, *Altnordisches etymologisches Wörterbuch*, 224–25, s.v. "herr."

61. de Vries, *Altnordisches etymologisches Wörterbuch*, 610–11, s.v. "þing"; Alexandra Sanmark, *Viking Law and Order: An Investigation of Norse Thing Sites* (Edinburgh, 2017).

62. *AWB*, s.v. "fâra"; Schützeichel, *Althochdeutsches Wörterbuch*, 317, s.v. "strīt."

63. But see above, pp. 111–12, on the case of the *tumultus* at Tours in 801.

64. Whitley Stokes and John Strachan, eds., *Thesaurus Palaeohibernicus*, 2 vols. (London, 1901–10). The most famous set of glosses is from a manuscript of Priscian (in Stokes and Strachan, *Thesaurus Palaeohibernicus*, vol. 2, 49–224), completed in the middle of the ninth century, now St. Gall, Stiftsbibliothek, MS 904. See also the recent edition of the first set of glosses from this manuscript: Rijcklof Hofman, ed., *The Sankt Gall Priscian Commentary: Part 1*, 2 vols. (Münster, 1996). I am grateful to Jo Wolf for their assistance with the Old Irish material.

65. Electronic Dictionary of the Irish Language (hereafter eDIL), https://dil.ie/, s.v. "drong."

66. eDIL, s.v. "popul"; Whitley Stokes, ed., *Three Irish Glossaries* (London, 1862), 42.

67. J. Vendryes, *Lexique étymologique de l'Irlandais ancien: Lettres R S* (Paris, 1974) 136–37.

68. Stokes and Strachan, ed., *Thesaurus Palaeohibernicus*, vol. 2, 70.

69. Pádraig Bambury, Stephen Beechinor, Julianne Nyhan, ed., *Táin Bó Cúalnge*, trans. Cecile O'Rahilly, 127 (Recension 1, lines 63–106), (https://celt.ucc.ie/published/T301012/index.html).

70. Irina Liusen, *Grechesko-staroslavianskiĭ konkordans k drevneĭshim spiskam slavianskogo perevoda evangeliĭ: Codices Marianus, Zographensis, Assemanianus, Ostromiri* [Greek-Old Church Slavic concordance to the oldest versions of the translation of the Gospel texts: Codices Marianus, Zographensis, Assemanianus, Ostromiri] (Uppsala, 1995), 174 (s.v. "ὄχλος"), 189 (s.v. "πλῆθος"); cf. Horace G. Lunt, *Old Church Slavonic Glossary*, ed. Michael S. Flier (Department of Slavic Languages and Literatures, Harvard University, 1959, corrected 2011). Another major source for early Slavonic is Antonín Dostál, ed., *Clozianus: Codex Palaeoslovenicus Glagoliticus, Tridentinus et Oenipontanus* (Prague, 1959). I am very grateful to Kuba Kabala and Jake Ransohoff for their guidance in questions of Slavonic philology.

71. Colette Sirat, *Hebrew Manuscripts of the Middle Ages* (Cambridge, UK, 2002), 61.

72. Sirat, *Hebrew Manuscripts*, 74.

73. Eva Haverkamp, ed., *Hebräische Berichte über die Judenverfolgungen während des Ersten Kreuzzugs*, MGH Hebräische Texte aus dem mittelalterlichen Deutschland 1 (Hanover, 2005); Avraham Fraenkel, Abraham Gross, and Peter S. Lehnardt, eds., *Hebräische liturgische Poesien zu den Judenverfolgungen während des Ersten Kreuzzugs*, MGH Hebräische Texte aus dem mittelalterlichen Deutschland 3 (Wiesbaden, 2016).

74. In the sixth century, Gregory of Tours reported that the Jews of Orléans shouted acclamations to King Guntramn in their own language: Gregory of Tours, *Hist.* 8.1, ed. Krusch and Levison, 370–71; Noël Coulet, "De l'intégration à l'exclusion: La place des juifs dans les cérémonies d'entrée solennelle au Moyen Âge," *Annales: Économies, Sociétés, Civilisations* 34 (1979): 672–83.

75. The earliest dated *medieval* Hebrew manuscript (a copy of Ruth and Nehemiah) hails from early tenth-century Iran: Cambridge, University Library, T-S NS 246.26.2; Sirat, *Hebrew Manuscripts*, 46.

76. James Strong, *The Comprehensive Concordance of the Bible* (New York, 1890), s.vv.

77. Robert Browning, *Medieval and Modern Greek* (London, 1969); Geoffrey Horrocks, *Greek: A History of the Language and Its Speakers*, 2nd ed. (Chichester, 2010).

78. Hans Georg Beck, *Res Publica Romana: Vom Staatsdenken der Byzantiner* (Munich, 1970); Anthony Kaldellis, *The Byzantine Republic: People and Power in New Rome* (Cambridge, MA, 2015).

79. Leontios Presbyteros, *Life of Gregory of Agrigento* (*BHG* 707), ed. Albrecht Berger, *Leontios Presbyteros von Rom: Das Leben des Heiligen Gregorios von Agrigent: Kritische Ausgabe, Übersetzung und Kommentar* (Berlin, 1995): πλῆθος (c. 34, p. 186); ὄχλος (c.39(39), p. 191); λαός (c. 80 (72), p. 239); στάσις (c.39(40), p. 192).

80. Bernhard Bischoff, "Das griechische Element in der abendländischen Bildung des Mittelalters," in *Mittelalterliche Studien: Ausgewählte Aufsätze zur Schriftkunde und Literaturgeschichte* (Stuttgart, 1967), vol. 2, 246–74; Pascal Boulhol, *La connaissance de la langue grecque dans la France médiévale VIe-XVe s.* (Aix-en-Provence, 2008), 21–48.

81. Many thanks to Arafat Razzaque for guidance.

82. See Paul M. Cobb, *White Banners: Contention in 'Abbāsid Syria, 750–880* (Albany, NY, 2001), 103–24, for armed urban crowds in 'Abbasid Syria, including discussion of the language of crowds.

83. Paul Alvar, *Indiculus Luminosus*, c. 35, ed. J. Gil, *Corpus Scriptorum Muzarabicorum*, 2 vols. (Madrid, 1973), vol. 1, 313–15. A very similar complaint was made (in a tenth- or eleventh-century Arabic text purporting to be from the late seventh century) about Coptic speakers forgetting their language and religion: "A Monk Deploring the Assimilation of the Christians to the Hagarenes" (from the Apocalypse of Samuel of Qalamum) translated by Arietta Papaconstantinou in Nimrod Hurvitz, et al., eds., *Conversion to Islam in the Premodern Age: A Sourcebook* (Oakland, 2020), 167–71, at 169–70.

84. *Diccionario de la lengua española*, 22nd ed. (Madrid, 2001), s.v. "alcavela."

85. Louis II (dict. Anastasius Bibliothecarius), *Epistola ad Basilium I. imperatorem* (871), ed. Walter Henze, MGH Epp 7 (Berlin, 1928), 393: "Ita ut facta videatur Neapolis Panormus vel Africa."

86. Walter Pohl, *The Avars: A Steppe Empire in Central Europe, 567–822* (Ithaca, NY, 2018), 270–73.

87. The Peshitta (the Syriac Bible) endowed Syriac hagiographical and historiographical writings with a rich vocabulary of crowds. The Anbandidi Gospel offers similar insight for ninth or tenth-century Georgian.

88. Isidore, *De differentiis verborum*, c. 369, PL 83, col. 48: "Inter multitudinem et numerum. Multitudo numero fit, turba loco posita. Possunt enim pauci in angusto turbam facere."

89. Only much later was this built upon by Huguccio of Pisa: Uguccione da Pisa, *Derivationes*, 2, T 78 [=*tero*] [38], ed. Enzo Cecchini (Florence, 2004), 1214: "Item a turbo hec turba -e, idest turbatio: et turba populi multitudo, sed multitudo numero fit, turba vero tantum in loco; possunt enim pauci in angusto turbam facere; unde turbella, idest turbatio; Augustinus De civitate Dei 'omnem motum cordis et salum omnesque turbellas fluitare asserit.'"

90. For the classical semantic range, see *TLL* 1: 1339, s.v. "agmen."

91. *TLL* 6.2: 1842–72, s.v. "gēns" (esp. 1862).

92. *Vita Aichardi seu Aichadri abbatis Gemeticensis* (*BHL* 181), c. 46, AASS Sep. 5.15.94F: "Coram cunctis fratribus." For this life, see Charles Mériaux, *Gallia irradiata: Saints et sanctuaires dans le nord de la Gaule du haut Moyen Âge* (Stuttgart, 2006), 345. A vision involving a whole monastic community in a ninth-century *translatio* imagines "all of the brothers of that monastery

sitting in the right part of the choir, decked in white clothing": *Translatio Germani Parisiensis anno 846* (*BHL* 3479), c. 29, in "Translatio S. Germani Parisiensis anno 846 secundum primævam narrationem, e codice Namucensi," *Analecta Bollandiana* 2 (1883): 69–99, at 91: "cunctos hujus monasterii fratres in dextera parte consistere chori, indutos candidissimis vestimentis." Similarly, *omnis* or *omnes* may be used to describe representative gatherings: *Vita Hugonis* (*BHL* 4032a), c. 30, ed. J. Van der Straeten, in "La vie inédite de S. Hughes," *Analecta bollandiana* 87 (1969): 232–60, at 257–58: "occurrit omnis sancta plebs omnisque familia cum omni ornatu eecclesiae [*sic*]."

93. *Translatio SS. Chrysanti et Dariae a. 844* (*BHL* 1793), c. 8, AASS Oct. 11.25.491D–E: "Cum vero jam decerneremus in locum, ubi nunc adorantur, Sanctorum deduci corpora; multitudo innumerabilis processit mundare vias, per quas reliquiæ deducendæ erant Martyrum. Cum igitur quædam succideretur arbor, quidam non præcavens casum, cecidit super eum. Cum itaque putaretur mortuus, amota arbore, ut credimus orationibus Sanctorum, ita incolumis repertus est, ac si nil pertulisset læsionis"; *Vita Geremari* (*BHL* 3441), c. 10, ed. B. Krusch, MGH SRM 4 (Hanover, 1902), 630: "Erat autem ibidem in monasterio multitudo maxima monachorum."

94. *TLL* 10.1: 2713–36, s.v. "populus."

95. *TLL* 10.1, s.v. "populus," lines 22–23.

96. *Multitudo* was always polysemic and all encompassing (*TLL* 8:1600–1603). For its extension into nonhuman collectivities, see, e.g., *Vita Bertini* I (*BHL* 763), c. 21, ed. W. Levison, MGH SRM 5 (Hanover, 1910), 768 (fish); *Vita Sulpicii episcopi Biturigi*, Recensio A (*BHL* 7927), c. 2, ed. B. Krusch, MGH SRM 4 (Hanover, 1902), 374 (a "multitude" of waters).

97. *Vita Bertini* II (*BHL* 1290), praef., AASS Sept. 2.5.590E: "duodecim Apostolos de turba totius generis humani electos." For this text, see Mériaux, *Gallia irradiata*, 351.

98. Daniëlle Slootjes, "Crowd Behavior in Late Antique Rome," in *Pagans and Christians in Late Antique Rome: Conflict, Competition, and Coexistence in the Fourth Century*, ed. Michele Renee Salzman, Marianne Sághy, and Rita Lizzi Testa (Cambridge, UK, 2016), 178–94, at 179–81.

99. H. G. Liddell and Robert Scott, *A Greek-English Lexicon*, revised ed. (Oxford, 1996), s.v. "ὄχλος," 1281.

100. E.g., Mark 3:20; Luke 19:48.

101. Alan Cameron, *Circus Factions: Blues and Greens at Rome and Byzantium* (Oxford, 1976), 28–35. See also Jamie Kreiner, "Gaul's Insiders: Hagiography and Entitlement," in *Hagiography and the History of Latin Christendom, 500–1500* (Leiden, 2020), 211–31, at 222–24.

102. Manu Leumann, J. B. Hofmann, and A. Szantyr, *Lateinische Grammatik* (Munich, 1972–77), 21 (no. 32).

103. Cameron, *Circus Factions*, 28–35.

104. Lucius Cornelius Sisenna, *Fragment* no. 80, ed. H. Peter, *Historicorum Romanorum reliquiae*, 2nd ed. (Leipzig, 1967), vol. 1, 288 (not a likely source for most authors of the earlier Middle Ages); Cicero, *De officiis*, 2.18.63, ed. C. Atzert (Leipzig, 1963), 76.

105. Luke 1:10, ed. Weber-Gryson, 1605: "et omnis multitudo populi erat orans foris hora incensi"; Acts 21:36, ed. Weber-Gryson, 1736: sequebatur enim multitudo populi clamans tolle eum."

106. 2 Chronicles 13:8, ed. Weber-Gryson, 602: "nunc ergo vos dicitis quod resistere possitis regno Domini quod possidet per filios David habetisque grandem populi multitudinem atque vitulos aureos quos fecit vobis Jeroboam in deos"; 2 Chronicles 33:25, ed. Weber-Gryson, 631: "porro reliqua populi multitudo caesis his qui Amon percusserant constituit regem Iosiam filium eius pro eo"; Proverbs 14:28, ed. Weber-Gryson, 969: "in multitudine populi dignitas regis et in paucitate plebis ignominia principis"; Sirach 42:11, ed. Weber-Gryson, 1082–83: "super filiam luxuriosam confirma custodiam nequando faciat te in opprobrium venire inimicis a detractione in civitate et abiectione plebis et confundat te in multitudine populi."

107. Genesis 28:3, ed. Weber-Gryson, 40: "Deus autem omnipotens benedicat tibi et crescere te faciat atque multiplicet ut sis in turbas populorum."

108. E.g., Alcuin, *Vita Vedasti* (*BHL* 8506-8), c. 3, c. 9, ed. Christiane Veyrard-Cosme, *L'œuvre hagiographique en prose d'Alcuin: Vitae Willibrordi, Vedasti, Richarii: Édition, traduction, études narratologiques* (Florence, 2003); *AB*, s.a. 830, ed. Grat et al., 2: "Ibique ueniens Pippinus cum multitudine populi...."; Einhard, *Translatio Marcellini et Petri*, 4.14, ed. Waitz, 261; *Translatio Viti martyris* (*BHL* 8718–19), ed. Schmale-Ott, 581, 582, 583, 584, 585; Willibald, *Vita Bonifatii* (*BHL* 1400), c. 6, ed. W. Levison, MGH SRG 57 (Hanover, 1905), 34. Compare *Vita Leucii* (*BHL* 4894), *Bibliotheca casinensis* 3 (Monte Cassino, 1877), 358–65, at 361 (column A), where *omnis turba populorum* is made the equivalent of *omnis populus*.

109. Gregory of Tours, *Liber Vitae Patrum* 8, ed. Krusch, MGH SRM 1.2, 247.

110. Paul H. Freedman, *Images of the Medieval Peasant* (Stanford, 1999).

111. *TLL* 10.1, s.v. "populus" (caput prius.I.D.3.c: plebes), col. 2727, lines 28–53.

112. Gregory the Great, *Moralia in Job*, 1.27.25, ed. Adriaen, 38.

113. Jensen, *Old French and Comparative Gallo-Romance Syntax*, 43 (c. 90).

114. Henry Kahane and Renée Kahane, "Abendland und Byzanz: Sprache," *Reallexikon der Byzantinistik* 1 (1976): 345–640, at 565–66, 583.

115. Anne-Marie Bautier, "'Popularis' et la notion de 'populaire,'" *Acta Antiquae Academiae Scientiarum Hungaricae* 23 (1975): 285–303. For the more amenable first / second declension *popularius*, see Stotz 8§12.8.

116. Hilary of Arles, *Sermo de Vita Honorati Episcopi Arelatensis* (*BHL* 3975), 39.2, ed. Marie-Denise Valentin, *Hilaire d'Arles: Vie de Saint Honorat; Introduction, texte critique, traduction, et notes*, SC 235 (Paris, 1977), 176.

117. For instance, in reference to a populace as a whole: Aigradus of Fontenelle, *Vita Lantberti* (*BHL* 4675), c. 3, 4, ed. Wilhelm Levison, MGH SRM 5 (Hanover, 1910), 610, 612.

118. Jamie Kreiner, "About the Bishop: The Episcopal Entourage and the Economy of Government in Post-Roman Gaul," *Speculum* 86 (2011): 321–60, at 328.

119. *TLL* 8, s.v. "multitudo," col. 1601, lines 12–33.

120. John of Biclar, *Chronica*, MGH AA 11, 213; Gregory of Tours, *Liber in gloria confessorum* 2.2, ed. Krusch, 299; Fredegar, *Chronicarum libri IV*, 2.41, ed. Krusch, MGH SRM 2, 65.

121. *TLL* 10.1, s.v. "plebes," at col. 2379–80.

122. E.g., *ARF*, s.a. 826, ed. Kurze, 171; Hrabanus Maurus, *Carm*. 19.3, ed. Ernst Dümmler, MGH Poetae 2 (Hanover, 1884), 184.

123. The word's derivations—*vulgo*, *vulgaris*, *vulgalis*, *vulgarie*, *vulgarice*, *vulgariter*, *vulgarizare*—referred to "vernaculars" spoken by common folk.

124. E.g., *Vita Vigoris* (*BHL* 8608–13), c. 8, AASS Nov. 1.1.301B: "Consurgens omnis multitudo rusticorum vulgus cum injuria ejecerunt eum."

125. Joshua 9:18, ed. Weber-Gryson, 298; 2 Kings 3:37, ed. Weber-Gryson, 421; 2 Chronicles 23:20, ed. Weber-Gryson, 615; Jeremiah 50:37, ed. Weber-Gryson, 1242.

126. *AWB*, s.v. "folc." The term *balgheri* (*AWB*, s.v. "balgheri"), literally "sack-army," was sometimes glossed as *vulgus*; this Old High German term referred to the "common lot" or "camp followers" of an army.

127. Chrodegang of Metz, *Regula canonicorum*, c. 31 (lines 22–23), ed. Wilhelm Schmitz, *Regula canonicorum: Aus dem Leidener Codex Vossianus Latinus 94 mit Umschrift der tironischen Noten* (Hanover, 1889), 21. Cf. Aug. Civ. dei, 19.21; 19.24. For Chrodegang's *Regula canonicorum*, see M. A. Claussen, *The Reform of the Frankish Church: Chrodegang of Metz and the Regula Canonicorum in the Eighth Century* (Cambridge, UK, 2004), 58–113.

128. Paul the Deacon, *Liber de episcopis Mettensibus*, ed. and trans. Damien Kempf, Dallas Medieval Texts and Translations 19 (Paris, 2013), 50–54. Concerning the interpolation, see Paul the Deacon, *Liber de episcopis Mettensibus*, 35–36, and, for the arguments, J.-C. Picard, "Le recours

aux origines: Les vies de saint Clément, premier évêque de Metz, composées autour de l'an mil," in J.-C. Picard, *Évêques, saints et cites en Italie et en Gaule: Études d'archéologie et d'histoire* (Rome, 1998), 367–84.

129. Paul the Deacon, *Liber de episcopis Mettensibus*, 48.

130. Paul the Deacon, *Liber de episcopis Mettensibus*, 49.

131. Alcuin, *Epistolae*, no. 132, c. 9, ed. Ernst Dümmler, MGH Epp. 4 (Berlin, 1895), 199; see Courtney M. Booker, "*Iusta Murmuratio*: The Sound of Scandal in the Early Middle Ages," *Revue Bénédictine* 126 (2016): 236–70, at 261–62; and Alcuin, *Epistolae*, no. 249, ed. Dümmler, 403. See Samuel W. Collins, *The Carolingian Debate over Sacred Space* (New York, 2012), 115–20. For Agobard, see especially Jean-Pierre Devroey, "La poudre du duc Grimoald: Une affaire criminelle au début du IXe siècle," *Revue belge de philologie et d'histoire* 96 (2018): 349–63. See also Shane Bobrycki, "The Flailing Women of Dijon: Crowds in Ninth-Century Europe," *Past & Present* 240 (2018): 3–46.

132. Compare Ramsay MacMullen, "Roman Bureaucratese," *Traditio* 18 (1962): 364–78, at 369: "Confusion, however, has its uses."

133. Autun, Bibliothèque municipale, MS 19bis, fol. 173v. For this manuscript, see Roger E. Reynolds, "The Portrait of the Ecclesiastical Officers in the Raganaldus Sacramentary and Its Liturgico-Canonical Significance," *Speculum* 46 (1971): 432–42; cf. Marie-Pierre Laffitte and Charlotte Denoël, eds., *Trésors carolingiens: Livres manuscrits de Charlemagne à Charles le Chauve* (Paris, 2007), 46.

134. For Latin: Stotz 1§24.1–6.

135. *TLL* 10.1: 2389–91, s.v. "plebes" (II.A.3.a–b).

136. *TLL* 4: 288–89, s.v. "congregātio." See 289, lines 11–29, for its use for monks and clerics in Late Antique times.

137. MLW 3: 1081–84, s.v. "ecclesia."

138. Alternative spellings include *conctio* (CIL 1.384.18) and *concio* in antiquity (Gudeman, "contio," *TLL* 4, 429). Medieval Latin admits of even further orthographical variation: *concio, cuntio, comptio, conctio*, and *conscio*. MLW, vol. 2 ("C"), 1742, lines 49–50. By the high Middle Ages, as with most *-tio* nouns, *concio* is at least as common as *contio*.

139. Theodor Mommsen, *Römisches Staatsrecht* (Leipzig, 1871–88), vol. 1, 191–209; Adolf Berger, *Encyclopedic Dictionary of Roman Law* (Philadelphia, 1953), s.v. "contio," 413.

140. Mommsen, *Römisches Staatsrecht*, vol. 3, 305.

141. Quoted in *TLL*, s.v. "contio": "contio significat conventum, non tamen alium quam eum qui a magistratu vel a sacerdote publico per praeconem convocatur." The source is the second century epitome (S. Pompeius Festus) of a lost first-century work on the signification of words (M. Verrius Flaccus) that survives in an eighth-century summary (Paul the Deacon) attested by a single eleventh-century fragmentary manuscript (the so-called *Codex Farnesianus*), which has, in turn, been badly burned and disassembled since its rediscovery in the early modern period. The standard edition is Festus, *De verborum significatu, Sexti Pompei Festi De verborum significatu quae supersunt cum Pauli epitome*, ed. W. M. Lindsay (Leipzig, 1913). For the manuscript, see A. Moscadi, ed., *Il Festo farnesiano (Cod. Neapl. 4.A.3)* (Florence, 2001). Incidentally, Giorgio Agamben's celebrated figure of the *homo sacer* derives from this battered source. Giorgio Agamben, *Homo Sacer: Sovereign Power and Bare Life* (Stanford, 1998), 72.

142. *The Oxford Classical Dictionary*, ed. Simon Hornblower and Antony Spawforth, 4th ed. (Oxford, 2012), s.v. "contio" (Piero Treves and Andrew William Lintott), 385. See also A. M. Ward, "How Democratic Was the Roman Republic?," *New England Classical Journal* 31 (2004): 101–19. Magistrates could call off a *contio* summoned by an inferior, while tribunes could use their power of veto to prevent a *contio* from taking place.

143. *OLD*, s.v. "contio," meaning 1.

144. Lucan, *De bello civili*, 1.1, ed. Shackleton Bailey, 1.

145. *New Pauly*, vol. 3, 747.

146. *New Pauly*, vol. 3, 747; F. Pina Polo, "Procedures and Functions of Civil and Military *Contiones* in Rome," *Klio* 77 (1995): 203–16. Cf. Caesar, *Bellum Civile*, 2.32.1, ed. A. Klotz, *C. Iuli Caesaris Commentarii*, vol. 2, *Commentarii belli civilis*, revised ed. (Leipzig, 1969), 74. Idiomatically, the word could mean "public opinion." *OLD*, s.v. "contio," meaning 2.

147. *OLD*, s.v. "contio," meaning 3.

148. *OLD*, s.v. "contionor," meaning 1.

149. *OLD*, s.v. "contionor," "contionalis"; *TLL*, s.v. "contionor," "contionalis."

150. *OLD*, s.v. "contio," meaning 1a.

151. Cicero, *Epistulae ad Atticum*, 4.2.3, ed. D. R. Shackleton Bailey, *M. Tulli Ciceronis Epistulae ad Atticum*, 2 vols. (Stuttgart, 1987), vol. 1, 128; Cicero, *Post reditum in senatu*, c. 12, *M. Tulli Ciceronis scripta quae manserunt omnia*, ed. T. Maslowski (Leipzig, 1981), fasc. 21, 7; Aulus Gellius, *Noctes Atticae*, 18.7.5–8, ed. C. Hosius, *A. Gellii Noctium Atticarum Libri XX* (Leipzig, 1903), 244–45 (acknowledging two other meanings).

152. Tertullian, *De spectaculis* 5.13, ed. E. Dekkers, CCSL 1 (Turnhout, 1954).

153. Acts 12:21: "Statuto autem die Herodes vestitus veste regia sedit pro tribunali, et concionabatur ad eos." Orosius used *contio* in the historical sense, describing how Gracchus was cut down by a mob at a *contio*. See C. Zangemeister, ed., *Pauli Orosii Historiarum adversum paganos libri VII*, CSEL 5 (Leipzig, 1889), 304.

154. Venantius Fortunatus, *Vita Martini* (*BHL* 5624), book 2, line 394, ed. F. Leo, MGH AA 4.1 (Berlin, 1881) 327.

155. MLW 2.4: 1744, s.v. "contio" (II.A.2).

156. Isidore, *Et.*, 10.38: "consolator, adlocutor."

157. Isidore, *Et.*, 6.2.18: "Latine Contionator dicitur, eo quod sermo eius non specialiter ad unum, sicut in Prouerbiis, sed ad uniuersos generaliter, quasi ad totam contionem et ecclesiam dirigatur." See also Hugh of St. Victor, *Didascalicon de studio legendi*, ed. Charles Buttimer (Washington, DC, 1939), 4, 80, which repeats this explanation verbatim.

158. MLW, vol. 2 ("C"), 1744, lines 53–54.

159. Rather of Verona, *Praeloquia*, 1.31, ed. P. Reid, CCCM 46A (Turnhout, 1984), 31.

160. R. E. Latham, ed., *Dictionary of Medieval Latin from British Sources* (Oxford, 1975), s.v. "contio."

161. *AWB*, s.v. "thingâri."

162. *ARF*, s.a. 800, ed. Kurze, 112–13.

163. Stefano Gasparri, "Venezia fra l'Italia bizantina e il regno italico: La *civitas* e l'assemblea," in *Venezia Itinerari per la storia della città*, ed. S. Gasparri, G. Levi, and P. Moro (Bologna, 1997), 61–82, at 61.

164. *Codex Udalrici*, no. 84, ed. Philipp Jaffé, *Bibliotheca rerum Germanicarum* (Berlin, 1869), vol. 5, 166: "cum contione sibi comissa." This letter survives in the twelfth-century formulary-book compiled by the Bamberg cleric Udalric, designed mainly as a primer for school exercises. For the sources of this collection, see Carl Erdmann, "Zu den Quellen des Codex Udalrici," *Neues Archiv der Gesellschaft für ältere deutsche Geschichtskunde* 50 (1935): 445–53. For this use of *contio*, see J. F. Niermeyer et al., eds., *Mediae Latinitatis Lexicon Minus*, 2 vols. (Leiden, 2002), vol. 2, 309, s.v. "concio" (albeit not listing the full range of other meanings).

165. *AH* 7, no. 118, 132, 3a.

166. R. I. Moore, *The Origins of European Dissent*, revised ed. (New York, 1985), 76–78.

167. Cf. Herbert Grundmann, *Religious Movements in the Middle Ages*, trans. Steven Rowan (Notre Dame, 1995 [1935]).

168. Alan of Lille, *Anticlaudianus*, book 7, line 172, ed. R. Bossuat, *Alain de Lille: Anticlaudianus, texte critique*, Textes philosophiques du Moyen Age 1 (Paris, 1955), 177.

169. Festus, *De verborum significatu*, ed. W. M. Lindsay, *Sexti Pompei Festi De verborum significatu quae supersunt cum Pauli epitome* (Leipzig, 1913).

170. Paul the Deacon, *Carm.* 56, MGH Poetae 1, 85.

171. Paris, BnF, lat. 7691 (Spanish Glossarium), with, e.g., fol. 11r: "coors [=cohors]: Numerus militum."

172. Paschasius Radbertus, *De corpore et sanguine domini*, lines 1–5, ed. B. Paulus, CCCM 16 (Turnhout, 1969), 1: "Regis adire sacrae qui vis sollemnia mensae, / Almificum Christi corpus contingere votis, / Delicias vesci, roseum potare cruorem, / Bachica nostra velim, puero quae misimus olim, / Et niveos casto condas in pectore flores." Note that the MSS all had trouble with *bachica*, including the "oldest and best of our manuscripts" (Paulus, xii), Paris, BnF, lat. 2854, which reads "brachia nostra" (f. 1r). Other readings included "bacchica," "bachicha," "bachia," "brachia," and "munera."

173. David Ganz, "The 'Liber Glossarum': A Carolingian Encyclopedia," in *Science in Western and Eastern Civilization in Carolingian Times*, ed. P. L. Butzer and D. Lohrmann (Basel, 1993), 127–35; for the transmission of this text, see Paolo Gatti, "Liber Glossarum," in *La trasmissione dei testi latini del medioevo*, ed. Paolo Chiesa and Lucia Castaldi (Florence, 2004), vol. 1, 264–67. See also A. C. Dionisotti, "On the Nature and Transmission of Latin Glossaries," in *Les manuscrits des lexiques et glossaires de l'antiquité tardive à la fin du moyen âge*, ed. Jacqueline Hamesse (Louvain-la-Neuve, 1996), 205–50.

174. For this tradition, see Rosamond McKitterick, "Glossaries and Other Innovations in Carolingian Book Production," in *Turning Over a New Leaf: Change and Development in the Medieval Manuscript*, ed. E. Kwakkel, R. McKitterick, and R. Thomson (Leiden, 2012), 21–78.

175. Liber Glossarum: Paris, BnF, lat. 11529, fol. 72r.

176. In late Roman North Africa, *caterva* in one famous case served as a technical term for a kind of civic brawl: Augustine, *De doctrina christiana*, 4.24.53, ed. Paul Tombeur, CCSL 32 (Turnhout, 1982), 159. See Brent D. Shaw, *Sacred Violence: African Christians and Sectarian Hatred in the Age of Augustine* (Cambridge, UK, 2011), 18–28; Giovanni Alberto Cecconi, "Come finisce un rituale pagano: La 'Caterva' di Cesarea di Mauritania," in *Forme di aggregazione nel mondo romano*, ed. E. Lo Cascio and G. G. Merola (Bari, 2006), 345–61; Jerzy Rohoziński, "Ritual Violence and Society in Maghreb: Regarding a Passage of St. Augustine's *De Doctrina Christiana*," in *Euergesias Charin: Studies Presented to Benedetto Bravo and Ewa Wipszycka by Their Disciples*, ed. Tomasz Derda, Jakub Urbanik, and Marek Węcowski (Warsaw, 2002), 219–23.

177. *OLD*, s.v. "turba."

178. A. Ernout and A. Meillet, *Dictionnaire étymologique de la langue latine, histoire des mots*, 4th ed. (Paris, 1967), 707–8; Michiel de Vaan, *Etymological Dictionary of Latin and the Other Italic Languages* (Leiden, 2008), 634; cf. Greek τύρβη.

179. E.g., Horace, *Epode* 5, line 97, ed. D. R. Shackleton Bailey, *Q. Horati Flacci: Opera* (Stuttgart, 1995), 148 (throwing rocks). For the abstract usage of *vulgus* enshrined in the adverb *vulgo* / *volgo* ("commonly"), see Johann Sofer, "'Vulgo': Ein Beitrag zur Kennzeichnung der lateinischen Umgangs- und Volkssprache," *Glotta* 25 (1936): 222–29.

180. Seneca, *Ep.* 7.1, 3, *L. Annaei Senecae ad Lucilium Epistulae Morales*, ed. L. D. Reynolds (Oxford, 1965), vol. 1, 11, 12: "Quid tibi uitandum praecipue existimes quaeris? turbam.... Nihil uero tam damnosum bonis moribus quam in aliquo spectaculo desidere; tunc enim per uoluptatem facilius uitia subrepunt. Quid me existimas dicere? auarior redeo, ambitiosior, luxuriosior, immo uero crudelior et inhumanior, quia inter homines fui." For this letter, see Gregor Maurach, *Der Bau von Senecas Epistulae Morales* (Heidelberg, 1970), 45–47; Franz-Frieder Lühr, "Zur Darstellung und Bewertung von Massenreaktionen in der lateinischen Literatur," *Hermes* 107 (1979): 92–114, at 109–10.

181. *OLD*, s.v. "turba," 1a, 1b ("civil disorder"), 1c ("commotion," "upheaval").

182. It is important to distinguish between a *turba* here and a *tumultus*, which held a separate significance in Roman law. The *turba* in this particular case refers to violence done in the course of a riot. A *tumultus* was a *vis maior* against the state. See Berger, *Encyclopedic Dictionary of Roman Law*, 746.

183. *Dig.* 48.7.4.3: "Turbam autem ex quo numero admittimus? Si duo rixam commiserint, utique non accipiemus in turba id factum, quia duo turba non proprie dicentur: enimvero si plures fuerunt, decem aut quindecim homines, turba dicetur. Quid ergo, si tres aut quattuor? Turba utique non erit. Et rectissime Labeo inter turbam et rixam multum interesse ait: namque turbam multitudinis hominum esse turbationem et coetum, rixam etiam duorum."

184. Patrizia Arena, "*Turba quae in foro litigat, spectat in theatris* (Sen., *Cons. ad. Marc.* 11, 2): Osservazioni sull'utilizzo del sostantivo *turba* in Seneca, Tacito, e Svetonio," in *Forme di aggregazione nel mondo romano*, ed. Elio Lo Cascio and Giovanna D. Merola (Bari, 2007), 13–30.

185. Arena, "*Turba quae in foro litigat,*" 17 n. 14.

186. R. Winnington-Ingram, "Two Latin Idioms," *The Classical Review*, New Series 5 (1955): 139–41, at 140–41.

187. Arena, "*Turba quae in foro litigat,*" 30.

188. Pacatus, *Oratio* 2 (XII), *XII Panegyrici Latini*, ed. W. Baehrens (Leipzig, 1911), 104; Pacatus, *Oratio* 2 (XII), ed. Baehrens, 119, 138.

189. Ammianus 31.16.9; on the context of Ammianus's histories, see John Matthews, *The Roman Empire of Ammianus*, revised ed. (Ann Arbor, MI, 2007), esp. 8–32; Alan Cameron, "The Roman Friends of Ammianus," *The Journal of Roman Studies* 54 (1964): 15–28; Roger Pack, "The Roman Digressions of Ammianus Marcellinus," *Transactions and Proceedings of the American Philological Association* 84 (1953): 181–89.

190. For Ammianus's prose rhythm, see Steven Oberhelman, "The Provenance of the Style of Ammianus Marcellinus," *Quaderni urbinati di cultura classica*, n.s., 27 (1987): 79–89; Steven Oberhelman and Ralph Hall, "Meter in Accentual Clausulae of Late Imperial Latin Prose," *Classical Philology* 80 (1985): 214–27, at 215, 224–25.

191. Ammianus 14.6.25, ed. Seyfarth et al., 17.

192. Ammianus 25.9.5, ed. Seyfarth et al., 376.

193. Ammianus 14.7.15, ed. Seyfarth et al., 20: "militares auidi saepe turbarum."

194. Ammianus 29.1.5, ed. Seyfarth et al., 96: "turbarum cupiditati semper addictus."

195. Ammianus 30.1.1, ed. Seyfarth et al., 131: "Inter has turbarum difficultates, quas perfidia ducis rege Quadorum excitauit occiso per scelus, dirum in oriente committitur facinus Papa Armeniorum rege clandestinis insidiis obtruncato."

196. Ammianus 15.1.2, ed. Seyfarth et al., 37 (*igneus turbarum incentor*); 15.7.5, 56 (*turbarum acerrimus concitor*); 31.9.4, 182 (*metuendo . . . incensore turbarum*); 17.9.5, 118 (*turbarum . . . concitores*); 20.9.9, 205 (*nullas ciere potuit turbas*); 22.12.3, 277 (*ciere turbas intempestiuas*); 21.13.12, 241 (*invidia. . . . turbarum acerrima concitatrix*); 22.8.49, 270 (*auctores . . . turbarum*); 28.6.28, 93 (*deletoque tristium concitore turbarum*); 30.3.6, 139 (*turbarum rex artifex*).

197. Ammianus 20.4.6, ed. Seyfarth et al., 189.

198. Ammianus 25.3.23, ed. Seyfarth et al., 360.

199. Ammianus 27.12.17, ed. Seyfarth et al., 58: "Quae imperator doctus, ut concitandas ex hoc quoque negotio turbas consilio prudenti molliret, diuisioni acquieuit Hiberiae, ut eam medius dirimeret Cyrus et Sauromaces Armeniis finitima retineret et Lazis, Aspacures Albaniae Persis que contigua."

200. Ammianus 29.5.16, ed. Seyfarth et al., 117.

201. Ammianus 31.10.11, ed. Seyfarth et al., 184.

202. Ammianus 19.11.11, ed. Seyfarth et al., 177.

203. Ammianus 23.6.83, ed. Seyfarth et al., 323: "Sequiturque semper haec turba, tamquam addicta perenni servitio, nec stipendiis aliquando fulta nec donis."

204. Ammianus 25.3.13, ed. Seyfarth et al., 358.
205. Ammianus 29.6.15, ed. Seyfarth et al., 129: "Obsistentes fortissime turbas confluentes oppressit."
206. Ammianus 21.9.8, ed. Seyfarth et al., 229.
207. Ammianus 22.2.2, ed. Seyfarth et al., 251.
208. Ammianus 22.9.16, ed. Seyfarth et al., 273.
209. Symmachus, *Epistulae*, 10.2, ed. O. Seeck, MGH AA 6.1 (Berlin, 1883), 277: "tu nobis publicas turbas in tranquillum redegisti." Symmachus, *Relationes*, 49, ed. O. Seeck, MGH AA 6.1 (Berlin, 1883), 317: "gestorum ordinem sciscitamur: omnium convenit adsertio, nihil turbarum esse conflatum." For Symmachus's place in the cultural life of late Rome, see Alan Cameron, *The Last Pagans of Rome* (Oxford, 2011), 353–98.
210. E.g., Matthew 15:32 (Vulgate), ed. Weber-Gryson, 1550: "Iesus autem convocatis discipulis suis dixit misereor turbae...", translating the Greek in *Novum Testamentum Graece*, ed. E. Nestle, E. Nestle, B. Aland, K. Aland, et al., 28th ed. (Stuttgart, 2015), 49: "Ὁ δὲ Ἰησοῦς προσκαλεσάμενος τοὺς μαθητὰς αὐτοῦ εἶπεν Σπλαγχνίζομαι ἐπὶ τὸν ὄχλον..." Other readings: "Misereor turbae," in *Biblia sacra vulgatae editionis*, ed. Michael Hetzenauer (Innsbruck, 1906); Itala: "Contristatus sum super turbas," in *Portions of the Gospels According to St. Mark and St. Matthew from the Bobbio Ms. (k), Now Numbered G. VIII. 15 in the National Library at Turin*, ed. John Wordsworth et al., Old-Latin Biblical Texts 2 (Oxford, 1886), and J. Belsheim, ed., *Evangelium Palatinum reliqvias IV evangeliorum ante Hieronymum latine translatorum* (Christiania, 1896); Itala: "Misereor turbis," in *Codex Vercellensis*, ed. J. Belsheim (Christiania, 1894); Itala: "Misereor huic turbae," in *Codex Veronensis*, ed. J. Belsheim (Prague, 1904); Itala: "Misereor super turbam," in *A Full Collation of the Codex Sinaiticus with the Received Text of the New Testament*, ed. F. H. Scrivener (Cambridge, UK, 1864); Itala: "Misereor turbae," in *The Gospel According to St. Matthew*, ed. John Wordsworth, Old-Latin Biblical Texts 1 (Oxford, 1883). In every instance in the Beuron Card Index, the term in Matthew 15.32 is *turba* in some form. The one exception in the database is Juvencus's line: *Secreto adloquitur: Plebis miseratio multa est*, which shows how closely *plebs* and *turba* were linked during the fourth century: Juvencus, *Evangeliorum Libri IV*, 3.204, ed. J. Huemer, CSEL 24 (Vienna, 1891), 87.
211. Elizabeth Malbon, "Disciples / Crowds / Whoever: Markan Characters and Readers," *Novum Testamentum* 28 (1986): 104–30.
212. Augustine, *Ad catholicos de secta Donatistarum*, 11.29, 13.34, ed. M. Petschenig, CSEL 52 (Vienna, 1909).
213. Jerome, *Ep*. 1, ed. I. Hilberg, CSEL 54 (Vienna, 1910), 4: "totus ad spectaculum populus effunditur et, prorsus quasi migrare ciuitas putaretur, stipatis proruens portis turba densatur." Jerome, *Commentarii in euangelium Matthaei*, book 1, line 1396, ed. D. Hurst and M. Adriaen, CCSL 77 (Turnhout, 1969): "turba quoque iudaeorum non est turba credentium, sed turba tumultuantium."
214. E.g., Egeria, *Itinerarium*, c. 13.3, 24.7, 25.12, 36.2, 37.9, 49.1, ed. A. Franceschini and R. Weber, CCSL 175 (Turnhout, 1965), 54: "nunc autem in ipso uico turbae aliquantae commanent"; 68: "Et post hoc denuo tam episcopus quam omnis turba uadent denuo post Crucem et ibi denuo similiter fit sicuti et ante Crucem"; 72: "Pro sollemnitate autem et laetitia ipsius diei infinite turbae se undique colligent in Ierusolima, non solum monazontes, sed et laici, uiri aut mulieres"; 79–80: "Et iam inde cum ymnis usque ad minimus infans in gessamani pedibus cum episcopo descendent, ubi pre tam magna turba multitudinis et fatigati de uigiliis et ieiuniis cotidianis lassi, quia tam magnum montem necesse habent descendere, lente et lente cum ymnis uenitur in Gessamani"; 82: "Maxima autem turba peruigilant, alii de sera, alii de media nocte, qui ut possunt"; 90: "Nam ante plurimos dies incipiunt se undique colligere turbae non solum monachorum uel aputactitum de diuersis prouinciis, id est tam de Mesopotamia uel Syria uel de Egypto aut Thebaida, ubi plurimi monazontes sunt, sed et de diuersis omnibus locis uel

prouinciis; nullus est enim, qui non se eadem die in Ierusolima tendat ad tantam laetitiam et tam honorabiles dies; seculares autem tam uiri quam feminae fideli animo propter diem sanctum similiter se de omnibus prouinciis isdem diebus Ierusolima colligunt."

215. Victricius of Rouen, *De laude sanctorum*, 1, 3, 12.1, ed. J. Mulders and R. Demeulenaere, CCSL 64 (Turnhout, 1985), 69 (*inter turbas sanctorum*), 74 (*turba castorum*), 88 (*turba sanctorum*).

216. Gregory the Great, *Moralia in Job*, 1.30, ed. M. Adriaen, CCSL 143 (Turnhout, 1979), 47. Job's "very great family" (*familia multa nimis*) (Job 1.3) is interpreted exegetically as the "numberless thoughts held under the mastery of the mind" (*cogitationes innumeras sub mentis dominatione*). We "hold together" our thoughts just as the master of a household controls his kin, so that a "crowd of thoughts" (*cogitationum turba*) may be likened to a "great family." Gregory adds that when reason, the household's mistress (*domina = ratio*), departs, this community of "cogitations" (tellingly, this word is also feminine) falls into disorder (*clamor*). Irrational thoughts are an unruled household, "just as a chattering crowd (*turba*) of servingwomen increases in number." Here, *turba* is simply a term for a crowd, although an interestingly gendered one. It is the absence of restraint, the presence of "disorder," and the "chattering" that give the *turba* its negative stamp.

217. Sidonius Apollinaris, *Carm.* no. 1, line 13, ed. André Loyen, *Sidoine Apollinaire*, vol. 1, *Poèmes* (Paris, 1960), 2; Sidonius Apollinaris, *Carm.* no. 7, line 572, ed. Loyen, 76.

218. Cassiodorus, *Variae* 1.4.1, ed. Å. J. Fridh, CCSL 96 (Turnhout, 1958), 13: "optamus, ut Libertatis genius gratam uideat turbam senatus."

219. Cassiodorus, *Variae* 3.33.2, 9.7.6, ed. Fridh, 121, 355.

220. Cassiodorus, *Variae*, 11.39.2, ed. Fridh, 457: "[Nam quam] breui numero esse poterat, qui mundi regimina possidebat. Testantur enim turbas ciuium amplissima spatia murorum, spectaculorum distensus amplexus, mirabilis magnitudo thermarum et illa numerositas molarum, quam specialiter contributam constat ad uictum." Here Fridh conjectures (and prints) "numquam" for the manuscripts' "nam quam," which would make sense ("Never could she be small in number . . .") but lacks manuscript support. For the first two words of the text printed above, therefore, I have preferred the reading in the edition of the *Variae* by Theodor Mommsen, in MGH AA 12 (Berlin, 1894), 352–53, and Giardina et al., ed., *Varie*, vol. 5, 62.

221. Cf. Raymond Van Dam, *Rome and Constantinople: Rewriting Roman History during Late Antiquity* (Waco, TX, 2012), 1–46, esp. 16–24.

222. Roberto Meneghini and Riccardo Santangeli Valenzani, *Roma nell'Altomedioevo: Topografia e urbanistica della città dal V al X secolo* (Rome, 2004), 21–27.

223. E.g., Alcuin, *Ep.* no. 249, ed. Dümmler, 402. See above, p. 111.

224. Stephen of Auxerre, *Vita S. Amatoris* (BHL 356), AASS Maii 1.1.58. Compare the slippage between the concrete term *manus* and the abstract term *multitudo* made explicit in the gloss to the early tenth-century *Gesta Berengarii*, book 1, line 145, ed. P. von Winterfeld, MGH Poetae 4.1 (Berlin, 1899), 364 (*manus multitudo*). On the glossator, see E. Bernheim, "Der Glossator der *Gesta Berengarii imperatoris*," *Forschungen zur deutschen Geschichte* 14 (1874): 138–54.

225. Archanaldus of Angers, *Vita Maurilii ep. Andegavensis* (BHL 5731), 16.94, ed. B. Krusch, MGH AA 4.2 (Berlin, 1885), 94: "Taliterque propriam regressus ad urbem, nimirum spectantibus turbis, de domini promissione securus venit ad pueri tumulum." This life, which purports to be by Fortunatus, is in fact the work of a deacon of Angers named Archanaldus, who wrote it in 905.

226. In an eighth-century life: Donatus, *Vita Ermenlandi* (BHL 3851), c. 1, ed. W. Levison, MGH SRM 5 (Hanover, 1910), 685: "Ipse vero gaudens, quia Dei virum in domum suam suscipere meruit, convocatis amicorum turbis, hilariter omnibus iussit cum pauperibus et peregrinis supervenientibus ex eodem vino ubertim distribui."

227. In a ninth-century saint's life, Saint Condedus draws in crowds (*turbae*) to hear his preaching on the Old and New Testament: *Vita Condedi anachoretae Belcinnacensis* (BHL 1907),

c. 7, ed. W. Levison, MGH SRM 5 (Hanover, 1910), 649: "O quam felix et beata insula Belcinnaca, beluarum quondam nutrix, nunc quoque servorum Christi secretissima quies! Hic namque vir sanctus fervore sanctae conversationis accensus, artiori animi studio se ipsum macerando constringebat et confluentium ad se turbas suavi fovebat alloquio, pandens de thesauro sui cordis nova et vetera." A subsequent epitome designed for liturgical use depicts the same scene: *Vita Condedi* (BHL 1908), c. 2, AASS Oct. 9.21.355A. For these lives, see Felice Lifshitz, *The Norman Conquest of Pious Neustria: Historiographic Discourse and Saintly Relics, 684–1090* (Toronto, 1995), 94–96. Compare a late tenth-century life of the Carolingian saint Ida: Uffingus, *Vita s. Idae* (BHL 4143), c. 12, AASS Sep. 2.4.265E: "Superveniente quadam sacrosancta Pentecostes solennitate, quando plus solito conflua turba eumdem locum annuatim frequenta..."

228. A crowd of monks in Ambrosius Autpertus (mid-eighth-century, Volturno), *Vita sanctorum patrum Paldonis, Tatonis et Tasonis* (BHL 6415), c. 14, *Ambrosii Autperti Opera*, ed. Robert Weber, part 3, CCCM 27B (Turnhout, 1979), 901: "Interea turba fratrum succrescente, coeperunt contra uotum habere per quod possent eisdem quod regebant subuenire. Dumque praedicti uenerabilis patris Thomae immemores dicti, multos per eos in hoc loco esse saluandos, amicam paupertatem sollicite requirentes, abicere conantur ea quae possidere uidebantur. Sed resistente eis diuino iudicio turba fratrum, studuerunt magis secundum Apostolum non sua singuli, sed quae alterius sunt quaerere." A "faithful *turba*" deposits the relics of Saint Audomar: *Vita Audomari* III (BHL 768, 769, 771), 4.37, AASS Sep. 3.9.414D: "Fidelis vero turba, per vim apertis januis, sanctas reliquias introduxit, easque super altare, prout dignum erat, constituit." In the ninth-century life of abbess Anstrudis of Laon, the term *turba* is used for a crowd of sisters: *Vita Anstrudis abbatissae Laudunensae* (BHL 556), c. 21, ed. B. Krusch and W. Levison, MGH SRM 6 (Hanover, 1913), 74 (*turbam sororum*). A crowd of "girls": *Karolus Magnus et Leo Papa*, line 258, MGH Poetae 1, 372: "Turba puellarum circumstrepit agmine denso."

229. *Translatio Viti martyris* (BHL 8718–19), c. 5, ed. I. Schmale-Ott, *Ubertragung des heiligen Martyrers Vitus*, Vertöffentlichungen der historischen Kommission für Westfalen 41 (Münster, 1979), 48: "habens secum turbam copiosam tam suorum monachorum quam aliorum virorum."

230. W. Horn and E. Born, *The Plan of St. Gall: A Study of the Architecture and Economy of, and Life in a Paradigmatic Carolingian Monastery*, 3 vols. (Berkeley, 1979), vol. 3, 17.

231. Horn and Born, *Plan of St. Gall*, vol. 3, 81. A facsimile of the Saint Gall Plan can now be consulted online at: http://www.stgallplan.org/en/.

232. Though it should be remembered that early medieval scribes copied Seneca's text: Claudia Villa, "La tradizione delle *Ad Lucilium* e la cultura di Brescia dell'età carolingia ad albertano," *Italia medioevale e umanistica* 12 (1969): 9–51.

233. E.g., *Miracula Audoeni* (BHL 761), AASS Aug. 4.24.839A: "in vigiliis ejusdem solennitatis fidelium turbis se immiscuit"; "omni spectante turba"; 839D: "ad cujus novitatem miraculi, velut ad spectaculum, populosæ civitatis confluentibus turbis." Milo of Saint-Amand, *Vita Amandi episcopi* II (Suppletio Milonis) (BHL 339–43b), c. 6, 8, ed. B. Krusch and W. Levison, MGH SRM 5 (Hanover, 1910), 473, 482. For this ninth-century text, see Mériaux, *Gallia irradiata*, 347–48. See also Heiric of Auxerre, *Miracula Germani* (BHL 3462, 3463, 3464), AASS Jul. 7.31.266E, for a saint's cure of an invalid who was "among the crowds of people coming forth" (*inter turbas properantium*); *Vita Genovefae* (BHL 3335), c. 42, ed. B. Krusch, MGH SRM 2 (Hanover, 1888), 233: "Et magnificavit universa turba Deum pro repentina incolomitate meritis Genovefae Claudiae reddita." See also the use of the *turba* in the ninth-century poetic hagiography of Heiric of Auxerre, *Vita Germani Autissiodorensis* (BHL 3458), c. 1.248, 2.160, 3.301, 4.52, 57, 4.189, 4.251, ed. L. Traube, MGH Poet. 3 (Berlin, 1886), 445, 457, 477, 480, 481. On Heiric's lengthy verse epic, see Wolfgang Kirsch, *Laudes Sanctorum: Geschichte der hagiographischen Versepik vom IV bis X Jahrhundert*, 2 vols. (Stuttgart, 2004), vol. 2.2, 843–61.

234. In the eighth-century *Translatio Heliani Beneventum a. 763* (BHL 3799), c. 2, ed. G. Waitz, MGH SRL 1 (Hanover, 1878), 582: "Cumque Beneventi meniis propinquasset, cum cereis

et lampadibus ac diverso thimiamatum genere omnis turba confluxit per stadiorum aliqua spatia; et sic cum ymnis et canticis introductum sanctissimum corpus, honorifice situm est in basilica, quam ille antequam iret construxerat."

235. *Translatio Regnoberti et Zenonis* (*BHL* 7063), c. 5, AASS Mai 3.16.621B, dated to the ninth century.

236. *Translatio Regnoberti et Zenonis* (*BHL* 7063), c. 8, AASS Mai 3.16.622D: "Quantus Monachorum aderat ordo! Canonicorum quam plurima turba! Videlicet ex vicinis provinciis ibi confluxerat omnis multitudo populi . . ."

237. *Translatio Regnoberti et Zenonis* (*BHL* 7063), c. 8, AASS Mai 3.16.622D–E: "Pluvia enim totam illam regionem instar fluviorum irrigaverat, sed in loco, quo populus ad festivitatem celebrandam convenerat, nihil omnino pluit."

238. *Missale Gothicum*, ed. Els Rose, *Missale Gothicum: e codice Vaticano Reginensi Latino 317 editum*, CCSL 159D (Turnhout, 2005), rubric 677.

239. *Missale Gothicum*, ed. Rose, rubric 341: "Deus quem . . . angelorum multitudo conlaudat."

240. E.g., *Missale Gothicum*, ed. Rose, ordo 4, oratio 17 (p. 356): "Omnes denique turba exultabat angelorum, quia terra regem suscepit aeternum."

241. *AH* 27, no. 184, 260: "Te sacra cleri populique turba . . . poscit."

242. Henry Miller Martin, "Some Phases of Grammatical Concord in Certain Merovingian Charters," *Speculum* 4 (1929): 303–14, at 309 (with *congregatio* and *caterva* discussed at 307–9).

243. *Marculfi Formulae* 1.2, 2.3, ed. K. Zeumer, MGH Formulae 1 (Hanover, 1886), 41 (line 16), 75 (lines 7–8). *Formulae Augienses*, Collectio A, c. 13, ed. K. Zeumer, MGH Formulae 1 (Hanover, 1886), 344 (line 41). On the formulary of Marculf, see K. Zeumer, "Zur Herkunft der Markulfischen Formeln," *Neues Archiv der Gesellschaft für ältere deutsche Geschichtskunde* 30 (1905): 716–19; Wilhelm Levison, "Zu Marculfs Formularbuch," *Neues Archiv der Gesellschaft für ältere deutsche Geschichtskunde* 50 (1935): 616–19; Alice Rio, *Legal Practice and the Written Word in the Early Middle Ages: Frankish Formulae, c. 500–1000* (Cambridge, UK, 2009), 81–103. At 20–26, Rio argues forcefully for the historical utility of the formularies as evidence for social, economic, and legal life in the early Middle Ages. For the so-called *Formulae Augienses*, see Karl Zeumer, "Über die alamannischen Formelsammlungen," *Neues Archiv der Gesellschaft für ältere deutsche Geschichtskunde* 8 (1883): 473–553, who divides the formulary into three collections (A, B, and C); Rio, *Legal Practice*, 144–50, provides a lucid critique of this division, with an overview of the manuscripts.

244. D Mer. no. 192, ed. T. Kölzer, MGH DD Mer. 1 (Hanover, 2001), 478; D Pippin no. 17, ed. E. Mühlbacher, MGH DD Kar. 1 (Hanover, 1906), 25 (line 40); D Charlemagne, ed. E. Mühlbacher, MGH DD Kar. 1 (Hanover, 1906), 137 (line 17).

245. Einhard, *Vita Karoli* (*BHL* 1580), c. 22, ed. O Holder-Egger, MGH SRG 25 (Munich, 1911), 27.

246. Anastasius Bibliothecarius, *Miracula S. Demetrii* (*BHL* 2123), PL 129, col. 722A–B: "Eusebius Thessalonicae civitatis archiepiscopus visionem vidit quam narrare cupio vobis. Antequam super civitatem Thessalonicam barbarici irruerent nimbi, vidit se praedictus pontifex in somnis sedere in theatro civitatis cum magna turba famulorum." For this text, see Benedetta Valtorta, *Clavis scriptorum Latinorum Medii aevi: Auctores Italiae (700–1000)* (Florence, 2006), 29.

247. Anastasius Bibliothecarius, *Miracula S. Demetrii* (*BHL* 2123), PL 129, col. 722B: "Innumerabilis barbarorum multitudo."

248. J. Castro Sánchez, ed., *Hymnodia hispanica*, CCSL 167 (Turnhout, 2010), 195: "Non ut fallax discipulus, / qui pacem ferens osculo / et dolum tenens pectore / turbis magistrum tradidit."

249. Castro Sánchez, ed., *Hymnodia hispanica*, 581: "tenebrosis dominare turbisque demonicis."

250. Hilduin of St-Denis, *Passio Dionysii* (BHL 2174), c. 32, 33, PL 106, col. 47A (*Tantaque multitudo fidelium*), 47B (*multitudo coelestis exercitus*), 47D ([*Larcia*] *prosiluit in infidelium turbas*). For an invading *turba* of pagans in an eighth-century hagiographical text, see Anso of Lobbes, *Vita Erminonis episcopi et abbatis Lobbiensis* I (BHL 2614), c. 7, ed. W. Levison, MGH SRM 6 (Hanover, 1913), 466.

251. *Vita Alcuini* (BHL 242), c. 2, ed. W. Arndt, MGH SS 15.1 (Hanover, 1887), 185: "malorum subito disparuit turba."

252. Adrevald of Fleury, *Vita Aigulfi* (BHL 194), PL 124, col. 960A: "turba stipatus maligna."

253. *Vita Wandregiseli* (BHL 8805), c. 4, AASS Jul. 5.22.273A–B.

254. Amolo of Lyon, *Epistolae*, no. 1, c. 2, ed. Ernst Dümmler, MGH E5 (Berlin, 1899), 364: "admirantium et stupentium turba." See further in chapter 4.

255. Bobrycki, "Flailing Women," 11–12, 16.

256. *Passio Sancti Saturnini* (BHL 7491), c. 23, ed. Antonio Piras (Rome, 2002), 41: "Quo audito, ab uno de turba uel ab ipso nequissimo sacerdote memoratus beatissimus Saturninus martyr gladio grauiter uulneratus, Christum Dominum confitendo sanguinem effundens, spiritum tradidit beatorum conmartyrum suorum choris adiunctus III kalendarum Novembrium die." The *Passio Sancti Saturnini* was traditionally thought to have been compiled in the eleventh or twelfth century as a pastiche of elements drawn from the hagiographical dossier of the more famous Saturninus of Toulouse. The *passio*'s recent editor, Antonio Piras, argues for an earlier dating, between the end of the sixth century and the end of the eighth century, basing this assertion, not very compellingly, on the presence of language redolent of Cassiodorus, Gregory the Great, and Bede (d. 735) (*Passio Sancti Saturnini*, ed. Piras, 15–16). As Richard Gyug rightly notes in his review of the edition in *Journal of Medieval Latin* 13 (2003): 279–81, at 280, Piras's argument merely establishes a "terminus ante quem non," since authors such as Cassiodorus, Gregory the Great, and Bede continue to be quoted throughout the Middle Ages. Nevertheless, Gyug concedes, on the basis of the Latinity of the *passio*, that "there is little reason to doubt that the *Passio* is early." Further philological examination may shed light on the question. Note a possible reference (*ab uno de turba*) to Augustine's passage about Alypius in the *Confessions*.

257. *Passio Sancti Saturnini* (BHL 7491), c. 11, ed. Piras, 39: "Crescebat autem per singulos turba fidelium et multiplicabantur apud deum coronae iustorum"; c. 13, 39: "Ad quod sceleratorum turbae cum inmundis hostiis concurrebant."

258. A villain in an eighth-century saint's life smashes through a set of doors with the help of a "mighty crowd" (*multitudo*) of accomplices: *Vita Landiberti episcopi Traeiectensis vetustissima* (BHL 4677), c. 13, ed. B. Krusch and W. Levison, MGH SRM 6 (Hanover, 1913), 367: "Cum vero Dodo et plurima multitudo sodaliorum eius cum eo adpropinquassent et intrare cepissent ianuis, fractisque osteis et sepis disruptis, et supermontare cepissent, cumque vidisset hec memoratus puer [a certain boy of the saint's household named Baldoveus], subito currens nunciavit pontifici." Cf. *Vita Landiberti episcopi Traeiectensis vetustissima*, c. 24, ed. Krusch and Levison, 378: "Nam in modicum tempus post visionem revelata de multitudinem hostium, que cum Dodono domestico ad necem sancti Landiberti fuerunt, pauci ex eos infra annum remanserunt." It is typical of the lack of a specific positive or negative valence that the word *multitudo* also describes the "copious crowd of men" that elects Landibert (*Vita Landiberti episcopi Traeiectensis vetustissima*, c. 4, ed. Krusch and Levison, 356) and the "great crowd of Christians" that attends his funeral (*Vita Landiberti episcopi Traeiectensis vetustissima*, c. 25, ed. Krusch and Levison, 379).

259. E.g., ARF, s.a. 775, ed. Kurze, 41, 43; s.a. 780, 57; s.a. 783, 65; s.a. 788, 83; s.a. 828, 176.

260. AH 51, p. 359: "Timor, tremor / taetras turbas terreat."

261. This is Hucbald of Saint-Amand's alliterative *Ecloga de calvis* (ninth century), whose 146 verses famously all begin with the letter C. Here, Hucbald praises those bald saints who have cured "blind crowds" (*caecas . . . catervas*): Hucbald of Saint-Amand, *Ecloga de calvis*, ed. P. von

Winterfeld, MGH Poetae 4.1 (Berlin, 1899), 269. For Hucbald, see Franz Brunhölzl, *Histoire de la littérature latine du Moyen Âge*, trans. Henri Rochais with Jean-Paul Bouhot (Turnhout, 1990–96), vol. 2, 509–11; Wattenbach-Levison-Löwe, fasc. 5 (Weimar, 1973), 552–55.

262. But see R. I. Moore, "Family, Community and Cult on the Eve of the Gregorian Reform," *Transactions of the Royal Historical Society*, 6th ser., 30 (1980): 49–69, at 50, for the persistence of "comparatively neutral terms" alongside "an occasional *turba*."

263. Stokes, ed., *Three Irish Glossaries*, 42.

264. Laurent Waelkens, "L'origine de l'enquête par turbe," *Tijdschrift voor rechtsgeschiedenis* 53 (1985): 337–46; Jean-François Poudret, "Réflexions sur la preuve de la coutume devant les juridictions royales françaises aux XIIIe et XIVe siècles, notamment le rôle de l'enquête par turbe," in Jean-François Poudret, *Coutumes et libertés: Recueil d'articles* (Dijon, 2009 [1987]), 72–89.

265. *AH* 11, no. 32, 25 ("De Corpore Christi," fourteenth century): "Jam lucis orto sidere / Sacramenti mysterium / Corde, ore et opera / Psallat turba fidelium."

Chapter 6. Representations

1. E.g., witnesses: *Vita Germani ep. Parisiensis II brevior* (*BHL* 3469), c. 3, ed. B. Krusch and W. Levison, MGH SRM 7 (Hanover, 1920), 421 (*fratrum caterva mirans*); *Vita Alpini episcopi Cabilonensis* (*BHL* 310), c. 13, AASS Sep. 3.7.89A–B (a man blinded by demons is cured in the view of large crowds); *Virtutes Fursei* (*BHL* 3213), c. 6, ed. B. Krusch, MGH SRM 4 (Hanover, 1902), 442 (a "large crowd of men and women in lamentation" comes to the house of a man they believed dead, who has been resurrected by a saint); Herard of Tours, *Vita Chrodegangi episcopi Sagiensis, translationes et miracula* (*BHL* 1782, 1784), 2.16, AASS Sep. 1.3.771A (*multitudo supervenientum fidelium* [crowd drawn to a miraculous sound]); *Vita Genovefae* (*BHL* 3335), c. 25, ed. B. Krusch, MGH SRM 2 (Hanover, 1888), 226 (crowds exulting in the wake of a miracle). Entourages: *Karolus Magnus et Leo papa*, lines 153–76, ed. H. Beumann, F. Brunhölzl, and W. Winkelmann, *Karolus Magnus et Leo Papa: Ein paderborner Epos vom Jahre 799* (Paderborn, 1966), 70–72; Ermoldus Nigellus, *Carmen in honorem Hludowici Caesaris*, 4.2175–77, ed. E. Faral, *Ermold le Noir: Poème sur Louis le Pieux et Épitres au Roi Pépin*, Les Classiques de l'Histoire de France au Moyen Age 14 (Paris 1964), 166. Both texts draw on Vergil's much used hexametric line ending: *cominante caterva / stipante caterva* (Vergil, Aen., 2.40, 2.370, 4.136). Cf. Richard Heinze, *Virgils epische Technik*, 2nd ed. (Leipzig, 1908), 13–15. Rapt multitudes: Jonas of Bobbio, *Vita Columbani abbatis discipulorumque* (*BHL* 1898), 1.10, ed. B. Krusch, MGH SRG 37 (Hanover, 1905), 169: "Ibi residens vir egregius, monasterium construere coepit, ad cuius famam plebes undique concurrere et cultui religionis dicare curabant, ita ut plurima monachorum multitudo adunata, vix unius caenubii collegio sistere valeret." Crowds in search of aid: *Vita Amati* (*BHL* 362), c. 13, AASS Sep. 4.13.130C: "Præterea multi dæmoniaci, cæci, ad exequias Sancti convenientes, incolumes ad propria redierunt"; *Vita Boniti episcopi Arverni* (*BHL* 1418), c. 27, ed. B. Krusch and W. Levison, MGH SRM 6 (Hanover, 1913), 132: "Cumque post hec eum infirmantium turba ubique prosequeretur, sed ille iactantiae vicium cavens, ubicumque potuisset, semet ipsum ospitiolo trudebat et infirmos ex oleo, quod ex beati Petri sepulcro benedictione levari iusserat, ungi praecipiebat"; Aimoin, *Translatio sanctorum Georgii, Aurelii et Nathaliae* (*BHL* 3409), PL 115, col. 949C: "compressantibus se hinc inde turbis."

2. Alex Woloch, *The One vs. the Many: Minor Characters and the Space of the Protagonist in the Novel* (Princeton, NJ, 2003), 4–6, 246–54.

3. Joaquín Martínez Pizarro, "The King Says No: On the Logic of Type-Scenes in Late Antique and Early Medieval Narrative," in *The Long Morning of Medieval Europe: New Directions in Early Medieval Studies*, ed. J. R. Davis and M. McCormick (Aldershot, UK, 2008), 181–92, at 191–92.

4. Paul Lehmann, *Die Parodie im Mittelalter*, 2nd ed. (Stuttgart, 1963), 1: "Die lateinische Literatur des Mittelalters ist voller Entlehnungen und Nachahmungen. Oft bis zum Überdruß klingen uns aus ihr Gedanken, Verse und Sätze, Phrasen, Worte und Wörter der Antike, der Bibel, der Kirchenväter, okzidentaler und orientalischer Schriftstücke verschiedener Zeiten und Gattungen entgegen. Bewußt und unbewußt hat man die Autoritäten von Kirche und Schule immer wieder sprechen lassen. Der Erforscher der mittellateinischen Poesie und Prosa hat nicht allein die mühsame Aufgabe, die Zitate, die zahlreichen Nachahmungen und Anklänge auf ihre Quellen zurückzuführen und taktvoll—wie es leider oft nicht geschehen ist—zu unterscheiden, was wirklich Entlehnung, was unbewußte Herübernahme im ganzen oder einzelnen ist, sondern auch zu beurteilen, das Urteil darüber vorzubereiten, ob und inwieweit das Mittelalter trotz der gewollten und ungewollten Verkettung mit der Vergangenheitsliteratur sich in den Gefilden der Gedanken, des Wortes aufrecht und frei bewegt hat."

5. Franz Quadlbauer, "Topik," in *Lexikon des Mittelalters* (Munich, 1997), vol. 8, col. 864–67. A. J. Festugière, "Lieux communs littéraires et thèmes de folk-lore dans l'hagiographie primitive," *Wiener Studien* 73 (1960): 123–52, esp. 124; Jacques Fontaine, "Un cliché de la spiritualité antique tardive: *Stetit immobilis*," in *Romanitas—Christianitas: Untersuchungen zur Geschichte und Literatur der römischen Kaiserzeit: Johannes Straub zum 70. Geburtstag*, ed. K-H. Schwarte and G. Wirth (Berlin, 1982), 528–52, esp. 551–52; see also the definition in Thomas Pratsch, *Der hagiographische Topos: Griechische Heiligenviten in mittelbyzantinischer Zeit* (Berlin, 2005), 355: "Ein Topos ist ein relativ feststehendes literarisches Motiv, eine literarische Konstante, die innerhalb der byzantinischen hagiographischen Literatur breite Anwendung gefunden hat, stets neu aufgegriffen und auf diesem Wege tradiert wurde."

6. Ernst Robert Curtius, *European Literature and the Latin Middle Ages*, trans. W. R. Trask (Princeton, NJ, 1953), 70 (compare p. x, where he speaks of a "technique of philological microscopy"). These ideas reiterate Curtius's earlier "Zur Literarästhetik des Mittelalters II," *Zeitschrift für romanische Philologie* 58 (1938): 129–232, at 129–43, esp. 139–40. For the intellectual origins of Curtius's concept, see Stefan Goldmann, "Zur Herkunft des Topos-Begriffs von Ernst Robert Curtius," *Euphorion* 90 (1996): 134–45. In classical rhetoric, the term *topos* (or Latin *locus*) had a specific function as part of *inventio*: Aristotle, *Ars Rhetorica*, 2.22–23.1395b–1400b, ed. R. Kassel (Berlin, 1976), 121–38; Quintilian, *Institutio oratoriae*, 5.10.20–22, ed. M. Winterbottom, 2 vols. (Oxford, 1970), vol. 1, 257–58. See also Heinrich Lausberg, *Handbook of Literary Rhetoric: A Foundation for Literary Study*, ed. and trans. M. T. Bliss et al. (Leiden, 1998), 119–20 (§ 260), 171–96 (§§ 373–409); Leonid Arbusow, *Colores rhetorici: Eine Auswahl rhetorischer Figuren und Gemeinplätze als Hilfsmittel für akademische Übungen an mittelalterlichen Texten*, ed. Helmut Peter, 2nd revised ed. (Göttingen, 1963), 91–121.

7. Joaquín Martínez Pizarro, *A Rhetoric of the Scene: Dramatic Narrative in the Early Middle Ages* (Toronto, 1989), 19, defines "a scene in narrative" as "the representation of a transaction between particular characters in their own words and actions, without the mediation of authorial commentary." Pizarro contrasts scenic presentation, which he characterizes as fundamentally oral and fundamentally early medieval (cf. 36: "scenes" are "the basic unit of early medieval narrative") with "the narrative of classical historiography" which is "authorial, exemplary, and summarizing" (19). A type scene is thus a repeatable scene (35, cf. 96). See also Pizarro, "The King Says No," 181–82. For earlier biblical scholarship using type scenes, see Robert Alter, "Biblical Type-Scenes and the Uses of Convention," *Critical Inquiry* 5 (1978): 355–68. Classical scholarship had already pioneered the study of conventional scenes: Walter Arend, *Die typischen Scenen bei Homer* (Berlin, 1933), 1–27.

8. Pizarro, *Rhetoric of the Scene*, 35 (prophet), 87 (deathbed), 51–52 (healing). Cf. Pizarro, "The King Says No," 182–91 (access). See also Jamie Kreiner, *The Social Life of Hagiography in the Merovingian Kingdom* (Cambridge, UK, 2014), 92–104, for the "scenic style" in the context of hagiographic mnemonic techniques.

9. Peter Dronke, *Poetic Individuality in the Middle Ages: New Departures in Poetry, 1000–1150*, 2nd ed. (London, 1986), 1–22, esp. 11–22, for a devastating critique of Curtius's tendency to underestimate the diversity of medieval poetry, his underestimation of individual agency, and his claims to "empirical soundness" (11). See also Erich Auerbach, *Literatursprache und Publikum in der lateinischen Spätantike und im Mittelalter* (Bern, 1958), 69, for Auerbach's treatment of Curtius's concept of topos. For an overview, see Albrecht Classen, "Robert Curtius and the Topos of the Book: The Impact of an Idea on Modern Philological Research," *Leuvense Bijdragen* 87 (1998): 59–78.

10. For Auerbach's historicism, see Jan Ziolkowski, "Foreward," to Erich Auerbach, *Literary Language and Its Public in Late Latin Antiquity and in the Middle Ages*, trans. R. Manheim (Princeton, NJ, 1993), ix–xxxix; Pizarro, "The King Says No," 191–92.

11. For overviews, see Martin Heinzelmann, *Translationsberichte und andere Quellen des Reliquienkultes*, Typologie Des Sources 33 (Turnhout, 1979); René Aigrain, *L'Hagiographie: Ses sources—ses méthodes—son histoire* (Brussels, 1953). See also the ongoing multivolume series dedicated to hagiographical traditions on a regional basis, with nine volumes so far: Guy Philippart et al., eds., *Hagiographies: Histoire internationale de la littérature hagiographique latine et vernaculaire en Occident des origines à 1550* (Turnhout, 1994–). For an example of a common *topos* among relic translation accounts, the incorruptibility of the saint's body, see Arnold Angenendt, "*Corpus incorruptum*: Eine Leitidee der mittelalterlichen Reliquienverehrung," *Saeculum* 42 (1991): 320–48.

12. Erich Auerbach, *Mimesis: The Representation of Reality in Western Literature*, trans. W. R. Trask (Princeton, NJ, 1957), 52, discussing how, for Ammianus Marcellinus, riots were the result of mere "stupid effrontery." This builds on Ammianus 15.7.1, ed. Seyfarth et al., 55–56.

13. For Vergil's enduring influence, Jan M. Ziolkowski and Michael C. J. Putnam, eds., *The Virgilian Tradition: The First Fifteen Hundred Years* (New Haven, CT, 2008).

14. E.g., Baudonivia, *Vita Radegundis* (*BHL* 7049), book 2, c. 2, ed. B. Krusch, MGH SRM 2 (Hanover, 1888), 380: "Hoc audientes Franci universaque multitudo cum gladiis et fustibus vel omni fremitu diabolico conabantur defendere; sancta vero regina inmobilis perseverans, Christum in pectore gestans, equum quem sedebat in antea non movit, antequam et fanus perureretur, et, ipsa orante, inter se populi pacem firmarent." Baudonivia's depiction builds on the *stetit immobilis* topos (Fontaine, "Un cliché") but also on the ancient topos of the man (or, as here, woman) who controls the unruly crowd (quintessentially Vergil, *Aen.* 1.148–53). For another example, see the bilingual seventh- or eighth-century *Vita Brigitae* (*Bethu Brigte*), c. 40: Donncha Ó hAodha, ed. and trans., *Bethu Brigte* (Dublin, 1978), 31.

15. Vergil, *Aen.* 4.136: "magna stipante caterva."

16. Rachel Stone, *Morality and Masculinity in the Carolingian Empire* (Cambridge, UK, 2012); Andrew Romig, *Be a Perfect Man: Christian Masculinity and the Carolingian Aristocracy* (Philadelphia, 2017).

17. Peter Brunt, "The Roman Mob," *Past & Present* 35 (1966): 3–27; Z. Yavetz, "Vitellius and the 'Fickleness of the Mob,'" *Historia* 18 (1969): 557–69. Seneca's letter to Lucilius about the crowd (cited below) is a *locus classicus* for anti-crowd anxieties among the Greco-Roman elite. For the crowd as the site of just indignation, Livy, *Ab urbe condita*, 3.49.1–2, ed. R. M. Ogilvie, *Titi Livi Ab urbe condita*, vol. 1, *Libri I–V* (Oxford, 1974), 211: "Concitatur multitudo partim atrocitate sceleris, partim spe per occasionem repetendae libertatis" (in connection with the evil deeds of the decimvir Appius Claudius Crassus toward the plebeian virgin Verginia).

18. E.g., Beno, *Gesta Romanae ecclesiae contra Hildebrandum*, no. 1, c. 7, ed. K. Francke, MGH LdL 2 (Hanover, 1892), 372 (*vulgus indoctum*). See Alexander Murray, *Reason and Society in the Middle Ages* (Oxford, 1978), 234–57, on the rise of an anti-crowd polemics in the twelfth century. But there are Carolingian examples, such as Hrabanus Maurus, *Expositio in Matthaeum*, book 6, ed. B. Löfstedt, CCCM 174A (Turnhout, 2000), 582: "Turba simplex et uulgus indoctum per humilitatis uiam gradiens ad credendum Domino miracula ab eo facta uenerari cogebatur."

19. Gregory of Tours, *Hist.* 3.36, ed. Krusch and Levison, 131–32.

20. Gerd Tellenbach, "Die geistigen und politischen Grundlagen der karolingischen Thronfolge: Zugleich eine Studie über kollektive Willensbildung und kollektives Handeln im neunten Jahrhundert," in G. Tellenbach, *Ausgewählte Abhandlungen und Aufsätze*, 5 vols. (Stuttgart, 1988), vol. 2, 503–621. See also Matthias Becher, *Eid und Herrschaft: Untersuchungen zum Herrscherethos Karls des Grossen* (Sigmaringen, 1993), 16–17.

21. John Contreni, "The Patristic Legacy to c. 1000," in *The New Cambridge History of the Bible*, vol. 2, *From 600 to 1450*, ed. J. Carleton Paget and J. Schaper (Cambridge, UK, 2012), 505–35, at 525–26, for the influence of the Bible on early medieval culture. See also Pizarro, *Rhetoric of the Scene*, 50–53. For the Old Testament, see Raymund Kottje, *Studien zum Einfluss des Alten Testaments auf Recht und Liturgie des frühen Mittelalters (6.–8. Jahrhundert)* (Bonn, 1970).

22. E.g., 3 Kings 3:8, ed. Weber-Gryson, 461: "et servus tuus in medio est populi quem elegisti populi infiniti qui numerari et supputari non potest prae multitudine." This language is picked up in the ninth century by Rudolf of Fulda to describe crowds thickly packed into a small oratory: *Miracula sanctorum in Fuldenses ecclesias translatorum* (BHL 7044), c. 5, ed. G. Waitz, MGH SS 15.1 (Hanover, 1887), 334: "Erat autem ibi oratorium non grande, quod intrare et feretrum inferre volentes, prae multitudine turbarum, quae praeibant et quae sequebantur, minime potuimus, ac per hoc sub divo in loco editore altari erecto, ac feretro iuxta illud posito, rursus missarum solemnia celebravimus." See also Genesis 12:2, 13:16, 15:5, 17:6, 22:17, 24:60, 28:3; Hebrews 6:14, 11:12; Romans 4:13. For bad crowds: Judges 6:5, 7:12; Joshua 11:4; Jeremiah 46:23.

23. Genesis 22:17, ed. Weber-Gryson, 30: "benedicam tibi et multiplicabo semen tuum sicut stellas caeli et velut harenam quae est in litore maris."

24. Judges 7:12; cf. Judges 6:5, Joshua 11:4, Jeremiah 46:23.

25. See, e.g., the depiction of the handing-down of the laws in the Stuttgart Psalter, Württembergische Landesbibliothek Stuttgart, Bibl. fol. 23, at Psalm [Vulgate] 77.1 ("Adtendite populus meus legem meam . . ."), fol. 90r, with an isocephalic audience dressed as Carolingian aristocrats.

26. E.g., Psalm [Vulgate] 108.30, ed. Weber-Gryson, 912: "confitebor Domino nimis in ore meo et in medio multorum laudabo eum" (Iuxta LXX); 913: "confitebor Domino vehementer in ore meo et in medio populorum laudabo eum" (Iuxta Hebr.). See, e.g., the eighth-century life by Audoenus, *Vita Eligii Noviomagensis* (BHL 2474), 2.20, ed. B. Krusch, MGH SRM 4 (Hanover 1902), 712: "Venit ergo per medias populorum turbas, et stans in quodam eminenti loco ante basilicam, coepit instantius praedicare, vehementer obiurgans populum, eo quod monitis salutaribus terga parantes, diabolicis filacteriis tantopere essent intenti"; the seventh-century collection of homilies, Eusebius "Gallicanus," *Collectio homiliarum*, ed. F. Glorie, CCSL 101A (Turnhout, 1971), homily 39 (lines 13, 19); and the ninth-century Pseudo-Isidorian forger, Ps.-Clemens, *Ep.* I, c. 37, ed. P. Hinschius, *Decretales Pseudo-Isidorianae et Capitula Angilramni* (Leipzig, 1863), 42.

27. Gregory the Great, *Homily on Ezechiel*, 2.6.22, ed. C. Morel, *Homélies sur Ezéchiel: texte latin, introduction, traduction et notes*, SC 327 (Paris, 1990), vol. 2, 312.

28. J. Carnandet and J. Fèvre, *Les Bollandistes et l'hagiographie ancienne et moderne: Études sur la collection des Actes des Saints* (Lyon, 1966), 92; Theofried Baumeister, *Martyrium, Hagiographie und Heiligenverehrung im christlichen Altertum* (Rome, 2009), 238–39; Baudouin de Gaiffier, "Miracles bibliques et Vies de saints," *Nouvelle revue théologique* 88 (1966): 376–85.

29. Christoph Winterer, "Karolingische Apokalypsenzyklen als ekklesiologischer Kommentar," in *Tot sacramenta quot verba: Zur Kommentierung der Apokalypse des Johannes von den Anfängen bis ins 12. Jahrhundert*, ed. K. Huber, R. Klotz, and C. Winterer (Münster, 2014), 343–60. For early medieval apocalypticism generally, see James Palmer, *The Apocalypse in the Early Middle Ages* (Cambridge, UK, 2014); Wolfram Brandes, "'Tempora Periculosa Sunt': Eschatologisches im Vorfeld der Kaiserkrönung Karls des Grossen," in *Das Frankfurter Konzil von 794: Kristallisationspunkt karolingischer Kultur*, ed. Rainer Berndt (Mainz, 1997), vol. 1, 49–79.

30. The word ὄχλος appears 167 times in the New Testament (forty-seven times in Matthew, thirty-four times in Mark, forty-one times in Luke, nineteen times in John, twenty-two times in Acts, and four times in Revelation). For the crowd's depiction in Mark, see Elizabeth S. Malbon, "Disciples / Crowds / Whoever: Markan Characters and Readers," *Novum Testamentum* 28 (1986): 104–30; Joel F. Williams, "Discipleship and Minor Characters in Mark's Gospel," *Bibliotheca Sacra* 153 (1996): 332–43, at 333.

31. Matthew 4:23–25, ed. Weber-Gryson, 1531: "Et circumibat Iesus totam Galilaeam docens in synagogis eorum et praedicans evangelium regni et sanans omnem languorem et omnem infirmitatem in populo et abiit opinio eius in totam Syriam et obtulerunt ei omnes male habentes variis languoribus et tormentis conprehensos et qui daemonia habebant et lunaticos et paralyticos et curavit eos et secutae sunt eum turbae multae de Galilaea et Decapoli et Hierosolymis et Iudaea et de trans Iordanen." Cf. Luke 4:42, ed. Weber-Gryson, 1614.

32. Mark 8:1–3, ed. Weber-Gryson, 1587: "in illis diebus iterum cum turba multa esset nec haberent quod manducarent convocatis discipulis ait illis, misereor super turba quia ecce iam triduo sustinent me nec habent quod manducent, et si dimisero eos ieiunos in domum suam deficient in via quidam enim ex eis de longe venerunt." Cf. Matthew 15:32, ed. Weber-Gryson, 1550.

33. Christian of Stavelot, *Expositio in euangelium Matthaei*, c. 15:32, ed. R. Huygens, CCCM 224 (Turnhout, 2008), 309: "Utraque natura domini in hoc facto monstratur, et diuina qua miraculum facit et humana qua turbae misereretur." For miraculous reduplication of distributed coins: *Passio Praeiecti episcopi et martyris Averni* (*BHL* 6915–6916), c. 6, ed. B. Krusch, MGH SRM 5 (Hanover, 1910), 22; *Vita Hadriani II*, c. 2, ed. Duchesne, *LP*, vol. 2, 173; R. Ingoglia, "'I Have Neither Silver nor Gold': An Explanation of a Medieval Papal Ritual," *The Catholic Historical Review* 85 (1999): 531–40.

34. Christian of Stavelot, *Expositio in euangelium Matthaei*, c. 25 (9:33), ed. R.B.C. Huygens, CCCM 224 (Turnhout, 2008), 210: "Et ejecto daemone locutus est mutus, et miratae sunt turbae [Matthew 9:33]. Turbae, quae minus eruditae videbantur, admirabantur semper doctrinam Domini. Pharisaei autem et Sadducaei detrahebant, vel in malam partem convertebant propter invidiam, quia dolebant pro doctrina Domini, quia Christus a turbis et sanctior et sapientior credebatur."

35. Hedwig Röckelein, *Reliquientranslationen nach Sachsen im 9. Jahrhundert: Über Kommunikation, Mobilität und Öffentlichkeit im Frühmittelalter* (Stuttgart, 2002), 359–70. For their place in court culture, see R. Le Jan, "Les cérémonies carolingiennes: Symbolique de l'ordre, dynamique de la compétition," in *Le corti nell'alto medioevo* (Spoleto, 2015), 167–94, at 180. On assemblies, see T. Reuter, "Assembly Politics in Western Europe," in T. Reuter, *Medieval Polities and Modern Mentalities*, ed. J. Nelson (Cambridge, UK, 2006), 193–216.

36. Birger Munk Olsen, *I classici nel canone scolastico altomedievale* (Spoleto, 1991), 23. Especially important were the celebrations of the saints in Prudentius, *Liber Peristefanon*, ed. M. P. Cunningham, CCSL 126 (Turnhout, 1966).

37. E.g., Prudentius, *Carm*. 4, line 57, *Liber Peristephanon*.

38. A.A.R. Bastiaensen, ed., *Atti e passioni dei martiri*, 2nd ed. (Milan, 1990). For a (probably) seventh-century example, see *Passio Afrae vetustior* (*BHL* 107b), ed. B. Krusch and W. Levison, MGH SRM 7 (Hanover, 1920), 200–204.

39. See Ramsay MacMullen, "The Place of the Holy Man in the Later Roman Empire," *Harvard Theological Review* 112 (2019): 1–32, at 16 (table 1).

40. Athanasius, *Vita Antonii*, trans. Evagrius of Antioch (*BHL* 609), PL 73, col. 125–69; *Verba seniorum* (*BHL* 6527), 1.7, PL 73, col. 855c (flight from the crowd), and see Claudia Rapp, *Holy Bishops in Late Antiquity: The Nature of Christian Leadership in an Age of Transition* (Berkeley, 2005), 100–105; Sulpicius Severus, *Vita Martini* (*BHL* 5610), ed. J. Fontaine, *Vie de Saint Martin*, 3 vols., SC 133–35 (Paris, 1967–69); Sulpicius Severus, *Dialogi*, ed. J. Fontaine, *Gallus: Dialogues*

sur les "vertus" de Saint Martin, SC 510 (Paris, 2006); *Acta Sylvestri* (BHL 7725–31), ed. B. Monbritius, *Sanctuarium seu vitae sanctorum* (Hildesheim, 1978), vol. 2; Gregory the Great, *Dialogorum libri iv*, ed. A. de Vogüé, SC 251, 260, 265 (Paris, 1978–80), which also enjoyed great popularity in the Byzantine East thanks to the translation into Greek by Pope Zacharias (741–52).

41. E.g., *Verba seniorum* (BHL 6527), 1.7, PL 73, col. 855c: "Dicebant de abbate Theodoro, cui est praenomen de Pherme, quia haec tria capitula habuerit supra multos, id est, nihil possidendi, abstinendi, homines fugiendi" ("They used to say about abbot Theodore, who bore the name of Pherme, that he had held these three strictures above many other people, namely: to possess nothing, to remain abstinent, and to flee human company"); *Verba seniorum* (BHL 6527), 1.7, PL 73, col. 855c. Gerhart Ladner, *The Idea of Reform: Its Impact on Christian Thought and Action in the Age of the Fathers*, revised ed. (New York, 1967), 341–43.

42. Jerome, *Vita Hilarionis* (BHL 3879), ed. A.A.R. Bastiaensen, *Vite dei santi*, vol. 4, *Vita di Martino, Vita di Ilarione, In Memoria di Paola*, ed. Christine Mohrmann (Milan, 1975), 72–143.

43. Jerome, *Vita Hilarionis* (BHL 3879), 2.3, ed. Bastiaensen, 74: "non circi furoribus, non arenae sanguine, non theatri luxuria delectabatur, sed tota illi voluntas in ecclesiae erat congregatione."

44. Jerome, *Vita Hilarionis*, 2.6, ed. Bastiaensen, 76: "nec congruum esse ducens pati in eremo populos civitatum . . ."

45. Jerome, *Vita Hilarionis*, 30.6, ed. Bastiaensen, 136: ". . . quodammodo in ultionem sui saeviens . . ."

46. Günter Glauche, *Schullektüre im Mittelalter: Entstehung und Wandlungen des Lektürekanons bis 1200 nach den Quellen dargestellt* (Munich, 1970), 5–6, 18–19. See also Antonio Placanica, "Venantius Fortunatus (Carmina)," in *La trasmissione dei testi latini del medioevo*, ed. P. Chiesa and L. Castaldi (Florence, 2005), vol. 2, 526–38, for the transmission of Venantius's poetry. Venantius composed a group of saints' lives that were similar to Prudentius in their influence: *Vita Martini* (BHL 5624), ed. F. Leo, MGH AA 4.1 (Berlin, 1881), 293–370; *Vita et virtutes Hilarii* (BHL 3885, 3887), ed. B. Krusch, MGH AA 4.2 (Berlin, 1885), 7–11; *Vita Paterni* (BHL 6477), ed. Krusch, MGH AA 4.2 (Berlin, 1885), 33–37; *Vita et miracula Albini* (BHL 234–5), ed. Krusch, MGH AA 4.2 (Berlin, 1885), 27–33; *Vita Marcelli* (BHL 5248), ed. Krusch, MGH AA 4.2 (Berlin, 1885), 49–54; *Vita Radegundis* (BHL 7048), ed. B. Krusch, MGH SRM 2 (Hanover, 1888), 364–77; *Vita Severini episcopi Burdegalensis* (BHL 7652), ed. B. Krusch and W. Levison, MGH SRM 7 (Hanover, 1920), 219–24; *Vita Germani episcopi Parisiensis* (BHL 3468), ed. Krusch and Levison, MGH SRM 7 (Hanover, 1920), 372–418. For Venantius's construction of episcopal identity, see Simon Coates, "Venantius Fortunatus and the Image of Episcopal Authority in Late Antique and Early Merovingian Gaul," *The English Historical Review* 115 (2000): 1109–37.

47. Rosamond McKitterick. *History and Memory in the Carolingian World* (Cambridge, UK, 2004).

48. Hippolyte Delehaye, *Cinq leçons sur la méthode hagiographique* (Brussels, 1934), 24. See also Hippolyte Delehaye, *Les origines du culte des martyrs*, 2nd revised ed. (Brussels, 1933); Hippolyte Delehaye, *Les légendes hagiographiques*, 3rd revised ed. (Brussels, 1927); Heinzelmann, *Translationsberichte*, 63–66. For a helpful overview of the depiction of *miracula* in early medieval hagiography, see Hans-Werner Goetz, "Wunderberichte im 9. Jahrhundert: Ein Beitrag zum literarischen Genus der frühmittelalterlichen Mirakelsammlungen," in *Mirakel im Mittelalter: Konzeptionen, Erscheinungsformen, Deutungen*, ed. Martin Heinzelmann, Klaus Herbers, and Dieter R. Bauer (Stuttgart, 2002), 180–226.

49. Patrick Geary, *Furta Sacra: Thefts of Relics in the Central Middle Ages*, revised ed. (Princeton, NJ, 1990).

50. Adrevald, *Miracula Benedicti* (BHL 1123–24), ed. E. de Certain, *Les miracles de saint Benoit*, Société de l'histoire de France 96 (Paris, 1858); Aimoin, *Translatio Vincentii* (BHL 8644–46),

PL 126, col. 1011–27; Almann of Hautvillers, *Historia Translationis Helenae* (*BHL* 3773), AASS Aug. 3.18.599–611. See Geary, *Furta Sacra*, 118–24.

51. Theodor Bitterauf, ed., *Die Traditionen des Hochstifts Freising* (Munich, 1905), vol. 1, no. 275, 242 (May 30, 808) (*multis adstantibus*). See Warren Brown, *Unjust Seizure: Conflict, Interest, and Authority in an Early Medieval Society* (Ithaca, NY, 2001), 135–38.

52. Kreiner, *Social Life*, 172–73. The "crowd of paupers" survives into later hagiography as a subject of a saint's pious mercy: *Vita Ansberti* (*BHL* 520), c. 16, ed. W. Levison, MGH SRM 5 (Hanover, 1910), 629: "Contigit enim tunc pauperum turbam prae foribus conclamare elemosinam petendo." According to Charles Mériaux, *Gallia irradiata: Saints et sanctuaires dans le nord de la Gaule du haut Moyen Âge* (Stuttgart, 2006), 348, this life was composed in Fontanelle during the second half of the eighth century or the ninth century, building upon an earlier life from around the year 700, now lost. A similar expression appears in *Vita Ansberti episcopi Rotomagensis* (*BHL* 519), in E. P. Sauvage, ed., "Vita Sancti Ansberti Archiepiscopi Rotomagensis (*BHL* 519)," *Analecta Bollandiana* 1 (1882): 178–91, at 186 (lines 19–21): "Contigit enim tunc pauperum turbam pro foribus clamare eleemosynam petendo."

53. Theodulf of Orléans, *De vulpecula involante gallinam* (*Carm.* no. 50), ed. Ernst Dümmler, MGH Poetae 1 (Berlin, 1881), 551 ("His visis gaudet monachorum turba fidelis, / Admiranda videns signa favente deo"); *Inscriptiones Locorum Sacrorum*, no. 23, ed. Ernst Dümmler, MGH Poetae 1 (Berlin, 1881), 317 ("Haec, Benedicte, tibi, pius abba, dux monachorum, / Confessor vester, texta dicata manent. / Turba monachorum celebrat te sancta per orbem, / Quorum vita fuit famine scripta tuo. / Te quoque sancta cohors fratrum specialiter istic / Assiduis precibus laudat, honorat, amat"); the St. Gall Plan (W. Horn and E. Born, *The Plan of St. Gall: A Study of the Architecture and Economy of, and Life in a Paradigmatic Carolingian Monastery* (Berkeley, 1979), vol. 3, 81) has this caption written above the cloister: "Hinc pia consilium pertractet turba salubre" ("Through here let healthful counsel be debated by the pious crowd [*pia . . . turba*]"). Youth: *Karolus Magnus et Leo papa*, line 173, ed. Beumann, Brunhölzl, and Winkelmann, 72. See also Matthew Innes, "'A Place of Discipline': Carolingian Courts and Aristocratic Youth," in *Court Culture in the Early Middle Ages: The Proceedings of the First Alcuin Conference*, ed. Catherine Cubitt (Turnhout, 2003), 59–76.

54. E.g., Amalarius, *Liber officialis*, 3.2.6–10, ed. J. M. Hanssens, *Amalarii opera liturgica omnia*, vol. 2, 262–46, Studi e Testi 139 (Vatican City, 1948): "In conventu ecclesiastico seorsum masculi et seorsum feminae stant [. . .] Masculi stant in australi parte et feminae in boreali, ut ostendatur per fortiorem sexum firmiores sanctos semper constitui in maioribus temptationibus aestus huius mundi, et per fragiliorem sexum infirmiores aptiore loco."

55. Council of Nantes (895), c. 19, ed. Mansi, vol. 18, 171–72; Suzanne Fonay Wemple, *Women in Frankish Society: Marriage and the Cloister, 500 to 900* (Philadelphia, 1981), 105–6.

56. Joaquín Martínez Pizarro, "Crowds and Power in the *Liber Pontificalis Ecclesiae Ravennatis*," in *The Community, the Family and the Saint: Patterns of Power in Early Medieval Europe*, ed. J. Hill and M. Swann (Turnhout, 1998), 265–83, at 272.

57. Shane Bobrycki, "The Flailing Women of Dijon: Crowds in Ninth-Century Europe," *Past & Present* 240 (2018): 3–46, at 8–9, 38–41; Thomas Kohl, "Peasant Agency and the Supernatural," *Studia Historica: Historia Medieval* 38 (2020): 97–116, at 106.

58. *Karolus Magnus et Leo papa*, line 152, ed. Beumann, Brunhölzl, and Winkelmann, 369: "Sternere cornigeram nigraque sub arbore turbam."

59. Jonas of Bobbio, *Vita Columbani abbatis discipulorumque* (*BHL* 1898), 1.10, ed. B. Krusch, MGH SRG 37 (1905), 169: "solae ibi ferae ac bestiae, ursorum, bubalorum, luporum multitudo frequentabant." I am grateful to Patrick Meehan for stimulating discussions about this and other passages in Jonas of Bobbio's hagiographical works.

60. *ARF*, s.a. 758, ed. Kurze, 17 (*plurimam . . . multitudinem*); s.a. 775, ed. Kurze, 41 (*congregatam Saxonum multitudinem . . . et magnus eorum numerus ibidem interfectus est*); s.a. 775,

ed. Kurze, 43 (*non modicum . . . multitudinis caedem* and *magnam . . . multitudinem*); s.a. 776, ed. Kurze, 76 (*inmensam illius perfidi populi multitudinem*); 777, ed. Kurze, 49 (*maxima multitudo*); s.a. 778, ed. Kurze, 53 (*ex ingenti multitudine*); s.a. 780, ed. Kurze, 57 (*maxima . . . multitudo*); s.a. 783, ed. Kurze, 65 (*de innumerabili eorum multitudine* and *infinita multitude*); s.a. 788, ed. Kurze, 83 (*innumera multitudo* and *inmodicam . . . multitudinem*); s.a. 793, ed. Kurze, 93 (*magna hominum multitudine*).

61. Canetti, *Masse und Macht*, 14.

62. Isidore, *De differentiis verborum*, c. 369, PL 83, col. 48.

63. Einhard, *Translatio Marcellini et Petri* (BHL 5233), 2.4, ed. G. Waitz, MGH SS 15.1 (Hanover, 1887), 247.

64. *Translatio Viti*, c. 9, ed. I. Schmale-Ott, *Übertragung des heiligen Märtyrers Vitus*, Veröffentlichungen der historischen Kommission für Westfalen 41 (Münster, 1979), 52: "Quae cum non valeret cum ipso prae turba accedere ad feretrum."

65. Suger, *Libellus alter de consecratione ecclesiae Sancti Dionysii*, c. 2, ed. A. Lecoy de la Marche, *Oeuvres complètes de Suger* (Paris, 1867), 216–17, for the famous scene in which crowds are so thick that the women in church turn men's heads into their floor.

66. Karl Ferdinand Werner, "Heeresorganisation und Kriegführung im deutschen Königreich des 10. und 11. Jahrhunderts," in K. F. Werner, *Structures politiques du monde franc (VIe–XIIe siècles): Études sur les origines de la France et de l'Allemagne* (London, 1979), 791–843, at 813; Bernard Bachrach, *Early Carolingian Warfare: Prelude to Empire* (Philadelphia, 2001), esp. 57–59 (and endnotes at 294–96); Eric Goldberg, *Struggle for Empire: Kingship and Conflict under Louis the German, 817–876* (Ithaca, NY, 2006), 95–96, 124–26; by contrast, see Guy Halsall, *Warfare and Society in the Barbarian West, 450–900* (London, 2003), 119–33.

67. Ermoldus Nigellus, *Carmen in honorem Hludowici Caesaris*, 1.302–7, ed. Faral, 26–28: "Interea regis proceres populique phalanges, / Dudum commoniti, jussa libenter agunt. / Undique conveniunt Francorum more catervae / atque urbis muros densa corona tenet. / Convenit ante omnes Carolo satus [Louis the Pious] agmine pulcro; / Urbis ad exitium congregat ille duces."

68. Notker, *Gesta Karoli*, 2.17, ed. H. F. Haefele MGH SRG N.S. 12 (Berlin, 1959), 83.

69. *Passio SS. Prisci, Cotti, et sociorum* (BHL 6930), AASS Maii 6.26.365–67, at 366. See discussion in Kreiner, *Social Life*, 129–30.

70. *Passio SS. Prisci, Cotti, et sociorum* (BHL 6930), AASS Maii 6.26.365F: "Cumque venisset ad locum, qui Cociacus vocatur, reperit Christianum, Priscum nomine, cum immensa multitudine ejusdem religionis psallentem."

71. *Passio SS. Prisci, Cotti, et sociorum* (BHL 6930), AASS Maii 6.26.365F, 366A, 366B; Lausberg, *Handbook of Literary Rhetoric*, 144 (§ 257.2) for *variatio*.

72. *Passio SS. Prisci, Cotti, et sociorum* (BHL 6930), AASS Maii 6.26.366B (*omnes unica voce dixerunt*).

73. Kreiner, *Social Life*, 129.

74. E.g., *Libellus de mirabili revelatione S. Corcodemi M., et conversione S. Mamertini ab idololatria* (BHL 5200–5201), AASS Jul. 7.31.210D: "Tunc ait turbæ, quæ cum eo erat." For this under-studied early medieval dream vision, see Wolfert van Egmond, "Een weinig bekende, zesde-eeuwse visioenstekst: Aard en doel van de *Revelatio Corcodemi seu conversio Mamertini*," in *Rondom Gregorius van Tours*, ed. Mayke de Jong, Els Rose, and Henk Teunis (Utrecht, 2001), 74–81. For further on this text, see Wolfert van Egmond, *Conversing with the Saints: Communication in Pre-Carolingian Hagiography from Auxerre* (Turnhout, 2006), 97–107.

75. *Passio SS. Prisci, Cotti, et sociorum* (BHL 6930), AASS Maii 6.26.366B (*omnes unica voce dixerunt*).

76. For the cult of Cassius, Victorinus, and Antholianus, promoted by Praeiectus in the late seventh century, see the *Passio Praeiecti episcopi et martyris Averni* (BHL 6915–16), c. 9,

ed. Krusch, 230–31 and c. 17, ed. Krusch, 236. Wattenbach-Levison-Löwe, fasc. 1 (Weimer, 1952), 129; see also Barbara Rosenwein, *Emotional Communities in the Early Middle Ages* (Ithaca, NY, 2006), 165–66.

77. *Passio Salvii* (BHL 7472), c. 15, ed. M. Coens, "La passion de saint Sauve, martyr à Valenciennes," *Analecta bollandiana* 87 (1969): 133–87, at 181–83.

78. Jürgen Hannig, *Consensus fidelium: Frühfeudale Interpretationen des Verhältnisses von Königtum und Adel am Beispiel des Frankenreiches* (Stuttgart, 1982).

79. As expressed in Pseudo-Isidore: Hinschius, ed., *Decretales Pseudo-Isidorianae*, 152.

80. E.g., *Vita Gaugerici* (BHL 3286), c.8, ed. B. Krusch, MGH SRM 3 (Hanover, 1896), 654: "Quoddam itaque tempore, cum triduano conventu rogationis, quas cunctos excolit populus veneratione plenissima . . ."; *Passio Desiderii episcopi et martyris Viennensis* (BHL 2149), c. 6, ed. B. Krusch, MGH SRM 3 (Hanover, 1896), 640: "Nam et hoc cunctus populus, populo dicente, cognovit, non unum ibidem dextera Christi per confessoris ipsius interventu leprae macula vulneratus, suam imminentem misericordiam, fuisse sanatus." For debates on the dating of this text, see José Carlos Martín Iglesias, "Una posible datación de la *Passio sancti Desideni* BHL 2149," *Euphrosyne*, n.s., 23 (1995): 439–56. Universal agreement was sometimes expressed abstractly too: Dracontius, *De laudibus dei*, 3.394, ed. C. Moussy and C. Camus, *Dracontius: Œuvres*, vol. 2, *Louanges de Dieu* (Paris, 1988); Venantius Fortunatus, *Ad Chilpericum regem*, lines 13–16, ed. F. Leo, MGH AA 4.1 (Berlin, 1881), 201: "Te nascente patri lux altera nascitur orbi, | nominis et radios spargis ubique novos, | que praefert Oriens, Libyes, Occasus et Arctus: | quo pede non graderis, notus honore venis."

81. E.g., *Vita Arnulfi* (BHL 692), c. 10, ed. B. Krusch, MGH SRM 2 (Hanover, 1888), 245: "Per idem namque tempus, quo triduanum ieiunium universalis celebrare consuevit aecclesia, vir sanctus extra civitatem cum crucibus adque promiscuo populi genere orandi gratia secundum mos ex urbe processit . . ." A curious use of this topos in a probably late eighth-century saint's life envisions the saint's body interred in a stable, where a large bull guards it from the other cattle, imagined as a promiscuous crowd. *Passio Salvii* (BHL 7472), c. 10, ed. Coens, 177: "Nempe, ut dictum est, si aliqua ex eis ire voluisset ad locum illum, taurus quidem diversis calcibus et cornuum ictibus eisdem resistebat omnem multitudinem bucularum promiscui sexus in circuitu stare faciebat, ut eumdem locum sanctum coinquinare non valerent." Martínez Pizarro, "Crowds and Power," 266, notes that, despite referring to the crowds of combatants in the annual mock-battle at Ravenna as being of *promiscui sexus*, Agnellus of Ravenna only ever mentions men as participants. Agnellus, *Liber pontificalis ecclesiae Rauennatis*, c. 126, ed. Otto Holder-Egger, MGH SRL 1 (Hanover, 1878), 361: "Die omni dominico vel apostolorum die Ravennensis cives non solum illustres, sed homines diversae aetatis, iuvenes et ephibi, mediocres et parvuli, promiscui sexus, ut diximus, post refectionem per diversas portas aggregatim egredientes, ad pugnam procedunt."

82. *Vita Audoeni* (BHL 753), 23.57, ed. E. P. Sauvage, "*Vita S. Audoeni Rotomagensis episopi auctore Anonymo* (BHL 753)," *Analecta Bollandiana* 5 (1886): 67–146, at 133: "Tota civitas exultabat; et ad tanti patris visionem omnis sexus, ætas universa, dignitas omnis, omnis conditio gaudents occurrebat." This text is possibly from the ninth or tenth century, although it survives in later manuscripts: Felice Lifshitz, *The Norman Conquest of Pious Neustria: Historiographic Discourse and Saintly Relics, 684–1090* (Toronto, 1995), 87–88.

83. Modoin, *Eclogue*, lines 40–41, ed. Ernst Dümmler, "Nasos (Modoins) Gedichte an Karl den Grossen," *Neues Archiv der Gesellschaft für ältere deutsche Geschichtskunde* 11 (1886): 77–91, at 83: "Quo caput orbis erit, Romam vocitare licebit / Forte locum: omnis erit huc, omnis sexus et aetas."

84. *Translatio Alexandri et Iustini* (BHL 271), c. 1, ed. W. Wattenbach, MGH SS 15.1 (Hanover, 1887), 287: "Densabatur nichilominus constipatio catervarum; vulgus simul ac nobiles, omnes in commune pergebant, una voce Dei laudes canebant, sanctorum suffragia postulantes."

85. *Sermo de relatione corporis beati Vedasti* (*BHL* 8516), c. 7, ed. O. Holder-Egger, MGH SS 15.1 (Hanover, 1887), 403: "Quippe aderat non parva monachorum caterva; aderat multiplex conventus canonicorum, presbiterorum reliquorumque clericorum; aderant viri cum mulieribus et parvulis, iuvenes et virgines; senes cum iunioribus ibi laudabant nomen Domini."

86. *Vita Gaugerici* (*BHL* 3286), c. 8, ed. B. Krusch, MGH SRM 3 (1896), 654.

87. Baltherus, *Vita Fridolini confessoris Seckingensis* (*BHL* 3170), c. 30, ed. B. Krusch, MGH SRM 3 (Hanover, 1896), 368: "Illuc ergo ad suam basilicam undique sexus innumerabili populorum caterva pro sua inpetranda clementia properante, allatus est idem paralyticus a suis parentibus in eandem ecclesiam."

88. E.g., *Vita Rimberti* (*BHL* 7258), c. 22, ed. G. Waitz, MGH SRG 55 (Hanover, 1884), 98; *Translatio S. Vincentii* (*BHL* 8644–46), book 2, c. 3, PL 126, col. 1019C–1020A; from the tenth century, *Sermo de Adventu Sanctorum Wandregisili, Ansberti et Vulframni in Monte Blandinium Vocato* (*BHL* 8810), c. 4, ed. N. Heyghebaert, *Une Translation de Reliques à Gand en 944: Le Sermo de Adventu Sanctorum Wandregisili, Ansberti et Vulframni in Monte Blandinium* (Brussels, 1978): "Cui translationi sollempniter celebrandae occurrit pari affectu omnis clerus, omne vulgus, omnis quoque sexus et aetas."

89. This is true even when a candidate is selected by an individual. E.g., *Vita Amandi episcopi* I (*BHL* 332), c. 18, ed. B. Krusch, MGH SRM 5 (Hanover, 1910), 442: "Tunc vero rex sanctum arcessivit Amandum, congregataque multitudine sacerdotum populique turbam non modicam, ad regendam Treiectensium ecclesiam eum praeposuit." Mériaux, *Gallia irradiata*, 347, discusses possible authors for this text, likely written by a "clerc septentrional" in the seventh or eighth century.

90. E.g., *Vita Hadriani II*, c. 4, ed. Duchesne, 173–74. Every single person desired him, except for those who did not. "Sed cum apostolicae memoriae sanctissimus papa Nicolaus rebus excessisset humanis et iste in presbiterio quintum et vigesimum annum transiret, omnes urbis Romanae concives, simul et hi quos extrinsecus adesse contigerat, tam pauperes quam divites, tam clericalis ordo quam cunctum populi vulgus, omnis scilicet etatis, professionis et sexus, contemptis omnibus excusationibus, Hadrianum desiderant, Hadrianum dari sibi presulem ac pastorem exoptant; nullusque in totius Urbis amplissimo spatio repertus est, nisi vel se vel suum quemque provehi voluisset, qui non Hadrianum promoveri ad hoc culmen medullitus exoptaret." See P. Daileader, "One Will, One Voice, and Equal Love: Papal Elections and the *Liber Pontificalis* in the Early Middle Ages," *Archivum Historiae Pontificiae* 31 (1993): 11–31.

91. E.g., *Passio Praeiecti episcopi et martyris Averni* (*BHL* 6915–16), c. 14, ed. Krusch, 234.

92. Louis Hamilton, *A Sacred City: Consecrating Churches and Reforming Society in Eleventh-Century Italy* (Manchester, 2010), 56–88. Hamilton here disputes the claim of Diana Webb, *Patrons and Defenders: The Saints in the Italian City-States* (London, 1996), 33–34, that the liturgical figure of the *plebs* or the *populus* in the liturgy is undifferentiated (see esp. 34–36).

93. Hamilton, *A Sacred City*, 61.

94. Philip Jones, *The Italian City-State: From Commune to Signoria* (Oxford, 1997), 334, for a logic "not of representation, the subordinate, class-divided parliaments of a hierarchic Ständestaat, but of common participation, government by all (*cunctus populus, universitas civium*)," which will "regenerate republicanism."

95. Bede, *HE* 4.2.1, ed. Lapidge, vol. 2, 200–202: "Et quia litteris sacris simul et saecularibus, ut diximus, abundanter ambo erant instructi, congregata discipulorum caterua scientiae salutaris cotidie flumina irrigandis eorum cordibus emanabant, ita ut etiam metricae artis, astronomiae et arithmeticae ecclesiasticae disciplinam inter sacrorum apicum uolumina suis auditoribus contraderent."

96. E.g., *Translatio SS. Chrysanti et Dariae a. 844* (*BHL* 1793), c. 27, AASS Oct. 11.25.493E: "Cum itaque frequens Sanctorum virtutem et miracula opinio circumquaque diffunderet, habitatores etiam præfatæ replevit villæ. Hac excitati fama, facta conventione ad locum omnes pariter oratum disponebant ire." Alternatively, the crowd itself may be contiguous with rumor.

See, for instance, the mid ninth-century life by Anskar of Bremen, *Miracula Willehadi* (BHL 8899), ed. G. H. Pertz, MGH SS 2 (Hanover, 1829), 385: "in ecclesia Bremensi coeperunt divinitus agi miracula, et de die in diem semper multiplitius crescere, ita ut iam longe lateque per populos rumor increbresceret plurimus." See also Courtney Booker, "*Iusta Murmuratio*: The Sound of Scandal in the Early Middle Ages," *Revue Bénédictine* 126 (2016): 236–70.

97. *Miracula S. Genesii* (BHL 3314), praef., ed. Wattenbach, 9: "Quae [reliquiae sancti Genesii martyris Christi] in brevi postquam in praedio praefati viri in secessu cuiusdam montis, quem Skinam aetas prior appellavit, haud longe a Rheno fluvio habitaculum sibi a deo, ut ad magnam aedificationem ecclesiae fideles circumquaque Christo laudem concinentes, permoti miraculis adcurrere festinarent."

98. *Vita Audomari* II (BHL 765, 767), 2.20, AASS Sept. 3.9.405F: "De quo pene innumerabiles testes promiscui sexus virorum feminarumque adhuc manent, qui ad hoc spectaculum presentes adstiterunt."

99. *Vita Eleutherii Tornacensis* I (BHL 2455), c. 1, AASS Feb. 3.20.187B: "Quid plura? Denique multi per eum crediderunt; multi ab eo baptizati sunt; multi cum eodem Martyre pro Christi nomine interempti sunt."

100. Einhard, *Translatio Marcellini et Petri* (BHL 5233), 2.4, ed. G. Waitz, MGH SS 15.1 (Hanover, 1887), 247: "In illa vero processione nostra, quam de basilica usque ad oratorium nostrum nos fecisse dixi, quid miraculi acciderit, censeo non esse tacendum."

101. Einhard, *Translatio Marcellini et Petri* (BHL 5233), ed. G. Waitz, MGH SS 15.1 (Hanover, 1887). Other *translationes* show the same thing. *Translatio Viti martyris* (BHL 8718–19), c. 27, ed. Schmale-Ott, 60: "Tandem igitur Christo propitio finito cepto itinere monasterium, quod Corveia Nova dicitur, multitudine populi utriusque sexus de nobilissimo Saxonum genere nobiscum comitante pervenimus pridie ante vigiliam sancti Viti, quod est Idus Iunias." Cf. Röckelein, *Reliquientranslationen*, 279. Aimoin, *Translatio S. Vincentii* (BHL 8644–46), book 2, c. 3, PL 126, col. 1019C–1020A: "Intrantesque quamdam ejusdem provinciae villam, quae a priscis cultoribus nomen Albis accepit, imposuerunt illud super altare ecclesiae beatae Mariae Virginis. Quo innumera multitudine utriusque sexus per biduum confluente, reperti sunt inter eos, contracti genibus duo, et una debilis mulier, caecus unus, ac febricitantes seu energumeni, ejus sanctis meritis ab omni infirmitatum gravedine liberati."

102. For death culture, see Frederick S. Paxton, *Christianizing Death: The Creation of a Ritual Process in Early Medieval Europe* (Ithaca, NY, 1990); Cécile Treffort, *L'église carolingienne et la mort: Christianisme, rites funéraires et pratiques commémoratives* (Lyon, 1996).

103. Verus of Orange, *Vita Eutropii* (BHL 2782), ed. P. Varin, "Vie de saint Eutrope, évêque de l'Orange," *Bulletin de la comité historique des monuments écrits de l'histoire de France* 1 (1849): 51–64, at 63: "communi universorum planctu."

104. *Vita Wandregiseli* (BHL 8804), c. 20, ed. B. Krusch and W. Levison, MGH SRM 5 (Hanover, 1910), 23: "Ad ultimum vero exitus suae congregata est omnis multitudo monachorum."

105. *Vita Balthildis* A (BHL 905), c. 15, ed. B. Krusch, MGH SRM 2 (Hanover, 1888), 502: "Omnibusque stupefactis pariter prostratisque ilico super humum, multisque ibi profusis lacrimis, cum inmenso doloris gemitu flentes et pio Domino gratias agentes et conlaudantes, commendaverunt eius sanctam animam pio regi Christo, ut ipse eam in sanctae Mariae choro vel sanctorum consortio perduceret, et, ut tunc erat decus ipsius, sepelientes eam cum magno honore et multa reverentia."

106. *Vita Bavonis confessoris Gandavensis* (BHL 1049), c. 7, ed. B. Krusch, MGH SRM 4 (Hanover, 1902), 540: "Videns eum turba iam mortuum, cum fletu corpus eius in navi deduxerunt ad memoratum castrum Gandavum, ut tumularetur illic, sicut mos est mortuos sepelire." For this life, see Mériaux, *Gallia irradiata*, 349.

107. E.g., the eighth-century *Vita Audoini episcopi Rotomagensis* (BHL 750), c. 17, ed. W. Levison, MGH SRM 5 (Hanover, 1910), 564: "Dum vero conventione facta plurimorum

episcoporum una cum abbatibus eorum vel sacerdotum seu clericorum multitudine seu inlustrium virorum et turba populorum Villiocasinensium opido ingressi sunt, cum magno favore beatum corpus humeribus deportantes, convenerunt cum laudibus et hymnis Deo canentes, cum grandi fletu pastoris feretrum praestolantes." Other examples: the *Vita Geremari* (*BHL* 3437), 2.19, AASS Sept 6.24.702D, where a "crowd of people weeping and lamenting" (*multitudo populi flens atque lugens*) follows the body of the saint to its inhumation in the church he had constructed; the *Vita Bertae abbatissae Blangiacensis* (*BHL* 1266), 2.24, AASS Jul. 2:4.53E, where Bertha's funeral rites are conducted "with a great crowd of people standing by" (*multa turba circumstante populi*).

108. *Vita et miracula Austrebertae* (*BHL* 832), 3.18, AASS Feb. 2.10.423C: "Superueniente porro die Dominico, quia iam eius bonitatis ac virtutum fama per Galliam longe lateque claruerat, confluxerunt ad eius transitum cateruatim Sacerdotes & Clerici, Abbates & monachi, necnon & vtriusque sexus populi multitudo." For this text, see Mériaux, *Gallia irradiata*, 348–49.

109. Carl Albrecht Bernoulli, *Die Heiligen der Merowinger* (Tübingen, 1900), 84; Anne-Marie Helvétius, "Le saint et la sacralisation de l'espace en Gaule du Nord d'après les sources hagiographiques (VIIe–XIe siècle)," in *Le sacré et son inscription dans l'espace à Byzance et en Occident: Études comparées*, ed. Michel Kaplan (Paris, 2001), 137–61, at 158, for the ubiquity of this widely spread topos.

110. *Vita Filiberti* (*BHL* 6805–6), c. 26, ed. W. Levison, MGH SRM 5 (Hanover, 1910), 597: "Egressus de carcere per litteras beati Audoini, adiit ad Ansoaldo viro nobile, Pectavorum pontifice ob monasterii gratiam construendi, quia multitudo hominum, qui per praedicationem illius ad Dominum confluebant, uno in loco capere non poterant." For the case of a female monastery outgrowing its original size, see *Vita Segolenae* (*BHL* 7570), c. 2.12.13, AASS Jul. 5.24.633B: "Cumque jam multarum monacharum societate densaretur, instituitur dies, qua se Sancta intra septa monasterii (ut mos virginum est) deliberaverat retrudi. Adfuit etiam plebium multitudo: omnes gaudent, omnes exsultant de ejus glorioso proposito."

111. Jonas of Bobbio, *Vita Columbani abbatis discipulorumque* (*BHL* 1898), 1.10, ed. B. Krusch, MGH SRG 37 (1905), 169: "Cumque iam multorum monachorum societate densaretur, coepit cogitare, ut potioris loci in eodem heremo quereret, quo monasterium construxisset"; Bobolenus, *Vita S. Germani abbatis Grandivallensis* (*BHL* 3467), c. 7, ed. Bruno Krusch, MGH SRM 5 (Hanover, 1910), 36: "Cernens vero Deo plenus, Spiritu sancto repletus, sacerdos Dei Waldebertus certatim undique catervas monachorum coadunari, anhelare coepit de tam plurima multitudine, si forte ubi et ubi inveniri possint loca uberrima, ubi de suis monachis ad habitandum adunaret."

112. *Passio Praeiecti episcopi et martyris Averni* (*BHL* 6915–16), c. 16, ed. Krusch, 235. This passage appears to build on the *Vita Germani* (*BHL* 3467), c. 7, ed. Krusch, 36, quote above in previous note (284, n. 111).

113. *Passio Praeiecti episcopi et martyris Averni* (*BHL* 6915–16), c. 34, ed. Krusch 244. Cf. Aimoin, *Translatio S. Vincentii* (*BHL* 8644–46), book 2, c. 4, PL 126, col. 1020A–C.

114. Donatien de Bruyne, "L'origine des processions de la Chandeleur et des Rogations à propos d'un sermon inédit," *Revue bénédictine* 34 (1922): 14–26; Geoffrey Nathan, "The Rogation Ceremonies of Late Antique Gaul: Creation, Transmission and the Role of the Bishop," *Classica et mediaevalia* 49 (1998): 275–303; Ian Wood, "Topographies of Holy Power in Sixth-Century Gaul," in *Topographies of Power in the Early Middle Ages: The Transformation of the Roman World*, ed. Mayke de Jong, Frans Theuws, and Carine van Rhijn (Leiden, 2001), 137–55, 150–54. For the interplay of architecture and processional liturgy, see Carol Heitz, "Architecture et liturgie en France de l'époque carolingienne à l'an Mil," *Hortus Artium Medievalium* 1 (1995): 57–73. For processions in Greco-Roman Antiquity, see Marion True et al., "Processions," in *Thesaurus Cultus et Rituum Antiquorum* (Los Angeles, 2004), vol. 1, 1–58.

115. Nathan J. Ristuccia, *Christianization and Commonwealth in Early Medieval Europe: A Ritual Interpretation* (Oxford, 2018).

116. Gregory of Tours, *Hist.* 4.5, ed. Krusch and Levison, 138–39; Gregory of Tours, *Liber vitae patrum* 6.6, ed. B. Krusch, MGH SRM 1.2, 234–35; Ian Wood, "Liturgy in the Rhône Valley and the Bobbio Missal," in *The Bobbio Missal: Liturgy and Religious Culture in Merovingian Gaul*, ed. Y. Hen and R. Meens (Cambridge, UK, 2004), 206–218, at 208; Rob Meens, *Penance in Medieval Europe, 600–1200* (Cambridge, UK, 2014), 31. For other examples of the careful construction of cults through liturgy and hagiographical memory, see Ian Wood, "Constructing Cults in Early Medieval France: Local Saints and Churches in Burgundy and the Auvergne 400–1000," in *Local Saints and Local Churches in the Early Medieval West*, ed. Alan Thacker and Richard Sharpe (Oxford, 2002), 155–87.

117. *Vita Arnulfi* (*BHL* 692), c. 10, ed. B. Krusch, MGH SRM 2 (Hanover, 1888), 245.

118. *Translatio Viti martyris* (*BHL* 8718–19), c. 5, ed. Schmale-Ott, 48. Cf. another ninth-century vita, emphasizing the universal nature of an audience: Liutgar, *Vita Gregorii abbatis Traiectensis* (*BHL* 3680), c. 4, ed. O. Holder-Egger, MGH SS 15.1 (Hanover, 1887), 71: "coram universo senatu populi Francorum."

119. *Translatio Viti martyris* (*BHL* 8718–19), c. 5, ed. Schmale-Ott, 48: "coram innumerabili multitudine populorum, tam monachorum quam canonicorum, virorum ac mulierum."

120. Or the moral valence of a witness crowd can shift. Kate Cooper, "Vetriloquism and the Miraculous: Conversion, Preaching, and the Martyr Exemplum in Late Antiquity," in *Signs, Wonders, Miracles: Representations of Divine Power in the Life of the Church*, ed. Kate Cooper and Jeremy Gregory (Woodbridge, UK, 2005), 22–45, at 24, gives the example of the martyr whose audience comes to observe a saint for the wrong reasons, only to be educated by the saint's martyrdom. This narrative audience is, in turn, a model for the audience of the sermon in which it is likely to appear.

121. *Vita Vulframni* (*BHL* 8738), c. 8, ed. W. Levison, MGH SRM 5 (Hanover, 1910), 667 (*aspicientibus gentilium turbis*). For this text, see Stéphane Lebecq, "Vulfran, Willibrord et la mission de Frise: Pour une relecture de la *Vita Vulframni*," in S. Lebecq, *Hommes, mers et terres du Nord au début du Moyen Âge* (Villeneuve d'Ascq, 2011), vol. 1, 75–94.

122. Malbon, "Disciples / Crowds / Whoever," 123–26.

123. Sara Lipton, *Dark Mirror: The Medieval Origins of Anti-Jewish Iconography* (New York, 2014), 240–81.

124. But see Röckelein, *Reliquientranslationen*, 342–43.

125. Cf. Mark 2:13, ed. Weber-Gryson, 1577: "Et egressus est rursus ad mare omnisque turba veniebat ad eum et docebat eos."

126. Interpretations of the gospel crowds were incorporated into the liturgy. See, e.g., Jesse D. Billett, "*Sermones ad diem pertinentes*: Sermons and Homilies in the Liturgy of the Divine Office," in *Sermo Doctorum: Compilers, Preachers and Their Audiences in the Early Middle Ages*, ed. Maximilian Diesenberger, Yitzhak Hen, and Marianne Pollheimer (Turnhout, 2013), 339–73, at 356–58.

127. Fulgentius of Ruspe, *Contra Fabianum*, fragment 34, ed. J. Fraipont, CCSL 91A (Turnhout, 1968) ("si quis autem quaerit, cui deo, illa statim angelica multitudo respondet: sedenti in solio et agno"); Alcuin, *Carm.* 27, ed. Ernst Dümmler, MGH Poetae 1 (Hanover, 1881), 247 ("Omnis ubique simul populus respondeat 'amen'"); *Translatio Sancti Calixti Cisonium* (*BHL* 1525), c. 5, ed. O. Holder-Egger, MGH SS 15.1 (Hanover, 1887), 420 ("Et dum, data oratione, una voce populus respondisset: 'Amen,' elevantes eum a loco in quo iacebat, nullo gravati pondere, efferebant cum ymnis et laudibus usque in atrium aecclesiae, ubi antea gressum fixerat"). For a crowd that turns from weeping to exulting in the wake of a miracle, see the ninth- or tenth-century *Vita Eremberti ep. Tolosani* (*BHL* 2587), c. 4, ed. W. Levison, MGH SRM 5 (Hanover, 1910), 655.

128. As in the ninth-century *Vita Aldegundis* II (*BHL* 245), c. 12, AASS Jan. 2.30.1037. For the ninth-century dating of this rewriting of an earlier, perhaps eighth-century life—*Vita Aldegundis*

I (*BHL* 244), ed. Luc d'Achéry and Jean Mabillon, *Acta Sanctorum ordinis Sancti Benedicti*, 9 vols. (Paris, 1669), vol. 2, 807–15—see Mériaux, *Gallia irradiata*, 346.

129. *Miracula S. Genesii* (*BHL* 3314), c. 4, in Wilhelm Wattenbach, ed., "Die Übertragung der Reliquien des h. Genesius nach Schienen," *Zeitschrift für die Geschichte des Oberrheins* 24 (1872): 8–21, at 13–14.

130. *Miracula S. Genesii* (*BHL* 3314), c. 4, ed. Wattenbach, 13–14: "Non aliud signum, inquit, illic modo diffamatum audivi, nisi quod mulier quaedam per secretam alvi naturam sonitum protulit inpudenter."

131. *Miracula S. Genesii* (*BHL* 3314), c. 4, ed. Wattenbach, 13. See also below at p. 156.

132. Cf. *Vita Maximini* (*BHL* 5822), c. 5, AASS Mai 7.29.22A, where an assembled multitude (*collecta multitudo*) of clerics and people seeks out the body of the saint, and they encounter a young boy who shows them the way.

133. See Kreiner, *Social Life*, 162, on the power of saints to control populations. Compare Peter Brown, *Power and Persuasion in Late Antiquity: Towards a Christian Empire* (Madison, WI, 1992), 148, for the bishop as "controller of crowds"; Michael Moore, *A Sacred Kingdom: Bishops and the Rise of Frankish Kingship, 300–850* (Washington, DC, 2011), 41–42, 87.

134. *Miracula S. Genesii* (*BHL* 3314), c. 5, 6, 15, ed. Wattenbach, 14, 15, 18.

135. Almann of Hautvillers, *Historia Translationis Helenae* (*BHL* 3773), 2.13, AASS Aug. 3.18.602C.

136. *Annales Mettenses priores*, s.a. 690, ed. B. von Simson, MGH SRG 10 (Hanover, 1905), 10: "Nam Theodericus in innumerabilis populi multitudine magis quam in consiliis prudentiae confidens traditum sibi iam Pippinum cum universo exercitu suo inanibus verbis gloriabatur." Irene Haselbach, *Aufstieg und Herrschaft der Karolinger in der Darstellung der sogenannten Annales Mettenses priores: Ein Beitrag zur Geschichte der politischen ideen im Reich Karls des Großen* (Lübeck, 1970), 166, places this depiction of Theuderic III within the context of other intentional contrasts between good Carolingian rulership and bad Merovingian rulership. See Rosamond McKitterick, *Charlemagne: The Formation of a European Identity* (Cambridge, UK, 2008), 48, for these annals' commitments and possible place of origin. Yitzhak Hen, "The Annals of Metz and the Merovingian Past," in *The Uses of the Past in the Early Middle Ages*, ed. Y. Hen and M. Innes (Cambridge, UK, 2000), 175–90, downplays the text's anti-Merovingian streak, though he notes that Theuderic III is one of the Merovingian rulers targeted especially by the authors of the annals (esp. 189–90). See also Norbert Schröer, "Die *Annales Mettenses priores*: Literarische Form und politische Intention," in *Geschichtsschreibung und geistiges Leben im Mittelalter: Festschrift für Heinz Löwe zum 65. Geburtstag*, ed. K. Hauck and H. Mordek (Cologne, 1978) 139–58, 139–42.

137. Laurent Jégou, "Compétition autour d'un cadavre: Le procès du pape Formose et ses enjeux (896–904)," *Revue Historique* 675 (2015): 499–524, at 520–21.

138. Philippe Buc, *The Dangers of Ritual: Between Early Medieval Texts and Social Scientific Theory* (Princeton, NJ, 2001), 259. See also Philippe Buc, "Postface," in Philippe Buc, *Pułapki rytuału Między wczesnośredniowiecznymi tekstami a teorią nauk społecznych*, trans. Michał Tomaszek (Warsaw, 2011), 308–29.

139. Bede, *HE* 1.17.2, ed. Lapidge, vol. 1, 174 (*Ex diuersis partibus multitudo*).

140. Lisi Oliver, *The Body Legal in Barbarian Law* (Toronto, 2011), 41.

141. E.g., DD Lo 15, ed. T. Schieffer, MGH DD Karol. 3 (Berlin, 1966), 407; DD Karl 172, 178, 184, ed. P. Kehr, MGH DD Karl (Berlin, 1937), 243, 257, 266–67.

142. Theodulf of Orléans, *Contra iudices*, line 153, ed. E. Dümmler, MGH Poetae 1 (Berlin, 1881), 498: "Magna catervatim nos contio saepe frequentat." On the language of this poem, see M. Fuhrmann, "Philologische Bemerkungen zu Theodulfs *Paraenesis ad iudices*," in *Das Profil des Juristen in der europäischen Tradition: Symposion aus Anlaß des 70. Geburtstages von Franz Wieacker*, ed. K. Luig and D. Liebs (Ebelsbach, 1980), 257–77.

143. The text of the *HE* was reedited by Michael Lapidge for Sources Chrétiennes: M. Lapidge, trans. P. Monat and P. Robin, eds., *Histoire ecclésiastique du peuple anglaise*, SC 489–91 (Paris, 2005); this expands upon the text in the Oxford Medieval Texts series: B. Colgrave and R. Mynors, ed. and trans., *Bede's Ecclesiastical History of the English People* (Oxford, 1969). For an orientation to the large literature, see Alan Thacker, "Bede and History," in *The Cambridge Companion to Bede*, ed. Scott DeGregorio (Cambridge, UK, 2010), 170–89.

144. Bede, *HE* 1.17–18, ed. Lapidge, vol. 1, 170–78. When the saint heals the child, "the parents rejoice as the crowd trembles at the miracle." Bede, *HE* 1.18.1, ed. Lapidge, vol. 1, 178: "Exultant parentes; miraculum populus contremescit." In the same passage, the evil opinion (*suasio iniqua*) of heresy has been pushed away from "the minds of all" (*ex animis omnium*).

145. Bede, *HE* 1.21.2, ed. Lapidge, vol. 1, 188 (*In conspectu omnium*).

146. Bede, *HE* 1.21.2, ed. Lapidge, vol. 1, 188, describes the crowd as an *inscia multitudo*.

147. *Vita Willehadi* (*BHL* 8898), ed. H. Pertz, MGH SS 2 (Hanover, 1829), 381, for a pagan multitude (*multitudo gentilium*) that is converted and baptized.

148. E.g., *Passio SS. Prisci, Cotti, et sociorum* (*BHL* 6930), AASS Mai 6.26.365–67, at 366.

149. *Sermo seu narratio de miraculo S. Genesii martyris Arelatensis* (*BHL* 3307), PL 50, col. 1273A–1276A.

150. Influenced by biblical precedent, when Jesus conducts healing miracles but commands beneficiaries to conceal the miracle from others (which they never do): Matthew 8.4, ed. Weber-Gryson, 1536: *Vide nemini dixeris* (leprosy); Matthew 9:30, ed. Weber-Gryson, 1539: *Videte ne quis sciat* (blindness).

151. Stephen of Auxerre, *Vita S. Amatoris* (*BHL* 356), AASS Mai 1.1.58A: "Accurrit catervatim turba languentium, et ante vestibulum Antistis prosternuntur"; see also 59E: "Accedunt hi propius qui portabant; viri Dei sospitatem inquirunt; cognoscunt ipsius fuisse, quam catervatim ex urbe proficisci viderant, pompam funeris deducendam."

152. Stephen of Auxerre, *Vita S. Amatoris* (*BHL* 356), AASS Mai 1.1.57E: ". . . & ne ei aliquo modo quorumdam Christianorum conventus furenti resisteret, turbam secum agrestem coadunans civitati improvisus advenit."

153. Bobrycki, "Flailing Woman," 7–8.

154. H. Campbell and J. Heyman, "Slantwise: Beyond Domination and Resistance on the Border," *Journal of Contemporary Ethnography* 36 (2007): 3–30; Cam Grey, *Constructing Communities in the Late Roman Countryside* (Cambridge, UK, 2011), 239; Bobrycki, "Flailing Women," 31.

155. Report of Ibrāhīm ibn Yaʿqūb, *Relacja Ibrahim Ibn Jakuba z podróży do krajów słowiańskich w przekładzie Al Bekriego*, ed. T. Kowalski (Cracow, 1946).

156. Hans Delbrück, *Geschichte der Kriegskunst im Rahmen der politischen Geschichte*, part 3, *Das Mittelalter* (Berlin, 1907), e.g., 193, 233, 290, 413.

157. *Annales Laureshamenses*, s.a. 791, s.a 796, MGH SS1, 34, 37 (*innumerabilis multitudo*); *ARF*, s.a. 783, MGH SRG 6, 65 (*innumerabilis multitudo*), 65 (*infinita multitudo*).

158. *ARF*, s.a. 828, ed. Kurze, 176.

159. *ARF*, s.a. 828, ed. Kurze, 176: "hoc facto ingentem Afris timorem incussit."

160. Louis II (dict. Anastasius Bibliothecarius), *Epistola ad Basilium I. imperatorem* (871), ed. Walter Henze, MGH Epp 7 (Berlin, 1928), 391: "Vestri autem sicut bruchi prae multitudine apparentes et sicut locustae primum impetum dantes, eo ipso quo conatum suum in prima fronte monstraverunt, pusillanimitate superati protinus infirmati sunt et more locustarum repente quidem salierunt, set confestim fatigati quasi a nisibus volandi deciderunt ac per hoc neque intuendo neque prandendo neque bellando quibuslibet insignibus triumphi monstratis motu subitaneo et clandestino recesserunt et inefficaces, nonnullis, et contra christianos, solummodo captivatis ad propria repedaverunt." Cf. Joel 1:4.

161. Louis II (dict. Anastasius Bibliothecarius), *Epistola ad Basilium I*, ed. Henze, 391.

162. CETEDOC, parameters sixth century to tenth century; search for "innumerabil* multitud*" and "multitud* innumerabil*."

163. Thietmar of Merseburg, *Chronicon* 7.45, ed. Robert Holtzmann, MGH SRG Nova Series 9 (Berlin, 1935), 453–54. See Paolo Squatriti, *Landscape and Change in Early Medieval Italy: Chestnuts, Economy, and Culture* (Cambridge, UK, 2013), 194–97.

164. Gustave Le Bon, *La psychologie des foules* (Paris, 1894), 36–37; Robert A. Nye, *The Origins of Crowd Psychology: Gustave Le Bon and the Crisis of Mass Democracy in the Third Republic* (London, 1975), 21.

165. Clark McPhail, *The Myth of the Madding Crowd* (New York, 1991).

166. Gregory of Tours, *Hist.* 3.36, ed. Krusch and Levison, 131–32 (the tax collector Parthenius).

167. Agobard of Lyon, *De grandine et tonitruis*, c. 2, in *Agobardi Lugdunensis Opera omnia*, ed. L. van Acker, CCCM 52 (Turnhout, 1981), 4. See Jean-Pierre Devroey, *De la grêle et du tonnerre: Histoire médiévale des imaginaires paysans* (Paris, 2024), chapter 1.

168. *Annales Fuldenses*, MGH SS rer. Germ. 7, ed. Kurze (Hannover, 1891), 109, s.a. 883 (Bavarian Continuator). See also Veronika Unger, ed., *Regesta Imperii I: Die Regesten des Kaiserreichs unter den Karolingern 751–918 (987)*, vol. 4, *Papstregesten 800–911*, part 3, 872–882 (Weimar, 2013), no. 727, 413–14. This is the sole contemporary description of John's death as murder. Scholars are divided as to its veracity. For the politics of the Bavarian Continuator of the *Annals of Fulda*, see Hagen Keller, "Zum Sturz Karls III," *Deutsches Archiv* 22 (1966): 333–84, and Simon MacLean, *Kingship and Politics in the Late Ninth Century: Charles the Fat and the End of the Carolingian Empire* (Cambridge, UK, 2003), 26–27.

169. For a mid-ninth-century case, see *Historia translationis Gorgonii* (BHL 3622), c. 10, AASS Mart. 2.11.59C.

170. Sisebut, *Vita et Passio Sancti Desiderii* (BHL 2148), c. 18, ed. Juan Gil, *Miscellanea Wisigothica* (Seville, 1972), 65: "Sic ait et ecce subito rabientium stipata caterua furens aduenit, homines funesti et uultu teterrimo, quorum erat frons torua, truces oculi, aspectus odibilis, motus orrendus; erantque mente sinistri, moribus praui, lingua mendaces, uerbis obsceni, foris tugidi, interius uacui, utrobique deformes, de bonis indigui, de pessimis opulenti, delictis obnoxei, inimici Dei, amici sane diabulo perpetui, ad mortem nimis ultronei." Gil's edition is preferable to Bruno Krusch, ed., MGH SRM 3 (Hanover, 1896), 630–37 (the above appears on 636). For Sisebut's *Vita*, see E. Dekkers, *CPL* no. 1298, 430; Díaz y Díaz, no. 86, 24; Max Manitius, *Geschichte der lateinischen Literatur des Mittelalters*, 3 vols, Handbuch der klassischen Altertumswissenschaft 9.2 (Munich, 1911–31), 1.188. King Sisebut (r. 612–21), ruler in the time of Isidore of Seville, also composed letters, a poem about eclipses, and possibly a hymn on the reckoning of time (Dekkers, *CPL*, nos. 1298–1301, 430–31). See Yitzhak Hen, "A Visigothic King in Search of an Identity—*Sisebutus Gothorum gloriosissimus princeps*," in *Ego Trouble: Authors and Their Identities in the Early Middle Ages*, ed. R. Corradini, R. McKitterick, I. Renswoude, and M. Gillis (Vienna, 2010), 89–99. Desiderius himself is probably best known for Gregory the Great's admonition to him that he turn away from classical frivolities in Gregory the Great, *Ep.* 11.34, ed. L. M. Hartmann, MGH E2 (Berlin, 1899), 303.

171. An "enormous gathering" (*plebs maxima*) is supplied in New Testament fashion with miraculous wine by the saint (Sisebut, *Vita*, c. 12).

172. See Jacques Fontaine, "King Sisebut's *Vita Desiderii* and the Political Function of Visigothic Historiography," in *Visigothic Spain: New Approaches*, ed. Edward James (Oxford, 1980), 93–129. See also Jamie Kreiner, "Gaul's Insiders: Hagiography and Entitlement," in *Hagiography and the History of Latin Christendom, 500–1500* (Leiden, 2020), 211–231, at 223, for the transmutation of this story.

173. Augustine, *Confessiones*, 6.8.13, ed. M. Skutella and L. Verheijen, CCSL 27 (Turnhout, 1981). See chapter 1, pp. 29–31 for discussion.

174. Agnellus of Ravenna, *Liber pontificalis ecclesiae Rauennatis*, c. 126–29, ed. Deborah M. Deliyannis, CCCM 199 (Turnhout, 2006), 300–303 (= O. Holder-Egger, ed., MGH SRL (1878), 361–63). For discussion, see Martínez Pizarro, "Crowds and Power"; Joaquín Martínez Pizarro, *Writing Ravenna: The Liber Pontificalis of Andreas Agnellus* (Ann Arbor, MI, 1995), 141–58; Thomas S. Brown, "Urban Violence in Early Medieval Italy: The Cases of Rome and Ravenna," in *Violence and Society in the Early Medieval West*, ed. Guy Halsall (Woodbridge, UK, 1998), 76–89, at 82–86; Judith Herrin, "Urban Riot or Civic Ritual? The Crowd in Early Medieval Ravenna," in *Raum und Performanz: Rituale in Residenzen von der Antike bis 1815*, ed. D. Boschung, K.-J. Hölkeskamp, and C. Sode (Stuttgart, 2015), 219–240, esp. 221–29; Judith Herrin, *Ravenna: Capital of Empire, Crucible of Europe* (Princeton, NJ, 2020), 297–305; Veronica West-Harling, *Rome, Ravenna, and Venice, 750–1000: Byzantine Heritage, Imperial Present, and the Construction of City Identity* (Oxford, 2020), 449–51.

175. Agnellus of Ravenna, *Liber pontificalis*, c. 126, 301.

176. Agnellus of Ravenna, *Liber pontificalis*, c. 128, 302.

177. Agnellus of Ravenna, *Liber pontificalis*, c. 129, 304.

178. Pizarro, "Crowds and Power," 277–79.

179. West-Harling, *Rome, Ravenna, and Venice*, 449–51.

180. Pizarro, "Crowds and Power," 282, here building explicitly on Elias Canetti.

181. Compare Pizarro, "Crowds and Power," 279.

182. See the essays collected in Sylvie Joye and Régine Le Jan, eds., *Genre et compétition dans les sociétés occidentales du haut Moyen Âge, IVe–XIe siècle* (Turnhout, 2018); Geneviève Bührer-Thierry, Régine Le Jan, Régine, and Vito Loré, *Acquérir, prélever, contrôler: Les ressources en compétition (400–1100)* (Turnhout, 2017); Philippe Depreux, François Bougard, and Régine Le Jan, eds., *Compétition et sacré au haut Moyen Âge: Entre médiation et exclusion* (Turnhout, 2015); François Bougard, Régine Le Jan, and Thomas Lienhard, eds., *Agon: La compétition, Ve–XIIe siècle* (Turnhout, 2012).

183. Suetonius alleged that Nero had hired a claque of professional acclaimers: Suetonius, *Nero* 20.

184. Buc, *The Dangers of Ritual*, 102.

185. E.g., Gregory of Tours, *Hist.* 8.20, ed. Krusch and Levison, 387.

186. Gregory of Tours, *Hist.* 4.11, ed. Krusch and Levison, 141–42. For this episode, see Buc, *The Dangers of Ritual*, 102–3; Sandrine Linger, "Puissance sociale des *domini* d'après l'œuvre de Grégoire de Tours," in *Aux sources de la gestion publique*, vol. 3, *Hommes de pouvoir, ressources et lieux du pouvoir (Ve–XIIIe siècles)*, ed. E. Magnou-Nortier (Villeneuve d'Ascq, 1997), 51–69, at 58; Allen E. Jones, *Social Mobility in Late Antique Gaul: Strategies and Opportunities for the Non-Elite* (Cambridge, UK, 2009), 230, building on the suggestion by Michel Rouche, "La matricule des pauvres: Évolution d'une institution de charité du Bas Empire jusqu'à la fin du Haut Moyen Âge," in *Études sur l'histoire de la pauvreté (Moyen Âge–XVIe siècle)*, ed. Michel Mollat, 83–110 (Paris, 1974), 93, that these *pauperes* may have included the *matricularii* of Saint-Martin. Herrin, "Urban Riot or Civic Ritual?," 229 n. 21, cites this case as "typical of the manipulation of crowds by unscrupulous rulers." See also Margarete Weidemann, *Kulturgeschichte der Merowingerzeit nach den Werken Gregors von Tours* (Mainz, 1982), vol. 1, 203–4; Ian Wood, *The Merovingian Kingdoms, 450–751* (London, 1994), 80–83.

187. Gregory of Tours, *Hist.* 4.11, ed. Krusch and Levison, 142: "At ille, ut erat vanae gloriae cupidus, adunata pauperum caterva, clamorem dari praecepit his verbis: 'Cur nos deseris, bone pater, filios, quos usque nunc edocasti? Quis nos cibo potuque reficiet, sit u abieris? Rogamus, ne nos relinquas, quos alere consuesti.'" For this use of *clamor*, see *TLL*, vol. 3, 1255, s.v. "clāmor," I.A.1 (Hoppe).

188. Gregory of Tours, *Hist.* 4.11, ed. Krusch and Levison, 142: "Tunc ille conversus ad clerum Turonicum, ait: 'Videtis nunc, fratres dilectissimi, qualiter me haec multitudo pauperum diligit;

non possum eos relinquere et ire vobiscum.'" For the depiction of *pauperes* in Gregory of Tours, see Johannes Schneider, "Die Darstellung der Pauperes in den Historiae Gregors von Tours: Ein Beitrag zur sozialökonomischen Struktur Galliens im 6. Jahrhundert," *Jahrbuch Für Wirtschaftsgeschichte* 4 (1966): 57–74. Lutz Raphael, "Royal Protection, Poor Relief, and Expulsion: Types of State and Modes of Inclusion / Exclusion of Strangers and Poor People in Europe and the Mediterranean World since Antiquity," in *Strangers and Poor People: Changing Patterns of Inclusion and Exclusion in Europe and the Mediterranean World from Classical Antiquity to the Present Day*, ed. A. Gestrich, L. Raphael, H. Uerlings (Frankfurt, 2009), 17–34, at 29–30, links the care of the poor by church institutions with weakened royal power in the early Middle Ages, but kings also made a habit of giving to the poor in numbers.

189. Gregory of Tours, *Hist.* 5.18, ed. Krusch and Levison, 219: "Convocabo enim populum Toronicum et dicam eis: 'Voceferamini contra Gregorium, quod sit iniustus et nulli hominum iustitiam praestit.'"

190. *Vita Stephani III*, c. 3, LP 1, 468: "aggregantes tam ex eadem Nepesina quamque ex aliis Tusciae civitatibus multitudinem exercitus atque catervam rusticorum."

191. *Vita Stephani III*, c. 10, LP 1, 470–71.

192. *Vita Stephani III*, c. 11, LP 1, 471.

193. *Vita Stephani III*, c. 14, LP 1, 472: ". . . quidam iniqui Campanini qui hic Roma advenerant, adortati ab aliis nequioribus se et impiissimis . . ."

194. Alcuin, *Ep.* no. 245–49, ed. Ernst Dümmler, MGH Epp 4 (Berlin, 1895), 393–404; Samuel W. Collins, *The Carolingian Debate over Sacred Space* (New York, 2012), 91–120.

195. Livy, *Ab urbe condita*, 24.25.8, ed. T. A. Dorey, *Titi Livi ab vrbe condita libri XXIII–XXV* (Leipzig, 1976), 71: "<e>a natura multitudinis est: aut servit humiliter aut superbe dominatur."

196. See chapter 3, 81–89.

197. E. P. Thompson, "The Moral Economy of the English Crowd in the Eighteenth Century," *Past & Present* 50 (1971): 76–136, at 78.

198. Thompson, "Moral Economy," 136.

199. Paul Cobb, *White Banners: Contention in 'Abbāsid Syria, 750–880* (Albany, NY, 2001), 105–6.

200. Thomas Walsingham, *Historia Anglicana*, ed. H.T. Riley, *Thomæ Walsingham, quondam monachi S. Albani, historia anglicana* (1862–64), vol. 2, 32: "When Adam dalf and Eve span, / Wo was thanne a gentilman?" Sylvia Resnikow, "The Cultural History of a Democratic Proverb," *Journal of English and Germanic Philology* 36 (1937): 391–405.

201. Thompson, "Moral Economy," 130–31.

202. O. G. Oexle, "Conjuratio und Gilden im frühen Mittelalter: Ein Beitrag der sozialen Kontinuität zwischen Antike und Mittelalter," in *Gilden und Zünfte: Kaufmännische und gewerbliche Genossenschaften im frühen und hohen Mittelalter*, ed. B. Schwineköper (Sigmaringen, 1985), 151–214, at 152–53.

203. *AB*, s.a. 859, ed. Grat et al., 80; See Chris Wickham, *Framing the Early Middle Ages: Europe and the Mediterranean, 400–800* (Oxford, 2005), 580–81; Wolfgang Eggert, "Rebelliones servorum: Bewaffnete Klassenkämpfe im Früh- und frühen Hochmittelalter und ihre Darstellung in zeitgenössischen erzählenden Quellen," *Zeitschrift für Geschichtswissenschaft* 23 (1975): 1147–1264, at 1152; Siegfried Epperlein, *Herrschaft und Volk im karolingischen Imperium: Studien über soziale Konflikte und dogmatisch-politische Kontroversen im fränkischen Reich* (Berlin, 1969), 49; Karl Brunner, *Oppositionelle Gruppen im Karolingerreich* (Vienna, 1979), 11–12, 131–32; and for an alternative view, see Oexle, "Conjuratio und Gilden," 152–53.

204. Janet Nelson, *King and Emperor: A New Life of Charlemagne* (London, 2019), 177.

205. The best study on the coordination of political and religious gatherings is M. Sierck, *Festtag und Politik: Studien zur Tagewahl karolingischer Herrscher* (Cologne, 1995). See also McKitterick, *Charlemagne*, 222–24, for information exchange at assemblies.

206. See above, pp. 76–77. Key texts include *Indiculus superstitionum et paganiarum*, c. 21, ed. Alfred Boretius, MGH Capit 1 (Hanover, 1883), 223 (shouting at the moon); c. 28, 223 (idols); Boniface, *Epistolae*, no. 59, ed. Michael Tangl, MGH Epp. sel. 1 (Berlin, 1916), 111; on bonfires, see *Concilium Germanicum* (742), c. 5, ed. Albert Werminghoff, MGH Conc. 2.1 (Hanover, 1906), 3–4; on shouting to the moon, see also Hrabanus Maurus, *Homilia*, no. 42 ["Contra eos qui in lunae defectu clamoribus se fatigabant"], *PL* 110, cols. 78C–80A: a new edition is in preparation by C. Woods for the CCCM. On sky people, see Agobard of Lyon, *De grandine et tonitruis*, c. 2, ed. L. van Acker, *Agobardi Lugdunensis Opera omnia*, CCCM 52 (Turnhout, 1981), 4. See Bernadette Filotas, *Pagan Survivals, Superstitions, and Popular Cultures in Early Medieval Pastoral Literature* (Toronto, 2005), 365–86, for the early medieval sources for pagan and superstitious practices.

207. Gregory of Tours, *Hist.* 10.25, ed. Krusch and Levison, 517–19. See also *Hist.* 9.6, ed. Krusch and Levison, 417–20, for another false saint, Desiderius.

208. Boniface, *Epistolae*, no. 59, ed. Tangl, 111; Nicole Zeddies, "Bonifatius und zwei nützliche Rebellen: Die Häretiker Aldebert und Clemens," in *Ordnung und Aufruhr im Mittelalter*, ed. Marie Theres Fögen (Frankfurt, 1995), 217–63, at 262–63.

209. Amolo, *Ep.* 1, ed. Ernst Dümmler, MGH Epp. 5 (Berlin, 1899), 363–68. On this episode, see Francesco Veronese, *Reliquie in movimento: Politiche della mobilità e rappresentazioni agiografiche in epoca carolingia (VIII–X secolo)* (Rome, 2023), 462–79; Bobrycki, "Flailing Women," 3–46; Charles West, "Unauthorised Miracles in Mid-Ninth-Century Dijon and the Carolingian Church Reforms," *Journal of Medieval History* 36 (2010): 295–311.

210. *AF*, s.a. 847, ed. Kurze, 36–37. See Wemple, *Women in Frankish Society*, 144–45; Julia Smith, "The Problem of Female Sanctity in Carolingian Europe, c. 780–920," *Past & Present* 146 (1995): 3–37, at 35; J. Schulenburg, "Female Sanctity: Public and Private Roles, ca. 500–1100," in *Women and Power in the Middle Ages*, ed. M. Erler and M. Kowaleski (Athens, GA, 1988), 102–25, at 116; Janet L. Nelson, "Women and the Word in the Earlier Middle Ages," in Janet L. Nelson, *The Frankish World, 750–900* (London, 1996), 199–221, at 218; Richard Landes, *Heaven on Earth: The Varieties of the Millennial Experience* (Oxford, 2011), 37–49, 61–66, 81–83.

211. *AF*, s.a. 847, ed. Kurze, 36–37: "Per idem tempus mulier quaedam de Alamanniae partibus nomine Thiota pseudoprophetissa Mogontiacum venit, quae Salomonis episcopi parroechiam suis vaticiniis non minime turbaverat. Nam certum consummationis seculi diem aliaque perplura Dei solius notitiae cognita quasi divinitus sibi revelata scire se fatebatur et eodem anno ultimum diem mundo imminere praedicabat. Unde multi plebeium utriusque sexus timore perculsi ad eam venientes munera illi offerebant seque orationibus illius commendabant; et, quod gravius est, sacri ordinis viri doctrinas ecclesiasticas postponentes illam quasi magistram caelitus destinatam sequebantur. Haec in praesentiam episcoporum apud sanctum Albanum deducta et diligenter de suis assertionibus requisita presbyterum quendam sibi ea suggesisse et se talia questus causa narrasse professa est. Quapropter synodali iudicio publicis caesa flagellis ministerium praedicationis, quod inrationabiliter arripuit et sibi contra morem ecclesiasticum vindicare praesumpsit, cum dedecore amisit suisque vaticiniis tandem confusa finem inposuit."

212. *AX*, s.a. 867 (866), ed. von Simson, 24: "Et confluebat ad eos multitudo magna gentis huius, tam divitum quam etiam ceterorum, diversa munera deferentes."

213. Bobrycki, "Flailing Women," 45–46.

214. Amolo, *Ep.* 1, c. 3, ed. Dümmler, 364.

215. Campbell and Heyman, "Slantwise."

216. For the term, see Elias Canetti, *Masse und Macht* (Düsseldorf, 1978), 15–16. Cf. Susanna Elm, "Captive Crowds: Pilgrims and Martyrs," in *Crowds*, ed. J. Schnapp and M. Tiews (Stanford, 2006), 133–48.

217. Amolo, *Ep.* 1, c. 8, ed. Dümmler, 367: "ita ut si forte aliqui obstinatiores in tali facto apparere voluerint, duris omnino verberibus coerciti ad confessionem veritatis compellendi nobis esse videantur."

218. Marc Bloch, *Feudal Society*, trans. L. A. Manyon (London, 1965), 69.

219. Florian Mazel, *Féodalités, 888–1180* (Paris, 2010), 387.

220. Christopher Loveluck, *Northwest Europe in the Early Middle Ages* (Cambridge, UK, 2013), 302–27.

221. R. I. Moore, "Family, Community and Cult on the Eve of the Gregorian Reform," *Transactions of the Royal Historical Society*, 6th ser., 30 (1980): 49–69, at 49. See also Gioacchino Volpe, *Movimenti religiosi e sette ereticali nella società medievale italiana, secolo XI–XIV* (Florence, 1961), 5–15; Cinzio Violante, *La società Milanese nell'età precomunale* (Bari, 1953), 196–213. For the Patarines, see also Olaf Zumhagen, *Religiöse Konflikte und kommunale Entwicklung: Mailand, Cremona, Piacenza und Florenz zur Zeit der Pataria* (Cologne, 2002). On the political environment leading into the Peace of God movement, see Thomas Head, "Peace and Power in France Around the Year 1000," *Essays in Medieval Studies* 23 (2007): 1–17; Richard Landes, "La vie apostolique en Aquitaine en l'an mil: Paix de Dieu, culte des reliques, et communautés hérétiques," *Annales. Histoire, Sciences Sociales* 46 (1991): 573–93; Theo Riches, "The Peace of God, the 'Weakness' of Robert the Pious and the Struggle for the German Throne, 1023–5," *Early Medieval Europe* 18 (2010): 202–22. For the historiography of the Peace of God, see the useful essay by F. S. Paxton, "The Peace of God in Modern Historiography: Perspectives and Trends," *Historical Reflections* 14 (1987): 385–404. For the people's new role in Italian Christianity, see the essays in Agostino Paravicini Bagliani and Neslihan Şenocak, eds., *A People's Church: Medieval Italy and Christianity, 1050–1300* (Ithaca, NY, 2023).

222. For the heretics of Orléans, see Heinrich Fichtenau, "Die Ketzer von Orléans (1022)," in *Ex Ipsis Rerum Documentis: Beiträge zur Mediävistik: Festschrift für Harald Zimmermann zum 65. Geburtstag*, ed. K. Herbers, H. Henning Kortüm, and C. Servatius (Sigmaringen, 1991), 417–27. For those at Arras as well, see Michael Frassetto, "Reaction and Reform: Reception of Heresy in Arras and Aquitaine in the Early Eleventh Century," *The Catholic Historical Review* 83 (1997): 385–400. For the relationship between the Peace of God and the First Crusade, see Jean Flori, "L'Église et la Guerre Sainte: De la 'Paix de Dieu' à la 'croisade,'" *Annales: Histoire, Sciences Sociales* 47 (1992): 453–66.

223. See Robert Chazan, "1007–1012: Initial Crisis for Northern European Jewry," *Proceedings of the American Academy for Jewish Research* 38 (1970): 101–17, at 117, for the influence of earlier eleventh-century violence on the paroxysms of violence that erupted at the time of the First Crusade. See also Michael Frassetto, "Heretics and Jews in the Writings of Ademar of Chabannes and the Origins of Medieval Anti-Semitism," *Church History* 71 (2002): 1–15, at 13–14, for the violent language directed against the Jews in early eleventh-century sermons.

224. E.g., a typical late eleventh-century example of a crowd (*turba*) of witnesses to a posthumous miracle: Fulbertus of St. Ouen, *Miracula Audoeni* (*BHL* 760), c. 26, AASS Aug. 4.24.830D; or a "crowd of faithful standing by" (*asstante fidelium turba*) amid the sufferings of Saint Dionysius in an eleventh-century hagiographic text from Regensburg: *Translatio S. Dionysii Areopagitae* (*BHL* 2195), ed. Veronika Lukas, *De jüngere Translatio s. Dionysii Areopagitae*, MGH SRM 80 (Wiesbaden, 2013), 282.

225. Alban Gautier, "Les activités compétitives au sein des bandes armées de l'Europe du Nord au haut Moyen Âge," in *Agôn: La compétition, Ve–XIIe siècle*, ed. F. Bougard, R. Le Jan, and T. Lienhard (Turnhout, 2012), 75–91, at 88–91, for the outbreak of violence in northern European armed bands before the tenth century.

226. On Flodoard, see especially Michel Sot, *Un historien et son église au Xe siècle: Flodoard de Reims* (Paris, 1993); Martina Stratmann, "Die *Historia Remensis Ecclesiae*: Flodoards Umgang mit seinen Quellen," *Filologia mediolatina* 1 (1994): 111–27. For Richer, see Justin Lake, *Richer of*

Saint-Rémi: The Methods and Mentality of a Tenth-Century Historian (Washington, DC, 2013); Jason Glenn, *Politics and History in the Tenth Century: The Work and World of Richer of Reims* (Cambridge, UK, 2004); Hartmut Hoffmann, "Die Historien Richers von Saint-Remi," *Deutsches Archiv* 54 (1998): 445–532.

227. Aimoin, author of the eleventh-century *Vita sancti Abbonis* (*BHL* 3), describes seditious crowds (*turbę*) who resist the saintly abbot of Fleury, Abbo, himself the victim of a violent death in 1004: Aimoin, *Vita sancti Abbonis* (*BHL* 3), c. 20, ed. and trans. R.-H. Bautier and Gillette Labory, *L'Abbaye de Fleury en l'an mil*, Sources d'histoire médiévale 32 (Paris, 2004), 124.

228. Michael Sizer, "Storming the Palace: Crowd Incursions into Aristocratic Spaces in Medieval Revolts," in *Art, Architecture, and the Moving Viewer, c. 300–1500 CE: Unfolding Narratives*, ed. Gillian Elliott and Anne Heath (Leiden, 2022), 446–68.

229. See especially Anne-Marie Helvétius, "Ermites ou moines: Solitude et cénobitisme du Ve au Xe siècle (principalement en Gaule du Nord)," in *Ermites de France et d'Italie XIe–XVe siècle*, ed. P. Vauchez (Rome, 2003), 1–27; Diana Webb, *Privacy and Solitude in the Middle Ages* (London, 2007); Peter-Damian Beslisle, *The Language of Silence: The Changing Face of Monastic Solitude* (Maryknoll, NY, 2003). For the complicated theological significance of solitude in the subsequent period, see Giles Constable, "The Ideal of Inner Solitude in the Twelfth Century," in Giles Constable, *Culture and Spirituality in Medieval Europe* (Aldershot, UK, 1996), 28–34.

230. Rainald of the Melinais, *De vita monachorum*, ed. Germain Morin, "Rainaud l'Ermite et Ives de Chartres: Un épisode de la crise du cénobitisme au XIe–XIIe siècle," *Revue bénédictine* 40 (1928): 99–115, at 109: "Quid dicemus de his, qui in urbibus commorantes saepius audiunt ab ipso dormitorio ipsas mulierum cantilenas, et earum strepitus, et choreas, et inquirunt principum et vulgi rumores, et aliquando videntur, et locuntur cum mulieribus, et habitant inter fumantes coquinas?" For the urban monasteries of northern Europe, see Hartmut Atsma, "Les monastères urbains du nord de la Gaule," *Revue d'histoire de l'Église de France* 62 (1976): 163–87. For the monastic regulation of conversation and noise in the early medieval period, see Scott G. Bruce, "The Tongue Is a Fire: The Discipline of Silence in Early Medieval Monasticism (300–1100)," in *The Hands of the Tongue: Essays on Deviant Speech*, ed. Edwin D. Craun (Kalamazoo, MI, 2007), 3–32, at 10–13.

231. Cf. Bede Lackner, *The Eleventh-Century Background of Cîteaux* (Washington, DC, 1972), 93–94, for Rainald's career in context.

232. For Odo of Cambrai, solitary celebrants of the mass addressed the "whole body" of the church when they read the words *et omnium circumstantium*. Odo of Cambrai, *Expositio in canonem missae*, PL 160, col. 1057B–C: "Cum primitus missae sine collecta non fierent, postea mos inolevit Ecclesiae, solitarias et maxime in coenobiis fieri missas. Et cum non habeant quam pluraliter collectam salutent, nec plurales mutare possunt salutationes, convertunt se ad Ecclesiam, dicentes se Ecclesiam in Ecclesia salutare, et in corpore totum corpus alloqui, et virtute totius communionis in Ecclesia confici sancta mysteria per gratiam Dei, nec esse quemquam alicubi infidelium, qui vivificorum non fiat particeps et cooperatorius sacrosanctorum, dum in corpore Ecclesiae adhaeret capiti, velut utile membrum." Cf. Giles Constable, *The Reformation of the Twelfth Century* (Cambridge, UK, 1996), 20–21.

233. Hrotsvit of Gandersheim, *Pafnutius*, 2.6, line 20, ed. P. von Winterfeld, MGH SRG 34 (Berlin, 1902), 169 (*Malo ire solus*).

234. For Hrotsvit's reimagining of Terence, see, among others, Keith A. Bate, "Hrotsvitha, Térence et les conventions scéniques romaines," in *Hommages à Carl Deroux*, vol. 5, *Christianisme et Moyen Âge: Néolatin et survivance de la latinité*, ed. P. Defosse (Brussels, 2003), 292–300; Carole Newlands, "Hrotswitha's debt to Terence," *Transactions of the American Philological Association* 116 (1986): 369–91; Judith Tarr, "Terentian elements in Hrotsvith," in *Hrotsvith of Gandersheim, rara avis in Saxonia? A Collection of Essays*, ed. K. M. Wilson (Ann Arbor, MI, 1987), 55–62.

235. F.J.E. Raby, *A History of Secular Latin Poetry in the Middle Ages*, 2nd ed. (Oxford, 1957), 302–3: "The most famous of all the Cambridge Songs." For the influence of the Song of Songs on this poem, see Peter Dronke, "The Song of Songs and Medieval Love-Lyric," in *The Bible and Medieval Culture*, ed. W. Lourdaux and D. Verhelst (Leuven, 1979), 236–62, at 247.

236. *Carmina Cantabrigensia*, no. 27, ed. K. Strecker, MGH SRG 40 (Hanover, 1926), 71; see also Jan Ziolkowski, ed. and trans., *The Cambridge Songs* (Tempe, AZ, 1998), 92–94 (edition) and 251–60 (commentary). The Cambridge Songs survive in a famous eleventh-century manuscript with the modern shelfmark Cambridge, University Library, MS Gg.5.35, where this poem has been almost entirely erased. This poem is also preserved in two other manuscripts, both of which provide neumes (musical annotation): Vienna, Österreichische Nationalbibliothek, MS Vindobonensis 116, fol. 157v (tenth-century); Paris, BnF, MS lat. 1118, fol. 247v (late tenth-century). For the poem's meter, see Wilhelm Meyer, *Gesammelte Abhandlungen zur mittellateinischen Rythmik* (Berlin, 1905–36), vol. 1, 228.

Conclusion

1. R. I. Moore, "Family, Community and Cult on the Eve of the Gregorian Reform," *Transactions of the Royal Historical Society*, 6th ser., 30 (1980): 49–69, at 49. For nuanced reassessments of the eleventh-century Pataria crowds, see James Norrie, "Rites of Resistance: Urban Liturgy and the Crowd in the Patarine Revolt of Milan, c. 1057–75," *The English Historical Review* 137 (2022): 1575–1605; Piroska Nagy, "Collective Emotions, History Writing and Change: The Case of the Pataria (Milan, Eleventh Century)," in *Emotions: History, Culture, Society* 2 (2018): 132–52.

2. Anna Komnene, *Alexiad*, 10.5–6, ed. D. R. Reinsch and A. Kambylis, *Annae Comnenae Alexias*, Corpus Fontium Historiae Byzantinae 40 (Berlin, 2001), vol. 1, 297–98.

3. Johanne Autenrieth, Dieter Geuenich, and Karl Schmid, eds., *Das Verbrüderungsbuch der Abtei Reichenau*, MGH Libri mem. N.S. I (Hanover, 1979), xlii.

4. Chris Wickham, "Consensus and Assemblies in the Romano-Germanic Kingdoms: A Comparative Approach," in *Recht und Konsens im frühen Mittelalter*, ed. Verena Epp and Christoph Meyer (Ostfildern, 2017), 389–424. See also the essays in Philippe Depreux and Steffen Patzold, eds., *Versammlungen im Frühmittelalter* (Berlin, 2023).

5. Chris Wickham, *Framing the Early Middle Ages: Europe and the Mediterranean, 400–800* (Oxford, 2005), 574–75.

6. Thomas S. Brown, "Urban Violence in Early Medieval Italy: The Cases of Rome and Ravenna," in *Violence and Society in the Early Medieval West*, ed. Guy Halsall (Woodbridge, UK, 1998), 76–89; Veronica West-Harling, *Rome, Ravenna, and Venice, 750–1000: Byzantine Heritage, Imperial Present, and the Construction of City Identity* (Oxford, 2020), 449–51; Thomas S. Brown, "Justinian II and Ravenna," *Byzantinoslavica* 56 (1995): 29–36; Judith Herrin, "Urban Riot or Civic Ritual? The Crowd in Early Medieval Ravenna," in *Raum und Performanz: Rituale in Residenzen von der Antike bis 1815*, ed. Dietrich Boschung, Karl-Joachim Hölkeskamp, and Claudia Sode (Stuttgart, 2015), 219–40, esp. 224.

7. Elias Canetti, *Masse und Macht* (Düsseldorf, 1978), 12–14.

8. Hendrick W. Dey, *The Afterlife of the Roman City: Architecture and Ceremony in Late Antiquity and the Early Middle Ages* (Cambridge, UK, 2015), 136.

9. Paolo Squatriti, "Barbarizing the *Bel Paese*: Environmental History in Ostrogothic Italy," in *A Companion to Ostrogothic Italy*, ed. Jonathan J. Arnold, M. Shane Bjornlie, and Kristina Sessa (Leiden, 2016), 390–421, at 392–98. For thoughtful examples of both approaches, see Isabelle Catteddu, *Archéologie médiévale en France: Le premier Moyen Âge (Ve–XIe siècle)* (Paris, 2009), 159–61; and Richard Hodges, *Dark Age Economics: A New Audit* (London, 2012), 67–90, 91–115.

10. Peregrine Horden and Nicholas Purcell, *The Corrupting Sea: A Study of Mediterranean History* (Oxford, 2000), 89–122, esp. 90–108, with quote at 90. For criticism, see Wickham, *Framing*, 591 n. 1; and James Fentress and Elizabeth Fentress, "The Hole in the Doughnut," *Past & Present* 173 (2001): 203–19.

11. Horden and Purcell, *The Corrupting Sea*, 91: "Urban history is far from being mere 'superstructure' on a microecological base. The point is precisely that is it indivisible from the broader canvas."

12. Bonnie Effros, "The Enduring Attraction of the Pirenne Thesis," *Speculum* 92 (2017): 184–208, at 200.

13. Effros, "Enduring Attraction," 200.

14. Dey, *The Afterlife of the Roman City*; Caroline Goodson, *Cultivating the City in Early Medieval Italy* (Cambridge, UK, 2021).

15. Cyprian Broodbank, *The Making of the Middle Sea: A History of the Mediterranean from the Beginning to the Emergence of the Classical World* (Oxford, 2013), 358 (estimating a Mediterranean population around fifteen million people during the second millennium BCE), 506–7 (estimating a growing population around twenty million by c. 800 BCE).

16. Clemens Gantner, Rosamond McKitterick, and Sven Meeder, eds., *The Resources of the Past in Early Medieval Europe* (Cambridge, UK, 2015).

17. Moore, "Family, Community and Cult on the Eve of the Gregorian Reform," 49.

18. Samuel Cohn, *Lust for Liberty: The Politics of Social Revolt in Medieval Europe, 1200–1425; Italy, France, and Flanders* (Cambridge, MA, 2006).

19. Norrie, "Rites of Resistance," 1597.

20. Philippe Depreux and Steffen Patzold, "Einleitung," in *Versammlungen im Frühmittelalter*, ed. Depreux and Patzold, 1–18, at 4. For parliaments, see John R. Maddicott, *Origins of the English Parliament, 924–1327* (Oxford, 2010); Sören Kaschke, "Politische Versammlungen im angelsächsischen England," in *Versammlungen im Frühmittelalter*, ed. Depreux and Patzold, 103–15, esp. 112–13.

21. Ernst Kantorowicz, *The King's Two Bodies: A Study in Mediaeval Political Theology* (Princeton, NJ, 1957), 476 (and n. 65); Lisi Oliver, *The Body Legal in Barbarian Law* (Toronto, 2011), 190; Gaines Post, "Plena Potestas and Consent in Medieval Assemblies: A Study in Romano-Canonical Procedure and the Rise of Representation, 1150–1325," *Traditio* 1 (1943): 355–408; Gaines Post, "Roman Law and Early Representation in Spain and Italy, 1150–1250," *Speculum* 18 (1943): 211–32; Stephen C. Yeazell, *From Medieval Group Litigation to the Modern Class Action* (New Haven, CT, 1987).

22. Laurent Waelkens, "L'origine de l'enquête par turbe," *Tijdschrift voor rechtsgeschiedenis* 53 (1985): 337–46. See also the discussion at p. 141 above.

23. Vasileios Syros, "The Sovereignty of the Multitude in the Works of Marsilius of Padua, Peter of Auvergne, and Some Other Aristotelian Commentators," in *The World of Marsilius of Padua*, ed. Gerson Moreno-Riaño (Turnhout, 2006), 227–48, at 240–41; Michael Sizer, "Storming the Palace: Crowd Incursions into Aristocratic Spaces in Medieval Revolts," in *Art, Architecture, and the Moving Viewer, c. 300–1500 CE: Unfolding Narratives*, ed. Gillian Elliott and Anne Heath (Leiden, 2022), 446–68, at 447–49.

24. Robert Bartlett, *Why Can the Dead Do Such Great Things? Saints and Worshippers from the Martyrs to the Reformation* (Princeton, NJ, 2013), 333–409.

25. Dante, *Paradiso*, canto 22, line 7, ed. G. Petrocchi, *La Commedia secondo l'antica vulgata*, 4 vols. (Milan, 1967), vol. 4, 357.

26. The ability of crowds to alter mental states has been an enduring question. See S. B. Patten and J. A. Arboleda-Flórez, "Epidemic Theory and Group Violence," *Social Psychiatry and Psychiatric Epidemiology* 39 (2004): 853–56; L. Nummenmaa, J. Hirvonen, and R. Parkkola, "Is Emotional Contagion Special? An fMRI Study on Neural Systems for Affective and Cognitive

Empathy," *Neuroimage* 43 (2008): 571–80; Stefan Stürmer and Bernd Simon, "Pathways to Collective Protest: Calculation, Identification, or Emotion? A Critical Analysis of the Role of Group-Based Anger in Social Movement Participation," *Journal of Social Issues* 65 (2009): 681–705; Elisabeth M. J. Huis in 't Veld and Beatrice de Gelder, "From Personal Fear to Mass Panic: The Neurological Basis of Crowd Perception," *Human Brain Mapping* 36 (2015): 2338–51; Sigal G. Barsade, "The Ripple Effect: Emotional Contagion and Its Influence on Group Behavior," *Administrative Science Quarterly* 47 (2002): 644–75; Tibor Bosse et al., "Agent-Based Analysis of Patterns in Crowd Behaviour Involving Contagion of Mental States," in *Modern Approaches in Applied Intelligence*, ed. Kishan G. Mehrotra et al. (Berlin, 2011), 566–77; Elaine Hatfield, John T. Cacioppo, and Richard L. Rapson, "Emotional Contagion," *Current Directions in Psychological Science* 2 (1993): 96–99; J. Tsai, E. Bowring, and S. Marsella, "Empirical Evaluation of Computational Emotional Contagion Models," *Intelligent Virtual Agents* (2011): 384–97. A. Kramer, J. Guillory, and J. Hancock, "Experimental evidence of massive-scale emotional contagion through social networks," *PNAS* 111 (2014): 8788–90, was a controversial study of emotional contagion across the online social network Facebook, which generated concern when it did not inform participants that they were being subjected to a study. See also Tony D. Sampson, *Virality: Contagion Theory in the Age of Networks* (London, 2012).

27. Victor Turner, *The Ritual Process: Structure and Anti-Structure* (London, 2009 [1969]), 128.

28. I am grateful to Elliott Colla for sharing and discussing with me post-2011 and post-2013 Egyptian poems on themes of dangerous unity and violence.

29. Philip Pettit, "Five Elements of Group Agency," *Inquiry* 66 (2023): 1–21; Christian List and Philip Pettit, *Group Agency: The Possibility, Design, and Status of Corporate Agents* (Oxford, 2011).

30. Mary Douglas, *Natural Symbols: Explorations in Cosmology*, revised ed. (London, 2003 [1970]), 8: "The first thing is to break through the spiky, verbal hedges that arbitrarily insulate one set of human experiences (ours) from another set (theirs)."

INDEX

Aachen, 47, 108, 140, 151; archaeology of, 213n162, 214n164; miraculously dense crowds of, 149, 153; palace capacity of, 62

Abbo (abbot of Fleury), seditious crowd resisted by, 293n227

Abbo of Saint-Germain-des-Prés, 54

Abd al-Rahman III (Umayyad caliph of Córdoba), 47

Abraham (biblical figure): numberless descendants of, 145; three hundred eighteen servants of, 52

Acts of Saint Sylvester (BHL 7725–43), as hagiographical model, 146

Adorno, Theodor, 6; on phoniness of totalitarian crowds, 182n23

Adrevald of Fleury (author of the *Miracula Benedicti* (BHL 1123–24)): topoi copied from Einhard by, 147; villainous crowd depicted by, 140, 272n253

Adso (abbot of Montier-en-Der): on crowds as signs of divine will, 71; on rustics, 69–70

Ælfric (abbot of Eynsham), 66

Æthelstan (English king), 57; assemblies of, 187n64

Aethicus Ister, *Cosmographia*, fantastic numbers of, 52

Agamben, Giorgio, 264n141

Agnellus of Ravenna (ninth-century historian): on amphitheater of Ravenna, 32; inflated figures of, 52; on mock-battles in Ravenna leading to violence, 162–63, 281n81

Agobard (archbishop of Lyon): crowd discourse of, 132; on peasant superstitions, 77, 161, 167, 291n206

agriculture, implications for peasant gatherings, 66–69

Aimoin (author and monk of Fleury, tenth and eleventh centuries), 147, 283n101, 293n227

Alcuin (English scholar, courtier to Charlemagne, abbot of St-Martin, Tours), 52, 91; conflict with Theodulf of Orléans over tumult at Tours, 111–12, 165; Latin style of, 252n205; negative crowd depictions of, 111–12, 132; unanimous crowd depicted by, 285n127

Aldebert (heretical eighth-century preacher with large crowds), 167

Aldhelm of Malmesbury: literary influence of, 147

Alexandria, 19, 21, 23

Althoff, Gerd: on deliberative vs. celebratory assemblies, 59, 115

Alvar, Paul, 128

Alypius (bishop of Thagaste, friend of Augustine), addiction to crowd entertainments of, 29–31, 162, 272n256

Amalarius (archbishop of Lyon, exegete of liturgy), 106, 279n54; on gender separation in church, 279n54

Amator (saint, bishop of Auxerre), child resurrected by, 2, 158

Ambrose (saint, bishop of Milan), 21

Ambrosius Autpertus, monastic crowd depicted by, 270n228

Ammianus Marcellinus (author of *Res Gestae*), 6, 21, 29, 275n12; negative use of term *turba* by, 136–37, 138

Amolo (archbishop of Lyon): advice to use blows against misbehaving crowds of women, 100, 168, 292n217; on crowds behaving exuberantly before unauthorized relics at Dijon, 53, 76, 78, 100, 167; on crowd size, 51, 217n203, 219n225
Amram Gaon (ninth-century Jewish sage), 126–27
Anastasius Bibliothecarius: on Byzantine numbers at joint-siege of Bari, 54, 159–60; negative crowd depiction of, 140; small numbers of council defended by, 53. *See also* Louis II
Andernach, battle of (876), 53
Ando, Clifford, on acclamations, 18; on Roman trial procedure, 189n22
angaria (peasant hauling labor), 72
Angilbert (abbot of Saint-Riquier): collective liturgical arrangements of, 48, 91, 95–96, 100; *Institutio de diversitate officiorum*, 95–96
Angles (people), 22
Annales Bertiniani (*Annals of Saint Bertin*; Prudentius of Troyes and Hincmar of Reims): on mass deaths in a tsunami, 53; on peasant *coniuratio* (859), 64, 87, 235n199, 235n199; on *Stellingas*, 84–85
Annales Fuldenses (*Annals of Fulda*), on Viking numbers, 53–54, 84–85, 167
Annales Mettenses priores, 156
Annales Regni Francorum (*Royal Frankish Annals*), 147; multiplying gaze in, 159; word *multitudo* in, 149; word *turba* avoided by, 140
Annales Xantenses (*Annals of Xanten*), 84
annona (Roman grain dole), 24, 26, 193n90
Anskar of Bremen, 282–83n96
Anstrudis of Laon (abbess), 270n228
Antholianus (martyr), 151, 280–81n76
Antioch, 23, 26
Antonine Constitution (212), 19
Antonine Plague, 38, 202n35
Anthony of Egypt (saint), 146, 147
Arabic: crowds denoted in, 166; crowd words of, 127–28

araturas (peasant plowing labor), 72
Arcadius (Roman emperor), 29–30
Archanaldus of Angers, 269n225s
Arena, Patrizia, 25; on classical polysemy of *turba*, 136
Arezzo, 45, Siena's jurisdictional conflict with, 46, 55, 74, 95
Armenian language, 129
armies, 84, 109–10, 117, 137, 150; angelic, 2, 102; crowds or peoples denoted as, 113, 123, 124, 125, 126, 220n239, 264n126; episcopal entourages lamented as, 56; Roman, 25, 137, 164; size of, 53–55, 159–60, 219n229; taxes for, 73, 74
Arras, eleventh-century heretics of, 169, 292n222
art, 6; isocephalic crowds in, 98, 172, 175, 276n25
assemblies, secular, 2, 3, 9, 10, 55, 56, 105, 107, 145, 171, 173; information and, 116; non-elite, 71, 86; oaths and, 74–75; parliaments and, 186–87n64; politics of, 113, 114–15, 176; in Roman era, 16–17, 20, 21; size of, 58–59, 62–63; sites of, 115, 117; "solemn assemblies," 93, 112–16; visual representations of, 186n58; words for, 122–25, 134. *See also* thing
Asturias, 41; non-elite revolt (c. 770) in, 81, 83, 87, 165, 234n164
Athanasius of Alexandria: *Life of Anthony*, 146; on number of fathers at Nicaea I, 72
Audo (sixth-century Frankish *iudex*), home burned by crowd, 80
Audoenus (Audoin; seventh-century saint and bishop), as hagiographer, 217n211, 276n26
Audomar (saint), 270n228
Auerbach, Erich, 6–7, 10, 28; on Curtius's concept of topos, 275n9; on representativeness of classicizing texts, 121
Augustine of Hippo (saint, bishop, and author), 29, 111; on the *caterva*, 266n176; on the crowd's lure and power, 29–31, 162, 195n122; sermon audiences of, 94, 239n34; word *turba* used by, 138. *See also* Alypius

INDEX   299

Augustus (Roman emperor), 28, 29, 116
Aurelian Walls (Rome), 24
Avars, 53, 54, 128

bacaudae (bagaudae), 19
Bacon, Roger, on hypnotic crowd leaders, 6
Bad Neuheim (salt production site), 49
Baghdad, 1, 4
Bailey, Lisa, 67–68
Baker, John, 115
Bakhtin, Mikhail, 5, 29
Baltherus (Balderich) of Säckingen (tenth-century hagiographer), 152, 282n87
Banerjee, Abhijit, 75, 290n98
Banniard, Michael, 121
Barbiera, Irene, 37. *See also* demography
Barcelona, 41, 53, 150, 207n86
Bari, Franco-Byzantine siege of (871), 53, 54, 159–60
barley, 66, 67, 227n22
Basel, 45
Basil I, Byzantine emperor, 54, 159–60. *See also* Bari, Franco-Byzantine siege of
Basque language, 128
Basra, 44
Baudonivia (nun and hagiographer), 275n14
Bauer, Franz, on "liturgical fragmentation," 97
Bavaria, 39, 74, 103,
Beck, Hans Georg, 127
Bede (saint and author): on crowd of students, 152; on demographic decline, 43; dispute between saint and heretic before a crowd described by, 157–58; *Historia Ecclesiastica gentis Anglorum*, 157; on retinue size, 56–57
Benedict VIII (pope), 160
Bernardino da Feltre (preacher), 62
Bernardino da Siena (preacher), 62
Bertin (saint), 129
Biddle, Martin, on settlement typologies, 45, 211n135
Biraben, Jean-Noël, 39–40
birds: crowds of, 5, 70; as pests, 66, 67, 70
Birka, 46

Bisson, Thomas: on celebratory character of assemblies, 114–15
blinding, 79, 165
blindness, 157, 272n261, 273n1, 287n150
Bloch, Marc: on churches as sites of gathering and business, 99; on demography, 36, 168; on peasants, 71, 78, 91–92
Blumer, Herbert (crowd theorist), 184n40
Bodo and Ermentrude (early ninth-century peasant couple), 77
Boethius: on psychological limits of crowds, 114; on public recognition by circus crowds, 27
Bohstedt, John: critique of E. P. Thompson, 185n44
Boniface (Carolingian count), 159
Boniface (saint, bishop of Mainz), 167; feast day of, 57, 102
Bordeaux, 42, 61
Boserup, Ester: on population and technology, 201n24
Bowes, Kim, 37
Brescia, memorial book (*liber memorialis*) of, 103
Brioude (Saint-Julian's), 154
British Isles, 56–57, 157; demographic trends in, 37, 40, 42–43; in Roman era, 22, 25
Brookes, Stuart, 115
Brown, Peter, 10, 23, 198n2
Brunhild (Merovingian queen), 161–62
Bruttium (Calabria), 138
Buc, Philippe: on texts and ritual, 157, 163, 237n4
Bührer-Thierry, Geneviève, 110
Burgundians, 22, 123
Byzantium (Byzantines), ix, 1, 3, 44, 52, 55, 79, 135, 159–160, 165, 171, 220n246; acclamations in, 254n233; ancient Roman civilization linked to, 17, 21, 166, 188n9; Greek crowd vocabulary of, 119, 127, 131, 142; Italian cities influenced by, 10; politics and spectacle in crowd culture of, 22, 32–33, 54, 166, 197n146; topoi in the literature of, 274n5

Caesar, Julius, 29, 208n90
Caesarius of Arles (saint, author), superstition criticized by, 76–77
Calpurnius Siculus, Titus (Roman poet), 24
Cameron, Alan, 194n113, 195n124, 195–96n127
Canetti, Elias: as crowd theorist, ix; on "open" vs. "closed" crowds, 4, 10, 64, 93, 94, 117, 163, 168, 173, 256n264, 289n180. *See also* closed crowds
caplim (peasant wood-cutting labor), 72
Caracalla (Roman emperor): baths of, 19, 24
carropera (peasant carting labor), 70
carrying capacities, 44–51. *See also* demography
Carthage, 23, 159, 218n213
Cassiodorus, Senator (sixth-century author), 32; "Catos don't go to the circus," 23, 194n114; on "excess" permitted by the circus crowd, 28–29, 194nn114–17; on food supply, 19; on Rome's *turbae*, 138–39
Cassius (martyr), 151, 280–81n76
Castiglioni, Maria, 37. *See also* demography
Çatalhöyük, 16
Cato (sixth-century priest and episcopal pretender), 163–64
cattle, 115, 167, 282n81; bulls, 281n81; oxen, 66, 70, 72, 151, 228n55
Catullus, Gaius Valerius (poet), 16
cave paintings, 16
Celtic fringe, 15
Celtic languages, 121, 126
Cenwald (bishop of Worcester), 57, 63
Ceolfrith (abbot of Warmouth-Jarrow), 56–57
cereals: production of, 67–68; in Roman era, 24; threats to, 70
Chang'an (Chinese city), 23
chariot racing: Byzantine, 32–33; non-western, 16; Roman, 25, 29. *See also* circuses
Charlemagne (Charles; Frankish king and emperor), 54–55, 79, 91, 151, 214n164; army of, 150; canal project of, 74; *Life* of, 57, 147; oaths required by, 75; party to Alcuin's and Theodulf's dispute, 111–12; peasants' legal recourse sought by, 166; retinue of, 56, 108, 140
Charles the Bald (Frankish king and emperor), 47, 56, 59
Charles III ("the Fat," Frankish emperor), 57, 113
chestnuts, 66, 67, 68; as metaphor, 160
Chilperic I (Merovingian king), 31, 80, 164
China, 16, 23, 27
Chlothar III (Merovingian king), 106–7
Christianity: discourse of crowds shaped by, 119, 132–35, 137–38, 141; in late antique crowds, 19, 21–22, 25
Christian of Stavelot: on ethnic dancing preferences, 232n122; on wisdom of crowds, 146
Chrodegang (saint, bishop of Metz), 131
churches: ambitions and limitations of, 94–95; archaeology of, 12; architecture and art of, 97–98; as asylums, 80; capacity of, 53; cities and, 46; festival days at, 46, 95–96; consensus building in, 99; as gathering sites, 13, 94–96; hierarchical and gender differentiation in, 96; liturgical fragmentation of, 97–98, 99–100; local identity bound up with, 95; pastoral care at, 95; peasants' attendance at, 75–76; slantwise behavior at, 77; use of space in, 97–100
Cicero, Marcus Tullius, 17, 25, 133
circumcelliones, 17, 19, 24
circuses, 5, 18, 28–29, 30, 41, 55, 100, 136, 173; "bread and circuses," 1, 26, 28, 32; churchgoing as competition to, 195–96n127; collapse of, 15, 190n12; factions (*demoi*) and, 17, 24, 27, 130; Merovingian, 31; pious disdain for, 147. *See also* chariot racing
Circus Maximus, 18, 23, 25; capacity of, 23
Cividale, memorial book of, 103
cities and towns: early medieval decline of, 35, 38, 39; early medieval unrest in, 78–81; historiographical importance of, 174–75;

in Roman Antiquity, 16, 23–25. *See also* demography
Clermont, 45, 70, 79, 99, 154, 163; plague outbreak at, 217n211
closed crowds, 4–6, 8–10, 27, 65, 93–118, 168, 173. *See also* Canetti, Elias
Clovis I (Frankish king), 195n126
Cobb, Paul, 166, 261n82
coemptio (compulsory Roman purchase of provisions), 24
Coleman, Edward, on assemblies, 113
Coleman, Emily, on infanticide, 37
Coleman, Kathleen, on audiences and sponsors at Roman games, 27
Collins, Samuel, on Alcuin's depiction of the crowd, 111
Cologne, 45
Colosseum, 1, 18; capacity of, 179n1; ominous lightning strikes of, 189n12; post-classical use of, 32, 196n135, 197n140
Columbanus, 154, 273n1; alone among animals, 279n59
Comacchio, 46
Commodus (Roman emperor), 29
Compiègne, 61, 213n161; site of *placitum* for peasants of Mitry, 47, 73, 74, 89
concilii (lay collectives in Lombard law), 71–72. *See also* gilds
Condedus (saint, preacher to *turbae*), 269–70n227
coniurationes, 68, 72, 87
conspirationes, 72
Constance, 45
Constantine (antipope in 768), 164
Constantinople, 1, 20, 23, 26, 44
Constantius II (Roman emperor), 137
contio (*concio*): alternative spellings of, 264n238; ancient and late antique meanings of, 133–34; antiquarian use of, 134–35; Christianization of, 134; negative Roman meanings of, 133. *See also* words for crowds
Coptic language, 128
Corbie, 47
Córdoba, 1; population of, 42, 208n89

corvadas (corvées), 72
Corvey, 103
councils, ecclesiastical, 21–22, 41, 56, 115, 117, 171; churches as venues for, 99; Germanic word for, 122; numbers of, 52–53, 58–62
Council of Chalcedon (451), 22, 52
Council of Chalon (647–53), 61
Council of Constantinople I (381), 52
Council of Constantinople II (553), 22
Council of Douzy (871), 57
Council of Ephesus (432), 22
Council of Nicaea (325), 22, 52
Council of Orléans (549), 59
Council of Paris (614), 59–60
Council of Piacenza (1095), 61–62
Council of Toledo (646), 56, 58
Council of Toulouse (844), 56
Courtisols, *placitum publicum* of (847), 50–51, 55, 217n201
courts, 18, 50–51, 74–75
Cremona, 79
crowd psychology, approaches to, 4, 295–96n26
crowd regime, early medieval, 10–12, 116–17, 172–75
crowds, historiography and social science of, 3–8. *See also* gathering
Curtius, Ernst Robert, 144
Cyprian Plague, as demographic factor, 38

Dacians, 18
Dalla Zuanna, Gianpiero, 37. *See also* demography
Damasus (pope), 21
Damian (archbishop of Ravenna), crowd control by, 162–63
Danes, 64, 87. *See also* Vikings
Daniel (book of the Bible), for apocalyptic number of ten billion, 52, 218n218
Dante Alighieri, on crowds, 176, 183n30
Davies, Wendy, on peasant coordination, 71
Davis, Natalie Zemon, x, 7–9, 10, 69, 88; on concept of "repertory," 8–9, 10, 64–65; criticism of, 185n44

deer, 70, 149
Delbrück, Hans: criticism of, 54, 219n237: on estimation of historical military figures, 53–54, 159
delegitimation of crowds, 158–68; fear, 167–68; fury, 161–63; gender, 168; greed, 167–68; numerousness, 159–60; otherness, 159–60; phoniness, 163–65; rusticity, 165–68
Demetrius (saint), 140
demography, 36–51, 174; archaeological evidence for, 37–38, 201n19, 201n24; of the British Isles, 43; carrying capacity of large pools, 45–46; carrying capacity of mid-sized pools, 47–49; carrying capacity of smaller pools, 49–51; causes of change in, 38–39; d index (demographic mortality index), 202n33, 204n51; effective population (N_e), 202n34; of Gaul, 42; gross estimated population change, 39–40; of Iberia, 41–42; of Italy, 40–41; logistical consequences of, 51; methods for measuring carrying capacity, 44–45; of Northern Europe, 42–43; scientific evidence for (osteological, isotopic, genetic, etc.), 38; of the Slavlands, 43–44; written evidence for, 36–47, 199–200n9, 200n12. *See also* depopulation
Deodatus (monk), accused by peasants of Mitry of mistreatment, 73
depopulation, late antique and early medieval, 1–2, 25, 32, 37, 38, 39–40; effects of, 22, 51, 174; limited explanatory power of, 171, 175. *See also* demography
Desan, Suzanne, 9; on the crowd historiography of E. P. Thompson and Natalie Davis, 185n44
De Seta, Vittorio (filmmaker), 69
Desiderius (Lombard king), 54, 150
Desiderius of Vienne (saint, bishop of Vienne), martyrdom at hands of crowd of, 161–62
Devroey, Jean-Pierre: on demography, 37; on fertility, 205n57; on peasants, 69
Dey, Hendrik, on "urban armature," 23, 48

Dickson, Gary, on high and late medieval crowd theory, 6
dies (peasant labor), 72
Diesenberger, Maximilian, 97
Dio Chrysostom, on autarkic rustics in the Roman empire, 24
Diocletian, Roman emperor, 19, 116
Dodilo (*missus* of the archbishop of Reims in the Courtisols case), 50–51
Donatists (late antique Christian sect), 21; *circumcelliones* of, 17
Dorestad (emporium): multitudes of poor at, 98; seasonal population of, 46; size estimate of, 213n151; as Viking target, 109
Douglas, Mary (anthropologist), 177, 182n17, 296n30
Dublin, 43
Duisburg, 47
Duflo, Esther, 75, 290n98
Durham, *Liber vitae*, 103
Durkheim, Émile, 4–6; on "anomie," 8; on "collective effervescence," 5, 182n16

Ebroin (Frankish magnate, mayor of the palace), 106–7, 248n149
"Edict" of Milan (313), 21
Edict of Rothari (Lombard law), 89
Edict of Thessalonica (380), 21
Effros, Bonnie, argument against Pirenne Thesis, 175
Egeria (fourth-century traveler to the Holy Land), *turba* used by, 138, 268–69n214
eggs: as dues exacted from peasants, 70; as rations for retinues, 58, 223n281
Einhard, 47; as Charlemagne's biographer (*Vita Karoli*), 56, 104, 140, 147; relics of Petrus and Marcellinus translated by, 104, 149, 153, 156, 164–65; style of, 121
Elafius (father of a boy healed before crowd by a saint), 157
elections, 79, 96, 106–7, 110, 114, 164, 248n145; consensus important in, 151–52, 282n90; contested, for papacy, 233n140; topos of reluctant elected official, 144

Eleutherius of Tournai (saint), praised by many (*multi*), 153
elites, ix, 65, 73–75, 93–118; approaches to, 186n63
Emma (Frankish queen), 247n128
Ems River, 42
Ennen, Edith, urban typologies of, 45
entourages (retinues), 55–58, 105–6, 124, 125
epidemics, 15, 80; in European demographic decline, 38–39. *See also* Antonine Plague; plague, bubonic; *Yersinia pestis*
Ermentrude (peasant woman). *See* Bodo and Ermentrude
Ermoldus (Ermold) Nigellus (poet), *In honorem Hludowici Caesaris*, 150, 280n67
euergetism, 18, 22, 188n5. *See also* circuses
Ethiopic language, 128
Eusebius (archbishop of Thessaloniki), 140
Evagrius (translator), 146

Fagan, Garrett, 27
famine, 38, 41, 67, 79
feast days, 57, 69–70, 76, 77–78, 91, 95, 116, 162; collecting dues on, 73–74; visiting monasteries on, 102
fertility rates (demographic), 37, 39, 204n50, 205n57. *See also* demography
Festus, Sextus Pompeius, 133, 264n141
fish, 5, 66, 69, 228n55, 259n51
flax, 66
Fleming, Robin, 115, 193n90
Flodoard of Reims, 169
floods, 69, 155
Fontenoy, battle of (841), 53
Francia, Franks, 22, 47, 53, 54–55, 124; councils in, 58–62
Frankfurt, 47; failed ritual in assembly at, 113; palace's capacity in, 62
Frechulf (historian, bishop of Lisieux), 52
Fredegar (chronicle), 109
Fredegund (Frankish queen), 80
Freud, Sigmund, crowd theory of, 4, 181n10, 182n11
Fridolin (saint), 152
Frisia, 42; dune-flattening tsunami in, 53

Fulda monastery, 57, 100, 102; number of monks in, 48
Fulk (archbishop of Reims): assassination of, 106
funerary practices: among early Frankish kings, 198n2; gild arrangements for, 71; Roman, 15–16; for saints, 153

gambling, 27
Garigliano, battle of (915), 53
gathering, as value-neutral term for crowd, 10, 186n55–56
Gaul, 15, 19, 22, 42, 63, 172
Gellius, Aulus, on the *contio*, 133
gender, 4, 27–28, 90, 95, 101, 144, 159, 168, 173, 193n97, 269n216
Genesius (saint, bishop of Lyon), 106; miracle story of, 158
Genesius of Jerusalem (saint), relics of, 155–56
Gennep, Arnold van, on liminality, 5
Genoa, 41, 45
Georgian language, 128
Gerbert of Aurillac, 247n128
Germanic languages, 122–26
Germanus of Auxerre, 157, 158
gilds, 68, 71–72, 166; as context for Stellingas, 85; defensive, 88, 92, 100; other words for (*concilius, coniuratio, collecta*), 72, 120
gladiators, 25, 26–27, 33, 117, 187–88n4; as addictive spectacle, 29–31; large numbers of, 18–19; as quintessential spectator sport, 117
Gniezno (Poland), 49
goats, 70, 73
Godo (eighth-century centenarian cleric), 55
Goldberg, Eric, 10, 102; on hunting, 107; on peasant vulnerability, 87, 102
Goodson, Caroline, 41
Goslar (Germany), 49
Gothic language, 123
Goths, 22, 28–29, 31, 42, 123
Gowers, Bernard, on Norman peasants' "revolt," 86
grain, 66, 67. *See also* cereals

grapes, 66, 67; harvest of, 68
Gratian (Roman emperor), 137
Gray, Thomas (poet), "Elegy Written in a Country Churchyard," 65
Greater Moravia, 43, 49
Greek language, 127
Gregory I ("the Great," pope), 25, 36, 81, 88, 97, 138, 146; *Dialogues*, 146; *Moralia in Job*, 131
Gregory of Tours (bishop, historian, and hagiographer), 48, 111, 115, 165; Clermont church described by, 99; on Clovis I, 195n126; on false holy men, 167, 291n207; on harvesters, 50, 179n4, 216n194; on Jews, 260n74; on lynching, 241n55; on Merovingian-era circuses, 195n125; on nuns' revolt at Poitiers (589–90), 101, 243n83; on plague, 217n211; on the poor, 290n188; on royal burning of tax documents, 200n11; on size of a mob in Carthage, 218n213; small cities idealized by, 45, 212n142; on staged rituals, 163–64, 289n186; town uprisings recounted by, 79–80, 87, 88, 161; writing style of, 121, 130, 131
Grundmann, Herbert, on semantic history as "seismograph," 119
guilds. *See* gilds
Gundobad, Burgundian king, 114
Gunteram (notary of Pavia in Siena), 55
gynaecea (women's workshops), 72
Gyug, Richard, 272n256

Habermas, Jürgen, 105, 186n59, 246–47n124
hadith, 127
Hadrian I (pope), 79
Hadrian II (pope), 152
Hadrian of Canterbury, saint, 152
Hagia Sophia, 62
hagiography, 108, 143–48, 153, 157, 159, 169
hagiography, works of
    Historia Translationis Helenae (BHL 3773), 147
    Passio Desiderii episcopi et martyris Viennensis (BHL 2149), by Sisebut, 161, 281n80

Passio Praeiecti (BHL 6915–16), 98
Passio Prisci et sociorum (BHL 6930), 150
Passio Saturnini (BHL 7491), 141, dating of, 272n256
Translatio Genesii (BHL 3314), 156, 283n97
Translatio Marcellini et Petri (BHL 5233), by Einhard, 47, 104, 147, 153, 156. *See also* Einhard
Translatio Vincentii (BHL 8644–8646), by Aimoin, 147, 283n101, 293n227
Translatio Viti martyris (BHL 8718–19), 149, 154, 283n101
Vita Amatoris (BHL 356), by Stephen of Auxerre, 158
Vita Arnulfi (BHL 692), 153, 281n81
Vita Gaugerici (BHL 3286), 152, 281n80
Vita Hilarionis (BHL 3879), by Jerome, 147; for Hilarion's distaste for circus, arena, and theater, 278n43. *See also* Jerome
Vita Leudegari (BHL 4849b), 106–7; authorship and dating of, 248n148
Vita Martini (BHL 5610), by Sulpicius Severus, 146
Hailstone, Catherine, on fear, 99
Halsall, Guy, on army sizes, 54, 219n229
Hamilton, Louis, on eleventh-century Italian crowds, 152
Hamwic, size of, 46
Han dynasty (China), 16, 23
Hannig, Jürgen, on consensus, 113, 114
Hardy, Thomas, *Far from the Madding Crowd*, 65
Hartmann, Wilfried, 115
harvests: gatherings affected by, 67–68; in Roman period, 24
Hastings, battle of (1066), 53
hay, 24, 66–68; harvest of, 68; haylofts, 50
Hebrew language, 126–27
Hedeby, size of, 46
Heitz, Carol, on liturgy and space, 97–98
Helen, saint, 147, 156

Helianus, saint, 139
Herod Agrippa, king of Judea, 133, 265n153
Herrin, Judith, 10
Hilarion, saint, flight from crowd by, 147
Hildesheim, 46
Hilduin (abbot of Saint-Denis), 104, 140, 154–55
Hilton, Rodney, 7, 10
Hincmar (archbishop of Reims), 50, 51 56, 59, 110, 115, 156; *Collectio de ecclesia et capellis* of, 56; on illicit revels, 77–78; on palace "multitude," 108
Hincmar (bishop of Laon), 57
Hippodrome, 22, 32–33, 197n146. *See also* chariot racing; circuses
Honoratus (saint), 158
Honorius (Roman emperor), 26
Horace (Roman poet), 105, 121; word *vulgus* used by, 266n179
Horden, Peregrine, on urbanism, 174–75
Hrotsvit of Gandersheim (author of *Pafnutius*), 169–70
Hucbald of Saint-Amand, 272–73n261
Huguccio (Uguccione) of Pisa, 231n89
Hungarian language, 128
hunter-gatherers, 16, 204n50
hunting, 107–8; staged theatrical hunts (*venationes*), 26, 195n124
Hypatia, 19

ibn Ya'qūb, Ibrāhīm (Jewish traveler from Umayyad Spain), 43
incastellamento (spread of fortified sites), 49
Indiculus superstitionum et paganiarum, 77, 291n206
Ine (West Saxon king), 54
Ingelheim, 47, 225n304; palace size of, 62
insects, 5, 70; in insulting comparisons, 54, 159–60
Ireland, 43, 126,
Isidore of Seville (bishop and author): on *contio* and derivations, 133–34, 265n157; games criticized by, 31–32, 195n123; *multitudo* and *turba* distinguished by (in *De differentiis verborum*), 128, 130, 134, 149; on numbers, 217n208; Old High German texts of, 259n45
Islamic Mediterranean, ix, 2, 3, 55, 165; army sizes in, 220n248; demography of, 41–42, 44, 207n81, 208n89
Italy, 10, 15, 22, 32, 39, 63, 79, 113, 123, 128, 134; demography of, 40–41; urbanization and deurbanization in, 37, 78, 172

Jay, Martin, "discourse" defined by, 182–83n25
Jericho, 16
Jerome (saint and author), 111, 136, 268n213; *contio* used by, 133; topos of saintly flight from the crowd (in *Life of Hilarion, BHL* 3879), 147; *turba* used by, 138
Jesus Christ, 101–2, 287n150; in *Christ Stopped at Eboli*, 24, 73 193n83; crowds as witnesses to miracles of, 130; logion of, 113–14; preaching before crowds by, 21, 145–46; pseudo-Christ of Bourges, 167; vulnerability of away from crowds, 106
Jews, 6, 44, 126–27, 160, 175; medieval manuscripts of, 261n75; medieval persecution of, 1, 169
John VII (pope), as patron of Santa Maria Antiqua at Rome, 98
John VIII (pope), death of, 161
Jonas of Bobbio (hagiographer), 273n1, 279n59, 284n111, on animals, 228n55
Jones, A.H.M., on homogeneity of Roman cities, 23; army size estimated by, 193n89
Joseph (bishop of Tours), 111–12
Joseph Tov-Elem, 127
Judas Iscariot, 140; crowdless Christ betrayed by, 106
Julian ("the Apostate," Roman emperor), 29, 137
Jumièges, number of monks at, 48
Justinian II (Byzantine emperor): public vengeance of, 33
Juvenal (Roman satirist), on "bread and circuses," 1, 26, 28, 32
Juvencus, Caius Vettius Aquilinius (Christian poet), 146; alternative text of Matthew 15:32 (*plebs* for *turba*), 268n210

Kaldellis, Anthony: on republican ideology, 17, 127, 188n9; on Roman-Byzantine continuities, 17, 189n19

Kazhdan, Alexander, on capacity of Hagia Sophia, 62

Kempf, Damien, 131–32

Kohl, Thomas: on peasant coordination, 69; on peasant mobility, 50; on risks of peasants' choices, 77

Kolberg (Kołobrzeg, Poland), 49

Komnene, Anna (Byzantine princess and author), on mass crusaders, 171

Kreiner, Jamie: on collective solidarity, 150; on episcopal access, 108; on episcopal entourage's size, 57–58, 59

Krüger, Astrid, on litany of Lorsch Rotulus, 102

Kufa, 44

Larcia (woman in hagiography of Saint Denis), 140, 272n250

Late Antique Little Ice Age (LALIA), as demographic factor, 38–39; scholarship on, 203n40

Latham, Jacob, on *pompa circensis*, 25

latifundia, 24, 192n80

Latin language, 120–22

Latium, 49

Latvia, 44

Le Bon, Gustave (crowd theorist), 4–7, 9, 181–82nn10–13; antidemocratic, misogynistic, and racist premises of, 4

Lechfeld, battle of (955), 53

Lefebvre, Georges (historian of French Revolution), 7

Lehmann, Paul, 144, 274n4

Le Jan, Régine, 110

Leo I (pope), on angelic consensus of councils, 114

Leo III (pope), ambushed by enemies, 161

Leoba (saint, abbess of Tauberbischofsheim), nuns in mass ritual ritually vindicated by, 2, 101–2, 153

Leovigild (Visigothic king), 41

Leudegar (saint, bishop of Autun), 106

Levi, Carlo, 24, 73, 193n83

Liber Glossarum, 135, 266n173

Liber Pontificalis (papal biographies), 32, 79, 107, 148, 152, 164–165, 254n236

libri memoriales (commemoration books, confraternity books), 49, 63, 102–3, 172

Lifshitz, Felice, on pastoral care by nuns, 102

Lipton, Sara, on crowds in late medieval depiction of Jews, 6

Liutprand (bishop of Cremona), in Constantinople, 57

Liutprand (Lombard king), legal decree on women in brawls, 90

Livy (Roman historian): on just indignation of crowds, 275n17; on "nature of the multitude" to serve or dominate, 165, 290n195

locusts: in disparaging metaphor for human numbers, 54, 145, 150, 159, 160, 171; as pests, 70

Loire River, 42, 64, 87

Lombardic language, 122, poor survival of, 123

Lombards, 22, 32, 55, 74, 83, 150, 174; assemblies of, 113; crowd-related laws of, 71–2, 89–91; the *thing* as institution of, 123, 192n66

London, 45; early medieval Lundenwic, 43, 46; modern riots in, 88; size of, 46

Lorsch Rotulus (Rogationtide litany with 534 saints' names), 102

Lot, Ferdinand: heterodox interpretation of peasant *coniuratio* (859), 235n199; population estimates of, 37, 42

Lothar I (Frankish emperor), role in *Stellingas*, 84–85

Lothar II (Frankish king), 56, 59

Louis the German (East Frankish king), 56, 59, 113; language used by, 122; Lorsch Rotulus and, 102, 244n100; *Stellingas* suppressed by, 84–85, 235n183

Louis the Pious (Frankish emperor): Field of Lies (833) and, 117; hunts of, 249n162; penitential assemblies of, 93, 113, 253n225

INDEX 307

Louis II (Frankish emperor of Italy): ghost-written letter to Basil I of, 54, 159–60; *liber memorialis* of Brescia possibly linked to, 245n108. *See also* Anastasius Bibliothecarius; Bari, Franco-Byzantine siege of

Louis III (West Frankish king): retinue of (*githigini*), 53; Vikings defeated at Saucourt by (881), 53–54, 219n233

Louis XIV (king of France), 37

Low Countries, 42, 209n106, 223n281; emporia of, 46, 98, 109

Lucania: in sixth century, 138; in twentieth century, 24

Lucca, 45, 200n12

Lucilius (addressee of Seneca's *Moral Epistles*), 28, 135, 275n17

Luoyang (China), 23

Lupus of Troyes, 157–58

lynching, 145, 165; ambivalence of, 233n148; of disparagers of saints, 241n55; diverted threat of, 80–81; historiographical approach to, 8; of sixth-century tax-collectors, 79–80, 88; of suspected witches and magicians, 81, 167

Lyon, 42, 59, 60

MacMullen, Ramsay: on number of church councils, 22; on performance time of Roman acclamations, 20; on Peter Brown, 192n55; on sermon audience sizes, 62, 99

Magalhães de Oliveira, Júlio César: on crowds in Late Antiquity, 19; late antique crowd violence catalogued by, 20, 82

Magdeburg, 47

Magennis, Hugh, on crowds in Old English hagiography, 6

Mainz, 45, 101

malaria, 39, 203n43

manopera (peasant hand-work labor), 70

Mansuetus (saint), 69–70

Marcus Aurelius (Roman emperor), 29

Marseille, 37, 42, 45, 60, 79, 80; plague at, 212n142; polyptychs of, 200n11

Martin (saint, bishop of Tours): crowds defending honor of, 76, 81, 91, 111–12, 241n55, 252n207; feast day of, 74; influential *Life* of (*BHL* 5610) by Sulpicius Severus, 146

Martínez Pizarro, Joaquín, 6: on Agnellus of Ravenna's depiction of violent crowds, 162–63; on type scenes, 144, 274n7–8

Mauck, Marchita, on Paschal I's decoration of S. Prassede, 241n52

Maurice, saint, 151

Mauricius, bishop in Istria, blinded by his flock, 79

Maurya empire (India), 16

Maya civilization: ballgame of, 16; cities of, 33

McCormick, Michael: on crowd in rituals, 188n9; on elite retinues, 105; entourage sizes extrapolated by, 58–59, 61; on Plea of Rižana, 242n68; spatial estimates of churches and palaces by, 62

McCune, James, on sermons, 97

McPhail, Clark (crowd theorist), concept of "gatherings," 10, 186n55–56

Meens, Rob, on Alcuin's and Theodulf's dispute, 112

Mehmet II (Turkish sultan), 17

Melve, Leidulf, on "public sphere," 105, 247n125

Metz, 45; many churches of, 46; *turbae* of, in Paul the Deacon's *Liber episcopis Mettensibus*, 131–32

Mieszko I (Polish ruler), 43

Milan, 21, 32, 41, 172; as large city in Latin Europe, 45; revolt at (983), 79; monastery of Sant'Ambrogio at, 73; Pataria (Patarines) of, 292n221, 294n1

Milkulčice (Greater Moravian site), 49

millet, 69; metaphorical use of, 160

mills, milling, 66, 69, 139, 243n84; as site and occasion for gathering, 104

mining, 38, 49

Mitry, peasants of, 47, 73, 89

mob (rabble; riot) in discourse: early medieval persistence of, 131; early medieval use of, 125, 130–31, 135; later medieval ideas of, 6; Roman ideas of, 3, 27–28, 121; as unruly and non-elite by nature, 7

Modoin (Frankish poet), 151, 281n83

Mohenjo-Daro, 16

Mollat, Michel, 7

monks, monasteries, 47–49, 56–58, 76, 81, 100–103, 154

Moore, R. I.: early medieval continuities acknowledged by, 175, 273n262; on return of "the crowd" (c. 1000) to the "public stage," 10, 127, 168–69, 171, 175, 256n267

Moses (biblical figure), 145

multiplying gaze, 159–60. *See also* locusts

multitudo: in the *Annales Regni Francorum*, 141; numerical associations of, 51; plebeian associations with, 121, 131; polysemy of, 129. *See also* words for crowds

Murray, Alexander, 6

Muschiol, Gisela, on pastoral care by nuns, 102

Muzzarelli, Maria Giuseppina, on later medieval preachers, 62

Naismith, Rory: on money, 215n187; on peasant agency, 69

Naples, 41, 45, 79, 128, 172; uprising of *mancipia* near, 81, 88

Nebelivka, 16

Nelson, Janet: on entourage size, 57, on peasant *coniuratio* (859), 87

Nero, Roman emperor, 18, 29, 32; claque hired by, 289n183

Nigel of Canterbury, 257n3

Nithard (author of ninth-century *Histories*), 84

noctes (peasant labor duties), 72

non-elites, 9, 12, 64–92, 117, 121, 125, 130–31, 141, 144, 158–59, 165–68, 172, 176

Norrie, James, 176

North Africa, 15, 17, 19, 21, 22, 24, 30, 128, 266n176; Frankish raid in, 159

Notker (late ninth-century author, biographer of Charlemagne), 57, 150, 220n245

Nuffelen, Peter van, on "virtue-based" crowd behavior, 20

nuns, nunneries, 2, 48, 79, 94, 148; lay crowds and, 101–2, 154; *turbae* of, 139

oats, 66

Odo of Cambrai, 293n232

Oexle, Otto Gerhard, 69

Old Church Slavonic language, 126

Old English language, 124–25

Old High German language, 124, 125, 131, 134

Old Irish language, 126

Old Norse language, 125

Old Saint Peter's church, Rome, 98

Old Saxon language, 124

olives, 66, 67, 68, 73

Orléans, 42; acclamations by sixth-century Jews of, 260n74; councils at, 60–61; eleventh-century heretics of, 169; Tours assault on men from, 91, 111–12, 165

Ostrów Lednicki (Poland), 49

Ottink, Marijke, on *populus*, 129

Ottonian dynasty, 47, 49, 214n164

Oviedo, 41

Pacatus Drepanius (fourth-century panegyrist), 136

Paderborn, 47, capacity of palace at, 62

Paris, 42, 45, 49, 53, 59–61; Merovingian circuses at, 31; Merovingian tax collector's home burned at, 80; sieges of (845, 885–86), 53, 54

Parthenius, 79–80

Paschal I (pope), 98

Passau, 45

passive resistance, 92, 173

Paulinus (missionary), 94

Paul the Deacon, 134; *Liber de episcopis Mettenibus*, 131–32

Pavia, 39, 45, 76

peasants, 64–92; agrarian labors of, 66–68; collective labor by, 68–69; definitions of, 65–66, 226n11; dues and taxes as gatherings for, 73–74; horizontal coordination among, 71–72; Latin terms for, 226n10; revolts and resistance by, 81–83, 85–92, 165; royal exactions upon, 74–75; spirituality of, 75–78; vertical coordination by lords of, 72–74

Pekáry, Thomas, catalogue of Roman-era uprisings by, 20, 82

Persian language, 129

Persians, 16, 27, 128; armies of, disparaged by Ammianus Marcellinus as *turbae*, 137

Pfäfers, *Liber Viventium* of, 103

Philip (antipope, 768), 164

Philip the Arab (Roman emperor), 19

Philo of Alexandria, on crowds, 27

Phocas (East Roman emperor), 33

Photios I (patriarch of Constantinople), accusations against, 114

Piacenza, 62; *xenodocium* at, 76

pigs, 31, 58, 66, 70; counterfeit relics and, 77

Pippin II (Frankish mayor of the palace), 156

Pippin III (Frankish king), 140

Pirenne, Henri, 36, 45

Pisa, 45

placitum ("plea," judicial assembly), 50, 55, 56, 95, 134. *See also* Arezzo; Courtisols; Mitry; Siena

plague, bubonic, 38–39, 217n211; demographic significance of, 203n41, 204n46, 204n51

Plea of Rižana (804), 74, 242n68

pleonasm, 130, 132

pluralization, 120; of early medieval crowd vocabulary, 130

Pohansko (Czechia), 43, 49

Poitiers, 60; battle of (732), 53; nuns' revolt (589–90) at, 48, 79, 101

Poland, 43–44, 49

polyptychs, 36–37, 49, 199–200n9, 200n12; as demographic evidence, 37, 50; as evidence for peasant obligations, 66, 73–74; landless individuals within, 227n26; *placitum* of Courtisols preserved in, 217n201; of Saint-Germain-des-Prés, 37, 42. *See also* demography

pompa circensis, 25. *See also* circuses

Pompey, 28

population. *See* demography

populus, 12, 28, 91, 94, 173; in liturgy, 75; non-Latin equivalents of, 124, 126, 130; polysemy of, 128–132, 142; plebeian associations with, 131; Roman, 16, 88; Romance evolution of, 122. *See also* words for crowds

Pössel, Christina, 107, 249n152, 253n223

Power, Eileen, 77

Poznań (Poland), 49

Praeiectus (saint): guard dogs' attacks avoided by, 108; shrine of, 98

Pratsch, Thomas, on topoi, 274n5

Priscian, 126, 260n64

Priscus (saint), 150

Proba (Christian poet), 146

Protoromance languages, 121–22

Prudentius (bishop of Troyes, part-author of *Annals of Saint Bertin*): on massacre of the *coniuratio* (859), 87–88; on tsunami, 53

Prudentius (late antique Christian poet), 146, 277n36

Puglia (Apulia): signs of decline in, 37; signs of growth in, 206n70

pulses, 66

Purcell, Nicholas, on urbanism, 174–75

Quierzy (Frankish palace), 47

Qur'an, 127; crowd words in, 127–28

rabble. *See* mob

Radegund (saint, queen, and monastic founder), 48

Rainald of the Melinais (preacher and hermit), 169, 293n230

Rammelsberg ore deposits, 49, 215n187

Rashi (Schlomo Yitzchaki), 127

Ratger of Fulda, 102, 223n275

Ravenna, 39, 41, 78, 172; Agnellus of Ravennas's account of eighth-century massacre in, 78, 162–63

Reccopolis, 37, 207n84

reduplication, as linguistic feature of crowd language, 130
Regensburg, 45, 47, 292n224
Regino of Prüm: on the slaughtered peasants of Prüm, 57; on the *Stellingas*, 53–54
Regnobertus (saint), 139
Reichenau, 156; confraternity book of, 63, 103, 172
relics, 21, 66, 75, 96, 99, 144, 147, 149, 156, 157, 168; counterfeit, 77; cult of, 13, 76, 103–4, 164–65; draw of, 48, 76, 94, 152–53; illicit, 53, 77, 167; and processions, 154–55; translation of, 2, 98, 139, 151
religious gatherings, 94–104
Rembold, Ingrid, 10, 85
Remiremont: *liber memorialis* of, 103; nunnery of, 48
rents, 73–74
repertory, 8–10, 11. *See also* Davis, Natalie Zemon
Rhine River, 42, 137, 170; Charlemagne's canal project and, 74
Rhône River, 42
Richard II (duke of Normandy), 85–86
Richer of Saint-Rémy, 169
riga (peasant piecework labor), 72
riots, 2, 7, 34; in ancient Rome, 18–19; as deterrent, 117; over food, 8; medieval decline of, 142; social scientific criticism of concept of, 7; over taxes, 80, 87; words for, 18, 111, 135–36. *See also* mob; *tumultus*; *turba*
Röckelein, Hedwig, 104
rodents, 70
Roman Antiquity, 1, 15–34; riots in, 18; urbanism in, 16, 17, 39
Roman law, 16, 18, 111, 135–36, 141
Romano, John, 94
Rome (city): ancient, 17–19, 20, 21, 24–25, 26, 29–30, 136, 138–39; early medieval, 32, 45, 57, 97–98, 104, 127, 152, 164; as hotspot for crowd politics, 79, 148, 173; size of, 1, 23, 41, 45, 63, 99, 207n77
Roncevaux, 53

Roscius Gallus, Quintus (actor), 17
Rothari (Lombard king), laws about gatherings of, 89–90
Rudé, George (crowd historian), 7–8, 88
Rudolf of Fulda, 101, 276n22
Russell, Josiah (demographer), 36, 39–40; causal importance of plague for, 202n39
rye, 66, 67

Saint-Denis, monastery, 48, 49, 109
Saint Donatus, Arezzo (cathedral church), 55, 269n226
Saint-Gall monastery, 48, 57, 102, 103, 139
Saint-Germain-des-Prés monastery, polyptych of, 37, 42
salt production, 38
Salvius (saint, bishop of Amiens), 151
Salzburg, 47, 103
Samarra, 44
Santa Maria Maggiore basilica, Rome, 97, 98
Santa Sabina basilica, Rome, 97
San Vincenzo al Volturno, monastery, 48
Saracens, 54, 148, 159, 160
Saturnius of Cagliari (saint), 141
Saucourt, battle of (881), 53
Savonnières, summit at (862), 59, 115
Saxons (Saxony), 22, 53, 124, 160; mass execution of, 54–55; *Stellingas* among, 84–85
Scandinavia, 15, 43, 255n246
Schofield, John, 45, 46
Schleswig-Holstein, 42
Schroeder, Nicholas, 69, 70
Scott, James: on passive resistance, 93, 236n207; on "public transcript," 93, 117
Sedulius, Scotus, 146
sheep, 70
Scheldt River, 42, 87
Seine River, 37, 42, 64, 87, 109, 166
Sen, Amartya, on causes of famine, 38
Seneca, Lucius Annaeua (the Younger), 28, 117–18, 135, 139; on moral danger of crowds, 29
Sergius I (pope), defended by Roman crowd, 79

sermons, 9, 70, 96–97; high and late medieval, 13, 62
Severus, Septimus (Roman emperor), 19
Shaw, Brent, on late antique collective violence, 24
Sidonius Apollinaris (bishop and author), 138
Sieben, Hermann, on conciliar logic, 114
Siena, 40, 45; Arezzo's jurisdictional conflict with, 46, 55, 74, 95
Sigloardus (*missus* of the archbishop of Reims), 50–51
Sisebut (Visigothic king and author), on violent mob, 161–62, 163, 288n170
slantwise resistance, ix, xiv, 13, 14, 92, 159, 166–68, 176; defined, 88, 166–68, 187n68
slavery, slaves, Roman, 15, 27. See also unfreedom
Slavic languages, 126
Slavlands, 15, 43–44, 159
Slootjes, Daniëlle, 191n54, 262n98
Soissons, 31, 61, 102
solitude: eleventh-century interest in, 169–70; entourages and, 105–6; in Stoic training, 28
Spain (Iberian Peninsula), 15, 19, 22, 41–42, 63, 71, 128, 140, 172
Spanish language, 122, 128
spectaculum, spectacula (Roman entertainment), 26–32; as metaphor for "spectacle," 101
spelt, 66, 67, 69
Speyer, 45
Stamford Bridge, battle of (1066), 53
Stará Kouřim (Czechia), 49
Stellingas (Saxon peasant revolt, 840s), 81, 84–85, 86, 165; explanations for, 85; gilds and, 85; meaning of name, 85; significant timing and location of, 87
Stephen (saint and protomartyr), 21, 145, 161; festival of (December 26), 75
Stephen of Auxerre, 287nn151–52, 269n224
Stephen III (pope), 164

Stettin (Szczecin, Poland), 49
Steuer, Heiko, 45, 46
Stewart, Potter (Supreme Court justice), 6
Strasbourg, 45, Oaths of (842), 122
strikes, 7
Suetonius, 24
Sueves, 22
Suger (abbot of Saint-Denis), 109, 149
Sulpicius Severus (hagiographer), 146
Sünskes Thompson, Julia, catalogue of Roman-era uprisings by, 20, 82
"superstition," 76–77, 166–68, as slur for gatherings, 141, 144, 159
Symmachus, Quintus Aurelius, 268n209
Syriac language, 128

Tacitus, Cornelius, 28
Táin Bó Cúailnge (Irish epic), 126
T'ang dynasty (China), 23
Tarquimpol, 45
taxation, 73–74, 80, 87
Ten Thousand Martyrs, 151
Terence, 170; as model for Hrotsvit, 293n234
Tertry, battle of (687), 53
Tertullian, on desire to be seen at spectacles, 27, on *contiones*, 133
Theoderic, Ostrogothic king, 28–29, 123; on circuses, 31
Theodore of Tarsus (saint, archbishop of Canterbury), 152
Theodosian Code, ceremonial Western approval of (438), 20–21
Theodosius I, Roman emperor, 29, 136, 137
Theodulf (bishop of Orléans): Alcuin's conflict with, 91, 111–12; on crowd (*turba*) of pious monks, 279n53; on crowds offering bribes, 74, 286n142; on hostile crowds, 80–81
Theudebert I, Merovingian king, 80
Theuderic II, Merovingian king, Desiderius persecuted by, 161–62
Theuderic III, Merovingian king, 106, trust in the multitude, 156

Thietmar of Merseberg, story of the chestnuts and the millet, 160
thing (*Ding, thinx*), 22, 122–23, 125; and the verb *thingare*, 71, 113, 123, 192n66. *See also* assemblies, secular; words for crowds
Thiota (woman preacher), 167–68, 291n211
Thompson, E. P., 28, 85; as crowd historian, 7–9; on "moral economy" of the crowd, x, 8, 87, 165–66; on official acknowledgment of rioters' reasons, 88, 112, 165–66; on riots as deterrents, 117; scholarly critiques of, 185n44
Tiberius (Roman emperor), disliked for spurning games, 29
Tilleda, 47
Tilly, Charles, x, 78, 256n263
Toledo, 37, 41; as council site, 56, 58
topoi (literary commonplaces), 12, 143–70; biblical models for, 146–46; classical models for, 144–45; definition and historical use of, 144–45; early medieval models for, 147; late antique models for, 146–47. *See also* type scenes
Toto (duke of Nepi), in contested papal election of 768, 164
Toubert, Pierre, 37; on *incastellamento*, 49
Toulouse, battle of (721), 53, 56
Tours, 45, 53, 76, 80, 111–12, 163
Trajan (Roman emperor), 18
Treaty of Meersen (870), 59
Trier, 32, 45, 79–80, 122, 196n134, 212n140
tumultus, 101, 111–12, 125–26; persistent negative connotation of, 131. *See also* words for crowds
turba: Ammianus Marcellinus's use of, 136–37; Christianization of, 137–39; Isidore of Seville's use of, 128; lost technical and negative connotations of, 3, 48, 11, 130, 131–32, 139–40; non-Latin equivalents of, 124, 126; persistence of negative connotations of, 140–41; in Roman law, 135–36; Roman meanings of, 18, 28, 31, 135–36. *See also* riots; words for crowds

Turin, revolt at (897), 79
Turner, Victor (anthropologist): on "communitas," 5, 182n19; on crowds that "flood their subjects with affect," 5–6, 177
type scenes, 7, 143, 153, 173; defined, 144, 274n7; monastic foundation scene, 154; sources of, 144–47. *See also* topoi

Udalric (twelfth-century formulary compiler), 265n164
Ulfilas (biblical translator), 123
Ullmann, Walter, 187n67
Ulpianus (Ulpian), Domitius, 136
unfreedom, 66, 67, 73, 81, 83, 88–90; peasant disputes focused on, 50–51; numerous forms of, 229n70. *See also* slavery, slaves
uprisings. *See* peasants; riots
Urban II (pope), 62
urbanism. *See* cities and towns
Uruk, 16
Utrecht, 45, 47

Valentinian III, Roman emperor, 29
Valle Trita (Abbruzzo, Italy): efficacy of passive resistance exemplified by, 88; as site of peasant conflict with San Vincenzo al Volturno, 81, 83–84, 86
Vandals, 22, 32, 42, 123; universal agreement in poetry of (Dracontius), 281n80
Venantius Fortunatus, 147
Venice, 41, 45, 46; crowd politics in, 79
Vergil: *Aeneid*, 145, 257n8, 273n1, 275n14, 275n15; on crowds and masculinity, 28, 145; influence of, 146, 273n1, 275n13; man (*vir*) calming the raging crowd simile (*Aen.* 1.148–53), 28, 121, 145, 194n109; on vulgarity of crowds, 121, 130
Verona, 41, 45; high medieval demographic growth of, 226n7; revolt at (968), 79
Verus of Orange (saint), collective lament for, 153
Vico, Giambattista, 6. *See also* Auerbach, Erich
Victorinus (martyr), 151, 280–81n76

Victricius of Rouen (fourth-century missionary and author), 146, *turba* used for saints by, 138, 269n215
Vienna, 45
Vigilius (pope), mocked and pelted by disgruntled Romans, 79
Vikings (Northmen), 43, 53–54, 64, 72, 87, 92, 103, 110, 166; peasant resistance against, 64, 87, 110, 235n199, 235n199; population pressure and, 43, 210n108
Visigoths, 22, 37, 41, 123, 174; assemblies and, 113; church councils and, 41–42, 56. *See also* Spain
Vitus (saint), 154
Vouillé, battle of (507), 53
vulgus (quintessential Latin word for non-elite crowd), 28, 121, 130–31. *See also* mob; non-elites; words for crowds

Wace, 86
Waldipert (faction leader in ninth-century Rome), 164
Wamba (Visigothic king), 31–32
Wandrille (saint), 140
Warin (abbot), as leader of relic procession, 154–55
Weber, Max, 45
Werla, 47
Werner, Karl Ferdinand, on army size, 54, 220n243
Weser River, 42
West, Charles, 50; on entourage size, 57; on peasants, 69
West-Harling, Veronica, 10

wheat, 66, 67, 69; in wheat and chaff metaphor, 25. *See also* cereals
Wickham, Chris, 10, 69, 89, 113; on defining peasants, 226n386; on peasant mode and demography, 39, 204n48, 204n50; on peasant resistance, 81, 82, 84, 236n200
Wilkin, Alexis, 50
William of Jumièges, 85–86
Wolff, Philippe, 7
Wollin, 49
wolves, 70
words for crowds, 3, 119–42; Arabic, 127–28; Celtic, 126; Germanic, 122–26; Greek, 27, 127, 130; Hebrew, 126–27; Latin, 120–21, 128–42; Protoromance, 121–22; Slavic, 126. *See also contio*; *multitudo*; *populus*; *thing*; *tumultus*; *turba*; *vulgus*
Worms, 45, 102
Wright, Roger, 121
WUNC (worthiness, unity, numbers, commitment), 256n263. *See also* Tilly, Charles

xenodochium (plural *xenodochia*), 76

Yersinia pestis, genetic evidence for, 203n41, 204n51, 210n111. *See also* plague, bubonic
York, 43

Zeno (saint), 139
Zerner-Chardavoine, Monique, 37
Zosimus (historian), 28, 194n113
Zürich, 47

Milton Keynes UK
Ingram Content Group UK Ltd.
UKHW040953051224
451775UK00001B/1/J